Phil Edmonston

LEMON-AID

2006

NEW CARS
and MINIVANS

Published in Canada by Fitzhenry & Whiteside, 195 Allstate Parkway, Markham, Ontario L3R 4T8

www.fitzhenry.ca   godwit@fitzhenry.ca

1   3   5   7   9   10   8   6   4   2

Library and Archives Canada has catalogued this publications as follows:

Edmonston, Louis-Philippe, 1944–
Lemon-aid new cars and minivans / Phil Edmonston.

Annual.
2002–
Imprint varies.
Continues: Edmonston, Louis-Philippe, 1944– . Lemon-aid new cars, ISSN 1481-4188.
ISSN 1700-7593
ISBN 1-55041-574-3 (2006 edition)

1. Automobiles—Purchasing—Periodicals. I. Title.

TL162.E3396   629.2'222'05   C2001-903607-8

Fitzhenry & Whiteside acknowledges with thanks the Canada Council for the Arts, the Government of Canada through the Book Publishing Industry Development Program (BPIDP), and the Ontario Arts Council for their support of our publishing program.

Printed in Canada by Webcom Limited
Packaged by Colborne Communications, Toronto
Publications manager: Greg Ioannou
Project co-ordinator: Andrea Battiston
Layout and production: Jack Steiner
Editing: Heather Ball, Andrea Battiston, Stacey Curtis, Andrea Douglas,
Greg Ioannou, Josie Malevich, Rachel Rosen
Illustrations: Rachel Rosen
Design: Ingrid Paulson

CONTENTS

KEY DOCUMENTS

Lemon-Aid is a feisty owner's manual that has no equal anywhere. We don't want you stuck with a lemon, or to wind up paying for repairs that are the automaker's fault and are covered by secret "goodwill" warranties. That's why we are the only book that includes many hard-to-find, confidential, and little-known documents that automakers don't want you to see.

In short, we know you can't win what you can't prove.

The following photos, charts, documents, and service bulletins are included in this index so that you can stand your ground and be treated fairly. Photocopy and circulate whichever document will prove helpful in your dealings with automakers, dealers, service managers, insurance companies, or government agencies. Remember, most of the hundreds of summarized service bulletins outline repairs or replacements that should be done for free.

Part One

THE BEST OF TIMES; THE WORST OF TIMES

Part Two

DOING RIGHT WHEN THINGS GO WRONG

Part Three

NEW-VEHICLE RATINGS

Appendix II

CALLING ALL CHEAPSKATES

Appendix III

TWENTY *REAL* WAYS TO SAVE ON FUEL COSTS

Appendix IV

SERVICE BULLETINS YOU AREN'T SUPPOSED TO HAVE

LIARS AND BUYERS

Supreme Justice

...In this case, the quantum ought to be sufficiently high as to correct the defendants' behaviour. In particular, Chrysler's corporate policy to place profits ahead of the potential danger to its customers' safety and personal property must be punished. And when such corporate policy includes a refusal to comply with the provisions of the Act and a refusal to provide any relief to the plaintiff, I find an award of $25,000 for exemplary damages to be appropriate. I therefore order Chrysler and Dodge City to pay: Damages in the sum of $41,969.83; Exemplary damages in the sum of $25,000; Party and party costs...

PREBUSHEWSKI V. DODGE CITY AUTO (1985) LTD. AND CHRYSLER CANADA LTD.
SUPREME COURT OF CANADA
MARCH 9, 2005
(www.lexum.umontreal.ca/csc-scc/en/com/2005/html/05-03-09.4.wpd.html)

Hybrid Hokum

David Champion tests cars for *Consumer Reports*. The government says the popular Toyota Prius gets 60 miles a gallon [4L/100 km] in the city and 51 [4.6L/100 km] on the highway. But in real-world driving, Champion got less.

"We found very similar results on the highway," said Champion, "But instead of 60 miles per gallon we only got 35 miles per gallon [6.7L/100 km] in the city."

NBC NIGHTLY NEWS
AUGUST 16, 2005

Fuel-Economy Fantasies

Consumer Reports magazine has discovered that the mileage promised on car stickers is grossly inflated, sometimes by as much as 40 percent. *CR* says that hybrids alone account for mileage discrepancies that average 12L/100 km (19 mpg) below the city rating given by the U.S. Environmental Protection Agency and Transport Canada.

But the average motorist doesn't know this. Consequently, drivers who see gasoline prices headed to $1.50 a litre are being stampeded into buying what they believe are fuel-frugal hybrids and diesels—then finding out they have been duped. Not only are the costs of running vehicles equipped with special engines much higher than advertised, but poor reliability and higher servicing costs also give these "green" vehicles a decidedly "lemony" flavour.

Once again, we have to beware of the lies. Toyota, for example, seldom mentions the fact that its hybrid battery packs can cost $8,000 U.S. to replace, or that *Lemon-Aid*, *Consumer Reports*, *Car and Driver*, and *Edmunds.com* have found that diesel and hybrid fuel-economy figures can be 30–40 percent less than advertised.

Smart drivers should ignore automaker gas-saving hype, hunker down, and keep their paid-for, reliable, gas-guzzling used vehicles, because the depreciation savings will more than offset the increased cost of fuel. Additionally, *Lemon-Aid's* 20 fuel-saving tips, found in Appendix III, will help you reduce fuel consumption without getting another vehicle. If you're searching for something that's both reliable and fuel-efficient, look up *Lemon-Aid's* list of recommended fuel-efficient vehicles, also in Appendix III.

False mileage claims targeted

Canadian courts are cracking down on lying dealers and deceptive sales practices. Ontario's new *Consumer Protection Act* (*www.e-laws.gov.on.ca/DBLaws/Statutes/English/02c30_e.htm*), for example, lets consumers cancel a contract within one year of entering into an agreement if the dealer makes a false, misleading, deceptive, or unconscionable representation.

This means dealers cannot make the excuse that they were fooled or that they were simply providing data supplied by the manufacturer. The law clearly states that both parties are jointly liable and that dealers are *presumed* to know the history, quality, and true performance of what they sell.

Even details like fuel economy can lead to a contract's cancellation if the dealer gives a higher-than-actual figure. In *Sidney v. 1011067 Ontario Inc.* (c.o.b. Southside Motors), a precedent-setting case filed before Ontario's *Act* was toughened this year, the buyer was awarded $11,424.51 plus prejudgment interest because of a false representation made by the defendant regarding fuel efficiency. The plaintiff claimed that the defendant advised him that the vehicle had a fuel efficiency of 800–900 km per tank of fuel, when in fact the maximum efficiency was only 500 km per tank.

This consumer victory is particularly important as fuel prices soar and everyone from automakers to sellers of ineffective gas-saving gadgets makes outlandishly false fuel-economy claims.

Consumer rights have also been strengthened this year as small claims courts have been given higher claim limits throughout Canada, with some provinces (Alberta and British Columbia) allowing claims up to $25,000. Another major development this year was the Supreme Court's $25,000 punitive damages award against Chrysler Canada. The Court allowed aggrieved car owners to sue for much more than the depreciated value of what they bought under provincial consumer protection statutes. If a manufacturer treats its customer unfairly, the Court reaffirmed the power of lower courts to assess an additional financial penalty to punish the automaker's past conduct and ensure that it doesn't repeat the offense (*Prebushewski v. Dodge City Auto Ltd. and Chrysler Canada Ltd.*).

End of the Showroom Shakedown

As new-car sales stagnated and 2005-model inventory piled up, 2005 started out as a lacklustre year for Detroit-built cars and trucks. By mid-year, Chrysler, Ford, and General Motors dealerships were tracking far behind Asian automakers as rebates failed to ignite shopper enthusiasm for unsold American cars. Out of desperation, GM made an announcement in June that stunned the auto industry. For the first time in its history the giant automaker told the truth: Its products were grossly overpriced—sometimes inflated by more than 30 percent.

GM then immediately cut prices between 20 and 30 percent under the guise of extending employee discounts to everyone. Ford and Chrysler reluctantly responded with their own successful "employee discount" programs. Leftover 2005 cars and trucks practically disappeared, along with buyers' confidence in the "suggested retail price." GM, Ford, and Chrysler now want to ditch discounting with their 2006 models, claiming future prices will be set at a more realistic level. Don't you believe it.

America's Big Three automakers want to put the price genie back in the bottle, but shoppers are too smart to believe the same lie twice. Therefore, although the 2006 models will initially have slightly higher prices than last year's versions, these increases will be rolled back and rebates added by December as Canadians demand prices equal to or lower than the 2005s.

In the end, buyers win; liars lose.

2006 New Car Guide Improvements

Going into my 35th year writing *Lemon-Aid*, I'm happy to see that new- and used-car prices are becoming more competitive and that consumers have more rights before our courts—two changes *Lemon-Aid* has been advocating since 1971. But these changes won't mean much if Canadians aren't given the easily accessible, unbiased information that they deserve.

That's why *Lemon-Aid* exists.

We've made a number of changes to the 2006 edition of *Lemon-Aid New Cars and Minivans* to make it easier to read, more content-rich, and more affordable. It's on the shelves earlier, it's $2 cheaper, its pages are larger, it's longer, and it features a new, user-friendly layout.

In this year's edition, you'll find a description of the best and worst vehicles for new drivers and seniors; tips on getting dealers to bid for your business; reasons why hybrid and diesel savings are illusory; steps to follow to get your money back when things go wrong; and information on finding the safest, most reliable, and most fuel-thrifty vehicle for your budget.

This year's guide also combines test results with owner feedback to provide a critical comparison of 2005–06 cars and minivans. If improvements and additional

safety features don't justify the higher costs of newer models (and most don't), we say so. We give safer, more reliable, and often cheaper alternatives for each vehicle. Front, offset, side, and rollover crash test results are also included, along with an exhaustive list of useful and useless accessories and safety features, and guidelines for how much profit dealers make on each vehicle.

Lemon-Aid is a feisty owner's manual that has no equal anywhere. We don't want you to get stuck with a lemon, or to wind up paying for repairs that are the automaker's fault and that are covered by secret "goodwill" warranties. That's why we're the only book that includes many hard-to-find, confidential, and little-known documents that automakers don't want you to see.

In short, no ads, no favourites, and no fluff.

Phil Edmonston
November 2005

Part One

THE BEST OF TIMES;
THE WORST OF TIMES

Wake Up and Smell the Sake!

For too many years, Detroit companies' primary tactic for fighting back has been to shift consumers' attention to the future, while leveraging their past as a sentimental weapon that they have used to obscure the deficiencies of the present.

MICHELINE MAYNARD
THE END OF DETROIT

5

Beware of Hurricane Katrina "Demos"

Sooner or later, Canada will be "flooded" with water-damaged vehicles shipped from the southern United States, where up to 500,000 vehicles were submerged after the passage last August of Hurricane Katrina. It won't be the first time that U.S. wrecks will be sold to unsuspecting Canadians.

Damaged cars are often repaired cosmetically, and moved across the border with "doctored" titles that have been cleansed through multi-state registrations. They can never be repaired to function safely, inasmuch as floodwaters can cause vehicle computer and electrical system shorts, as well as lead to anti-lock braking and airbag system malfunctions....

CARFAX AND *AUTOMOTIVE NEWS*
SEPTEMBER 2005

For Canadian auto owners and shoppers, 2005 was the best of times and the worst of times. The Big Three automakers' deep discounting cut prices by more than 30 percent and drove used-car prices to historically low levels with plenty of supply. Conversely, fuel prices have practically doubled to over $1.50 a litre, sending large car and truck sales plummeting and cutting the resale values of most trade-ins.

But some things haven't changed. Detroit Big Three automakers continue to build poor-quality cars and trucks, although this year there appears to be some improvement. The gap between Asian and American automobile quality may be narrowing for 2005–06; however, this may only reflect a lowered benchmark following recent Honda, Nissan, and Toyota powertrain, electrical system, and body fit

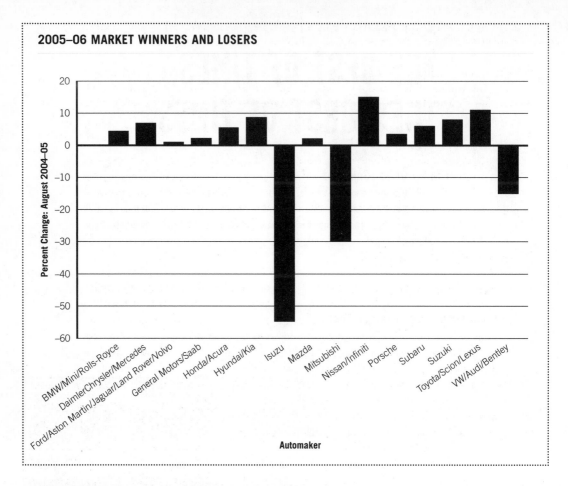

2005–06 MARKET WINNERS AND LOSERS

Nissan's 2004–05 Quest has become the poster child for poor quality control and bizarre styling. Its engineers and stylists are working overtime to staunch hemorrhaging sales.

glitches. Nevertheless, Toyota and Lexus continue to dominate J.D. Power's latest dependability surveys, while American and European makes are mostly ranked below the industry average.

The estimated sales figures above apply to the American market. Canadian sales have been very similar, with the following exceptions:

• GM sales fell almost 3.6 percent from August 2004, when sales weren't discounted. If losses continue, GM will likely extend its discounts to cover all 2006 models, and Chrysler and Ford will follow.

- DaimlerChrysler Canada sales are up 23 percent, despite Mercedes' sales losses. Expect sales to decline substantially, though, as fuel costs hit Chrysler's large trucks and SUVs hard.
- Ford Canada sales were up 2.6 percent. Ford attributed the increase to its fuel-efficient vehicles. The company neglected to mention, however, that August was the first month it was outsold by DaimlerChrysler, General Motors, and Honda.

On the one hand, sales trends in both countries indicate that higher fuel prices are breathing new life into hybrids, diesel-engine-equipped models, and gas-sipping small cars made by GM (Daewoo), Honda, Hyundai, Kia, Mazda, Nissan, Subaru, Suzuki, and Toyota. On the other hand, Audi, Isuzu, Jaguar, Mitsubishi, Saab, and Volkswagen have remained poor sales performers through the month of August.

Buying a New Car or Minivan

First, keep in mind that you are going to spend much more money than you might have anticipated—a bit over $30,000 for the average vehicle transaction, according to Dennis DesRosiers, a Toronto-based auto consultant. This is because of the many hidden fees like freight charges and so-called administrative costs that are added to the bottom line. But that's just the beginning of your real costs.

According to the Canadian Automobile Association (CAA), the average household owns two vehicles, which are each driven about 20,000 kilometres annually and cost an average of $800 annually for maintenance. Insurance will cost $1,777 a year for a 2005 Chevrolet Cavalier compact, or $1,652 for a 2005 Chrysler Caravan. CAA also estimates in its 2005 "Driving Costs" study (*www. caa.ca/PDF/3708-EN-2005.pdf*) that the per-kilometre expense of

Buyers who pay the "list price," or manufacturer's suggested retail price, always pay too much. This Coquitlam, British Columbia, GM dealership placed the above ads in April 2005, listing new 2005s for almost half the price set six months earlier. And this was before GM announced discount prices in June. Hmm...wonder how the customers who paid full list felt?

driving that same minivan 24,000 kilometres would be 49.2 cents, or $11,811.30 a year. The owner of a 2005 Chevrolet Cavalier compact would pay 45.3 cents per kilometre, or $10,872.55 for the year—almost $1,000 less than what the minivan would cost.

Keep in mind that it's practically impossible to buy a bare-bones car or minivan, because automakers cram them with costly, non-essential performance and convenience features in order to maximize profits. Nevertheless, money-wasting gadgets like electronic navigation and sophisticated entertainment systems can easily be passed up with little impact on safety or convenience. Full-torso curtain side airbags, however, are important safety options that are well worth the extra expense.

 Before paying big bucks, though, you should know what your real needs are and how much you can afford to spend. Don't confuse *needs* with *styling* (do you have a bucket bottom to conform to those bucket seats?) or *trendy* with *essential* (will a cheaper Mazda5 mini-minivan or Chrysler's Caliber hatchback suit you as well as or better than a Caravan or mid-sized car?). Visiting the showroom with your spouse or a level-headed relative or friend will help you steer a truer course through all the non-essential options you'll be offered.

Women don't receive the same welcome at auto showrooms as men get because they make the salesmen (yes, usually less than 10 percent of the sales staff are women) work too hard to make a sale. Most sales agents admit that female shoppers are far more knowledgeable about what they want and patient in negotiating the contract's details than men, who tend to be mesmerized by many of the techno-toys available and often skip over the fine print and bluff their way through the negotiations.

Knowing that women often approach their purchases differently than men, you would think that smart dealerships would cater to this difference. But this is not the case. Marion W., a volunteer *Lemon-Aid* regional reporter from British Columbia, writes of her showroom experience:

> As a new young widow, shopping alone for the first time, I am totally shocked at the treatment I am receiving at the hands of car salespeople. Whatever happened to sexual equality?
>
> One salesperson had the gall to ask me if I had my husband's permission to buy a car! Another salesperson cornered my 12-year-old son and asked him on the sly if I had the money to buy that particular vehicle. Many dealerships don't even bother to approach me to ask if I would like help, and several have refused to let me drive their vehicles, giving me some pretty flaky reasons why I can't. I have a perfect driving record, so there should be no excuse....

In increasing numbers, women have discovered that minivans and SUVs are more versatile than passenger cars and station wagons. And, having spotted a profitable trend, automakers are offering increased versatility combined with unconventional styling in so-called "crossover" vehicles. These blended cars are part sedan and part station wagon, with a touch of sport-utility added for function and fun. For example, the Chrysler Pacifica is a smaller, sporty crossover vehicle that looks like a miniature SUV. It has been a competent performer during the past few years, but sales have been slow despite sizeable rebates.

What Can I Afford?

Determine how much money you can spend, and then decide which vehicles in that price range interest you. Have several models in mind so that the overpriced one won't tempt you too much. As your benchmarks, use the ratings, alternative models, estimated purchase costs, and residual value figures shown in Part Three of this guide. Remember, logic and prudence are the first casualties of showroom hype, so carefully consider your actual requirements and how much you can budget to meet them before comparing models and prices at a dealership. Write down your first, second, and third choices relative to each model and the equipment offered. Browse the automaker websites and *www.carcostcanada.com/en* for the manufacturer's suggested retail price (MSRP), promotions, and package discounts. Look for special low prices that may only apply to Internet-generated referrals. Once you get a good idea of the price variations, get out the fax machine or PC at home or work (a company letterhead is always impressive) and make the dealers bid against each other (see page 72). Then call the lowest-bidding dealership, ask for an appointment to be assured of getting a sales agent's complete attention, and take along the downloaded info from the automaker's website to avoid arguments.

 ## Can I Get More for Less?

Sure. Sometimes a cheaper twin will fill the bill. Twins are nameplates made by different auto manufacturers or different divisions of the same company that are virtually identical in body design and mechanical components, such as the Chevrolet Cobalt and Pontiac Pursuit.

American manufacturers are a wily bunch. While beating their chests over the need to "buy American," they have joined Asian automakers in co-ventures where they know they can't compete on their own. This has resulted in manufacturing partnerships whose parentage isn't always easy to nail down, but that incorporate a higher degree of quality control than the American company's efforts alone. For example, Toyota and Pontiac churn out identical Matrix and Vibe compacts in Ontario and the United States; however, the cheaper, Ontario-built Matrix has the better reputation for quality. And Suzuki dealers are still selling GM-Daewoos, despite some grumblings about Daewoo's poor quality.

Sometimes choosing a higher trim line will cost you less when you take all the standard features into account. It's hard to compare value prices with the manufacturer's base price, though, because the base prices are inflated and can be negotiated downward, while value-priced cars are usually offered "take it or leave it" with bundled options.

Vehicles that will soon be discontinued, like the Chrysler Neon compact and GM's Astro/Safari minivans, can be bought rather cheaply, thanks to discounting, rebates, and end-of-production bonuses. As long as the vehicles weren't limited-production models, parts and servicing will likely remain unaffected.

And speaking of minivans, they often come in two versions: a base commercial, or cargo, version and a more luxurious model for private use. The commercial versions don't have as many bells and whistles, but they're more likely to be in stock and will probably cost much less. And if you're planning to convert one, there's a wide choice of independent customizers who will likely do a better job than the dealer for less money. Of course, you will want a written guarantee that no changes will invalidate the manufacturer's warranty.

Representing about one-fifth of the new-vehicle market, leasing is an alternative used to make vehicles seem more affordable. Be careful, though—it's really more expensive than buying, and for most people the pitfalls will far outweigh any advantages. If you have to lease, keep your losses to a minimum by leasing for the shortest time possible and by making sure that the lease is close-ended (meaning that you walk away from the vehicle when the lease period ends). CAA estimates that 75 percent of lessees return their vehicles when the lease expires.

Instead of leasing, consider purchasing used. Look for a 3- to 5-year-old vehicle with 60,000–100,000 kilometres on the clock and some of the original warranty left. Such a vehicle will be just as reliable, at less than half the cost of one bought new or leased. Parts will be easier to find, independent servicing should be a breeze, insurance premiums will come down from the stratosphere, and your financial risk will be lessened considerably if you get a lemon. Among compact cars, Honda, Hyundai, Mazda, and Toyota offer you the most value for what you pay. Look in Part Three for detailed ratings.

On both new and used purchases, be wary of unjustified hidden costs, like a $495 "administrative" or "disposal" fee, an "acquisition" charge, and boosted transport and freight costs that can collectively add several thousand dollars to the retail price. You can find out which automakers charge excessive freight and preparation fees at *www.carcostcanada.com*.

What Are My Driving Needs?

Our driving needs are influenced by where we live, our lifestyles, and our ages (see pages 13–16 for a discussion of vehicles best suited for Baby Boomers and mature drivers). The ideal car should be crashworthy and easy to drive, have minimal high-tech features to distract and annoy you, and not cost much to maintain.

In the city, a small wagon or hatchback is more practical and less expensive than a mid-sized car like a Honda Accord or a Toyota Camry. However, if you're going to be doing a lot of highway driving, transporting small groups of people, or loading up on accessories, a medium-sized sedan, wagon, or small sport-utility could be the logical choice for price, comfort, and reliability.

If you travel less than 20,000 kilometres per year, mostly in the city, choose a small car equipped with a 4-cylinder engine that produces between 120 and 140 horsepower to get the best fuel economy without sacrificing performance. Anything more powerful is just a waste. Extensive highway driving, however, demands the cruising performance, extra power for additional accessories, and durability of a larger 6-cylinder engine. Believe me, fuel savings will be the last thing on your mind if you buy an underpowered vehicle.

Pushrod versus overhead cam

Most North American automakers prefer overhead valve engines (or pushrods) because they cost about $800 less, provide better low-end power, use fewer parts, and weigh less than the overhead cam (multi-valve) engines favoured by automakers globally. Still, the more popular overhead cam configuration is used extensively by Japanese manufacturers because this configuration offers more power at higher rpm, provides a smoother idle, and uses variable valve timing for a better torque range, increased fuel economy, and cleaner emissions.

Be especially wary of the towing capabilities bandied about by automakers. They routinely exaggerate towing capability and seldom mention the need for expensive optional equipment, or that the top safe towing speed may be only 72 km/h (45 mph), as is the case with some Japanese minivans.

Remember, you may have to change your driving habits to accommodate the type of vehicle you purchase. Front-drive braking is quite different from braking with a rear drive, and braking efficiency on ABS-equipped vehicles is compromised if you pump the brakes. Also, rear-drive minivans handle like trucks, and will scrub the right rear tire during sharp right-hand turns until you get the hang of making wider turns. Limited rear visibility is another problem with larger vans, forcing drivers to carefully survey side and rear traffic before changing lanes or merging with traffic.

Front-drives

Front-drives direct engine power to the front wheels, which pull the vehicle forward while the rear wheels simply support the rear. The biggest benefit of front-drives is foul-weather traction. With the engine and transmission up front, there's lots of extra weight pressing down on the front-drive wheels, increasing tire grip in snow and on wet pavement. But when you drive up a steep hill or tow a boat or trailer, the weight shifts and you lose the traction advantage.

Although I recommend a number of front-drive vehicles in this guide, I don't like them as much as rear-drives. Granted, front-drives provide a bit more interior room (no transmission hump), more carlike handling, and better fuel economy than do rear-drives, but damage from potholes and fender-benders is usually more extensive, and maintenance costs (especially premature front tire and brake wear) are much higher than with rear-drives.

Rear-drives

Rear-drives direct engine power to the rear wheels, which push the vehicle forward. The front wheels steer and also support the front of the vehicle. With the engine up front, the transmission in the middle, and the drive axle in the rear, there's plenty of room for larger and more durable drivetrain components. This makes for less crash damage, lower maintenance costs, and higher towing capacities than front-drives.

On the downside, rear-drives don't have as much weight over the front wheels as do the front-drives, and therefore they can't provide as much traction on wet and icy roads and tend to fishtail unless they're equipped with an expensive traction-control system.

Four-wheel drive (4X4)

Four-wheel drive (4×4) directs engine power through a transfer case to all four wheels, which pull and push the vehicle forward, giving you twice as much traction. On most models, when four-wheel drive isn't engaged, the vehicle reverts to rear-drive. The large transfer case housing makes the vehicle sit higher, giving you additional ground clearance.

Keep in mind that extended driving over dry pavement with 4×4 engaged will cause the driveline to bind and result in serious damage. Some buyers are turning instead to rear-drive pickups equipped with winches and large, deep-lugged rear tires.

Many 4×4 customers have been turned off by the typically rough and noisy driveline, a tendency for the vehicle to tip over when cornering at moderate speeds (a Ford Bronco and Isuzu Rodeo specialty), vague or trucklike handling, high repair costs, and poor fuel economy.

All-wheel drive (AWD)

Essentially, this is four-wheel drive *all* the time. Used mostly in sedans and minivans, all-wheel drive (AWD) never needs to be de-activated when running over dry pavement and doesn't require the heavy transfer case that raises ground clearance and cuts fuel economy. AWD-equipped vehicles aren't recommended for off-roading because of their lower ground clearance and fragile driveline parts, which aren't as rugged as 4×4 components. Anyhow, you shouldn't be off-roading in a car or minivan in the first place.

Cars for Older Drivers

According to the Canada Safety Council, almost 30 percent of Canada's population was over age 50 in 2002, and half of Canadians 65 and older living in private households drive motor vehicles—though most drive only a few times a week. Furthermore, drivers over 80 are the fastest-growing segment of the driving population. Husbands do the bulk of family driving, which usually involves short trips (11–17 km per day, on average) for medical appointments and visits to family, friends, and shopping malls. This puts older women, who tend to outlive their husbands, in a serious bind because of their lack of driving experience—particularly in rural areas, where driving is a necessity rather than a choice.

Best Choices

Older drivers, like most of us, want cars that are reliable, relatively inexpensive, and fuel-efficient. Additionally, they require vehicles that compensate for some of the physical challenges associated with aging and that provide protection for accidents more common with mature drivers (side impacts, for example). Furthermore, as drivers get older, they find that the very act of getting in a car (sitting down while moving sideways, without bumping their heads or twisting their necks) demands considerable acrobatic skill.

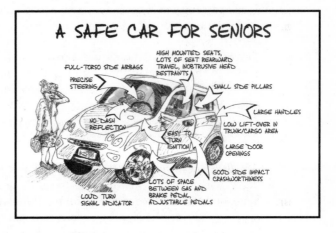

No wonder small wagons set on car platforms are so popular with senior drivers with limited mobility.

Access and comfort

Some drivers with arthritic hands have to insert a pencil into their key ring to twist the key in the ignition. Make sure your ignition lock doesn't require that much effort. Power locks and windows are a must, especially if the vehicle will be operated with hand controls. A remote keyless entry will allow entry without having to twist a key in the door lock. A vehicle equipped with a buttonless shifter will be less difficult to activate for arthritis sufferers and drivers with limited upper-body mobility. Cruise control can be helpful for those with lower-body mobility challenges.

Get a vehicle that's easy to enter and exit. Check for door openings that are wide enough to get in and out of easily, both for you and for any wheelchairs or scooters that may need to be loaded. If necessary, your trunk or rear cargo area should have a low liftover and room to stow a wheelchair or scooter. Bench seats are preferable because they're roomier and easier to access; a power-adjustable driver seat is also a good idea. Make sure the seat is comfortable—rent your choice and take a trip of several hours—and has plenty of side bolstering.

Forget minivans, unless you invest in a step-up, choose one with an easily reached inside grip handle, and don't mind bumping the left-side steering column stalk with your knee each time you slide into the driver's seat. Incidentally, General Motors' minivans offer a Sit-N-Lift option, which is a motorized, rotating lift-and-lower passenger seat that's accessed through the middle door and can be taken out when not needed.

Drivers with limited mobility or those who are recovering from hip surgery give kudos to the Buick LeSabre, Cadillac Escalade, and GM Venture/Montana minivans; Toyota's Echo, Yaris, Matrix, and Avalon; and small SUVs like the Honda CR-V, Hyundai Santa Fe, or Toyota RAV4.

Safety

The driver seat should be mounted high enough to give a commanding view of the road (with slower reaction times, seniors need earlier warnings). Driver seats must offer enough rearward travel to attenuate the force of an exploding airbag, which can be particularly hazardous to older, small-statured occupants, children, and anyone recovering from surgery. Adjustable gas and brake pedals are a must for short-legged drivers.

And, while we're discussing airbags, remember that they are calibrated to *explode* during low-speed collisions (at less than 10 km/h), and reports of injuries caused by their deployment are commonplace. Therefore, always put at least 25 centimetres between your upper torso and the steering wheel. Also, since most intersection collisions involving mature drivers occur when drivers are making a turn into oncoming traffic, head-protecting side airbags are crucial.

Look for handles near the door frame that can be gripped for support when entering or leaving the vehicle, bright dashboard gauges that can be seen in sunlight, and instruments with large-sized controls.

Remote-controlled mirrors are a must, along with adjustable, unobtrusive head restraints and a non-reflective front windshield (many drivers put a cloth on the dash top to cut the distraction). Make sure that the brake and accelerator pedals aren't mounted too close together.

As far as safety features are concerned, a superior crashworthiness rating is essential, as well as torso- and head-protecting side airbags. The extra head protection can make a critical difference in side impacts. For example, Toyota's 2004 RAV4, with $680 head-protecting side airbags earned a "best pick" designation from the Insurance Institute for Highway Safety (IIHS). When tested without the head protection, it received a Poor rating in the side test.

Don't be overly impressed by anti-lock brakes, since their proper operation (no tapping on the brakes) runs counter to everything you have been taught, and they aren't that reliable. Look for headlights that give you a comfortable view at night, as well as easily seen and heard dash-mounted turn signal indicators. Ensure that the vehicle's knobs and switches are large and easy to identify. An easily accessed, full-sized spare tire and user-friendly lug wrench and jack stand are also important.

Trip Tips

Before you begin a—perhaps oxymoronic—driving vacation, make sure that the vehicle is properly serviced, that baggage and occupants don't exceed a safe weight limit, and that visibility is unobstructed. Above all, don't treat the trip as an endurance marathon. Plan your route with rest stops scheduled every two hours or 200 km, don't drive at night (even with glasses, your night vision can be poor) or during weekends (lots of impaired, crazy drivers), and if you fall behind schedule, call ahead to say you'll be a bit late.

Sooner or later, you'll find that everyone on the highway is going much faster than you. Although the speed limit says 100 km/h, most drivers will speed by at 120 km/h. It will also seem like every vehicle in your rear-view mirror is a huge commercial truck hugging your rear bumper. All the more reason to stay in the middle lane and let the speeders pass you by. Why not simply stay all the way to the right? Too many exits that cut off the right lane, or merging cars entering the highway. Your slow speed will likely cause them to speed up and cut you off as they dart from the far-right lane to the middle lane.

When to Stop Driving

Most older drivers know when it's time to stop driving, but many continue driving because they have to. The Ontario Ministry of Transportation lists the following five warning signs that tell you to stop driving:

1. Frequent near collisions
2. Direct involvement in minor collisions
3. Difficulty seeing pedestrians, objects, and other vehicles
4. Difficulty coordinating hand and foot movements
5. Increased nervousness behind the wheel

Safety and Comfort

Do I Feel Comfortable in This Vehicle?

The advantages of many sports cars and minivans quickly pale in direct proportion to your tolerance for a harsh ride, noise, a claustrophobic interior, and limited visibility. Minivan owners often have to deal with a high step-up, a cold interior, lots of buffeting from wind and passing trucks, and poor rear visibility. With these drawbacks, many buyers find that after falling in love with the showroom image, they end up hating their purchase—all the more reason to test-drive your choice over a period of several days to get a real feel for its positive and negative characteristics.

 Check to see if the vehicle's interior is user-friendly. For example, can you reach the sound system and AC controls without straining or taking your eyes off the road? Are the controls just as easy to operate by feel as by sight? What about dash glare onto the front windshield and headlight aim and brightness? Can you drive with the window open and not be subjected to an ear-splitting roar? Do rear-seat passengers have to be contortionists to enter or exit, as is the case with many two-door vehicles?

To answer these questions, you need to drive the vehicle over a period of time to test how well it responds to the diversity of your driving needs, without having some impatient sales agent yapping in your ear. If this isn't possible, you may find out too late that the handling is less responsive than you'd wanted.

You can conduct the following showroom tests: Adjust the seat to a comfortable setting, buckle up, and settle in. Can you sit 25 centimetres away from the steering wheel and still reach the accelerator and brake pedals? When you look out the windshield and use the rear- and side-view mirrors, do you detect any serious blind spots? Will optional mirrors give you an unobstructed view? Does the seat feel comfortable enough for long trips? Can you reach important controls without moving off the seatback? If not, shop for something that better suits your needs.

What Safety Features Are Best?

Automakers are loading 2006–07 models with features that wouldn't have been imagined several decades ago, because safety devices appeal to families and some, like airbags, can be marked up by 500 percent. Yet some safety innovations, such as anti-lock brakes, don't deliver the safety payoffs promised by automakers and may create additional dangers. Some of the more effective safety features are head-protecting side and de-powered airbags, electronic stability control, adjustable brake and accelerator pedals, standard integrated child safety seats, seat belt pre-tensioners, adjustable head restraints, and sophisticated navigation and communication systems.

Seat belts provide the best means of reducing the severity of injury arising from both low- and high-speed frontal collisions. In order to be effective, though, seat belts must be adjusted properly and feel comfortably tight without undue slack. Owners often complain that seat belts don't retract enough for a snug fit, are too tight, chafe the neck, and don't properly fit children. Some automakers have corrected these problems with adjustable shoulder-belt anchors that allow both tall and short drivers to raise or lower the belt for a snug, more comfortable fit. Another important seat belt innovation is the pretensioner (not found on all seat belts), a device that automatically tightens the safety belt in the event of a crash.

More Safety Considerations

There are no more easy safety solutions. According to the National Highway Traffic Safety Association's (NHTSA) 2003 figures, 50 percent of car occupants and 70 percent of pickup crash fatalities weren't wearing seat belts. This statistic is all the more troubling because everyone knows safety belt use saves lives. Clearly, half of us don't give a damn.

Although there has been a dramatic reduction in fatalities and injuries over the past three decades, safety experts feel that additional automobile safety features will henceforth pay small dividends. They say it's time to target the driver, after reviewing NHTSA's studies that show 76 percent of almost 7 million annual crashes on North American highways are caused by driver error, 14 percent are attributed to driver impairment (drugs, alcohol, or illness), and 8 percent are caused by the environment (roads and weather). Just 2 percent are caused by vehicle problems such as tires or poor design.

This means that safety programs that concentrate primarily on motor vehicle standards won't be as effective as measures that target the driver, such as stricter licence requirements, including graduated licensing and de-licensing directed at teens and seniors, and stricter law enforcement.

Incidentally, police studies have shown an important side benefit to arresting traffic law scofflaws: They often net dangerous career criminals and seriously impaired drivers before they harm others. Apparently, sociopaths and substance abusers don't care which laws they break.

Active Safety

Advocates of active safety stress that accidents are caused by the proverbial "nut behind the wheel," and believe that safe driving can best be taught through schools or by private driving courses. Active safety components are generally those mechanical systems, such as anti-lock brake systems (ABS), high-performance tires, and traction control, that may help avoid accidents if the driver is skillful and mature.

The theory of active safety has several drawbacks. First, many fatal accidents are caused by drivers who are under the influence of alcohol or drugs. All the high-performance options and specialized driving courses in the world will not make these criminals safer drivers. Second, because active safety components get a lot of use—you're likely to need anti-lock brakes 99 times more often than an airbag—they have to be well designed and easily serviced to remain effective. Finally, consider that independent studies show that safe driving taught to young drivers doesn't reduce deaths and injuries (the most relevant study can be found in the *Lancet*, July 2001; 1978 DeKalb County, Georgia).

Passive Safety

Passive safety assumes that you will be involved in life-threatening situations and should be warned in time to avoid a collision or automatically protected from rolling over, losing traction, or bearing the brunt of collision forces. Enhanced stability control, daytime running lights, and a third, centre-mounted brake light are three passive safety features that have paid off handsomely in reduced injuries and lives saved.

Passive safety features also assume some accidents aren't avoidable and that, when those accidents occur, vehicles should provide as much protection as possible to drivers, passengers, and other vehicles that may be struck—without depending on the driver's reactions. Passive safety components that have consistently been proven to reduce vehicular deaths and injuries are seat belts, vehicle structures that enhance crashworthiness by absorbing or deflecting crash forces away from the vehicle's occupants, and laminated windshields.

Rollovers

Although rollovers represent only 3 percent of crashes (10,000 annual U.S. road accidents), they cause a third of all traffic deaths from what are usually single-vehicle accidents.

Rollovers occur less frequently with passenger cars and minivans than with SUVs, trucks, and full-sized vans (especially the 15-passenger variety). That's why electronic vehicle stability systems aren't as important a safety feature on passenger cars as on vans, pickups, and SUVs. All of the rollover ratings for prior years and models can be found at *www.nhtsa.dot.gov/ncap*.

Crashworthiness

A vehicle with a high crash protection rating is a lifesaver. In fact, crashworthiness is the one safety improvement over the past 40 years that everyone agrees has paid off handsomely without presenting any additional risks to drivers or passengers. By surrounding occupants with a protective cocoon and deflecting crash forces away from the interior, auto engineers have successfully created safer vehicles without increasing vehicle size or cost. And purchasing a vehicle with the idea that you'll be involved in an accident some day is not unreasonable. According to IIHS, the average car will likely have two accidents before ending up as scrap and is twice as likely to be in a severe front-impact crash as a side-impact crash.

Since some vehicles are more crashworthy than others, and since size doesn't always guarantee crash safety, it's important to buy a vehicle that gives you the best protection from a frontal, a frontal offset, and a side collision, while keeping rollover potential to a minimum.

For example, the Chrysler Caravan and Ford Windstar minivans are similarly designed, but your chances of surviving a high-speed collision are far greater with the Windstar than they are with a Caravan or any other Chrysler minivan. The chance that your Windstar will survive a trip to the service bay is less certain.

Two Washington-based agencies monitor how vehicle design affects crash safety: NHTSA and IIHS. Crash information from these two groups doesn't always correspond because, while IIHS's results incorporate all kinds of accidents, including offset crashes and bumper damage sustained from low-speed collisions, NHTSA's figures relate only to 56 km/h (35 mph) frontal and some side collisions. The frontal tests are equivalent to two vehicles of equal weight hitting each other head-on while travelling at 56 km/h or to a car slamming into a parked car at 114 km/h (70 mph). Bear in mind that a vehicle providing good injury protection may also cost more to repair because its structure, not the occupants, absorbs most of the collision forces. That's why safer vehicles don't always have lower insurance rates.

Don't get taken in by the five-star crash rating hoopla touted by automakers. There isn't any one vehicle that can claim a prize for being safest. Vehicles that do well in NHTSA side and front crash tests may not do very well in IIHS offset crash tests, or may have poorly designed head restraints that can increase the severity of neck injuries. Or a vehicle may have a high number of airbag failures, such as the bags deploying when they shouldn't or not deploying when they should.

Before making a final decision on the vehicle you want, look up its crashworthiness and overall safety profile in Part Three.

Cars versus trucks (size matters, sometimes)

Occupants of large vehicles have fewer severe injury claims than do occupants of small vehicles. This was proven conclusively in a 1996 NHTSA study, which showed that collisions between light trucks or vans and small cars resulted in an 81 percent higher fatality rate for the occupants of the small cars than occupants of the light trucks or vans.

Vehicle weight offers the most protection in two-vehicle crashes. In a head-on crash, for example, the heavier vehicle drives the lighter one backward, which decreases forces inside the heavy vehicle and increases forces in the lighter one. All heavy vehicles, even poorly designed ones, offer this advantage in two-vehicle collisions. However, they may not offer good protection in single-vehicle crashes.

Crash test figures show that SUVs, vans, and trucks also offer more protection to adult occupants than do passenger cars in most crashes because their higher set-up allows them to ride over other vehicles (Ford's 2002 4×4 Explorer lowered its bumper height to prevent this hazard). Conversely, because of their high centre of gravity, easily overloaded tires, and unforgiving suspensions, these vehicles have a disproportionate number of single-vehicle rollovers, which are far deadlier than frontal or side collisions. In the case of the early Ford Explorer, Bridgestone/Firestone CEO John Lampe testified August 2001 that 42 of 43 rollovers involving Ford Explorers in Venezuela were on competitors' tires—shifting the rollover blame to the Explorer's design and crashworthiness.

Interestingly, a vehicle's past crashworthiness rating doesn't always guarantee that subsequent model years will be just as safe or safer. Take Ford's 1991 Escort as an example. It earned five stars for front passenger collision protection and then earned fewer stars every year thereafter, until the model was discontinued in 2002. The 2000 Dodge Caravan is another example. It was given five stars for driver side protection and has earned four stars ever since.

Safety Features That Kill

In the late '60s, Washington forced automakers to include essential safety features like collapsing steering columns and safety windshields in their cars. As the years have passed, the number of mandatory safety features has increased to include seat belts, airbags, and crashworthy construction. These improvements met with public approval until quite recently, when reports of deaths and injuries caused by ABS and airbag failures showed that defective components and poor engineering negated the potential life-saving benefits associated with these devices.

For example, one out of every five ongoing NHTSA defect investigations concerns inadvertent airbag deployment, deactivation of the front passenger airbag, failure of the airbag to deploy, or injuries suffered when the bag did go off. In fact, airbags are the agency's single largest cause of current investigations, exceeding even the full range of brake problems, which runs second.

Anti-Lock Brake Systems (ABS)

I am not a fan of ABS brakes. They are often ineffective, failure-prone, and expensive to service.

Essentially, ABS prevents a vehicle's wheels from locking when the brakes are applied in an emergency situation, thus reducing skidding and the loss of directional control. When braking on wet and dry roads, your stopping distance will be about the same as with conventional braking systems. But in gravel, slush, or snow, your stopping distance will be greater.

The most important feature of ABS is that it preserves steering control. As you brake in an emergency, ABS will release the brakes if it senses wheel lock-up. Braking distances will lengthen accordingly, but at least you'll have some steering control. But if you start sliding on glare ice, don't expect ABS to help you out very much. The laws of physics (no friction, no stopping!) still apply on ABS-equipped vehicles. You can decrease the stopping distance, however, by removing your all-season tires and installing four snow tires that are the same make and size.

Transport Canada studies show ABS effectiveness is highly overrated. IIHS—an American insurance research group that collects and analyzes insurance claims data—says that cars with ABS brakes are actually more likely to be in crashes where no other car is involved but a passenger is killed. Other insurance claim statistics show that ABS brakes aren't producing the overall safety benefits that were predicted by the government and automakers. One IIHS study found that a passenger has a 45 percent greater chance of dying in a single-vehicle crash in a car with anti-lock brakes than in the same car with old-style brakes. On wet pavement, where ABS supposedly excels, that figure rises to a 65 percent greater chance of being killed. In multi-vehicle crashes, ABS-equipped vehicles have a passenger death rate 6 percent higher than vehicles not equipped with ABS.

The high cost of ABS maintenance is another problem that few safety advocates mention, but consider the following: original parts can cost five times more than regular braking components, and many dealers prefer to replace the entire ABS unit rather than troubleshoot a very complex system.

Keep in mind that anti-lock brakes are notoriously unreliable on all makes and models. They often fail completely, resulting in no braking whatsoever, or they may extend stopping distance by 30 percent. This phenomenon is amply documented throughout NHTSA's complaint database.

Airbag Dangers (Unsafe at Any Speed?)

First the good news: It is estimated that airbags have reduced head-on crash fatalities by up to 30 percent and moderate-to-severe injuries by 25 to 29 percent. Injury claims at hospitals resulting from traffic crashes have dropped 24 percent as a result of airbags.

But there is a downside to airbag use. To begin with, no airbag is safe, although some model years are safer than others. Pre-'97 airbags explode too forcefully and can seriously injure or kill occupants vulnerable to injury. Later de-powered "smart" devices are less hazardous, but they're not smart enough. Many systems will turn off the airbag if a seat is covered, or if an occupant weighs less than 120 pounds.

Inadvertent airbag deployment

Airbags frequently go off for no apparent reason, usually because of faulty sensors. Causes of sudden deployment include passing over a bump in the road; slamming the car door; having wet carpets; or, in some Chrysler minivans, simply putting the key in the ignition.

This happens more often than you might imagine, judging by the frequent recalls and thousands of complaints recorded on NHTSA's website at *www-odi.nhtsa.dot.gov/cars/problems/complain/complaintsearch.cfm*. Incidentally, dealers and manufacturers are routinely denying claims by alleging that airbags don't go off without a collision. They usually back down if the insured presses the issue.

> On June 17, 2004, after dropping my son off for baseball practice in Toronto, I decided to run a couple of errands. Upon returning to the ball field, I put my 1998 Dodge Grand Caravan in park and turned off the ignition. Immediately thereafter my airbag deployed. I was struck on the left side of my face and neck and my left ear received some trauma. The *bang* from the air bag deploying was so loud that people from three surrounding ball fields heard the blast....

•

> Our airbags on our 2003 Volkswagen Jetta TDI deployed for no reason on a smooth surface July 3, 2004. We were denied warranty because the Calgary Volkswagen field technician found two small dents on the bottom of the car. We met another Volkswagen Jetta TDI driver who experienced basically the same as us on July 1, 2004, and was also denied warranty. An employee at the dealership stated that another customer had an airbag deploy on a Jetta one month earlier causing $5,600 in damage...The deployment of our airbag tore open the ceiling along the passenger side of the car, ruptured the seat, damaged the panel beside the passenger seat, and immobilized the front passenger seat belt...These airbags instead of bringing safety are more of a danger. If we had been aware of this or the way Volkswagen would respond to this problem, we never would have bought from them....

If you are hit from the rear and thrown within 25 centimetres of the steering wheel as the airbag deploys, you risk severe head, neck, or chest trauma, or even death. If you are making a turn, with your arms crossing in front of the steering wheel, you are out of position and risk fractures to both arms. If you drive with your thumbs extended a bit into the steering hub area, as I often do, you risk losing both thumbs when the housing cover explodes.

Sometimes, just being female is enough to get you killed. Two startling 1996 and 1998 Transport Canada–financed studies were uncovered in October 1999 as part of a CBC *Marketplace* investigation into airbag safety. The consumer TV show unearthed research that showed that airbags reduce the risk of injury by only an additonal 2 percent for adults who wear seat belts, while *increasing* the risk of injury to women by 9 percent and the risk of death for children by 21 percent.

Airbag benefits generally outweigh their shortcomings, and they shouldn't be disabled without good reason. If you feel vulnerable, you'll want to choose a vehicle with adjustable brake and accelerator pedals or an adjustable seat that can travel backward far enough to keep you at a safe distance (about 25 cm, or one foot) from the front airbag's explosive force. Children's safety can be assured by getting a vehicle with an airbag shut-off switch, or by having the children sit in the rear middle seat position, away from front seatbacks, which frequently collapse in rear-enders.

Side airbags—good and bad

In crashes with another passenger vehicle, 51 percent of driver deaths in recent model cars during 2000–01 occurred in side impacts, up from 31 percent in 1980–81.

Side airbags and side curtains are designed to protect drivers and passengers in rollovers and side-impact crashes, which are estimated to account for almost a third of vehicular deaths. They also have been shown to help keep unbelted occupants from being ejected in rollovers. Head-protecting side airbags can reduce serious crash injuries by 45 percent. Side airbags without head protection reduce injuries by only 10 percent. Ideally, you want a side airbag system that protects both the torso and head.

Because side airbags aren't required by federal regulation in Canada or the States, neither government has developed any tests to measure their safety for children and small adults. IIHS hopes its test results will goad government regulators and automakers into standardizing the design of side airbags and increasing their effectiveness and safety.

There is a downside to increased side airbag protection: Sit properly in your seat, or face serious injury from the deploying side airbag. Preliminary safety studies show side airbags may be deadly to children or to any occupant sitting too close to the airbag, resting his or her head on the side pillar, or holding onto the roof-mounted assist handle. Research carried out in 1998 by safety researchers (Anil Khadikar, Biodynamics Engineering Inc., and Lonney Pauls, Springwater Micro Data Systems, "Assessment of Injury Protection Performance of Side Impact Airbags") shows there are four hazards that have yet to be addressed by automakers:

1. Inadvertent airbag firing (short circuit, faulty hardware or software)
2. Unnecessary firing (sometimes the opposite-side airbag will fire; the airbag may deploy when a low-speed side-swipe wouldn't have endangered occupant safety)
3. A three-year-old restrained in a booster seat could be seriously injured
4. Out-of-position restrained occupants could be seriously injured

The researchers conclude with the following observation: "Even properly restrained vehicle occupants can have their upper or lower extremities in harm's way in the path of an exploding [side] airbag."

The 1998 study and dozens of other scientific papers confirm that small and tall restrained drivers face death or severe injury from frontal and side airbag deployments for the simple reason that they are outside of the norm of the 5'8", 180 lb., male test dummy.

These studies also debunk the safety merits of ABS brakes, so it's no surprise they go unheralded by Transport Canada and other government and private safety groups. With a bit of patience, though, you can find this research at *www.nhtsa.dot.gov/esv.*

In the meantime, don't forget NHTSA's side airbag warning issued on October 14, 1999:

> Side impact airbags can provide significant supplemental safety benefits to adults in side impact crashes. However, children who are seated in close proximity to a side airbag may be at risk of serious or fatal injury, especially if the child's head, neck, or chest is in close proximity to the airbag at the time of deployment.

Protect yourself

Because not all airbags function, or malfunction, the same way, *Lemon-Aid* has done an exhaustive analysis of U.S. and Canadian recalls, crash data, and owner complaints to determine which vehicles and which model years use airbags that may seriously injure occupants or deploy inadvertently. That data can be found in Part Three's model ratings.

Additionally, you should take the following steps to reduce the danger from airbag deployment:

- Buy a vehicle with head-protecting side airbags for front and rear passengers.
- Make sure that seat belts are buckled and all head restraints are properly adjusted (about ear level).
- Make sure the head restraints are rated Good by IIHS in Part Three.
- Insist that passengers who are frail, short, or have recently had surgery sit in the back and are properly positioned away from side airbags.
- Make sure that the driver's seat can be adjusted for height and has tracks with sufficient rearward travel to allow short drivers to remain a safe distance (over 25 centimetres) away from the bag's deployment and still reach the accelerator and brake.
- If you are short-statured, consider buying pedal extensions to keep you a safe distance away from a deploying airbag.

Top 20 Safety Defects

The U.S. federal government's online safety complaints database contains well over 100,000 entries, going back to vehicles made in the late '70s. Although the database was originally intended to record incidents of component failures that only relate to safety, you will find every problem imaginable dutifully recorded by clerks working for NHTSA.

A perusal of the listed complaints shows that some safety-related failures occur more frequently than others and often affect one manufacturer more than another. Here is a summary of some of the more commonly reported failures, in order of frequency:

1. Airbags not deploying when they should or deploying when they shouldn't
2. ABS total brake failure; wheel lock-up
3. Tire tread separation
4. Electrical or fuel system fires
5. Sudden acceleration
6. Sudden stalling
7. Sudden electrical failure
8. Transmission failing to engage or suddenly disengaging
9. Transmission jumping from Park to Reverse or Neutral; vehicle rolling away when parked
10. Steering or suspension failure
11. Seat belt failures
12. Collapsing seatbacks
13. Defective sliding door, door locks, and latches
14. Poor headlight illumination
15. Dash reflecting onto windshield

16. Hood flying up
17. Wheel falling away
18. Steering wheel lifting off
19. Transmission lever pulling out
20. Exploding windshields

Other Buying Considerations

When New Isn't "New"

Nothing will cause you to lose money more quickly than buying a new car that's older than advertised, has previously been sold and taken back, has accident damage, or has had the odometer disconnected or turned back.

Even if the vehicle hasn't been used, it may have been left outdoors for a considerable length of time, causing the deterioration of rubber components, premature body and chassis rusting, or severe rusting of internal mechanical parts, which leads to brake malfunction, fuel line contamination, hard starting, and stalling.

 You can check a vehicle's age by looking at the date-of-manufacture plate found on the driver-side door pillar. If the date of manufacture is 7/05, your vehicle was probably one of the last 2005 models made before the September changeover to the 2006s. Redesigned vehicles or those new to the market are exceptions to this rule. They may arrive at dealerships in early spring or mid-summer, and are considered to be next year's models. They also depreciate more quickly, owing to their earlier launching, but this difference narrows over time.

Sometimes, a vehicle can be too new, and cost you more in maintenance because redesign glitches haven't yet been worked out. As Honda's North American manufacturing chief, Koki Hirashima, so ably put it, carryover models generally have fewer problems than vehicles that have been significantly reworked or just introduced to the market. Newly redesigned vehicles get quality scores that are, on average, 2 percent worse than vehicles that have been around for a while, says J.D. Power. Some surprising poor performers: the 2002 Jaguar X-Type, the 2002 Nissan Altima, the 2002 Toyota Avalon and Camry, and the 2001 Honda Civic. More recently, the 2004 Nissan Quest and the Toyota Sienna failed to live up to expectations.

Because they were the first off the assembly line for that model year, most vehicles assembled between September and February are called "first-series" cars. "Second-series" vehicles, made between March and August, incorporate more assembly-line fixes and are better built than the earlier models, which may depend on ineffective "field fixes" to mask problems until the warranty expires. Second-series vehicles will sell for the same price or less, but they will be a far better buy because of their assembly-line upgrades and more generous rebates. Chrysler's new Caliber and Charger, GM's Solstice, Torrent, and Sky roadsters, and the Ford Fusion, Zephyr, and Milan are all prime candidates for second-series shopping.

There's also the very real possibility that the new vehicle you've just purchased was damaged while being shipped to the dealer and was later fixed in the service bay during the pre-delivery inspection. It's estimated that this happens to about 10 percent of all new vehicles. Although there's no specific Canadian legislation allowing buyers of vehicles damaged in transit to cancel their contracts, B.C. legislation says that dealers must disclose damages of $2,000 or more. In a more general sense, Canadian common-law jurisprudence *does* allow for cancellation or compensation whenever the delivered product differs markedly from what the buyer expected to receive. Ontario's revised *Consumer Protection Act* is particularly hard-nosed in prohibiting this kind of misrepresentation.

Fuel-Economy Follies

The hidden expense of poor gas mileage is one of the top complaints among owners of new cars and minivans. Drivers say gas mileage is seldom as high as it's hyped to be; in fact, it's likely to be 10–20 percent *less* than advertised. *Consumer Reports* magazine estimates that 90 percent of vehicles sold don't get the gas mileage advertised, and targeted hybrids built by Honda and Toyota as the worst offenders.

This is not a new phenomenon. Environment Canada's independent research confirms that 2003–04 models were much less fuel efficient than vehicles built 15 years ago. At that time, cars and trucks averaged 10.5L/100 km; now it's estimated by independent analysis to be 11.2L/100 km, once all of the gas-guzzling SUVs and pickups were factored into the study. Even more astounding, a Ford Model T got 7.8–11.5L/100 km (25–30 mpg)

C'mon Toyota, 'fess up. *Canadian Driver, Car and Driver, Consumer Reports, Edmunds.com,* EPA, and SAE can't all be wrong...hybrid fuel-economy is much less than advertised.

nearly a century ago. Today, the average Ford gets 12.5L/100 km (23 mpg).

Why such a contradiction between promise and performance?

It's simple: Automakers cheat on their tests. They submit their own test results to the government after testing under optimum conditions. Transport Canada then publishes these self-serving "cooked" figures as its own research. One Ford service bulletin is remarkably frank in discounting the validity of these tests:

In theory this kind of misrepresentation is actionable, but no successful consumer lawsuit has been reported in Canada. Most people simply live with the fact that they were fooled.

And that's understandable. Although good fuel economy is important, it's hardly worth a harsh ride, excessive highway noise, side-wind buffeting, anemic acceleration, and a cramped interior. You may end up with much worse gas mileage than advertised and a vehicle that's underpowered for your needs.

FUEL ECONOMY CONVERSION TABLE

L/100 KM	MPG	L/100 KM	MPG	L/100 KM	MPG
5.0	56	7.4	38	12.5	23
5.2	54	7.6	37	13.0	22
5.4	52	7.8	36	13.5	21
5.6	50	8.0	35	14.0	20
5.8	48	8.5	33	15.0	19
6.0	47	9.0	31	15.0	18
6.2	46	9.5	30	17.0	17
6.4	44	10.0	28	18.0	16
6.7	43	10.5	27	19.0	15
6.8	42	11.0	26	20.0	14
7.0	40	11.5	25	21.0	13
7.2	39	12.0	24	23.0	12

If you never quite got the hang of metric fuel economy measurements, use this fuel conversion table to establish how many miles to a gallon of gas your vehicle provides.

Finally, let's not leave the subject of fuel economy fantasies without mentioning the Pogue Carburetor, Canada's own fuel economy urban legend.

In 1935, Canadian inventor Charles Nelson Pogue tried to patent a "miracle" carburetor that he said produced fuel economy in the range of 200-plus mpg (1.17L/100 km). This claim was supported in the May 1936 issue of *Canadian Automotive Trade* magazine, which reported that a 1,879-mile (3,000 km) trip used only 14.5 gallons (55L) of fuel. Pogue later denied the story.

On *Snopes.com*, the Pogue carburetor's performance is further debunked:

No one reputable was allowed to see the mechanical miracle in action, let alone have a chance to measure its results. After the initial excitement over Pogue's 1936 announcement had faded, more serious types began to openly doubt that the carburetor would work as described....

Pogue's miracle carburetor was heard of no more. Faced with the choice of believing that Pogue had made false claims about his invention or that a moneyed bad guy had bought up the technology to forever keep it off the market, some chose to believe the suppression theory.

Excessive Maintenance Fees

Maintenance inspections and parts represent hidden costs that are usually exaggerated by dealers and automakers to increase their profits on vehicles that rarely require fixing or that are sold in insufficient numbers to support a service bay. Both Mazda and Honda owners suspect this to be the case, and a CBC *Marketplace* survey confirms the accusations against Mazda dealers.

In an investigative report shown on February 18, 2003, CBC TV's *Marketplace* surveyed 12 Mazda dealers across the country to determine how much they charged for a "regularly scheduled maintenance inspection" as listed in the owner's manual of a 2001 Mazda MPV with 48,000 km (*www.cbc.ca/consumers/market/files/cars/mazda_warranty*). Even with different labour rates, Mazda says the check-up should not cost more than about $280 anywhere in Canada. Here are the prices they were quoted:

- $400 (Montreal)
- $546 (Burlington)
- $225 (Toronto)
- $300 (Toronto)
- $271 (Winnipeg)
- $700 (Winnipeg)
- $253 (Calgary)
- $340 (Calgary)
- $450 (Calgary)
- $350 (Vancouver)
- $500 (Vancouver)
- $525 (Vancouver)

The first quote for service in Winnipeg was $700. A service technician told *Marketplace*'s producer that the price varied between $400 and $500 and warned that the work was needed to maintain the warranty. However, a check of the owner's manual didn't show any connection between the service and keeping the warranty in place. Gregory Young, director of Corporate Public Relations for Mazda Canada said, "There's nothing in the owner's manual that says if you don't have this work done in its entirety at a prescribed time that automatically your warranty is void."

Alan Gelman, a well-known Toronto garage owner and host of CFRB radio's *Car Talk*, warns drivers:

> There are actually two maintenance schedules handed out by car companies and dealers. The dealer inspection sheets often call for far more extensive and expensive routine maintenance checks than what's listed in the owner's manual. Most of those checks are padding; smart owners will stick with the essential checks listed in the manual and have them done by cheaper, independent garages.

Getting routine work done at independent facilities will cost about a third to one-half the price usually charged by dealers. Just be sure to follow the automaker's suggested schedule so no warranty claim can be tied to botched servicing. Additionally, a $25 ALLDATA service bulletin subscription (see Appendix I) will keep you current as to your vehicle's factory defects, required check-ups, recalls, and what's covered by little-known "goodwill" warranties (see Chrysler, Ford, and GM bulletin summaries on pages 51–54) and will save you valuable time and money when troubleshooting common problems (I just *hate* it when mechanics replace all of the good parts to get to that one defective component).

Who Can You Trust?

Very few people or agencies, it appears.

The government lies to us about fuel economy and airbag dangers. Automakers lie to us about the reliability and "real" prices of their products. Car dealers routinely charge us for services covered by "goodwill" extended warranties and put pricing information in such small print in newspapers that no one can read it. And most car journalists lie to us when they say that they're unbiased.

Most investigative stories done on the auto industry in Canada (such as exposés on secret car warranties, dangerous airbags, and car company shenanigans) have been written by business columnists, freelancers, or "action line" troubleshooters rather than by reporters on the auto beat. This is because most auto beat reporters are regularly beaten into submission by myopic editors and greedy publishers who don't give them the time nor the encouragement to do hard-hitting investigative exposés. In fact, it's quite impressive that we do have a small cadre of reporters who won't be cowed. Links to some of the best Canadian and American sites can be found at *www.lemonaidcars.com* or in Appendix I.

Here are some examples:

- The non-profit Automobile Protection Association (*www.apa.ca*) is a consumer protection website. The group specializes in exposing unsafe and unreliable cars and trucks. Presently, it is in the middle of a campaign to get Ford Canada to recall 1997–2004 F-Series trucks with defective tie-rod ends that may suddenly throw the truck out of control. After almost two years of APA pressure, Ford's only reponse has been to send a service letter reminding owners to inspect or repair their truck—at the owners' expense, of course.
- *Straight-six.com* is an Ottawa-based independent car enthusiast website that offers a unique and entertaining voice to the dedicated car zealot. The editorial content, mostly written by publisher John LeBlanc, focuses on topics ranging from automaker marketing strategies to product and business trends. Readers of *straight-six.com* get unbiased, no BS, non-PR reviews and commentary on automotive issues related to the love of driving cars. LeBlanc is at his best when

he gives no-nonsense reviews of high-performance vehicles and proves that dollar power doesn't always convert to performance power.

- Toronto-based Kurt Binnie's *onthehoist.com* is a well-written weblog replete with auto information from a consumer advocacy and car enthusiast perspective (not an easy balance). Binnie buttresses information files and real price quotes with zillions of URLs from around the world that run the gamut from the well known to the obscure. Take, for example, Chrysler's decision to drop its 7-year powertrain warrant on 2006 models. Kurt quotes an Edmunds *Inside Line* article that had this to say:

> Chrysler, realizing their cars suck, cancels 7-year/70,000 mile warranty. Will instead offer free breadcrumb trail of auto parts back to the dealership as you drive off.

ONTHEHOIST.COM
MAY 5, 2005

- The *Canadian Driver* website (*www.canadiandriver.com*) offers a cornucopia of Canadian car critics who are relatively independent of industry influence.

Jeremy Cato and Michael Vaughn, who host the *Globe and Mail*–affiliated *Report on Business* daily TV show out of Toronto, epitomize the best combination of auto journalism and business reporting. This duo asks the tough questions that automakers hate to answer. On Saturday nights, Toronto's CityPulse24 goes after dishonest or incompetent dealers and automakers as Mohamed Bouchama, president of Car Help Canada, shakes up the industry by rating new and used cars, providing legal advice, and teaching consumers the art of complaining. The *Vancouver Sun*'s Linda Bates does an outstanding job without compromising her integrity and was the first to blow the whistle on "bad gas" in B.C. There's also the *Toronto Star*'s Ellen Roseman, one of Canada's foremost consumer advocates and business columnists who recently skewered Mazda Canada over its $40,000 RX-8 sports cars that won't start:

> We did our own search and found many similar stories, including one from [an] owner who gave the car a one-star rating (out of five) at *Consumer Reports* magazine's website. "A nightmare for any woman," she wrote. "Cannot move to wash, etc., or engine will flood."
>
> Mazda put out a service bulletin in February, which can be found online, covering repair techniques for flooded 2004 and 2005 RX-8 models that have to be towed into dealerships. (The title: "Engine cranks, no start.")

TORONTO STAR
MAY 28, 2005

Maryanna Lewyckyj is another crusading consumer advocate and journalist. She is a *Toronto Sun* business and consumer columnist who is more car-savvy than most automaker PR stuffed shirts. Recently, Chrysler press honchos had the Toronto motoring press fawning over their announcement they were extending low-interest financing throughout Canada as a service to buyers everywhere. When Lewyckyj took a close look at the numbers, she came away unimpressed, and effectively torpedoed Chrysler's pro-consumer pretensions.

And then there's my fellow Montrealer, Phil Bailey, a Lachine, Quebec, garage owner with over four decades of experience with European, Japanese, and American cars. In his insightful comments on the car industry, he's as skillful with his pen as he is with a wrench; plus, he's got the everyday garage experience that make him and Toronto CFRB broadcaster Alan Gelman such unimpeachable auto-industry critics.

Here's what Bailey has to say about hybrid vehicles, the *enfant cherie* of most car journalists and tree-huggers (*www.baileycar.com/baileyblog.html*):

Everybody in the hybrid market is losing money. The current units, which are very complex, cost about $5,000 more than a normal IC engine. The buyer is paying about a $3,000 premium, which means the manufacturer is upside-down for about $2,000... [F]uel economy gains are less than people think, what with winter when the heater and defroster are used and summer when the A/C is in operation. Yes, there is a small improvement in city mpg, but it's negligible on the open road. Couple that with the still-undetermined cost of maintenance of the Rube Goldberg power units and the unknown life cycle of the battery packs, and the economic advantages become hazy at best. A great deal depends on the future price of gasoline or if the government radically increases fuel mileage standards. But as it stands now, the average customer is going to stay with a conventional automobile because the mpg cost factor makes obvious economic sense. The price of fuel and lower cost technology will govern the market, and the role hybrids will play remains doubtful at best....

These reporters and advocates are the exception, not the rule. Even the most ardent reporters frequently have to jump through hoops to get their stories out simply because their editors or station managers have bought into many of the fraudulent practices so common to the auto industry. Haranguing staff for more "balance" is the pretext *du jour* for squelching hard-hitting stories implicating dealers and automakers. News editors don't want truth, they want copy and comfort. They'll spend weeks sifting through Paul Martin's or Belinda Stronach's trash cans looking for conflicts of interest or love letters, while ignoring the auto industry scams threaded throughout their own classified ads.

Want proof? Go ahead and try to decipher the fine print in *the Globe and Mail* or *Toronto Star* leasing ads or, better yet, try to decipher the fine print scrolled at breakneck speed on television new-vehicle commercials. Think about this: Dealers selling used cars from residences, posing as private parties ("curbsiders"), are periodically exposed by dealer associations and "crusading" auto journalists. Yet these scam artists place dozens or more ads weekly in the classified section of local newspapers, where the same phone numbers and billing addresses constantly reappear, sometimes merely days after the scam has been featured in local news reports. The ad order-takers know who these crooks are. News editors know that their own papers are promoting these scammers. But classified ad sellers care only about selling ads. And although car columnists claim that their integrity is not for sale, there's no doubt that it can be rented. Travel junkets and public relations and advertising contracts all sweeten the pot for these pseudo-journalists.

Two of my favourite auto journalists, Dan Neil, automotive writer for the liberal *Los Angeles Times,* and Robert Farago, a long-time auto critic and creator of *The Truth About Cars*, a British-based website, were both punished this past year for writing the truth.

Neil's paper was hit by a $10 million (U.S.) loss after General Motors and its dealers pulled their ads in response to his sharp criticism of GM for a series of poor management decisions that lead to the flop of its 2005 G6 model:

> GM is a morass of a business case, but one thing seems clear enough, and Lutz's mistake was to state the obvious and then recant: The company's multiplicity of divisions and models is turning into a circular firing squad...someone's head ought to roll, and the most likely candidate would be the luminous white noggin of Lutz...[the G6] is not an awful car. It's entirely adequate. But plainly, adequate is not nearly enough...

> *LOS ANGELES TIMES*
> APRIL 6, 2005

The *Times* stood by Neil, a Pulitzer Prize–winning automobile columnist. GM's ads eventually returned after a hiatus of several months.

Farago didn't fare as well. In late August 2005, he was canned and stayed canned. His column was permanently axed, without explanation, by the uber-liberal *San*

The Subaru Tribeca.

Francisco Chronicle after his criticism of Subaru's Tribeca, an SUV wannabe that never will be:

I'm not sure if the *Chronicle* removed my description of the SUV's front end as a "flying vagina" (the editors ignored my request for a copy of the published review), but even without it my analysis of the B9 was not bound to please its manufacturer....

In fact, the Subaru B9 Tribeca is both subjectively (to the best of my knowledge and experience) and empirically a dreadful machine that besmirches the reputation of its manufacturer. Sure, the B9 handles well. The review pointed this out. But to suggest that it's an SUV worthy of its manufacturer's hype ("The end of the SUV as we know it" and "The ideal balance of power and refinement") is to become a co-conspirator in Subaru's attempts to mislead the public....

And here's the thing: I believe the media in general, and newspapers in particular, have an obligation to tell the truth about cars. You know all those puff pieces that fill up the odd blank spot in every single automotive section in this great country of ours?...And that's why so many car enthusiasts have turned to the web. Other than Dan Neil at the *Los Angeles Times*, there are no print journalists ready, willing and able to directly challenge the auto manufacturers' influence with the plain, unvarnished truth (including the writers found in the happy clappy buff books). Car lovers yearn for the truth about cars. Sites like *www.jalopnik.com* are dedicated to providing it. And that's why the mainstream press' cozy little Boys' Club is doomed....

The "Car of the Year" Scam

Once you've established a budget and selected some vehicles that interest you, the next step is to ascertain which ones have high safety and reliability ratings. Be wary of the ratings found in some enthusiast magazines and car enthusiast websites; their supposedly independent tests are a lot of baloney (see "Auto Quality Rankings" on page 38).

You want proof of how misleading these ratings can be? Take *Car and Driver* as an example. It rated the Ford Focus as a "Best Buy" during its first three model years, while government and consumer groups decried the car's dozen or so recall campaigns and the huge number of owner safety and reliability complaints. *Consumer Reports* made the same mistake with the 2006 Focus and recanted the following day.

There are dozens of organizations and magazines that rate cars for everything from their overall reliability and frequency of repairs (J.D. Power and *Consumer*

Reports) to their crashworthiness and appeal to owners (NHTSA, IIHS, and Strategic Visions Total Quality Survey [TQS]). These ratings don't always match. For instance, BMW's Mini ranked 25th of 28 brands in J.D. Power's Initial Quality Survey (IQS). But the popular British import ranks second of 30 brands included in the TQS. And, as fuel prices hit record levels, Mini dealers are tacking on extra charges. Such is the popularity of their little car.

Getting Reliable Info

Funny, as soon as they hear that you're shopping for a new car, everybody wants to tell you what to buy—relatives, co-workers, friends, and even bank robbers.

After a while you'll get so many conflicting opinions that it'll seem as if any choice you make will be wrong. Before making your decision, remember that you should invest a month of research into your $30,000-plus new-car-buying project. This includes two weeks for basic research and another two weeks to actually bargain with dealers to get the right price and equipment. The following sources provide a variety of useful information that will help you ferret out what vehicle best suits your needs and budget.

Clyde Barrow wrote to Henry Ford praising the automaker's vehicles: "For sustained speed and freedom from trouble the Ford has got every other car skinned, and even if my business hasent been strickly legal it don't hurt enything to tell you what a fine car you got in the V8."

Auto shows

Auto shows are held from January through March throughout Canada, starting in Montreal and ending in Vancouver. Although you can't buy or drive a car at the show, you can easily compare prices and the interior and exterior styling of different vehicles. In fact, show officials estimate that about 20 percent of auto show visitors are actively seeking info for an upcoming new-car purchase. Interestingly, while the shows are open, dealer traffic nosedives, making for much more generous deals in showrooms. Business usually picks up following the show.

Online services

Anyone with access to a computer and a modem can now obtain useful information relating to the auto industry in a matter of minutes at little or no cost. This is accomplished in two ways: subscribing to an online service, like America Online (AOL), that offers consumer forums and easy Internet access; or going directly to the Internet through a low-cost Canadian Internet service provider (ISP) and a search engine like Google that helps you find thousands of helpful sites. An extensive listing of informative and helpful sites can be found in Appendix I; however, I've listed a few of my favourite sites below. Many of them are a bit offbeat and highly critical of the auto industry:

American Car Fans
www.americancarfans.com

Auto Extremist
www.autoextremist.com/index.shtml

Auto Spies
www.autospies.com

Auto Week
www.autoweek.com

Auto Wonder
www.autowonder.com

Autoblog
www.autoblog.com

Automobile Magazine
www.automobilemag.com

AutoMuse
www.vehicleinfo.com/AutoMuse

Car Connection
www.thecarconnection.com

Car Design News
www.cardesignnews.com

Cars! Cars! Cars!
www.carscarscars.blogs.com

Cartype
www.cartype.com

Detroit News
www.detnews.com/autosinsider/index.htm

eMercedesBenz—The Unofficial Mercedes-Benz Weblog
www.emercedesbenz.com

Gearhead Magazine
www.gearheadmagazine.com

GermanCarFans.com
www.germancarfans.com

Green Car Congress
www.greencarcongress.com

Jalopnik
www.jalopnik.com

JapaneseCarFans.com
www.japanesecarfans.com

Jason on Cars
www.jasononcars.com

Kit Car Mag
www.kitcarmagazine.com

Le Blog Auto
www.leblogauto.com

Low Rider
www.lowridermagazine.com

Modern Racer
www.modernracer.com

On The Hoist
www.onthehoist.com

Roadfly
www.roadfly.com

Serious Wheels
www.seriouswheels.com

Sports Car Market
www.sportscarmarket.com

Straight-Six
www.straight-six.com

Supercars.net
www.supercars.net

The Auto Prophet
www.theautoprophet.blogspot.com

The Car Blog
www.thecarblog.com

The Truth About Cars
www.thetruthaboutcars.com

Tuning News
www.tuningnews.net

Turbo Magazine
www.turbomagazine.com

 Shopping on the Internet

The key word here is "shopping," because *Consumer Reports* magazine has found that barely 2 percent of Internet surfers actually buy a new or used car online. Yet over 80 percent of buyers admit to using the Internet to get prices and specifications before visiting the dealership. Apparently, few buyers want to purchase a new or used vehicle without seeing what's offered and knowing all money paid will be accounted for.

New-vehicle shopping through automaker and independent websites is a quick and easy way to compare prices and model specifications, but you will have to be careful. Many so-called independent sites are merely fronts for dealers and automakers and tailor their information to steer you into their showroom or convince you to buy a certain brand of car. One independent Canadian site for real discounted prices is *onthehoist.com*.

Shoppers now have access to information they once were routinely denied or had trouble finding, such as dealer price markups and incentive programs, the book value for trade-ins, and considerable safety data. Canadian shoppers can get Canadian invoice prices and specs by contacting APA by phone or fax, or online from *www.carcostcanada.com*.

Other advantages to online shopping: Some dealers offer a lower price to online shoppers, and the entire transaction, including financing, can be done on the Internet. Buyers don't have to haggle; they merely post their best offer electronically to a number of dealers in their area code (for more convenient servicing of the vehicle) and await counteroffers. Three caveats: 1) You will have to go to a dealer to finalize the contract and be preyed upon by the financing and insurance (F&I) sales agents; 2) as far as bargains are concerned, *Consumer Reports* says its test shoppers found that lower prices are more frequently obtained by visiting the dealer showroom and concluding the sale there; and 3) only a third of online dealers respond to customer queries.

Auto Quality Rankings

There are two major surveyors of automobile quality: J.D. Power and Associates, a private American automobile consulting organization, and Consumers Union, an American non-profit consumer organization that publishes *Consumer Reports*.

J.D. Power

Each year, J.D. Power and Associates publishes the results of two important surveys measuring vehicle quality and owners' customer service satisfaction (CSI). Interestingly, these two polls often contradict each other. For example, its Dependability Index places Saturn near the bottom of the list; however, Saturn placed sixth from the top in the Power Service Index. This leads one to conclude that the car isn't very reliable, but service is given with a smile!

Power does have influence in the auto industry. Its criticism of Nissan's 2004 Quest minivan had that company's engineers working overtime fixing or replacing faulty sliding doors, power window switches, interior reading lights, second-row seat levers, and airbag sensors after the group's 2004 Initial Quality Study rated the Quest last among minivans in consumer perceptions of quality during the first 100 days of ownership. Nissan's Titan full-sized pickup and Armada full-sized SUV also placed last in their segments for other problems.

Consumer Reports

Consumer groups and non-profit auto associations like APA and Car Help Canada (see Appendix I) are your best bets for the most unbiased auto ratings for Canadians. They're not perfect, though, so it's a good idea to consult both groups and look for ratings that match.

Consumer Reports (CR) is an American publication that once had a tenuous affiliation with the Consumers Association of Canada. Its ratings, extrapolated from Consumers Union's annual U.S. member survey, don't quite mirror the Canadian experience. Components that are particularly vulnerable to our harsh climate usually don't perform as well as the *CR* reliability ratings indicate, and poor servicing caused by a weak dealer body in Canada can make some service-dependent vehicles a nightmare to own in Canada, whereas the American experience may be less problematic.

Based on 851,000 American and Canadian member responses, *CR* lists used vehicles that, according to owner reports, are significantly better or worse than the industry average. Statisticians agree that *CR*'s sampling method leaves some room for error, but with a few notable exceptions, the ratings are fair, conservative, and consistent guidelines for buying a reliable new vehicle. My only criticisms of the ratings are that many Asian models, like Toyota and Honda, are not as harshly scrutinized as their American counterparts, despite the fact that service bulletins and extended "goodwill" warranties show they also have serious engine, transmission, and electrical problems. Also, older vehicles are excluded from *CR*'s ratings, just as statistics show owners are keeping their vehicles a decade or longer. Many of the ratings about the frequency of repair of certain components aren't specific enough. For example, don't just mention that there are problems with the fuel or electrical system. Rather, be specific about which components are likely to fail—is it the fuel pumps that are failure-prone, or the injectors that clog up, or the battery that suddenly dies?

Lemon-Aid versus *Consumer Reports*

I have a lot of respect for *Consumer Reports*, having been an elected member of its Board almost 30 years ago. Therefore, it's not surprising that *CR* and *Lemon-Aid* ratings are often in agreement. Where they differ is in *Lemon-Aid*'s greater reliance upon NHTSA safety complaints, service bulletin admissions of defects, and owner complaints received through the Internet (rather than from *CR*'s subscriber base, which may simply attract owners singing from the same hymnal).

CR's best new- and used-vehicle picks for 2003, as published in its December 2002 edition, included a number of recommended vehicles that defied all logic.

Foremost was the Ford Windstar, followed by the Saturn Vue. It is inconceivable that *CR* wasn't aware of the multiplicity of powertrain, body, and suspension failures affecting these vehicles. Then there's the assorted Chrysler lineup. Now, you'd have to live on another planet not to know that Chryslers are afflicted by chronic automatic transmission, ball joint, body, brake, and AC defects. In fact, *Consumer Reports*' "Frequency of Repair" tables in the same edition gave out plenty of black marks to the aforementioned models and components. Yet sloppy research and editing failed to pick up on these contradictions.

CR has done a better job with its 2005–06 ratings. But once again Ford trips them up. This time they gave a Recommended rating to the Focus, one of the worst Fords ever built. (*CR* retracted the day after it published its ratings, when NHTSA government crash tests showed the Focus to be dangerously vulnerable to side impacts.)

 ## Leasing Losses

Leasing Traps

Leasing means paying more than you have to. Lessees usually pay the full MSRP on a vehicle loaded with costly options, plus hidden fees and interest charges that wouldn't be included if the vehicle were purchased instead. Researchers have found that some fully loaded entry-level cars leased with high interest rates and deceptive "special fees" could cost more than what some luxury models would cost to *buy*. A useful website that takes the mystery out of leasing is at *www.federalreserve.gov/pubs/leasing*, run by the United States Federal Reserve Board. It goes into incredible detail, comparing leasing versus buying, and has a handy dictionary of terms you're most likely to encounter.

The Devil *Is* in the Details

Take a close look at the small print found in most leasing ads. Pay particular attention to the "weasel" words relating to the model year, kind of vehicle (demonstration or used), equipment, warranty, interest rate, buy-back amount, down payment, security payment, monthly payment, transportation and preparation charges, administration fee ("acquisition" and "disposal" fees), insurance premium, number of free kilometres, and excess kilometre charge.

When and Where to Buy

When to Buy

A good time to buy a new car or minivan that hasn't been redesigned is in the winter, between January and March, when you get the first series of rebates and dealer incentives and production quality begins to improve. Try not to buy when there's strike action—it will be especially tough to get a bargain because there's less product to sell and dealers have to make as much profit as possible on each vehicle remaining in their diminishing stock. Furthermore, work stoppages increase the chances that assembly-line defects will go uncorrected and the vehicle will be delivered as is to product-starved dealers.

Instead, lie low for a while and then return in force in the summer and early fall, when you can double-dip from additional automakers' dealer incentive and buyer rebate programs, which can mean thousands of dollars in additional savings. Remember, too, that vehicles made between March and August offer the most factory upgrades, based on field complaints from those unfortunate fleet managers and rental car agencies who bought the vehicles when they first came out.

Allow yourself at least two weeks to finalize a deal if you're not trading in your vehicle, and longer if you sell your vehicle privately. Visit the showroom at the end of the month, just before closing, when the salesperson will want to make that one last sale to meet the month's quota. If sales have been terrible, the sales manager may be willing to do some extra negotiating in order to boost sales-staff morale.

Where to Buy

Large towns have more of a selection and a variety of payment plans that will likely suit your budget. On the downside, servicing is likely to be hit or miss, because of the transient nature of the customers and mechanics. And you can forget about individual service.

Good dealers aren't always the ones with the lowest prices, though. Buying from someone you know who gives honest and reliable service is just as important as getting a good price. Check a dealer's honesty and reliability by talking with motorists who drive vehicles purchased from that dealer (identified by the nameplate on the trunk). If these customers have been treated fairly, they'll be glad to recommend their dealer. You can also ascertain the quality of new-vehicle preparation and servicing by renting one of the dealer's cars or minivans for a weekend or by getting your trade-in serviced.

How can you tell which dealers are the most honest and competent? Well, judging from the thousands of reports I receive each year, dealerships in small suburban and rural communities are fairer than big-city dealers because they're more vulnerable to negative word-of-mouth advertising and to poor sales—when their vehicles aren't selling, good service takes up the slack. Their prices may also be more competitive, but don't count on it.

Dealers who sell more than one manufacturer's product line present special problems. Overhead can be quite high, and cancellation of a dual dealership by an automaker in favour of an exclusive franchise elsewhere is an ever-present threat. Parts availability may also be a problem, because a dealer with two separate vehicle lines must split the inventory and may therefore have an inadequate supply on hand.

The quality of new-vehicle service is directly linked to the number and competence of dealerships within the network. If the network is weak, parts are likely to be unavailable, repair costs can go through the roof, and the skill level of the mechanics may be questionable. Among foreign manufacturers, Asian automakers have the best overall dealer representation across Canada, except for Mitsubishi and Kia.

Kia's dealer network is very weak, having been left by its owner, Hyundai, to fend for itself for many years. The company's new 2006 Sportage SUV will decide Kia's future. Mitsubishi is almost bankrupt, with a handful of its top executives headed for the slammer for concealing manufacturing defects that killed owners. Its Canadian dealers are piggybacked onto existing Chrysler franchises, which have their own sales problems, so don't expect the alliance to last for long.

BMW and Porsche are leading the European automakers in sales profits this year. Sure, their cars are highly dealer-dependent for service and for parts that tend to be pricier than Japanese and American components, but their popularity continues to grow. Servicing by other European makes in Canada is still woefully inadequate, with VW's lack of a Canadian customer assistance office making a bad situation worse.

And, talking about bad situations, Mercedes-Benz has gained a reputation for poor-quality vehicles encompassing its SUVs, C-Series, and E-Series cars (complaints include engine sludge and electrical system problems).

You can always get better treatment by patronizing dealerships that are accredited by auto clubs such as the CAA or consumer groups like APA or Car Help Canada. Auto club accreditation is no ironclad guarantee of courteous, honest, or competent business practices, but if you're insulted, cheated, or given bad service by one of their recommended garages (look for the accreditation symbol in their phone book ads or on their shop windows), the accreditor is one more place to take your complaint and apply additional mediation pressure. And as you'll see under "Repairs" in Part Two, plaintiffs have won substantial refunds by pleading that the auto club is legally responsible for the actions of the garage it recommends.

Automobile Brokers and Vehicle-Buying Services

Brokers are independent agents who act as intermediaries to find the new or used vehicle you want at a price below what you'd normally pay. They have a Rolodex full of contacts, speak the sales lingo, know all of the angles and scams, and generally can quickly cut through the bull to find a fair price, usually within a matter of days. Their services may cost a few hundred dollars; your savings may be a few thousand. Additionally, you save the stress and hassle associated with the dealership experience, which for many people is like a trip to the dentist.

Brokers get new vehicles through dealers. The broker's job is to find a vehicle to meet the client's expressed needs, and then negotiate its purchase (or lease) on behalf of the client. The majority of brokers tend to deal exclusively in new vehicles, with a small percentage dealing in both new and used vehicles. Ancillary services vary among brokers, and may include such things as comparative vehicle analysis and price research.

The cost of hiring a broker ranges anywhere from a flat fee of a few hundred dollars to a percentage of the value of the vehicle (usually 1–2 percent). A flat fee is usually best because it encourages the broker to keep the selling price low. Reputable brokers are not beholden to any particular dealership or make, and will disclose their flat fee up front or tell the buyer the percentage amount they will charge on a specific vehicle.

 Finding the right broker

This is a tall order, because good brokers are hard to find, particularly in Western Canada and British Columbia. Buyers who are looking for a broker should first ask friends and acquaintances if they can recommend one. Your local credit union or the regional CAA office is also a good place to get a broker referral from people who see their work every day.

Toronto's Metro Credit Union (contact David Lawrence or Rob LoPresti at 1-800-777-8507 or 416-252-5621) has a vehicle counselling and purchasing service (Auto Advisory Services Group) where members can hire an expert "car shopper" who will do the legwork—including the tedious and frustrating dickering with sales staff—and save members time and hassle. This program can also get that new or used vehicle at a reduced (fleet) rate, arrange top-dollar prices for trade-ins, provide independent advice on options like rustproofing and extended warranties, carry out lien searches, and even negotiate the best settlement with insurance agents. The credit union also holds regular car-buying seminars throughout the year in the Greater Toronto Area.

Choosing a Reliable, Cheap Vehicle

Quality Is Not Job 1

Overall vehicle safety and body fit and finish on both domestic and imported vehicles has improved among all automakers during the past three decades. Premature rusting is less of a problem and reliability is improving. Repairs, however, are outrageously expensive and complicated. Owners of cars and minivans made by GM, Ford, and Chrysler still report serious powertrain deficiencies, often during the first year in service. These defects include electrical system failures caused by faulty computer modules; malfunctioning ABS systems, brake rotor warpage, and early pad wearout; failure-prone air conditioning and automatic transmissions; and defective engine head gaskets, intake manifolds, fuel systems, suspensions, steering, and paint.

If an automaker doesn't care if the trunk lid and other body parts are aligned, imagine how well the mechanical components are assembled.

Nothing shows the poor quality control of Detroit's Big Three automakers as much as the poor fit and finish of body panels. Next time you are stuck in traffic, look at the trunk lid or rear hatch alignment of the vehicle in front of you.

Chances are, if it's a Chrysler, Ford, or GM model, the trunk or hatch will be so misaligned that there will be a large gap on one side. Then look at most Asian products: Usually you will see perfectly aligned trunks and hatches, without any large gaps on either side.

That, in a nutshell, is Detroit's problem.

Chrysler

Chrysler has made some progress in improving the overall dependability of its vehicles on a model-by-model basis, although Mercedes, its parent company, continues to struggle with its own electronic and other generic deficiencies. Imbued

Chrysler's Mitsubishi-based Caliber will replace the Neon in the spring of 2006. Smart shoppers should snap up bargain-priced Neons or wait for the Caliber's better-built second-series to hit the streets sometime next fall.

with the confidence that its vehicles are now better built than previous models, Chrysler enters the 2006 model year without a 7-year powertrain warranty, once considered essential to protect owners from the automaker's biodegradable automatic transmissions. So far, owner complaints have indeed moderated, but it's still early, since powertrain glitches usually crop up after five years or 100,000 km—just when the new reduced warranty expires.

Nevertheless, service bulletins cross-referenced with owner complaints confirm the Dodge Neon, PT Cruiser, Sebring, and Caravan are generating fewer complaints than did previous models built five years ago. Stay tuned.

Unlike Ford and GM, Chrysler won't be launching many new cars this year, concentrating instead on a redesigned Ram pickup and a larger Jeep Cherokee, called the Commander. One new 2006 car that has been much anticipated, though, is the Charger, a rear-drive muscle car equipped with a 250-hp, 3.5L V6 or three optional Hemi V8 engines: a 340-hp 5.7L, a 350-hp variant, and a 425-hp 6.1L. These powerful engines will delight high-performance aficionados, but they are notorious fuel-guzzlers and have not been very reliable. Nevertheless, Chrysler's return to rear drives has produced better reliability scores, so if the Hemi's kinks can be worked out and fuel prices moderate, the Charger may do quite well.

Inexplicably, the Neon will be axed early next year to make way for the 2007 Caliber, a small four-door hatchback co-developed with Mitsubishi. Quality-wise, this is a disappointment because the Neon, despite its early deficiencies, has turned into a fairly reliable, fuel-efficient, and competent performer.

Ford

Ford is in chaos. Its management is dysfunctional—going through its second major restructuring in three years—and its products are pathetically bad. Since the early '90s, the company has built vehicles that are grossly unsafe and particularly unreliable, like Explorers that suddenly accelerate or roll over, trucks and SUVs that catch fire while parked overnight in your garage, and vehicles that suddenly go out of control when their coil-spring suspension collapses. As if this weren't enough, the company is also saddled by problem-plagued European models, like Jaguar, which it paid billions to acquire.

Ford just doesn't get it. In the winter of 2002, stung by owner complaints about frequent V6 engine and automatic transmission failures, Ford USA convened an urgent meeting with its suppliers. After ripping through the supplier body, telling them how shoddy their engines and transmissions were, Ford was told that the parts suppliers were only supplying what Ford procurement had ordered and then reordered, with constantly changing specs. They reminded Ford that Nissan, Honda, and Toyota—companies that were at the top of J.D. Power's quality surveys—were their best customers.

Too bad Ford pulled in its horns. In the three-year interval since that "crisis" meeting with suppliers, Nissan, Honda, and Toyota have suffered their own supplier-related powertrain failures and subsequently set up publicly disclosed 7- to 8-year "goodwill" engine and transmission warranty extensions affecting 1997–2004 model cars, trucks, SUVs, and minivans.

In 2006, Ford's quality shortcomings may be alleviated by its closer partnership with Mazda and Volvo. The new 2006 Fusion, Milan, and Zephyr (one car sold as three), for example, is a Mazda6 spin-off, slightly smaller than the Five Hundred (which replaced the Taurus), competing with the Chevrolet Malibu, the Honda Accord, the Hyundai Sonata, and the Toyota Camry. Volvo's platform was used for the first time on the 2005 Five Hundred, Freestar, and Montego. Several new front-drive Lincolns, based on Volvo's D3 architecture, will arrive as 2007 models (I smell another front-drive Continental goof). Lincoln's reliable and proftable Town Car will likely remain for a few more years as Ford's only rear-drive Lincoln, such is its popularity with seniors and fleet managers.

General Motors

GM has eight divisions selling over 70 models, many of which are higher cost duplicates that nobody wants to buy. Sure, this method of throwing everything against the wall and seeing what sticks sells a broad range of vehicles, but it is terribly inefficient and costly in contrast to the tightly focused niche-driven marketing by Honda and Toyota. In fact, Wall Street analysts have downgraded GM bonds to junk status after concluding that the automaker may be losing $1,227 per car. When you are losing money on this scale, you can't invest much in quality control.

GM's quality deficiencies affect most of its lineup, notably American-built front-drives and pickups. Owners cite unreliable powertains, poor braking performance, electrical problems, and subpar fit and finish as the main offenders.

Unlike Ford, which has few new models this year, GM hopes to improve quality by launching lots of new cars, many of which are simply refurbished existing models. The company is returning to its rear-drive roots with the new Solstice/Torrent/Sky roadsters, and will continue churning out thrifty small cars through its partnerships with Daewoo and Toyota.

The new Pontiac Solstice.

The Pontiac Solstice is nearly 400 pounds heavier than the Mazda Miata MX-5 and uses GM's loud and wimpish Ecotec engine. Selling the same car as the Saturn Sky doesn't fool anyone and simply dilutes the brand. Although the Toyota link is a proven asset, GM's Daewoo offerings, also marketed through Suzuki, have been widely criticized as ho-hum, albeit fuel-thrifty, performers with serious quality issues themselves. Suzuki's chairman confirmed this fact last August, when he publicly lashed out at GM-Daewoo as the reason for Suzuki's dead-last ranking in a recent J.D. Power Initial Quality Study. Power gave this rating to the Suzuki Forenza, built by GM-Daewoo and marketed by GM Canada as the Chevrolet Optra.

Asian automakers

Don't buy into the myth that parts for imports are overpriced or hard to find. It's actually easier to find parts for Japanese vehicles than for domestic vehicles because of the large number of units produced, the presence of hundreds of independent suppliers, the ease with which relatively simple parts can be interchanged among different models, and the large reservoir of used parts stocked by junkyards. Incidentally, when a part is hard to find, the *Mitchell Manual* is a useful guide to substitute parts that can be used for many different models. It's available in some libraries, most auto parts stores, and practically all junkyards.

Sadly, customer relations have been the Japanese automakers' Achilles heels. Dealers are spoiled rotten by decades of easy sales and have developed a "take it or leave it" showroom attitude, which is often accompanied by a woeful ignorance of their own model lineups. This was once a frequent complaint of Honda and Toyota shoppers, though recent APA undercover surveys show a big improvement among Toyota dealers.

Where it has gotten worse is in the service bay, where periodic maintenance visits and warranty claims are like sessions with Liberal bagmen. Well-known factory-related defects (Honda engine oil leaks, Nissan exhaust manifolds, and Toyota engine and tranny problems) are corrected under extended warranties, but you always have the feeling you owe the family.

There's no problem with discourteous or ill-informed South Korean automakers. Instead, poor quality has been their bugaboo. Yet, like Honda and Toyota's recovery following start-up quality glitches, Hyundai, South Korea's biggest automaker, has made considerable progress in bringing up quality almost to Toyota and Honda's level.

The same can't be said for Kia, a struggling, low-quality, small South Korean compact automaker bought by Hyundai in October 1998. Since then, it has languished under Hyundai's "benign neglect," as Hyundai spent most of its resources on its own cars and SUVs. Hyundai says it will work hard to improve 2006 Kia models by using more Hyundai parts in the redesigned Kia Sportage SUV (absent since 2002) and the improved Sedona minivan.

Up to the mid-'90s, South Korean vehicles were merely cheap, poor-quality knock-offs of their Japanese counterparts. They would start to fall apart after their third year because of subpar body construction, unreliable automatic transmission and electrical components, and parts suppliers who put low prices ahead of reliability and durability. This was particularly evident with Hyundai's Pony, Stellar, Excel, and early Sonata models. During the past several years, though, Hyundai's product lineup has been extended and refined and quality is no longer a worry. Also, Hyundai's comprehensive base warranty protects owners from most of the more expensive breakdowns that may occur.

Kia's 2006 Sedona is a small, fuel-efficient minivan that can be a winner if quality is improved and gas prices remain high.

Hyundais are easily repaired by independent garages, and their rapid depreciation doesn't mean much because they cost so little initially and entry-level buyers are known to keep their cars longer than most, thereby easily amortizing the higher depreciation rate.

European models

Lemon-Aid doesn't recommend many European cars; there are way too many with serious and expensive quality and servicing problems. Heck, even the Germans have abandoned their own products. For example, a 2002 J.D. Power survey of 15,000 German car owners found that German drivers are happiest at the wheel of a Lexus, a Japanese car. This survey included compact and luxury cars as well as off-roaders. Toyota won first place on quality, reliability, and owner satisfaction, while Nissan's Maxima headed the luxury class standings. BMW was the first choice among European offerings.

For those who feel the German survey was a fluke, there's also a 2003 study of 34,000 car owners with vehicles up to eight years old, published by Britain's Consumers' Association. It found that less than half of British owners would recommend a British-made Rover or Vauxhall to a friend. The most highly rated cars in the study were the Japanese Subaru, Isuzu, and Lexus. Over 85 percent of drivers would recommend them.

Here's another surprise: Although it builds some of the most expensive cars and SUVs in the world, Mercedes-Benz quality isn't first-class. After stumbling badly when it first launched its rushed-to-production American-made SUV for the 1998 model year, the automaker has sent out many urgent service bulletins that seek to correct a surprisingly large number of production deficiencies affecting its entire lineup, including C-Class and E-Class models. Judged by its own confidential bulletins, Mercedes' many factory-related defects have overwhelmed the company's resources at a time when much of its energies are directed at a dramatic mid-year administrative shake-up, following the resignation of its CEO.

Mercedes executives admit that the company's cars and SUVs have serious quality shortcomings and have vowed to correct them. But such a turnaround is complicated by M-B's huge financial losses (its Smart division has lost billions and won't hit the States before 2007) and management chaos where the most secure jobs are with the Chrysler group.

While Mercedes sorts through its woes, shoppers who can't resist a German nameplate on their car should buy a BMW 3- or 5-series and take special courses to learn how to manage the cars' iDrive multifunctional cockpit controller.

Volkswagen's quality is just as bad as Mercedes', and its sales have been equally dismal. True, VW has always been early on the scene with great concepts, but they have always been accompanied by poor execution and a weak servicing network.

With its failure-prone and under-serviced Eurovan and Camper, the company hasn't been a serious minivan player since the late '60s, and VW's Rabbit and Golf small cars have been resounding duds. Even the company's forays into luxury cruisers have been met by underwhelming enthusiasm and general derision.

With European models, your service options are limited and customer-relations staffers can be particularly insensitive and arrogant. You can count on lots of aggravation and expense because of the unacceptably slow distribution of parts and their high markup. Because these companies have a quasi-monopoly on replacement parts, there are few independent suppliers you can turn to for help. And auto wreckers, the last-chance repository for inexpensive car parts, are unlikely to carry European parts for vehicles that are more than three years old or were manufactured in small numbers.

These vehicles also age badly. The weakest areas remain the drivetrains, electronic control modules, electrical and fuel systems, brakes, accessories (including the sound system and AC), and body components.

Cutting Costs

Watch the Warranty

There's a big difference between warranty promise and warranty performance. Most automakers offer bumper-to-bumper warranties good for at least the first 3 years/60,000 km, and some problem-prone models and luxury makes get additional base coverage up to 5 years/100,000 km. DaimlerChrysler and South Korean automakers are also using more comprehensive 5- to 7-year warranties as important marketing tools to give their cars luxury cachet, or to allay buyers' fears of poor quality and reliability. It's also becoming an industry standard for car companies to pay for roadside assistance, a loaner car, or hotel accommodations if your vehicle breaks down while you're away from home and it's still under warranty. *Lemon-Aid* readers report few problems with these ancillary warranty benefits.

Warranty costs vary enormously among manufacturers and are often a good indication of how well the company stands behind its product. In the chart on the following page, it is interesting to note that both General Motors and Cummins had higher claim costs than Ford. Does this show that Ford has fewer claims, or that it has simply stonewalled owner refund requests?

Ford's automotive costs increased by $1.4 billion in the first half of 2005, with about $300 million coming from worse-than-expected warranty repairs for old models still under warranty.

WARRANTY CLAIMS FOR SEVERAL MAJOR COMPANIES

COMPANY	WARRANTY CLAIMS FOR FIRST HALF OF 2005 (IN MILLIONS)	CLAIMS AS PERCENTAGE OF PRODUCT SALES	PERCENTAGE CHANGE SINCE 2004
Lexmark International	$ 83	8.3%	−1.6%
Maxtor Corp.	$ 90	4.6%	−1.4%
Deere & Co.	$ 186	1.5%	−0.7%
Hewlett-Packard Co.	$1,213	3.6%	−0.1%
Whirlpool Corp.	$ 167	2.7%	+0.1%
Apple Computer Inc.	$ 93	1.7%	+0.1%
Dell Inc.	$ 669	2.8%	+0.2%
Maytag Corp.	$ 68	3.1%	+0.2%
Ford Motor Co.	$1,965	2.5%	+0.2%
General Motors Corp.	$2,366	3.0%	+0.3%
Caterpillar Inc.	$ 380	2.3%	+0.3%
IBM Corp.	$ 409	3.3%	+0.5%
Cummins Inc.	$ 139	3.0%	+0.8%

Source: *Warranty Week*, September 3, 2005
www.warrantyweek.com

Don't buy more warranty than you need

If you pick a vehicle recommended by *Lemon-Aid*, you don't need additional bumper-to-bumper protection and can pocket $2,000 in savings. But you may get a good price on a vehicle known for some engine or transmission problems with past models. In that case, you may want a $1,000 extended powertrain warranty. If you are picking up a vehicle that has a sorry repair history, you will likely need a full $2,000 comprehensive warranty. But first ask yourself this question: "Why am I buying a vehicle that's so poorly made that I need to spend several thousand dollars to protect myself until the warranty company grows tired of seeing my face?"

Just like the weight-loss ads you see on TV, what you see isn't always what you get. For example, bumper-to-bumper coverage usually excludes stereo components, brake pads, clutch plates, and many other expensive components. And automakers will pull every trick in the book to make you pay for their factory screw-ups. This includes blaming your driving or poor maintenance, penalizing you for using an independent garage or the wrong fuel, or simply stating that the problem is "normal," and it's really you who is out of whack.

Part Two has all the answers to the above bullcrap excuses. It will arm you with court decisions and sample claim letters that would make any lawyer proud and make automakers and their dealers think twice about turning you away.

Don't pay for repairs covered by "secret" warranties

Automobile manufacturers are reluctant to publicize their secret warranty programs because they feel that such publicity would weaken consumer confidence in their products and increase their legal liability. The closest they come to an admission is to send out a "goodwill policy," "special policy," or "product update" service bulletin for dealers' eyes only. These bulletins admit liability and propose free repairs for defects that include faulty paint, air conditioning malfunctions, and engine and transmission failures on Chrysler, Ford, and GM vehicles (see Part Three).

If you're refused compensation, keep in mind that secret warranty extensions are, first and foremost, an admission of manufacturing negligence. You can usually find them in technical service bulletins (TSBs) that are sent daily to dealers by automakers. Your bottom-line position should be to accept a pro rata adjustment from the manufacturer, whereby you share a third of the repair costs with the dealer and automaker. If polite negotiations fail, challenge the refusal in court on the grounds that you should not be penalized for failing to make a reimbursement claim under a secret warranty that you never knew existed!

Service bulletins are written by automakers in "mechanic-speak" because service managers relate better to them that way. They're great guides for warranty inspections (especially the final one), and they're useful in helping you decide when it's best to trade in your car. Manufacturers can't weasel out of their obligations by claiming that they never wrote such a bulletin.

If your vehicle is out of warranty, show these bulletins to less expensive independent garage mechanics, so they can quickly find the trouble and order the most recent *upgraded* part, ensuring that you don't replace one defective component with another.

The following three bulletin summaries show the types of problems GM, Chrysler, and Ford minivans are likely to have:

2005 GM MONTANA SV6, RELAY, TERRAZA, AND UPLANDER

NUMBER	DATE	TITLE
05539	04/11/2005	Recall—Emissions/PCM/ECM Replacement
05015	03/29/2005	Recall—Second Row Seat Latch Release Handle Removal
05-06-02-001	02/24/2005	Cooling System—Aluminum Radiator/Heater Core Info.
NHTSA05V061000	02/16/2005	Recall 05V061000: Seat Release Latch Lever Defect
04-08-46-003A	02/14/2005	OnStar®—Unable to Connect (Alaska Vehicles)
01-08-42-001B	02/11/2005	Lighting—Replacement Guidelines for Condensation
05-09-40-001	02/11/2005	Restraints—Third Row Center Seat Belt Retractor Locks Up
05-08-44-005	02/11/2005	Audio System—Rear Headphone Ear Pads Worn/Damaged

02-08-58-005B	02/09/2005	Body—Wind Noise from Windshield Base
00-08-46-003B	02/09/2005	Instruments—GPS System Performance Degradation
05-06-01-005	02/08/2005	Engine—Whistling at Idle or on Light Acceleration
99-04-20-002C	01/31/2005	Drivetrain—Normal Clunk Shifting Between D & R
00-09-40-001C	01/31/2005	Restraint Systems—Excessive Child Seat Movement
04-07-30-013A	01/25/2005	A/T—Shift/Driveability Concerns/SES Lamp ON
05-08-64-002	01/20/2005	Body—Door Latches Freeze in Extreme Cold
04-08-48-001A	01/19/2005	AC—Rear Defogger Heating Grid Damage Detection
05-00-89-002	01/13/2005	Interior—Rear Seat Removal/Installation
04-08-49-018E	01/05/2005	Fuel System—Cranks but No-Start/Inaccurate Fuel Gauge
02-07-30-013C	01/03/2005	A/T—4T65E SES Lamp ON/Slipping/DTCs Set/Harsh Shifts
04-08-46-005	12/21/2004	OnStar®—System Inoperative/No LED Lamp ON
04-08-44-024	12/14/2004	Audio—Fuse Removal Prior to Module Programming
04-06-04-047C	12/14/2004	Fuel System—"Top Tier" Gasoline Information
04-06-03-016	12/13/2004	Battery—Specification Label Clarification
00-07-30-022C	12/10/2004	A/T—4L60/65E No Reverse/Second or Fourth Gear
04-08-44-023	12/09/2004	Audio—CD Player Won't Play Above a Certain Track
01-07-30-041A	12/03/2004	A/T—Fluid Leak Diagnostics
04-03-10-001A	11/30/2004	Tires—Puncture Repair Procedures
04-08-46-003	11/29/2004	OnStar®—Unable to Connect to OnStar (Alaska Only)
02-08-46-010E	11/23/2004	OnStar®—French Canadian Voice Recognition
99-08-51-007B	11/22/2004	Wheels—Aluminum Wheel Refinishing
01-04-18-001C	11/18/2004	Drivetrain—AWD/4WD Driveline Characteristics
04-08-44-022	11/17/2004	Audio System—CD Eject Button Sticks
04-08-42-014	11/12/2004	Lighting—Tail Lamp Retaining Bolt Loosening Information
03-07-29-004A	11/12/2004	M/T—Operational Characteristics
02-06-03-006B	11/10/2004	Electrical—Testing Prior to Alternator/Battery R&R
02-07-30-052C	09/01/2004	A/T—Fluid Flushing Procedure/Tool
01-01-38-006D	09/01/2004	A/C—R-134a System Flushing Procedures
04-03-10-012	09/01/2004	Wheels—Chrome Wheel Pitting/Brake Dust Accumulation
01-07-30-036D	09/01/2004	Transmission Controls—DTC P0756 Diagnostic Tips
04-08-68-002	09/01/2004	Cruise Control—Increasing Set Speed
99-09-40-005B	09/01/2004	Restraint System—Seat Belt Extender Availability
01-07-31-002A	09/01/2004	M/T—Improved Hydraulic Clutch Bleeding Procedure
01-07-30-010A	08/06/2004	A/T—Torque Converter Replacement Guideline
02-06-03-008A	07/28/2004	Charging System—Operational Characteristics
01-03-10-009A	07/27/2004	Wheels—Plastic Wheel Nut Covers Loose/Missing
00-00-89-027B	07/21/2004	Interior—Odour Elimination
02-06-03-010A	07/02/2004	Battery—Parasitic Drain
04-06-00-047	06/24/2004	Fuel—Top Tier Detergent Gasoline Information
00-06-01-026A	06/14/2004	Engine—New Long Block Installation Precaution
02-08-44-007A	06/14/2004	XM Radio/OnStar®—Problems w/ Cloth or Vinyl Roofs

2005 DODGE CARAVAN

NUMBER	DATE	TITLE
23-022-05	04/02/2005	Interior—Low Gloss Interior Trim Care
08-020-05	03/23/2005	Instruments—Parking Assist Tones Not Loud Enough
02-003-05	03/16/2005	Suspension—Front Suspension Rattle/Knocking Sound
18-010-05A	03/04/2005	Engine Controls—MIL ON/DTC P0135 Set
08-015-05	03/02/2005	Engine Controls—PCM Initialization After Replacement
08-014-05	02/17/2005	Accessories—MOPAR(R) Remote Starter Inoperative
08-013-05	02/16/2005	Cell Phone—Hands-Free Phone Inoperative
08-008-05	02/04/2005	Engine Controls—MIL ON/DTC P0135 (O2 Sensor)
05-002-05	01/29/2005	Brakes—Vibration/Pulsation Felt in Steering Wheel
19-001-05	01/26/2005	Steering—Steering Wheel Tilt Mechanism Inoperative
23-002-05	01/14/2005	Body—Water Leaks to Interior from Roof Seam
08-040-04	12/09/2004	Electrical—Locks Inoperative/Liftgate Triggers Alarm
19-011-04	12/07/2004	Steering—Moaning Noise on Low Speed Turns
05-004-04A	12/02/2004	Brakes—Rear Wheel Speed Sensor Replacement Guidelines
19-010-04	11/29/2004	Power Steering—Additive Prohibition
23-017-04C	11/01/2004	Interior—Third Row Seat Front Leg Will Not Retract
21-008-04A	10/16/2004	A/T—MIL ON/DTC P1776 Set
21-005-04A	10/09/2004	A/T—Coastdown Ticking Noise
19-008-04	10/05/2004	Steering—In and Out Steering Column Movement
14-001-04	09/28/2004	Fuel System—Fuel Tank Removal Precaution
18-006-04B	09/13/2004	Engine Control—Generic PCM Programming Procedure
09-013-04	08/06/2004	Engine—Oil Quality/Viscosity Requirements
08-027-04	07/30/2004	Safety Systems—Inadvertent Damage/Disabling
08-022-04	05/25/2004	Entertainment System—Crackling Noise from Headphones
18-018-04	04/27/2004	Engine Controls/Ignition—MIL ON/Misfire DTCs Set
18-016-04	04/13/2004	Engine Controls—Warm Engine Rough Idle
21-004-04	03/16/2004	A/T—ATF Usage List
05-002-04	02/17/2004	Brakes—Rear Drum Water/Snow Ingestion/Freezing
NHTSA04V047000	02/03/2004	Recall 04V047000: Seat Belt Retractor Defect
D04	02/01/2004	Recall—Right Front Seat Belt Retractor Inspection
08-001-04	01/06/2004	Airbag System—Passenger Airbag Service Precautions

2005 FORD FREESTAR

NUMBER	DATE	TITLE
05-6-17	04/04/2005	ABS/TCS—Lamps ON/ABS Self Activation/DTC C1288
05-6-4	04/04/2005	Instruments—False Parking Aid Warnings
05-3-1	02/21/2005	Engine Controls—MAF Sensor Diagnostic Service Tip
05-3-10	02/21/2005	Restraints—Seat Belt Stop Button Service
05-2-1	02/07/2005	Interior—Glove Box Latch Replacement
04-26-10	12/31/2004	Brakes—Accelerated Rear Brake Pad Wear
04-26-16	12/31/2004	Body—Weld Bonding Procedure

04-25-15	12/27/2004	Restraint System—SRS Lamp ON/DTC B1342 Set
04-25-10	12/27/2004	Body—Power Sliding Door/Liftgate Inoperative/DTC C1999
04-24-14	12/13/2004	Engine Controls—General PCM Programming Procedures
04-24-5	12/13/2004	AC/Audio—Defroster/Antenna Grid Diagnosis/Repair
04-24-3	12/13/2004	Steering—Leather Coming Loose from Steering Wheel
04-24-21	12/13/2004	Restraint System—Seat Belts Slow to Retract
04-23-1	11/29/2004	Electrical—ABS/TCS/Park Brake Lamps Flickering
04-22-9	11/15/2004	Interior—Under Column Access Door Warped/Broken
04-21-17	11/01/2004	Interior—Third Row Seat Strap Breakage
04-20-7	10/18/2004	Interior—Trim Paint Application Procedures
04-19-9	09/22/2004	Body—Exterior Door Trim Moldings Loose
04-17-10	09/06/2004	A/T—4F50N No. 1–2 Upshift/DTC P0732 Set
04-17-6	09/06/2004	Body—Cowl Panel Grille Breakage
04-14-8	07/26/2004	AC—Front Blower Motor Whistle Noise
04-14-7	07/26/2004	Electrical—Wiring Harness Replacement Guidelines/Tips
04-12-5	06/01/2004	ABS—Module Replacement Service Tip

Because these bulletins are sent out by U.S. automakers, Canadian service managers and automakers may deny at first that the bulletins even exist, or may shrug their shoulders and say that they only apply in the States. However, when they're shown a copy, they usually find the appropriate Canadian part number or bulletin in their files. The problems and solutions don't change from one side of the border to another. Imagine American and Canadian tourists being towed across the border because each country's technical service bulletins were different. Mechanical fixes do differ in cases where a bulletin is for California only, or relates to a safety or emissions component used only in the States. But these instances are rare indeed. What is quite gratifying is to see some automakers, like Honda, candidly admit in their bulletins that "goodwill" repair refunds are available (see following page). What a shame other automakers aren't as forthcoming.

The best way to get bulletin-related repairs carried out is to visit the dealer's service bay and attach the specific ALLDATA-supplied service bulletin covering your vehicle's problems to a work order.

Getting your vehicle's service bulletins

Free summaries of automotive recalls and technical service bulletins listed by year, make, model, and engine can be found at the ALLDATA (*www.alldata.com/TSB*) and NHTSA (*www.safercar.gov*) websites. Like the NHTSA summaries, ALLDATA's summaries are so short and cryptic that they're of limited use. You can download the complete contents of all the bulletins applicable to your vehicle from ALLDATA at *www.alldatadiy.com* if you pay the $24.95 (U.S.) annual subscription fee. Bulletins for Acura and BMW are not available, since these automakers have requested that ALLDATA keep their service bulletin information confidential.

Trim Insurance Costs

Insurance premiums can average between $900 and $2,000 per year, depending on the type of vehicle you own, your personal statistics and driving habits, and whether you can obtain coverage under your family policy.

 There are some general rules to follow when looking for insurance savings. For example, vehicles older than five years do not necessarily need collision coverage, and you may not need loss-of-use coverage or a rental car. Other factors that should be considered:

- A low damageability rating and an average theft history also can reduce rates by 10–15 percent. These rankings can be checked at *www.ibc.ca/vehinfo_pub_howcarsmeasureup.asp*. Don't be surprised, though, if there appears to be no rhyme or reason for the disparity in the ratings of similar vehicles. Insurance statistics aren't as scientific as insurers pretend—they often charge whatever the market will bear.

- When you phone for quotes, make sure you have your serial number in hand. Many factors, such as the make of the car, the number of doors, if there's a sports package, and the insurer's experience with the car, affect the quote. And be honest, or you'll find your claim denied, the policy cancelled, or your premium cost boosted.
- Where you live and work also determine how much you pay. Auto insurance rates are 25–40 percent lower in London, Ontario, than in downtown Toronto because there are fewer cars in the city and fewer kilometres to drive to work. Similar disparities are found in B.C. and Alberta.
- A driver-training course can save you thousands of premium dollars. For example, a policy on a '98 Honda Civic for a schooled driver under 25 may be $3,000 less than the regular premium price.
- You may be able to include your home or apartment insurance as part of a premium package eligible for additional discounts.

The Consumer's Guide to Insurance website (*www.insurancehotline.com*), based in Ontario but with quotes for other provinces, says that it pays to shop around for cheap auto insurance rates. In February 2003, the group discovered that the same insurance policy could vary in cost by a whopping 400 percent. For example, a 41-year-old married female driving a 2002 Honda Accord and a 41-year-old married male driving a 1998 Dodge Caravan, both with unblemished driving records, should pay no more than $1,880, but some companies surveyed asked as much as $7,515.

The Consumer's Guide to Insurance service can be accessed by telephone at 416-686-0531. There is a small service fee for some referrals.

"Hidden" Costs

Depreciation

Depreciation is the biggest—and most often ignored—expense you encounter when you trade in your vehicle or when an accident forces you to buy another vehicle before the depreciated loss can be amortized. Most new cars depreciate a whopping 30–40 percent during the first two years of ownership. The best way to use depreciation rates to your advantage is to choose a vehicle listed as being both reliable and economical to own and keep it for five to 10 years. Alternatively, you may buy insurance to protect you from depreciation's bite. Generally, by choosing a lower-depreciating vehicle—such as one that keeps at least half its value over three years—you are storing up equity that will give you a bigger down payment and less loan costs with your next purchase.

Gas Pains

With gas prices jumping between $1.00 and $1.50 a litre, motorists are scratching their heads to find easy ways to cut gas consumption. Here are three simple suggestions (20 more tips are found in Appendix III):

1. Buy a used compact car for half its original price. Savings on taxes, freight fees, and depreciation: $15,000.
2. Buy low-octane fuel from Internet-referred gas stations. You can save about 15 cents a litre.
3. Keep your vehicle properly tuned for a 10-percent savings from improved fuel economy.

How about gas-saving gadgets and government mileage figures? Don't trust 'em. Ottawa hoodwinks us with gas mileage figures that are impossible to achieve.

Stephen Akehurst, a senior manager at Natural Resources Canada, which tests vehicles and publishes the annual *Fuel Consumption Guide*, admits that his lab tests vehicles under ideal conditions. He says that actual driving may burn about 25 percent more fuel than what the government tests show. Too bad we never see this fact hyped in the automaker fuel economy ads.

Ottawa's *Fuel Consumption Guide* is a work of fiction intended to make automakers, bureaucrats, and motorists feel "green" and empowered.

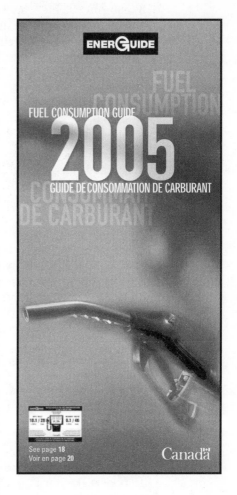

Some examples: One of the biggest gas-guzzlers tested, the Lincoln Aviator, burned 44 percent more than the *Fuel Consumption Guide*'s estimate, and a Nissan Quest burned twice as much fuel as was advertised. Only the Hyundai Elantra did well. It burned a full litre less than predicted by the guys in the white coats.

Diesels

Diesel engines are 30 percent more efficient than gasoline engines, and they become more efficient as the engine load increases (whereas gasoline engines become less efficient). This is the main reason diesels are best used in situations where the driving cycle includes a lot of city driving, with slow speeds, heavy loads, frequent stops, and long idling times. At full throttle, both engines are essentially equal from a fuel-efficiency standpoint. The gasoline engine, however, leaves the diesel in the dust when it comes to high-speed performance. Many owners of diesel-equipped vehicles are frustrated by excessive repair costs and poor road performance on vehicles that lack turbo. Bear in mind that before the fuel savings can outweigh the high cost of a diesel purchase, the average owner would have to drive 40,000–50,000 km per year.

Diesel engines aren't all equally reliable, either. For passenger cars, Mercedes-Benz and Volkswagen diesels perform extraordinarily well during their first three years on the market. Thereafter, electronic modules, injectors, and other high-cost electrical and emissions-related components drive up servicing costs and degrade overall reliability. But when it comes to Ford and GM diesels, owners report subpar performance, frequent breakdowns, and poor dealer servicing.

Hybrid cars

Automakers are offering hybrid vehicles like the Toyota Prius and Honda Civic and Accord Hybrids that use an engine/electric motor for maximum fuel economy and low emissions while providing the driving range of a comparable small car. Yet this latest iteration of the electric car still has serious drawbacks, which may drive away even the most green-minded buyers:

- Real world fuel consumption may be 40 percent higher than advertised.
- Cold weather can cut fuel economy by almost 10 percent.
- AC and other options can increase fuel consumption by 20 percent.
- The electrical system can deliver a life-threatening 275–500 volts if tampered with through incompetent servicing or during an emergency rescue.
- Battery packs can cost up to $8,000 U.S., and fuel savings equal the hybrid's extra costs only after about 200,000 km of use.
- Hybrids cost more to insure and depreciate as much as non-hybrid vehicles.
- Hybrids make you a captive customer where travel is dependent upon available service facilities.

If you find the limitations of an electric hybrid too daunting, why not simply buy a more fuel-efficient small car? Here are the top eight environmentally friendly cars recommended by Toronto-based Environmental Defence Canada (starred vehicles are recommended by *Lemon-Aid* for their reliability and fuel economy):

1. *Toyota Echo
2. *Honda Civic
3. *Toyota Corolla
4. Saturn SC
5. *Nissan Sentra
6. Ford Focus
7. *Hyundai Accent

Surviving the Options Jungle

 The best options for your buck are a 5-speed automatic transmission, an anti-theft immobilizer, air conditioning, a premium sound system, and higher quality tires—features that may bring back a third to half their value. Rustproofing makes cars easier to sell in some provinces with salt on the roads, but paint protection and seat sealants are a waste of money. Most option packages can be cut by 20 percent. Extended warranties are overpriced by about 75 percent. And what will happen when the warranty runs out...?

Dealers make more than three times as much profit selling options as they do selling most cars (50 percent profit versus 15 percent profit). No wonder their eyes light up when you start perusing their options list. If you must have some options, compare prices with independent retailers and buy where the price is lowest and the warranty is the most comprehensive. Buy as few options as possible from the dealer, since you'll get faster service, more comprehensive guarantees, and lower prices from independent suppliers. Remember, extravagantly equipped vehicles hurt your pocketbook in three ways: They cost more to begin with and return only a fraction of what they cost when the car is resold, they drive up maintenance costs, and they often consume extra fuel.

A heavy-duty battery and suspension and perhaps an upgraded sound system will generally suffice for American-made vehicles; most imports already come well equipped. An engine block heater with a timer—favoured by 39 percent of new car shoppers—isn't a bad idea, either. It's an inexpensive investment that ensures winter starting and reduces fuel consumption by allowing you to start out with a semi-warm engine.

When ordering parts, remember that purchases from American outlets can be slapped with a small customs duty if the part isn't made in the United States. Then you'll pay the inevitable GST levied on the part's cost and customs duty. Finally, your freight carrier may charge a $15–$20 brokerage fee for representing you at the border

Smart Options

The problem with options is you often can't refuse them. Dealers sell very few bare-bones cars and minivans, and they option-pack each vehicle with features that can't be removed. You'll be forced to dicker over the total cost of what you are offered, whether you need the extras or not. So it's not a case of "yes or no," but more a decision of "at what cost?"

Adjustable Pedals and Extensions

A safety feature available from most automakers, this device moves the brake and accelerator pedals forward or backward about 10 cm (4 in.) to accommodate short-statured drivers and protect them from airbag-induced injuries.

If the manufacturer of your vehicle doesn't offer optional power-adjustable pedals, there are several companies selling inexpensive pedal extensions by mail order through the Internet; go to *stores.yahoo.com/hdsmn/pedex.html*. If you live in Toronto or London, Ontario, check out *www.kinomobility.com*.

Adjustable Steering Wheel

This option makes access to the driver's seat easier and permits a more comfortable driving position. It's particularly useful if a vehicle will be driven by more than one person.

Air Conditioning

Why not? AC systems are far more reliable than they were a decade ago and they have a lifespan of five to seven years. Sure, replacement and repair costs can hit $1,000, but that's very little when amortized over an eight- to ten-year period. AC also makes your car easier to resell.

Does AC waste or conserve fuel when a vehicle is driven at highway speeds? Interestingly, *Mythbusters,* a popular Discovery TV program, concluded that driving with the air conditioning on and the windows up saved the most fuel. Other AC benefits: It provides extra comfort, reduces wind noise (from not having to roll down the windows), and improves window defogging. Buy a factory-installed unit. You'll get a longer warranty and reduce the chance that other mechanical components will be damaged during installation.

Anti-Theft Systems

You'd be a fool not to buy an anti-theft system, including a lockable fuel cap, for your much-coveted-by-thieves Japanese compact or sports car. Auto break-ins and thefts cost Canadians more than $400 million annually, meaning that there's a one in 130 chance that your vehicle will be stolen and only a 60 percent chance that you'll ever get it back. Chrysler minivans are also theft-prone because of to their rudimentary door lock assemblies.

Since most vehicles are stolen by amateurs, the best theft deterrent is a visible device that complicates the job while immobilizing the vehicle and sounding an alarm. For less than $150, you can install both a steering-wheel lock and a hidden remote-controlled ignition disabler. Satellite tracking systems like GM's OnStar feature are also very effective.

Battery (Heavy-Duty)

The best battery for northern climates is the optional heavy-duty type offered by many manufacturers for about $80. It's a worthwhile purchase, especially for vehicles equipped with lots of electric options. Most standard batteries last only two winters; heavy-duty batteries give you an extra year or two for about 20 percent more than the price of a standard battery.

Central Locking Control

With a price tag of around $200, this option is most useful for families with small children, car-poolers, or drivers of minivans who can't easily slide across the seat to lock the other doors.

Child Safety Seat (Integrated)

Integrated safety seats are designed to accommodate any child more than one year old or weighing over 9 kg (20 lb.). Since the safety seat is permanently integrated into the seatback, the fuss of installing and removing the safety seat and finding some place to store it vanishes. When not in use, it quickly folds out of sight, becoming part of the seatback. Two other safety benefits: You know that the seat has been properly installed, and your child gets used to having his or her "special" seat in back, where it's usually safest to sit.

Electronic Stability Control (ESC)

A life-saving $500–$1,000 option that is slowly becoming a standard feature, ESC helps prevent loss of control in a turn, on slippery roads, or when drivers must make a sudden steering correction. It is particularly useful in maintaining stability with SUVs, but is less useful with passenger coupes and sedans.

An NHTSA study released in September 2004 found that cars with ESC were involved in 30 percent fewer fatal single-vehicle crashes than those without and that SUVs with ESC were involved in 63 percent fewer such crashes. An IIHS study released a month later concluded that cars and SUVs with ESC were involved in 56 percent fewer fatal single-vehicle crashes than comparable models without ESC.

Presently, there is no federal standard governing the performance of these systems, which is worrisome, considering that not all electronic stability control systems work as they should. In tests carried out by *Consumer Reports* magazine on 2003 models, the stability control system used in the Mitsubishi Montero was rated "unacceptable," BMW's X5 3.0i system provided poor emergency handling, and Acura's MDX and Subaru's Outback VDC stability systems left much to be desired.

Engines

Choose the most powerful 6- or 8-cylinder engine available if you're going to be doing a lot of highway driving, plan to carry a full passenger load and luggage on a regular basis, or intend to load up the vehicle with convenience features like air conditioning. Keep in mind that multipurpose vehicles with larger engines are easier to resell and retain their value the longest. For example, Honda's '96 Odyssey minivan was a sales dud in spite of its bulletproof reliability, mainly because buyers didn't want a minivan with an underpowered 4-cylinder power plant. Some people buy underpowered vehicles in the mistaken belief that increased fuel economy is a good trade-off for decreased engine performance. It isn't.

Cylinder Deactivation

Keep your fingers crossed. This was a scary fuel saver when it was used for a short time by GM in its 1981–82 Cadillacs. The company promptly dropped the option when owners complained the eight cylinders would often default to 4-cylinder power when accelerating. A variation of this feature is found on the Cadillac Northstar V8. It can run on four or eight cylinders. If the water pump fails, the engine can cycle air through half the engine while running on the other half, then switch back and forth. This way, the engine won't overheat, and you can limp home.

Honda fuel consumption will be cut by 20 percent by powering the 2005 Odyssey with a 3.5L V6 that runs on all six cylinders when accelerating and three cylinders when cruising. So far there have been no complaints, and Honda has expanded the technology in its 2006 Accord Hybrid.

Engine and Transmission Cooling System (Heavy-Duty)

This relatively inexpensive option provides extra cooling for the transmission and engine. It can extend the life of these components by preventing overheating when heavy towing is required.

Flat-Folding Rear Seats

Fold-down rear seats give sedans and coupes additional room to carry long or bulky items. Split-folding rear seats are the most useful because they allow you to carry another passenger in the rear with one of the seats folded.

Keyless Entry (Remote)

An essential option for the 30 percent of cars that don't come with a passenger-side manual door lock. With this safety and convenience option, you don't need to fiddle with the key in a dark parking lot or take off a glove in cold weather to unlock or lock the vehicle. Best bet: A keyless entry system combined with anti-theft capability, such as an ignition kill switch or some other disabler.

 ## Paint Colour

Choosing a popular colour can make your vehicle easier to sell at a good price. DesRosiers Automotive Consultants says that blue is the preferred colour overall, but green and silver are also popular with Canadians. Manheim Auctioneers says that green-coloured vehicles brought in 97.9 of the average auction price, while silver ones sold at a premium 105.5 percent. Remember that certain colours require particular care. For example:

BLACK (AND OTHER DARK COLOURS): These are most susceptible to sun damage because of their heavy absorption of ultraviolet rays.

PEARL-TONED COLOURS: These are the most difficult to work with. If the paint needs to be retouched, it must be matched to look right from both the front- and side-angle views.

RED: This also shows sun damage, so keep your car in a garage or shady spot whenever possible.

WHITE: Although grime looks terrible on a white car, white is the easiest colour to care for.

Power-Assisted Sliding Doors, Mirrors, Windows, and Seats

Merely a convenience feature with cars, power-assisted windows and doors are a necessity with minivans—crawling across the front seat a few times to roll up the passenger-side window or lock the doors will quickly convince you of their value. Power seats with memory are particularly useful if a vehicle is driven by more than one person. Automatic window and seat controls currently have few reliability problems, and they're fairly inexpensive to install, troubleshoot, and repair. As a safety precaution, make sure the window control has to be lifted. This will ensure no child is strangled from pressing against the switch. Power-sliding doors are even more of a danger. They are failure-prone on all makes and shouldn't be purchased by families with children.

Side Airbags

A worthwhile feature if you are the right size and properly seated, side airbags are presently way overpriced and aren't very effective unless the head and upper torso are protected. Side airbags are often featured as a $500 add-on to the sticker price, but you would be wise to bargain aggressively; insiders say automakers pay only about $100 for a pair of side curtain airbags.

Stow-N-Go Seating

Pioneered by Chrysler in its minivans, Stow-N-Go seating allows the second- and third-row seats to be folded into, not onto, the floor. Folding the seats is a one-hand operation and the head restraints don't need to be removed. Pop the spring-loaded seats back up, and there's an in-floor storage bin under each seat. One caveat: These seats sacrifice comfort for versatility. But check them out.

Suspension (Heavy-Duty)

Always a good idea, this inexpensive option pays for itself by providing better handling, allowing additional ride comfort (though a bit on the firm side), and extending shock life an extra year or two.

Tires

There are three rules to remember when purchasing tires. First, neither brand nor price is a reliable gauge of performance, quality, or durability. Second, choosing a tire recommended by the automaker may not be in your best interest, since traction and long tread life are often sacrificed for a softer ride and maximum EPA mileage ratings. And third, don't buy any new tire that's older than two years, since the rubber compound may have deteriorated because of poor handling and improper storage (if they've been stored near electrical motors). You can check the date of manufacture on the side wall.

There are two types of tires: all-season and performance. Touring is just a fancier name for all-season tires. All-season radial tires cost between $90 and $150 per tire. They're a compromise, since according to Transport Canada, they won't get you through winter with the same margin of safety as snow tires will, and they don't provide the same durability on dry surfaces as do regular summer tires. In areas with low to moderate snowfall, however, these tires are adequate as long as they're not pushed beyond their limits.

Mud or snow tires provide the best traction on snowy surfaces, but traction on wet roads is actually decreased. Treadwear is also accelerated by the use of softer rubber compounds. Beware of using wide tires for winter driving; 70-series or wider give poor traction and tend to float over snow.

Self-sealing and run-flat tires

Today, there are two technologies available to help maintain vehicle mobility when a tire is punctured: self-sealing and self-supporting, or run-flat, tires.

SELF-SEALING: Ideal if you drive long distances. Punctures are fixed instantly and permanently with a sealant that seals most punctures from nails, bolts, or screws up to 3/16 of an inch in diameter. A low air pressure warning system isn't required.

Expert testers say a punctured self-sealing tire can maintain air pressure for up to 200 kilometres—even in freezing conditions. The Uniroyal Tiger Paw NailGard ($85–$140, depending on size) is the overall winner in a side-by-side test conducted by the Tire Rack.com.

SELF-SUPPORTING/RUN-FLAT: Priced from $175 to $350 per tire, 25 to 50 percent more than the price of comparable premium tires, Goodyear's Extended Mobility Tire (EMT) run-flat tires were first offered as an option on the 1994 Chevrolet Corvette, and then became standard on the 1997 model. These tires reinforce the side wall, so it can carry the weight of the car for 90 kilometres, or about an hour's driving time, even after all air pressure has been lost. You won't feel the tire go flat and must depend upon a $250–$300 optional tire pressure monitor to warn you before the sidewall collapses and you begin riding on your rim. Also, not all vehicles can adapt to run-flat tires; you may need to upgrade your rims. Experts say run-flats will give your car a harder ride and you'll likely notice more interior tire and road noise. The car might also track differently. The 2004 Sienna Dunlop Run Flat Tech tires have a terrible reputation for premature wear. At 25,000 km, one owner complained that her Sienna needed a new set at $200 each. You can expect a backlog of over a month to get a replacement, and Toyota doesn't include any type of spare. Goodyear has had their EMT and Pirelli, their P-Zero tires for some time now, and they seem to perform adequately. Don't make a final choice before talking with an auto manufacturer rep as to what's recommended and how your warranty will be affected.

 ## Which tires are best?

There is no independent Canadian agency that evaluates tire performance and durability. However, the U.S.-based NHTSA rates treadwear, traction, and resistance to sustained high temperatures and etches them onto all tires sold in the States and Canada, and also regularly posts its findings on the Internet (*www.nhtsa.dot.gov*). The treadwear grade is fixed at a base 100 points and the tire's wear rate is measured after the tire is driven through a course that approximates most driving conditions. A tire rated 300 will last three times as long as one rated 100.

I've come up with the following tire ratings after researching government tests, consumer comments, and industry insiders. Remember, some of the brand names are subject to change.

DUNLOP D65 TOURING AND SP20 AS: Treadwear rated 520. These tires are the bargain of the group. They provide excellent wet and dry cornering and good steering response.

GOODRICH CONTROL TA M65: Treadwear rated 360. This tire excels at snowbelt performance.

GOODYEAR AQUATRED #3: Treadwear rated 340. This tire is a bit noisy and its higher-rolling resistance cuts fuel economy. Still, it's an exceptional performer on wet roads and works especially well on front-drive cars where the weight is over the front tires. Average performance on dry pavement.

GOODYEAR REGATTA #2: Treadwear rated 460. This tire does everything well, including keeping tire noise to a minimum.

MICHELIN MX4: Treadwear rated 320. This tire gives a smoother ride and a sharper steering response than the Aquatred. MX1 is also an excellent winter performer.

PIRELLI P300 AND P400: Treadwear rated 460 and 420. These are two of the best all-around all-season tires.

YOKOHAMA TC320: Treadwear rated 300. This is an Aquatred knock-off that performs almost as well for half the price.

REPLACEMENTS FOR HIGH-PERFORMANCE TIRES

VEHICLE	ALTERNATE TIRE BRAND
2003 BMW X5 3.0i	Continental 4X4 Contact
2003 Nissan Maxima GXE	Continental ContiTouring Contact CH95
2005 Chrysler 300C	Pirelli P6 Four Seasons
2003 Lexus IS 300	Pirelli P6 Four Seasons

OTHER GOOD TIRE CHOICES

WINTER ALL-SEASON	GRAND TOURING ALL-SEASON
Dunlop Winter Sport M2	Continental ContiPremierContact
Dunlop Winter Sport M3	Continental ContiTouringContact CV
*Goodyear Ultra Grip	*Dayton Grenadier PLE
Mastercraft Glacier Grip II	*Goodyear Assurance Triple Tred
Michelin Pilot Alpin PA2	*Hankook Mileage Plus II
Michelin Pilot Alpin	Kumho HP4 716
*Michelin X-Ice	Kumho ECSTA HP4 716
Pirelli Winter 240 SnowSport	Michelin Energy MXV4-A Plus
Pirelli Winter 210 SnowSport	*Michelin Hydro Edge
*Viking Snow Tech	*Michelin X-Radial
	*Yokohama Avid TRZ

*Best-performing tires in this category

OTHER GOOD TIRE CHOICES (CONTINUED)

STANDARD TOURING ALL-SEASON	PASSENGER CAR ALL-SEASON
BFGoodrich Touring T/A TR4	Goodyear Assurance ComforTred
BFGoodrich Touring T/A VR4	Goodyear Assurance TripleTred
Dunlop D65 T Touring	Michelin Harmony
Dunlop D65 T Touring Elite	Michelin HydroEdge
Goodyear Regatta 2	Uniroyal Laredo AWR
Kumho Touring A/S 795	Yokohama Aegis LS4
Kumho Touring Plus 732	
Michelin MXV4	
Pirelli P400 Touring	
Pirelli P4000 Super Touring	
Yokohama AVID Touring	
Yokohama AVID TRZ	
Yokohama Y376B	

Traction Control

This option limits wheelspin when accelerating. It is most useful with rear-drive vehicles and provides surer traction in wet or icy conditions.

Trailer-Towing Equipment

Just because you need a vehicle with towing capability doesn't mean that you have to spend big bucks. The first things you should determine before choosing a towing option are whether you need a pickup or small van to do the job and whether your tires will handle the extra burden. For most towing needs (up to 900 kilograms/2,000 pounds), a passenger car, small pickup, or minivan will work just as well as a full-sized pickup or van (and cost much less). If you're pulling a trailer that weighs more than 900 kilograms, most passenger cars won't handle the load unless they've been specially outfitted according to the automaker's specifications. Pulling a heavier trailer (up to 1,800 kilograms/4,000 pounds) will likely require a compact passenger van. You may, however, have to keep your speed at 72.4 km/h (45 mph) or less as Toyota suggests with the 2004 Sienna.

Automakers reserve the right to change limits whenever they feel like it, so make any sales promise an integral part of your contract (see "False Advertising" in Part Two). A good rule of thumb is to reduce the promised tow rating by 20 percent. In assessing towing weight, factor in the cargo, passengers, and equipment of both the trailer and the tow vehicle. Keep in mind that five people and luggage add 450 kilograms (1,000 lb.) to the load, and that a full 227-litre (50-gallon) water tank adds another 225 kilograms (500 lb.). The manufacturer's gross vehicle weight rating (GVWR) takes into account the anticipated average cargo and supplies that your vehicle is likely to carry.

Automatic transmissions are fine for trailering, although there's a slight fuel penalty. Manual transmissions tend to have greater clutch wear caused by towing than do automatic transmissions. Both transmission choices are equally acceptable. Remember, the best compromise is to shift the automatic manually for maximum performance going uphill and to maintain control while not overheating the brakes when descending mountains.

Unibody vehicles (those without a separate frame) can handle most trailering jobs as long as their limits aren't exceeded. Front-drives aren't the best choice for pulling heavy loads in excess of 900 kilograms, since they lose some steering control and traction with all the weight concentrated in the rear.

Whatever vehicle you choose, keep in mind that the trailer hitch is crucial. It must have a tongue capacity of at least 10 percent of the trailer's weight; otherwise it may be unsafe to use. Hitches are chosen according to the type of tow vehicle and, to a lesser extent, the weight of the load.

Most hitches are factory-installed, even though independents can install them more cheaply. Expect to pay about $200 for a simple boat hitch and a minimum of $600 for a fifth-wheel version.

Equalizer bars and extra cooling systems for the radiator, transmission, engine oil, and steering are a prerequisite for towing anything heavier than 900 kilograms. Heavy-duty springs and brakes are a big help, too. Separate brakes for the trailer may be necessary to increase your vehicle's maximum towing capacity.

Transmissions

Despite its many advantages, the manual transmission is an endangered species in North America, where manuals equip only 12 percent of all new vehicles (mostly econocars, sports cars, and budget trucks). European buyers opt for a manual transmission almost 90 percent of the time.

A transmission with four or more forward speeds is usually more fuel efficient than one with three forward speeds, and manual transmissions are usually more efficient than automatics, although this isn't always the case.

Unnecessary Options

Anti-Lock Brakes (ABS)

ABS is another safety feature that's fine in theory but impractical under actual driving conditions. The system maintains directional stability by preventing the wheels from locking up. This will *not* reduce the stopping distance, however. In practice, ABS makes drivers overconfident. Many still pump the brakes and render them ineffective, total brake failure is common, and repairs are frequent, complicated, and expensive to perform.

Cruise Control

Automakers provide this $250–$300 option, which is mainly a convenience feature, to motorists who use their vehicles for long periods of high-speed driving. The constant rate of speed saves some fuel and lessens driver fatigue during long trips. Still, the system is particularly failure-prone and expensive to repair, can lead to driver inattention, and can make the vehicle hard to control on icy roadways. Malfunctioning cruise control units are also one of the major causes of sudden acceleration incidents. At other times, cruise control can be very distracting, especially to inexperienced drivers who are unaccustomed to sudden speed fluctuations.

Electronic Instrument Readout

If you've ever had trouble reading a digital watch face or resetting your VCR, you'll feel right at home with this electronic gizmo. Gauges are presented in a series of moving digital patterns that are confusing, distracting, and unreadable in direct sunlight. This system is often accompanied by a trip computer and vehicle monitor that determine fuel use and how many kilometres until the tank is empty, indicate average speed, and signal component failures. Figures are frequently in error or slow to catch up.

Foglights

A pain in the eyes for other drivers, foglights aren't necessary for most drivers with well-aimed original-equipment headlights.

Gas-Saving Gadgets and Fuel Additives

The accessory market has been flooded with hundreds of gas-saving gadgets and fuel additives that purport to make these vehicles less fuel-thirsty. There isn't one on the Canadian market that works, according to Transport Canada, and the use of any of these products is a quick way to render your warranty invalid.

GPS Navigation Systems (Portable)

This $1,500–$2,000 navigation aid links a GPS satellite unit to the vehicle's cellular phone and electronics. For a monthly fee, the unit connects drivers to live operators who will help them with driving directions, give repair or emergency assistance, or relay messages. If the airbag deploys or the car is stolen, satellite-transmitted signals are automatically sent from the vehicle to operators who will notify the proper authorities of the vehicle's location.

Many of the systems' functions can be performed by a cellular telephone, and the navigation screens may be obtrusive, distracting, washed out in sunlight, and hard to calibrate. A portable Garmin GPS unit is more user-friendly and much cheaper.

High-Intensity Headlights

These headlights are much brighter than standard headlights, and they cast a blue hue. Granted, they provide additional illumination of the roadway, but they are also annoying to oncoming drivers, who will flash their lights at you, thinking your high beams are on. These lights are easily stolen and expensive to replace.

ID Etching

This $150–$200 option is a scam. The government doesn't require it, and thieves and joyriders aren't deterred by the etchings. If you want to etch your windows for your own peace of mind, several private companies will sell you a $15–$30 kit that does an excellent job (*www.autoetch.net*), or you can wait for your municipality or local police agency to conduct one of their periodic free VIN ID etching sessions in your area.

Paint and Fabric Protectors

Selling for $200–$300, these "sealants" add nothing to a vehicle's resale value. Although paint lustre may be temporarily heightened, this treatment is less effective and more costly than regular waxing, and it may also invalidate the manufacturer's guarantee at a time when the automaker will look for any pretext to deny your paint claim.

Auto fabric protection products are nothing more than variations of Scotchguard, which can be bought in aerosol cans for a few dollars—a much better deal than the $50–$75 charged by dealers.

Power-Assisted Minivan Sliding Doors

Not a good idea if you have children. These doors have a high failure rate, opening or closing for no apparent reason and injuring children caught between the door and post.

Reverse-Warning System

Selling for about $500 as part of an option package, this safety feature warns the driver of any objects in the rear when backing up. Although a sound idea in theory, in practice the device often fails to go off or sounds an alarm for no reason. Drivers eventually either disconnect or ignore it.

Rollover Detection System

This feature makes use of sensors to determine if the vehicle has leaned beyond a safe angle. If so, the side airbags are automatically deployed and remain inflated to make sure occupants aren't injured or ejected in a rollover accident. This is a totally new system that has not been proven. It could have disastrous consequences if the sensor malfunctions, as has been the case with front and side airbag sensors over the past decade.

Rooftop Carrier

Although this inexpensive option provides additional baggage space and may allow you to meet all your driving needs with a smaller vehicle, a loaded roof rack can increase fuel consumption by as much as 5 percent. An empty rack cuts fuel economy by about 1 percent.

Rustproofing

Rustproofing is no longer necessary, since automakers have extended their own rust warranties. In fact, you have a greater chance of seeing your rustproofer go belly up than having your untreated vehicle ravaged by premature rusting. Even if the rustproofer stays in business, you're likely to get a song and dance about why the warranty won't cover so-called internal rusting, or why repairs will be delayed until the sheet metal is actually rusted through.

 Be wary of electronic rustproofing. Selling for $425 to $665.99, these electrical devices claim to inhibit vehicle corrosion by sending out a pulse current to the grounded body panels, protecting areas that conventional rust-inhibiting products can't reach. There is much debate as to whether these devices are worth the cost, or work at all.

If you live in an area where roads are heavily salted in winter, or in a coastal region, have your vehicle washed every few weeks and undercoated annually, paying particular attention to rocker panels (door bottoms) and wheelwells. Also, don't use a heated garage in winter; Canadian studies show that a heated garage will accelerate the damage caused by corrosion.

Sunroof

Unless you live in a temperate region, the advantages of a sunroof are far outweighed by its disadvantages. You're not going to get better ventilation than a good AC system would provide, and a sunroof may grace your environment with painful booming wind noises, rattles, water leaks, and road dust accumulation. A sunroof increases gas consumption, reduces night vision because overhead highway lights shine through the roof opening, and can lose you several inches of headroom.

Tinted Glass

On the one hand, tinting jeopardizes your safety by reducing your night vision. On the other hand, it does keep the interior cool in hot weather, reduces glare, and hides the car's contents from prying eyes. Factory applications are worth the extra cost, since cheaper aftermarket products (costing about $100) distort visibility and peel away after a few years. Some tinting done in the United States can run afoul of provincial highway codes that require more transparency.

Cutting the Price

 ### Bidding by Fax or Email

Dealers are more receptive to fax and email bidding this year because showroom traffic has dwindled without "employee" discount programs. The process is quite easy: Simply fax or email an invitation for bids to area dealerships, asking them to give their bottom-line price for a specific make and model. Be clear that all final bids must be sent within a week. When all the bids are received, the lowest bid is sent to the other dealers to give them a chance to beat that price. After a week of bidding, the lowest price gets your business.

Dozens of *Lemon-Aid* readers have told me how this approach has cut thousands of dollars from the advertised price and saved them from the degrading song-and-dance routine between the buyer, sales agent, and sales manager ("you said, he said, the sales manager said").

A *Lemon-Aid* reader sent in the following suggestions for buying by fax:

> First, I'd like to thank you for writing the *Lemon-Aid* series of books, which I have used extensively in the fax-tendering purchase of my '99 Accord and '02 Elantra. I have written evidence from dealers that I saved a bare minimum of $700 on the Accord (but probably more) and a whopping $900 on the Elantra through the use of

fax-tendering, over and above any deals possible through Internet-tendering and/or showroom bargaining.

Based on my experience, I would suggest that in reference to the fax-tendering process, future *Lemon-Aid* editions emphasize:

- Casting a wide geographical net, as long as you're willing to pick the car up there. I faxed up to 50 dealerships, which helped tremendously in increasing the number of serious bidders. One car was bought locally in Ottawa, the other in Mississauga.
- Unless you don't care much about what car you end up with...be very specific about what you want. If you are looking at just one or two cars, which I recommend, specify trim level and all extended warranties and dealer-installed options in the fax letter. Otherwise, you'll end up with quotes comparing apples and oranges, and you won't get the best deal on options negotiated later. Also, specify that quotes should be signed—this helps out with errors in quoting.
- Dealerships are sloppy—there is a 25–30 percent error rate in quotes. Search for errors and get corrections, and confirm any of the quotes in serious contention over the phone.
- Phone to personally thank anyone who submits a quote for their time. Salespeople can't help themselves, they'll ask how they ranked, and often want to then beat the best quote you've got. This is much more productive than faxing back the most competitive quote (I know, I've tried that too).

Another reader, in British Columbia, was successful with this approach:

I purchased your 2005 edition *SUVs, Vans, and Trucks* earlier this year from Chapters. Thanks for all the information that helped me decide to purchase a new Honda Odyssey EX-L for a super price from a good dealer. After completing my research (and vacillating for a few weeks) I ended up issuing a faxed "request for quotation" (RFQ) from several dealerships. I can tell you that some of them were not happy and tried to tell me that Honda Canada was clamping down on this activity. In the end, one dealership did not respond and one "closer" salesperson called to attempt to get me in their dealership so he could "assess my needs." I told him that my needs were spelled out very specifically in my request but he refused to give me a price. In the end, I received five quotations by phone, fax, and email. I purchased my van in Chilliwack for about $2,200 off list. It turned out that the salesperson just started selling cars two months ago and was very appreciative of my business. The whole deal was completed in half an hour. I was in full control but treated every respondent fairly. I did not play dealers off one another and went with the lowest first offer.

Here is the fax bid request I sent to the dealers:

SAMPLE FAX BID REQUEST

WITHOUT PREJUDICE

Date: _____

Dear Sir or Madam,

I will be purchasing a new 2005 Toyota Sienna or a new 2005 Honda Odyssey and am issuing a request for quotation to several dealerships. I am willing to travel to complete a deal.

The quoted price is to *include* my requested options as well as any applicable pre-delivery inspection, administration, documentation, freight, and delivery fees. I understand that tire tax, air conditioning tax, battery tax, and provincial and federal sales tax are extra and are not required on your quotation. The dealer may sell off the lot or order the vehicle.

Please complete the attached form and either fax or email it back to me before the deadline of *5:00pm, April 14, 2005*. All respondents will be contacted after the deadline to confirm their bid. The winning bidder will then be contacted soon after to complete the transaction.

I will accept an alternate price quotation for a demonstration model with similar options, but this is not a mandatory requirement.

Please direct any questions via email to me at _____ and I will respond promptly. Alternately you may call me at my office at _____.

Sincerely,
Joe Buyer

Getting a Fair Price

"We Sell Below Cost"

No dealers sell below their cost. If they did, they wouldn't be in business for long. This is just part of the sorry spectacle seen every day in dealerships as sellers use any argument to achieve the average $1,500-U.S.-per-new-car profit that *Automotive News* says they make. It's not surprising that "real" prices and "true sales commissions" are shrouded in mystery. However, we can easily see the the profit margins by comparing the list price with discounted prices offered in the spring and summer. I've listed the percentage difference below, excluding freight, PDI, and administrative fees, which you should bargain down.

DEALER MARKUP

DEALER MARKUP (AMERICAN VEHICLES)		DEALER MARKUP (JAPANESE VEHICLES)	
small cars:	12–18%	small cars:	10–15%
mid-sized cars:	15–20%	mid-sized cars:	15–20%
large cars:	20+%	large cars:	20+%
sports cars:	25%	sports cars:	20+%
high-end sports cars:	25+%	high-end sports cars:	25+%
luxury cars:	25+%	luxury cars:	25+%
high-end luxury cars:	25–30+%	high-end luxury cars:	25+%
minivans:	20%	minivans:	20%
high-end minivans:	25+%	high-end minivans:	25+%

South Korean prices are the most negotiable, while Japanese and European vehicle prices are much firmer. In addition to the dealer's markup, some vehicles may also have a 3 percent carryover allowance paid out in a dealer incentive program. Finance contracts may also tack on a 3 percent dealer commission.

Holdback

Ever wonder how dealers who advertise vehicles for "a hundred dollars over invoice" can make a profit? They are counting mostly upon the manufacturer's holdback.

In addition to the MSRP, the invoice price, dealer incentives, and customer rebates (available to Canadians at *www.apa.ca*), another key element in every dealer's profit margin is the manufacturer's holdback—quarterly payouts dealers depend upon when calculating gross profit.

The holdback was set up almost 40 years ago by General Motors as a guaranteed profit for dealers tempted to bargain away their entire profit to make a sale. It usually represents 1–3 percent of the sticker price (MSRP) and is seldom given out by Asian or European automakers, who use dealer incentive programs instead. There are several free Internet sources for holdback information: The most recent and comprehensive are *www.edmunds.com* and *www.kbb.com*, two websites geared toward American buyers. Although there may be a difference in the holdback percentage between American automakers and their Canadian subsidiaries, it's usually not significant.

Some GM dealers maintain that they no longer get a holdback allowance. They are being disingenuous—the holdback may have been added to special sales "incentive" programs, which won't show up on the dealer's invoice. Options are the icing on the cake, with their average 35–65 percent markup.

Can You Get a Fair Price?

Yes, but you'll have to keep your wits about you and time your purchase well into the model year—usually in late winter or spring.

New-car negotiations aren't wrestling matches where you have to pin the sales agent's shoulders to the mat to win. If you feel that the overall price is fair, don't jeopardize the deal by refusing to budge. For example, if you've brought the contract price 10 percent or more below the MSRP and the dealer sticks you with a $200 "administrative fee" at the last moment, let it pass. You've saved money and the sales agent has saved face.

Of course someone will always be around to tell you how he or she could have bought the vehicle for much less. Let that pass, too.

To come up with a fair price, subtract one-half the dealer markup from the MSRP and trade the carryover and holdback allowance for a reduced delivery and transportation fee. Compute the options separately and sell your trade-in privately. Buyers can more easily knock $2,000–$3,000 off a $20,000 base price if they wait until January or February when sales are stagnant, choose a vehicle in stock, and resist unnecessary options.

Beware of Financing and Insurance Traps

Once you and the dealer have settled on the vehicle's price, you aren't out of the woods yet. You'll be handed over to an F&I (financing and insurance) specialist, whose main goal is to convince you to buy additional financing, loan insurance, paint and seatcover protectors, rustproofing, and extended warranties. These items will be presented on a computer screen as costing only "a little bit more each month."

 Compare the dealer's insurance and financing charges with those from an independent agency that may offer better rates and better service. Often the dealer gets a kickback for selling insurance and financing, and guess who pays for it? Additionally, remember that if the financing rate looks too good to be true, you're probably paying too much for the vehicle. The F&I closer's hard-sell approach will take all your willpower and patience to resist, but when he or she gives up, your trials are over.

Add-on charges are the dealer's last chance to stick it to you before the contract is signed. Dealer pre-delivery inspection (PDI) and transportation charges, "documentation" fees, and extra handling costs are ways that the dealer gets extra profits for nothing. Dealer preparation is often a once-over-lightly affair, with a car seldom getting more than a wash job and a couple of dollars of gas in the tank. It's paid for by the factory in most cases and, when it's not, should cost no more than 2 percent of the car's selling price. Reasonable transportation charges are acceptable, although dealers who claim that the manufacturer requires the payment often inflate them.

"No Haggle" Pricing Means "Price-Fixing"

All dealers bargain. They hang out the "No dickering, one price only" sign simply as a means to discourage customers from asking for a better deal. Like parking lots and restaurants that claim they won't be responsible for lost or stolen property, they're bluffing. Still, you'd be surprised by how many people believe that if it's posted, it's non-negotiable.

No-haggle pricing is not only a deceptive practice, it's also illegal under federal price-fixing statutes. Several *Lemon-Aid* readers say some Honda dealers refuse to negotiate prices via email or fax (see page 72) because Honda Canada threatened to yank their franchise if they did so. Following *Lemon-Aid*'s formal complaint, the feds opened a formal investigation of Honda's practice.

In June 2004, Toyota Canada abandoned its Access no-haggle price strategy sales system after settling out of court a price-fixing probe undertaken by the federal Competition Bureau. Toyota is still the target of class-action lawsuits in Quebec and British Columbia, however, and the Automobile Protection Association says Toyota's actions have changed little since the settlement.

If you bought your Toyota in B.C. and feel you paid too much under Access, contact Leslie Mackoff at *lmackoff@mackoff.ca*. Mackoff's class-action lawsuit alleges dealers set prices unlawfully, refused to offer discounts from the Access price, and would not offer free options or extra features. Quebec buyers may file a similar claim with Daniel Belleau of *www.apa.ca*, a Montreal lawyer who has also filed a class-action claim in that province.

Price Guidelines

When negotiating the price of a new vehicle, remember there are several price guidelines, and dealers use the one that will make them the most profit on each transaction. Two of the more common prices quoted are the MSRP (what the automaker advertises as a fair price) and the dealer's invoice cost (which is supposed to indicate how much the dealer paid for the vehicle). Both price indicators leave considerable room for the dealer's profit margin, along with some extra padding in the form of inflated transportation and preparation charges. If you are presented with both figures, go with the MSRP, since it can be verified by calling

the manufacturer. Any dealer can print up an invoice and swear to its veracity. If you want an invoice price from an independent source, contact *Carcostcanada.com* (at 1-800-805-2270).

Buyers who live in rural areas and in Western Canada are often faced with grossly inflated auto prices compared to those charged in major metropolitan areas. A good way to get a more competitive price without buying out of province is to buy a couple of out-of-town newspapers (the Saturday *Toronto Star* "Wheels" section is especially helpful) and demand that your dealer bring his selling price, preparation charges, and transportation fees into line with the prices advertised.

Another tactic is to take a copy of a local competitor's car ad to a competing dealer selling the same brand and ask for a better price. Chances are they've already lost a few sales due to the ad and will work a little harder to match the deal; if not, they're almost certain to reveal the tricks in the competitor's promotion to make the sale.

Dealer Incentives and Customer Rebates

Automobile incentives have been around ever since Henry Ford offered $40–$60 rebates on the Model T in 1914. However, rebates were first used as a sales incentive in Canada and the States during Super Bowl Sunday in 1975, just after Detroit automakers raised prices 10 percent and lost sales because of what would later be called "sticker shock." Backpedalling furiously to regain sales, automakers cut some prices immediately, and added cash rebates of a few hundred dollars as an additional inducement. Sports broadcaster Joe Garagiola became the Chrysler rebate pitchman with his unforgettable tag line: "Buy a car. Get a check [$400]."

Sales incentives haven't changed much in the past 30 years. When vehicles are first introduced in the fall, they're generally overpriced; early in the new year, they'll sell for about 30 percent less. In the summer, many models will sell for almost half their original retail price through a combination of dealer sales incentives (manufacturer-to-dealer), cash rebates (manufacturer-to-customer), zero-percent interest financing (manufacturer-finance-company-to-customer), and discounted prices (dealer-to-customer).

The enormity of these discounts came to light this year as Detroit's Big Three engaged in cutthroat discounting early in 2005 and followed up with even more generous "employee discounts for all" during the summer.

Smart shoppers who delay their purchases for about six months routinely shave $10,000 to $13,000 off the dealer's list price.

In most cases, the manufacturer's rebate is straightforward and mailed directly to the buyer from the automaker. There are other rebate programs that require a financial investment on the dealer's part, however, and these shared programs tempt dealers to offset losses by inflating the selling price or pocketing the manufacturer's rebate. Therefore, when the dealer participates in the rebate program, demand that the rebate be deducted from the MSRP, and not from some inflated invoice price concocted by the dealer.

Some rebate ads will include the phrase "from dealer inventory only." If your dealer doesn't have the vehicle in stock, you won't get the rebate.

Sometimes automakers will suddenly decide that a rebate no longer applies to a specific model, even though their ads continue to include it. When this happens, take all brochures and advertisements showing your eligibility for the rebate plan to provincial consumer protection officials. They can use false advertising statutes to force automakers to give rebates to every purchaser who was unjustly denied one.

If you are buying a heavily discounted vehicle, be wary of "option packaging" by dealers who push unwanted protection packages (rustproofing, paint sealants, and upholstery finishes), or who levy excessive charges for preparation, filing fees, loan guarantee insurance, and credit life insurance.

Rebates and Quality

Forget the old adage, "you get what you pay for." Many reliable, top-performing vehicles come with rebates—they just aren't as generous as what you'll find with more mediocre choices. For example, rarely will Toyota and Honda offer more than $1,000 rebates, whereas Chrysler, Ford, and GM routinely hand out $3,000 discounts and other sales incentives. To come out ahead, you have to know how to play this rebate game by choosing quality first.

Customer and dealer incentives are frequently given out to stimulate sales of year-old models that are unpopular, scheduled to be redesigned, or headed for the axe. By choosing carefully which rebated models you buy, it's easy to realize important savings with little risk. For example, GM's $2,000 incentives are good deals when applied to its reasonably reliable compact cars, but not worth it when applied to the company's glitch-prone front-drive minivans. Ford's F-150 pickup and Freestar minivan rebates ($3,000+) also aren't sufficient to offset the greater risk of factory-related defects afflicting these failure-prone models. DaimlerChrysler rebates can be a good deal when applied to minivans, but not advisable as a reason to buy the company's less reliable SUVs.

Inflated or Deflated Prices

Generally, vehicles are priced according to what the market will bear and then are discounted as the competition heats up (Chrysler and GM minivans and Ford trucks are prime examples). A vehicle's stylishness, scarcity, or general popularity can inflate its value considerably. For example, Chrysler's rear-drive Hemi-engine-equipped 2005 Magnum has a prevailing market value higher than its suggested selling price, mainly because it's in a hot market niche and in short supply. Once sales slow down later in the new year, popular but overpriced vehicles usually sell at a discount (VW's New Beetle, for example). With vehicles that have an inflated value, wait two years for their popularity to subside or purchase the previous year's version. If your choice has a deflated market value (like underpowered first-year Odysseys or overly maligned South Korean models), find out why it's so unpopular and then decide if the savings are worth it. Vehicles that don't sell because of their weird styling are no problem, but poor quality control (think Chrysler Concorde and Ford Focus) can cost big bucks.

Chrysler is dropping its 7-year powertrain warranty on 2006 models, and this will also be a big factor in the perceived value of its vehicles. Expect the company to be forced to add an extra $1,000 to its usual $2,000 rebates, igniting a rebate war more brutal than what was seen last year.

 **Leftovers**

In the fall, at the beginning of each new model year, most dealers still have a few of last year's vehicles left. Some are new, and some are demonstrators with a few thousand kilometres on them. The factory gives the dealer a 3–5 percent rebate on late-season vehicles, and dealers will often pass on some of these savings to clients. But are these leftovers really bargains?

They might be, if you can amortize the first year's depreciation by keeping the vehicle for eight years. But if you're the kind of driver who trades every two or three years, you're likely to come out a loser by buying an end-of-the-season vehicle. The simple reason is that as far as trade-ins are concerned, a leftover is a used vehicle that has depreciated at least 20 percent. The savings the dealer gives you may not equal that first year's depreciation (a cost you'll incur without getting any of the first year's driving benefits). If the dealer's discounted price matches or exceeds the 20 percent depreciation, then you're getting a pretty good deal. But if the next year's model is only a bit more expensive, has been substantially improved, or is covered by a more extensive, comprehensive warranty, it could represent a better buy than a cheaper leftover.

Ask the dealer for all work orders relating to the vehicle, including the PDI checklist, and make sure that the odometer readings follow in sequential order. Remember as well that most demonstrators should have less than 5,000 kilometres on the ticker, and that the original warranty has been reduced from the day the vehicle was first put on the road. Have the dealer extend the warranty or lower the price accordingly—about $100 for each month of warranty that has expired. If the vehicle's file shows that it was registered to a leasing agency or any other third party, you're definitely buying a used vehicle disguised as a demo. You should walk away from the sale—you're dealing with a crook.

Cash versus Financing

Let's clear up one myth right away: Dealers won't treat you better if you pay cash. They want you to buy a fully loaded vehicle and finance the whole deal. Paying cash is not advantageous to the dealer, since kickbacks on finance contracts represent an important part of the F&I division's profits. Actually, barely 8 percent of new-car buyers pay cash.

Those buyers may be making a big mistake. Financial planners say it can be smarter to borrow the money to purchase a new vehicle even if you can afford to pay cash, because if you use the vehicle for business, a portion of the interest may be tax-deductible. The cash that you free up can then be used to repay debts that aren't tax-deductible (mortgages or credit card debts, for example).

Rebates versus Low or Zero Percent Financing

If you are buying an expensive vehicle, like a luxury car or an SUV, and going for longer financing, the low-rate financing will be a better deal than the rebate. A zero percent loan will save you $80 per $1,000 financed over 24 months, or $120 per $1,000 financed over 36 months, compared with 7.5 percent financing. If you were financing a $30,000 car for two years, you'd multiply $80 × 30 and save about $2,400.

Low-financing programs have the following disadvantages:

• The buyer must have exceptionally good credit.
• A shorter financing period means higher payments.
• Cash rebates are excluded.
• Only fully equipped or slow-selling models are eligible.
• The buyer pays full retail price.

Remember, to get the best price, whether you're paying cash or financing the purchase, first negotiate the price of the vehicle without disclosing whether you are paying cash or financing the purchase (say you haven't yet decided). Once you have a fair price, then take advantage of the financing.

Getting a Loan

Borrowers must be at least 18 years old (age of majority), have a steady income, prove that they have discretionary income sufficient to make the loan payments, and be willing to guarantee the loan with additional collateral or their parent or spouse as a co-signer.

Before applying for a loan, you should have established a good credit rating via a paid-off credit card and have a small savings account with your local bank, credit union, or trust company. Prepare a budget listing your assets and obligations. This will quickly show whether or not you can afford a car. Next, pre-arrange your loan with a phone call. This will protect you from much of the smoke-and-mirrors showroom shenanigans.

Incidentally, if you do get in over your head and require credit counselling, contact Credit Counselling Service (CCS), a non-profit organization located in many of Canada's major cities (*www.creditcanada.com*).

Hidden Loan Costs

Don't trust anyone. The APA's undercover shoppers have found that most deceptive deals involve major banking institutions rather than automaker-owned companies.

In your quest for an auto loan, remember that the Internet offers help for people who need an auto loan and want quick approval, but don't want to face a banker. The Bank of Montreal (*www.bmo.com*) was the first Canadian bank to allow vehicle buyers to post a loan application on its website, and it promises to send a loan response within 20 seconds. Other banks, such as RBC, are offering a similar service. Loans are available to any web surfer, including those who aren't current Montreal or RBC customers.

 Be sure to call various financial institutions to find out the following:

- The annual percentage rate on the amount you want to borrow and for the duration of your repayment period
- The minimum down payment that the institution requires
- Whether taxes and licence fees are considered part of the overall cost and thus are covered by part of the loan
- Whether lower rates are available for different loan periods or for a larger down payment
- Whether discounts are available to depositors and, if so, how long you must be a depositor before qualifying

When comparing loans, consider the annual rate and calculate the total cost of the loan offer; that is, how much you'll pay above and beyond the total price of the vehicle.

Dealers can finance your purchase at interest rates that are competitive with the banks' because of the rebates they get from the manufacturers and some lending institutions. Some dealers, though, mislead their customers into thinking they can borrow money at as much as five percentage points below the prime rate. Actually, they're jacking up the retail price to more than make up for the lower interest charges. Sometimes, instead of boosting the price, dealers reduce the amount they pay for the trade-in. In either case, the savings are illusory.

When dealing with banks, keep in mind that the traditional 36-month loan has now been stretched to 48 or 60 months. Longer payment terms make each month's payment more affordable, but over the long run, they increase the cost of the loan considerably. Therefore, take as short a term as possible.

Be wary of lending institutions that charge a "processing" or "document" fee ranging from $25 to $100. Sometimes consumers will be charged an extra 1–2 percent of the loan up front in order to cover servicing. This is similar to lending institutions adding "points" to mortgages, except that with auto loans, it's totally unjustified. In fact, dealers in the States are the object of several state lawsuits and class actions for inflating loan charges.

Some banks will cut the interest rate if you're a member of an automobile owners' association or if loan payments are automatically deducted from your chequing account. This latter proposal may be costly, however, if the chequing-account charges exceed the interest-rate savings.

Finance companies affiliated with GM, Ford, and Chrysler have been offering low-interest loans many points below the prime rate. In many cases, this low rate is applicable only to hard-to-sell models or vehicles equipped with expensive options. The low rate frequently doesn't cover the entire loan period. If vehicles recommended in this book are covered by low-interest loans, however, then the automaker-affiliated finance companies become a useful alternative to regular banking institutions.

Loan Protection

Credit insurance guarantees that the vehicle loan will be paid if the borrower becomes disabled or dies. There are three basic types of insurance that can be written into an installment contract: credit life, accident and health, and comprehensive. Most bank and credit union loans are already covered by some kind of loan insurance, but dealers sell the protection separately at an extra cost to the borrower. For this service, the dealer gets a hefty 20 percent commission. The additional cost to the purchaser can be significant. The federal 7 percent GST is applied to loan insurance, but PST may be exempted in some provinces.

Collecting on these types of policies isn't easy. There's no payment if your illness is caused by some condition that existed prior to your taking out the insurance. Nor will the policy cover situations like strikes, layoffs, or being fired. Generally, credit insurance is unnecessary if you're in good health, you have no dependents, and your job is secure.

Personal loans from financial institutions now offer lots of flexibility. Most offer financing (with a small down payment), fixed or variable interest rates, a choice of loan terms, and no penalties for prepayment. Precise conditions depend on your personal credit rating. Finally, credit unions can also underwrite new vehicle loans that combine a flexible payment schedule with low rates.

Leasing contracts are less flexible. There's a penalty for any prepayment, and rates aren't necessarily competitive.

 **Financing Scams**

Financing was turned down

This scam usually begins after you have purchased the car and left your trade-in with the dealer. A few days later you are told that your loan was rejected and that you now must put down a larger down payment and accept a higher monthly payment. Of course, your trade-in has already been sold.

Protect yourself from this rip-off by getting a signed agreement that stipulates the financing has been approved and that monthly payments can't be readjusted. Don't give up your trade-in until that agreement has been reached.

Dealer offers to pay off your existing lease or loan

The dealer will. And then the dealer will add what was paid to your new loan at a much higher interest rate. Early termination of your lease will also likely expose you to substantial penalty costs.

Negotiating the Contract

How likely are you to be cheated when buying a new car? APA staffers posing as buyers visited 42 dealerships in four Canadian cities in early 2002. Almost half the dealers they visited (45 percent) flunked their test, and (hold onto your cowboy hats) auto buyers in Western Canada are especially vulnerable to dishonest dealers.

In Vancouver and Edmonton, dealer ads either left out important information or vehicles in the ads weren't available or were selling at higher prices. Fees for paperwork and vehicle preparation were frequently excessive, with Chrysler dealerships in Vancouver and Toronto charging the most ($299–$632). In some cases, the dealers may have double-billed the buyer. In Toronto, pre-delivery charges of $343 and $89 were levied on top of Chrysler's $955 PDI/transport fee.

Chrysler and Ford dealerships performed the worst overall, Toyota and General Motors performed best, and Mazda and Hyundai dealers were mediocre (they charged extra for items other automakers include in the base price). APA found that Toyota dealers demonstrated a superior level of product knowledge, covered all the bases more consistently, and applied the least pressure to make a sale. But Toyota dealers in the regions with Access-fixed selling prices appeared to charge substantially more.

The Devil's in the Details

Watch what you sign, since any document that requires your signature is a contract. Don't sign anything unless all the details are clear to you and all the blanks have been filled in. Don't accept any verbal promises that you're merely putting the vehicle on hold. And when you are presented with a contract, remember it doesn't have to include all the clauses found in the dealer's pre-printed form. You and the sales representative can agree to strike some clauses and add others.

ADDITIONAL CONTRACT CLAUSES

1. **Original contract:** This is the ONLY contract; i.e., it cannot be changed, retyped, or rewritten, without the specific agreement of both parties.

2. **Financing:** This agreement is subject to the purchaser obtaining financing at _____% or less within _____ days of the date below.

3. **"In-service" date and mileage:** To be based on the closing day, not the day the contract was executed, and will be submitted to GM for warranty and all other purposes. The General dealership will have this date corrected by GM if it should become necessary.

4. **Delivery:** The vehicle is to be delivered by _____, failing which the contract is cancelled and the deposit will be refunded.

5. **Cancellation:**

   (a) The purchaser retains the right to cancel this agreement without penalty at any time before delivery of the vehicle by sending a notice in writing to the vendor.

   (b) Following delivery of the vehicle, the purchaser shall have two days to return the vehicle and cancel the agreement in writing, without penalty. After two days and before thirty-one days, the purchaser shall pay the dealer $25 a day as compensation for depreciation on the returned vehicle.

   (c) Cancellation of contract can be refused where the vehicle has been subjected to abuse, negligence, or unauthorized modifications after delivery.

   (d) The purchaser is responsible for accident damage and traffic violations while in possession of the said vehicle.

6. **Protected Price:** The vendor agrees not to alter the price of the new vehicle, the cost of preparation, or the cost of shipping.

7. **Trade-in:** The vendor agrees that the value attributed to the vehicle offered in trade shall not be reduced, unless it has been significantly modified or has suffered from unreasonable and accelerated deterioration since the signing of the agreement.

8. **Courtesy Car:**

   (a) In the event the new vehicle is not delivered on the agreed-upon date, the vendor agrees to supply the purchaser with a courtesy car at no cost. If no courtesy vehicle is available, the vendor agrees to reimburse the purchaser the cost of renting a vehicle.

   (b) If the vehicle is off the road for more than five days for warranty repairs, the purchaser is entitled to a free courtesy vehicle for the duration of the repair period. If no courtesy vehicle is available, the vendor agrees to reimburse the purchaser the cost of renting a vehicle of equivalent or lesser value.

9. **Work Orders:** The purchaser will receive duly completed copies of all work orders pertaining to the vehicle, including warranty repairs and the pre-delivery inspection (PDI).

10. **Dealer Stickers:** The vendor will not affix any dealer advertising, in any form, on the vehicle.

11. **Fuel:** Vehicle will be delivered with a free full tank of gas.

12. **Excess Mileage:** New vehicle will not be acceptable and the contract will be void if the odometer has more than 50 km at delivery/closing.

13. **Tires:** Original equipment Firestone, Bridgestone, or Goodyear tires are not acceptable.

_____ _____ _____
Date   Vendor's Signature   Buyer's Signature

When the sales agent asks for a deposit, make sure that it's listed on the contract as a deposit and try to keep it as small as possible (a couple hundred dollars at the most). If you decide to back out of the deal on a vehicle taken from stock, let the seller have the deposit as an incentive to cancel the contract (believe me, it's cheaper than a lawyer and probably equal to the dealer's commission).

Scrutinize all references to the exact model (there is a heck of an upgrade from base to LX or Limited), prices, and delivery dates. Delivery can sometimes be delayed three to five months, and you'll have to pay all price increases announced during the interim (1–2 percent) unless you specify a delivery date in the contract that protects the price.

Make sure that the contract indicates that your new vehicle will be delivered to you with a full tank of gas. Once this was the buyer's responsibility, but now, with drivers spending over $30,000 for the average new vehicle, dealers usually throw in the tank of gas.

 ## Clauses You Should Change

You can put things on a more equal footing by negotiating the inclusion of as many clauses as possible from the sample additional contract clauses found on the previous page. To do this, write in a "Remarks" section on your contract and add "See attached clauses, which form part of this agreement." Then attach a photocopy of the "Additional Contract Clauses" page and persuade the sales agent to initial as many of the clauses as possible. Although some clauses may be rejected, the inclusion of just a couple of them can have important legal ramifications later on if you want a full or partial refund.

"We Can't Do That"

Don't take the dealer's word that "we're not allowed to do that"—heard most often in reference to your reducing the PDI or transportation fee. Some dealers have been telling *Lemon-Aid* readers that they are "obligated" by the automaker to charge a set fee and could lose their franchise if they charge less. This is pure hogwash. No dealer has ever had their franchise licence revoked for cutting prices. Furthermore, the automakers clearly state that they don't set a bottom price, since doing so would violate Canada's *Competition Act*—that's why you always see them putting disclaimers in their ads saying the dealer can charge less.

The Pre-delivery Inspection

The best way to ensure that the PDI (written as PDE in some regions) will be done is to write in the sales contract that you'll be given a copy of the completed PDI sheet when the vehicle is delivered to you. Then, with the PDI sheet in hand, verify some of the items that were to be checked. If any items appear to have been missed, refuse delivery of the vehicle. Once you get home, check out the vehicle more thoroughly and send a registered letter to the dealer if you discover any incomplete items from the PDI.

Selling Your Trade-In

When Is the Right Time?

It doesn't take a genius to figure out that the longer one keeps a vehicle, the less it costs to own—up to a point. The Hertz Corporation has estimated that a small car equipped with standard options, driven 16,000 km (10,000 mi.), and traded each year costs approximately 6 cents/km more to run than a comparable compact traded after five years. A small car kept for 10 years and driven 16,000 kilometres a year would cost 6.75 cents/km less than a similar vehicle kept for five years, and a whopping 12.75 cents/km less than a comparable vehicle traded in each year. That would amount to savings of $20,380 over a 10-year period.

If you're happy with your vehicle's styling and convenience features, and it's safe and dependable, there is no reason to get rid of it. But when the cost of repairs becomes equal to or greater than the cost of payments for a new car, then you need to consider trading it in. Shortly after your vehicle's fifth birthday (or whenever you start to think about trading it in), ask a mechanic to look at it to give you some idea of what repairs, replacement parts, and maintenance work it will need in the coming year. Find out if dealer service bulletins show that it will need extensive repairs in the near future (see Appendix I for how to order bulletins from ALLDATA). If it's going to require expensive repairs, you should trade the vehicle right away; if expensive work isn't necessary, you may want to keep it. Auto owner associations provide a good yardstick. They estimate that the annual cost of repairs and preventive maintenance for the average vehicle is between $700 and $800. If your vehicle is five years old and you haven't spent anywhere near $3,500 in maintenance, it would pay to invest in your old vehicle and continue using it for another few years.

Consider whether your vehicle can still be serviced easily. If it's no longer on the market, the parts supply is likely to dry up and independent mechanics will be reluctant to repair it.

Don't trade for fuel economy alone. Most fuel-efficient vehicles, such as front-drives, offset the savings through higher repair costs. Also, the more fuel-efficient vehicles may not be as comfortable to drive because of their excessive engine noise, lightweight construction, stiff suspension, and torque steer.

Reassess your needs. Has your family grown to the point that you need a new vehicle? Are you driving less? Are you taking fewer long trips? Let your truck or van show its age and pocket the savings if its deteriorating condition doesn't pose a safety hazard and isn't too embarrassing. If you're in sales and are constantly on the road, it makes sense to trade every few years—in that case, the vehicle's appearance and reliability become a prime consideration, particularly since the increased depreciation costs are mostly tax deductible.

Getting the Most for Your Trade-in

Customers who are on guard against paying too much for a new vehicle often sell their trade-ins for too little. Before agreeing to any trade-in amount, read Part Three of *Lemon-Aid Used Cars and Minivans*. The guide will give your vehicle's dealer and private selling price and offer a formula to figure out regional price fluctuations.

Now that you've nailed down your trade-in's approximate value, here are some tips on selling it with a minimum of stress:

- Never sign a new vehicle sales contract unless your trade-in has been sold—you could end up with two vehicles.
- Negotiate the price from *retail* (dealer price) down to *wholesale* (private sales).
- If you haven't sold your trade-in after two weekends, you might be trying to sell it at the wrong time of year or have it priced too high.

Private Sales

If you must sell your vehicle and want to make the most out of the deal, consider selling it yourself and putting the profits toward your next purchase. You'll likely come out hundreds of dollars ahead—buyers will pay more for your vehicle because they won't have to pay the 7 percent GST on a private sale. The most important thing to remember is that there's a large market for used vehicles in good condition in the $4,000–$5,000 range. Although most people prefer buying from individuals rather than from used car lots, they may still be afraid that the vehicle is a lemon. By using the following suggestions, you should be able to sell your vehicle quite easily:

1. Know its value. Study dealers' newspaper ads and compare them with the prices listed in this book. Undercut the dealer price by $300–$800 and be ready to bargain down another 10 percent for a serious buyer. Remember, prices can fluctuate wildly depending on which models are trendy, so watch the want ads carefully.
2. Enlist the aid of the salesperson who's selling you your new car. Offer her a few hundred dollars if she finds you a buyer. The fact that one sale hinges on the other along with the prospect of making two commissions may work wonders.

3. Post notices on bulletin boards at your office or local supermarkets and place a "For Sale" sign in the window of the vehicle itself. Place a newspaper ad only as a last resort.

4. Don't give your address right away to a potential buyer responding to your ad. Instead, ask for the telephone number where you may call that person back.

5. Be wary of selling to friends or family members. Anything short of perfection and you'll be eating Christmas dinner alone.

6. Don't touch the odometer. You may get a few hundred dollars more—and a criminal record.

7. Paint the vehicle. Some specialty shops charge only $300 and give a guarantee that's transferable to subsequent owners.

8. Make minor repairs. This includes a minor tune-up and patching up the exhaust. Again, if any repair warranty is transferable, use it as a selling point.

9. Clean the vehicle. Go to a reconditioning firm or spend the weekend scrubbing the interior and exterior. First impressions are important. Clean the chrome, polish the body, and peel off old bumper stickers. Remove butts from the ashtrays and clean out the glove compartment. Make sure all tools and spare parts have been taken out of the trunk. Don't remove the radio or speakers—the gaping holes will lower the vehicle's worth much more than the cost of radio or speakers. Replace missing or broken dash knobs and window cranks.

10. Change the tires. Recaps are good buys.

11. Let the buyer examine the vehicle. Insist that it be inspected by an independent garage, and accompany the prospective buyer to the garage. This gives you protection if the buyer claims you misrepresented the vehicle.

12. Don't mislead the buyer. If the vehicle was in an accident, or some financing is still to be paid, admit it. Any misleading statements may be used later against you in court. It's also advisable to have someone witness the actual transaction in case of a future dispute.

13. Keep important documents handy. Show prospective buyers the sales contract, repair orders, owner's manual, and all other documents that show how the vehicle has been maintained. Authenticate your claims about fuel consumption.

14. Write an effective ad.

Selling to Dealers

Selling to a dealer means that you're likely to get 20 percent less than if you sold your vehicle privately, unless the dealer agrees to participate in an accommodation sale. Most sellers will gladly pay some penalty to the dealer, however, for the peace of mind that comes with knowing that the eventual buyer won't lay a claim against them. This assumes that the dealer hasn't been cheated by the seller—if the vehicle is stolen, isn't paid for, has had its odometer spun back (or forward to a lower setting), or is seriously defective, the buyer or dealer can sue the original owner for fraud. Sell to a dealer who sells the same make. He or she will give you more because it's easier to sell your trade-in to customers who are interested only in that make of vehicle.

Drawing up the Contract

The province of Alberta has prepared a useful bill of sale applicable throughout Canada that can be accessed at *www3.gov.ab.ca/gs/pdf/registries/reg3126.pdf.* Your bill of sale should identify the vehicle (including the serial number) and include its price, whether a warranty applies, and the nature of the examination made by the buyer. The buyer may ask you to put in a lower price than what was actually paid in order to reduce the sales tax. If you agree to this, don't be surprised when a Revenue Canada agent comes to your door. Although the purchaser is ultimately the responsible party, you're an accomplice in defrauding the government. Furthermore, if you turn to the courts for redress, your own conduct may be put on trial.

Summary

Purchasing a used vehicle and keeping it at least five years saves you the most money. It takes about eight years to realize similar depreciation savings when buying new. Giving the biggest down payment you can afford, using zero percent financing programs, and piling up as many kilometres and years as possible on your trade-in are the best ways to save money with new vehicles. Remember that safety is another consideration that depends largely on the type of vehicle you choose.

Buy Safe

Safety features to look for:

1. A high NHTSA and IIHS crashworthiness rating for front, offset, and side collisions and low rollover potential; pay particular attention to the side rating if you are a senior driver
2. Good-quality tires; be wary of "all-season" tires and Bridgestone/Firestone makes
3. Three-point belts with belt pretensioners and adjustable shoulder belt anchorages
4. Integrated child safety seats and seat anchors, safety door locks, and override window controls
5. De-powered dual airbags with a cut-off switch, side airbags with head protection, unobtrusive, effective head restraints, and pedal extenders
6. Front driver's seat with plenty of rearward travel and a height adjustment
7. Good all-around visibility; a dash that doesn't reflect onto the windshield
8. An ergonomic interior with an efficient heating and ventilation system
9. Headlights that are adequate for night driving and don't blind oncoming traffic
10. Dash gauges that don't wash out in sunlight or produce windshield glare
11. Adjustable head restraints for all seating positions
12. Delaminated side window glass

13. Easily accessed sound system and climate controls
14. Navigation systems that don't require an MIT degree to calibrate
15. Manual sliding doors in vans (if children are transported)

Buy Smart

1. Buy the vehicle you need and can afford, not the one someone else wants you to buy, or one loaded with options that you'll probably never use. Take your time. Price comparisons and test-drives may take a month, but you'll get a better vehicle and price in the long run.
2. Buy in winter or later in the new year to double-dip from dealer incentives and customer rebate or low-cost financing programs.
3. Sell your trade-in privately.
4. Arrange financing before buying your vehicle.
5. Test-drive your choice by renting it overnight or for several days.
6. Buy through the Internet or by fax, or use an auto broker if you're not confident in your own bargaining skills, you lack the time to haggle, or you want to avoid the "showroom shakedown."
7. Ask for at least a 5 percent discount off the MSRP, and cut PDI and freight charges by at least 50 percent. Insist on a specific delivery date written in the contract, as well as a protected price in case there's a price increase between the time the contract is signed and when the vehicle is delivered. Also ask for a free tank of gas.
8. Order a minimum of options and seek a 20–30 percent discount on the entire option list. Try not to let the total option cost exceed 15 percent of the vehicle's MSRP.
9. Avoid leasing. If you must lease, choose the shortest time possible, drive down the MSRP, and refuse to pay an "acquisition" or "disposal" fee.
10. Japanese vehicles made in North America, co-ventures with American automakers, and re-badged imports often cost less than imports and are just as reliable. However, some Asian and European imports may not be as reliable as you might imagine—Kia's Sportage and Mercedes' M-Class sport-utilities, for example. Get extra warranty protection from the automaker if you're buying a model that has a poorer-than-average repair history. Use auto club references to get honest, competent repairs at a reasonable price.

Now that you know how to get the best for less, Part Two will show you how to get your money back when that "dream car" turns into a nightmare.

DOING RIGHT WHEN THINGS GO WRONG

The Insurer from Hell

The jury's award of punitive damages, though high [$1 million], was within rational limits. The respondent insurer's conduct towards the appellant was exceptionally reprehensible. It forced her to put at risk her only remaining asset (the $345,000 insurance claim) plus $320,000 in costs that she did not have. The denial of the claim was designed to force her to make an unfair settlement for less than she was entitled to. The conduct was planned and deliberate and continued for over two years, while the financial situation of the appellant grew increasingly desperate. The jury evidently believed that the respondent knew from the outset that its arson defence was contrived and unsustainable. Insurance contracts are sold by the insurance industry and purchased by members of the public for peace of mind. The more devastating the loss, the more the insured may be at the financial mercy of the insurer, and the more difficult it may be to challenge a wrongful refusal to pay the claim.

WHITEN. V. PILOT INSURANCE CO.
SUPREME COURT OF CANADA
FEBRUARY 22, 2002

93
—

There's One Chance in Ten It's a Lemon

Runzheimer Consultants says that one out of every 10 American vehicles produced by the Detroit Big Three is a lemon. I would guess that the owners of Ford and GM vehicles with faulty plastic engine intake manifold gaskets or of Toyotas with stinky exhaust would double that figure.

If you've bought an unsafe vehicle or one that was misrepresented, or you've had to pay for repairs to correct factory-related defects, this section's for you. Its intention is to help you get your money back—without going to court or getting frazzled by the dealer's broken promises or "benign neglect." But if

---

EXCESSIVE SULFUR DIOXIDE ODORS

BULLETIN NO.: EG010-04   DATE: MAY 7, 2004

2004 RAV4
Some customers may complain of excessive sulfur dioxide odor under the following conditions:
- Stop and go driving.
- Heavy acceleration.

In order to reduce the sulfur dioxide odor, a new catalytic converter has been developed.

Toyota's not alone with its "body odour" problems. Most of the major automakers report that rotten-egg odours caused by malfunctioning emissions and exhaust-system components are quite common. Most owners don't know that the fix is free.

going to court is your only recourse, you'll find the jurisprudence you need to cite in your complaint to get an out-of-court settlement or to win your case without spending a fortune on lawyers and research.

Four Ways to Get Your Money Back

Remember the "money-back guarantee"? Well, that's long gone. Automakers are reluctant to offer any warranty that requires them to take back a defective car or minivan because they know that there are a lot of lemons out there. Fortunately, our provincial consumer protection laws have filled the gap when the base warranty expires, so that now any sales contract for a new or used vehicle can be cancelled—or free repairs can be ordered—if the vehicle:

- Is unfit for the purpose for which it was purchased;
- Is misrepresented;
- Is covered by a secret warranty or a "goodwill" warranty extension; or
- Hasn't been reasonably durable, considering how well it was maintained, the mileage driven, and the type of driving done (this is particularly applicable to engine, transmission, and paint defects).

The four legal concepts enumerated above can lead to the contract being cancelled, the purchase price partially refunded, and damages awarded. For example, if the seller says that a minivan can pull a 900-kg (2,000-lb.) trailer, and you discover that it can barely tow half that weight, or won't reach a reasonable speed while towing, you can cancel the contract for misrepresentation. The same principle applies to a seller's exaggerated claims concerning a vehicle's fuel economy or reliability, as well as to "demonstrators" that are in fact used cars with false (rolled-back) odometer readings. GM's and Chrysler's secret paint warranties and Ford's Windstar engine and transmission "goodwill" programs have all been successfully challenged in small claims court. And reasonable durability is an especially powerful legal argument that allows a judge to determine what the dealer and auto manufacturer will pay to correct a premature failure long after the original warranty has expired.

Unfair Contracts

Sales contracts aren't fair, nor are they meant to be. Dealers' and automakers' lawyers spend countless hours making sure their clients are well protected with ironclad contracts.

Called "standard form contracts," or "contracts of adhesion," these agreements are looked upon by judges with a great deal of skepticism. They know these are contracts in which you have little or no bargaining power, such as loan documents, insurance contracts, and automobile leases. So when a dispute arises over terms or language, provincial consumer protection statutes require that judges interpret these contracts in the way most favourable to the consumer.

"Hearsay" Not Allowed

It's essential that printed evidence and/or witnesses (relatives are not excluded) are available to confirm that a false representation actually occurred, that a part is failure-prone, or that its replacement is covered by a secret warranty. Stung by an increasing number of small claims court defeats, automakers are now asking small claims court judges to disallow evidence from *Lemon-Aid*, service bulletins, or memos on the pretext that such evidence is hearsay (not proven), unless confirmed by an independent mechanic or unless the document is recognized by the automaker's or dealer's representative at trial ("Is this a common problem? Do you recognize this service bulletin? Is there a case-by-case 'goodwill' plan covering this repair?"). This is why you should bring in an independent garage mechanic or body expert to buttress your allegations. Sometimes, though, the service manager or company representative will make key admissions if questioned closely by you, a court mediator, or the trial judge. That questioning can be particularly effective if you call for the exclusion of witnesses until they're called (let them mill outside the courtroom wondering what their colleagues have said).

Automakers often blame owners for having pushed their vehicle beyond its limits. Therefore, when you seek to set aside the contract or get a repair reimbursed, it's essential that you get the testimony of an independent mechanic and co-workers in order to prove that the vehicle's poor performance isn't caused by negligent maintenance or abusive driving.

It Should Have Lasted Longer!

The reasonable durability claim is your ace in the hole. It's probably the easiest allegation to prove, since all automakers have benchmarks as to how long body components, trim and finish, and mechanical and electronic parts should last (see the durability chart on pages 107–08). Vehicles are expected to be reasonably durable and merchantable. What "reasonably durable" means depends on the price paid, the kilometres driven, the purchaser's driving habits, and how well the vehicle was maintained by the owner. Judges carefully weigh all these factors in awarding compensation or cancelling a sale.

Whatever the reason you use to get your money back, don't forget to conform to the "reasonable diligence" rule that requires you to file suit within a reasonable time after purchase or after you've discovered the defect. If there have been no negotiations with the dealer or automaker, this period cannot exceed a few months. If either the dealer or the automaker has been promising to correct the defects for some time, or has carried out repeated unsuccessful repairs, the delay for filing the lawsuit can be extended.

Refunds for Other Expenses

It's a lot easier to get the automaker to pay to replace a defective part than it is to obtain compensation for a missed day of work. Manufacturers seldom pay for consequential expenses like a ruined vacation, the vehicle not living up to its advertised hype, or the owner's mental distress because they can't control the amount of the refund. Courts, however, are more generous, having ruled that all expenses (damages) flowing from a problem covered by a warranty or service bulletin are the manufacturer's or dealer's responsibility under both common law (which covers all provinces except Quebec) and Quebec civil law. Fortunately, when legal action is threatened—usually through small claims court—automakers quickly up their ante to include most of the owner's expenses because they know the courts will be more generous.

One precedent-setting judgment (cited in *Sharman v. Ford,* found on page 131) giving generous damages to a motorist fed up with his "lemon" Cadillac was rendered in 1999 by the British Columbia Supreme Court in *Wharton v. Tom Harris Chevrolet Oldsmobile Cadillac Ltd.,* [2002] B.C.J. No. 233, 2002 BCCA 78d. In that case, Justice Leggatt threw the book at GM and the dealer in awarding the following amounts:

(a) Hotel accommodations: $ 217.17

(b) Travel to effect repairs at 30 cents per kilometre: The plaintiff claims some 26 visits from his home in Ucluelet to Nanaimo. Some credit should be granted to the defendants since routine trips would have been required in any event. Therefore, the plaintiff is entitled to be compensated for mileage for 17 trips (approximately 400 km from Ucluelet to Nanaimo return) at 30 cents per kilometre.

$2,040.00

TOTAL: $2,257.17

[20] The plaintiff is entitled to non-pecuniary damages for loss of enjoyment of their luxury vehicle and for inconvenience in the sum of $5,000.

Warranties

The manufacturer's or dealer's warranty is a written legal promise that a vehicle will be reasonably reliable, subject to certain conditions. Regardless of the number of subsequent owners, this promise remains in force as long as the warranty's original time/kilometre limits haven't expired. Unfortunately, these warranties are full of so many loopholes ("you abused the car; it was poorly maintained; it's normal wear and tear") that they may be useless when a vehicle breaks down.

Thankfully, car owners get another kick at the can. As clearly stated in *Frank v. GM*, every vehicle sold new or used in Canada is also covered by an *implied* warranty—a collection of federal and provincial laws and regulations that protect you from hidden defects, misrepresentation, and a host of other scams. Furthermore, Canadian law presumes that car dealers, unlike private sellers, are aware of the defects present in the vehicles they sell. That way, they can't just pass the ball to the automakers and walk away from the dispute. For instance, in British Columbia, a new-car dealer is required to disclose damage requiring repairs costing more than 20 percent of the price (the *Motor Dealer Act Regulations*).

Treacherous Tires

Consumers have gained additional rights following Bridgestone/Firestone's massive tire recall in 2001. Because of the confusion and chaos surrounding Firestone's handling of the recall, Ford's 575 Canadian dealers stepped into the breach and replaced the tires with any equivalent tires dealers had in stock, no questions asked.

This is an important precedent that tears down the traditional liability wall separating tire manufacturers from automakers in product liability claims. In essence, whoever sells the product can now be held liable for damages. In the future, Canadian consumers will have an easier time holding the dealer, automaker, and tiremaker liable, not just for recalled products, but for any defect that affects the safety or reasonable durability of that product.

This is particularly true now that the Supreme Court of Canada (*Winnipeg Condominium v. Bird Construction* [1995] 1S.C.R.85) has ruled that defendants are liable in negligence for any designs that resulted in a risk to the public for safety or health. The Supreme Court reversed a long-standing policy and provided the public with a new cause of action that had not existed before in Canada. Prior to this Supreme Court ruling, companies dodged liability for falling bridges and crashing planes by warranty exclusion and "entire-agreement" contract clauses. In the *Winnipeg Condominium* case, the Supreme Court held that repairs made to prevent serious damage or accidents could be claimed from the designer or builder for the cost of repair in tort, from any subsequent purchaser. Consumers with tire or other claims relating to the safety of their vehicles would be wise to insert the above court decision (with explanation) in their claim letter and mail or fax it to the automaker's "legal affairs" or "product liability" department. A copy should also be deposited with the clerk of the small claims court if you have to use that recourse.

Other Warranty Items

Safety features

Safety restraints, such as airbags and seat belts, have warranty coverage extended for the lifetime of the vehicle, following an agreement made between U.S. automakers and importers. In Canada, though, some automakers try to dodge this responsibility because they are incorporated as separate Canadian companies. That distinction didn't fly with B.C.'s Court of Appeal in the 2002 *Robson* decision (*www.courts.gov.bc.ca/jdbtxt/ca/02/03/2002bcca0354.htm*). In that class action petition, the court declared that both Canadian companies *and* their American counterparts can be held liable in Canada for deceptive acts that violate the provincial *Trade Practices Act* (in this case, Chrysler and GM paint delamination):

> At this stage, the plaintiffs are only required to demonstrate that they have a "good arguable case" against the American defendants. The threshold is low. A good arguable case requires only a serious question to be tried, one with some prospect of success: see *AG Armeno Mines, supra,* at para. 25 [*AG Armeno Mines and Minerals Inc. v. PT Pukuafu Indah* (2000), 77 B.C.L.R.(3d) 1 (C.A.)].

Aftermarket products and services—such as gas-saving gadgets, rustproofing, and paint protectors—can render the manufacturer's warranty invalid, so make sure you're in the clear before purchasing any optional equipment or services from an independent supplier.

How fairly a warranty is applied is more important than how long it remains in effect. Once you know the normal wear rate for a mechanical component or body part, you can demand proportional compensation when you get less than normal durability—no matter what the original warranty said.

Some dealers tell customers that they need to have original equipment parts installed in order to maintain their warranty. A variation on this theme requires that routine servicing—including tune-ups and oil changes (with a certain brand of oil)—be done by the selling dealer, or the warranty is invalidated.

Nothing could be further from the truth.

Canadian law stipulates that whoever issues a warranty cannot make that warranty conditional on the use of any specific brand of motor oil, oil filter, or any other component, unless it's provided to the customer free of charge.

Sometimes dealers will do all sorts of minor repairs that don't correct the problem, and then after the warranty runs out they'll tell you that major repairs are needed. You can avoid this nasty surprise by repeatedly bringing your vehicle into the dealership before the warranty ends. During each visit, insist that a written work order include the specific nature of the problem as *you* see it and that the work order carry the notation that this is the second, third, or fourth time the same problem has been brought to the dealer's attention. Write it down yourself, if need be. This allows you to show a pattern of non-performance by the dealer during the warranty period and establishes that it's a serious and chronic problem. When the warranty expires, you have the legal right to demand that it be extended on those items consistently reappearing on your handful of work orders. *Lowe v. Fairview Chrysler* (see page 131) is an excellent judgment that reinforces this important principle. In another lawsuit, *François Chong v. Marine Drive Imported Cars Ltd. and Honda Canada Inc.* (see page 141), a Honda owner forced Honda to fix his engine six times—until they got it right.

 A retired GM service manager gave me another effective tactic to use when you're not sure a dealer's warranty "repairs" will actually correct the problem for a reasonable period of time after the warranty expires. Here's what he says you should do:

> When you pick up the vehicle after the warranty repair has been done, hand the service manager a note to be put in your file that says you appreciate the warranty repair; however, you intend to return and ask for further warranty coverage if the problem reappears before a reasonable amount of time has elapsed—even if the original warranty has expired. A copy of the same note should be sent to the automaker.... Keep your copy of the note in the glove compartment as cheap insurance against paying for a repair that wasn't fixed correctly the first time.

Extended (Supplementary) Warranties

Supplementary warranties providing extended coverage may be sold by the manufacturer, dealer, or an independent third party, and are automatically transferred when the vehicle is sold. They cost $1,500 or more and should be purchased only if the vehicle you're buying has an iffy reputation for quality (see Part Three) or is in its first year on the market, or if you're reluctant to use the small claims courts when factory-related trouble arises.

Don't let the dealer pressure you into deciding right away. Generally, you can purchase an extended warranty anytime during the period in which the manufacturer's warranty is in effect. An automaker's supplementary warranty is the best choice, but will likely cost about a third more than warranties sold by independents. And in some parts of the country, notably British Columbia, dealers have a quasi-monopoly on selling warranties with little competition from the independents.

Because up to 60 percent of the warranty's cost represents dealer markup, dealers love to sell extended warranties, whether you need them or not. Out of the remaining 40 percent comes the sponsor's administration costs and profit margin, calculated at another 15 percent. What's left to pay for repairs is a minuscule 25 percent of the original amount. The only reason that automakers and independent warranty companies haven't been busted for operating this warranty Ponzi scheme is that only half of the car buyers who purchase an extended service contract actually use it.

It's often difficult to collect on supplementary warranties because independent companies frequently go out of business or limit the warranty's coverage through subsequent mailings. Provincial laws cover both situations. If the bankrupt warranty company's insurance policy won't cover your claim, take the dealer to small claims court and ask for the repair cost and the refund of the original warranty payment. Your argument for holding the dealer responsible is a simple one: By accepting a commission to act as an agent of the defunct company, the dealer took on the obligations of the company as well. As for limiting the coverage after you have bought the warranty policy, this is illegal, and allows you to sue both the dealer and the warranty company for a refund of both the warranty and repair costs.

Emissions Control Warranties

These little-publicized warranties can save you big bucks if major engine or exhaust components fail prematurely. They come with all new vehicles and cover major components of the emissions control system for up to 8 years/130,000 km. Unfortunately, although owner's manuals vaguely mention the emissions warranty, most don't specify which parts are covered. Fortunately, the U.S. Environmental Protection Agency has intervened on several occasions with hefty fines against Chrysler and Ford for stonewalling emission-system claims and ruled that all major motor and fuel-system components are covered. These include fuel metering, ignition spark advance, restart, evaporative emissions, positive crankcase ventilation, engine electronics (computer modules), and catalytic converters, as well as hoses, clamps, brackets, pipes, gaskets, belts, seals, and connectors. Canada, however, has no government definition, and it's up to each manufacturer and the small claims courts to decide which components are covered.

Many of the confidential technical service bulletins listed in Part Three show parts failures that are covered under the emissions warranty, even though motorists are routinely charged for their replacement. This Ford bulletin, applicable to the 2002–05 Taurus and Sable, shows that the automaker will pay for fuel gauge repairs under the emissions warranty. Other companies with similar emission-component problems, like General Motors, follow the same guidelines.

FUEL GAUGE DOES NOT READ FULL AFTER FILLING TANK

BULLETIN NO.: 04-14-14   **DATE: MAY 2002**

FORD TAURUS, SABLE

ISSUE: Some 2002–05 Taurus/Sable vehicles may exhibit a fuel gauge which indicates the tank is only 7/8 full after filling the fuel tank. This may be due to the the calibration of the fuel level indication unit.

ACTION: To service, remove the fuel delivery module and replace the fuel level indication unit. DO NOT REPLACE THE ENTIRE FUEL DELIVERY MODULE FOR THIS CONDITION.

WARRANTY STATUS: Eligible under provisions of new vehicle limited warranty coverage and emissions warranty coverage.

Operation	Description	Time
041414A	Replace Fuel Gauge tank unit (includes time to remove tank, drain and refill)	1.3hrs

SULFER (ROTTEN EGG) SMELL COMING FROM EXHAUST (REPLACE PCM AND CATALYTIC CONVERTER)

BULLETIN NO.: 04-06-05-0011A   **DATE: MARCH 17, 2005**

2003–05 PONTIAC VIBE (AUTOMATIC TRANSMISSION ONLY)

CONDITION: Some customers may comment on a sulfur or rotten egg odor coming from the exhaust. Vehicle conditions such as extended idling, hard braking, aggressive acceleration and long wide open throttle maneuvers or driving in reverse may intensify the odor.

CAUSE: Sulfur level in the fuel. Sulfur is a natural component of crude oil from which gasoline is refined and the amount of sulfur can vary between different sources.

Unfortunately, few owners will ever see these bulletins; most will end up paying $300 to $1,000 to replace the fuel gauge or catalytic converter because they didn't know that the emissions warranty applied.

Make sure you get your emissions system checked out thoroughly by a dealer or independent garage before the emissions warranty expires and before having the vehicle inspected by provincial emissions inspectors.

 ## The Wacky World of "Secret" Warranties

Few vehicle owners know that secret warranties exist. The closest automakers come to an admission is sending a "goodwill policy," "product improvement program," or "special policy" technical service bulletin (TSB) to dealers or first owners of record. Consequently, the only motorists who find out about these policies are the original owners who haven't moved or leased their vehicles. The other motorists who get compensated for repairs are the ones who read *Lemon-Aid* each year, wave TSBs, and yell the loudest.

Remember, second owners and repairs done by independent garages are included in these secret warranty programs. Large, costly repairs, such as blown engines, burned transmissions, and peeling paint, are often covered.

Here are a few examples of the latest, most comprehensive secret warranties that have come across my desk in the last several years.

All Years, All Models
Automatic transmissions

Problem: Faulty automatic transmissions that self-destruct, shift erratically, gear down to "limp mode," are slow to shift in or out of Reverse, or are noisy. **Warranty coverage:** If you have the assistance of your dealer's service manager, expect an offer of 50–75 percent (about $1,500). File the case in small claims court and a full refund will be offered up to 7 years/160,000 km. Acura, Honda, Hyundai, Lexus, and Toyota coverage varies between seven and eight years.

Brakes

Problem: Premature wearout of brake pads, calipers, and rotors, especially on SUVs, trucks, and vans. **Warranty coverage:** *Calipers and pads:* Goodwill settlements confirm that brake calipers and pads that fail to last 2 years/40,000 km will be replaced for 50 percent of the repair cost; components not lasting 1 year/20,000 km will be replaced for free. *Rotors:* If they last less than 3 years/60,000 km, they will be replaced at half price; replacement is free up to 2 years/40,000 km. Interestingly, early brake wearout, once mainly a Detroit failing, is now quite common with Asian makes as well.

Apparently, brake suppliers to all automakers are using cheaper calipers, pads, and rotors that can't handle the heat generated by normal braking on heavier passenger cars, trucks, and vans. Consequently, drivers find routine braking causes rotor warpage that produces excessive vibrations, shuddering, noise, and pulling to one side when braking.

Engines

Problem: Around 60,000–100,000 km, the engine may overheat, lose power, burn extra fuel, and possibly self-destruct. Under the best of circumstances, the repair will take a day and cost about $800–$1,000. **Warranty coverage:** If you have the assistance of your dealer's service manager, expect a 100 percent refund up to 7 years/160,000 km.

Exhaust systems

Problem: A nauseating "rotten-egg" exhaust smell permeates the interior. **Warranty coverage:** At first owners are told they need a tune-up. Then they are told to change fuel and to wait a few months for the problem to correct itself. When this fails, the catalytic converter will likely be replaced and the power control module recalibrated.

Chrysler, Ford, General Motors, and Hyundai

Paint

Problem: Faulty paint jobs that cause paint to turn white and peel off horizontal panels. **Warranty coverage:** Automakers will offer a free paint job or partial compensation up to six years with no mileage limitation. Thereafter, all three manufacturers offer 50–75 percent refunds on the small claims courthouse steps.

In *Frank v. GM*, the Saskatchewan small claims court set a 15-year benchmark for paint finishes, and three other Canadian small claims judgments have extended the benchmark to seven years, second owners, and pickups.

I wanted to let you and your readers know that the information you publish about Ford's paint failure problem is invaluable. Having read through your "how-to guide" on addressing this issue, I filed suit against Ford for the "latent" paint defect. The day prior to our court date, I received a settlement offer by phone for 75 percent of what I was initially asking for.

This settlement was for a 9-year-old car. I truly believe that Ford hedges a bet that most people won't go to the extent of filing a lawsuit because they are intimidated or simply stop progress after they receive a firm no from Ford.

M.P.

12 Service Bulletins That Give You Extra Rights

CHRYSLER RIGHT LEAD/REVISED ALIGNMENT SPECIFICATIONS

BULLETIN NO.: 02-002-05   **DATE: MARCH 12, 2005**

OVERVIEW: This bulletin involves adjusting the alignment to revised specifications.
2005–**2006** (LX) 300/CHARGER/MAGNUM
SYMPTOM/CONDITION: The vehicle operator states the vehicle leads to the right.
DIAGNOSIS: Drive the car on a FLAT road. If the car tracks straight, the vehicle operator is experiencing crown sensitivity. If the vehicle tracks to the right, perform the Repair Procedure. Crown sensitivity can not be eliminated in all the cases.

CHRYSLER UPPER BODY SEAM SEAL APPEARANCE CONCERN/ WATER LEAK

BULLETIN NO.: 23-002-05   **DATE: JANUARY 14, 2005**

THIS BULLETIN SUPERSEDES SERVICE BULLETIN 23-001-03 DATED JANUARY 17, 2003, WHICH SHOULD BE REMOVED FROM YOUR FILES. THIS IS A COMPLETE REVISION AND NO ASTERISKS HAVE BEEN USED TO HIGHTLIGHT REVISIONS.
OVERVIEW: This bulletin involves repairing a crack/split in the upper body seam sealer at the "B" or "C" pillar.
2003–05 (RS) TOWN AND COUNTRY/CARAVAN/VOYAGER

CHRYSLER TRANSFER GEAR WHINE SOUND BETWEEN 68 MPH AND 84 MPH, EITHER ACCELERATING OR DECELERATING

BULLETIN NO.: 21-003-05   **DATE: JANUARY 19, 2005**

OVERVIEW: This bulletin involves inspecting and properly seating the low steering column boot.
2003–05 (JR) SEBRING CONVERTIBLE/SEBRING SEDAN/STRATUS SEDAN
SYMPTOM/CONDITION: Vehicle operator may experience a transfer gear whine sound while vehicle is either accelerating or coasting down between 68 mph (109 kph) and 84 mph (135 kph). This condition may also be described as a whistling sound.

FORD FUEL FILL SLOW, OR DIFFICULT TO FILL— VEHICLE BUILT BEFORE 4/26/2005

BULLETIN NO.: 05-15-12

FORD: 2005 MUSTANG
ISSUE: Some 2005 Mustang vehicles built before 4/26/2005, may exhibit the fuel tank being slow or difficult to fill. The condition may be described as repeated rapid shut-offs of the filling station pump nozzle, or multiple nozzle shut-offs when attempting to fill the fuel tank. The condition may be due to the fuel tank venting system inside the fuel tank.
ACTION: Install a new fuel tank. Refer to Section 310-01 of the Workshop Manual. The new fuel tank has a revised internal venting system to improve fuel filling.

GM ENGINE WILL NOT CRANK (REPROGRAM ECM)

BULLETIN NO.: 05-06-04-016   **DATE: MARCH 7, 2005**

2005 BUICK LA CROSSE, ALLURE (CANADA ONLY)
2004–05 BUICK RENDEZVOUS
2004–05 CADILLAC CTS, SRX
2005 CADILLAC STS, WITH 2.8L OR 3.6L V-6 ENGINE

PART TWO • DOING RIGHT WHEN THINGS GO WRONG

Frank M. Ligon
Director
Service Engineering Operations
Ford Customer Service Division

FORD MOTOR COMPANY
P.O. Box 1904
Dearborn, Michigan 48121

September 12, 2005

TO: All U.S. Ford and Lincoln Mercury Dealers

SUBJECT: Customer Satisfaction Program 05B31—INFORMATION ONLY
Certain 1995 through 2006 Lincoln Town Car with Limo Prep Package
Limo Package Upgrade Kit Offering

PROGRAM TERMS
THIS BULLETIN IS BEING POSTED FOR DEALER INFORMATION ONLY. There is no action required of dealers to administer this Customer Satisfaction Program. This program will be in effect until March 15, 2006. There is no mileage restriction on this program.

AFFECTED VEHICLES
Certain 1995 through 2006 Lincoln Town Car vehicles built at the Wixom Assembly Plant from September 12, 1994 through September 5, 2005, equipped with the Limo Prep Package. Affected vehicles are **not** identified in OASIS.

REASON FOR THIS PROGRAM
In all of the affected vehicles, Ford has determined that there is a possibility that during a high speed/high energy rear collision, certain components have an increased risk of puncturing the fuel tank. The increased risk is due to the added weight and stiffness of a Town Car stretch limousine. There is no defect of any component or system in these vehicles and they meet or exceed all federal standards. This action is being taken to enhance the rear collision impact performance of the Town Car stretch limousine.

SERVICE ACTION
No further action is required of dealers. Upon vehicle owner request, Ford Company will provide a Shield Kit at no charge directly to the owner. The owner of the vehicle will be responsible for installation of the kit.

Beginning in September 2005, this same kit will be included with the vehicle as shipped from the assembly plant. The shield kit that will be provided contains the same components used on the Crown Victoria Police Interceptor.

GM ENGINE HARMONIC BALANCER NOT SEATED

BULLETIN NO.: 05548B   DATE: AUGUST 2, 2005

2005 CHEVROLET UPLANDER   2005–06 CHEVROLET MALIBU, MALIBU MAXX
2005 PONTIAC MONTANA SV6   2005–06 PONTIAC G6
2005 BUICK TERRAZA   2006 BUICK RENDEZVOUS
2005 SATURN RELAY

CONDITION: Certain 2005 Chevrolet Uplander; Pontiac Montana SV6; Buick Terraza; Saturn Relay; 2005–06 Chevrolet Malibu, Malibu Maxx; Pontiac G6 and 2006 Buick Rendezvous model vehicles, equipped with a 3.5L V6 (RPO LX9-VIN L) engine, may have a condition in which the engine harmonic balancer is not completely seated. An engine harmonic balancer that is not completely seated may cause crackshaft key failure. Crankshaft key failure will cause damage to the sprocket and timing gears, cylinder head and valves, pistons and residual internal engine damage. All of these failures may lead to engine repair or replacement.

GM GENERAL WINDNOISE/WATERLEAK DIAGNOSTIC GUIDE

BULLETIN NO.: 05-08-58-001   DATE: MARCH 31, 2005

2005 BUICK TERRAZA
2005 CHEVROLET UPLANDER
2005 PONTIAC MONTANA
2005 SATURN RELAY

This bulletin contains information on various windnoise and waterleak conditions starting from front of vehicle to the rear of the vehicle. Refer to the following table for a quick reference to the conditions and the corresponding illustrations:

CONDITION	BEST DESCRIBED IN
Buzz type noise in front end.	#1
Road noise, Windnoise or the windshield fogs up.	#2
Windnoise around the top of the door.	#3
Windnoise from the sliding side door.	#4
Windnoise from the sliding side door glass.	#5
Windrush from the sliding side door glass.	#6
Water running down the "A" pillar.	#7
Water at bottom of the door.	#8
Water settles in the trim around the rear door striker.	#9
Headliner is wet or water is coming out of the "D" pillar trim to rear quarter trim.	#10
Water may be dripping from "D" pillar trim to rear quarter trim or the rear carpet is wet.	#11

GM WATER LEAK ON FRONT PASSENGER FLOOR (INSTALL WATER DEFLECTOR)

BULLETIN NO.: 03-08-57-006B   DATE: FEBRUARY 25, 2005

2005 BUICK LA CROSSE, ALLURE (CANADA ONLY)
2004–05 PONTIAC GRAND PRIX

CAUSE: Water may be getting past the rubber water deflector located under the air inlet grille panel. During diagnosis, the technician may note that the passenger compartment air filter is wet.

NISSAN LACK OF POWER A/T IN FAIL SAFE (3RD GEAR)

BULLETIN NO.: AT04-013A, NTB04-144A   DATE: FEBRUARY 7, 2005

2004–05 QUEST (V42)

IF YOU CONFIRM:

A customer reports the following:

• The engine has low power, and/or the transmission doesn't shift (stays in 3rd gear),

and

• The incident occurs just after the engine is started,

and

• When the engine is turned OFF then restarted, the engine and transmission return to normal operation.

ACTION: Replace the A/T Control Module (TCM) with the new one listed in the parts information.

How Long Should a Part or Repair Last?

How do you know when a part or service doesn't last as long as it should and whether you should seek a full or partial refund? Sure, you have a gut feeling based on your use of the vehicle, how you maintained it, and the extent of work that was carried out on it. But you'll need more than emotion to win compensation from garages and automakers.

You can definitely get a refund if a repair or part lasts longer than its guarantee but not as long as is generally expected. But you'll have to show what the auto industry considers to be reasonable durability. Automakers, mechanics, and the courts all have their own benchmarks as to what's a reasonable period of time or amount of mileage one should expect a part or adjustment to last. Consequently, I've prepared this table to show what most automakers consider is reasonable durability, as expressed by their original and "goodwill" warranties.

REASONABLE PART DURABILITY

ACCESSORIES		BRAKE SYSTEM	
Air conditioner	7 years	Brake drum	120,000 km
Cruise control	5 years/ 100,000 km	Brake drum linings	35,000 km
		Brake rotor	60,000 km
Power doors, windows	5 years	Brake calipers/pads	30,000 km
Radio	5 years	Master cylinder	100,000 km
		Wheel cylinder	80,000 km
BODY			
Paint (peeling)	7–11 years		
Rust (perforations)	7–11 years		
Rust (surface)	5 years		
Water/wind/air leaks	5 years		

ENGINE AND DRIVETRAIN

CV joint	6 years/160,000 km
Differential	7 years/160,000 km
Engine (diesel)	15 years/350,000 km
Engine (gas)	7 years/160,000 km
Motor	7 years/112,000 km
Radiator	4 years/80,000 km
Transfer case	7 years/160,000 km
Transmission (auto.)	7 years/160,000 km
Transmission (man.)	10 years/250,000 km
Transmission oil cooler	5 years/100,000 km

EXHAUST SYSTEM

Catalytic converter	5 years/100,000 km or more
Muffler	2 years/40,000 km
Tailpipe	3 years/60,000 km

IGNITION SYSTEM

Cable set	60,000 km
Electronic module	5 years/80,000 km
Retiming	20,000 km
Spark plugs	20,000 km
Tune-up	20,000 km

SAFETY COMPONENTS

Airbags	life of vehicle
ABS brakes	7 years/160,000 km
ABS computer	10 years/160,000 km
Seatbelts	life of vehicle

STEERING AND SUSPENSION

Alignment	1 year/20,000 km
Ball joints	10 years/160,000 km
Coil Springs	10 years/160,000 km
Power steering	5 years/80,000 km
Shock absorber	2 years/40,000 km
Struts	5 years/80,000 km
Tires (radial)	5 years/80,000 km
Wheel bearing	3 years/60,000 km

VISIBILITY

Halogen/fog lights	3 years
Sealed beam	2 years
Windshield wiper	5 years

Many of the preceding guidelines were extrapolated from Chrysler and Ford pay-outs to thousands of dissatisfied customers over the past decade, in addition to Chrysler's original 7-year powertrain warranty (applicable from 1991 to 1995 and re-applied from 2001 to 2004). Other sources for this chart were the Ford and GM transmission warranties outlined in their secret warranties; Ford, GM, and Toyota engine "goodwill" programs laid out in their internal service bulletins; and court judgments where judges have given their own guidelines as to what is reasonable durability.

Safety features—with the exception of ABS—generally have a lifetime warranty, which is usually considered part of normal maintenance. Nevertheless, the Chrysler 10-year "free-service" program portion of its ABS recall, announced seven years ago, can serve as a handy benchmark as to how long one can expect these components to last.

Airbags are a different matter. Those that are deployed in an accident—and the personal injury and interior damage their deployment will likely have caused—are covered by your accident insurance policy. However, if there is a sudden deployment for no apparent reason, the automaker and dealer should be held jointly responsible for all injuries and damages caused by the airbag. You can prove their liability by downloading data from your vehicle's data recorder. This will likely lead to a more generous settlement from the two parties and prevent your insurance premiums from being jacked up.

Use the manufacturer's emissions warranty as your primary guideline for the expected durability of high-tech electronic and mechanical pollution control components, such as powertrain control modules (PCM) and catalytic converters. Look first at your owner's manual for an indication of which parts on your vehicle are covered. If you come up with few specifics, ask the auto manufacturer for a list of specific components covered by the emissions warranty.

Recall Repairs

Vehicles are recalled for one of two reasons: Either they are unsafe or they don't conform to federal pollution control regulations. Whatever the reason, recalls are a great way to get free repairs—if you know which ones apply to you and you have the patience of Job.

More than 500 million unsafe vehicles have been recalled by automakers for the free correction of safety-related defects since American recall legislation was passed in 1966 (a weaker Canadian law was enacted in 1971). During that time, NHTSA estimates that about 28 percent of the recalled vehicles never made it back to the dealership for repairs because owners were never informed, they just didn't consider the defect that hazardous, or they gave up waiting for corrective parts.

Subsequent American legislation targets automakers who drag their feet in making recall repairs. Owners on both sides of the border may wish to cite the following NHTSA guidelines for support:

 If you've moved, it's smart to pay a visit to your local dealer, give him your address, and get a "report card" on which recalls, free-service campaigns, and warranties apply to your vehicle. Simply give the service advisor your vehicle identification number (VIN)—found on the dash just below the windshield on the driver's side, or on your insurance card—and have the number run through the automaker's computer system. Make sure that your new address is listed in the automaker's computer. This ensures that you'll receive notices of warranty extensions and emissions and safety recalls.

In the U.S., recall campaigns force automakers to pay the entire cost of fixing a vehicle's safety-related defect for as long as that vehicle remains in service. Getting repairs when the automaker says you are too late often takes a small claims court filing. But these cases are easy to win and are usually settled out of court. Recalls may be voluntary or ordered by the U.S. Department of Transportation and can be nationwide or regional. In Canada, all recalls are considered voluntary. Transport Canada can only order automakers to notify owners that their vehicles may be unsafe; it can't force them to correct the problem. Fortunately, most U.S.-ordered recalls are carried out in Canada, and when Transport Canada makes a defect determination on its own, automakers generally comply with an owner notification letter and a recall campaign.

Voluntary recall campaigns, frequently called Special Service or Safety Improvement Campaigns, are a real problem. The government does not monitor the notification of owners; dealers and automakers routinely deny there's a recall, thereby dissuading most claimants; and the company's so-called fix, not authorized by any governing body, may not correct the hazard at all. Also, the voluntary recall may leave out many of the affected models or unreasonably exclude certain owners.

Wherever you live or drive, don't expect to be welcomed with open arms when your vehicle develops a safety or emissions-related problem that's not yet part of a recall campaign. Automakers and dealers generally take a restrictive view of what constitutes a safety or emissions defect and frequently charge for repairs that should be free under federal safety or emissions legislation. To counter this tendency, look at the following list of typical defects that are clearly safety related. If you experience similar problems, insist that the automaker fix the problem at no expense to yourself, including a car rental:

- Airbag malfunctions
- Corrosion affecting safe operation of vehicle
- Disconnected or stuck accelerators
- Electrical shorts
- Faulty windshield wipers
- Fuel leaks
- Problems with original axles, drive shafts, seats, seat recliners, or defrosters
- Seat belt problems
- Stalling or sudden acceleration
- Sudden steering or brake loss
- Suspension failures
- Trailer coupling failures

Regional recalls

Don't let any dealer refuse you recall repairs because of where you live. In order to cut recall costs, many automakers try to limit a recall to vehicles in a certain designated region. This practice doesn't make sense, since cars are mobile and an unsafe, rust-cankered steering unit can be found anywhere—not just in certain rust-belt provinces or American states.

In 2001, Ford attempted to limit to five American states its recall of faulty Firestone tires. Public ridicule of the company's proposal led to an extension of the recall throughout North America.

In July 2004, Ford announced a regional recall to install protective spring shields on almost one million 1999, 2000, and 2001 model-year Taurus and Sable sedans to correct defective front springs that can break and puncture a tire. As it did for Windstars and Aerostars recalled earlier for the same problem, Ford says it will send recall letters only to owners whose vehicles are registered in high-corrosion areas, or where salt is used on roads.

Safety Defect Information

If you wish to report a safety defect or want recall info, you may access Transport Canada's website at *www.tc.gc.ca/roadsafety/recalls/search_e.asp*. You can get recall information in French or English, as well as general information relating to road safety and importing a vehicle into Canada. Web surfers can now access the recall database for 1970–2005 model vehicles but, unlike NHTSA's website, owner complaints aren't listed, defect investigations aren't disclosed, voluntary warranty extensions (secret warranties) aren't shown, and service bulletin summaries aren't provided. You can also call Transport Canada at 1-800-333-0510 (toll-free within Canada) or 613-993-9851 (within the Ottawa region or outside Canada) to get additional information.

If you're not happy with Ottawa's treatment of your recall inquiry, try NHTSA's website. It's more complete than Transport Canada's (NHTSA's database is updated daily and covers vehicles built since 1952). You can search the database for your vehicle or tires at *www.nhtsa.dot.gov/cars/problems*.

You'll get immediate access to four essential database categories applicable to your vehicle and model year: the latest recalls, current and closed safety investigations, defects reported by other owners, and a brief summary of TSBs.

NHTSA's fax-back service provides the same info through a local line that can be accessed from Canada—although long-distance charges will apply (most calls take 5–10 minutes to complete). The following local numbers get you into the automatic response service quickly and can be reached 24 hours a day: 202-366-0123 (202-366-7800 for the hearing impaired).

"Black Box" Recorders

Forget privacy rights. If your car has an airbag, it's probably spying on you. Event 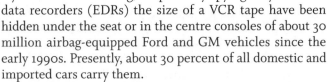 data recorders (EDRs) the size of a VCR tape have been hidden under the seat or in the centre consoles of about 30 million airbag-equipped Ford and GM vehicles since the early 1990s. Presently, about 30 percent of all domestic and imported cars carry them.

These devices operate in a fashion similar to flight data recorders used in airplanes—they record data during the last five seconds before impact, including the force of the collision, the airbag's performance, when the brakes were applied, engine and vehicle speed, gas pedal position, and whether the driver was wearing a seat belt.

Apart from the "invasion of privacy" aspect of hiding recorders in customers' vehicles, Ford and GM have systematically hidden their collected data from U.S. and

Canadian vehicle safety researchers investigating thousands of complaints relating to airbags that don't deploy when they should (or deploy when they shouldn't) and anti-lock brakes that don't brake.

This refusal to voluntarily share data with customers and researchers is unfortunate, because the recorders are collecting critical information that could lead to better-functioning safety devices. In fact, experts say that highway safety could be vastly improved if black boxes that record information about car crashes were installed in all cars, just as similar devices are placed in all airplanes.

To find out if your car or truck carries an EDR, go to *www.cbc.ca/consumers/ market/files/cars/blackboxes*.

Fortunately, it has become impossible for automakers to hide recorder data now that Vetronix Corporation sells a $2,500 (U.S.) portable download device that accesses the data and stores it on any PC. It's presently marketed to accident reconstructionists, safety researchers, law enforcement agencies, and insurance companies. Furthermore, litigants can subpoena the info through an automaker's dealer if the data is needed in court. Car owners who wish to dispute criminal charges, oppose their insurer's decision, or hold an automaker responsible for a safety device's failure (airbags, seat belts, or brakes) will find this data invaluable.

Safety benefits

Enthusiastically promoted by government and law enforcement agencies around the world, these data recorders have actually had a positive effect in accident prevention: A 1992 study by the European Union cited by the Canada Safey Council found that EDRs reduced the collision rate by 28 percent and costs by 40 percent in police fleets where drivers knew they were being monitored.

The recorders are also sending people to jail, helping accident victims reap huge court awards, and prompting automaker recalls of unsafe vehicles. In October of 2003, Montreal police won their first dangerous driving conviction using EDR data (*R. v. Gauthier*, [2003-05-27] QCCQ 500-01-013375-016; Source: *www.canlii. org/qc/jug/qccq/2003/2003qccq17860.html*). In June 2003, Edwin Matos of Pembroke Pines, Florida, was sentenced to 30 years in prison for killing two teenage girls after crashing into their car at more than 160 km/h (100 mph). The recorder's speed data convicted him. Two months earlier, an Illinois police officer received a $10 million (U.S.) settlement after data showed the driver of an empty hearse, who was supposedly unconscious from a diabetes attack, actually accelerated and braked in the moments before slamming into the officer's patrol car. In July of 2002, New Brunswick prosecutors sent a dangerous driver to jail for two years based on his car's EDR data. (*R. v. Daley*, 2003 NBQB 20 Docket(s): S/CR/7/02 Source: *www.canlii.org/nb/cas/nbqb/2002/2003nbqb20.html*). GM was forced to recall more than 850,000 Cavaliers and Sunfires when its own data recorders showed that the cars' airbags often deployed inadvertently. Incidentally, California is the only jurisdiction where EDR data cannot be downloaded unless the car owner agrees or a court order is issued. Traffic accident reconstructionists Harris Technical Services have prepared a chronological list of dozens of Canadian and American court cases related to automotive Event Data Recorders. It is available at *www.harristechnical.com.*

Three Steps to a Settlement

Step 1: Informal Negotiations

If your vehicle was misrepresented, has major defects, or wasn't properly repaired under warranty, the first thing you should do is give the seller (the dealer and automaker) a written summary (by registered mail or fax) of the outstanding problems and stipulate a time period in which they will need to be corrected or your money will be refunded. Keep a copy for yourself, along with all your repair records. Be sure to check all of the sales and warranty documents you were given to see if they conform to provincial laws. Any errors, omissions, or violations can be used to get a settlement with the dealer in lieu of making a formal complaint.

At the beginning, try to work things out informally and, in your attempt to reach a settlement, keep in mind the cardinal rule: Ask only for what is fair and don't try to make anyone look bad.

Speak in a calm, polite manner and try to avoid polarizing the issue. Talk about how "we can work together" on the problem. Let a compromise slowly emerge—don't come in with a hardline set of demands. Don't demand the settlement offer in writing, but make sure that you're accompanied by a friend or relative who can confirm the offer in court if it isn't honoured. Be prepared to act upon the offer without delay so your hesitancy won't be blamed for its withdrawal.

The dealer and service manager

Service managers have more power than you may have realized. They make the first determination of what work is covered under warranty or through post-warranty "goodwill" programs and are directly responsible to the dealer and manufacturer for that decision (dealers hate manufacturer audits that force them to pay back questionable warranty decisions). Service managers are paid to save the dealer and automaker money and to mollify irate clients—an almost impossible balancing act. Nevertheless, when a service manager agrees to extend warranty coverage, it's because you've raised solid issues that neither the dealer nor automaker can ignore. All the more reason to present your argument in a confident, forthright manner with your vehicle's service history and *Lemon-Aid*'s reasonable durability chart. Also bring as many technical service bulletins and owner complaint printouts as you can find from websites like NHTSA's. It's not important that they apply directly to your problem: They establish parameters for giving out after-warranty assistance or "goodwill." Don't use your salesperson as a runner, since the sales staff are generally quite distant from the service staff and usually have less pull than you do. If the service manager can't or won't set things right, your next step is to convene a mini-summit with the service manager, the dealership principal, and the automaker's rep. By getting the automaker involved, you run less risk of having the dealer fob you off on the manufacturer and you can often get an agreement where the seller and automaker pay two-thirds of the repair cost.

Step 2: Sending a Registered Letter, Fax, or Email

This is the next step to take if your claim is refused. Send the dealer and manufacturer a polite registered letter or fax (see sample on following page) that asks for compensation for repairs that have been done or need to be done, insurance costs while the vehicle is being repaired, towing charges, supplementary transportation costs like taxis and rented cars, and damages for inconvenience.

Specify five days (but allow 10) for either party to respond. If no satisfactory offer is made, file suit in small claims court. Make the manufacturer a party to the lawsuit, especially if the emissions warranty, a secret warranty extension, a safety recall campaign, or extensive chassis rusting is involved.

Step 3: Mediation and Arbitration

If the formality of a courtroom puts you off or you're not sure that your claim is all that solid and don't want to pay legal costs to find out, consider using mediation or arbitration. These services are sponsored by the Better Business Bureau, the Automobile Protection Association, the Canadian Automobile Association, the Canadian Automobile Manufacturers Vehicle Arbitration Program at *www.camvap. ca*, small claims court (mediation is often a prerequisite to going to trial), and consumer mediation services set up by provincial and territorial governments.

Incidentally, several owners have reported back to me that CAMVAP has forced the automaker to buy back their vehicles. The first buyback was a 2004 Toyota Echo (see: *camvap.blogspot.com*), and the second was a Dodge Ram truck:

> I just won my case with Chrysler Canada over my 2003 Ram SLT 4X4 quad cab truck. I've been having PCV valves freezing up (5 PCVs in 9,000 km). After one month in the shop, I went to CAMVAP to put in my claim, went to arbitration, and won. They have agreed to buy back my truck.

NEW VEHICLE COMPLAINT LETTER/FAX/EMAIL

WITHOUT PREJUDICE

Date: _____

Name: _____

Please be advised that I am dissatisfied with my vehicle, a _____, bought from you on _____.

It has had the following recurring problems that I believe are factory-related defects, as confirmed by internal service bulletins sent to dealers, and are covered by your "goodwill" policies:

1. _____
2. _____
3. _____

If your "goodwill" program has ended, I ask that my claim be accepted nevertheless, inasmuch as I was never informed of your policy while it was in effect and should not be penalized for not knowing it existed.

I hereby formally put you on notice under federal and provincial consumer protection statutes that your refusal to apply this extended warranty coverage in my case would be an unfair warranty practice within the purview of the above-cited laws.

Your actions also violate the "implied warranty" set down by the Supreme Court of Canada (*Donoghue v. Stevenson* and *Longpre v. St. Jacques Automobile*) and repeatedly reaffirmed by provincial consumer protection laws (*Lowe v. Chrysler*, *Dufour v. Ford du Canada*, and *Frank v. GM*).

I have enclosed several estimates (my bill) showing that this problem is factory related and will (has) cost $_____ to correct. I would appreciate your refunding me the estimated (paid) amount, failing which, I reserve the right to have the repair done elsewhere and claim reimbursement in court without further delay. I also reserve the right to claim up to $1 million for punitive damages, pursuant to the Supreme Court of Canada's February 22, 2002, ruling in *Whiten v. Pilot*.

A positive response within the next five (5) days would be appreciated.

(signed with telephone number, fax number, or email address)

Getting Outside Help

Don't let poor preparation scuttle your case. Ask government or independent consumer protection agencies to evaluate how well prepared you are before going to your first hearing. Also, use the Internet to ferret out additional facts and gather support (*www.lemonaidcars.com* is a good place to start). Ontario consumers may file an online claim with the Ontario Motor Vehicle Industry Council at *https://ewconsumers.omvic.on.ca/complaint/complaint.asp*). Sure, OMVIC is the dealer's self-defence lobby—made up of 9,000 registered dealers and 20,000 registered salespeople—but it has a mandate to maintain a "fair, safe, and informed marketplace in Ontario by protecting the rights of consumers, enhancing industry professionalism, and ensuring fair, honest, and open competition for registered motor vehicle dealers." The way your complaint is handled will test the veracity of their above-stated goals.

Classified ads and television exposés

Put an ad in the local paper describing your plight, and ask for information from people who may have experienced a problem similar to your own. This alerts others to the potential problem, helps build a base for a class action or group meeting with the automaker, and puts pressure on the local dealer and manufacturer to settle. Sometimes the paper's news desk will assign someone to cover your story after your ad is published or you set up a website.

Television producers and their researchers need articulate consumers with issues that are easily filmed and understood. If you want media coverage, you must summarize your complaint and have visual aids that will hold the viewer's interest. (Viewers should be able to understand the issues with the sound turned off.) Paint delamination? Show your peeling car. Bought a lemon vehicle? Show your repair bills. Holding a demonstration? Make it a "lemon" parade: Target one of the largest dealers, give your group a nifty name, and make sure the vehicles are decorated with "lemon" signs.

Federal and provincial consumer affairs

The wind left the sails of the consumer movement over two decades ago, leaving consumer agencies understaffed and unsupported by the government. This has created a passive mindset among many staffers, who are tired of getting their heads kicked in by businesses, deadwood bosses, and budget cutters.

Consumer affairs offices can still help with investigation, mediation, and some litigation. Strong and effective consumer protection legislation has been left standing in most of the provinces, and resourceful consumers can use these laws in conjunction with media coverage to prod provincial consumer affairs offices into action. Furthermore, provincial bureaucrats aren't as well shielded from criticism as their federal counterparts. A call to your MPP or MLA, or to their executive assistants, can often get things rolling.

Federal consumer protection is a government-created PR myth. Don't expect the staffers in the reorganized Office of Consumer Affairs to be very helpful—they've been de-fanged and de-gummed through budget cuts and a succession of ineffective ministers. Although the beefed-up *Competition Act* has some bite with regards to misleading advertising and a number of other illegal business practices, the federal government has been more reactive than proactive in applying the law.

Nevertheless, you can lodge a formal complaint with Ottawa for misleading advertising, odometer tampering, or price fixing at *https://strategis.ic.gc.ca/ sc_mrksv/competit/complaint/form.html*. An online complaint sent to the address above made Toyota cease its Access price-fixing practices and pay out almost $2 million as a settlement fee. (See page 145 for more info on lodging a formal complaint.)

Invest in protest

You can have fun and put additional pressure on a seller or garage by putting a lemon sign on your car and parking it in front of the dealer or garage, creating a lemon website, or forming a self-help group, like the Chrysler Lemon Owners Group (CLOG) or the Ford Lemon Owners Group (FLOG). After forming your group, you can have the occasional parade of creatively decorated cars visit area dealerships as the local media are convened. Just remember: Keep your remarks pithy and factual, don't interfere with traffic or customers, and remain peaceful.

One other piece of advice from this consumer advocate with hundreds of pickets and mass demonstrations over the past 34 years under his belt: Keep a sense of humour and never break off negotiations.

Finally, don't be scared off by threats that it's illegal to criticize a product or company. Unions, environmentalists, and consumer groups do it regularly (it's called "informational picketing"), and the Supreme Court of Canada in *R. v. Guinard* reaffirmed this right in February 2002. In that judgment, an insurance policyholder posted a sign on his barn claiming the Commerce Insurance Company was unfairly refusing his claim. The municipality of St-Hyacinthe told him to take the sign down. He refused, maintaining that he had the right to state his opinion. The Supreme Court agreed. This judgment means that consumer protests, signs, and websites that criticize the actions of corporations cannot be banned simply because they say unpleasant things.

➤ Fighting Back Successfully

Sudden Acceleration, Chronic Stalling, and ABS and Airbag Failures

Incidents of sudden acceleration or chronic stalling are quite common. However, they are very difficult to diagnose and are treated quite differently by federal safety agencies. Sudden acceleration is considered to be a safety-related problem— stalling isn't. Never mind that a vehicle's sudden loss of power on a busy highway puts everyone's lives at risk. VW and Audi 2001–03 ignition coil failures are an example. The same problem exists with engine and transmission powertrain failures, which are only occasionally considered to be safety related. ABS and airbag failures are universally considered to be life-threatening defects. If your vehicle manifests any of these conditions, here's what you need to do:

1. Get independent witnesses to the fact that the problem exists. This includes verification by an independent mechanic, passenger accounts, downloaded data from your vehicle's data recorder and lots of Internet browsing using *www.lemonaidcars.com* and Google's browser as your primary tools. Notify the dealer and manufacturer by fax, email, or registered letter that you consider the problem to be a factory-induced, safety-related defect. Make sure you address your correspondence to the manufacturer's product liability or legal affairs department. At the dealership's service bay, make sure that every work order clearly states the problem, as well as the number of previous attempts to fix it. (This should result in you having a few complaint letters and a handful of work orders, confirming that this is an ongoing deficiency.) If the dealer won't give you a copy of the work order because the work is a warranty claim, ask for a copy of the order number "in case your estate wishes to file a claim, pursuant to an accident." (This will get the service manager's attention.) Leaving this kind of "paper trail" is crucial for any claim you may have later on because it shows your concern and persistence, and clearly indicates that the dealer and manufacturer have had ample time to correct the defect.

2. Note on the work order that you expect the problem to be diagnosed and corrected under the emissions warranty or a "goodwill" program. It also wouldn't hurt to add the phrase on the work order or in your claim letters that any deaths, injuries, or damage caused by the defect will be the dealer's and manufacturer's responsibility since this work order (or letter, fax, or email) constitutes your putting them on "formal notice."

3. If the dealer does the necessary repairs at little or no cost to you, send a follow-up confirmation that you appreciate the assistance. Also, emphasize that you'll be back if the problem reappears, even if the warranty has expired, because the repair renews your warranty rights applicable to that defect. In other words, the warranty clock is set back to its original position. Understand that you won't likely get a copy of the repair bill, either, because dealers don't like to admit that there was a serious defect present. You can, however, get your complete vehicle file from the dealer and manufacturer by issuing a subpoena (this costs about $40) if the case goes to small claims or a higher court.

This request has produced many out-of-court settlements when the internal documents show extensive work was carried out to correct the problem.

4. If the problem persists, send a letter, fax, or email to the dealer and manufacturer saying so, look for ALLDATA service bulletins to confirm that your vehicle's defects are factory related, and call Transport Canada or NHTSA or log onto NHTSA's website to report the failure. Also, call the Nader-founded Center for Auto Safety in Washington, D.C., (Tel: 202-328-7700) for a lawyer referral and an information sheet covering the problem.

5. Now come two crucial questions: Repair the defect now or later? Use the dealer or an independent? Generally it's smart to use an independent garage if you know the dealer isn't pushing for free corrective repairs from the manufacturer, if weeks or months have passed without any resolution of your claim, if the dealer keeps repeating that it's a maintenance item, and if you know an independent mechanic who will give you a detailed work order showing the defect is factory related and not caused by poor maintenance. Don't mention that a court case may ensue, since this will scare the dickens out of your only independent witness. An added bonus is that the repair charges will be about half of what a dealer would demand. Incidentally, if the automaker later denies warranty "goodwill" because you used an independent repairer, use the argument that the defect's safety implications required emergency repairs, carried out by whomever could see you first.

6. Dashboard-mounted warning lights usually come on prior to airbags suddenly deploying, ABS brakes failing, or engine glitches causing the vehicle to stall out. (Sudden acceleration usually occurs without warning.) Automakers consider these lights to be critical safety warnings and generally advise drivers to *immediately* have the vehicle serviced to correct the problem (advice found in the owner's manual) when any of the above lights come on. This bolsters the argument that your life was threatened, emergency repairs were required, and your request for another vehicle or a complete refund isn't out of line.

7. Sudden acceleration can have multiple causes, isn't easy to duplicate, and is often blamed on the driver mistaking the accelerator for the brakes or failing to perform proper maintenance. Yet NHTSA data shows that with the 1992–2000 Explorer, for example, a faulty cruise control or PCV valve and poorly mounted pedals are the most likely causes of the Explorer's sudden acceleration. So how do you satisfy the burden of proof showing that the problem exists and it's the automaker's responsibility? Use the legal doctrine called "the balance of probabilities" by eliminating all of the possible dodges the dealer or manufacturer may employ. Show that proper maintenance has been carried out, you're a safe driver, and the incident occurs frequently and without warning.

8. If any of the above defects causes an accident or the airbag fails to deploy or you're injured by its deployment, ask your insurance company to have the vehicle towed to a neutral location and clearly state that neither the dealer nor the automaker should touch the vehicle until your insurance company and Transport Canada have completed their investigation. Also, get as many witnesses as possible and immediately go to the hospital for a check-up, even if

you're feeling okay. You may be injured and not know it because the adrenalin coursing through your veins is masking your injuries. A hospital exam will easily confirm that your injuries are accident related, which is essential in court or for future settlement negotiations.

9. Peruse NHTSA's online accident and service bulletin database to find reports of other accidents caused by the same failure, bulletins that indicate part upgrades, current defect investigations, and reported failures that have resulted in recalls or closed investigations.

10. Don't let your insurance company bully you. Refuse to let them settle the case if you're sure the accident was caused by a mechanical failure. Even if an engineering analysis fails to directly implicate the manufacturer or dealer, you can always plead the aforementioned balance of probabilities. If the insurance company settles, your insurance premiums will soar and the manufacturer has committed the perfect crime.

Defective Tires

Tire companies are far easier to deal with than automobile manufacturers because under the legal doctrine of *res ipsa loquitor* (liability is shown by the failure) tires aren't supposed to fail. And when they do, smart claimants can use the *Robson* decision to bring in the American corporation and refer to our Supreme Court judgment (*Winnipeg Condominium v. Bird Construction* [1995] 1S.C.R.85), which ruled that defendants are liable in negligence for any designs that result in a risk to the public for safety or health. This 10-year-old decision reversed a long-standing policy and provided the public with a new cause of action that had not existed before in Canada.

No wonder tire and auto companies routinely avoid liability by imputing blame to someone or something else, like punctures, impact damage, overloading, over-inflating, or under-inflating.

If you have any failure (tire or otherwise) that conceivably put your life in peril, consider the 10 steps outlined previously, and add the following:

1. Access NHTSA on the Internet (see Appendix I) for current data on which tires are failure prone and which companies are under investigation, conducting recalls, or carrying out "silent recalls."

2. Keep the tire. If the tiremaker says an analysis must be done, permit only a portion of the tire to be taken away.

3. Plead the balance of probabilities, using friends and family to refute the tire company's contention that you caused the failure.

4. Ask for damages that are adequate for the replacement of all the tires on your vehicle, including mounting costs.

5. Include in your damage claim any repairs needed to fix body damage caused by the tire's failure.

Paint and Body Defects

The following settlement advice applies mainly to paint defects, but you can use these tips for any other vehicle defect that you believe is the automaker's or dealer's responsibility. If you're not sure that the problem is a factory-related deficiency or a maintenance item, have it checked out by an independent garage or get a technical service bulletin summary for your vehicle. The summary may include specific bulletins relating to the diagnosis, correction, and ordering of upgraded parts needed to fix your problem.

Four good examples of favourable paint judgments are *Shields v. General Motors of Canada, Bentley v. Dave Wheaton Pontiac Buick GMC Ltd. and General Motors of Canada, Maureen Frank v. General Motors of Canada Limited,* and the most recent, *Dunlop v. Ford of Canada.*

Dunlop v. Ford of Canada, No. 58475/04, Ontario Superior Court of Justice (Richmond Hill Small Claims Court), January 5, 2005, Deputy Judge M. J. Winer. The owner of a 1996 Lincoln Town Car, purchased used in 1999 for $27,000, was awarded $4,091.64. Judge Winer cited the *Shields* decision (below) and gave the following reasons for finding Ford of Canada liable:

> Evidence was given by the Plaintiff's witness, Terry Bonar, an experienced paint auto technician. He gave evidence that the [paint] delamination may be both a manufacturing defect and can be caused or [sped] up by atmospheric conditions. He also says that [the paint on] a car like this should last ten to 15 years, [or even for] the life of the vehicle....

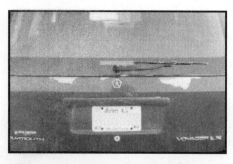

> It is my view that the presence of ultraviolet light is an environmental condition to which the vehicle is subject. If it cannot withstand this environmental condition, it is defective....

Shields v. General Motors of Canada, No. 1398/96, Ontario Court (General Division), Oshawa Small Claims Court, 33 King Street West, Oshawa, Ontario L1H 1A1, July 24, 1997, Robert Zochodne, Deputy Judge. The owner of a 1991 Pontiac Grand Prix purchased the vehicle used with over 100,000 km on its odometer. Beginning in 1995, the paint began to bubble and flake, and eventually peeled off. Deputy Judge Robert Zochodne awarded the plaintiff $1,205.72 and struck down every one of GM's arguments that the peeling paint was caused by acid rain, UV rays, or some other

Paint delamination is a common defect that automakers often blame on everything from bird droppings to ultraviolet light. Chrysler usually settles out of court, while Ford and General Motors often blame the environment or simply say the warranty has expired. The courts haven't been very receptive to these kinds of excuses.

environmental factor. Other important aspects of this 12-page judgment that GM did not appeal:

1. The judge admitted many of the technical service bulletins referred to in *Lemon-Aid* as proof of GM's negligence.
2. Although the vehicle had 156,000 km when the case went to court, GM still offered to pay 50 percent of the paint repairs if the plaintiff dropped his suit.
3. Deputy Judge Zochodne ruled that the failure to protect the paint from the damaging effects of UV rays is akin to engineering a car that won't start in cold weather. In essence, vehicles must be built to withstand the rigours of the environment.
4. Here's an interesting twist: The original warranty covered defects that were present at the time it was in effect. The judge, taking statements found in the GM technical service bulletins, ruled that the UV problem was factory related, existed during the warranty period, and represented a latent defect that appeared once the warranty expired.
5. The subsequent purchaser was not prevented from making the warranty claim, even though the warranty had long since expired from a time and mileage standpoint and he was the second owner.

Bentley v. Dave Wheaton Pontiac Buick GMC Ltd. and General Motors of Canada, Victoria Registry No. 24779, British Columbia Small Claims Court, December 1, 1998, Judge Higinbotham. This small claims judgment builds upon the *Ontario Shields v. General Motors of Canada* decision and cites other jurisprudence as to how long paint should last on a car. If you're wondering why Ford and Chrysler haven't been hit by similar judgments, remember that they usually settle out of court.

Maureen Frank v. General Motors of Canada Limited, No. SC#12 (2001), Saskatchewan Provincial Court, Saskatoon, Saskatchewan, October 17, 2001, Provincial Court Judge H.G. Dirauf:

> On June 23, 1997, the Plaintiff bought a 1996 Chevrolet Corsica from a General Motors dealership. At the time, the odometer showed 33,172 km. The vehicle still had some factory warranty. The car had been a lease car and had no previous accidents.
>
> During June of 2000, the Plaintiff noticed that some of the paint was peeling off from the car and she took it to a General Motors dealership in Saskatoon and to the General Motors dealership in North Battleford where she purchased the car. While there were some discussions with the GM dealership about the peeling paint, nothing came of it and the Plaintiff now brings this action claiming the cost of a new paint job.
>
> During 1999, the Plaintiff was involved in a minor collision causing damage to the left rear door. This damage was repaired. During this repair some scratches to the left front door previously done by vandals were also repaired.

The Plaintiff's witness, Frank Nemeth, is a qualified auto body repairman with some 26 years of experience. He testified that the peeling paint was a factory defect and that it was necessary to completely strip the car and repaint it. He diagnosed the cause of the peeling paint as a separation of the primer surface or colour coat from the electrocoat primer. In his opinion no primer surfacer was applied at all. He testified that once the peeling starts, it will continue. He has seen this problem on General Motors vehicles. The defect is called delamination.

Mr. Nemeth stated that a paint job should last at least 10 years. In my opinion, most people in Saskatchewan grow up with cars and are familiar with cars. I think it is common knowledge that the original paint on cars normally lasts in excess of 15 years and that rust becomes a problem before the paint fails. In any event, paint peeling off, as it did on the Plaintiff's vehicle, is not common. I find that the paint on a new car put on by the factory should last at least 15 years.

It is clear from the evidence of Frank Nemeth (independent body shop manager) that the delamination is a factory defect. His evidence was not seriously challenged. I find that the factory paint should not suffer a delamination defect for at least 15 years and that this factory defect breached the warranty that the paint was of acceptable quality and was durable for a reasonable period of time.

There will be judgment for the Plaintiff in the amount of $3,412.38 plus costs of $81.29.

Some of the important aspects of the *Frank* judgment are:

1. The judge accepted that the automaker was responsible, even though the car had been bought used. The subsequent purchaser was not prevented from making the warranty claim, even though the warranty had long since expired from a time and mileage standpoint and she was the second owner.
2. The judge stressed that the provincial warranty can kick in any time the automaker's warranty has expired or isn't applied.
3. By awarding full compensation to the plaintiff, the judge didn't feel that there was a significant "betterment" or improvement added to the car that would warrant reducing the amount of the award.
4. The judge decided that the paint delamination was a factory defect.
5. The judge also concluded that without this factory defect, a paint job should last up to 15 years.
6. GM offered to pay $700 of the paint repairs if the plaintiff dropped the suit; the judge awarded five times that amount.
7. Maureen Frank won this case despite having to confront GM lawyer Ken Ready, who had argued other paint cases for GM and Chrysler.

Other paint and rust cases

Martin v. Honda Canada Inc., March 17, 1986, Ontario Small Claims Court (Scarborough), Judge Sigurdson. The original owner of a 1981 Honda Civic sought compensation for the premature "bubbling, pitting, cracking of the paint, and rusting of the Civic after five years of ownership." Judge Sigurdson agreed and ordered Honda to pay the owner $1,163.95.

Thauberger v. Simon Fraser Sales and Mazda Motors, 3 B.C.L.R., 193. This Mazda owner sued for damages caused by the premature rusting of his 1977 Mazda GLC. The court awarded him $1,000. Thauberger had previously sued General Motors for a prematurely rusted Blazer truck and was also awarded $1,000 in the same court. Both judges ruled that the defects could not be excluded from the automaker's express warranty or from the implied warranty granted by ss. 20, 20(b) of the B.C. *Sale of Goods Act*.

Whittaker v. Ford Motor Company (1979), 24 O.R. (2d), 344. A new Ford developed serious corrosion problems in spite of having been rustproofed by the dealer. The court ruled that the dealer, not Ford, was liable for the damage for having sold the rustproofing product at the time of purchase. This is an important judgment to use when a rustproofer or paint protector goes out of business or refuses to pay a claim, since the decision holds the dealer jointly responsible.

See also:

- *Danson v. Chateau Ford* (1976) C.P., Quebec Small Claims Court, No. 32-00001898-757, Judge Lande.
- *Doyle v. Vital Automotive Systems*, May 16, 1977, Ontario Small Claims Court (Toronto), Judge Turner.
- *Lacroix v. Ford*, April 1980, Ontario Small Claims Court (Toronto), Judge Tierney.
- *Marinovich v. Riverside Chrysler*, April 1, 1987, District Court of Ontario, No. 1030/85, Judge Stortini.

Going to Court

Sue as a Last Resort

If the seller you've been negotiating with agrees to make things right, set a deadline and then have an independent garage check the repairs. If no offer is made within 10 working days, file suit in court. Make the manufacturer a party to the lawsuit only if the original, unexpired warranty was transferred to you; your claim falls under the emissions warranty, a TSB, a secret warranty extension, or a safety recall campaign; or there is extensive chassis rusting because of poor engineering.

Choosing the Right Court

Most claims can be handled without a lawyer in small claims court, especially now that the court's jurisdiction varies between $10,000 and $25,000. Still, it's up to you to decide what remedy to pursue; that is, whether you want a partial refund or a cancellation of the sale. To determine the refund amount, add the estimated cost of repairing existing mechanical defects to the cost of prior repairs. Don't exaggerate your losses or claim for repairs that are considered routine maintenance. A suit for cancellation of sale involves practical problems. The court requires that the vehicle be "tendered" or taken back to the seller at the time the lawsuit is filed. This leaves you without transportation for as long as the case continues, unless you purchase another vehicle in the interim. If you lose the case, you must then take back the old vehicle and pay storage fees. You could go from having no vehicle to having two, one of which is a clunker.

Generally, if the cost of repairs or the sales contract amount falls within the small claims court limit (discussed later), file the case there to keep costs to a minimum and get a speedy hearing. Small claims court judgments aren't easily appealed, lawyers aren't necessary, filing fees are minimal (about $125), and cases are usually heard within a few months. In fact, your suit should almost always be argued in the provincial small claims court to keep costs and frustrations down and to get a quick resolution within a few months.

> Mr. Edmonston, I emailed you earlier in the year seeking help on my small claims case against Ford. I'm happy to report that I won my case and received a $1,900 settlement cheque from Ford in the mail yesterday! As you may recall I have a 1991 Explorer that has a significant paint peel problem.
>
> I followed all the steps recommended by your website—ultimately I ended up in small claims court. Ford had indicated in court documents that they were going to send a representative to the hearing, but nobody showed. The judge made a quick ruling in my favour and I was out the door. I didn't even get a chance to show the load of material I had brought to make my case.
>
> MARK G.

Another reason not to be greedy: If you claim more than the small claims court limit, you'll have to go to a higher court—where costs quickly add up, lawyers routinely demand 30 percent of your winnings or settlement, and delays of a few years or more are commonplace.

Small Claims Courts

Small claims courts are efficient and effective. That's why they scare car dealers and automakers alike. No, they can't issue million-dollar judgments, or force litigants to spend millions in legal fees, but they can award sizeable sums to individual, unrepresented plaintiffs and make jurisprudence that other judges on the same bench will consider.

For example, in *Dawe v. Courtesy Chrysler*, Dartmouth Nova Scotia Small Claims Court SCCH #206825, July 30, 2004, Judge Patrick L Casey, Q.C., rendered an impressive 21-page decision citing key automobile product liability judgments rendered over the past 80 years. He awarded $5,037 to the owner of a new 2001 Cummins-equipped Ram pickup that wandered all over the road; lost power, or jerked and bucked; shifted erratically; lost braking ability; bottomed out when passing over bumps; allowed water to leak into the cab; emitted a burnt-wire and oil smell in the interior as lights would dim; and produced a rear-end whine and wind noise around the doors and under the dash.

Interestingly, "small claims" court is quickly becoming a misnomer, now that Alberta and British Columbia allow claims of up to a limit of $25,000 and most other provinces permit $10,000 filings.

There are small claims courts in most counties of every province, and you can make a claim in the county where the problem happened or where the defendant lives and conducts business. Simply go to the small claims court office and ask for a claim form. Instructions on how to fill it out accompany the form. Remember, you must identify the defendant correctly, which may require some help from the court clerk (look for other recent lawsuits naming the same party). Crooks often change their company's name to escape liability; for example, it would be impossible to sue Joe's Garage (1999) if your contract is with Joe's Garage Inc. (1984).

At this point, it wouldn't hurt to hire a lawyer or a paralegal for a brief walk-through of small claims procedures to ensure that you've prepared your case properly and that you know what objections will likely be raised by the other side. If you'd like a lawyer to do all the work for you, there are a number of law firms around the country that specialize in small claims litigation. Small claims doesn't means small legal fees, however. In Toronto, some law offices charge a flat fee of $1,000 for the basic small claims lawsuit and trial.

Remember that you're entitled to bring to court any evidence relevant to your case, including written documents such as a bill of sale or receipt, contract, or letter. If your car has developed severe rust problems, bring a photograph (signed and dated by the photographer) to court. You may also have witnesses testify in court. It's important to discuss a witness's testimony prior to the court date. If a witness can't attend the court date, he or she can write a report and sign it for representation in court. This situation usually applies to an expert witness, such as an independent mechanic who has evaluated your car's problems.

If you lose your case in spite of all your preparation and research, some small claims court statutes allow cases to be retried, at a nominal cost, in exceptional circumstances. If a new witness has come forward, additional evidence has been discovered, or key documents (that were previously not available) have become accessible, apply for a retrial. In Ontario, this little-known provision is Rule 18.4 (1).B.

Alan MacDonald, a *Lemon-Aid* reader who won his case in small claims court, gives the following tips on beating Ford over a faulty automatic transmission:

> I want to thank you for the advice you provided in my dealings with the Ford Motor Company of Canada, Limited and Highbury Ford Sales Limited regarding my 1994 Ford Taurus wagon and the problems with the automatic transmission (Taurus and Windstar transmissions are identical) ... (*MacDonald v. Highbury Ford Sales Limited*, Ontario Superior Court of Justice in the Small Claims Court London, June 6, 2000, Court File #0001/00, Judge J.D. Searle).

> In 1999, after only 105,000 km, the automatic transmission went. I took the car to Highbury Ford to have it repaired. We paid $2,070 to have the transmission fixed, but protested and felt the transmission failed prematurely. We contacted Ford, but to no avail: Their reply was we were out of warranty, period. The transmission was so poorly repaired (and we went back to Highbury Ford several times) that we had to go to Mr. Transmission to have the transmission fixed again nine months later at a further $1,906.02.

> It is at that point that I contacted you, and I was surprised, and somewhat speechless (which you noticed) when you personally called me to provide advice and encouragement. I am very grateful for your call. My observations with going through small claims court involved the following: I filed in January of 2000, the trial took place on June 1 and the judgment was issued June 6.

> At pretrial, a representative of Ford (Ann Sroda) and a representative from Highbury Ford were present. I came with one binder for each of the defendants, the court and one for myself (each binder was about 3 inches thick—containing your reports on Ford Taurus automatic transmissions, ALLDATA Service Bulletins, Taurus Transmissions Victims (Bradley website), Center for Auto Safety (website), Read This Before Buying a Taurus (website), and the Ford Vent Page (website).

> The representative from Ford asked a lot of questions (I think she was trying to find out if I had read the contents of the information I was relying on). The Ford representative then offered a 50 percent settlement based on the initial transmission work done at Highbury Ford. The release allowed me to still sue Highbury Ford with regards to the necessity of going to Mr. Transmission because of the faulty repair done by the dealer. Highbury Ford displayed no interest in settling the case, and so I had to go to court.

> For court, I prepared by issuing a summons to the manager at Mr. Transmission, who did the second transmission repair, as an expert witness. I was advised that unless you produce an expert witness you won't win in a car repair case in small claims

court. Next, I went to the law school library in London and received a great deal of assistance in researching cases pertinent to car repairs. I was told that judgments in your home province (in my case Ontario) were binding on the court; that cases outside of the home province could be considered, but not binding, on the judge.

The cases I used for trial involved *Pelleray v. Heritage Ford Sales Ltd.*, Ontario Small Claims Court (Scarborough) SC7688/91 March 22, 1993; *Phillips et al. v. Ford Motor Co. of Canada Ltd. et al,* Ontario Reports 1970, 15th January 1970; *Gregorio v. Intrans-Corp.*, Ontario Court of Appeal, May 19, 1994; *Collier v. MacMaster's Auto Sales,* New Brunswick Court of Queen's Bench, April 26, 1991; *Sigurdson v. Hillcrest Service & Acklands* (1977), Saskatchewan Queen's Bench; *White v. Sweetland*, Newfoundland District Court, Judicial Centre of Gander, November 8, 1978; *Raiches Steel Works v. J. Clark & Son*, New Brunswick Supreme Court, March 7, 1977; *Mudge v. Corner Brook Garage Ltd.*, Newfoundland Supreme Court, July 17, 1975; *Sylvain v. Carroseries d'Automobiles Guy Inc. (1981)*, C.P. 333, Judge Page; *Gagnon v. Ford Motor Company of Canada, Limited et Marineau Automobile Co. Ltée.* (1974), C.S. 422–423.

In court, I had prepared the case, as indicated above, had my expert witness and two other witnesses who had driven the vehicle (my wife and my 18-year-old son). As you can see by the judgment, we won our case and I was awarded $1,756.52, including pre-judgment interest and costs.

Key Court Decisions

The following Canadian and U.S. lawsuits and judgments cover typical problems that are likely to arise. Use them as leverage when negotiating a settlement or as a reference should your claim go to trial. Legal principles applying to Canadian and American law are similar; however, Quebec court decisions may be based on legal principles that don't apply outside that province.

You can find a comprehensive listing of Canadian decisions from small claims courts all the way to the Supreme Court of Canada at *www.canlii.org* and *legalresearch.org/docs/internet3.html*. Additional court judgments can be found in the legal reference section of your city's main public library or at a nearby university law library. The Canadian version of the Consumer Clearing House (CCH) updated binders has lots of judgments relative to contract, product liability, insurance law, and consumer protection. Ask the librarian for help in choosing the legal phrases that best describe your claim.

 My favourite reference book, which will give you plenty of tips on filing, pleading, and collecting your judgment, is Judge Marvin Zuker's *Ontario Small Claims Court Practice 2002–2003* (Carswell, 2002). Judge Zuker's book is easily understood by non-lawyers and uses court decisions from across Canada to help you effectively plead your case in almost any Canadian court.

Product Liability

Almost three decades ago, before *Robson* and just after *Bird*, the Supreme Court of Canada in *Kravitz v. GM* clearly affirmed that automakers and their dealers are jointly liable for the replacement or repair of a vehicle if independent testimony shows that it is afflicted by factory-related defects that compromise its safety or performance. The existence of a secret warranty extension or technical service bulletins also help prove that the vehicle's problems are the automaker's responsibility. For example, in *Lowe v. Fairview Chrysler* (see page 133), technical service bulletins were instrumental in showing in 1989 that Chrysler had a history of automatic transmission failures similar to what we see in Ford and GM today.

In addition to replacing or repairing the vehicle, an automaker can also be held responsible for any damages arising from the defect (see *Wharton*). This means that loss of wages, supplementary transportation costs, and damages for personal inconvenience can be awarded. However, in the States, product liability damage awards often exceed millions of dollars, while Canadian courts are far less generous.

When a warranty claim is rejected on the pretext that you "altered" the vehicle, failed to carry out preventive maintenance, or drove abusively, manufacturers *must* prove a link between their allegation and the failure (see *Julien v. General Motors of Canada Ltd.* (1991), 116 N.B.R. (2d) 80).

Before settling any claim with GM or any other automaker, download the latest information from dissatisfied customers who've banded together and set up their own self-help websites. Follow the links at *www.lemonaidcars.com*.

Implied Warranty

Reasonable durability

This is that powerful "other" warranty that they never tell you about. It applies during and after the expiration of the manufacturer's or dealer's expressed or written warranty and requires that a part or repair will last a "reasonable" period of time. Look at the reasonable durability chart on pages 107–08 for some guidelines as to what you should expect.

Judges usually apply the implied or legal warranty when the manufacturer's expressed warranty has expired and the vehicle's manufacturing defects remain uncorrected. The landmark Canadian decisions upholding implied warranties in auto claims have been *General Motors Products of Canada Ltd. v. Kravitz*, [1979] 1 S.C.R. 790 and *Donoghue v. Stevenson*, [1932] A. C. 562 (H.L.).

In *Donoghue*, the court had to determine if the manufacturer of a bottle of ginger beer owed a duty to a consumer who suffered injury as a result of finding a decomposed snail in the bottle after consuming part of the contents of the bottle. Lord Atkin, in finding liability against the manufacturer, established the principle of negligence. His reasons have been followed and adopted in all the common law countries:

> The rule that you are to love your neighbour becomes in law, you must not injure your neighbour; and the lawyer's question, who is my neighbour? receives a restricted reply. You must take reasonable care to avoid acts or omissions which you can reasonably foresee would be likely to injure your neighbour. Who, then, is my neighbour?
>
> The answer seems to be—persons who are so closely and directly affected by my act that I ought reasonably to have them in contemplation as being so affected when I am directing my mind to the acts or omissions which are called in question....

Forty-five years later in Quebec, *Kravitz* said essentially the same thing. In that case, the court said the seller's warranty of quality was an accessory to the property and was transferred with it on successive sales. Accordingly, subsequent buyers could invoke the contractual warranty of quality against the manufacturer, even though they did not contract directly with it. This precedent is now codified in articles 1434, 1442, and 1730 of Quebec's *Civil Code* (see *Tardif v. Hyundai Motor America* at *www.canlii.org/qc/jug/qccs/2004/2004qccs12258.html* for a full analysis of warranties, hidden defects, and misrepresentation relating to Hyundai's inability to be truthful about its horsepower ratings).

Windstar Doors and Engines

In the following judgments, Ford was forced to pay for the mental distress it created and reimburse the cost of Windstar engine head gasket repairs carried out under the *implied warranty*—long after the *expressed warranty* had expired.

Windstar "mental distress"

In *Sharman v. Formula Ford Sales Limited, Ford Credit Limited, and Ford Motor Company of Canada Limited*, Ontario Superior Court of Justice, No. 17419/02SR, 2003/10/07, Justice Shepard awarded the owner of a 2000 Windstar $7,500 for mental distress resulting from the breach of the implied warranty of fitness, plus $7,207 for breach of contract and breach of warranty. The problem with the Windstar was that its sliding door wasn't secure and leaked air and water after many attempts to repair it. The judge cited the *Wharton* decision as support for his award for mental distress.

> The plaintiff and his family have had three years of aggravation, inconvenience, worry, and concern about their safety and that of their children. Generally speaking, our contract law did not allow for compensation for what may be mental distress, but that may be changing. I am indebted to counsel for providing me with the decision of

the British Columbia Court of Appeal in *Wharton v. Tom Harris Chevrolet Oldsmobile Cadillac Ltd.*, [2002] B.C.J. No. 233, 2002 BCCA 78. This decision was recently followed in *T'avra v. Victoria Ford Alliance Ltd.*, [2003] B, CJ No. 1957.

This Court upheld an award of damages of $1,000 in *Wilson v. Sooter Studios* (1988), 42 B.L.R. 89 (C-A.), where a photographer arrived late to take wedding photographs; instead of 102 photographs contracted for, only 10 photographs of acceptable quality were produced. The award was for the bride's "direct and inevitable" (p. 92) disappointment resulting from the breach of contract.

In *Farley* (at para-19), Lord Steyn described the "peace of mind" cases as "not the product of Victorian contract theory but the result of evolutionary developments in case law from the 1970s." He cited *Jarvis v. Swans Tours Ltd.*, [1973] Q.B. 233 (C.A.) and *Jackson v. Horizon Holidays Ltd.*, [1975] 1 W.L.R. 1468 (C.A.), in which damages were awarded to "disappointed vacationers."

Free engine repairs

Dufour v. Ford Canada Ltd., April 10, 2001, Quebec Small Claims Court (Hull), No. 550-32-008335-009, Justice P. Chevalier. Ford was forced to reimburse the cost of engine head gasket repairs carried out on a 1996 Windstar 3.8L engine.

Schaffler v. Ford Motor Company Limited and Embrun Ford Sales Ltd., Ontario Superior Court of Justice, L'Orignal Small Claims Court, Court File No. 59-2003, July 22, 2003, Justice Gerald Langlois. The plaintiff bought a used 1995 Windstar in 1998. The engine head gasket was repaired for free three years later under Ford's 7-year extended warranty. In 2002, at 109,600 km, the head gasket failed again, seriously damaging the engine. Ford refused a second repair.

Justice Langlois ruled that Ford's warranty extension bulletin listed signs and symptoms of the covered defect that were identical to the problems written on the second work order ("persistent and/or chronic engine overheating; heavy white smoke evident from the exhaust tailpipe; flashing 'low coolant' instrument panel light even after coolant refill; and constant loss of engine coolant"). The judge concluded that the dealer knew of the problem well within the warranty period and was therefore negligent. The plaintiff was awarded $4,941, plus 5 percent interest. This included $1,070 for two months' car rental.

John R. Reid and Laurie M. McCall v. Ford Motor Company of Canada, Superior Court of Justice, Ottawa Small Claims Court, Claim No. 02-SC-077344, July 11, 2003, Justice Tiernay. A 1996 Windstar bought used in 1997 experienced engine head gasket failure in October 2001 at 159,000 km. Judge Tiernay awarded the Plaintiffs $4,145 for the following reasons:

A Technical Service Bulletin dated June 28, 1999, was circulated to Ford dealers. It dealt specifically with "undetermined loss of coolant" and "engine oil contaminated with coolant" in the 1996–98 Windstar and five other models of Ford vehicles. I conclude that Ford owed a duty of care to the Plaintiff to equip this vehicle with a cylinder head gasket of sufficient sturdiness and durability that would function trouble-free for at least seven years, given normal driving and proper maintenance conditions. I find that Ford is answerable in damages for the consequences of its negligence.

You can use these judgments as a guide for complaints relating to premature engine failure involving any automaker.

Automatic Transmission Failures

Lowe v. Fairview Chrysler-Dodge Limited and Chrysler Canada Limited, May 14, 1996, Ontario Court (General Division), Burlington Small Claims Court, No. 1224/95. This judgment, in the plaintiff's favour, raises important legal principles relative to Chrysler:

- Internal dealer service bulletins are admissible in court to prove that a problem exists and certain parts should be checked out.
- If a problem is reported prior to a warranty's expiration, warranty coverage for the problematic component(s) is automatically carried over after the warranty ends.
- It's not up to the car owner to tell the dealer or automaker what the specific problem is.
- Repairs carried out by an independent garage can be refunded if the dealer or automaker unfairly refuses to apply the warranty.
- The dealer or automaker cannot dispute the cost of the independent repair if it fails to cross-examine the independent repairer.
- Auto owners can ask for and win compensation for their inconvenience, which in this judgment amounted to $150.
- Court awards quickly add up. Although the plaintiff was given $1,985.94, with the addition of court costs and pre-judgment interest, plus costs of inconvenience fixed at $150, the final award amounted to $2,266.04.

New-Vehicle Defects

Bagnell's Cleaners v. Eastern Automobile Ltd. (1991), 111 N.S.R. (2nd), No. 51, 303 A.P.R., No. 51 (T.D.). This Nova Scotia company found that the new van it purchased had serious engine, transmission, and radiator defects. The dealer pleaded unsuccessfully that the sales contract excluded all other warranties except for those contained in the contract. The court held that there was a fundamental breach of the implied warranty and that the van's performance differed substantially from what the purchaser had been led to expect. An exclusionary clause could not protect the seller, who failed to live up to a fundamental term of the contract.

Burridge v. City Motor, 10 Nfld. & P.E.I.R., No. 451. This Newfoundland resident complained repeatedly of his new car's defects during the warranty period, and stated that he hadn't used his car for 204 days after spending almost $1,500 for repairs. The judge awarded all repair costs and cancelled the sale.

Davis v. Chrysler Canada Ltd. (1977), 26 N.S.R. (2nd), No. 410 (T.D.). The owner of a new $28,000 diesel truck found that a faulty steering assembly prevented him from carrying on his business. The court ordered that the sale be cancelled and that $10,000 in monthly payments be reimbursed. There was insufficient evidence to award compensation for business losses.

Fox v. Wilson Motors and GM, February 9, 1989, Court of Queen's Bench, New Brunswick, No. F/C/308/87. A trucker's new tractor-trailer had repeated engine malfunctions. He was awarded damages for loss of income, excessive fuel consumption, and telephone charges under the provincial *Sale of Goods Act*.

Gibbons v. Trapp Motors Ltd. (1970), 9 D.L.R. (3rd), No. 742 (B.C.S.C.). The court ordered the dealer to take back a new car that had numerous defects and required 32 hours of repairs. The refund was reduced by mileage driven.

Johnson v. Northway Chevrolet Oldsmobile (1993), 108 Sask. R., No. 138 (Q.B.). The court ordered the dealer to take back a new car that had been brought in for repairs on 14 different occasions. Two years after purchase, the buyer initiated a lawsuit for the purchase price of the car and for general damages. General damages were awarded.

Julien v. GM of Canada (1991), 116 N.B.R. (2nd), No. 80. The plaintiff's new diesel truck produced excessive engine noise. The dealer claimed that the problem was caused by the owner's engine alterations. The plaintiff was awarded the $5,000 cost of repairing the engine through an independent dealer.

Magna Management Ltd. v. Volkswagen Canada Inc., May 27, 1988, Vancouver (B.C.C.A.), No. CA006037. This precedent-setting case allowed the plaintiff to keep his new $48,325 VW while awarding him $37,101—three years after the car was purchased. The problems were centred on poor engine performance. The jury accepted the plaintiff's view that the car was practically worthless with its inherent defects.

Maughan v. Silver's Garage Ltd., Nova Scotia Supreme Court, 6 B.L.R., No. 303, N.S.C. (2nd), No. 278. The plaintiff leased a defective backhoe. The manufacturer had to reimburse the plaintiff's losses because the warranty wasn't honoured. The Court rejected the manufacturer's contention that the contract's exclusion clause protected the company from lawsuits for damages resulting from a latent defect.

Murphy v. Penney Motors Ltd. (1979), 23 Nfld. & P.E.I.R., No. 152, 61 A.P.R., No. 152 (Nfld. T.D.). This Newfoundland trucker found that his vehicle's engine problems took his new trailer off the road for 129 days during a 7-month period. The judge awarded all repair costs, as well as compensation for business losses, and cancelled the sale.

Murray v. Sperry Rand Corp., Ontario Supreme Court, 5 B.L.R., No. 284. The seller, dealer, and manufacturer were all held liable for breach of warranty when a forage harvester did not perform as advertised in the sales brochure or as promised by the sales agent. The plaintiff was given his money back and reimbursed for his economic loss, based on the amount his harvesting usually earned. The court held that the advertising was a warranty.

Oliver v. Courtesy Chrysler (1983) Ltd. (1992), 11 B.C.A.C., No. 169. This new car had numerous defects over a three-year period, which the dealer attempted to fix to no avail. The plaintiff put the car in storage and sued the dealer for the purchase price. The court ruled that the car wasn't roadworthy and that the plaintiff couldn't be blamed for putting it in storage rather than selling it and purchasing another vehicle. The purchase price was refunded minus $1,500 for each year the plaintiff used the car.

Olshaski Farms Ltd. v. Skene Farm Equipment Ltd., January 9, 1987, Alberta Court of Queen's Bench, 49 Alta. L.R. (2nd), No. 249. The plaintiff's Massey-Ferguson combine caught fire after the manufacturer had sent two notices to dealers informing them of a defect that could cause a fire. The judge ruled under the *Sale of Goods Act* that the balance of probabilities indicated that the manufacturing defect caused the fire, even though there was no direct evidence proving that the defect existed.

Western Pacific Tank Lines Ltd. v. Brentwood Dodge, June 2, 1975, B.C.S.C., No. 30945-74, Judge Meredith. The court awarded the plaintiff $8,600 and cancelled the sale of a new Chrysler New Yorker with badly adjusted doors, water leaks into the interior, and electrical short circuits.

Leasing

Ford Motor Credit v. Bothwell, December 3, 1979, Ontario County Court (Middlesex), No. 9226-T, Judge Macnab. The defendant leased a 1977 Ford truck that had frequent engine problems, characterized by stalling and hard starting. After complaining for one year and driving 35,000 km (22,000 mi.), the defendant cancelled the lease. Ford Credit sued for the money owing on the lease. Judge Macnab cancelled the lease and ordered Ford Credit to repay 70 percent of the amount paid during the leasing period. Ford Credit was also ordered to refund repair costs, even though the corporation claimed that it should not be held responsible for Ford's failure to honour its warranty.

Schryvers v. Richport Ford Sales, May 18, 1993, B.C.S.C., No. C917060, Justice Tysoe. The court awarded $17,578.47, plus costs, to a couple who paid thousands of dollars more in unfair and hidden leasing charges than if they had simply purchased their Ford Explorer and Escort. The court found that this price difference constituted a deceptive, unconscionable act or practice, in contravention of the *Trade Practices Act*, R.S.B.C. 1979, c. 406.

Judge Tysoe concluded that the total of the general damages awarded to the Schryvers for both vehicles would be $11,578.47. He then proceeded to give the following reasons for awarding an additional $6,000 in punitive damages:

> Little wonder Richport Ford had a contest for the salesperson who could persuade the most customers to acquire their vehicles by way of a lease transaction. I consider the actions of Richport Ford to be sufficiently flagrant and high-handed to warrant an award of punitive damages.
>
> There must be a disincentive to suppliers in respect of intentionally deceptive trade practices. If no punitive damages are awarded for intentional violations of the legislation, suppliers will continue to conduct their businesses in a manner that involves deceptive trade practices because they will have nothing to lose. In this case I believe that the appropriate amount of punitive damages is the extra profit Richport Ford endeavoured to make as a result of its deceptive acts. I therefore award punitive damages against Richport Ford in the amount of $6,000.

Salvador v. Setay Motors/Queenstown Chev-Olds, Hamilton Small Claims Court, Case No. 1621/95. Robert Salvador was awarded $2,000 plus costs from Queenstown Leasing. The court found that the company should have tried harder to sell the leased vehicle, and at a higher price, when the "open lease" expired.

Incidentally, about 3,700 dealers in 39 American states paid between $3,500 and $8,000 each in 2004 to settle an investigation of allegations that they and Ford Motor Credit Co. overcharged customers who terminated their leases early.

See also:

- *Barber v. Inland Truck Sales*, 11 D.L.R. (3rd), No. 469.
- *Canadian-Dominion Leasing v. Suburban Super Drug Ltd.* (1966), 56 D.L.R. (2nd), No. 43.
- *Neilson v. Atlantic Rentals Ltd.* (1974), 8 N.B.R. (2nd), No. 594.
- *Volvo Canada v. Fox*, December 13, 1979, New Brunswick Court of Queen's Bench, No. 1698/77/C, Judge Stevenson.
- *Western Tractor v. Dyck*, 7 D.L.R. (3rd), No. 535.

Dealers routinely keep much of their lease customers' security deposits when the leases expire. However, that action can always be challenged. In the following claim, settled out of court, Ontario lawyer, Harvey Goldstein forced GMAC and a GM dealer to refund his $525 security deposit:

1. The Plaintiff Claims:
   (A) Return of his security deposit of $525.00; and a finding that no amount is owing to the Defendants;
   (B) Alternatively, damages in the above amount;
   (C) Prejudgment interest on $525.00 at the rate of 2% per month (24% per annum) from June 22, 2005, to the date of this Claim, and thereafter on the date of payment or Judgment at the rate of 4% per annum, pursuant to Section 128 of the *Courts of Justice Act*, R.S.O. (1990) as amended;
   (D) Post-judgment interest at the post-judgment rate of interest, pursuant to Section 129 of the Courts of Justice Act, R. S. O. (1990) as amended;
   (E) His costs of this action;
   (F) Punitive damages in an amount to be determined; and
   (G) Such further and other relief as this Honorable Court deems just and proper.

   . . .

4. On or about June 10, 2005, the Plaintiff advised the Defendant North York Chevrolet Oldsmobile Ltd that he wanted it to inspect the said vehicle for chargeable damage prior to its return or that he be present when it was inspected after its return to the said Defendant.
5. The said Defendant advised that it had no control over the inspection process and that the Defendant GMAC Leaseco Limited would inspect the vehicle only after the lease expired, the vehicle was returned to the dealer and the Plaintiff was not present.
6. The Plaintiff sent an email on June 10, 2005 to the Defendant GMAC Leaseco Limited asking it for an inspection prior to the vehicle being returned.
7. The said Defendant did not respond to the request.
8. The Plaintiff called and spoke with a representative of the said Defendant on June 17, and wrote her a letter sent by fax the same day, again asking that an inspection be scheduled in his presence. The said Defendant did not respond to the letter.
9. On June 23, 2005, the Plaintiff again called the said Defendant. He was told that it had no record of the vehicle being returned to the dealership.
10. Shortly thereafter, the Plaintiff called the Defendant North York Chevrolet Oldsmobile Ltd to enquire as to the status of his security deposit. The said Defendant advised that it had no record of the vehicle being returned to it.
11. Not having heard from either Defendant, the Plaintiff called the Defendant GMAC Leaseco Limited on July 15, 2005. He was advised that he owed the said Defendant $550.00, less the amount of the security deposit held by it. He was further advised that details of its claim to that amount could be found on the said Defendant's website. He was told that it did not inspect the said vehicle until July 7, 2005, 15 days after it was left in the dealership's service bay. He

was told that the vehicle was at an auction and that he could not inspect the alleged damages for which the Defendants claimed compensation. He was advised that no adjustment would be made to their claim even though the vehicle was returned with 20,000.00 kilometers less than allowed by the lease agreement. Further, he was told that the alleged damages to the vehicle were not repaired prior to sending it to auction.

12. The Plaintiff denies that the vehicle required repairs claimed by the Defendants and puts them to the strict proof thereof.

13. The Plaintiff further claims that the process by which the Defendants seek to claim compensation from him is unfair open to abuse and contrary to the principles of natural justice. The Defendants pay the fee of the alleged independent inspectors and deny the Plaintiff the opportunity to dispute the charges in any meaningful fashion. Further, its delay in inspecting the vehicle for 15 days, leaves open the question of when, if ever, the damages occurred.

Repairs

Faulty diagnosis

Davies v. Alberta Motor Association, August 13, 1991, Alberta Provincial Court, Civil Division, No. P9090106097, Judge Moore. The plaintiff had a used 1985 Nissan Pulsar NX checked out by the AMA's Vehicle Inspection Service prior to buying it. The car passed with flying colours. A month later, the clutch was replaced and numerous electrical problems ensued. At that time, another garage discovered that the car had been involved in a major accident, had a bent frame and a leaking radiator, and was unsafe to drive. The court awarded the plaintiff $1,578.40 plus three years of interest. The judge held that the AMA set itself out as an expert and should have spotted the car's defects. The AMA's defence—that it was not responsible for errors—was thrown out. The court held that a disclaimer clause could not protect the association from a fundamental breach of contract.

Insurance repairs

Is your insurance company obliged to provide new parts, or old? Original equipment parts, or cheaper knock-offs? A number of class actions are presently working their way through the courts to decide both those questions. *Albert Hague and Terrance O'Brien v. Liberty Mutual Insurance Company,* Ontario Superior Court, Case No. 01-CV-204787CP, June 14, 2004, is a class action petition filed by attorney Harvin Pitch (*hpitch@teplitskycolson.com*). It was recently certified by Justice Ian Nordheimer. The lawsuit asks for general damages plus $3 million in punitive damages. Pitch has also filed actions against State Farm, CGU, Zurich, Wawanesa, and Royal Insurance. As of January 3, 2000, similar Quebec class actions were been filed by other law firms against Group Desjardins, ING Canada, and AXA Canada relating to their use of non-OEM parts.

False Advertising

Vehicle not as ordered

When you're buying a new vehicle, the seller can't misrepresent the vehicle through a lie or a failure to disclose important information. Anything that varies from what one would commonly expect, or from the seller's representation, must be disclosed prior to signing the contract. Typical scenarios are odometer turn-backs, accident damage, used or leased cars sold as new, new vehicles that are the wrong colour and the wrong model year, or vehicles that lack promised options or standard features.

Goldie v. Golden Ears Motors (1980) Ltd, Port Coquitlam, June 27, 2000, British Columbia Small Claims Court, Case No. CO8287, Justice Warren. In a well-written eight-page judgment, the court awarded plaintiff Goldie $5,000 for engine repairs on a 1990 Ford F-150 pickup in addition to $236 court costs. The dealer was found to have misrepresented the mileage and sold a used vehicle that didn't meet Section 8.01 of the provincial motor vehicle regulations (unsafe tires, defective exhaust, and headlights).

In rejecting the seller's defence that he disclosed all information "to the best of his knowledge and belief," as stipulated in the sales contract, Justice Warren stated:

> The words "to the best of your knowledge and belief" do not allow someone to be wilfully blind to defects or to provide incorrect information. I find as a fact that the business made no effort to fulfill its duty to comply with the requirements of this form…. The defendant has been reckless in its actions. More likely, it has actively deceived the claimant into entering into this contract. I find the conduct of the defendant has been reprehensible throughout the dealings with the claimant.

This judgment closes a loophole that sellers have used to justify their misrepresentation, and it allows for cancellation of the sale and damages if the vehicle doesn't meet highway safety regulations.

Lister v. Scheilding (c.o.b. Kar-Lon Motors), [1983] O.J. No. 907 (Co. Ct.). Here, the plaintiff was entitled to rescind the contract because of the defendant's false representation. The defendant failed to state that the motor had been changed and was not the original motor.

MacDonald v. Equilease Co. Ltd., January 18, 1979, Ontario Supreme Court, Judge O'Driscoll. The plaintiff leased a truck that was misrepresented as having an axle stronger than it really was. The court awarded the plaintiff damages for repairs and set aside the lease.

Seich v. Festival Ford Sales Ltd. (1978), 6 Alta. L.R. (2nd), No. 262. The plaintiff bought a used truck from the defendant after being assured that it had a new motor and transmission. It didn't, and the court awarded the plaintiff $6,400.

Bilodeau v. Sud Auto, Quebec Court of Appeal, No. 09-000751-73, Judge Tremblay. This appeals court cancelled the contract and held that a car can't be sold as new or as a demonstrator if it has ever been rented, leased, sold, or titled to anyone other than the dealer.

Chenel v. Bel Automobile (1981) Inc., August 27, 1976, Quebec Superior Court (Quebec), Judge Desmeules. The plaintiff didn't receive his new Ford truck with the Jacob brakes essential to transporting sand in hilly regions. The Court awarded the plaintiff $27,000, representing the purchase price of the vehicle less the money he earned while using the truck.

Lasky v. Royal City Chrysler Plymouth, February 18, 1987, Ontario High Court of Justice, 59 O.R. (2nd), No. 323. The plaintiff bought a 4-cylinder 1983 Dodge 600 that was represented by the salesman as being a 6-cylinder model. After putting 40,000 km on the vehicle over a 22-month period, the buyer was given her money back, without interest, under the provincial *Business Practices Act*.

Rourke v. Gilmore, January 16, 1928, (Ontario Weekly Notes, vol. XXXIII, p. 292). Before discovering that his new car was really used, the plaintiff drove it for over a year. For this reason the contract couldn't be cancelled. However, the appeals court instead awarded damages for $500, which was quite a sum in 1928!

Sidney v. 1011067 Ontario Inc. (c.o.b. Southside Motors), [1999] O.J. No. 1822 (Sup. Ct.). The plaintiff was awarded $11,424.51 plus prejudgment interest because of a false representation made by the defendant regarding fuel efficiency.

Secret Warranties

It's common practice for manufacturers to secretly extend their warranties to cover components with a high failure rate. Customers who complain vigorously get extended warranty compensation in the form of "goodwill" adjustments.

François Chong v. Marine Drive Imported Cars Ltd. and Honda Canada Inc., May 17, 1994, British Columbia Provincial Small Claims Court, No. 92-06760, Judge C. L. Bagnall. Mr. Chong was the first owner of a 1983 Honda Accord with 134,000 km on the odometer. He had six engine camshafts replaced—four under Honda "goodwill" programs, one where he paid part of the repairs, and one via a small claims court judgment. (Please note that Honda's earlier engine problems and its arrogant attitude have since moderated a bit.)

In his ruling, Judge Bagnall agreed with Chong and ordered Honda and the dealer to each pay half of the $835.81 repair bill, for the following reasons:

> The defendants assert that the warranty which was part of the contract for purchase of the car encompassed the entirety of their obligation to the claimant, and that it expired in February 1985. The replacements of the camshaft after that date were paid for wholly or in part by Honda as a "goodwill gesture." The time has come for these gestures to cease, according to the witness for Honda. As well, he pointed out to me that the most recent replacement of the camshaft was paid for by Honda and that, therefore, the work would not be covered by Honda's usual warranty of 12 months from date of repair. Mr. Wall, who testified for Honda, told me there was no question that this situation with Mr. Chong's engine was an unusual state of affairs. He said that a camshaft properly maintained can last anywhere from 24,000 to 500,000 km. He could not offer any suggestion as to why the car keeps having this problem.
>
> The claimant has convinced me that the problems he is having with rapid breakdown of camshafts in his car is due to a defect, which was present in the engine at the time that he purchased the car. The problem first arose during the warranty period and in my view has never been properly identified nor repaired.

Damages (Punitive)

Punitive damages (also known as exemplary damages) allow the plaintiff to get compensation that exceeds his or her losses, as a deterrent to those who carry out dishonest or negligent practices. These kinds of judgments, common in the U.S., sometimes reach hundreds of millions of dollars.

Punitive damages are rarely awarded in Canadian courts and are almost never used against automakers. When they are given out, it's usually for sums less than $100,000. In *Prebushewski v. Dodge City Auto (1985) Ltd. and Chrysler Canada Ltd.* (2001 SKQB 537; Q.B. No. 1215) the plaintiff got $25,000 in a judgment handed down December 6, 2001, in Saskatoon, Saskatchewan, and confirmed by the Supreme Court of Canada on May 19, 2005. It followed testimony from Chrysler's expert witness that the company was aware of many cases where daytime running lights shorted and caused 1996 Ram pickups to catch fire. The plaintiff's truck had burned to the ground and Chrysler refused the owner's claim, in spite of its knowledge that fires were commonplace.

Angered by Chrysler's stonewalling, Justice Rothery rendered the following judgment:

> Not only did Chrysler know about the problems of the defective daytime running light modules, it did not advise the plaintiff of this. It simply chose to ignore the plaintiff's requests for compensation and told her to seek recovery from her insurance company. Chrysler had replaced thousands of these modules since 1988. But it had also made a business decision to neither advise its customers of the problem nor to recall the vehicles to replace the modules. While the cost would have been about $250 to replace each module, there were at least one million customers. Chrysler was not prepared to spend $250 million, even though it knew what the defective module might do.
>
> Counsel for the defendants argues that this matter had to be resolved by litigation because the plaintiff and the defendants simply had a difference of opinion on whether the plaintiff should be compensated by the defendants. Had the defendants some dispute as to the cause of the fire, that may have been sufficient to prove that they had not wilfully violated this part of the *Act*. They did not. They knew about the defective daytime running light module. They did nothing to replace the burned truck for the plaintiff. They offered the plaintiff no compensation for her loss. Counsels' position that the definition of the return of the purchase price is an arguable point is not sufficient to negate the defendants' violation of this part of the *Act*. I find the violation of the defendants to be willful. Thus, I find that exemplary damages are appropriate on the facts of this case.
>
> In this case, the quantum ought to be sufficiently high as to correct the defendants' behaviour. In particular, Chrysler's corporate policy to place profits ahead of the potential danger to its customer's safety and personal property must be punished. And when such corporate policy includes a refusal to comply with the provisions of the *Act* and a refusal to provide any relief to the plaintiff, I find an award of $25,000 for exemplary damages to be appropriate. I therefore order Chrysler and Dodge City to pay:
>
> 1. Damages in the sum of $41,969.83
> 2. Exemplary damages in the sum of $25,000
> 3. Party and party costs

The Supreme Court of Canada's confirmation of this judgment can be found at *www.lexum.umontreal.ca/csc-scc/en/rec/html/2005scc028.wpd.html.*

Vlchek v. Koshel (1988), 44 C.C.L.T. 314, B.C.S.C., No. B842974. The plaintiff was seriously injured when she was thrown from a Honda all-terrain cycle on which she had been riding as a passenger. The Court allowed for punitive damages because the manufacturer was well aware of the injuries likely to be caused by the cycle. Specifically, the Court ruled that there is no firm and inflexible principle of law stipulating that punitive or exemplary damages must be denied unless the defendant's acts are specifically directed against the plaintiff. The Court may apply punitive damages "where the defendant's conduct has been indiscriminate of focus, but reckless or malicious in its character. Intent to injure the plaintiff need not be present, so long as intent to do the injurious act can be shown."

See also:

- *Granek v. Reiter*, Ont. Ct. (Gen. Div.), No. 35/741.
- *Morrison v. Sharp*, Ont. Ct. (Gen. Div.), No. 43/548.
- *Schryvers v. Richport Ford Sales*, May 18, 1993, B.C.S.C., No. C917060, Judge Tysoe.
- *Varleg v. Angeloni*, B.C.S.C., No. 41/301.

Provincial business practices acts cover false, misleading, or deceptive representations, and allow for punitive damages should the unfair practice toward the consumer amount to an unconscionable representation (see C.E.D. (3d) s. 76, pp. 140–45). "Unconscionable" is defined as "where the consumer is not reasonably able to protect his or her interest because of physical infirmity, ignorance, illiteracy, or inability to understand the language of an agreement or similar factors."

- Exemplary damages are justified where compensatory damages are insufficient to deter and punish. See *Walker et al. v. CFTO Ltd. et al.* (1978), 59 O.R. (2nd), No. 104 (Ont. C.A.).
- Exemplary damages can be awarded in cases where the defendant's conduct was "cavalier." See *Ronald Elwyn Lister Ltd. et al. v. Dayton Tire Canada Ltd.* (1985), 52 O.R. (2nd), No. 89 (Ont. C.A.).
- The primary purpose of exemplary damages is to prevent the defendant and all others from doing similar wrongs. See *Fleming v. Spracklin* (1921).
- Disregard of the public's interest, lack of preventive measures, and a callous attitude all merit exemplary damages. See *Coughlin v. Kuntz* (1989), 2 C.C.L.T. (2nd) (B.C.C.A.).
- Punitive damages can be awarded for mental distress. See *Ribeiro v. Canadian Imperial Bank of Commerce* (1992), Ontario Reports 13 (3rd) and *Brown v. Waterloo Regional Board of Comissioners of Police* (1992), 37 O.R. (2nd).

In the States, punitive damage awards have been particularly generous. Do you remember the Alabama fellow who won a multi-million dollar damages award because his new BMW had been repainted before he bought it and the seller didn't tell him so? The case was *BMW of North America, Inc. v. Gore*, 517 U.S. 559, 116 S. Ct. 1589 (1996). In *Gore*, the Supreme Court cut the damages award and established standards for jury awards of punitive damages. Nevertheless, million-dollar awards are still quite common. For example, an Oregon dealer learned that a $1 million punitive damages award was not excessive under *Gore* and under Oregon law.

The Oregon Supreme Court determined that the standard it set forth in *Oberg v. Honda Motor Company*, 888 P.2d 8 (1996), on remand from the Supreme Court, survived the Supreme Court's subsequent ruling in *Gore*. The court held that the jury's $1 million punitive damages award, 87 times larger than the plaintiff's compensatory damages in *Parrott v. Carr Chevrolet, Inc.*, (2001 Ore. LEXIS 1, January 11, 2001) wasn't excessive. In that case, Mark Parrott sued Carr Chevrolet, Inc. over a used 1983 Chevrolet Suburban under Oregon's *Unlawful Trade Practices Act*. The jury awarded Parrott $11,496 in compensatory damages and $1 million in punitive damages because the dealer failed to disclose collision damage to a new car buyer.

See also:

- *Grabinski v. Blue Springs Ford Sales, Inc.*, 2000 U.S. App. LEXIS 2073 (8th Cir. W.D. MO, February 16, 2000).

Price-Fixing

Canadian car buyers have little-known kick-butt powers to force car dealers and automakers to negotiate fair prices.

Under the price maintenance provisions of the *Competition Act*, it is a criminal offence "to attempt to influence upward or discourage the reduction of prices by threat, promise, agreement, or other like means or to refuse to supply or otherwise discriminate against a person because of their low pricing policy."

Ottawa's price-fixing net has recently snared some pretty big fish: Toyota Canada settled for $2.3 million; John Deere gave back $1.191 million; RE/MAX changed its realtor policies and paid the government's lawyers; and The Stroh Brewery Company paid a $250,000 fine.

The RE/MAX and Toyota precedents

These settlements, registered in the Federal Court of Canada, raise the issue of the extent to which a manufacturer, distributor, franchisor, or licensor can set guidelines or policies that may raise the prices that a dealer or distributor may charge for the goods and services that are provided to the public by their dealers, franchisees, or licensees.

Section 61 of the *Competition Act*, "Prohibition of Resale Price Maintenance" is particularly interesting to questions of automakers' price-fixing: The first subsection of Section 61 provides:

> (1) No person who is engaged in the business of producing or supplying a product...or who has the exclusive rights and privileges conferred by a patent, trade-mark, copyright...shall, directly or indirectly, by agreement, threat, promise or any like means,

attempt to influence upward, or to discourage the reduction of, the price at which any other person engaged in business in Canada supplies or offers to supply or advertises a product within Canada.... "Product" is defined to include a service.

So let's recap for a moment: If a dealer or automaker jerks you around on pricing or misrepresents a vehicle in any way, you can ask for Ottawa's intervention online at *https://strategis.ic.gc.ca/sc_mrksv/competit/complaint/form.html* and obtain compensation by invoking the federal *Competition Act*. Presently, *Lemon-Aid* has lodged a formal complaint against Honda Canada for allegedly preventing its dealers from negotiating prices through email, faxes, or third-party website referrals.

Remember, it *is* a criminal offence to contravene Section 61. There is no dollar limit to the fines that a court may impose on a company or an individual convicted of a price-maintenance offence. Individuals convicted of an offence alternatively may be imprisoned for up to five years. In addition, Section 36 of the *Act* creates a civil remedy. As a result, any person who suffers loss or damage as a result of an act contrary to Section 61 may sue to recover the loss or damage. The usual method of suit in such cases is a class action, although small claims court relief isn't out of the question.

Now that we know how to get the best deal for less money and protect our rights, let's take a look in Part Three at which cars and minivans to pick and which ones to avoid.

Part Three
NEW-VEHICLE RATINGS

Not So Fast

"I really shouldn't say this because people aren't going to buy a new [redesigned] car in its first year," says Koki Hirashima, Honda's manufacturing chief in North America. After introduction, each new model makes a gradual improvement, he says, and "the car's quality is at its best toward the end of its model lifecycle."

THE WALL STREET JOURNAL
JUNE 4, 2002

Not So Smart

The only thing more challenging than holding the Smart on a steady bearing is changing speed. Mercedes can rightly claim to build some of the world's best automatic transmissions. Now they can claim to build the world's worst. The Smart's autobox doesn't "slur" its changes. It stops, thinks about it, thinks about it some more, then gives you the next gear....

THE TRUTH ABOUT CARS
DECEMBER 9, 2001

Driving a Smart mini-compact on Canada's highways is akin to taking a pea-shooter to a gunfight.

Rating the Ratings

Hirashima is right, but you'd never know it from reading most butt-kissing car journalists, who go into orgasmic fits over anything new from Detroit or Dusseldorf. For them, "new" means copy and copy means exposure. So what if the Smart rolled over at its press pre-view, hasn't made a penny since its 1998 European debut, and lost $792 million in 2004? As hyper-bole proliferates so do ad pages, and everyone profits—except, of course, for those readers who want independent, critical reviews.

Sure, it's tough rating new and used vehicles without prostituting yourself. Dozens of auto journalists who have interviewed me during my two annual cross-Canada book-promotion trips these past 34 years have told me so. It all begins when the smooth-talking suits come around to tell you how much they admire your work, but how much better it would be with more *balance*. Then they invite you on their trips to Japan and Europe, where they give you hats and jackets, specially prepared vehicles, and interviews with the top brass. Hell, they even concoct writing prizes for the best reports—the ones that repeat the industry's mantras.

You feel like nobility; they see you as a whore.

Lemon-Aid has managed to stay away from auto industry pimps and give honest, straight-talking reports for the past 34 years by following these simple rules:

- Ratings should be used primarily as a comparative database where rankings are similar in different driving tests and owner surveys. The best rating approach is to combine a driving test with an owners' survey of past models (only *Consumer Reports* and *Lemon-Aid* do this).
- The responses must come from a large owner pool (851,000 responses from *CR* subscribers, for example). Anecdotal responses should then be cross-referenced, updated, and given depth and specificity through NHTSA's safety complaint prism. Responses must again be cross-referenced through automaker internal service bulletins to determine the extent of a defect over a specific model and model-year range and to alert owners to problems likely to occur.
- Rankings should be predicated upon important characteristics measured over a significant period of time, unlike Car of the Year contests, owner-perceived value, or J.D. Power–surveyed problems (which are recorded after only three months of ownership).
- Ratings must come from unimpeachable sources. There should be no conflicts of interest, such as advertising, consultant ties, or self-serving tests done under ideal conditions.
- Tested cars must be bought or rented, not borrowed from the car company, and serviced, not pampered as part of a journalists' fleet lent out for ranking purposes. Also, all automakers need to be judged equally (Toyota at one time did not accept weekend car journalist "roundup" tests as valid, and refused to lend its vehicles to the events). Automakers must not be members of the ranking body.

Beware of self-administered fuel-economy ratings used by automakers in complicity with the federal government. *Automotive News* recently added its name to the skeptics when it found that Honda and Toyota hybrids get 20–40 percent less real-world gas mileage than advertised. The car industry publication discovered that hybrids require a particular style of driving in order to be fuel-efficient, that short trips and air conditioning penalize hybrids more than ordinary cars, and that colder climates increase fuel consumption way beyond what the ratings figures indicate.

Responsible auto raters shouldn't hit up dealers or manufacturers for free "test" vehicles under any circumstances, but most auto columnists and some consumer groups compromise their integrity by doing so. Test vehicles should be rented from a major rental agency or borrowed from an owner. I've adopted this practice from my early experience as a consumer reporter. Nissan asked me to test-drive its new 1974 240Z—no strings attached. I took the car for a week, had it examined by an independent garage, spoke with satisfied and dissatisfied owners, and accessed internal service bulletins. I came to the conclusion that the car's faulty brakes made it unsafe to drive, and said so in my report. Nissan sued me for $4 million, fixed the brakes through a "product improvement campaign," and dropped the lawsuit two years later. I never went back for another car.

What Makes a Good Car or Minivan?

Your new car or minivan should first live up to the promises made by the manufacturer and dealer. It *must* be reasonably priced, safe, crashworthy, fuel-efficient, and fairly durable (lasting at least 10 years); cost no more than about $800 a year to maintain; and provide you with a fair resale value a few years down the road. Parts should be affordable and easily available, and servicing shouldn't be hard to find or performed incompetently by a dealer network afflicted by a "what, me worry?" mindset.

And don't believe for one moment that the more you spend, the better the vehicle. For example, most Hondas are as good as more expensive Acuras, yet Acura charges thousands of dollars more for a luxury cachet. The same is true of Toyota and Lexus. Even more surprising, some luxury makes, like Jaguar, give you a dressed-up Ford at a luxo-car price. The extra money only buys you more features of dubious value and newer, unproven technology, like rear-mounted video cameras and failure-prone electronic gadgetry.

Lemon-Aid tries to publish up-to-date photographs of each new model rated, but some automakers disagree with our ratings and refuse to co-operate with us in any manner whatsoever—including sending us recent photos and current technical specifications. We regret any errors or omissions that may result. But our independence is more important to us than a book full of pretty pictures.

Definitions of Terms

Ratings

We rate vehicles on a scale of one to five stars, with five stars as our top ranking. This edition makes use of owner complaints, confidential technical service bulletins (TSBs), and test-drives to expose serious factory-related defects, design deficiencies, or servicing glitches. It should be noted that customer complaints alone do not make a scientific sampling, and that's why they are used in conjunction with other sources of information. Owner complaints combined with inside information found in technical service bulletins are a good starting point to cut through the automakers' hyperbole. Since ratings can change dramatically from one year to the next (take the Dodge Neon, for example), depending upon the manufacturer's warranty performance or incremental quality improvements, you will want to log on to *www.lemonaidcars.com* to keep abreast of these changes between editions.

This guide emphasizes important new features that add to a vehicle's safety, reliability, road performance, and comfort, and points out those changes that are merely gadgets and styling revisions. Also noted are important improvements to be made in the future, or the dropping of a model line. In addition to the "Recommended" or "Not Recommended" rating, each vehicle's strong and weak points are summarized.

Unlike most auto guides, *Lemon-Aid* isn't bedazzled by high-tech wizardry. Three decades of consumer advocacy in the auto industry have taught me that complex components are usually quite troublesome during their first few years on the market. Complexity drives up ownership costs, reduces overall reliability, and puts extra stress on such expensive major parts as the powertrain, fuel system, and emissions components.

It takes about six months to acquire enough information for a fair-minded evaluation of a car or minivan's first year on the market, unless the vehicle has been in service under another name or has only been re-badged. Most new cars hit the market before all of the bugs have been worked out, so it would be irresponsible to recommend them before they've been owner-driven, or before the quality of service from the dealer and manufacturer has been customer-tested.

 Recommended: This rating indicates a best buy. This category includes new vehicles that combine a high level of crashworthiness with good road performance, few safety-related complaints, decent reliability, and better-than-average resale value. Servicing must be readily available, and parts inexpensive and easy to find.

A vehicle may lose its "Recommended" rating from the previous edition of *Lemon-Aid* whenever complaints registered by NHTSA increase, its price becomes unreasonable, or its warranty performance falters.

Above Average: Vehicles in this class are pretty good choices. They aren't perfect, but they're often more reasonably priced than the competition. Most vehicles in this category have quality construction, good durability, and plenty of safety features as standard equipment. On the downside, they may have expensive parts and servicing, too many safety-related complaints, or only satisfactory warranty performance—one or all of which may have disqualified them from the Recommended category.

Average: Vehicles in this group have some deficiencies or flaws that make them a second choice. In many cases, certain components are prone to premature wear or breakdown, or lack some other positive aspect of long-term ownership. An "Average" rating can also be attributed to such factors as substandard assembly quality, lack of a solid long-term reliability record, a substantial number of safety-related complaints, or some flaw in the parts and service network.

Below Average: This rating category denotes an unreliable vehicle that may have also had a poor safety record. Improvements may have been made to enhance durability or safety. An extended warranty is advised.

Not Recommended: Chances of having major breakdowns or safety-related failures are omnipresent. Inadequate road performance and poor dealer service, among other factors, can make owning one of these vehicles a traumatic and expensive experience.

Vehicles that have not been on the road long enough to assess, or that are sold in such small numbers that owner feedback is insufficient, are also Not Recommended.

Cost Analysis and Best Alternatives

Fall prices for the 2006 models haven't risen much this year because GM and Chrysler have ramped up generous discounts and rebates. Only a few automakers, like BMW and Mazda (with hot new models), are bucking this trend with substantial price increases.

Each model's cost is analyzed in light of cheaper earlier models eligible for substantial rebates, PDI and destination charges, insurance costs, parts costs, depreciation, and fuel consumption. Federal government fuel-economy ratings are listed, but savvy readers will understand that actual mileage routinely undershoots these ratings by 15–20 percent. A listing of competing recommended new models is also included; good used alternatives can be found in *Lemon-Aid Used Cars and Minivans 2005–06*.

Quality, Reliability, and Safety

Lemon-Aid bases its quality and reliability evaluations on owner comments, confidential manufacturer service bulletins, and government reports from NHTSA safety complaint files. This year's edition also draws on the knowledge and expertise of professionals working in the automotive marketplace, including mechanics and fleet owners. The aim is to have a wide range of unbiased (and irrefutable) data on quality, reliability, durability, and ownership costs. Allowances are made for the number of vehicles sold versus the number of complaints, as well as for the seriousness of problems reported and the average number of problems reported by each owner.

Technical Service Bulletins (TSBs) listed in this section give the most probable cause of factory-related defects on 2005 models that will likely be carried over to the 2006 versions. TSBs are a reliable source of information because manufacturers depend on the dealer corrections outlined in their bulletins until a permanent, cost-effective engineering solution is found at the factory, which often takes several model years with lots of experimentation.

Most bulletins listed in this edition come from American sources and often differ from Canadian bulletins only where part numbers are concerned. Nevertheless, the problems and defects they treat are exactly the same on both sides of the border. Some vehicles have more TSBs than others, but this doesn't necessarily mean they're lemons. It may be that the listed problems affect only a small number of vehicles, or are minor and easily corrected. TSBs should also be used to verify that a problem was correctly diagnosed, the correct upgraded replacement part was used, and the billed labour time was fair.

As you read through the quality and reliability ratings (safety is more of a mixed bag) you'll quickly discover that most Japanese and South Korean manufacturers are far ahead of Chrysler, Ford, and GM in maintaining a high level of quality control in their vehicles (European makes are even worse performers).

Warranty Performance

A manufacturer's warranty is a legal commitment. It promises that the vehicle will perform in the normal and customary manner for which it is designed. If a part malfunctions or fails (unless it's because of owner negligence or poor maintenance), the dealer must fix or replace the defective part or parts and bill the automaker or warranty company for all of the part and labour costs. Warranties are an important factor in *Lemon-Aid*'s ratings. Unfortunately, it has been our experience that most automakers cheat on their warranty obligations and inflate the cost of scheduled maintenance work.

Most new-vehicle warranties fall into two categories: bumper-to-bumper for a period of 3 to 5 years, and powertrain for up to 5 years/100,000 km. Automakers sometimes charge an additional $50–$100 fee for repairs requested by purchasers of used vehicles with unexpired base warranties. For snowbirds, the federal and provincial governments can charge GST and sales tax on warranty and non-warranty repairs done south of the border—beware. Also, keep in mind that some automakers, like Honda, may not honour your warranty if a vehicle is purchased in Canada and registered in the United States.

Road Performance

The main factors considered in this rating are acceleration and torque, transmission operation, routine handling, emergency handling, steering, and braking.

At the very minimum, every vehicle must be able to merge safely onto a highway and have adequate passing power for two-lane roads. Steering feel and handling should inspire confidence. The suspension ought to provide a reasonably well-controlled ride on most road surfaces. Ideally, the passenger compartment will be roomy enough to accommodate passengers comfortably on extended trips. The noise level should not become tiresome and annoying. As a rule, handling and ride comfort are inversely proportional—good handling requires a stiff suspension, which pounds the kidneys. Variations from this pattern are reflected in the ratings.

Cost

We list the manufacturer's suggested retail price (MSRP) in effect at press time and applicable to standard models, as well as that price's negotiability, the range of the dealer's markup, and the vehicle's estimated residual value over the next five years (particularly helpful when leasing). Undoubtedly, the MSRP will be a bit higher when the fall prices are announced. However, ask for a copy of the manufacturer's notice to the dealer of the MSRP increase. If the dealer refuses, you can confirm the MSRP figure by accessing each manufacturer's website.

To help you negotiate the best price, this edition indicates those MSRP prices that are firm and those that are negotiable, and gives the approximate price markup percentage in parentheses (including assorted extra fees).

Destination charges and the pre-delivery inspection (PDI) are a "backdoor" into your wallet that can cost you almost $3,000 (in the case of a 2005 Dodge Sprinter). If you get tired of haggling with the dealer, agree to pay no more than 2 percent of a vehicle's invoice for these extra charges. Also, don't fall for the $99–$475 "administration fee" scam, unless the bottom-line price is so tempting that it won't make much difference. Principle is one thing; not losing an attractive deal is another.

Technical Data

Note that towing capacities differ depending on the kind of powertrain/suspension package or towing package you buy. Remember that there's a difference between how a vehicle is rated for cargo capacity or payload and how heavy a boat or trailer it can pull. Do not purchase any new vehicle without receiving from the dealer very clear information, in writing, about a vehicle's towing capacity and the kind of special equipment you'll need to meet your requirements. Have the towing capacity and necessary equipment written into the contract.

Load capacity is defined as the safe combined weight of occupants and cargo (such as luggage). It is taken from the manufacturers' rating or from *Consumer Reports'* calculated safe load. Exceeding this maximum weight can adversely affect the vehicle's handling, or make it unstable.

Safety Features and Crashworthiness

Some of the main features weighed in the safety ratings are a model's crashworthiness and the availability of seat belt pretensioners, de-powered airbags, airbag disablers, adjustable brake and accelerator pedals, integrated child safety seats, effective head restraints, assisted stability and traction control, and front and rearward visibility. Check marks indicate whether a safety feature is standard or optional; check marks in both columns show it is standard on a specific model only.

Frontal and side crash protection figures are taken from NHTSA's New Car Assessment Program. For the front crash test, vehicles are crashed into a fixed barrier, head-on, at 57 km/h (35 mph). NHTSA uses star rankings to show the likelihood, expressed as a percentage, of the belted occupants being seriously injured. The higher the number of stars, the greater the protection.

NHTSA's side crash test represents an intersection-type collision with a 1,368 kg (3,015 pound) barrier moving at 62 km/h (38.5 mph) into a standing vehicle. The moving barrier is covered with material that has "give" to replicate the front of a car.

IIHS rates head restraint and frontal, offset, and side crash protection as Good, Acceptable, Marginal, or Poor. In the Institute's 64 km/h (40 mph) offset test, 40 percent of the total width of each vehicle strikes a barrier on the driver side. The barrier's deformable face is made of aluminum honeycomb, which makes the forces in the test similar to those involved in a frontal offset crash between two vehicles of the same weight, each going just less than 64 km/h.

NHTSA COLLISION RATINGS: CHANCE OF SERIOUS INJURY

	FRONT	SIDE
5	10% or less	5% or less
4	11% to 20%	6% to 10%
3	21% to 35%	11% to 20%
2	36% to 45%	21% to 25%
1	46% or greater	26% or greater

Note: Two numbers indicate either driver or passenger injury risk (D/P) or front/rear occupant injury risk (F/R).

The IIHS 50 km/h (31 mph) side-impact test is carried out at a slower speed than the NHTSA test; however, the barrier uses a front end shaped to simulate the typical front end of a pickup or SUV. The Institute also includes the degree of head injury in its ratings.

NHTSA ROLLOVER RATINGS: CHANCE OF TIPPING OVER

	ROLLOVER RISK
[5]	Less than 10%
[4]	Between 10% and 20%
[3]	Between 20% and 30%
[2]	Between 30% and 40%
[1]	Greater than 40%

A vehicle's rollover resistance rating is an estimate of its risk of rolling over in a single-vehicle crash, not a prediction of the likelihood of a crash. As the chart at left indicates, the lowest-rated vehicles (one star) are at least four times more likely to roll over than the highest-rated vehicles (five stars), when involved in a single-vehicle crash.

After comparing crash-tests performed by IIHS with NHTSA government tests, the Government Accountability Office (GAO) admitted in 2005 what *Lemon-Aid* and safety groups have been saying for close to a decade: Government-run crash tests are outdated and in need of revision. Specifically, GAO concluded that NHTSA's system now gives too many vehicles a top ranking. A revision of the testing procedures is likely next year.

NHTSA DRIVER SIDE-IMPACT PROTECTION (2005 TOYOTA CAMRY)

Save vehicles	Vehicle	Frontal Star Rating based on risk of head & chest injury		Side Star Rating based on risk of chest injury		Rollover Rating	
		Driver	Passenger	Front Seat	Rear Seat	2 wheel drive	4 wheel drive
☐	2005 Toyota Camry 4-DR. (PC/Me)	★★★★★	★★★★★	★★★★	★★★	★★★★	

IIHS DRIVER SIDE-IMPACT PROTECTION (2002–05 TOYOTA CAMRY)

OVERALL EVALUATION: P

	Injury measures			Head protection	Structure/safety cage
	Head/neck	Torso	Pelvis/leg		
Driver	P	M	G	P	A
Rear passenger	G	P	G	M	

NHTSA gives 2005 Camrys an Above Average rating for driver side-impact protection, whereas IIHS gives 2002–05 Camrys a Poor rating for driver side-impact protection. The 2006 model-year Camry returns unchanged.

AMERICAN VEHICLES

Detroit's Big Three car companies have been caught flat-footed by high fuel prices that almost doubled during the summer of 2005. Since it takes almost three years for the automakers to shift their product mix and bring in more economical models, this year they will "talk the talk" but stick with huge V8 gas-guzzlers like the 2006 Dodge Charger, Chevrolet's Impala SS, and Ford's Crown Victoria and Mercury Marquis (the Marquis is sold only in the States). Sure, we will be told that "more is less," but don't believe it. These heavy, fuel-wasting, high-performance cars are throwbacks to an era when Detroit suits worshipped NASCAR and Budweiser.

Chevy's 2006 Impala SS will have a V8 engine, last used in the rear-drive Caprice, coupled to a front-drive platform. Ugh.

Most of the fuel-efficient 2006 cars will be co-productions with Japanese and South Korean automakers. This is a plus for reliability as well, because many of the Asian platforms and components, like the Mazda6 parts found in Ford's new Fusion, have been used and improved over many years and are much more dependable than their Detroit counterparts.

When Ford used Mazda components in the 1992 Escort, the car's rating went from "lemon" to "Recommended." Hopefully, the Fusion (above) will do as well.

Another trend that will be obvious this year is the ever-increasing number of Asian models that will employ hybrid powertains or engine cylinder deactivation. Both of these innovations are being used successfully by Japanese automakers, though the hybrid fuel-saving claims are more Harry Potter than Society of Automotive Engineers. Nevertheless, Ford has pledged that half of its lineup will offer hybrid vehicles by 2010.

This is an interesting development because historically, many of the Japanese products' most successful new powertrain features were once used in American cars and then dropped (think of GM's attempt to horseshoe a Wankle engine into its Vega, or its early misadventures with Cadillac engine cylinder deactivation).

So, what will this mean for the average buyer of Chrysler, Ford, and GM models this year?

Ford has recalled about five million fire-prone 1992–2002 cars, trucks, and SUVs to change a cruise-control switch ($50 for parts and labour). Eleven million other vehicles, including Taurus, Sable, Windstar, and assorted Lincolns, are still under investigation. Can you multiply $50 by 16 million?

Patience will pay off. Prices will nosedive in the new year as a bad economy, higher fuel costs and interest rates, and a lack of consumer confidence take a heavy toll on 2006 sales. Additionally, automaker revenue will take a huge hit from unsold large trucks, SUVs, and vans that no one wants, fewer profits from small car sales, hurricane losses, high employee costs, and massive recall charges.

2006 will be a critical "sink or swim" year for Detroit-based automakers. As inventory piles up and losses mount, don't be surprised if General Motors or Ford throws in the towel and merges with a coalition of Asian partners.

DaimlerChrysler

A case in point is an old joke being repeated alongside water coolers at Chrysler's Detroit headquarters. It goes like this: How do you pronounce the name of the German-American automaker? It's "Daimler"; the "Chrysler" is silent. Increasingly, the sentiment coming from the bride's side of the family is that the groom (Daimler-Benz) is an old-country boor; and worse, a control freak.

AUTOMOTIVE AFTERMARKET RETAILERS OF ONTARIO
www.aaro.ca/main_frame.php

It's ironic, but true: Chrysler's popular trucks and rear-drive cars pushed the automaker into the profit column for the first half of 2005; conversely, DaimlerChrysler (Mercedes), its parent company, struggles to cut two years of losses after dumping its CEO Jurgen Schrempp ("the little Shrempp that couldn't") and threatening to dump its money-losing Smart econocar.

DaimlerChrysler has lost a considerable amount of money with its Chrysler investment, and now Daimler is feeling the sting of stagnant sales affecting its own Mercedes lineup, while Chrysler sales pick up because of the popular Hemi engine and the rear-drive 300C and Magnum. Industry experts don't expect the Chrysler turnaround to continue, though, as higher fuel prices kill off sales of large vehicles and minivans.

Although lots of money could be saved by sharing components between the two divisions, Mercedes-Benz has always been fearful of losing its luxury cachet if it shared too many components with Chrysler products. This arrogance will probably fade as losses mount and production costs are slashed. Expect to see more parts-sharing between both automakers and the re-badging of some Mitsubishi models as "new" Chrysler and Mercedes offerings.

Daimler-Benz's $36-billion buyout of Chrysler in 1998 was widely hailed as a giant leap forward in the cost-efficient manufacture and development of cars and trucks (*Lemon-Aid* said it wasn't). Instead, it has become a case study in deception, corporate mismanagement, and greed. Daimler promised that the merger was a coming together of equals when it was really a shotgun wedding—the American and European cultures continually clashed until Daimler forced out most of the top American executives.

But don't feel sorry for Chrysler's head honchos: The top 30 executives divided among themselves nearly $500 million in cash, stock, and severance pay. Chrysler chairman Robert Eaton got the lion's share, with $3.7 million in cash and $66.2 million in stock. Chrysler vice-chairman and media darling Bob Lutz was subsequently hired as GM's product czar after piloting two companies that went bankrupt (Exide and Cunningham Motors). He got $1.3 million in cash, plus $25.7 million in stock from the Chrysler sale, while the media forgot all about his past ineptitude.

Chrysler's vehicles *do* look good. Whether it's the bold and quirky styling of its sports cars or PT Cruiser, or simply the sleek "cab forward" styling of the 300M, the automaker's vehicles seldom go unnoticed. And when it comes to convenience and savings, you can't beat the company's minivans for providing oodles of performance and convenience features at prices that usually beat the competition. Chrysler is also making better quality vehicles, though powertrain, electrical system, and fit and finish defects still dominate the list of owner complaints.

Don't believe Chrysler's press releases that say 2006 models will be sold without the generous rebates and low-cost financing programs used in the past. Nothing will change. GM's sales incentives, used throughout its lineup, are just too effective in attracting buyers. This means Chrysler vehicles will become substantially less costly by mid-2006, making patience more of a virtue than ever before.

Chrysler will launch two new cars in 2005–06: the Caliber and the Charger. As with all first-year cars, don't consider buying either vehicle until it has been on the market at least six months.

DODGE CALIBER ★

RATING: Not Recommended during its first year on the market. The $15,000 (before rebates and discounts) Caliber nevertheless has a great deal of potential as an inexpensive, fuel-sipping small car for short commutes and urban chores. A small five-door hatchback developed jointly with Mitsubishi and Hyundai, Caliber is

Chrysler's new Caliber will replace the fading Neon in early 2006.

competing with the Matrix/Vibe and Chevrolet's HHR. It will eventually replace the Neon sometime in 2006. The combination of the Japanese-built constantly variable transmission (CVT) and the new engine should make for a powertrain that's more reliable than the Neon's and that gives about 5 percent more fuel economy. Optional all-wheel drive will increase gas consumption by about ten percent. A 1.8L 140-hp 4-cylinder engine is a standard feature. There are two optional 4-cylinder powerplants: a 2.0L 150-hp version and a 170-hp 2.4L variant.

The Caliber will likely have staying power because of its low production cost and a shift by senior buyers from mid-sized vehicles to less costly and more fuel-efficient small cars.

The new Dodge Charger.

RATING: Not Recommended during its first year on the market. The $25,000–$40,000 (before rebates and discounts), four-door, rear-drive Dodge Charger doesn't look as muscular or as elegant as its 1960s two-door, rear-drive namesake. Nevertheless, credit Chrysler with giving this Dodge 300 clone more than ample power—if you don't mind the gas bills. SE and SXT base models come with a competent 250-hp 3.5L V6; however, the cars' extra weight puts their real-world fuel economy at the back of the pack. And this problem is exacerbated by the two Hemi V8s found on the R/T, the R/T with Road/Track or Daytona packages, or the SRT8. Expect a heavy gas penalty: the 340- and 350-hp 5.7L Hemi V8 get 254 fewer kilometres for every 100 litres of gas, and the 425-hp V6 with the 6.1L Hemi gets 425 fewer kilometres per 100L. It's doubtful the SRT8 V8-equipped 6.1L Hemi variant would ever have seen the light of day if DaimlerChrysler knew beforehand that fuel costs would almost double by early fall.

Although this car may be fun to drive and buys you entry into the high-performance crowd, it is destined to be a loser. High fuel, insurance, and depreciation costs will quickly thin out your wallet, and the absence of a comprehensive powertrain warranty is like performing a high-wire act without a net. The Charger, like Ford's resurrected Thunderbird, will likely have a short shelf life. Chrysler revived the Hemi name in 2002 with a 5.7L Hemi V8 engine used in its pickups, and then extended it to the 300 Ram Wagon sedan—a winning combination that revived lagging pickup, sedan, and wagon sales. But that was when fuel was relatively cheap. For 2006, all bets are off.

VIPER SRT-10 ★★★★★

best buy

RATING: Recommended. **Strong points:** Good acceleration and handling; slow depreciation; and only two minor safety-related complaints logged in the past three years. **Weak points:** Poor fuel economy. Passenger comfort is compromised by a hard ride, excessive wind noise, and limited storage room. No side airbags. **New for 2006:** The SRT-10 Coupe.

OVERVIEW: This $127,000, mid-sized, two-door, rear-drive roadster breaks all the marketing rules—and wins. Its awesome 500-hp 8.3L V10 engine, 6-speed manual gearbox, and "in your face" styling aren't equalled by any vehicle in its class. It features de-powered airbags and an airbag cut-off switch, though side airbags and a traction-control system aren't available. Service bulletins and owner comments paint a positive picture of the Viper's overall dependability. Some bulletins address poor idling and engine service light malfunctions. 2003s were revised from the ground up. With "500-500-500" as its slogan, the Viper engine now has 500 horsepower, torque, and displacement (50 more than the 2002). The new engine got a lower intake manifold to accommodate a flatter hood, the convertible was restyled, the coupe was dropped, and sidepipes were added. 2004s were given trunk carpeting and red brake calipers. The 2006 SRT-10 Coupe keeps the last generation integrated rear spoiler and double-bubble roof. **Best alternatives:** A base Porsche 911 or a 2005 Acura NSX (this is its last year).

NEON SX 2.0, SRT-4 ★★★

The Neon SX 2.0.

RATING: Average, but for its size, the best Detroit's Big Three has to offer. **Strong points:** Plenty of interior space; good handling; a thrifty, competent engine if not pushed unduly; impressive turbocharged power; and much-improved quality. **Weak points:** Base engine lacks power in the upper gear ranges; turbo's long-term reliability is still to be determined; imprecise manual shifter; and excessive engine, road, and body noise. Turbo's stiffer suspension may be too firm for some. Servicing for the high-performance SRT-4 may deteriorate once the Neon is taken off the market. Less service-intensive Neons will do okay, though. Log onto *www.neons.org* for updated servicing reports. Fit and finish on all models is decidedly subpar. **New for 2006:** Nothing.

OVERVIEW: Neon is Chrysler's homegrown small car. It's presently treading water until the Hyundai- and Mitsubishi-sourced lineup arrives sometime next year. The SX 2.0 is roomy and reasonably powered for urban use, and recent refinements have given it a softer, quieter ride while enhancing the car's handling and powertrain performance. Interior room easily accommodates six-footers.

Chrysler has tried to make these low-end cars more appealing by loading up on features that are usually seen only with higher-priced vehicles. One of those higher-priced entries is the $26,950 SRT-4 high-performance version, equipped with a turbocharged 215-hp 2.4L 4-cylinder engine hooked to a manual 4-speed transmission, a hood scoop, 17-inch wheels, a revised suspension, and four-wheel disc brakes.

COST ANALYSIS: This peppy econocar is a real bargain as Chrysler dealerships cut prices to make way for the Caliber. **Best alternatives:** Other cars worth looking at are the Honda Civic, the Hyundai Accent or Elantra, the Mazda3, the Suzuki Swift, and the Toyota Echo or Corolla. If you're in the market for a sport coupe, check out the Hyundai Tiburon. **Options:** Consider getting the height adjustment for the steering wheel (for short drivers). Optional front side airbags (without head protection) and ABS aren't the proven lifesavers they pretend to be and may simply add extra cost and complexity to maintenance repairs. **Rebates:** Generous discounts will apply to the SRT-4. Expect $2,000–$3,000 rebates on all models by early 2006. **Delivery/PDI:** $850. **Depreciation:** Average. **Insurance cost:** Average. **Parts supply/cost:** Average. **Annual maintenance cost:** Higher than average. **Warranty:** Bumper-to-bumper 3 years/60,000 km; powertrain 5 years/100,000 km; rust perforation 5 years/160,000 km. **Supplementary warranty:** Not necessary. **Highway/city fuel economy:** 7–9.5L/100 km with the base 2.0L engine.

Quality/Reliability/Safety

Pro: Quality control: Average. A perusal of owner comments confirms that there has been a dramatic drop in owner complaints during the past three years. Still, quality control is not up to what you get with Japanese and South Korean competitors. The 4-cylinder engine's faulty head gaskets, present since 1995, have been remedied with improved gaskets on 2001–05 models.

Con: Reliability: Airbag failures and transmission performance problems continue to impinge a bit upon the car's overall reliability. **Warranty performance:** Below average. **Owner-reported problems:** Problems mentioned relate to the premature replacement of the brake rotors and pads; rusty brake components; wheel bearing failures; and doors that lock inadvertently. Owners also complain that the front windshield pillars create a huge blind spot. **Service bulletin problems:** Acceleration stumble, engine snapping sound, and a clicking noise when turning. **NHTSA safety complaints:** Nothing serious.

 ## Road Performance

Pro: Better than average acceleration with plenty of low-end torque. The 2.0L engine's 132 horses and the Neon's low weight give it acceptable performance in lower gear ranges, but restrict it to mainly urban use. The 4-speed automatic provides relatively smooth performance, though it saps power in the upper ranges. **Emergency handling:** Better than average. **Steering:** Precise and easy to control on smooth roads.

Con: Acceleration/torque: Base engine runs out of steam in high gear and is buzzy from 4000 rpm on up. It runs particularly roughly after 5000 rpm. This is especially irritating because horsepower and torque peak at 5000 and 6000 rpm. Even with the manual transmission, highway passing requires downshifting from Fifth gear to Third, with the 2.0L engine crying all the way. **Transmission:** The manual transmission is harsh and noisy—no comparison with Honda and Toyota vehicles. The manual gearbox also requires lots of downshifting when going over small hills. **Routine handling:** The jittery ride becomes fairly rough when traversing anything but the smoothest roads. The ride deteriorates and the suspension bottoms with a vengeance with a full load. The turbo's stiffer suspension may be too firm for some. **Braking:** Disc/drum; average.

NEON SX 2.0, SRT-4

List Price (negotiable)	Residual Values (months)			
	24	36	48	60
Base: $15,195 (18%)	$ 9,500	$ 7,500	$ 6,000	$ 4,500
Sport: $18,195 (20%)	$11,500	$ 9,500	$ 7,500	$ 6,000
R/T: $20,995 (21%)	$13,000	$11,000	$ 9,000	$ 7,000
SRT-4: $26,950 (23%)	$16,000	$14,000	$12,000	$10,000

SAFETY FEATURES			CRASHWORTHINESS RATINGS		
	STD.	OPT.	Head restraints F/R	❶	❶
Anti-lock brakes	✓	✓	Visibility F/R	❸	❶
Seat belt pretensioners F/R	—	—	Crash protection (front) D/P	❹	❹
Side airbags F/R	✓	✓	Crash protection (side) F/R	❸	❸
Stability control	—	—	Crash protection (offset)	❷	—
Traction control	—	—	Rollover	❹	—

SEBRING, STRATUS ★★★★

The Sebring convertible.

RATING: Above Average. **Strong points:** Good V6 performance, comfortable ride, plenty of interior room, and few owner complaints. The convertible is especially attractive because of its reasonable price and slow depreciation. **Weak points:** Mediocre 4-cylinder engine performance and lots of engine and road noise. It isn't much more fuel-efficient than the V6. **New for 2006:** The Sebring sedan and convertible go into their last model year, while the Mitsubishi-sourced coupe gets the axe. Stratus gets a slightly restyled R/T sport package with attractive ground-effects trim, and a retuned suspension.

OVERVIEW: These front-drive sedans and convertibles are good buys mainly because they've had fewer new-model "teething" problems than other Chrysler-built vehicles. The Sebring is a reasonably priced luxury model equipped with standard amenities including AC, bucket seats, and a tilt steering wheel, while the Stratus fills the sporty coupe niche with standard tinted glass and an awesome sound system.

TECHNICAL DATA

POWERTRAIN (FRONT-DRIVE)

Engines: 2.4L 4-cyl. (150 hp) • 2.7L V6 (200 hp) • 3.0L V6 (200 hp); Transmissions: 5-speed man. • 4-speed auto.

DIMENSIONS/CAPACITY

Passengers: 2/3; Wheelbase: 106 in., 108 in.; H: 54.9/L: 190.7/W: 70.6 in.; Headroom F/R: 4.0/1.5 in.; Legroom F/R: 41.5/31.5 in.; Cargo volume: 13.1 cu. ft.; Fuel tank: 61L/regular; Tow limit: 1,000 lb.; Load capacity: 865 lb.; Turning circle: 40 ft.; Weight: 3,190 lb.

Powertrains and platforms are borrowed from the reasonably reliable Mitsubishi Eclipse and Galant models—thank goodness—freeing owners from the fear of breakdowns that have plagued Chrysler's home-grown components in the past. They also share most safety features and mechanical components, including standard dual airbags and a wimpy 150-hp 2.4L 4-banger along with a better-suited optional 200-hp 2.7L V6. In 2003, convertibles got a manual gearbox and coupes received a new front- and rear-end treatment.

COST ANALYSIS: The Sebring and Stratus have continued their sales slump throughout 2005, so look for hefty discounts throughout the 2006 model year. Consider buying a heavily discounted (at least 20 percent) 2005 version instead of this year's model; however, if you wait until next spring, the 2006s will be similarly discounted. **Best alternatives:** The Honda Accord, the Hyundai Elantra or Sonata, and the Toyota Camry or Solara. **Options:** You'll want the V6 engine for better all-around performance without much of a fuel penalty. It does have a checkered history for engine sludging through the 2002 model year, but that isn't expected to be a problem any longer. Be wary of the previously failure-prone ABS brakes. **Rebates:** $3,000–$5,000 rebates and discounts plus zero percent financing on all models. **Delivery/PDI:** $895. **Depreciation:** A bit slower than average. **Insurance cost:** Average. **Parts supply/cost:** Reasonably priced parts are easily found. **Annual maintenance cost:** Average. **Warranty:** Bumper-to-bumper 3 years/60,000 km; powertrain 5 years/100,000 km; rust perforation 5 years/160,000 km. **Supplementary warranty:** An extended warranty isn't needed. **Highway/city fuel economy:** 7.3–11.2L/100 km with the base 4-cylinder; 8–12L/100 km with the V6.

 ## Quality/Reliability/Safety

Pro: Quality control: Quality control is unusually good; body construction and assembly are solid, but with a few water leaks; body flexing and door creaking on convertible models. **Reliability:** Better than average. **Warranty performance:** Average.

Con: Owner-reported problems: Poor engine idling; vehicle shut down while on the freeway; slipping automatic transmission; excessive steering shake at idle; suspension glitches; rear brake grinding; early replacement of brake rotors; cricket sound produced when in First gear and a whistling is heard when cruise control is engaged; headlights and foglights go off for no reason; dash lights flicker on and off while driving; and water leaks into the vehicle. **Service bulletin problems:** Clicking noise when turning; intermittent loss of audio and inoperative steering-mounted audio switches; door rattles and clunks; incorrect fuel mileage display; and poor AC operation. **NHTSA safety complaints:** Sudden, unintended acceleration while stopped at a traffic light; engine overheating and stalling; steering failure; airbags failed to deploy; passenger-side seat heater started smoking; ineffective braking; and windshield wiper switch pulled away from the steering column.

 ## Road Performance

Pro: Emergency handling: Average. **Steering:** Steering is responsive and light. **Acceleration/torque:** Adequate, but far from sporty acceleration (0–100 km/h: 10 seconds with the V6). **Transmission:** Smooth and quiet operation in all gear ranges. **Routine handling:** Handling is acceptable with either engine, but the car isn't very agile when cornering under speed. Jarring is reduced as passengers are added.

Con: The base 2.4L engine is a buzzy fuel-burner. It loses power when mated to the 4-speed automatic and, when pushed, it's less responsive than the V6. Some front-end plow in turns. The ride is hard and deteriorates on bad surfaces. The car's large turning circle makes parking a chore. Entry and exit are a bit difficult. **Braking:** Disc/disc; unimpressive (100–0 km/h: 43 m).

SEBRING, STRATUS

List Price (very negotiable)	Residual Values (months)			
	24	36	48	60
Sebring 4d: $24,115 (20%)	$16,000	$15,000	$13,500	$12,000
Stratus: $23,380 (20%)	$16,000	$15,000	$13,500	$12,000
Sebring Cvt.: $39,195 (25%)	$24,000	$20,000	$16,000	$12,000

SAFETY FEATURES	STD.	OPT.
Anti-lock brakes	✓	✓
Seat belt pretensioners F/R	—	—
Side airbags	—	✓
Stability control	—	—
Traction control	—	✓

CRASHWORTHINESS

Sebring

Head restraints F/R	3	2
4d	5	5
Visibility F/R	4	5
Crash protection (front) D/P	4	4
4d	5	5
Convertible	3	3
Crash protection (side) F/R	5	5
4d	5	5
Convertible	3	3
Crash protection (offset)	3	—

Stratus

Head restraints F/R	4	3
Visibility F/R	5	5
Crash protection (front) D/P	4	4
4d	5	5
Crash protection (side) F/R	3	5
4d	3	3
Crash protection (offset)	3	—
Rollover (2d)	4	—
4d	5	—

300, 300C, MAGNUM ★★★

The Dodge Magnum.

All ratings on a numbered scale where 5 is good and 1 is bad. See page 153–154 for a more detailed description.

RATING: Average. The rear-drive configuration has been a winner in the past, and short-term dependability has been quite good. **Strong points:** Plenty of power with the V6; excellent high-speed handling; and a remarkably quiet and spacious interior along with a large trunk. **Weak points:** Way overpriced—$13,000 extra for a Hemi-equipped model is ridiculous. Excess weight and large engines drive up fuel costs. Consequently, resale value is dropping because buyers are shifting to smaller, more economical sedans. Standard towing capability is less than one would expect from a rear-drive. Some of the electronics derived from Mercedes luxury models have had serious reliability problems. The 2.7L V6 has a history of engine sludging. Windshield and windows appear small, though visibility isn't affected much, and the car's high waistline and tall doors make for a claustrophobia-inducing interior. It's less fuel-efficient than its front-drive predecessors, and premium fuel is recommended (though regular grade is acceptable). **New for 2006:** A Charger spin-off and two high-performance police vehicles join the lineup. An upgraded standard 5-speed automatic transmission will replace the 4-speed on 3.5L V6-equipped models during the second six months of production. Tire-pressure monitoring and a new DVD-based entertainment centre are also new this year.

OVERVIEW: Front-drives are out and rear-drives are in—again—along with all-wheel drive and a V8. Chrysler is selling more than twice as many models as it predicted. Starting at $29,995, the top-of-the-line 300 shares its platform with the sportier Dodge Magnum wagon and comes in three packages: the base model with a 190-hp V6; a Touring version with a 250-hp V6; and the high-performance 300C with a 340-hp V8 Hemi engine. The V8 is rather exceptional and scary. It features Chrysler's Multi-Displacement System, which theoretically uses 8 cylinders under load and then switches to 4-cylinder mode when cruising. This is unsettling because the last time this was offered by an American automaker (Cadillac, in the '80s), owners found their cars running on 4 cylinders along freeways and switching to 8 cylinders in traffic. After a torrent of lawsuits, GM went back to a conventional powertrain set-up. This year, a high-performance 425-hp 6.1L Hemi V8 was put into the Chrysler 300 SRT, the Dodge Magnum SRT-8, and the 2006 Dodge Charger.

AWD is available on Touring and 300C models. V6-equipped models have a 4-speed automatic transmission that will be replaced by a 5-speed later in the model year. AWD and V8 versions use a 5-speed automatic with manual shift gate. Four-wheel disc brakes, a tilt/telescope steering wheel, curtain side airbags, power

TECHNICAL DATA

POWERTRAIN (REAR-DRIVE)

Engines: 2.7L V6 (190 hp) • 3.5L V6 (250 hp) • 5.7L V8 (340 hp) • 5.7L V8 (425 hp) • 6.1L V8 (425 hp); Transmissions: 4-speed auto. • 5-speed auto.

DIMENSION/CAPACITY (BASE)

Passengers: 2/3; Wheelbase: 120 in.; H: 58.4/L: 196.8/W: 74.1 in.; Headroom F/R: 2.5/3.0 in.; Legroom F/R: 42/28.5 in.; Cargo volume: 29.5–71.6 cu. ft.; Fuel tank: 68L/regular; Tow limit: 2,000 lb.; Load capacity: 865 lb.; Turning circle: 41 ft.; Weight: 4,046 lb., 3,950 lb.

driver seat, and 18-inch wheels are standard. Available features include adjustable pedals, satellite radio, and Chrysler's UConnect, which uses the audio system as a hands-free, wireless link to cell phones.

After two decades of touting the handling virtues of front-drives, DaimlerChrysler has reversed its position, and now says rear-drives are best—especially when they have a 53/47 front-to-rear weight distribution ratio, standard traction control, electronic stability control, and ABS.

Overall reliability is expected to be better than average. Nevertheless, the 2.7L V6 may have long-term sludging problems. NHTSA has received over 400 complaints from owners of 1998–2002 Concorde, Intrepid, Sebring, and Stratus models plagued by seriously defective engines. The typical failure mode is engine seizure during highway driving. Many consumers report timing chain failure at well under Chrysler and Dodge's recommended 160,000 km (100,000 mi.) change level. Costs of repairs average $5,200 but can go as high as $9,500 for a replacement engine.

Interestingly, Mercedes-Benz recently settled a class action lawsuit for $32 million U.S. over engine sludge breakdowns affecting its 1998–2001 lineup of luxury cars (see *www.legalnewswatch.com/news_182.html*).

COST ANALYSIS: Best alternatives: Ford's Crown Victoria or a used Grand Marquis are credible rear-drive alternatives. **Options:** Consider the SXT model with the 3.5L V6 and traction/stability control. Don't pay the big bucks for an RT unless a Hemi engine is your dream and your company pays for your gas bills. **Rebates:** Expect $3000–$7,000 discounts or rebates once the cars' popularity wanes this winter. Low-interest financing programs will continue throughout the year. **Delivery/PDI:** $900. **Depreciation:** Higher than average. According to *Automotive Lease Guide*'s survey taken before fuel prices soared, the powerful Hemi engine is more a liability than an asset. For example, the 2005 Chrysler 300C with a Hemi V8 is predicted to retain 48 percent of its sticker price after three years, while the 300 Touring sedan, with no Hemi, will likely keep 52 percent of its sticker price in the same period. The Magnum wagon is expected to retain less value, which is not unusual with wagons. **Parts supply/cost:** Expect long delays and high costs. **Annual maintenance cost:** Average. **Warranty:** Bumper-to-bumper 3 years/60,000 km; powertrain 5 years/100,000 km; rust perforation 5 years/160,000 km. **Supplementary warranty:** A toss-up. **Highway/city fuel economy:** Mileage for the V8 is estimated at 13.8L/100 km city and 9.4L/100 km highway. For the V6, Chrysler estimates 12.4L/100 km city and 8.7L/100 km highway. Owners report that real-world fuel economy with both engines, however, is far less than the above estimates.

300, 300C, MAGNUM

List Price (firm at first)	Residual Values (months)			
	24	36	48	60
Magnum: $27,995 (22%)	$21,000	$14,500	$12,000	$10,000
300: $29,995 (24%)	$22,000	$15,500	$13,000	$11,000
Touring: $31,995 (25%)	$23,000	$16,500	$14,000	$12,000
300C: $42,995 (30%)	$30,000	$21,000	$18,000	$15,000

SAFETY FEATURES			CRASHWORTHINESS		
	STD.	OPT.			
Anti-lock brakes (4W)	✓	—	Visibility F/R	5	5
Seat belt pretensioners F/R	✓	—	Crash protection (front) D/P	5	5
Side airbags	✓	—	Crash protection (side) F/R	4	5
Stability control	—	✓	Rollover	4	—
Traction control	✓	✓			

PT CRUISER ★★★★

RATING: Above Average. This Neon spin-off's popularity is making a comeback because buyers want to save on fuel without sacrificing interior space. Cobbled together with Neon parts and engineering, the PT Cruiser is essentially a fuel- and space-efficient hatchback mini-minivan that uses the same nostalgic hot-rod flair

TECHNICAL DATA

POWERTRAIN (FRONT-DRIVE)

Engines: 2.4L 4-cyl. (150 hp) • 2.4L 4-cyl. turbo (180 hp) • 2.4L 4-cyl. turbo (230 hp); Transmissions: 5-speed man. • 4-speed auto.

DIMENSION/CAPACITY (BASE)

Passengers: 2/3; Wheelbase: 103 in.; H: 63.0/L: 168.8/W: 67.1 in.; Headroom F/R: 4.0/2.0 in.; Legroom F/R: 41.5/27 in.; Cargo volume: 64 cu. ft.; Fuel tank: 57L/regular; Tow limit: 1,000 lb.; Load capacity: 715 lb.; Turning circle: 40 ft.; Weight: 3,455 lb.

that was so successful with the Prowler. It is such a popular style that GM has copied it with the Chevrolet HHR, a downsized version of a 1949 Suburban truck. **Strong points:** Excellent fuel economy (regular fuel); nimble handling around town; good braking; an upgraded, versatile, and spacious interior; many thoughtful interior amenities; easy access; and slow depreciation. **Weak points:** Lethargic base engine (especially with the automatic transmission); rough downshifts; mediocre highway performance and handling; a firm ride; lots of engine, wind, and road noise; and limited rear visibility. Log on to *www.ptcruiser.org* for the latest owners' comments. **New for 2006:** This year's Cruiser will be lightly restyled with new front and rear ends, and an improved interior. Maximum turbo power is bumped to 230 hp.

OVERVIEW: The Cruiser is ideal for buyers tired of the trucklike handling of rear-drive minivans, and who want good passenger or cargo flexibility. Its bold styling is an attention-getter, but the basic configuration has been used in other countries for years by Asian and European automakers and in North America with the bland-looking Mitsubishi Expo LRV/Eagle Summit popular in the early '90s.

The Cruiser comes with a nice assortment of new parts that include attractive chrome door handles, a four-spoke steering wheel, and for the 5-speed manual, a cue-ball shifter that sits atop a chrome stalk with a vinyl boot. It carries a base 150-hp 2.4L 16-valve engine, and two turbocharged variants of the same powerplant that produce 180 and 230 hp, respectively. A convertible version joined the lineup in March 2005.

COST ANALYSIS: Get the 2006 PT for the interior upgrades. End-of-year discounts and competition from Chevy's new HHR will make dealers more than eager to haggle, though they are pretty hard-nosed in pricing the convertible PT. **Best alternatives:** In a pinch, you may wish to consider the Pontiac Vibe, the Toyota Matrix, or the Mazda5. Sport-utilities worth a gander are the Honda CR-V EX, the Hyundai Santa Fe, and the Toyota RAV4. **Options:** The optional front-folding rear seatback allows objects up to 2.4 m (8 ft.) long to fit inside the vehicle. The same option permits the back of the front passenger seat to be used as a table for the driver. The sunroof design causes excessive interior wind noise. Although the disc brakes have been improved, Chrysler's large number of ABS failures is worrisome. It would be a good idea to replace the rear drum brakes with discs; however, that option is only available with the more expensive packages. **Rebates:** Look for $3,000+ rebates and discounting on both model year vehicles. **Delivery/PDI:**

$810. **Depreciation:** Practically non-existent. Expect 10 percent depreciation per year to kick in after the second year. **Insurance cost:** Higher than average, because many insurance companies impose the higher rates they use for trucks. **Parts supply/cost:** Average, since many parts come from the Neon generic parts bin. Body parts are another matter. Expect long delays and high costs. **Annual maintenance cost:** Average. **Warranty:** Bumper-to-bumper 3 years/60,000 km; powertrain 5 years/100,000 km; rust perforation 5 years/160,000 km. **Supplementary warranty:** A toss-up; only needed if you plan to exceed base warranty. **Highway/city fuel economy:** 8.3–11.7L/100 km.

Quality/Reliability/Safety

Pro: Reliability: Better than average. Many of the Neon's generic deficiencies have been cleaned up or fixed under warranty. **Quality control:** Very few problems reported by owners. **Warranty performance:** Average. Apparently, DaimlerChrysler is much more sensitive to Cruiser complaints than to complaints on models that will soon get the axe, like the Neon.

Con: Owner-reported problems: Main complaint areas continue to be the automatic transmission, AC, and brakes. Other problems include excessive oil consumption caused by a faulty valve cover gasket, extremely rough idling, high-speed engine surging, drivetrain whine, an annoying wind noise when driving with the rear window or sunroof open, moisture between clearcoat and paint that turns the hood a chalky white colour, moisture accumulation in headlights, water leaks through the side passenger window, and leather splitting at the stitching area. **Service bulletin problems:** Squeaking, chirping engine; drivebelt clicking; irregular snapping sound in engine; whistling noise heard when turning; and intermittent loss of audio. **NHTSA safety complaints:** Ineffective brakes, sudden electrical shutdown, steering lockup, hard-to-read instrument panel, and power windows that may strangle children:

> My 6-year-old stuck her head out the window.... When she did, she accidentially kicked the power window button with her foot. The button was located near the floor in the backseat on the middle console. She rolled the window up on her own head and was stuck in the window. She only lived through the event because 1) her head was tilted at the time so the window rolled up on the side of her neck and not on her trachea; and 2) her 8-year-old sister in the back seat with her heard her screams and got her foot off the button and rolled the window back down. It was terrifying and painful and totally preventable. The button should be in a different place where it cannot be kicked or bumped so easily, and there should be a mechanism that allows the window to roll back down if it meets resistance.

Other problems: Sudden, unintended acceleration; gas pedal that went to floor with no acceleration; airbags that deployed for no reason or failed to deploy;

vehicle suddenly shifts into First gear while cruising; sudden brake lock-up; head-rests too high, blocking vision; optima battery leaks acid; white powder leaks from airbag; and speedometer is hard to read.

Road Performance

Pro: Steering: Acceptable, with good road feedback. **Acceleration/torque:** Blistering acceleration with the turbocharged engine. Competent acceleration with a manual transmission coupled to the base engine. **Transmission:** Precise manual shifter. Optional automatic gearbox works quite well. The AutoStick is no big deal. **Routine handling:** Getting around town is easy. **Braking:** Disc/drum; above average.

Con: Acceleration/torque: The 2.4L 150-hp 4-cylinder engine is not very smooth-running when matched to the automatic transmission; it struggles when going uphill or merging with freeway traffic. Going uphill or merging requires frequent down-shifting and lots of patience—accelerating to 100 km/h takes about 9 seconds. Automatic transmission doesn't have much low-end torque, forcing early kickdown shifting and deft manipulation of the accelerator pedal. Solution? Get a manual tranny or pay extra for a turbocharger and cross your fingers when the warranty expires. **Emergency handling:** Slow and sloppy. The turning diameter seems excessive for such a short vehicle. Hard cornering produces an unsteady, wobbly ride because of the car's height.

PT CRUISER

List Price (very negotiable)	**Residual Values** (months)			
	24	**36**	**48**	**60**
Classic: $24,800 (20%)	$18,000	$16,000	$13,000	$11,000
Convertible: $26,995 (22%)	$22,000	$19,000	$16,000	$14,000

SAFETY FEATURES

	STD.	OPT.
Anti-lock brakes (4W)	—	✓
Seat belt pretensioners F/R	—	✓
Side airbags	—	✓
Stability control	—	—
Traction control	—	✓

CRASHWORTHINESS

Head restraints F/R	[5]	[5]
Visibility F/R	[4]	[3]
Crash protection (front) D/P	[4]	[4]
Crash protection (side) F/R	[4]	[5]
Rollover	[4]	—

All ratings on a numbered scale where [5] is good and [1] is bad. See page 153–154 for a more detailed description.

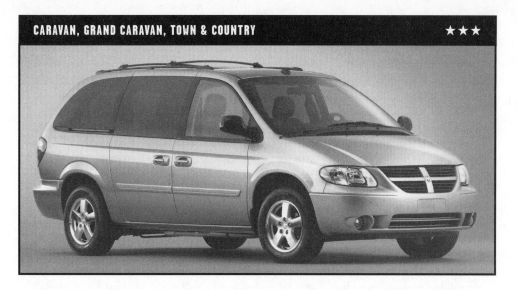

RATING: Average. These minivans are better built and more fuel-efficient than their failure-prone Ford Freestar/Windstar and GM front-drive competitors. Although the 4-cylinder engine promises better fuel economy, overall performance is seriously compromised by its meager 150 horses. **Strong points:** Very reasonably priced and subject to deep discounting. You get a comfortable ride, excellent braking, lots of innovative convenience features, user-friendly instruments and controls, two side sliding doors, easy entry and exit, and plenty of interior room. **Weak points:** Poor 4-cylinder acceleration and mediocre handling with the extended versions, though the ride is smoother over bumps. A sad history of chronic powertrain, AC, ABS, and body defects that are exacerbated by the automaker's hard-nosed attitude in interpreting its after-warranty-assistance obligations. No power doors on the regular length models. Get used to a cacophony of rattles, squeals, moans, and groans caused by the vehicle's poor construction and subpar components. Crashworthiness has declined a bit, though it's not bad. Fuel economy isn't as good as advertised for both the 4-cylinder and V6. **New for 2006:** Improved access to the second-row storage bins in the Stow-N-Go seating system.

OVERVIEW: These versatile minivans return with a wide array of standard and optional features that include anti-lock brakes, child safety seats integrated into the seatbacks, flush-design door handles, and front windshield wiper and washer controls located on the steering column lever for easier use. Childproof locks are standard and the front bucket seats incorporate vertically adjustable head restraints. The Town &

TECHNICAL DATA

POWERTRAIN (FRONT-DRIVE)

Engines: 2.4L 4-cyl. (150 hp) • 3.3L V6 (180 hp) • 3.8L V6 (205 hp); Transmission: 4-speed auto.

DIMENSION/CAPACITY (BASE)

Passengers: 2/2/3; Wheelbase: 119 in.; H: 68.5/W: 201/L: 79 in.; Headroom F/R1/R2: 4.5/3.5/2.5 in.; Legroom F/R1/R2: 38.5/31.0/26.5 in.; Cargo volume: 60 cu. ft.; Fuel tank: 76L/regular; Tow limit: 3,800 lb.; Load capacity: 1,185 lb.; Turning circle: 41 ft.; Weight: 3,985 lb.

Country, a luxury version of the Caravan, comes equipped with a 3.8L V6 and standard luxury features that make the vehicle more fashionable for upscale buyers.

COST ANALYSIS: This year, Chrysler is in a state of minivan sales euphoria after seeing its sales increase dramatically after applying big discounts last summer. Since the 2006 models are carried over practically unchanged, there is no reason to pay more than the earlier discounted price levied on the 2005s. Sales are waning somewhat as we go into the winter of 2006, so wait until then to start some hard bargaining. **Best alternatives:** The 2006 Honda Odyssey should be your first choice, but earlier versions will do quite nicely. Toyota's 2003 or earlier models are the best used choice. Mazda's 2006 Mazda5 is also a good alternative because of its frugal 4-cylinder and wagon-like configuration. GM and Ford front- and rear-drive minivans aren't credible alternatives because of their failure-prone powertrains; brake, suspension, and steering problems; electrical short-circuits; and subpar body work. However, full-sized GM and Chrysler rear-drive cargo vans are a more affordable and practical buy if you intend to haul a full passenger load, do regular heavy hauling, are physically challenged, use lots of accessories, or take frequent motoring excursions. Don't splurge on a new luxury Chrysler minivan: Chrysler's upscale Town & Country may cost up to $15,000 more than a base Caravan, yet be worth only a few thousand more after five years on the market. **Options:** As you increase body length, you lose manoeuvrability but gain ride comfort, except with the Sport Touring Group suspension, which makes for a firmer ride. Don't even consider the 4-cylinder engine—it has no place in a minivan. The 3.3L V6 is a better choice for most city-driving situations, but don't hesitate to get the 3.8L if you're planning lots of highway travel or carrying four or more passengers. Since its introduction, it's been relatively trouble-free, and it's more economical on the highway than the 3.3L, which wastes gas as it strains to maintain speed. Try to get 16-inch wheels and four-wheel disc brakes for a relatively cheap handling and safety upgrade. The sliding side doors make it easy to load and unload children, install a child safety seat in the middle, or remove the rear seat. On the downside, they expose kids to traffic and are a dangerous, failure-prone option. Child safety seats integrated into the rear seatbacks are convenient and reasonably priced, but Chrysler's versions have had a history of tightening up excessively or not tightening enough, allowing the child to slip out. Try the seat with your child before buying it. Other important features to consider are the optional defroster, power mirrors, power door locks, and power driver's seat (if you're shorter than 5'9" or expect to have different drivers using the minivan). You may wish to pass on the tinted windshields; they seriously reduce visibility. Ditch the failure-prone Goodyear original equipment tires and remember that a night drive is a prerequisite to check out headlight illumination, called inadequate by many. **Rebates:** 2005 and 2006 models will likely get $3,500–$4,000 rebates or discounting, plus zero percent financing throughout the year. **Delivery/PDI:** $995. **Depreciation:** Slightly slower than average. **Insurance cost:** About average for a minivan. **Parts supply/cost:** Higher than average, especially for AC, transmission, and ABS components, which are covered under a number of "goodwill" warranty programs and several recall campaigns. **Annual maintenance cost:** Repair costs are average during the warranty period. **Warranty:** Base warranty is inadequate if you plan to keep your minivan more than five years. Bumper-to-bumper 3 years/60,000 km; powertrain 5 years/100,000 km; rust perforation 5 years/160,000 km. **Supplementary warranty:** A wise buy. Bargain the price down to about one-third the $1,500 asking price. **Highway/city fuel economy:** *Caravan:* 9–13L/ 100 km; *Grand Caravan AWD:* 10–14L/100 km; *Town & Country:* 9–14L/100 km; *Town & Country AWD:* 10–15L/100 km.

Quality/Reliability/Safety

Pro: Dual airbags include knee bolsters to prevent front occupants from sliding under the seat belts. Side-impact protection has been increased with steel beams in door panels. Remote-control power door locks can be programmed to lock when the vehicle is put in gear. Chrysler has developed a mechanism that releases the power door locks and turns on the interior lights when the airbag is deployed.

Con: Quality control: You are not buyng a Mercedes minivan—thankfully, because Mercedes quality is also on the downswing. Nevertheless, 2006 Chrysler minivans can be expected to have some powertrain, electrical system, brake, suspension, AC, and body deficiencies similar to previous versions. *Consumer Reports* rates only the extended versions as worse than average, yet *Lemon-Aid* readers report that the base models are just as failure-prone. This isn't surprising— quality control has been below average since these vehicles were first launched 20 years ago, and surprisingly, got much worse after the '90 model year introduced limp-prone transmissions. **Reliability:** Somewhat improved, but inferior to the Asian competition. **Warranty performance:** Fair. **Owner-reported problems:** Owners say powertrain and sliding door failures make them afraid to drive these minivans. Their complaints also focus on electrical glitches, erratic AC performance, and early brake wear (*forum.chryslerminivan.net*). Premature wearout was reported on the cooling system, clutch, front suspension components, wheel bearings, air conditioning, and body parts (trim; weather stripping becomes loose and falls off; plastic pieces rattle and break easily). The front brakes need constant attention, if not to replace the pads or warped rotors after two years or 30,000 km, then to silence the excessive squeaks when braking.

Service bulletin problems: A rough idle, hesitation, and hard starts; accessory drivebelt chirping; front suspension rattling; transmission ticking; AC water leaks; the roof panel may be wavy or have depressions; and rusted, frozen rear brake drums. **NHTSA safety complaints:** NHTSA has recorded numerous complaints of airbags failing to deploy in an accident or deploying unexpectedly—when passing over a bump in the road or simply when turning on the vehicle. Chrysler continues to downplay the safety implications of its minivan defects, whether in the case of ABS failures, inadvertent airbag deployments, or sudden transmission breakdowns. Seat belts are another recurring problem: Belts may become unhooked from the floor anchor; buckles jam or suddenly release; and the child safety seat harness easily pulls out or over-retracts, trapping children. **Other safety problems:** The automatic transmission won't shift or suddenly drops into Reverse; chronic stalling; a faulty airbag clock spring may also cause the cruise control to malfunction; excessive steering vibration; a missing suspension bolt, which caused the right side to collapse; and wiper blades that stick together.

 ## Road Performance

Pro: Acceleration/torque: The most versatile (though a bit underpowered) powertrain for short-distance commuting is the 3.3L V6 engine (0–100 km/h in about 10.8 seconds with a 3.3L-equipped Grand Caravan). Chrysler's top-of-the-line 3.8L engine is a better choice if you intend to do a lot of highway cruising—it's smooth and quiet with lots of much-needed low-end torque. The AWD transfers 90 percent of the engine power to the front wheels during normal driving conditions. It's easy to use and performs well. As the front wheels lose traction, the rear wheels get additional power until traction has been stabilized or the 55/45 percent front-to-rear limit is reached. **Routine handling:** The regular-sized models are the closest thing to a passenger car when it comes to ride and handling. The redesigned chassis and improved steering provide a comfortable, no-surprise ride. Stiff springs greatly improve handling and comfort. Manoeuvrability around town is easy. **Emergency handling:** Slow, but acceptable. **Steering:** Generally precise and predictable. **Braking:** Acceptable ABS braking when it functions as it should.

Con: Transmission: The 41TE 4-speed automatic transmission with Overdrive shifts slowly and imprecisely. The transmission whines excessively. It's hard to use engine compression to slow down by gearing down. Downshifting from the electronic gearbox provides practically no braking effect. The AWD option is overrated and not worth the fuel penalty for most driving situations. **Routine handling:** The stretched wheelbase version gives less-than-nimble handling. A large turning radius and long nose can make parking difficult. **Steering:** Power steering is vague and over-assisted as speed increases. **Braking:** Brake pedal feels mushy and the brakes tend to heat up after repeated applications, causing considerable loss of effectiveness (fade) and warping of the front discs. The ABS system has proved unreliable on older vans, and repair costs are astronomical.

CARAVAN, GRAND CARAVAN, TOWN & COUNTRY

List Price (soft)	Residual Values (months)			
	24	36	48	60
Base Caravan: $27,825 (22%)	$20,000	$16,000	$14,000	$11,000
G. Caravan: $34,500 (25%)	$24,000	$18,000	$16,000	$13,000
Town & Country Touring: $44,595 (30%)	$29,000	$23,000	$20,000	$17,000

All ratings on a numbered scale where 5 is good and ❶ is bad. See page 153–154 for a more detailed description.

SAFETY FEATURES	STD.	OPT.
Anti-lock brakes (4W)	—	✓
Seat belt pretensioners F/R	✓	—
Side airbags	✓	—
Stability control	—	—
Traction control	✓	✓

CRASHWORTHINESS		
Head restraints F/R		
Caravan	2	1
G. Caravan	4	3
Town & Country	3	2/1
Visibility F/R	4	4
Crash protection (front) D/P		
Caravan	5	5
G. Caravan	5	5
Town & Country	5	5
Crash protection (side) F/R		
Caravan	5	5
G. Caravan	5	5
Town & Country	5	5
Crash protection (offset)	3	—
Rollover	4	—

Ford

Fusion Modesty

To tell the truth, I was kind of dreading this car. I thought it might be like the Ford Five Hundred, which is cousin to the Mercury Montego, which I found to be a floppy, shaky mess of a car. Instead, the Fusion is more like the Focus, which I love—a tight, lightweight piece that doesn't surpass in any one category but wins you with its well-rounded portfolio. The Fusion is a modest car for times when modesty, if not humility, is much in order.

DAN NEIL
LA TIMES
SEPTEMBER 7, 2005

Ford Rolls the Dice

Ford Motor Co., the No. 2 U.S. automaker, continues to lose billions of dollars annually and would lose millions more were it not for profits made from auto loans and last-minute summer discount sales. Nevertheless, the company's second-quarter profit fell 19 percent as its North American auto operations lost money for the third time in a year.

Rubbing salt in Ford's revenue wounds, Toyota, Honda, and Nissan are selling more cars and trucks than ever before, with Mazda's hot-selling Mazda3 and revamped Miata coming on strong. Add increased South Korean sales, and it comes as no surprise that Ford's second-quarter share of the U.S. market fell to 18.2 percent from 19.7 percent a year earlier.

Canadian market share hasn't done better. Independent industry analyst Dennis DesRosiers noted that August was the first month that Ford Canada was outsold not only by GM Canada, but also by DaimlerChrysler Canada and Honda Canada Inc.

For the past decade, Ford has had three problems that may end up bankrupting the company: bad products, bad quality, and bad management. In spite of the sales success of its Escape SUV and F-Series pickups, Ford is going downhill fast according to virtually every yardstick used to measure automotive success: profit, market share, quality, productivity, morale, bonuses, credit rating, public image, and relations with car owners, dealers, investors, and shareholders.

No one wants Ford's cars. In fact, car sales for August were the worst Ford has experienced since the end of World War II. Now, when you refer to the Big Three automakers, you are speaking of GM, Toyota, and Honda. Ford is a distant fourth.

Last year, Ford brought out a slew of new cars that it hoped would boost lagging sales, down 13.1 percent in Canada through August 2004. Unfortunately, except for the popular rear-drive Mustang (a sports car that was recommended by *Lemon-Aid,* but that really wasn't all that new), these new models missed their mark. The Five Hundred, a V6-powered large sedan; the Mercury Montego, another large sedan; and the Freestyle, a mid-sized crossover, have all been greeted with underwhelming enthusiasm. Additionally, high fuel costs are driving down sales of the company's profitable full-sized SUVs, trucks, and vans.

The Thunderbird gets the axe this year. Resurrected in August 2001, it just never caught on. Ford says it never intended the car to be in regular production. Other casualties are the Lincoln Aviator, Explorer Sport Trac, and Excursion. Both the Taurus family sedan and the Freestar minivan are living on borrowed time.

A Glimmer of Hope

Ford, like Chrysler and GM, is finally shifting its product mix to smaller vehicles that use more reliable Japanese components and that are assembled in Mexico or offshore. For example, the automaker's major launch this fall is the 2006 Ford Fusion, Mercury Milan, and Lincoln Zephyr mid-sized cars, all based on the successful Mazda6 and built in Hermosillo, Mexico. This move keeps production cost down and also quickly puts into the marketplace relatively fuel-efficient and highway-proven vehicles that follow the marketplace shift to downsized cars and trucks.

Whether it's called the Fusion, Milan (above), or Zephyr, Ford's Mazda6 spin-off should have a bright future.

There will also be a tripling of the company's hybrid SUV lineup over the next three years, led by this fall's launch of the Mercury Mariner (in the States only). A possible bottleneck in this plan, though, is the limited supply of hybrid transmissions built by Aisin Seiki Co. Ltd., a company minority-controlled by Toyota, Ford's primary hybrid competitor. Would Toyota choke off supply? You bet.

Now let's look at Ford's administration follies. Of course, no one wants to admit runnng a company into the ground through gross mismanagement. But Wall Street analysts and industry insiders all agree that the last decade's management, from Jac Nasser to Bill Ford, has seriously burned up the company's cash reserves, soured dealer relations, and alienated loyal customers. Dealer protests and successful lawsuits have killed the Blue Oval dealer reorganization program after it squandered millions of dollars; the company's "Ford 2000" attempt to centralize its global business spun out of control and was subsequently abandoned at a cost of millions more; and the Premier Automotive Group, which sells many of the company's European cars, is floundering, having lost its independence and the confidence of Ford's senior management in Dearborn.

What could Ford have been thinking when it bought the turkey called Land Rover—a company that nearly bankrupted BMW and sells fewer than 100 cars a month? Actually, Ford *was* thinking globally: Knowing that it couldn't sell luxury cars throughout the world with just its Lincoln models, it acquired companies that already had a worldwide luxury cachet. Land Rover became part of Ford's Premier Automotive Group, joining Aston Martin, Jaguar, Lincoln, and Volvo.

Like GM with its Jaguar purchase, Ford didn't realize that "luxury" and "lemon" aren't mutually exclusive terms. Except for Volvo, all the above auto divisions are sales duds.

Poor quality

Fire-prone cruise-control deactivation switches, powertrain defects, and premature brake wear and brake failures are the primary concerns of Ford owners. The company's engine and automatic transmission deficiencies affect most of its products and have existed for over a decade, judging by *Lemon-Aid* reader reports, NHTSA complaints, and confidential Ford internal documents cited by *www. blueoval.com*. The quality of body components also remains far below Japanese and European standards.

On top of this, Ford has managed to profoundly tick off its suppliers, dealer body, and customers. Parts suppliers have been berated by Ford management for simply following the company's insane cost-cutting orders. The dealer body no longer trusts the company that has shut down Mercury in Canada, cut warranty payouts with its Blue Oval program, and made dealers beg for after-warranty assistance for customers screwed by the automaker's abysmal quality control.

Over the past decade, *Lemon-Aid* has warned a succession of Ford Canada presidents that quality control and management had to improve dramatically, or sales and profits would plummet. That's exactly what has happened.

But it may not be too late. Ford can turn itself around by taking the following three steps:

• Work more closely with Mazda and Hyundai in new-product development and quality control.
• Sell its money-losing European operations and Hertz.
• Recognize that it has driven away many of its customers through unfair warranty denials and rotten customer-relations policies. Set up a 7-year/160,000 km retroactive warranty to compensate owners for powertrain breakdowns, and regain customer loyalty.

A better warranty worked for Chrysler, Hyundai, and Kia; it'll work for Ford.

FUSION, MILAN, ZEPHYR ★

The Ford Fusion.

RATING: Not Recommended during their first year on the market. Nevertheless, this trio of practically identical mid-sized sedans has a lot going for it—most of which comes from Mazda.

These cars will definitely give GM's Impala and Malibu a run for their money, but Honda's Accord, the Hyundai Sonata, and Toyota's Camry offer more performance, features, and quality. The Fusion should represent an acceptable buy once it has been on the market awhile, is discounted, is given more standard features, and rethinks its 6-speed automatic transmission. **Strong points:** Good acceleration and handling; Mazda's 4-cylinder engine is competent, thrifty, and dependable; steering is tight, precise, and vibration-free; impressively quiet cabin; comfortable rear seating. **Weak points:** Overpriced; Ford's V6 engine has a history of problems and relatively high fuel consumption, while Honda Accord's 240-hp engine is more powerful and smoother-running; less interior room than the Accord or Camry; Hyundai's Sonata provides more standard features; no stability control available and both traction control and ABS are extra-cost features; 6-speed automatic transmission shifts constantly; subpar fit and finish; predicted fast depreciation (it will likely lose 57 percent of its value after three years). **New for 2006:** Everything.

OVERVIEW: This four-door mid-sized sedan is an easy car to buy. There are only two engines available: a 2.3L 160-hp 4-cylinder made by Mazda and an optional Ford Duratec 3.0L 221-hp V6. The smaller engine can be coupled to either a 5-speed manual (highly recommended) or a 5-speed automatic transmission. There's no choice with the V6, which comes with a 6-speed automatic. Interestingly, the Fusion and its Milan and Zephyr brothers are the only vehicles in this segment that offer a standard 6-speed automatic. Furthermore, all-wheel drive will be added in the fall of 2006 and a hybrid variant is due in 2008.

Slightly smaller than the slow-selling Five Hundred, the Fusion is set on a Mazda6 platform that has been lengthened a couple of inches. Added rigidity and additional chassis tweaking have resulted in a car that will comfortably seat five passengers and handle quite well, particularly when cornering. Standard four-wheel disc brakes (ABS is optional) do a good job stopping the car, with little fading after repeated stops.

A word about the 6-speed automatic transmission: The driver can only choose "D" and "L." This results in constant up and down shifts that are not only annoying, but hazardous as well. (Are you listening, Ford?)

Although more spacious than the Mazda6, there is slightly less interior room than what you will find with the Accord and Camry. Nevertheless, this may be a minor point since the high, comfortable seats, abundant foot room under the front seats, and excellent outward visibility all add to the feeling of spaciousness. Drivers will also appreciate the standard tilt/telescope steering and seat-height adjustment to configure a comfortable driving position.

Interior appointments are unremarkable and apparently place more emphasis on function than style. Early reports indicate that fit and finish isn't impressive, with misaligned trim pieces and overall sloppy workmanship—not surprising on first series cars. The cabin, however, is remarkably quiet.

At $20,000–$24,000, Fusion prices are a bit on the high side and can be expected to drop once $2,000 to $3,000 discounts are applied by year's end. Without Ford discounts, Accord and Camry shoppers will have an edge of several thousand dollars. Hyundai's Sonata comes with more standard features, including a powerful 235-hp engine.

As far as estimated fuel economy is concerned, expect to be disappointed. Sure, Ford claims a highway rating of about 9.5L/100 km (30 mpg) with the four-banger; 11.5L/100 km would be more realistic.

From a quality standpoint, if anything goes wrong, it will likely be the automatic transmission, long a Mazda problem. However, with its new Aisin transmission, and with Toyota controlling the majority of that company's shares, the tranny problems of old may be long-gone.

FOCUS ★★

RATING: Below Average. Without a doubt, the 2005–06 Focus is a better quality vehicle than those built during the first four years. Nevertheless, from a reliability standpont, they are no way comparable to the Toyota Echo or even to Suzuki and Hyundai entry-level models. Performance-wise, this is a pretty good vehicle for urban use, but it's so poorly made that you risk your life, your wallet, and possibly your manhood if you drive one:

The cigarette lighter, after being pushed in and getting hot, popped out of the holder and landed either on the occupant's lap or on the carpeting. When this was shown to the rental company [Budget], and a demonstration was done, the lighter burned the representative's legs....

Strong points: Excellent handling and road holding, a commanding view of the highway, plenty of interior space for occupants and cargo, well appointed for an entry-level vehicle, user-friendly control layout, and impressive fuel economy. **Weak points:** Mediocre acceleration with base power plants, excessive engine and road noise, difficult rear-seat access with the hatchback version, and a large number of safety- and performance-related complaints. **New for 2006:** Nothing significant.

OVERVIEW: Ford's sleek Focus came to North America as an uplevel premium small car, positioning itself between the entry-level four-door Escort and the Contour. Ten centimetres taller and almost 18 centimetres longer than the Escort, and embodying Ford's "new edge" styling (less aero, more creases), the Focus features three body styles: a two-door hatchback in sporty ZX3 trim; LX, SE, and upscale ZTS four-door sedans; and a four-door SE wagon. The Escort's base engine, a 136-hp twin-cam 2.0L 4-banger, is carried over to the Focus LX and SE, while the 151-hp 2.3L is standard on the ST. Either engine can be hooked to a manual or an optional 4-speed automatic transmission.

TECHNICAL DATA

POWERTRAIN (FRONT-DRIVE)
Engines: 2.0L DOHC 4 (136 hp) • 2.3L DOHC 4 (151 hp); Transmissions: 5-speed man. • 4-speed auto.

DIMENSIONS/CAPACITY
Passengers: 2/3; Wheelbase: 103 in.; H: 56.3/L: 175.1/W: 67 in.; Headroom F/R: 5.0/2.0 in.; Legroom F/R: 39/26.5 in.; Cargo volume: 13 cu. ft.; Fuel tank: 53L/regular; Tow limit: 1,185 lb.; Load capacity: 825 lb.; Turning circle: 37 ft.; Weight: 2,800 lb.

COST ANALYSIS: Ford probably won't increase the 2006s' price by more than a few hundred dollars. If so, that model year represents the better buy because you'll stand a better chance of avoiding some of the car's quality glitches from the 2005 redesign. **Best alternatives:** Other viable alternatives include the Honda Civic, the Hyundai Accent, the Mazda3, and the Toyota Echo. **Options:** Go for the upgraded 2.3L twin-cam engine; the extra horsepower is sorely needed. **Rebates:** $2,000 and 0.9 percent financing. **Delivery/PDI:** $995. **Depreciation:** Average. **Insurance cost:** Average. **Parts supply/cost:** Average. **Annual maintenance cost:** Average. **Warranty:** Bumper-to-bumper 5 years/100,000 km; rust perforation 5 years/unlimited km. **Supplementary warranty:** A good idea for the powertrain. **Highway/city fuel economy:** 6.5–9.4L/100 km with the manual transmission; 6.9–9.4L/100 km with the automatic.

Quality/Reliability/Safety

Pro: Warranty performance: Ford Canada is attending to the Focus' quality problems under warranty, but once the warranty expires, plan on regular meetings with your bank's loan officer.

Con: Quality control: Mediocre in the past, and as Ford winds down Focus production, the company will likely invest most of its warranty dollars in the Fusion and Five Hundred. A disturbingly large number of life-threatening defects have been reported on previous year models. **Reliability:** Worse than average, particularly in view of the many stalling, powertrain, and brake complaints. **Owner-reported problems:** Automatic transmission failures:

> Vehicle was driven less than 70 miles [110 km] after being released from the manufacturer. Within that time, upon merging onto the highway, transmission failed. Transmission started slipping with engine revving to 3000 rpm, and vehicle slowly

accelerated onto the highway. Within a few seconds the transmission engaged, but only in the First gear. This entire incident occurred after the manufacturer had held the vehicle because of a quality control issue. The dealership wanted to replace the entire transmission.

Other complaints: Prematurely worn engine head and spark plugs; engine surges dangerously; hard starts caused by a defective mass airflow system (MAS), fuel pump, or fuel rail pressure sensor; PCM fails repeatedly; seized ignition cylinder lock prevents vehicle from starting; manual transmission Reverse and First gear failure; transmission suddenly downshifts; axle and transmission failures; cruise control disengages and Transmission Trouble light comes on; transmission makes a shuddering sound while in Reverse; loud rear-end popping; rear windshield stress cracks; electrical system shorts out; frequent replacement of the brake rotors and calipers; water leaks into the trunk compartment; inoperative power door locks; trunk won't close or fails to open; long delay for wheel delivery; and excessive suspension vibrations cause the rear end to wobble. **Service bulletin problems:** Rough-running engine; suspension creak, crunch, grind, or rattle; manual transmission rattling at idle with clutch depressed; and a deafening brake squeal corrected by changing rotors, callipers, and pads after only three months of use.

NHTSA safety complaints: Sudden acceleration and chronic stalling (likely caused by a defective fuel pump and covered by a "goodwill" warranty); wagon shakes violently when driven at 100 km/h with the windows down; airbags failed to deploy or deployed inadvertently; second-row middle seat belt buckle unlatched when brakes were applied; complete brake failure; while cruising, a loud rear-end bang is followed by excessive vibration and shimmy, making vehicle hard to control; rear window suddenly shattered (a service bulletin covers this); rear doors, trunk may open while driving; speedometer reading washes out in sunlight; and high-beam and turn-signal indicator lights are too dim.

 ## Road Performance

Pro: Acceleration/torque: Very good with the 151-hp optional engine and acceptable with the base 2.0L variant (some surging with both engines, however). **Emergency handling:** Better than average. **Transmission:** Automatic transmission is usually smooth and quiet; however, it does compromise performance a bit and long-term durability is still undecided since last year's redesign. **Steering:** Tight and responsive steering has good road feedback. **Routine handling:** Excellent. In spite of all of its quality problems, the Focus is one of the most fun-to-drive cars in its niche. Competent and predictable handling. Good tire grip and little body lean under power when going into corners. **Braking:** Good, but some brake fade.

Con: Acceleration/torque: 136-hp engine runs out of steam in the upper gear ranges. Expect a ho-hum 0–100 km/h time of about 10 seconds. **Transmission:** Manual's short gearing requires frequent shifting.

FOCUS

List Price (very negotiable)   **Residual Values** (months)

	24	36	48	60
ZX3 S: $17,555 (18%)	$14,500	$12,500	$11,000	$ 8,000
ZX5: $21,755 (19%)	$16,500	$13,500	$12,000	$ 9,500
ZXW SES: $22,605 (20%)	$17,500	$14,500	$13,000	$10,500

SAFETY FEATURES	STD.	OPT.
Anti-lock brakes	✓	✓
Seat belt pretensioners F/R	✓	—
Side airbags	—	✓
Stability control	—	—
Traction control	—	✓

CRASHWORTHINESS		
Head restraints F/R	4	4
Visibility F/R	5	5
Crash protection (front) D/P	4	4
4d	5	4
Crash protection (side) F/R	3	4
4d	3	4
Crash protection (offset)	5	—
Rollover	4	—

FIVE HUNDRED, FREESTYLE ★★

RATING: Below Average. Also sold as the Mercury Montego in the States, the Five Hundred and its Freestyle wagon spin-off are outclassed by Asian family sedans. **Strong points:** Wagon is longer and lower than most car-based SUVs, easy rear access, third-row seats stow into the floor, spacious rear compartment, high seating for a sedan, generous head and knee room, and optional adjustable pedals. **Weak points:** The 203-hp V6, which is also used in the Taurus, isn't powerful enough for a 1,860-kilogram (4,100 lb.) vehicle; very limited towing capability (450 kg, or 1,000 lb.); complicated and dealer-dependent CVT transmission; unproven self-levelling shocks; optional all-wheel-drive system that is part Volvo, part Ford—not the best combination for trouble-free performance; limited legroom for front occupants; 18-inch tires make for a stiff, choppy ride; and bland plastic interior. **New for 2006:** Carried over practically unchanged.

OVERVIEW: Bland but solid looking, the spacious Five Hundred is a spin-off of the Volvo S80 and will eventually replace the Crown Victoria as Ford's flagship sedan and wagon. Five Hundred uses a modified Volvo XC90 SUV and S80 wagon/sedan

The Ford Five Hundred.

TECHNICAL DATA

POWERTRAIN (FRONT/AWD)
Engine: 3.0L V6 (203 hp); Transmissions: CVT • 6-speed auto.
DIMENSIONS/CAPACITY
Passengers: 2/3; Wheelbase: 113 in.; H: 60.1/L: 201/W: 75 in.; Headroom F/R: 5.0/3.0 in.; Legroom F/R: 40/31 in.; Cargo volume: 21 cu. ft.; Fuel tank: 72L/regular; Tow limit: 1,000 lb.; Load capacity: 950 lb.; Turning circle: 41 ft.; Weight: 3,664 lb.

The Ford Freestyle.

TECHNICAL DATA

POWERTRAIN (FRONT/AWD)
Engine: 3.0L V6 (203 hp); Transmissions: CVT • 6-speed auto.
DIMENSIONS/CAPACITY
Passengers: 2/3/2; Wheelbase: 112.9 in.; H: 64.9/L: 199.8/W: 74.4 in.; Headroom F/R: 5.0/3.0 in.; Legroom F/R1/R2: 41.2/40.2/33.3 in.; Cargo volume: 85 cu. ft.; Fuel tank: 72L/regular; Tow limit: 1,000 lb.; Load capacity: 950 lb.; Turning circle: 40. ft.; Weight: 4,112 lb.

platform capable of giving the car the advantages associated with an SUV, such as higher seating, increased interior space, and optional 4×4 or all-wheel drive. There is more interior space and trunk capacity than in the full-sized Crown Victoria. Compared with the Taurus, the Five Hundred has blockier styling, but is about the same width and slightly longer and taller and sits on a longer wheelbase.

Power is supplied by a barely acceptable 203-hp 3.0L V6 Duratec engine that has proven problematic in the past. It will be coupled to either a 6-speed automatic or a continuously variable transmission. Note that the CVT transmission has never worked well when used to power Detroit iron; Saturn ditched the CVT last year after several years of breakdowns and mounting warranty claims.

Freestyle: Although Ford calls it a "crossover" car to cover every possible marketing niche, the Freestyle is essentially a taller wagon version of the Five Hundred. A mid-sized, six- or seven-passenger wagon/SUV that uses the same powertrain and platform as the Five Hundred, its third-row seating is roughly comparable to the Chrysler Pacifica's, with a weaker engine and some styling and interior differences. True to its car-based European heritage, the Freestyle handles twisting roadways with unusual aplomb.

COST ANALYSIS: Following last year's poor sales, Ford is already heavily discounting the identical 2006 models, which represent the best buy because you'll stand a better chance of avoiding some of the car's quality glitches from its first year production. **Best alternatives:** Other viable alternatives include the Honda Accord, the Hyundai Elantra, and the Toyota Camry. **Options:** Front side and curtain side airbags and power adjustable pedals. The rear-obstacle detection system may be more annoying than useful. **Rebates:** $4,000 and 0.9 percent financing. **Delivery/PDI:** $1,150. **Depreciation:** Faster than average. **Insurance cost:** Higher than average. **Parts supply/cost:** Average. **Annual maintenance cost:** Average. **Warranty:** Bumper-to-bumper 5 years/100,000 km; rust perforation 5 years/unlimited km. **Supplementary warranty:** A good idea for the powertrain. **Highway/city fuel economy:** 7.8–11.5L/100 km. Some owners report their gas consumption is about 20 percent higher than the official figures.

Quality/Reliability/Safety

Another reason to pass on these cars this year is Ford's internal memos that say they are seriously problem-plagued, according to BlueOvalNews at *www.blueovalnews. com/2004/cars/fivehundred.quality092804.htm:*

> Internal Ford Motor Company documents recently furnished to BlueOvalNews indicate that there are serious quality issues with the early build Ford Five Hundred, Freestyle and Mercury Montego models. While the documents detail everything from build costs to assembly concerns, the most troubling area that these documents detail are a high number of quality issues plaguing the D3 vehicles. According to the documents, these early D3s have possibly suffered from one or more of sixty-five (65) quality concerns, from defective platforms to faulty CVT gearbox and paint quality problems.

FIVE HUNDRED

List Price (negotiable)	Residual Values (months)			
	24	36	48	60
SE: $29,495 (25%)	$22,000	$17,000	$14,000	$11,000
Limited AWD: $38,845 (28%)	$26,000	$22,000	$19,000	$15,000

SAFETY FEATURES	STD.	OPT.
Anti-lock brakes	✓	—
Seat belt pretensioners F/R	✓	—
Side airbags	—	✓
Stability control	—	—
Traction control	✓	—

CRASHWORTHINESS		
Visibility F/R	5	5
Crash protection (front) D/P	5	5
Crash protection (side) F/R	5	5
Crash protection (offset)	5	—
Rollover	4	—

FREESTYLE

List Price (negotiable)	**Residual Values** (months)			
	24	36	48	60
SE: $33,495 (25%)	$24,000	$19,500	$15,000	$12,000
SEL AWD: $37,745 (30%)	$30,500	$22,000	$19,000	$15,000

SAFETY FEATURES	STD.	OPT.
Anti-lock brakes	✓	—
Seat belt pretensioners F/R	✓	—
Side airbags	—	✓
Stability control	—	—
Traction control	✓	—

CRASHWORTHINESS		
Visibility F/R	5	5
Crash protection (front) D/P	5	5
Crash protection (side) F/R	5	5
Rollover	4	—

MUSTANG ★★★★★

best buy

RATING: Recommended. **Strong points:** Base models come equipped with a host of luxury and convenience items. Fast acceleration, and impressive handling, braking, and resale value. Better-than-average past crashworthiness and good overall reliability. **Weak points:** Insufficient rear-seat room, limited cargo space, fishtails easily when accelerating on a wet surface or cornering under moderate speed. **New for 2006:** Nothing significant.

OVERVIEW: The perfect "back to the future" retro sports car, the Mustang's body panel creases reign supreme. Four decades after its debut, the original "pony car" concept is back, and it looks quite handsome. The new car arrives with V6 or V8 (in the GT) engines, both more powerful than current Mustang powerplants. The 4.0L SOHC V6 generates a respectable 210 hp and the 4.6L V8 is a 300-hp

All ratings on a numbered scale where 5 is good and 1 is bad. See page 153–154 for a more detailed description.

powerplant (40 more horses than the last generation 2004 Mustang). A 5-speed manual transmission is standard and a 5-speed automatic transmission, also used in the Lincoln LS and Ford Thunderbird, is an available option.

The Mustang's long wheelbase makes for a sleek car, though the grille, dashboard, tail lights, panels behind the doors, rear medallion on the trunk, and rear windows all harken back to the early Mustangs.

COST ANALYSIS: There are many unsold 2005 models around, so bide your time until discounts are announced for the 2006s early in the new year. **Best alternatives:** Other cars worth considering are the Acura RSX, this year's redesigned Mazda Miata, and Toyota's Celica. **Options:** Traction control—considering this rear-drive's tendency to spin out when pushed, and an anti-theft system that includes an engine immobilizer. **Rebates:** $3,000, plus 0.9 percent financing. **Delivery/PDI:** $1,050. **Depreciation:** Slower than average. **Insurance cost:** Way higher than average. **Parts supply/cost:** Inexpensive and easily found among independent suppliers; some delays getting engine and body components. **Annual maintenance cost:** Lower than average: Most mechanics will be able to fix a Mustang, although computer module powertrain glitches will drive them nuts. **Warranty:** Bumper-to-bumper 3 years/60,000 km; rust perforation 5 years/unlimited km. **Supplementary warranty:** Not necessary; put your money into handling options and theft protection. **Highway/city fuel economy:** 7.6–12.3L/100 km; 9.0–14.5L/100 km with the 4.6L.

TECHNICAL DATA

POWERTRAIN (REAR-DRIVE)
Engines: 4.0L V6 (210 hp) • 4.6L V8 (300 hp); Transmissions: 5-speed man. • 5-speed auto.

DIMENSIONS/CAPACITY
Passengers: 2/2; Wheelbase: 107.1 in.; H: 54.5/L: 187.6/W: 73.9 in.; Headroom F/R: 5.0/1.0 in.; Legroom F/R: 40.5/24 in.; Cargo volume: 12.3 cu. ft.; Fuel tank: 61L/regular; Tow limit: 1,000 lb.; Load capacity: 720 lb.; Turning circle: 39 ft.; Weight: 3,590 lb.

Quality/Reliability/Safety

Pro: Quality control: Average. Nevertheless, insiders report many factory-related problems with 4.6L engine cylinder heads. **Reliability:** Good. Body assembly since the 2005 redesign is much improved. If anything goes seriously wrong, it'll likely involve Ford's 4.6L engine interacting with the old transmission and revised suspension. **Warranty performance:** Unlike Ford's front-drives, few warranty complaints are lodged against the rear-drive Mustang.

Con: Owner-reported problems: The automatic transmission, fuel system, front suspension, brakes, electrical system, steering components, and fit and finish remain the primary weak spots. Sudden stalling with all models, but the Cobra is particularly affected. The automatic transmission rattles, clunks, and bangs, the AC fails, the engine computer can be temperamental, and electrical problems are common. Keep an eye on the 4.6L engine: Overheating, excessive oil burning, and head gasket failures may be frequent. Both engines produce an annoying "harmonic vibration." Body assembly quality is not up to the level of Japanese vehicles. Numerous complaints of convertible, door, and trunk water leaks and side windows leaking when it rains. **Service bulletin problems:** Engine overheating; rough-running (see Focus); loss of power and hard starting; supercharged engine may lack power; engine ticking when idling; difficulty troubleshooting transmission noise; gear whine in First, Third, and Reverse gears; driveline transmission clunk; noisy front suspension; instrument panel vent and hood scoop rattling; and exhaust leak. **NHTSA safety complaints:** Fire ignited in the wiring harness under dash area; airbags failed to deploy; hard starts; chronic stalling when coasting, braking, or when clutch is depressed; sudden, unintended acceleration; engine surging; Cobra pedal fractures easily; complete brake failure; seat belt doesn't retract properly; Goodyear tire blowout; serpentine belt came off, causing loss of power steering and brakes; wheel lug nuts fell off; sudden acceleration; sudden loss of steering when making a left-hand turn; car left on an incline with transmission in Park and motor shut off rolled down after 10 minutes and hit a tree; airbags failed to deploy in a frontal collision; driver's seat totally collapsed in a rear-ender; emergency brake ratchet assembly broke, making mechanism inoperable; gas spills out of fuel tank because clamps weren't sufficiently tightened; fuel smell in the cabin area; left front wheel fell off when the lower control arm and ball joint became loose; defective transmission spider gear; stuck gas pedal; seat ratchet assembly teeth broke; seat belt continually tightens up when worn; head restraints don't adjust up sufficiently; right side exhaust pipe leak; and a light rear end makes the car dangerously unstable on wet roads or when cornering at moderate speeds.

Road Performance

Pro: Emergency handling: Slow but predictable. **Steering:** Quick and responsive. **Acceleration/torque:** The V8 provides very quick acceleration and smooth power delivery (0–100 km/h: 7.1 sec.), while the V6 performs fairly well with the automatic 5-speed transmission. **Transmission:** The clutch is reasonably smooth and the automatic shifts reasonably well most of the time. **Routine handling:** Models equipped with the sport suspension (which includes larger tires) provide sure and predictable handling on dry roads. The base suspension also makes the car more stable and controllable on most roads. **Braking:** Disc/disc; excellent braking performance for a car this heavy (100–0 km/h: 36 m).

Con: Emergency handling: The 4.0L V6 is rough and noisy when pushed. The V8 is a bit too powerful for the amount of traction available to the rear wheels, making for lots of wheelspin and instability on slippery surfaces. **Transmission:** The manual transmission is notchy at times and the automatic sometimes hesitates between gears. **Routine handling:** The rear end tends to slip out under hard cornering. The GT rides harshly on rough roads.

MUSTANG

List Price (firm)	**Residual Values** (months)			
	24	**36**	**48**	**60**
Coupe: $23,995 (18%)	$17,500	$14,500	$12,000	$10,000
GT: $32,995 (22%)	$22,500	$19,500	$16,000	$14,000
Conv.: $36,995 (25%)	$25,500	$22,500	$19,000	$16,000

SAFETY FEATURES	STD.	OPT.
Anti-lock brakes	✓	✓
Seat belt pretensioners F/R	✓	—
Side airbags	—	✓
Stability control	—	—
Traction control	✓	✓

CRASHWORTHINESS		
Head restraints F/R	[4]	[4]
Visibility F/R	[5]	[5]
Crash protection (front) D/P	[5]	[5]
Crash protection (side) F/R	[4]	—
Convertible	[2]	[3]
Rollover	[5]	—

TAURUS ★★

RATING: Below Average. 2005 will be the last "official" model year for the Taurus, though it'll remain a fleet favourite for a little while longer. Wagons hold their value longer than sedans do, despite being outclassed by imports and most minivans for reliability and performance. **Strong points:** Quiet running, competent handling and road holding, comfortable ride, better-than-average crash protection, and bargain prices. **Weak points:** Insufficient storage space, limited rear headroom and access, and a history of serious mechanical and body deficiencies that can drive you straight to the poorhouse. **New for 2006:** Nothing.

TECHNICAL DATA

POWERTRAIN (FRONT-DRIVE)

Engines: 3.0L V6 (153 hp) • 3.0L V6 (201 hp); Transmissions: 5-speed man. • 4-speed auto.

DIMENSION/CAPACITY (LX)

Passengers: 3/3; Wheelbase: 108.5 in.; H: 56.1/L: 197.5/W: 73.1 in.; Headroom F/R: 6.5/3.0 in.; Legroom F/R: 41.5/30.5 in.; Cargo volume: 15.8 cu. ft.; Fuel tank: 68L/regular; Tow limit: 1,750 lb.; Load capacity: 1,100 lb.; Turning circle: 42 ft.; Weight: 3,350 lb.

OVERVIEW: Despite their past quality deficiencies, the Taurus and Sable are Ford's most popular family cars because of their attractive combination of a reasonable base price, good crashworthiness, impressive handling, and interior and ride comfort (except for the wagon's small rear seat). The base V6 is adequate, though it's outclassed by the optional 201-hp V6. Other nice standard features include heated outside mirrors, a 60/40 split-fold rear seatback for additional cargo space, a driver's foot rest, and reserve power to operate the power windows and moon roof after the engine is shut off. Wagons are equipped with four-wheel disc brakes.

COST ANALYSIS: A 2005 discounted by at least $4,000 is your best buy, but only if you get an extended bumper-to-bumper warranty and trade it in at the 5-year mark—just before the extra warranty expires. **Best alternatives:** Other sedans worth considering are the Honda Accord, the Mazda6, and the Toyota Camry. Wait a year to see if the Ford Fusion's price comes down and quality improves. Wagons worth considering are the Subaru Outback or Impreza and the Volvo V40. **Options:** Expect to spend about $300 more for the flexible-fuel Taurus (ethanol or methanol), currently sold only to fleets. The automatic climate control system, a rear integrated child safety seat, power seats, and a heavy-duty suspension are wise choices. Don't buy the optional leather seats; they're slippery and not all that durable. The gimmicky and distracting digital instrumentation is another useless option. Some more useful options are Ford's pedal extensions, which minimize the danger from airbag deployments, and the InstaClear windshield, which is a boon in Canadian winters. **Rebates:** Look for generous dealer incentives and customer rebates this fall as fleet sales fall off. Expect at least $3,500+ rebates and low-interest financing on all models. **Delivery/PDI:** $1,050. **Depreciation:** Higher than average as the Ford's Fusion replacement captures all the attention. **Insurance cost:** Average. **Parts supply/cost:** Parts are easily found and reasonably priced. **Annual maintenance cost:** Average to higher than average after five years or 100,000 km. **Warranty:** Bumper-to-bumper 3 years/60,000 km; rust perforation 5 years/unlimited km. **Supplementary warranty:** A wise investment, particularly when you replace the AC, automatic transmission, or fuel pump around the fifth year of use. **Highway/city fuel economy:** 7.7–12L/100 km with the base 3.0L.

Quality/Reliability/Safety

Pro: Important safety improvements once found only on luxury vehicles, have worked their way down to Ford's popular mid-sized family sedans. The Taurus, for example, has standard "thinking" seat belts and airbags that come in two parts to protect head and shoulders and upper torso separately. They can detect whether a driver has buckled the belt and prevent the airbag from deploying in fender-bender accidents, or cause it to deploy more slowly in high-speed impacts. Furthermore, the car's sides have been reinforced to prevent intrusion into the interior, and the Taurus' armrests have been redesigned to crumple, protecting passengers from possibly severe internal injuries in a side impact. Optional adjustable pedals, needed by short-statured drivers to avoid airbag injury, are also a worthwhile safety feature. Test-drive a vehicle with the extensions, though, before ordering the option.

Con: Reliability: There have been an inordinate number of reliability complaints recorded by government and private consumer protection agencies. The Taurus is in its final year, so don't expect many corrective improvements. **Quality control:** Way below average. As you will see below, owner complaints called into NHTSA still show a disturbing pattern of powertrain, brake, suspension, fuel and electrical system, and body component deficiencies. **Warranty performance:** Erratic and sometimes perverse. The same company that set up a generous 7-year/160,000 km after-warranty assistance program for 1994–95 engine failures won't admit that its automatic transmissions are also crap and merit a similar compensation program today. And engine problems still dog Ford's latest models, with intake manifold defects topping the list. **Owner-reported problems:** Engine failures; leaks; sudden shutdown; cold starting or surging; rough idle, running; automatic transmission shifts out of First gear too soon, shifts slowly, constantly bangs through the gears, and often chooses the wrong gear; AC, electrical system (lots of blown fuses), steering, fuel system, fuel pump, front suspension, warped brake rotor, and ignition problems; and constant wheel chirping. Vehicle has only one lock, which is located on the driver-side door. **Service bulletin problems:** Engine misfires (see Focus); deck lid opens as the dome light comes on and the chime sounds; automatic transmission torque-converter clutch fails to engage (this problem dates back to 1996 models); transmission may not go into Reverse; troubleshooting transmission malfunctions. Fuel-cap lamp illuminates when cap is on; engine-cooling-fan-induced body boom; rough engine idle sensation; unusual engine noise at idle; incorrectly installed gear-driven camshaft position sensor synchronizer assemblies may cause engine surge, loss of power, or MIL to light; no-start or hard starts; rattling, clunking front suspension; wipers won't shut off; erratic operation of AC blower motor; inaccurate fuel gauge; and power-window grunting noise. **NHTSA safety complaints:** Coil spring broke and punctured the tire (a problem seen on many other Ford models and model years); brake failure; airbags deploy for no reason or fail to deploy; airbag warning light stays lit; rear left wheel and rim flew off because of defective lug nuts; sudden acceleration; vehicle surges and then shuts off when fuel tank is filled; poor idle during a rolling stop; frequent stalling, hard starts, and hesitation caused by many factors, including chronic fuel pump failures or a contaminated fuel pressure sensor; strong fuel smell comes from the air vents; fuel gauge stuck on Full; fuel tank is easily punctured; engine had to be replaced because block heater was incorrectly mounted on the engine; engine belt tensioner shattered; excessive steering vibration; interior rear-view mirror location obstructs visibility; dash reflects upon the front windshield; seat belts may not reel out or retract; seat belt continually tightened around child and had to be cut off; adjustable brake and accelerator pedals are set too close together and are often too loose; right rear wheel almost fell off because of a faulty stabilizer bolt; rear brake lines rub together; high beam lights are too dim; and cigarette lighter pops out and falls under the passenger seat.

 ## Road Performance

Pro: Acceleration/torque: The optional 201-hp 3.0L engine is by far the better performer. It provides plenty of power in all gear ranges. **Emergency handling:** Better than average. **Steering:** The speed-sensitive variable-assist power steering makes the car easier to handle, but not as much as Ford claims. **Transmission:** The 4-speed automatic transmission shifts smoothly and responsively. **Routine handling:** The sedan's handling, both around town and on the highway, is better than average, primarily because of its solid suspension and stiff body construction.

Con: Ford's base 3.0L V6 is okay for rentals and city commuting, but it's unable to take full advantage of the car's handling characteristics and noisily protests as it struggles when merging with traffic or going up inclines. Wagons handle poorly in turns and over uneven terrain. **Braking:** Unimpressive braking (100–0 km/h: 41 m). ABS produces strong pedal pulsations.

TAURUS

List Price (very negotiable)

Residual Values (months)

	24	36	48	60
SE: $25,095 (22%)	$14,000	$12,000	$10,000	$ 7,500
SEL: $28,695 (25%)	$16,000	$14,000	$13,000	$ 9,500

SAFETY FEATURES	STD.	OPT.	CRASHWORTHINESS		
			Head restraints F/R	3	3
Anti-lock brakes	—	✓	Visibility F/R	5	5
Seat belt pretensioners F/R	✓	—	Crash protection (front) D/P	4	5
Side airbags	—	✓	Crash protection (side) F/R	3	3
Stability control	—	—	Crash protection (offset)	5	—
Traction control	—	✓	Rollover	4	—

All ratings on a numbered scale where 5 is good and ❶ is bad. See page 153–154 for a more detailed description.

best buy

The Grand Marquis.

RATING: Recommended. If you're going to buy a Lincoln, the Town Car can't be beat. These '50s-era behemoths are best suited for highway cruising, vacationing, and trailer towing. The Grand Marquis is the only Mercury still sold in Canada. **Strong points:** Lots of interior room, quiet running, easy entry and exit, reliable, and excellent resale value. A natural-gas V8 engine is available. **Weak points:** Difficult trunk access, terrible fuel economy, and some factory-related powertrain deficiencies that are carried over year after year. **New for 2006:** Nothing important.

OVERVIEW: The Grand Marquis and its discontinued Crown Victoria twin have always been favourites with police, taxi drivers, farmers, and retirees. With the addition of a 4.6L OHC V8 several years ago, the Grand Marquis GS and LS (a $3,000 upgrade) soldier on as Ford's rear-drive, full-sized sedans.

Although some fleets have replaced their Crown Victorias and Grand Marquis with 200-hp 3.8L V6-equipped Impalas following reports of rear-end collision fires and to save on fuel costs, the rank and file don't like the change. Never mind that acceleration tests conducted by the Michigan State Police found that Ford's additional 239-hp engine didn't result in significant performance improvements when compared with the more fuel-efficient and smaller front-drive Impala. The State Police found the rear-drive's pursuit performance hard to resist:

TECHNICAL DATA

POWERTRAIN (REAR-DRIVE)
Engine: 4.6L V8 (224–239 hp);
Transmission: 4-speed auto.
DIMENSION/CAPACITY
Passengers: 3/3; Wheelbase: 114.7/118 in.; H: 56.8/L: 212/W: 78.2 in.; Headroom F/R: 5.5/3.0 in., 3.0/3.5 in.; Legroom F/R: 40.5/27.5 in., 40.2/30.0 in.; Cargo volume: 20.6 cu. ft.; Fuel tank: 71L/ regular; Tow limit: 2,000 lb.; 1,100 lb.; Load capacity: 1,100 lb.;Turning circle: 42 ft.; Weight: 4,180 lb./4,415 lb.

We're adamant about a rear-drive car...especially for pursuit situations. On snow and ice, you can pull a rear-wheel car around; you can spin it around, but when you accelerate a 4X4 car, the front end will go right out from under you.... It will slide sideways and you will lose control.

Aside from the sheer wastefulness of the design and the high fuel cost of running one of these boats, they're fairly reliable and predictable highway cruisers. Handling isn't very precise, though it is more predictable than with front-drives, and everyone is going to be comfortable inside. The mechanical design is also straightforward and easy to troubleshoot (electronic and emission components excepted).

The Lincoln Town Car is still, to many people, the epitome of large-car, six-passenger luxury, and it's a popular rear-drive base for Ford's full-sized sedans. Essentially a stretched version of the Crown Victoria/Grand Marquis, the Town Car's air-spring rear suspension provides a comfortable ride and prevents tail dragging, even when the car is fully loaded. Its 4.6L V8 gives a quiet, smooth performance.

COST ANALYSIS: Look for a discounted 2005 or 2006. High fuel costs have created a serious inventory overload. Remember, a $10,000–$15,000 price cut can buy a lot of gas. **Best alternatives:** The redesigned Toyota Avalon is also a credible alternative. **Options:** Invest in the "Handling and Performance" option to reduce body roll and increase traction, and consider a power seat. **Rebates:** Throughout the year, expect $7,000+ rebates, hefty discounts, and a continuation of 0.9 percent financing. **Delivery/PDI:** $1,150. **Depreciation:** Much faster than average. **Insurance cost:** Higher than average. **Parts supply/cost:** Parts aren't hard to find; costs are about average when compared with other American cars in this class, but cheaper than the European equivalents. Asian parts are less expensive, however. **Annual maintenance cost:** A bit higher than average. Although repairs are relatively easy to carry out, these cars have complicated brake, fuel, and electronic systems that are a pain in the butt—and wallet—to troubleshoot. **Warranty:** *Grand Marquis*: Bumper-to-bumper 3 years/60,000 km; rust perforation 5 years/unlimited km. *Town Car*: Bumper-to-bumper 4 years/80,000 km; rust perforation 5 years/unlimited km. **Supplementary warranty:** Not needed. **Highway/city fuel economy:** 9.2–13.9L/100 km.

 ## Quality/Reliability/Safety

Pro: Quality control: Body components and construction are fairly good, thanks to several decades of incremental improvements. **Reliability:** Overall reliability is above average. **Warranty performance:** Better than average. Ford's luxury-car owners are treated like VIPs—at first (things go downhill from there). These cars have a nice array of safety features, such as adjustable pedals (optional on the Crown Victoria, standard with the Grand Marquis LS Premium), ABS, dual-stage airbags, crash-severity and seat-position sensors, and safety belt pretensioners.

Con: Owner-reported problems: Main problem areas are the 4.6L engine oil and coolant leaks (an Owner Notification Program covers engine intake manifolds that are cracked at the coolant crossover duct); constant stalling; automatic transmission glitches; excessive vibration in the driveshaft and differential assembly; prematurely worn brakes; and problems with the fuel and electrical systems. **Service bulletin problems:** Transmission failure; poor idle and hard or no-starts; engine knock and ticking noise; excessive engine vibration at idle; cracked lower control arm bushing; inoperative rear windshield defroster; slow or binding door glass operation; snapping noise when opening front doors; AC rattles and lack of cooling from vents; flickering electronic instruments; and intermittent horn self-activation. **NHTSA safety complaints:** Vehicle was struck from behind and exploded in flames; tire tread separation; missing upper control-arm bolt; brake booster failed; fan belt comes off in rainy weather, causing overheating and loss of power steering, water pump, and other accessories; horn "sweet spot" too small and takes too much effort to sound; sunlight causes a reflection of the defrost vents onto the windshield; poor dash panel illumination.

Road Performance

Pro: Emergency handling: A bit slow, but predictable and sure-footed. Less body lean in corners thanks to the upgraded suspension. **Steering:** Fairly accurate and responsive, with better road feel than previous models. **Acceleration/torque:** Respectable, though not impressive, acceleration with plenty of low-end torque (0–100 km/h: 10.2 seconds). The smooth, quiet-running 4.6L V8 provides more than enough power for a comfortable ride. Towing capacity is 2,250 kg (5,000 lb.) with the Class III Towing or Handling and Performance packages that are offered with the Grand Marquis. **Transmission:** Flawless, most of the time, although there is some gear hunting because of miscalibrated powertrain control modules. **Routine handling:** Ponderous, but acceptable for vehicles this size. Ride isn't overly soft. In effect, the rear end no longer sways when you turn the steering wheel. **Braking:** Better-than-average braking with the four-wheel disc brakes (100–0 km/h: 38 m).

Con: Transmission: Sometimes hesitates between gear changes. Handling still takes a back seat to ride quality.

GRAND MARQUIS, TOWN CAR

List Price (negotiable)	Residual Values (months)			
	24	36	48	60
Grand Marquis: $37,075 (26%)	$23,000	$17,000	$15,000	$13,000
Town Car Signature: $58,685 (35%)	$40,000	$32,000	$27,000	$23,000

SAFETY FEATURES	STD.	OPT.	CRASHWORTHINESS		
			Visibility F/R	5	2
Anti-lock brakes (4W)	✓	—	Crash protection (front) D/P		
Seat belt pretensioners F/R	✓	—	Crown Victoria and Gr. Marquis	5	5
Side airbags	✓	✓	Town Car	5	5
Stability control	—	—	Crash protection (side) F/R	4	5
Traction control	✓	✓	Crash protection (offset)	5	—
			Rollover	5	—

LINCOLN LS ★★

RATING: Below Average. Who wants to buy a luxury car that will no longer be manufactured after 2005? **Strong points:** Impressive V8 acceleration, comfortable ride, crisp handling, comfortable interior, and good warranty performance. **Weak points:** Erratic automatic transmission shifting; confusing climate controls; and poor-quality mechanical, electrical, and body components. Servicing will likely go downhill after the LS is taken off the market. **New for 2006:** Nothing significant in its last model year.

OVERVIEW: Lincoln's LS rear-drive mid-sized sedan comes with a high-performance 232-hp variant of the Taurus 3.0L V6 mated to an automatic gearbox. Also available: a 280-hp 3.9L V8 based on the Jaguar XK8 coupe coupled to a semi-automatic transmission. Both engines are identical but the one used in the LS produces fewer horses than the Jag equivalent.

TECHNICAL DATA

POWERTRAIN (REAR-DRIVE)
Engines: 3.0L V6 (232 hp) • 3.9L V8 (280 hp); Transmissions: 5-speed auto. • 5-speed auto./man.

DIMENSION/CAPACITY
Passengers: 2/3; Wheelbase: 114.5 in.; H: 56.1/L: 193.9/W: 73.2 in.; Headroom F/R: 3.5/2.5. in.; Legroom F/R: 41/28.5 in.; Cargo volume: 14 cu. ft.; Fuel tank: 68L/premium; Tow limit: 2,000 lb.; Load capacity: 900 lb.; Turning circle: 39 ft.; Weight: 3,655 lb.

The V6 version is priced in the territory of the BMW 3 Series, the Lexus ES 300, and the Mercedes C-Class, while delivering standard equipment and interior space that rivals the 5 Series, GS, and E-Class. The 2004 models were given reworked automatic transmissions to enhance performance and an improved suspension to reduce noise, vibration, and harshness.

COST ANALYSIS: It doesn't make much difference whether you buy a 2005 or 2006 model; they're both the same and eligible for huge rebates and discounts. **Best alternatives:** Alternative models include the Acura TL, the BMW 3 Series, the Infiniti G35, and the Lexus ES 300. **Options:** One option worth considering is the sports package, which includes thicker

All ratings on a numbered scale where 5 is good and 1 is bad. See page 153–154 for a more detailed description.

anti-roll bars, upgraded brake pads, re-calibrated variable-ratio steering, an auto-manual shifter (if ordered with an automatic), body-coloured bumper trim, a full-sized spare, and bigger wheels and tires. **Rebates:** Sales have been slow; expect rebates of $7,000+, plus zero percent financing. **Delivery/PDI:** $1,150. **Depreciation:** Faster than average. **Insurance cost:** Higher than average. **Parts supply/cost:** Parts availability hasn't been a problem and part costs have been reasonable. **Annual maintenance cost:** Predicted to be a bit higher than average as owners scurry around looking for competent servicing. **Warranty:** Bumper-to-bumper 4 years/80,000 km; rust perforation 5 years/unlimited km. **Supplementary warranty:** A good idea to ensure that Lincoln doesn't forget you after it has forgotten the ill-fated LS. **Highway/city fuel economy:** V6: 8.9–13.8L/100 km; V8: 9.1–14.2L/100 km.

 ## Quality/Reliability/Safety

Pro: Warranty performance: Better than average. Lincoln handles complaints well, but factory-related deficiencies are simply too numerous to recommend the LS.

Con: Reliability: In spite of Ford's good warranty performance noted above, powertrain, brake, and electrical problems still compromise the LS's overall reliability. **Quality control:** Below average. Apparently, Lincoln's return to rear-drive has opened up a Pandora's box of powertrain, AC, and body glitches. **Owner-reported problems:** Poor transmission shifting; excessive drivetrain and body noise and vibrations; inconsistent braking response; electrical system short circuits; and faulty AC performance. **Service bulletin problems:** High rolling idle; erratic transmission shifting; harsh 2–3 upshifts; transmission vent fluid leakage; suspension noise when accelerating; MIL indicator may stay on; inoperative power window and rear defroster; unintended opening of the side window and moon roof; sagging headliner; squeaking noise when switching climate control modes; steering squeak; repeat heater core failures; inadequate front seat cushion padding; and keyless entry won't work. **NHTSA safety complaints:** Airbag deployed for no reason or failed to deploy; curtain air canopy and side airbags injured occupant when deployed; vehicle suddenly shut down because of a computer glitch; failure to decelerate when foot taken off the gas pedal; lower ball joint failure caused accident (vehicle was not part of ball-joint recall); sudden acceleration in Forward or Reverse gear; lurching, hesitating automatic transmission shifting; chronic stalling; engine head gasket leaks oil on the AC compressor; brakes failed after a cold start; brake pedal becomes hard and resists application, or becomes mushy and goes to the floor without effect; defective steering causes violent swerving from side to side; automatic door locks engage by themselves, locking out driver; interior and exterior lights, dash panel lights, and gauges go haywire; and horn doesn't always blow.

Road Performance

Pro: Acceleration/torque: The V8 is the engine of choice for moving the LS (0–100 km/h: 7.3 seconds). **Emergency handling:** Traction control works quite well in emergency situations. **Steering:** Acceptable, but not as responsive as European and Japanese luxury vehicles. **Routine handling:** Pretty good, despite the soft suspension. **Braking:** Quite good.

Con: The V6's performance is seriously compromised by the Lincoln's heft, and turns in 0–100 km/h times that are one to two seconds slower than V6 competitors'. **Transmission:** The 5-speed automatic shifts slowly, not as decisively as competitors' gearboxes, and far less smoothly than Lexus drivetrains. A manual transmission (the first one since 1951) is available only with the V8-equipped LS. The suspension provides a soft ride and is not as sporty as the competition's.

LINCOLN LS

List Price (very negotiable)	Residual Values (months)			
	24	36	48	60
Lincoln LS: $50,595 (30%)	$35,000	$29,000	$25,000	$21,000

SAFETY FEATURES	STD.	OPT.	CRASHWORTHINESS		
Anti-lock brakes (4W)	✓	—	Head restraints F/R	5	5
Seat belt pretensioners F/R	✓	—	Visibility F/R	5	5
Side airbags	✓	—	Crash protection (front) D/P	4	4
Stability control	—	✓	Crash protection (side) F/R	4	5
Traction control	✓	—	Crash protection (offset)	5	—
			Rollover	5	—

THUNDERBIRD ★

RATING: Not Recommended. A lame-duck carryover, this is a textbook example of style and nostalgia overriding function and performance. Mercifully, Ford will drop this 'Bird in April 2006. **Strong points:** Good steering and handling (some handling is sacrificed for ride comfort) and better-than-average crashworthiness ratings. **Weak points:** Heavy, thirsty, and slow. Low-profile tires, which make for a firm ride; minimal trunk room even though the car is quite large for a two-seater; outrageously overpriced; and IIHS gives head restraints a Poor rating. Early reports note that the car's body construction is astonishingly poor, producing considerable creaks and rattles, and, when passing over bumps, it shakes its contents like a soda fountain's milkshake mixer (how's that for '50s nostalgia?). Long-term quality and reliability has yet to be determined. Also keep in mind the car's uncertain future (remember the Merkur XR4Ti?) and small dealer network, which can complicate servicing and warranty support. **New for 2006:** 2005 is its last model year.

OVERVIEW: After a brief hiatus, the Thunderbird name returned affixed to a $56,775 retro-styled, two-seat, rear-drive convertible that looks nothing like its 1955–57 namesake, or the $25,095 1997 model it replaces (now worth $4,500). This 'Bird shares variations of the engine and chassis used by the Lincoln LS and Jaguar S-Type, as well as their 5-speed automatic transmission. Power is supplied by a retuned 280-hp 3.9L V8.

Standard features include an independent suspension, four-wheel disc ABS brakes, side airbags, 17-inch alloy wheels, and a CD changer. The Premium package adds traction control (a good idea, considering that rear-drive rear ends tend to fishtail under a heavy load) and chrome wheels. The power-folding softtop houses a heated glass rear window; a removable hardtop with the T-Bird's signature side porthole windows is also available.

NHTSA frontal crash tests gave the Thunderbird a four-star rating for driver protection and five stars for the front passenger; side crash protection was given five stars for the driver only; rollover resistance was given five stars.

Sizzle over substance

The resurrected Thunderbird is a money-losing publicity ploy to show Ford's creativity, in much the same way that Honda's first cobbled-together Insight hybrid was developed mostly to show the company's "green" side. Neither vehicle was that exceptional, nor were they expected to earn back their development costs or be priced so that the average Joe or Jane can afford them. So, while most of the motoring press went gaga over the new Thunderbird, buyers saw it as simply a restyled Linc-Jag fuelled by tons of press releases.

The best Thunderbirds, in my opinion, other than the classic and unaffordable 1954–57 models, were those versions built from 1985–97. They were fairly reliable, relatively inexpensive, sporty, comfortable, and well equipped. They were fun to drive and easily maintained.

So why aren't the 2005 models a hit?

First off, this Thunderbird sequel is way overpriced. Sure, you get lots of bells and whistles for your $50,000+, but other cars offer just as much for far less money. Secondly, this is one dull-looking luxury roadster with few features that distinguish it from a half dozen imports of the same genre. Other minuses: a tiny, shallow trunk; a cheap-looking, boring instrument panel; limited headroom; an unwieldy folding top cover; and excessive air turbulence when driven with the top down.

Ford wants us to believe that the new Thunderbird is true to the heritage of its classic forebears and represents good value for its cost. Unfortunately, this Thunderbird proves just the opposite. Head restraints are rated Poor by IIHS, the official launch and delivery was delayed several times because of factory-related problems, the base MSRP is double what a Thunderbird cost just a few years ago, and the car will soon get the axe. Just the thing to boost our confidence in the product, eh?

Will Thunderbird 2 be a collector's car? Not likely. The only collectors I can imagine will be those Ford Oakville executives who are taking early retirement and were refused a Volvo.

FREESTAR, MONTEREY ★★

RATING: Below Average. The Freestar is essentially a renamed and reworked Windstar, one of the most unreliable minivans you'll find, last seen on the market in 2003. The Monterey is Freestar's Mercury twin. **Strong points:** Easily negotiated prices; nice array of cabin appointments; easier rear access; flat-folding third-row seats; good cargo capacity; large brakes that should improve pad and rotor durability; and impressive crashworthiness ratings. **Weak points:** Long-term reliability has yet to be determined. This is especially important because these minivans, under their Windstar moniker, have had serious failures that include engines, transmissions, brakes, electrical systems, and suspension components. Other minuses: a wimpy engine that doesn't inspire confidence; mediocre handling with lots of body lean when

The Ford Freestar.

cornering; a driver's seat that is uncomfortable for big, tall drivers, who complain of the lack of legroom, seat contouring, and lower back support; and an abundance of engine growl, clunks, rattles, wind, and road noise.

Owners also report self-destructing automatic transmissions, defective engine head gaskets and bearings, and failure-prone brakes and front coil springs, all of which can transform your dream minivan into Freddy Kruger's nightmare vehicle. And, as a counterpoint to Ford's high-crashworthiness boasting, take a look at the summary of safety-related complaints recorded by the U.S. Department of Transportation: coil spring breakage blowing the front tire, sudden acceleration, stalling, steering loss, windows exploding, wheels falling off, horn failures, sliding doors that open and close on children, and vehicles rolling away while parked.
New for 2006: Nothing.

TECHNICAL DATA

POWERTRAIN (FRONT-DRIVE)
Engines: 3.9L V6 (193 hp) • 4.2L V6 (201 hp); Transmission: 4-speed auto.
DIMENSION/CAPACITY
Passengers: 2/2/3; Wheelbase: 121 in.; H: 68.8/L: 201/W: 77 in.; Headroom F/R1/R2: 5.5/6.0/5.0 in.; Legroom F/R1/R2: 40/29/27.5 in.; Cargo volume: 61.5 cu. ft.; Fuel tank: 98L/regular; Tow limit: 3,500 lb.; Load capacity: 1,315 lb.; Turning circle: 42 ft.; Weight: 4,425 lb.

OVERVIEW: The Freestar is a re-engineered, restyled Windstar without any important dimensional changes. It features upgrades in safety, interior design, steering, ride, and performance. An optional "safety canopy" side curtain airbag system offers protection in side impact collisions and rollovers for all three rows of seating. There's also better access to the third row seat, which now folds flat into the floor.

Canadian Freestars are available with a 4.2L 201-hp V6 coupled to a 4-speed automatic transmission. In the States, Mercury will sell an upscale Freestar called the Monterey to replace that brand's defunct Nissan-based Villager.

COST ANALYSIS: Get the discounted 2006 version, if you feel lucky. The 2005s continue to be glitch-prone and may not be worth the extra savings. **Best alternatives:** Honda's Odyssey and the Toyota Sienna are recommended alternatives, although the new Hyundai and Kia minivans look quite promising. **Options:** Dual-integrated child safety seats for the middle bench seat and adjustable pedals are worthwhile options. Sliding side doors are an overpriced, failure-prone feature that is especially hazardous to children (see *Sharman v. Ford* in Part Two). **Rebates:** $7,000 discounts and rebates or zero percent financing on 2006 models. **Delivery/PDI:** $1,150. **Depreciation:** Average. **Insurance cost:** Average. **Parts supply/cost:** Reasonably priced parts are easy to find, mainly because of the entry of independent suppliers and the fact these minivans are recycled Windstars, which have been around for over a decade. **Annual maintenance cost:** Average while under warranty; outrageously higher than average thereafter, primarily because of powertrain breakdowns not covered by warranty or insufficiently covered by parsimonious "goodwill" gestures. **Warranty:** Bumper-to-bumper 3 years/60,000 km; rust perforation 5 years/unlimited km. **Supplementary warranty:** An extended bumper-to-bumper warranty is a good idea. **Highway/city fuel economy:** 9.5–13.3L/100 km.

Quality/Reliability/Safety

Pro: Adjustable pedals help protect drivers from airbag injuries. Be careful, though—some drivers have found them set too close together and say they often felt loose. Other nice safety features include airbags that adjust deployment speed according to occupant weight and a sliding door warning light.

Con: Warranty performance: Below average. Owners say Ford is unusually tight-fisted in giving out refunds for the correction of factory-related deficiencies. **Quality control:** Average. **Reliability:** The Windstar had serious problems affecting the automatic transmission, which shifted erratically and was historically failure-prone. Ford insiders and service bulletins confirm that this transmission problem is both hardware and software related and affects much of Ford's model lineup—it's a chronic complaint from owners reporting to NHTSA. Electrical system and brake defects also frequently sidelined the Windstar, and the same problems have been seen with the Freestar. **Owner-reported problems:** Transmission, suspension (coil springs), and power-sliding door malfunctions lead the list of factory-related problems, but there have also been many complaints concerning computer modules, engine oil leaks, timing cover gasket coolant leaks, and excessive brake noise.

Service bulletin problems: Transmission has no 1–2 upshift; false activation of parking assist (an optional safety device that will drive you nuts with false warnings); ways to find and fix sliding door's many failures; and loose rear door trim. **NHTSA safety complaints:** Sudden loss of steering; airbag light stays on or airbag may not deploy; driver heard a bang, then it felt like Freestar was running on a flat tire; the A-frame dropped out of the tie-rod collar; front axle suddenly broke while underway; left inner brake pad fell apart and locked up brake; dealer had to change pads and rotor; sliding door closed on a child, causing slight injuries; plastic running board broke, blocking sliding door operation, locking occupants inside the vehicle; and headliner-mounted DVD screen blocks rear-view mirror.

Road Performance

Pro: Emergency handling: High-speed handling is acceptably stable and predictable. **Steering:** Adequate; not as effortless as the Asian, Chrysler, and

GM competition. **Acceleration/torque:** The 3.8L V6 is usually competent and smooth, with lots of low-end torque (0–100 km/h: 10.7 seconds). **Transmission:** The electronic 4-speed automatic responds well and shifts smoothly, when it's working properly (see "Con"). **Routine handling:** Easy to drive. Smooth and supple ride under most driving conditions improves as the load increases.

Con: Engine known to stall because of fuel pump, computer module, and electrical system glitches. Erratically performing automatic gearbox may slip out of gear, lurch into gear, or simply refuse to engage whichever gear you choose. The Freestar's city manners aren't impressive: Excessive body swish and sway take their toll on tires and make the Freestar's highway driving less carlike than the Chrysler, Honda, and Toyota minivans'. **Steering:** Excessive torque steer tug on the steering wheel during rapid acceleration. It also has a large turning radius. **Quietness**: Lots of wind noise on the highway. **Braking:** Disc/drum; average braking that's a bit difficult to modulate.

FREESTAR (2004)

List Price (very negotiable)	Residual Values (months)			
	24	36	48	60
Wagon: $28,295 (30%)	$17,000	$15,000	$12,000	$ 9,000
Wagon Sport: $34,295 (30%)	$20,000	$18,000	$15,000	$11,000

SAFETY FEATURES	STD.	OPT.	CRASHWORTHINESS		
Anti-lock brakes (4W)	✓	—	Head restraints F/R	5	5
Seat belt pretensioners F/R	✓	—	Visibility F/R	5	5
Side airbags	—	✓	Crash protection (front) D/P	5	5
Traction control	—	✓	Crash protection (side) F/R	4	5
			Crash protection (offset)	5	—
			Rollover	4	—

General Motors

Selling the "Sizzle"

For 2006, GM is committed to returning to a bewildering combination of incentives, equipment packages, and finance deals, now called "value pricing." While the promise pleases GM's profit-squeezed dealers, it will piss away the one thing that money can't buy: customers' goodwill.

THE TRUTH ABOUT CARS
ROBERT FARAGO

North America's largest automobile manufacturer doesn't know what it's doing. It's on life-support as it lurches from discounts to rebates in an effort to "sell the deal" rather than sell its cars. Closing Oldsmobile and throwing money away on its Saturn, Pontiac, and Buick divisions is incredibly stupid, but buying Saab and promising to buy Fiat defies all explanation. Now that the company is propped up by its lending operations, GM's automobile business is going down the drain, thanks to its overpriced, gas-guzzling, and poor-quality vehicles.

How'd you like to pay $12,000 more than your neighbour for the same 2005 DeVille?

For example, how do you build customer confidence in your pricing when the average U.S. sticker price for a 2005 Cadillac DeVille was $54,193 in August 2004, but six months later, the discounted price dropped to $42,211—a 22 percent difference? Would you buy another GM after paying the high-end price—especially after learning that savvy buyers usually got additional discounts from the dealer?

General Motors' claim that it has a hybrid strategy to make its vehicles more fuel-efficient is just a bunch of bull. Sure, the company sold a few thousand "hybrid" Silverado and Sierra pickups in North America, but they don't have as powerful a battery, or the capability to run on only electric power, as the competition does. And get this: After paying a $2,500 premium, owners may get only another kilometre per litre. GM could have done better with a cylinder deactivation system similar to the one in Honda's Accord V6.

While paying lip service to hybrid engines, GM is gaining time and PR points by embracing fuel cells, an untested technology that uses hydrogen and oxygen to generate electricity and power a vehicle. GM promises a million fuel-cell vehicles in the future, ignoring questions of whether there is sufficient hydrogen available, whether it can be generated cheaply (it can't) and stored safely (can you say "kaboom"?), whether it can be distributed efficiently enough to give a vehicle sufficient range, and whether the technology is affordable. Reminds me of a Hydro-Quebec press conference 15 years ago when, with great fanfare, the Quebec utility boasted it would corner the North American market for electrically powered vehicles. It never happened and never will. *D'accord?*

New Models and New Partners

General Motors is desperate to get more attractive, fuel-efficient, reliable, and profitable products onto the market this year as it tries to shake its reputation for making look-alike, low-quality vehicles. Consequently, a handful of new models will be introduced along with some carryovers masquerading as new.

The company is calling 2006 its "breakthrough" year for new models, but if I were a GM executive up against the surging Asian competiton, I'd be checking my Canada Pension Plan benefits.

I can't help being so critical. Car execs want us to forget the bullcrap they fed us years ago, but I won't. I remember GM's last so-called breakthrough model lineup in the late 1980s, when its GM10 variants (Grand Prix, Regal, Lumina, and Cutlass) incarnated mediocre performance and poor quality.

Ironically, the company is counting on its Asian and European competitors to save its hide through new manufacturing and marketing alliances that will quickly put into the marketplace fuel-efficient small cars that generate reasonable profits. In fact, the automaker is much further along in these worldwide co-ventures than Chrysler and Ford, who are just now getting new small cars on the market. Ironically, Ford came within a hair of buying Daewoo less than five years ago. GM's also making up for stagnant car sales by concentrating on a few new cars like the Buick Lucerne (the LeSabre's replacement), the Pontiac Solstice two-seater, the Pontiac Torrent sport wagon, and the Chevrolet HHR wagon—a downsized 1949 Suburban truck. The company, however, is running in the oppo-

Buick's new Lucerne is a competent front-drive family car that replaces the venerable LeSabre. Two engines are offered with this new 2006 model: a 197-hp 3.8L V6 and a 275-hp V8. Look for a $30,995 base price before discounts of at least 20 percent in 2006. Furthermore, wait at least six months for the price to come down substantially and the first-series glitches to be corrected.

site direction with a January launch of a bevy of mid-sized and full-sized SUV gas-guzzlers that no one will want to buy or fuel.

If you wonder how GM could so badly misjudge the market, keep in mind that Detroit product planners are like a huge oil tanker trying to shift direction. Just as it takes a tanker 16 km to change course, Detroit usually takes three years to do so, while Asian automakers are getting their response time down to almost two years. Hence, we have a 2006 and 2007 model lineup that was planned when gasoline was relatively cheap. Get ready for huge discounts early in the new year.

The rear-drive STS gives Cadillac its best chance to recapture market share.

Cadillac STS—Carrying a pricetag of $56,275 for the 255-hp 3.6L V6 (coupled to a 5-speed automatic transmission) and $68,725 for the 320-hp 4.6L V8 (AWD), this rear-drive/AWD Seville replacement is quite attractive and has plenty of power and performance. The V6 is more powerful than the BMW 5 Series or Mazda E-Class 6-cylinder engines, while the V8 has a bit less horsepower than the comparable BMW and more than the Mercedes or Lexus. Undoubtedly, Cadillac's switch to rear-drive enhances the STS's balance, handling, overall performance, and hopefully, reliability. The interior is first class, and rear-seat room is larger than most of the competition. Standard features include StabiliTrak stability enhancement, a Bose sound system with CD player, leather seats, Keyless Access with push-button ignition start, Adaptive Remote Start, and Panic Brake Assist. STS has lots of potential as Cadillac fights a volatile market where price, fuel-economy, reliability, and cachet rule.

Chevrolets' new HHR.

Chevrolet HHR—A mini version of GM's 1949 Suburban, this $18,995 (LS) five-passenger retro trucklet targets the Chrysler PT Cruiser crowd. Although it's almost 8 inches longer than the Cruiser, the HHR ("Heritage High Roof") doesn't match Chrysler for power, with a top rating of only 172 hp compared to the Cruiser's 230. GM hopes to overcome its horsepower deficit by undercutting the Cruiser's selling price by several thousand dollars.

The HHR is basically a compact wagon that uses GM's Cobalt/Pursuit platform and 4-cylinder engines: a base 143-hp 2.2L and the aforementioned 172-hp 2.4L variant, mated to either a manual or automatic transmission. Air conditioning is a standard feature.

Drivers moving from a minivan or SUV will appreciate the HHR's high seating position and commanding view of the road. There's also plenty of rear legroom and storage space. Additionally, the vehicle's interior is easily accessed through wide-opening doors and easy-entry seats. Drivers over six feet tall, however, will likely find their heads grazing the headliner, especially if a sunroof is installed.

On the road, the HHR handles quite well, although shoppers would be well advised to get the better-performing 2.4L powerplant, especially since there isn't very much difference in fuel consumption. Steering is accurate and responsive, and the brakes perform well even after repeated stops. Surprisingly, ABS and curtain airbags are optional on the base model, a serious omission for an automaker that wants to attract both young and old.

Granted, the Cobalt and Pursuit are going into their second year on the market and have performed reasonably well. Nevertheless, the HHR/Cobalt package has too many variables to ignore, so prudent shoppers should wait until at least next summer when the first-series quality problems have been worked out and prices have come down even more.

Alternative vehicles worth considering: the Chevrolet SSR (another retro truck), the Chrysler PT Cruiser, and the Honda Element.

Pontiac Solstice/Saturn Sky—

Mainly targeting Mazda's revamped 2006 Miata, GM's first budget-priced roadster is scheduled to debut in the late fall after several delays caused by production glitches. It will be followed by the 2007 Sky, a fully loaded clone. These two-passenger, rear-drive roadsters are powered by a 170-hp

Don't look for discounts on GM's hot little Solstice; the car is back-ordered and selling for full MSRP. Wait a year and you'll save a bundle.

2.4L 4-cylinder engine mated to a 5-speed manual or an optional 5-speed automatic transmission promised for early 2006. Estimated price for the Solstice is $25,695; the Sky will sell at a $5,000 premium (I don't know why).

What is there to like? The Solstice looks good at first glance, as any roadster should. Its low profile and snug passenger compartment are no different from the configuration used for years by Alfa Romeo, Triumph, and MG. The Pontiac's wide, poised stance and low dual-port grille quickly set the Solstice apart from the crowd.

Steering is precise and fairly responsive, with excellent road feel. Braking is easy with the four-wheel disc brakes; however, anti-lock brakes are optional. Electronic stability control should be available in 2006. The suspension doesn't punish you, like we remember with the MG and Triumph.

This new roadster is practically the same length as the 2006 Mazda Miata, but the Solstice's 95.1-inch wheelbase is 3.4 inches longer, and the vehicle is 3.6 inches wider, enhancing high-performance handling.

The Solstice is impressively quiet, allowing very little wind or road noise to enter the cabin—another change from the roadsters we once drove.

The car features three cupholders, but only one—a magnesium engineer's delight mounted on the passenger side of the transmission tunnel—is of much use. The other two pop out of a shoulder-dislocating ergonomic nightmare of a slot in the cabin's rear bulkhead. Interior storage space is also limited, but that's not much of a surprise in such a small car.

What are the car's weak points? First, the Solstice is nearly 180 kg (400 lb.) heavier than the Mazda Miata, and it drags that hoary and roary old Ecotec engine around for one last hurrah. And what's with the Saturn Sky? Who in their right mind wants to spend top-dollar for a Saturn twin? Alfred P. Sloan, maybe.

Tall drivers and passengers need not apply; occupants taller than 6′2″ will feel cramped. Furthermore, the interior is more functional than stylish (why can't American automakers make attractive interiors?). The 3.8 cubic feet of enclosed cargo space called a trunk is also a disappointment. There's room for two very soft-sided bags with the top down.

This Torrent is the Aztek's replacement.

Pontiac Torrent—Pontiac's 2006 Torrent is a warmed-over Chevy Equinox and Saturn Vue, with a bit firmer suspension, some styling freshening, and a slightly higher price ($26,585 before rebates and discounting).

Unlike Ford, GM's dealer network isn't in turmoil and relations are cordial and respectful, despite some bad blood and lawsuits related to the Oldsmobile franchise phase-out (most dealers feel Saturn or Pontiac should have gotten the axe). This dealer truce may not last for long though, if GM's Saturn division doesn't start making real profits soon to make up for all the money GM has blown on it. Another looming problem is that General Motors' Daewoo subterfuge (it sells Daewoos as re-badged Suzukis and Chevys) will inevitably cut into GM's own compact car sales, ticking off dealers who have invested heavily in Cobalt and Pursuit inventory.

In Canada, Chevrolet dealers sell the entry-level Aveo; the Optra, a compact based on the Daewoo Lacetti; and the Epica, a mid-sized vehicle based on Daewoo's Magnos. Suzuki sells the subcompact Swift, based on the Kalos, and the Verona for GM.

Warranty Performance, Quality Control

It is estimated that GM loses about $2,000 per vehicle on mid-sized cars. Nevertheless, the company has put more money into warranty repairs and continues to let its dealers make most post-warranty decisions. So it's not surprising to see that GM warranty complaints have lessened a bit over the years. This being said, GM's quality is still nowhere near that of the high-quality cars and trucks sold by the Japanese automakers.

GM's quality control needs serious improvement. Its engines and automatic transmissions still aren't as reliable or as durable as the Asian competition, who've been embarrassed over the recent disclosure of their own spate of powertrain defects. Furthermore, GM brake and electronic components often fail prematurely and cost owners big bucks to diagnose and repair. The quality and assembly of body components also remain far below Japanese and European standards.

Interestingly, these problems are shared by all three Detroit-based auto manufacturers and will hopefully diminish as Chrysler, Ford, and GM move back to rear-drives and merge operations and divisions with Japanese manufacturers.

In other words, if you can't beat them, join then.

CAVALIER, COBALT, PURSUIT, SUNFIRE

RATING: Average. The 2005 Cavalier and Sunfire were sold alongside the Cobalt and Pursuit last year, but only the Cobalt and Pursuit remain as 2006s. **Strong points:** Very reasonably priced; good acceleration; plenty of front passenger and cargo room; comfortable riding; well appointed for an entry-level vehicle; and split rear seatbacks that add to storage capacity. **Weak points:** Steering and handling are only average; limited rear passenger room; cheap interior; mediocre fit and finish; small trunk opening; and problematic rear entry and exit (on the

The Chevrolet Cobalt.

coupe). Real world fuel economy is much less than what's advertised. Crash safety and quality control still need improvement. **New for 2006:** Nothing.

OVERVIEW: Both the Cobalt and Pursuit use GM's Opel Astra platform and offer a base 2.2L 145-hp 4-cylinder engine (five more horses than the Cavalier) that is a good performer, although noisy and relatively fuel-thirsty. A more powerful super-charged 2.0L 4-cylinder is standard on the SS version.

The Cavalier and Sunfire twins have been around for decades. They have a good powertrain set-up, exceptional styling (especially the Sunfire coupe), and lots of interior room. The Sunfire is identical to the Cavalier except for its more rakish look. The Cavalier LS Sport and 1SC-equipped Sunfire are performance versions of the base compacts.

TECHNICAL DATA (COBALT AND PURSUIT)

POWERTRAIN (FRONT-DRIVE)
Engines: 2.2L 4-cyl. (145 hp) • 2.0L SC 4-cyl. (205 hp); Transmissions: 5-speed man. OD • 4-speed auto.

DIMENSION/CAPACITY
Passengers: 2/3; Wheelbase: 103 in.; H: 54.8/L: 180/W: 68 in.; Headroom F/R: 3.5/3.0 in.; Legroom F/R: 41.5/27 in.; Cargo volume: 13.2 cu. ft.; Fuel tank: 49L/regular; Tow limit: 1,000 lb.; Load capacity: 890 lb.; Turning circle: 37 ft.; Weight: 2,850 lb.

COST ANALYSIS/BEST ALTERNATIVES: With competitors like the redesigned 2006 Honda Civic, Toyota's Echo and Corolla, and the Mazda3, this quartet of small cars doesn't compete from both a quality and a price standpoint. Even Hyundai, Kia, and GM's Daewoo-sourced Aveo look good in comparison. **Options:** There's very little worthwhile, except for the side air-bags, enhanced suspension, power windows and locks, and remote keyless entry. Forget about the rear spoiler; it looks silly and doesn't add to the car's performance. The LS, LS Sport, and performance packages aren't worth the extra cost. **Rebates:** Don't bother looking for 2005 leftovers. GM's summer discount frenzy cleaned most of them out. Expect to see $3,000 rebates and other incentives on 2006 models in the late fall. **Delivery/PDI:** $995. **Depreciation:** Slower than average. **Insurance cost:** Average. **Parts supply/cost:** Parts are easy to find and reasonably priced, with heavy discounting by independent suppliers. **Annual maintenance cost:** Average. **Warranty:** Bumper-to-bumper 3 years/60,000 km; powertrain 5 years/100,000 km; rust perforation 6 years/160,000 km. **Supplementary warranty:** Yes, but only for the powertrain if you'll be keeping the car for more than five years. **Highway/city fuel economy:** 6.7–10L/100 km with the base engine and a 4-speed automatic.

Quality/Reliability/Safety

Pro: Warranty performance: Better than average. **Safety:** Important safety features include a remote keyless entry with a panic button, top child-seat anchors for all three rear positions, and side airbags that protect the head and upper torso.

Con: Reliability: Not as reliable as the Asian competition and on a par with what's offered by Ford and DaimlerChrysler. **Quality control:** A history of early powertrain and brake failures. Cheap body hardware is fragile and often poorly assembled. **Owner-reported problems:** *Cobalt and Pursuit:* Automatic transmission failures, prematurely worn clutches, AC blows warm air, driver's seat rocks back and forth, inaccurate fuel gauge, third brake light stays lit, steering wheel doesn't return to the centre position after making a left-hand turn, steering and suspension noises, and the undercarriage is easily damaged when passing over potholes. *Cavalier and Sunfire:* Historically, engine head gasket failures have been a frequent problem, made worse by GM's denials that the problem exists and refusal to admit that a "secret warranty" covers the defect. This dishonesty infuriates customers like this 2003 Cavalier owner:

> I was informed by a customer service rep that my vehicle was covered for head gasket repair under a "Special Policy" recall. At the urging of a customer service rep from Chevrolet, I took my vehicle to the dealer for repair. I was notified by their service department that this "Special Policy" had expired July 2003 and that it would cost over $1,400 to fix.

Many complaints of automatic transmission failures and grinding when shifting. PCM computer modules have also been one of the most common sources of complaints; symptoms include stalling and a shaky idle. Fuel injection and cooling systems are temperamental as well. The power steering may lead or pull, and the steering rack tends to deteriorate quickly, usually requiring replacement sometime shortly after 80,000 km. The front MacPherson struts also wear out rapidly, as do the rear shock absorbers. Many owners complain of rapid front-brake wear and warped brake discs after a year or so. One owner reported the following brake repairs to NHTSA:

Front brake rotors are warping and had to be turned at 1,600 miles [2,575 km] and 1,800 miles [2,897 km]. They then were replaced at 2,800 miles [4,506 km]. They would cause the vehicle to jump when braking.

More recent owner-reported problems include front vacuum leaks, causing the vehicle to lose power; hard starts; chronic stalling; slipping transmission; a grinding noise when shifting gear; a rattling noise when shifting from First to Second gear; frequent steering failures and noisy steering; excessive pulsation when braking; airbag warning light comes on continuously; dashboard noise; fuel sloshing in fuel tank; water leaks through the windshield; and window may fall off its track and slide between the door panels. **Service bulletin problems:** *Cobalt and Pursuit:* Voluntary Customer Satisfaction Program to correct AC malfunctions and 2.2L engine stalling. *Cavalier and Sunfire:* No starts, hard starts, and poor idling may be caused by clogged fuel injectors; firm shifts and shudder; transmission slips, or no shift; Neutral or rpm flare while in Drive; no 1–2 upshift; momentary loss of steering assist; rattle and knocking; steering or suspension popping, creaking sound when turning; front-end clunks; rattling or thumping sound heard from the passenger side floorboard when vehicle passes over rough roads; grinding or growling in Park; wheel squeaking; dash rattle; instrument panel lens cracks or discolours; faulty heater; inaccurate fuel gauge tied to faulty fuel module, fuel level sensor, or other defects; and hard-to-change temperature settings. **NHTSA safety complaints:** *Cobalt and Pursuit:* If driver's knee bumps the underside of the steering column, the vehicle suddenly shuts down; chronic stalling; and air-bags failed to deploy.

I was driving about 40 mph [64 km/h] with my two kids in the car, and then the vehicle slowed down and wouldn't accelerate. I was able to pull over to the side of the road and then the car just stalled. I then put the car in Park and waited a few minutes. I then tried starting the car again and it did start. My vehicle has 600 miles [965 km]. Today, I received a notice from Chevrolet Motor Division central office stating that they are conducting a voluntary customer satisfaction program that affects certain 2005 model year Chevrolet Cobalt vehicles equipped with a 2.2L engine and air conditioning. I called the dealership service department and also the 800-number on my letter and told them about my vehicle stalling and to let them know I received the letter. I'm scheduled for an appointment to correct the problem and to look into why my vehicle stalled. Although they state this is "voluntary customer statisfaction program," I think they should just call it a recall and have all customers who purchased this model bring their vehicle in now rather than when they experience a problem.

Cavalier and Sunfire: Tire jack suddenly collapsed; driver's door opens when vehicle passes over uneven terrain; engine fires; Reverse bulbs exploded, causing back light area to catch fire; leaking fuel tank; plastic fuel tank easily punctured; fuel spews out when refuelling; seatback broke when vehicle was rear-ended; seatback spring assembly suddenly snapped for no reason; right and left wheel axle broke off vehicle; chronic hesitation, stalling, and surging; sudden acceleration; clutch will not disengage, causing sudden acceleration; faulty ABS; brake failure caused by leaking master cylinder fluid; ABS locked up, causing vehicle to go into a skid; air-bags failed to deploy; seat belt failed to retract; automatic transmission wouldn't go into Reverse; suddenly shifted into Neutral on the highway; failed to engage upon start-up; locks up in Second gear; vehicle rolled away even though parked with parking brake engaged; vehicle rolls backward when stopped on an incline; when foot is on the brake with vehicle in Drive, it lurches forward, stalls, and produces a crashing sound; during highway driving the vehicle suddenly accelerated without steering control; rear leaf-spring U-bolts broke, causing entire rear end to drop; front right side of the vehicle collapsed after wheel bolts sheared off, causing the wheel to detach completely; springs are too weak, causing poor stability and con-trol; floor mat impedes clutch pedal travel; sudden brake cable breakage while driving; brake grinding noise; warping of the front and rear brakes; thumping noise when stopping; when driving with door locked, door came ajar; hood flew up while driving; misaligned driver's door; windshield water leaks; side window exploded; sunroof shattered; defogger doesn't correct chronic windshield fogging; loose fuel cap caused the Check Engine light to come on; horn wouldn't work in an emer-gency; early burnout of the turn signal and brake light bulbs; prematurely worn Goodyear tire blew out; plastic bumper fell apart, causing front wheel damage; and the trunk lid remains open at such a low angle that it's easy to hit your head.

 ## Road Performance

Pro: Acceleration/torque: The fuel-injected 2.2L 4-cylinder engine provides adequate power, if not pushed too hard. The supercharged 2.0L is an impressive performer, but one wonders how long it'll last. The optional suspension package offers better handling at highway speeds and the best ride control on bad roads. **Braking:** Disc/drum; acceptable.

Con: Emergency handling: Excessive lean when cornering under power and standard tires corner poorly. **Steering:** Power steering feels over-assisted, resulting in insufficient road feel. **Transmission:** The 5-speed manual transaxle has an abrupt clutch. **Routine handling:** Base models don't handle as well as do most other vehicles in this class.

CAVALIER (2005), COBALT, PURSUIT, SUNFIRE (2005)

List Price (very negotiable)	Residual Values (months)			
	24	36	48	60
Cobalt LS $15,710 (15%)	$12,000	$ 9,000	$ 7,500	$ 5,500
Cobalt LT: $19,795 (18%)	$14,000	$11,000	$ 9,000	$ 7,000
Cobalt SS: $22,195 (20%)	$15,500	$13,000	$11,000	$ 9,500

SAFETY FEATURES (COBALT AND PURSUIT)			CRASHWORTHINESS (COBALT AND PURSUIT)		
	STD.	OPT.			
Anti-lock brakes (4W)	—	✓	Head restraints F/R	1	1
Seat belt pretensioners F/R	✓	—	Visibility F/R	5	5
Side airbags	—	✓	Crash protection (front) D/P		
Stability control	—	—	2d	4	5
Traction control	—	✓	4d	4	5
			Crash protection (side) F/R		
			2d	—	—
			4d	3	4
			Crash protection (offset)	5	—
			Rollover	4	—

SAFETY FEATURES (CAVALIER AND SUNFIRE)			CRASHWORTHINESS (CAVALIER AND SUNFIRE)		
	STD.	OPT.			
Anti-lock brakes (4W)	—	✓	Head restraints F/R	1	1
Seat belt pretensioners F/R	✓	—	Visibility F/R	5	5
Side airbags	—	✓	Crash protection (front) D/P		
Stability control	—	—	2d	4	4
Traction control	—	✓	4d	4	4
			Crash protection (side) F/R		
			2d	1	2
			4d	1	3
			Crash protection (offset)	1	—
			Rollover	4	—

G6 ★★

RATING: Below Average. This car offers a number of standard safety and convenience features, though outward visibility isn't one of them. **Strong points:** Decent acceleration and a smooth-shifting automatic transmission combine to give sufficient power when you need it. There's no real need for the GT's sportier manual shift gate, firmer suspension, and 17-inch tires. However, the GT's standard ABS, traction control, and power-adjustable pedals will enhance handling. Adequate room for front occupants, if the seats are pushed way back. Standard tilt/telescope steering wheel, height-adjustable seat, and adjustable pedals are quite handy for seniors and drivers who don't fit Detroit's "norm" to configure a comfortable driving position. Interior appointments, instrumentation, and controls are well laid out and of average quality for this price level. Seats have ample side bolstering. Large doors enhance entry and exit, but may be difficult to handle for some. **Weak points:** The ride is a bit stiff and jerky. Steering doesn't give much road feedback, and steering wheel grip isn't ideal. GT suspension is

much firmer, but at an onerous price. Mushy brake feel and annoying brake pulsations when ABS is engaged. Optional front torso side airbags, and head-protecting curtain side airbags. Difficult rear access. Claustrophobic rear seating, with limited head room for average-sized occupants, and practically no side visibility thanks to the sloping roofline. Visibility is further impinged by tall front head restraints and thick front and rear roof pillars. Seats lack sufficient padding for long trips. Convertible tops have been glitch-prone and there have been some reports of serious body fit problems. Engine and road noise intrusion into the cabin is evident, though tolerable; not as quiet as the Honda Accord, the Hyundai Sonata, the Mazda6, or the Toyota Camry. Small trunk also has a narrow opening. Fuel economy is nowhere near what GM pretends it to be. **New for 2006:** A hardtop and convertible. Performance range is shifted higher with the addition of the GTP variants which offer a more powerful, though fuel-thirsty, 240-hp 3.9L V6.

OVERVIEW: Selling for $23,160, this mid-sized Grand Am replacement is built on GM's front-drive Epsilon platform and is offered as a coupe, sedan, and convertible. It is powered by a standard 2.4L 4-cylinder engine, which is rated at 167 hp—one more horse than the Honda Accord and a bit more than most of the competition's family sedans. GM brags that the convertible features a retractable hardtop that is the longest in the industry; however, operating glitches with the opening and retracting mechanism have delayed the convertible's launching several times. The automaker promises it will be ready early in 2006.

TECHNICAL DATA

POWERTRAIN (FRONT-DRIVE)

Engines: 2.4L 4-cyl. (167 hp) • 3.5L V6 (201 hp) • 3.9L V6 (240 hp); Transmissions: 4-speed auto. • 6-speed man.

DIMENSION/CAPACITY

Passengers: 2/3; Wheelbase: 112 in.; H: 55.1/L: 189/W: 71 in.; Headroom F/R: 4.0/2.0 in.; Legroom F/R: 42/31 in.; Cargo volume: 14/15 cu. ft.; Fuel tank: 64L/regular; Tow limit: 1,000 lb.; Load capacity: 890 lb.; Turning circle: 41 ft.; Weight: 3,475 lb.

COST ANALYSIS: The G6 has been a slow seller, despite the hundreds of cars given away last year on the *Oprah* TV show in the States. Look for a discount of at least 15–20 percent. **Best alternatives:** Performance and quality control are no match for the Honda Accord, the Mazda6, and the Toyota Camry. Chrysler's Sebring is a credible alternative both as a coupe and convertible. Ford's Fusion might do, if its automatic transmission is recalibrated for smoother and less-frequent shifting and first-year factory-induced defects are corrected. The Hyundai Elantra is also worth considering. **Options:** Don't get a sunroof, unless severe wind buffeting and noise are your cup of tea. **Rebates:** $3,000+, plus zero percent financing. **Delivery/ PDI:** $1,150. **Depreciation:** Average. **Insurance cost:** Average. **Parts supply/ cost:** Easy-to-find parts at reasonable prices. **Annual maintenance cost:** Average. **Warranty:** Bumper-to-bumper 3 years/60,000 km; rust perforation 6 years/160,000 km. **Supplementary warranty:** A toss-up. **Highway/city fuel economy:** 6.7–10.5L/100 km with the 3.5 L V6 and a 4-speed automatic.

 ## Quality/Reliability/Safety

Pro: Warranty performance: Average, so far. Most of these cars are still covered by the original warranty.

Con: Quality control: Mediocre. Insiders say the car's hardtop has flunked durability tests. A poor fit between the deck lid and rear fenders is another problem. Service bulletins are replete with instructions on correcting water leaks, severe wind noise, and dash, suspension, and steering squeaks and rattles. **Reliability:** The automatic transmission, engine, steering, and electrical system have proven to be troublesome on last year's model. **Owner-reported problems:** Short circuits; noisy suspension struts; and a substandard body assembly that produces many annoying squeaks and rattles. Owners say car cannot be driven at highway speeds with the window down without creating a pounding noise and severe vibration. **Service bulletin problems:** A Customer Satisfaction Program will correct a malfunctioning engine harmonic balancer for free; no-starts and long cranking time; remote starter doesn't work; ignition key cannot be removed from the ignition lock cylinder; engine flares at idle; Service Engine Soon and airbag warning light stay on; troubleshooting a damaged transmission tailshaft bushing; increased steering effort; vibration at all speeds; reasons why the carpet may be wet; water intrusion into the cabin from the doors; water causes a short circuit, leading to unintended door and trunk locking and unlocking; inoperative rear defogger; dash clicking, ticking; rear fascia bows out where tail lights and rear quarter panels meet; and servicing tips for a cracked exhaust at the catalytic converter mount.

NHTSA safety complaints: Sudden steering lockup caused vehicle to veer off the road and crash; vehicle cannot be driven with windows open; automatic transmission jerks into gear; proceeding up a driveway incline may damage the undercarriage and engine cradle; brake lights remain lit.

Steering system locked. This occured on the highway, going around a right turn at 50 mph [80 km/h] (uphill). It resulted in a collision with the concrete barrier on the side of the road. The ability to steer returned after the driver yanked the wheel hard. The driver felt a pop and the steering returned, but there was no time to regain control of the car.

•

Steering on this vehicle has locked up multiple times, causing the vehicle to go off the road. GM has investigated the car after the previous incident and claimed there was no problem and will not check the car again. Most recent steering lockup occured at 8,400 miles [13,500 km].

•

Open rear window or windows at speed of 40 mph [64 km/h] and above creates a safety problem as the noise from the rear of the car becomes so intense that you either have to close the window or stop the car... The faster you go over 40, the louder it becomes.... I reported this to GM and they told me it's the nature of the beast, [a] totally unacceptable answer.

Road Performance

Pro: Emergency handling: Average. **Steering:** Steering is predictably responsive, when it is working properly. **Acceleration/torque:** Fair acceleration with the 4-cylinder engine. V6 acceleration is quite good, delivering power smoothly. **Transmission:** Well suited to the V6. **Routine handling:** Acceptable. **Braking:** Average, with minimal brake fade after repeated stops.

Con: The base model isn't very agile on the highway and original equipment tires are subpar performers. Many complaints of sudden steering lockup. Base model is hard-riding.

G6

List Price (very negotiable)	Residual Values (months)			
	24	36	48	60
G6 Sedan: $23,160 (17%)	$17,000	$14,000	$11,000	$ 8,500
V6 GT: $27,995 (19%)	$19,500	$16,500	$13,500	$10,500

SAFETY FEATURES			CRASHWORTHINESS		
	STD.	OPT.	Visibility F/R	❸	❶
Anti-lock brakes (4W)	✓	✓	Crash protection (front) D/P	❺	❹
Seat belt pretensioners F/R	✓	—	Crash protection (side) F/R	❸	❺
Side airbags	—	✓	Rollover	❹	—
Traction control	✓	✓			
Head restraints F/R	—	—			

MALIBU, MAXX, SS ★★★

The Malibu Maxx SS.

RATING: Average. The Malibu's performance strengths are compromised by the car's overall poor reliability. **Strong points:** Good V6 powertrain set-up. Well appointed, comfortable though firm ride, very responsive handling, plenty of passenger and luggage space, and few squeaks and rattles. Excellent crashworthiness ratings. **Weak points:** Base 4-cylinder engine is barely adequate for highway driving with a full load and an automatic transmission. Bland interior. Expect lots of factory-related engine, transmission, and brake problems. Short 3-year powertrain warranty. **New for 2006:** The addition of an SS model, equipped with a 3.9L 240-hp V6, an automatic transmission, an upgraded interior, and a sportier suspension; all other models get a 4-speed automatic/manual transmission and a restyled exterior.

TECHNICAL DATA (MALIBU)

POWERTRAIN (FRONT-DRIVE)

Engines: 2.2L 4-cyl. (145 hp) • 3.5L V6 (200 hp) • 3.9L V6 (240 hp); Transmissions: 4-speed auto. • 4-speed auto./man.

DIMENSION/CAPACITY

Passengers: 2/3; Wheelbase: 106 in.; H: 57.5/L: 188/W: 70 in.; Headroom F/R: 5.5/3.0 in.; Legroom F/R: 41.5/29 in.; Cargo volume: 15.4 cu. ft.; Fuel tank: 61L/regular; Tow limit: 1,000 lb.; Load capacity: 915 lb.; Turning circle: 39.0 ft.; Weight: 3,297 lb.

OVERVIEW: Malibu is a relatively new front-drive, mid-sized sedan distinguished by its nice array of standard features. It is joined by the Malibu Maxx and SS. The Maxx is a five-door hatchback—6 inches longer than the sedan—that features a skylight over the rear passengers and a rear seat with 18 centimetres of forward-and-back travel to provide increased passenger and cargo space. This year's SS addition carries a more powerful V6 and handling enhancements.

The base Malibu is "powered" by GM's wimpy 145-hp 2.2L 4-cylinder power plant, found on many of its compact cars. Most buyers will be tempted to pay extra for the torquier and smoother 200-hp 3.5L V6.

The optional 4-speed manual/automatic transmission is a major improvement this year.

The Malibu's styling is quite conservative and uncluttered. A fold-flat passenger seat and a 60/40-split rear folding bench seat maximizes the interior room. Other useful standard amenities include a driver-seat power height adjuster; a telescoping steering column that also tilts; power windows, door locks, and outside mirrors; and power adjustable brake and accelerator pedals (LS and LT).

From a safety perspective, these cars offer almost everything. The LT sedan and Maxx have four-wheel disc brakes, and ABS and traction control are standard on the LS and LT and optional on the base sedan. A side curtain airbag is optional on all models.

COST ANALYSIS: Go for the upgraded 2006 Malibu. **Best alternatives:** The Honda Accord has more usable interior space and quicker and more accurate steering, and the Toyota Camry is plushier, though not as driver-oriented. Both Japanese competitors are also far more reliable. Other cars worth considering: the Hyundai Elantra or Tiburon, the Mazda6, or the Nissan Sentra. **Options:** The LS package, side curtain airbags, and premium tires. **Rebates:** $3,000 rebates and zero percent financing. **Delivery/PDI:** $1,150. **Depreciation:** Average. **Insurance cost:** Higher than average. **Parts supply/cost:** Malibu uses GM generic parts that are found everywhere and are reasonably priced. **Annual maintenance cost:** Average. **Warranty:** Bumper-to-bumper 3 years/60,000 km; rust perforation 6 years/160,000 km. **Supplementary warranty:** A wise investment. **Highway/city fuel economy:** *2.2L 4-cylinder:* 6.6–9.8L/100 km; *V6:* 6.7–10.5L/100 km. Interestingly, the V6 isn't much thirstier than the 4-cylinder.

Quality/Reliability/Safety

Pro: Warranty performance: Average. **Safety:** Excellent crashworthiness scores. Optional curtain side airbags are effective in protecting the head and upper torso.

Con: Quality control: Below average. **Reliability:** Below average. Engine failures, electrical system glitches, the frequent replacement of brake and suspension components, AC malfunctions, and very poor fit and finish. **Owner-reported problems:** Premature engine piston failure caused "piston slap" noise; chronic stalling; erratic transmission shifting; pervasive odour of oil burning on the exhaust; driver's seat rocks back and forth; and frequent brake repairs. **Service bulletin problems:** Automatic transmission growl or howl; slipping automatic transmission; ignition key is hard to remove from the ignition lock cylinder in cold weather; rattle or buzz from the instrument panel; and poor radio reception. **NHTSA safety complaints:** Airbags deployed inadvertently or failed to deploy; sudden brake loss; premature warpage of the brake rotors; steering loss; sudden steering lock-up; chronic steering shimmy; frequent stalling for unexplained reasons; stalling caused by leaking fuel line; hit a small bump in road and vehicle stalled with a complete loss of electrical power; tire blew and cruise control wouldn't disengage; fuel-tank filler tube is loosely connected to the frame; excessive vibration at any speed; brake, steering wheel pulsation; engine rattle caused by defective piston; automatic transmission jumped from Park to Reverse; transmission doesn't lock when the key is in the accessory position; very loose steering; faulty high-beam switch; original equipment tires don't have gripping power and fail prematurely; outside mirrors are too small; interior rear-view mirror vibrates; inaccurate fuel gauge; and door flies open when vehicle is underway:

> Driver-side rear door did not latch properly when closed. No Door Ajar light was indicated and door swung open upon turning a corner even with doors locked. We were experiencing a cold snap at the time, but this has happened another time when there was cold weather. No one was injured, but an unbuckled child or passenger could have been thrown from the vehicle. I am not sure if this is a defect with the latch mechanism. I took the vehicle to the dealer and they advised that it was caused by a frozen lock. They treated it with silicon spray and lube. Hopefully this will solve the problem but I am now worried the door will open again. This is a 2005 car with only 700 miles [1,100 km].

> •

> At approximately 5 mph [8 km]...our back seat passenger rested his arm against the rear driver-side door, the door swung open (latch failure). The door would not re-latch despite approximately 50 attempts to close the door. We rotated the latch assembly trying to see what was wrong and it would still not latch. If this was a child or if I was travelling at a higher speed, this could have been catastrophic and could have resulted in injury or death. Finally, we were able to get the door to stick closed halfway, the whole drive home it rattled and door ajar was listed. It was 9°F [−12°C] according to the onboard computer at the time. The next morning, at 22 degrees [−6°C], we opened it and it latched properly on the first attempt. On January 21st, also at 9 degrees, I opened the rear door and attempted to close it. This would not latch at all, and after 30 minutes of trying, I drove 5 miles [8 km] to the dealership with my hand extended to the back seat, holding the door closed manually so that it would not swing out and cause an accident or property damage. The service manager looked at this, and duplicated the problem for approximately 5 minutes, at which time the car was warmed up slightly due to it being indoors, and it closed properly. The dealer asked if I had any children and when I said no, they released the vehicle to me and said they'd be in contact with GM.

Road Performance

Pro: Emergency handling: Cornering under speed is well controlled, with little front-end plowing or excessive body roll. **Steering:** Acceptable for everyday driving. **Acceleration/torque:** Acceptable with the 4-cylinder, but the V6 does a much better job without much of a fuel penalty. Brisk acceleration and plenty of low-end torque with the V6 engine; the V6 delivers power in a smooth, quiet manner. **Transmission:** Smooth and predictable shifting, most of the time. **Routine handling:** Better than average, thanks to an independent suspension that doesn't sacrifice solid handling for passenger comfort.

Con: Hard cornering produces considerable body lean and numb steering. Pushrod V6 is a bit rougher than the overhead-cam V6 used by the competition. Downshifting is a bit slow when passing other vehicles. **Braking:** Antiquated rear drum brakes provide mediocre braking with standard ABS. Some brake fade after repeated stops.

MALIBU

List Price (negotiable)   **Residual Values** (months)

	24	36	48	60
LS Sedan: $19,995 (21%)	$15,500	$14,000	$11,000	$ 8,000
LT: $22,470 (23%)	$17,000	$15,000	$12,000	$ 9,500

SAFETY FEATURES	STD.	OPT.	CRASHWORTHINESS	2	1
Anti-lock brakes	✓	✓	Head restraints F/R	2	1
Seat belt pretensioners F/R	✓	—	Visibility F/R	5	5
Side airbags	—	✓	Crash protection (front) D/P	5	5
Traction control	✓	✓	Crash protection (side) F/R	4	5
			Crash protection (offset)	5	—
			Rollover	4	—

GRAND PRIX, IMPALA, LACROSSE/ALLURE, MONTE CARLO ★★★

The Chevrolet Impala.

TECHNICAL DATA (GRAND PRIX)

POWERTRAIN (FRONT-DRIVE)
Engines: 3.5L V6 (211 hp) • 3.6L V6 (240 hp) •
3.8L V6 (200 hp) • 3.8L V6 (260 hp) • 3.9L V6 (242
hp) • 5.3L V8 (303 hp); Transmission: 4-speed auto.

DIMENSION/CAPACITY
Passengers: 2/3; Wheelbase: 111 in.; H: 56.6/L:
198/W: 72 in.; Headroom F/R: 2.0/2.0 in.; Legroom
F/R: 41.5/28 in.; Cargo volume: 16/17 cu. ft.; Fuel
tank: 64L/reg./prem.; Tow limit: 1,000 lb.; Load
capacity: 915 lb.; Turning circle: 41 ft.; Weight:
approx. 3,400 lb.

TECHNICAL DATA (LACROSSE/ALLURE)

POWERTRAIN (FRONT-DRIVE)
Engines: 3.8L V6 (200 hp) • 3.6L V6 (240 hp);
Transmission: 4-speed auto.

DIMENSION/CAPACITY
Passengers: 2/3; Wheelbase: 111 in.; H: 57.4/L:
198/W: 73 in.; Headroom F/R: 2.0/1.5 in.; Legroom
F/R: 41/27 in.; Fuel tank: 64L/reg./prem.; Cargo
volume: 16 cu. ft.; Tow limit: 1,000 lb.; Load
capacity: 915 lb.; Turning circle: 40 ft.; Weight:
approx. 3,565 lb.

RATING: Average. **Strong points:** Nice array of standard features, good choice of powertrains, comfortable ride, easily accessed and roomy interior. LaCrosse/Allure provides additional rear legroom and a front bench seat. The restyled Impala has a convenient flip-down centre console in the middle of the bench seats, and rear seatbacks fold flat, opening up cargo storage space. **Weak points:** Rear seating uncomfortable for three; bland styling; and obstructed rear visibility because of the high-tail rear end. These cars have been hobbled by a chintzy 3-year powertrain warranty that's clearly insufficient, knowing GM's past engine and transmission deficiencies. **New for 2006:** *Impala:* Restyled and re-engineered, about 75 percent of the car's components have been changed. *LaCrosse/Allure:* Standard side airbags. *Monte Carlo:* New engine lineup that includes a base 211-hp 3.5L V6, a 240-hp 3.9L V6, and an SS-only 303-hp 5.3L V8, equipped with cylinder de-activation (also called "Displacement on Demand"). Additionally, the front end has been restyled, with bigger headlights, new spoilers, a taller hood, and a more aggressive stance. Interior comfort and convenience have been enhanced with better seats and an improved dash. Front end and suspension improvements also make this year's model much quieter and smoother-riding.

OVERVIEW: The Buick Allure (called the LaCrosse in the United States) is a substantially upgraded and stiffened version of the recently discontinued Century and Regal. Its four-wheel independent suspension is 80 percent retuned—including stiffer springs, thicker stabilizer bars, and longer rebound damper bumpers—for improved ride and handling qualities. The rack-and-pinion steering and four-wheel disc braking system is completely new. Selling for $26,295 before discounting, the Allure features a sleek exterior, a 200-hp 3.8L V6 and a 240-hp 3.6L V6, a quiet-riding chassis, remote keyless entry, power driver seat, power door locks, power windows, and a six-speaker stereo with the CD player. Base models are sold with a full complement of standard safety features, along with optional Ultrasonic Rear Parking Assist (of doubtful value) and factory-installed remote starting system. Allure is considered an Average buy since it's on par with the cars it replaces.

A cousin to the Impala, the Monte Carlo is a mid-sized sport coupe that incorporates more creases in its styling, along with round tail lights, a longer wheelbase, and shorter length. Side airbags are optional on all models. The Monte Carlo also got an SS designation several years ago after it was fitted out with the Impala's supercharged engine, replaced this year by the 5.3L V8. Other new 2006 features include a base 211-hp 3.5L and a 242-hp 3.9L V6 (two more horses than last year's supercharged 3.8L). The only available transmission is a 4-speed automatic that wastes fuel and cuts overall performance.

COST ANALYSIS: Go for a second-series 2006 to minimize your chances of getting a problem-plagued re-engineered car. The new V8, cylinder de-activation, and other new features require a bit more time to be perfected. Premium fuel is "recommended" for the V8, but not "required." You figure it out. **Best alternatives:** Keep in mind that there are plenty of more reliable, better-performing vehicles available from the competition, including the Honda Accord, the Mazda6, the Hyundai Elantra, and the Toyota Camry or Avalon. Those wanting a bit more performance should consider the BMW 3 Series. **Options:** The rear-mounted child safety seat and head-protecting side curtain airbags are worth buying, but stay away from the Impala's rear spoiler, which obstructs rear visibility and is of doubtful utility. **Rebates:** This is where GM's fight for market share (instead of profits) becomes hand-to-hand combat. Its cars are in a marketing segment that's steadily losing ground to Japanese entries, and GM is throwing tons of cash around in the form of discounts, rebates, low-financing plans, extended 5-year-plus payment plans, balloon payments, and overnight test-drives. The longer you wait, the cheaper these cars will become. Expect generous $4,000+ rebates on all 2005 and 2006 models. **Delivery/PDI:** $1,150. **Depreciation:** Average. **Insurance cost:** Higher than average. **Parts supply/cost:** Moderately priced parts that aren't hard to find. **Annual maintenance cost:** Higher than average. Independent garages can perform most non-emissions servicing; however, cylinder de-activation makes you a prisoner of GM dealer servicing. Good luck. **Warranty:** Bumper-to-bumper 3 years/60,000 km; rust perforation 6 years/160,000 km. **Supplementary warranty:** Essential, especially after the third year of ownership. **Highway/city fuel economy:** *Base sedan with 3.5L:* 8–12.7L/100 km; *3.8L:* 7.6–12.3L/100 km.

Quality/Reliability/Safety

Pro: Warranty performance: Average. **Safety:** Good crashworthiness ratings.

Con: Tire-inflation monitor is unproven. **Quality control:** Below average for powertrain and body construction, which puts it on par with Chrysler and a bit ahead of Ford. **Reliability:** The 3.5L and 3.8L V6 engines have had more than their share of fuel system, intake manifold, and computer module problems that keep cars off the road. **Owner-reported problems:** Premature engine head gasket failures, piston slap noise, and early transmission breakdowns. Electrical system problems are common on cars loaded with power accessories. Front and rear brakes rust easily and wear out early, and the discs warp far too often. Shock absorbers and MacPherson struts wear out or leak prematurely. The power rack-and-pinion steering system degenerates quickly after three years and is characterized by chronic leaking. Poor body fit, particularly around the doors, leads to excessive wind noise and water leaking into the interior.

> Purchased the Allure in March of '05, have had it in a total of 24 days for service, on about 10 different occasions. The front doors leaked badly in the rain. They have since been adjusted, had new seals put in, Bondo applied at a body shop. Then Buick replaced both doors with new factory doors. These also leaked. They were adjusted and Bondo was applied to the new doors. They required multiple adjustments as well. Now the doors feel like they drop a quarter-inch when you open them and there is a lot of wind noise.

Service bulletin problems: All models: Here's the "smoking gun" GM internal service bulletin admitting to poor-quality engine intake manifolds (see following page). Note that this defect has existed over eight model years, and imagine how many owners have paid to fix this defect, which GM admits here is clearly its own fault. Other problems include a broken console lid latch and poor radio reception.

NHTSA safety complaints: (Keep in mind that the safety problems noted below may apply to any of the cars in this section.) *Allure:* Passenger side airbag is inadvertantly disabled; distracting mirror reflection.

> The consumer complained about a problem with the airbag on the passenger's side. The airbag sensor was de-activating when his wife was in the passenger-side seat. The passenger weighed 121 pounds. The airbag will stay on and activate when the owner was in the seat weighing about 50 pounds more than the passenger. The owner had the car taken to the dealership to be checked, and the dealership said it was the design of the vehicle, and it could be the magnetic field. The manufacturer was contacted, and they called the dealership to see what was going on and they said that it was the magnetic field. They could not help either. The owner said that he could not get It fixed because the dealer indicated there was nothing wrong with the car.

> •

> The glare from the chrome strip on the dash is blinding the driver. (The glare affected the 1/2-inch chrome strip across the dash and the rectangular strip around the gear selector.) This problem would occur when the sun reflects vertically or obliquely through the windows. The glare caused the consumer headaches...and the reflection of the silver trim on the driver and passenger front door windows is distracting and interferes with the view of the exterior mirrors.

Vehicle wanders all over the road; brake pad, caliper, and rotor failures. *Impala:* Airbags failed to deploy; frequent complaints of dash-area and engine-

ENGINE OIL OR COOLANT LEAK

BULLETIN NO.: 03-06-01-010A   DATE: APRIL 2003

ENGINE OIL OR COOLANT LEAK (INSTALL NEW INTAKE MANIFOLD GASKET)

2000–03	Buick Century	1996–2003	Oldsmobile Silhouette
2002–03	Buick Rendezvous	1999	Oldsmobile Cutlass
1996	Chevrolet Lumina APV	1999–2003	Oldsmobile Alero
1997–2003	Chevrolet Venture	1996–99	Pontiac Trans Sport
1999–2001	Chevrolet Lumina	1999–2003	Pontiac Grand Am
1999–2003	Chevrolet Malibu, Monte Carlo	2000–03	Pontiac Grand Prix, Montana
2000–03	Chevrolet Impala	2001–03	Pontiac Aztek

with 3.1L or 3.4L V6 engine (VINs J, E - RPOs LGB, LA1)

CONDITION: Some owners may comment on an apparent oil or coolant leak. Additionally, the comments may range from spots on the driveway to having to add fluids.

CAUSE: Intake manifold may be leaking, allowing coolant, oil, or both to leak from the engine.

CORRECTION: Install a new-design intake manifold gasket. The material used in the gasket has been changed in order to improve the sealing qualities of the gasket. When replacing the gasket, the intake manifold bolts must also be replaced and torqued to a revised specification. The new bolts will come with a pre-applied threadlocker on them.

Is it fair to presume that GM will continue to have similar engine problems now that the company has changed over to new power plants? You bet. As long as insane supplier price-cutting continues, car owners will end up paying for GM's folly.

compartment fires; front harness wires overheat; excessive current load from fuel pump may burn the ignition block wire terminal; inhalation injuries caused by the melting of the wiring harness plastic; electrically heated seat burned the driver's back; the connection that goes to the brake pedal piston collapsed, causing total brake failure; chronic stalling; engine sputters, hesitates; Service Engine and Battery lights come on (dealer unable to correct problem); when traction control is activated, wheel slip computer is also activated and security system kills the engine and prevents it from being restarted; driver-side wheel fell off; vehicle jerks when passing over rough pavement; car rolls back at a stop; excessive steering wheel vibration; excessive front-end vibration; fuel sloshes in tank when accelerating or stopping; brake rotors had to be replaced at 7,500 km; popping sound upon stopping, starting, and turning; transmission line broke and poured fluid all over the road; transmission centre support bearing was put in backwards, causing the transmission to fail; left and right control arm, lower control arm, ball joint, and steering failure; the rubber seal on the windows, which sometimes acts as a squeegee when lowering and raising the window, has been removed with a new design, which allows road salt to enter and short-circuit the window mechanism; and front driver-side windshield wiper doesn't clean the windshield completely. *Monte Carlo:* Engine cradle mounting welds came apart from the steering gear, and driver's and passenger's seat belts tighten up progressively to the point where they are extremely uncomfortable. *Century:* Sudden brake failure; car rolls backward when stopped in gear on an incline; constant reflection of curved dashboard in windshield with or without sunlight; front-seat head restraints won't stay in raised position; vent behind shifter handle becomes very hot when heater is on; gearshift lever continually sticks; water leaks onto the interior carpet; air dam deflector on the front of the vehicle is mounted too low and hits the road on dips; defective radio volume control; and horn is hard to find. *Grand Prix:* Chronic stalling; false airbag deployment; airbag failed to deploy; seatbacks designed with an inertia lock that only locks when braking aggressively, allowing unoccupied seatback to flop around and distract driver; ABS failure; prematurely worn rear brake pads create excessive metal-to-metal grinding noise; wheel lug nuts and bolts sheared off, causing wheel to fall off; windshield wipers malfunction; windshield wiper system freezes up in cold weather; lap and shoulder seat belts become twisted when reaching up and pulling down from the guide loop; cruise control suddenly engaged on its own and wouldn't release; sometimes cruise control causes the vehicle to suddenly accelerate and then slow down; engine coolant won't siphon back into radiator; and right door speaker and dash rattling. *Regal:* Vehicle was on a medium incline, with the ignition on and the shift indicator in the Drive position, when driver took foot off the brake pedal and the vehicle rolled backward; excessive shaking on smooth roads; audio speaker failure; loose power steering; and passenger-side airbag cover came loose.

 ## Road Performance

Pro: Emergency handling: Above average, thanks to standard traction control. **Steering:** Precise and predictable. **Acceleration/torque:** The V6 engines produce sufficient power for smooth acceleration and work well with the 4-speed automatic transmission, but could use more high-speed torque. For extended highway use, you'll find the 3.9L power plant better suited to your needs. Some torque steer is evident with the new V8, however, it seems to be easily handled. **Transmission:** The automatic transmission is quiet and smooth under most conditions. **Routine handling:** Handling and ride are better than average owing to recent suspension and steering refinements. **Braking:** Disc/drum, disc/disc; above average braking.

Con: The automatic 4-speed transmission is sometimes slow to downshift and the Overdrive is clunky; these cars cry out for a 5-speed automatic gearbox.

GRAND PRIX, IMPALA, LACROSSE/ALLURE, MONTE CARLO

List Price (negotiable)	Residual Values (months)			
	24	36	48	60
Grand Prix: $25,885 (23%)	$19,500	$14,500	$12,000	$ 8,500
Impala LS: $24,685 (23%)	$20,500	$16,000	$13,500	$10,500
Allure CX: $26,295 (21%)	$20,500	$15,500	$14,000	$11,000
Monte Carlo: $24,685 (23%)	$20,500	$16,500	$13,500	$11,000

All ratings on a numbered scale where ⑤ is good and ❶ is bad. See page 153–154 for a more detailed description.

SAFETY FEATURES			CRASHWORTHINESS		
	STD.	OPT.			
Anti-lock brakes (4W)	✓	✓	Head restraints F/R	1	1
Seat belt pretensioners F/R	✓	—	Grand Prix	3	1
Side airbags	✓	✓	Visibility F/R	5	3
Stability control	—	✓	Crash protection (front) D/P	5	5
Traction control	✓	✓	Grand Prix	5	4
			Impala	5	5
			Crash protection (side) F/R	3	3
			Monte Carlo	3	4
			Impala	4	4
			Crash protection (offset)	4	—
			Rollover	4	—

BONNEVILLE, LESABRE, PARK AVENUE, ULTRA (2005) ★★★

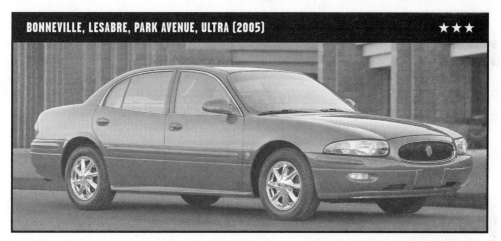

The Buick LeSabre.

RATING: Average. They aren't very fuel-efficient, but generous discounting has made them bargains. So, how much gas can you buy with an $8,000 discount? **Strong points:** Great powertrain performance; comfortable ride; and plush interior. *Bonneville:* Terrific styling; a number of powertrain choices; and rear-seat-to-trunk pass-through. *LeSabre:* Nice array of useful standard equipment at an affordable base price, but costs go up quickly as the options grow. *Park Avenue:* Quiet running; plenty of passenger and cargo room. Rear seating is a bit better than in the LeSabre. Low trunk liftover. **Weak points:** Fuel-thirsty; poor-quality mechanical and body components. The suspension is on the soft side; the cars are a bit jittery on rough roads and handling isn't all that responsive. *Bonneville:* Some torque-steer on the SSEi; braking sometimes hard to modulate; lots of wind and road noise; cramped seating for five; uncomfortable rear seating for the middle passenger; insufficient rear headroom for tall passengers; rear bench seat lacks

TECHNICAL DATA

POWERTRAIN (FRONT-DRIVE)

Engines: 3.8L V6 (205 hp) • 3.8L V6 (240 hp); Transmission: 4-speed auto.

DIMENSION/CAPACITY (LESABRE)

Passengers: 2/3; Wheelbase: 112 in.; H: 57/L: 200/W: 73.5 in.; Headroom F/R: 5.0/4.5 in.; Legroom F/R: 40.5/27.5 in.; Cargo volume: 18 cu. ft.; Fuel tank: 70L/regular; Load capacity: 1,075 lb.; Tow limit: 1,000 lb.; Turning circle: 42 ft.; Weight: 3,640 lb.

support; and the tacky-looking dash isn't well laid out. *LeSabre:* Climate controls aren't particularly user-friendly and not all gauges can be easily read. Rear seating is squeezed for three. Cushion is both too low and too soft to provide confident, supportive seating. Trunk hinges intrude into storage area. *Park Avenue:* Ponderous handling caused partly by a mediocre suspension and over-assisted steering with the base model; obstructed rear visibility; hard braking accompanied by severe nosedive; and interior gauges and controls aren't easily deciphered or accessed. Front bench seat is too narrow. Ultra requires premium fuel. **New for 2006:** All gone this year. The LeSabre is replaced by the Lucerne (see page 207).

OVERVIEW: Full-sized luxury-sedan aficionados love the flush glass, wrap-around windshield and bumpers, and clean body lines that make for an aerodynamic, pleasing appearance. But these cars are more than a pretty package; they provide lots of room, luxury, style, and—dare I say it—performance. Plenty of power is available with the 205-hp 3.8L V6 engine and the 240-hp supercharged version of the same power plant. It does 0–100 km/h in under 9 seconds—impressive, considering the heft of these vehicles—and improves low- and mid-range throttle response. Power is transmitted to the front wheels through an electronically controlled transmission that features "free-wheeling" clutches designed to eliminate abrupt gear changes. Although the Park Avenue is a bit larger and more expensive than the Bonneville and LeSabre, its mechanicals, performance, and overall reliability are quite similar to its smaller brethren. The Ultra version comes with a supercharged engine, StabiliTrak, larger 17-inch wheels, lower-profile tires, and a plushier interior.

COST ANALYSIS: Get a discounted 2005 model, if you can find one. **Best alternatives:** The Ford Mercury Grand Marquis, the Infiniti I30, and the Lexus ES 330. **Options:** Try to find a leftover with side airbags and traction control. **Rebates:** $7,000+ **Delivery/PDI:** $1,150. **Depreciation:** Faster than average. **Insurance cost:** Higher than average. **Parts supply/cost:** Parts aren't hard to find, but they can be pricey (particularly the supercharged engine components). **Annual maintenance cost:** Higher than average. **Warranty:** Bumper-to-bumper 3 years/60,000 km; rust perforation 5 years/160,000 km. **Supplementary warranty:** It'll come in handy going into the fourth year. **Highway/city fuel economy:** 7.8–12.4L/100 km; 7.7–13.2L/100 km with the High Output engine. The supercharged V6 sips fuel, unlike the V8-equipped competition.

Quality/Reliability/Safety

Pro: Quality control: Average. **Warranty performance:** Better than average. **Safety:** A personalized vehicle security system disables the starting and fuel systems if a non-matching key is used. Rear shoulder belts have a strap to pull the belt away from the neck of small passengers and children. Right-side mirror tilts down when Reverse is engaged. Safety belts mount to the outboard front seats for better neck protection.

Con: Reliability: Mediocre. **Owner-reported problems:** Engine, transmission, brake, and electronic module malfunctions. This 2003 LeSabre owner found out that GM's intake manifold fix was no fix at all:

> I recently received a letter from GM stating that there may be a problem with coolant leaks around gaskets at the upper intake manifold or at the lower intake manifold which might "cause high engine temperatures." The letter says it is a "voluntary customer satisfaction program." The suggested fix is to take the vehicle in to the local dealer and have them change some of the fasteners and then "add cooling system sealant" to the radiator. It seems to me that putting cooling system sealant in a brand new car (and thus reducing the life of the radiator) is an unacceptable fix for a possible gasket problem. I would think that the company needs to replace the intake manifold gaskets instead, if they are the faulty part. However, when I called the number that GM supplied, they said that they would not replace the gasket and that if we did not have the repair done as stated in their letter and the gasket subsequently failed after the warranty period was over, we would have to pay the full cost of the repairs.

Service bulletin problems: *Bonneville and LeSabre:* Firm shift, shudder; grinding, growling while in Park; rear seatback trim loose or sagging (LeSabre); and inoperative front heated seat. **NHTSA safety complaints:** *Bonneville:* Defogger was activated and fire ignited; fire erupted in the rear deck speaker; and the sun washes out gauge readings. *LeSabre:* Engine intake manifold failure; engine surging while driving on the highway; brake pedal goes almost to the floor without stopping the vehicle; trunk lid fell and struck driver's head; improper headlight illumination; and horn is difficult to activate owing to the hand pressure required. *Park Avenue:* Front outer tie-rod end failure (yet they are said to be lubricated for life).

Road Performance

Pro: Acceleration/torque: The 3.8L V6 engine is competent, quiet, and smooth running, with lots of low-end torque. Impressively fast with the supercharged engine (0–100 km/h: 8 seconds). **Transmission:** The F31 electronic 4-speed transmission works imperceptibly. Cruise control is much smoother without all those annoying downshifts we've learned to hate in GM cars. **Routine handling:** Acceptably predictable, though quite slow with variable-assist power steering and shocks that are a bit firmer than usual. Body roll has been reduced thanks to the retuned suspension. With its stiffer suspension, the Ultra performs well on winding roads, while the softly sprung Park Avenue is best for city use. **Emergency handling:** Fairly quick and sure-footed. **Braking:** Good braking with or without ABS (100–0 km/h: 41 m).

Con: Acceleration/torque: Acceleration isn't breathtaking with the base 3.8L engine; at higher revs torque falls off quickly. **Steering:** Power steering is a bit vague at highway speeds. Panic braking causes considerable nosediving, which compromises handling.

BONNEVILLE, LESABRE, PARK AVENUE, ULTRA

List Price (very negotiable)   **Residual Values** (months)

	24	36	48	60
Bonneville SE: $33,920 (26%)	$24,000	$18,000	$14,000	$12,000
LeSabre Custom: $34,710 (27%)	$25,500	$19,500	$15,500	$13,500
Park Avenue: $47,610 (30%)	$34,000	$27,000	$23,000	$18,000
Ultra: $53,210 (30%)	$37,000	$31,000	$26,000	$22,000

SAFETY FEATURES	STD.	OPT.	CRASHWORTHINESS		
			Head restraints F/R	5	5
			Park Avenue	1	1
Anti-lock brakes	✓	—	Visibility F/R	5	3
Seat belt pretensioners F/R	✓	—	Crash protection (front) D/P	4	5
Side airbags	✓	✓	Crash protection (side) F/R	4	4
Traction control	✓	✓	Crash protection (offset)	5	—
			Rollover	5	—

CORVETTE ★★★

RATING: Average; a brawny, bulky sport coupe that's slowly evolving into a more refined machine. But quality control continues to be subpar and safety-related engine and brake failures are legion. The Z06 delivers more performance-per-dollar than the Dodge Viper, which costs about $20,000 more, or the Ford GT, a speedster that will cost almost double the Corvette's price. Unfortunately, it also delivers lots of suspension kickback, numb steering, and an overpowering amount of road, engine, and transmission noise that forces you to yell at your passenger while cruising on the highway at 100 km/h. Overall, get the quieter and less tempermental base Corvette; it delivers the same cachet for lots less money.

All ratings on a numbered scale where 5 is good and 1 is bad. See page 153–154 for a more detailed description.

The Z06 is the fastest Corvette the company has ever produced. It redefines high-performance like Lance Armstrong redefines a bike ride.

Strong points: Powerful powertrain; easy handling; user-friendly instruments and controls; and lots of standard convenience features. **Weak points:** Poorly performing "skip shift" manual gearbox; unproven 6-speed automatic transmission; hard, jolting ride (Z51 or Z06 suspension); vague steering; limited rear visibility; no side airbags; inadequate storage space; poor-quality powertrain and brake components and mediocre fit and finish; excessive cabin noise; and cabin amenities and materials not up to the competition. No crashworthiness or rollover data, and seat belt pretensioners aren't offered. **New for 2006:** The standard Corvette gets an optional 6-speed automatic transmission with sequential paddle shifts. After a one-year absence, a more powerful and better-performing Z06 returns with a new high-performance 505-hp, 7.0L V8—a hundred horses more than the previous engine. Estimated Z06 production: 10,000 cars.

OVERVIEW: More than a million Corvettes have been sold since they were introduced in 1953, with an estimated 600,000 still on the roads. The car's peak year was 1984, when over 84,000 coupes and convertibles were sold in North America for about a third of today's price.

Completely revamped last year with the emphasis on a new body, an enhanced interior, and more horse-power, it's no surprise that changes are minimal on the 2006 Corvette. Standard models come with a 400-hp 6.0L V8 mated to a 6-speed manual or optional automatic transmission; Keyless Access with push-button start; large tires and wheels (18-inch front, 19-inch rear); HID xenon lighting; power hatch pull-down; AM/FM CD/MP3 player with seven

TECHNICAL DATA

POWERTRAIN (REAR-DRIVE)

Engines: 6.0L V8 (400 hp) • 7.0L V8 (505 hp); Transmissions: 6-speed man. • 6-speed auto.

DIMENSION/CAPACITY

Passengers: 2/1; Wheelbase: 105.7 in.; H: 49.1/L: 174.6/W: 72.6 in.; Headroom: 3.0 in.; Legroom: 42.7 in.; Cargo volume: 13.3 cu. ft.; Fuel tank: 68L/premium; Tow limit: N/A; Load capacity: N/A; Turning circle: 39 ft.; Weight: 3,179 lb.

speakers and in-dash six-CD changer; and heated seats. The base design is more flowing and muscular than previous stylings.

Z06 returns

Although not quite as fast as the Dodge Viper, this is the fastest (0–100 km/h in 3.6 to 4.2 seconds) and priciest ($89,900) model found in the Corvette lineup. It's also the lightest Z06 yet, thanks to the magic of Detroit re-engineering. Instead of just adding iron and components to carry extra weight, GM has reinforced the rear axle and 6-speed clutch, installed coolers everywhere (oh, my!), adopted a dry-sump oil system to keep the engine well oiled when cornering, and added wider wheels and larger, heat dissipating brakes. These improvements added about 50 kg of weight, which was trimmed by using cast-magnesium in the chassis struc-ture and installing lighter carbon-fibre floorboards and front fenders. Net result: a monster 'Vette that is rated for 300+ km/h and weighs about 75 kg less than the base model, more than 100 kg less than the all-aluminum Ferrari F430, and half a kilo more than Porsche's $450,000 carbon-fibre Carrera GT.

To be honest, the Z06 chassis isn't very communicative to the driver, so the car doesn't inspire as much driving confidence as does the European competition, although it does feature standard stability control for when you get too frisky.

COST ANALYSIS: Get a second-series 2005 base model for the many upgrades; however, if you want the *magna cum laude* Z06, you will have to dig deep into your billfold. Keep in mind that premium fuel and astronomical insurance rates will further drive up your operating costs. **Best alternatives:** Other sporty models worth considering: the Dodge Viper and the Porsche 911 or Boxster. The Nissan 350Z looks good on paper, but its quality problems carried over year after year make it a risky buy. **Options:** Remember, performance options rarely increase performance to the degree promised by the seller; the more performance options you buy, the less comfort you'll have, the more things can go wrong, and the more simple repairs can increase in complexity. Run-flat tires from Goodyear are an excellent investment. Forget about the head-up instrument display that projects speed and other data onto the windshield; it's annoyingly distracting and you'll end up turning it off. **Rebates:** The Corvette is so popular that GM normally doesn't have to offer rebates to boost sales, but there will be some discounting late in 2005 as sales slacken. **Delivery/PDI:** $1,300. **Depreciation:** Much slower than average, but nowhere near the resale prices promised by salespeople. **Insurance cost:** Astronomical. **Parts supply/cost:** Good availability, but parts are pricey. **Annual maintenance cost:** Higher than average. **Warranty:** Bumper-to-bumper 3 years/60,000 km; rust perforation 6 years/160,000 km. **Supplementary warranty:** A smart idea to protect you from drivetrain failures. **Highway/city fuel economy:** 8.8–14.1L/100 km with the base engine and an automatic transmission.

Quality/Reliability/Safety

Pro: Key-controlled lockout feature discourages joy riding by cutting engine power in half. Both Corvette versions are equipped with an impressively effective PASS KEY theft-deterrent system that uses a resistor pellet in the ignition to disable the starter and fuel system when the key code doesn't match the ignition lock. **Safety:** The tires have built-in low-pressure sensors that warn the driver by way of a light on the centre console. Run-flat tires eliminate the need for a spare tire.

Con: Warranty performance: Below average. **Quality control:** Below average, especially body construction. **Reliability:** Spotty. The Corvette's sophisticated electronic and powertrain components have low tolerance for real-world conditions. Expect lots of visits to the dealer's repair bays. Engine and brake failures routinely put Corvette occupants' lives in danger. **Owner-reported problems:** Excessive oil consumption; harsh transmission shifts; 2–4 band and 3–4 clutch damage; rear differential and transmission pump leaks; noisy transmission engagement; light brake drag; brake light remains lit; B-pillar wind noise; and dash reflects upon the windshield. Electronically controlled suspension systems have been plagued with glitches over the past several years. Squeaks and rattles are caused by the car's structural deficiencies. The car was built as a convertible, and therefore has too much body flex. Servicing the different sophisticated fuel-injection systems isn't easy, even (especially) for GM mechanics. **Service bulletin problems:** Engine knocking or lifter noise; cracked or broken transmission case; inoperative AC control; difficulty refuelling; seatback twisting; deck lid not flush with left-hand quarter panel; poor radio reception; and exhaust system noise. **NHTSA safety complaints:** *2005 models:* Sudden engine failure caused by defective crank pulley; brake-line failure:

> Less than 24 hours after purchasing the Corvette, the crank pulley "came loose" and the car threw its serpentine belt (learned after the incident) while driving on a crowded interstate. The first indication of a problem was when the driver information console (DIC) displayed a malfunction with the vehicle's charging system that needed service. Voltage displayed on DIC dropped quickly in .1 volt increments until roughly 11 volts were displayed. Then, the car became increasingly unresponsive to driver input for steering and throttle. Brakes felt "mushy" but continued to respond to driver input. Although the dash displayed a frightening number of error messages and alarms, the occupants had no idea what was the matter with the vehicle. Trying to cross five lanes of packed freeway traffic to get to a safe breakdown area, in a car that appears to have lost its mind and is spraying antifreeze all over the highway, could have easily resulted in injury or death. We were very fortunate that we did not cause an accident. Crank pulley, bolt(s), serpentine belt, and underhood insulation (damaged by flying belt) were replaced. A friction washer was added behind the crank pulley on the advice of GM tech support.

Car broke down again with the same problem. GM has ordered the motor replaced and the dealer is awaiting parts. This is not an isolated failure, there are other IS2 engines breaking down because of this crank pulley problem.

•

My 3-day-old Corvette shredded its serpentine belt, overheated, and lost its steering. Car had 300 miles [480 km] on it. From what I have been reading on Corvette Forum, this was not an isolated incident but has been occurring in too many new Corvettes. This problem could affect the operation of the vehicle as it not only affected the cooling system but more importantly, the steering and braking. To make matters worse, the repair of this problem was failing on many cars, and they were experiencing it for the second and third time.

•

Seven to eight thousand Chevrolet Corvettes built in late 2004 are in a batch being watched by GM because there have been dozens of instances of the crankshaft pulley belt backing out and allowing the pulley to loosen or fall off. When that happens, the car looses power steering and the rest of the functions run off the belts. The belt and pulley can also cause other damage under the hood. Production number Corvettes from over 3,000 to over 11,000 are in the group identified as problematic. Chevrolet has released a Technical Service Bulletin, TSB No. 05-06-01-001a, but says it cannot help buyers until after a failure. I own a Corvette in that group, and I fear that I can't trust the car to perform safely. I belong to several Corvette-related Internet forums, and I get reports of new failures every day. There are dozens of failures reported by members of just one forum. The failures have been occurring since November 2004.

•

A brakeline ruptured on my vehicle while I was driving it at 55 mph [100 km/h]. I needed to exit an interstate, and the car came to a halt very slowly, the remaining brakeline working much less effectively, of course. No warning light came on. After I stopped, clouds of pure white smoke billowed from the hood and into the passenger compartment. I assume this was brake fluid contacting a hot surface. There is some doubt whether a dealer can re-install a brake line safely and effectively: See the discussion at *forums.corvetteforum.com/showthread.php?t=1113860&forum_id=74* as the forum discussion indicates, this has happened to other new Corvette owners. No one knows, at this point, how to fix my Corvette and when it will be fixed. Had I had to stop short, I would have had a serious accident, as one of my brakelines had failed with no warning on a brand new car.

Right rear axle suddenly snapped in half. *Earlier models:* Catalytic converter caught fire; when fuel tank is full, fuel leaks from the top of the vent; steering wheel locked up upon start-up; steering wheel locked up in Reverse gear and was corrected only when transmission was put into Park and key re-inserted into the ignition; "Service Column Lock" indication has been a common problem; chronic stalling and engine surging; fuel-injector failures cause vehicle to shudder and stall; engine dies while driving in the rain and brakes don't work; brakes drag and lock up; brake pedal doesn't spring back; overheated rotors; car is nearly uncontrollable at time of brake lock-up; early failure of the engine serpentine belt and tensioner; intermittent electrical problems degrade computer operation; if one wheel loses traction, the throttle closes, starving the engine; excessive cabin heat, even with AC set to Max; driver's seat moves while driving; warped trunk door; seat belts twist easily and tend to pull down uncomfortably against the shoulder; passenger seat belt jams and won't extend or retract; smelly fumes enter the cabin, causing watery eyes and dizziness; dash reflects onto the windshield; the glass rear-view window limits rear vision; and front and rear wheel weights fly off the wheels.

 ## Road Performance

Pro: Acceleration/torque: Gobs of torque and horsepower with a top speed of 277 km/h (172 mph). Base engine is fast (0–100 km/h: 5 seconds), but the Z06 is faster (0–100 km/h: 3.9 seconds). **Transmission:** The 6-speed gearbox performs well in all gear ranges and makes shifting smooth, with short throws and easy entry into all gears. **Emergency handling:** Acceptable, but you don't always feel you're in control. Enhanced side-slip angle control helps to prevent skidding and provides better traction control. No oversteer, wheel spinning, breakaway rear ends, or nasty surprises. **Steering:** Predictable, though a bit numb. **Routine handling:** Above average. The car is so low that its front air dam scrapes over the smallest rise in the road, but it still gives no-surprise handling and responds quickly to the throttle. The Bilstein FX-3 Selective Ride Control suspension can be pre-set to Touring, Sport, or Performance. **Braking:** Disc/disc; better than average. The ABS-vented disc brakes are easy to modulate and fade-free.

Con: Suspension's ride is too firm for some, and the Z06 suspension is too firm for many. Car's jerky suspension and vague steering don't inspire confidence. True, the 6-speed manual does provide quicker acceleration and better fuel economy, but it's not particularly user-friendly. This is one large and heavy sports car, and its weight compromises its fuel economy. A lack of sound-deadening material is a serious oversight.

CORVETTE

List Price (negotiable)	Residual Values (months)			
	24	36	48	60
Corvette: $67,805 (30%)	$51,000	$41,000	$34,000	$26,000
Convertible: $79,905 (30%)	$58,000	$49,000	$39,000	$32,000

SAFETY FEATURES			CRASHWORTHINESS		
	STD.	OPT.			
Anti-lock brakes	✓	—	Head restraints F/R	③	③
Seat belt pretensioners F/R	—	—	Visibility F/R	③	②
Stability control	✓	—			
Traction control	✓	—			

DTS, DEVILLE ★★★

The Cadillac DTS.

RATING: Average. As Cadillac reinvents itself in a futile attempt to lure younger buyers, its cars are looking less and less like traditional Caddies and more like LEGO toys. One gets the impression that Cadillac designers aren't sure of their market, so they're trying angular, slab-panel styling just to be different. They are also loading up the cars with every gadget imaginable to project an image of daring innovation. **Strong points:** *DTS:* Brisk acceleration with the large V8, and handling that is fairly good for a car of this size. Impeccable road manners and a comfortable, spacious interior. The improved chassis, suspension, and running gear result in crisper handling and better roadholding than we have seen with the DeVille. **Weak points:** Excessive torque steer (twisting so much that the steering wheel is jerked to one side) when accelerating is remedied via the traction control system by reducing engine power and selectively applying the brakes (feeling confident?). Body and mechanical components aren't top quality and servicing can be complicated. **New for 2006:** A new name (DTS), a restyled exterior and interior, improved powertrain and suspension refinements. This year's base engine has been tuned for quicker acceleration and greater peak torque than last year's version. The optional 291-hp Northstar powerplant doesn't add any torque, but it does produce higher revs and more peak horsepower—in other words, less fuel economy. But who buys a Cadillac to save fuel?

TECHNICAL DATA

POWERTRAIN (FRONT-DRIVE)

Engines: 4.6L V8 (275 hp) • 4.6L V8 (291 hp); Transmission: 4-speed auto.

DIMENSION/CAPACITY

Passengers: 3/3; Wheelbase: 115 in.; H: 56.7/L: 207/W: 74 in.; Headroom F/R: 4.5/3.0 in.; Legroom F/R: 41.5/3.0 in.; Cargo volume: 19.1 cu. ft.; Fuel tank: 70L/premium; Tow limit: 2,000 lb.; Load capacity: 1,085 lb.; Turning circle: 40.2 ft.; Weight: 3,984 lb.

OVERVIEW: Cadillac's largest car (the Escalade is an SUV), the 2006 DTS is a $50,000 warmed-over version of the full-sized luxury DeVille (dimensions are little-changed). Hyped as a "new" Caddy sedan, it comes with fresh body lines, a redesigned interior, improved running gear, and suspension refinements. It still carries a 4.6L V8 4-speed automatic transmission and rear self-levelling suspension. Standard features include ABS, traction control, front torso side airbags and head-protecting curtain side airbags, a tire-pressure monitor, remote engine starter, xenon headlights, GM OnStar assistance, and leather upholstery. Offered as a single model, with no other interior, the DTS has a number of option packages (including a front bench seat), and two levels of Northstar V8 power. For example, a Performance Package option gives the base 275-hp engine 16 more horses, a firmer suspension with auto-adjusting shock absorbers, and larger wheels. Other options include a front bench seat that increases passenger capacity to six from five, anti-skid, front and rear obstacle detection, navigation system, satellite radio, cruise control designed to maintain a safe following distance, heated/cooled front seats, and a heated steering wheel.

Owner-reported problems: A persistent rotten-egg odour in the cabin; electrical failures causing hard starts; poor idling; constant stalling; right rear wheel fell off because of a broken axle; tire jack collapse; side-door airbag deployed while driving; airbag light stays lit; brake failures; faulty tire-pressure sensors; frequent tire blowouts; turn signals don't self-cancel; distorted windshields; front-seat shoulder strap crosses at the neck; and seat belts are too short. **Service bulletin problems:** Slipping transmission; steering and seat vibration; wind noise from right door; rear suspension noise; and poor radio reception. **NHTSA safety complaints:** Sudden, unintended acceleration with no brakes; loss of brakes; jack collapsed; chronic stalling; power steering failure; power window closed on child's head; sun visor is too large and exterior mirrors are mounted too high; and radio volume may suddenly increase fivefold without warning.

DTS, DEVILLE (2005)

List Price (very negotiable)	Residual Values (months)			
	24	36	48	60
Base: $52,680 (30%)	$40,000	$32,000	$27,000	$24,000

SAFETY FEATURES (DEVILLE)			CRASHWORTHINESS (DEVILLE)		
	STD.	OPT.	Head restraints F/R	❷	❷
Anti-lock brakes (4W)	✓	—	Visibility F/R	❺	❺
Seat belt pretensioners F/R	✓	—	Crash protection (front) D/P	❹	❹
Side airbags	✓	—	Crash protection (side) F/R	❹	❹
Stability control	✓	✓	Rollover	❺	—
Traction control	✓	✓			

ASTRO, SAFARI (2005) ★★★★

RATING: Above Average. Gone and sadly missed, these were GM's first minivans, launched several decades ago. More mini-truck than minivan, this duo is well suited for cargo hauling and light towing. Believe it or not, these simple minivans look quite good when compared to the problem-plagued GM front-drives, Chrysler and Ford minivans, and the more-expensive Asian competition. (VW? Not even in the running.) They have fewer safety-related problems reported to the government, are easy to repair, and cost little to acquire. Stay away from the unreliable AWD models; they're much more expensive to repair and not very durable.

The GMC Safari.

Strong points: Brisk acceleration; trailer-towing capability; lots of passenger room and cargo space; well laid-out instrument panel with easy-to-read gauges. Very low ground clearance enhances this minivan's handling, but precludes most off-roading. Good brakes. Rock-bottom used prices, and average reliability and quality control. **Weak points:** No side airbags or traction control. Tall drivers may find the pedals too close, and an obtrusive engine makes for very narrow front footwells. Difficult entry and exit because of the high step-up and intruding wheelwell. Harsh ride, limited front seat room, interior noise levels rise sharply at highway speeds, and excessive fuel consumption made worse by the AWD option. **New for 2006:** Nothing; 2005 is the last model year.

OVERVIEW: More a utility truck than a comfortable minivan, these boxy, rear-drive vehicles are built on a reworked S-10 pickup chassis. As such, they offer uninspiring handling, trouble-prone mechanical and body components, and relatively high fuel consumption. Both Astro and Safari come in a choice of either cargo or passenger van. The cargo van is used either commercially or as an inexpensive starting point for a fully customized vehicle. The Safari is identical to the Astro, except for a slightly higher base price.

The engine is a 4.3L 190-hp V6. Dual airbags are standard. Also offered are an optional rear door and rear bench seats that can be adjusted fore and aft. Carried-over standard features are a 4-speed automatic transmission with Overdrive, power steering, a front stabilizer bar, and four-wheel anti-lock disc brakes. All-wheel drive with a single-speed transfer case with viscous-controlled differential (no switches to throw) is available on the regular length and extended models. The Sport package includes louvred rear-quarter body panels, two-tone paint, foglights, and a front air dam. With the right options, and when equipped with heavy-duty suspension, the Astro and Safari have the advantage of being versatile cargo haulers. In fact, Astro's 2,500 kg (5,500 lb.) trailer-towing capability is 900 kg (2,000 lb.) more than that of the front-drive Chevrolet Uplander.

COST ANALYSIS: Get a heavily discounted 2005 leftover, or a cheaper cargo model (about $2,000 less than a passenger version). **Best alternatives:** Front-drive minivans made by Honda and Mazda have better handling, and are more reliable and economical people-carriers; unfortunately, they lack the Astro's considerable grunt, essential for cargo hauling and trailer towing. **Options:** Integrated child safety seats, rear AC, and rear Dutch doors. Be wary of AWD; it costs $3,000 more than the regular passenger version, exacts a high fuel penalty, and is unreliable. **Rebates:** About $3,000–$5,000 on all models, plus discounting. **Delivery/PDI:** $1,150. **Depreciation:** Average. **Insurance cost:** Slightly higher than average. **Annual maintenance cost:** Less than average. Any garage can repair these rear-drive minivans. **Parts supply/cost:** Good supply of cheap parts. A large contingent of independent parts suppliers keeps repair costs down. Parts are less expensive than for other minivans and aren't likely to dry up after the Astro and Safari are taken off the market. **Warranty:** Bumper-to-bumper 3 years/60,000 km; rust perforation 6 years/160,000 km. **Supplementary warranty:** A toss-up. Individual repairs won't cost a lot, but those nickels and dimes can add up. A powertrain-only warranty is a wise choice. **Highway/city fuel economy:** 10.6–14.6L/100 km for 4×2 and 11.3–15.3L/100 km with AWD.

TECHNICAL DATA

POWERTRAIN (REAR-DRIVE)
Engine: 4.3L V6 (190 hp); Transmissions: 4-speed auto. OD • AWD

DIMENSION/CAPACITY
Passengers: 2/3/3; Wheelbase: 111.2 in.; H: 75/L: 189.8/W: 77.5 in.; Headroom F/R1/R2: 5.0/4.0/4.0 in.; Legroom F/R1/R2: 41.6/36.5/38.5 in.; Cargo volume: 98 cu. ft.; Fuel tank: 95L/regular; Tow limit: 5,500 lb.; Load capacity: N/A; Turning circle: 40.5 ft.; Weight: 3,964 lb.

Quality/Reliability/Safety

Pro: Quality control: Average. **Reliability:** Average; most of the Astro and Safari's defects are easy to diagnose, leading to a minimum of downtime in the repair bay. **Warranty performance:** Average. Four-wheel disc brakes are an important improvement, considering this minivan's poor braking performance in the past.

Con: Owner-reported problems: Automatic transmission deficiencies; rear axle whine; steering, electrical system, heating, and defrosting system malfunctions; premature brake wear; faulty suspension components; and glitch-prone sliding doors. **Service bulletin problems:** Hard starts, rough idle, and intermittent misfiring. A transfer-case shudder can be fixed inexpensively. Automatic transmission malfunctions may be caused by debris in the transmission. Delayed gear engagement. GM says that a chronic driveline clunk can't be silenced and is a normal characteristic of its vehicles (yikes!). Silence a booming noise heard during engine warm-up by installing an exhaust dampener assembly. Right rear door handle breakage and tips for silencing a suspension pop. **NHTSA safety complaints/safety:** Rear driver-side window exploded; sudden acceleration; chronic stalling; hard starts; cranks, but would not start because of broken electrical connection; sudden total electrical failure, especially when going into Reverse; airbag failed to deploy; harsh, delayed shifting; on a slight incline, sliding door will unlatch and slam shut; driver's cargo door latch and hinge slipped off and door flew open; loss of power steering; sudden steering and brake loss when power-steering pump shaft snapped; when applying brakes, pedal stiffens and vehicle surges ahead; extended stopping distance with ABS, especially in rainy weather; brake pedal set too high; differential in transfer case locked up while driving; defective axle seals; vehicle rolls backward on an incline while in Drive (dealer adjusted transfer case to no avail); front passenger seat belt locked up; fuel gauge failure; faulty AC vents; intermittent windshield wiper failure; and water can be trapped inside the wheels and freeze, causing the wheels to be out of balance.

Road Performance

Pro: Acceleration/torque: The V6 engine is more than adequate for most driving chores and has plenty of reserve power for trailer towing and heavy hauling (0–100 km/h: 11.8 seconds). **Braking:** Disc/disc; excellent braking.

Con: The V6 is thirsty in city driving. **Emergency handling:** Ponderous, but still fairly predictable. **Steering:** Very light power steering, but still handles and manoeuvres like a large truck. **Transmission:** Clunky automatic transmission. **Routine handling:** Handling isn't very precise; overall behaviour is competent but sloppy. A heavy-duty suspension will improve both ride and handling. Busy, harsh ride caused by stiff springs.

ASTRO, SAFARI

List Price (very negotiable)	**Residual Values** (months)			
	24	**36**	**48**	**60**
Base: $28,895 (30%)	$19,000	$16,000	$13,000	$11,000

SAFETY FEATURES	**STD.**	**OPT.**
Anti-lock brakes (4W)	✓	—
Seat belt pretensioners F/R	✓	—

CRASHWORTHINESS		
Head restraints F/R	[1]	[1]
Visibility F/R	[5]	[2]
Crash protection (front) D/P	[3]	[4]
Crash protection (side) F/R	[5]	[5]
Crash protection (offset)	[1]	—

MONTANA SV6, RELAY, TERRAZA, UPLANDER ★★

The Buick Terraza.

RATING: Below Average; they may be an acceptable buy if the dealer will throw in a free extended powertrain warranty. These minivans are almost as bad as Ford's Windstar/Freestar and actually make Chrysler's so-so minivans look good. Furthermore, while Honda, Toyota, and Nissan push the envelope in engineering and styling, GM's restyled minivans join the Ford Freestar as also-ran, *pseudo-nouveau* entries. Don't get taken in by GM's "name game"; the biggest difference between these models is price.

TECHNICAL DATA

POWERTRAIN (FRONT-DRIVE)
Engines: 3.5L V6 (200 hp) • 3.9L V6 (240 hp); Transmissions: 4-speed auto. • AWD
DIMENSION/CAPACITY (UPLANDER)
Passengers: 2/2/3; Wheelbase: 112 in.; H: 67.4/L: 205/W: 72.0 in.; Headroom F/R1/R2: 5.0/4.0/3.5 in.; Legroom F/R1/R2: 40.5/26/28 in.; Cargo volume: 75 cu. ft.; Fuel tank: 94.6L/regular; Tow limit: 3,500 lb.; Load capacity: 1,290 lb.; Turning circle: 43 ft.; Weight: 4,380 lb.

This foursome has been downrated this year for the following reasons: They are overpriced when compared with the competition; serious automatic transmission and engine head gasket failures have become chronic occurrences; the base warranty is inadequate to deal with deteriorating reliability; and serious safety defects like sliding doors crushing and injuring children reappear year after year. Of course, Chrysler, Toyota, and Honda minivans have posed similar door dangers, hence *Lemon-Aid*'s admonition that you carefully re-think the need for automatic sliding doors if you're planning on transporting children. **Strong points:** A comfortable ride with the longer versions; acceptable routine handling; good braking; plenty of comfort and convenience features; flexible seating arrangements; good visibility fore and aft; lots of storage bins and compartments; good crash scores; and side airbags added to the 2006s. **Weak points:** Average acceleration with a light load and the 3.5L engine; slow, vague steering; poor emergency handling; unproven AWD; insufficient headroom for tall drivers, and short drivers may find it hard to see where the front ends; low rear seats force passengers into an uncomfortable knees-up position; narrow cabin makes front-to-rear access a bit difficult; seat cushions on the centre and rear bench seats are hard, flat, and too short, and the seatbacks lack sufficient lower back support; cargo may not slide out easily because the rear sill sticks up a few inches; a high number of safety-related failures where sliding door injuries are paramount; engine exhaust manifold defects; and disappointing real world fuel economy. **New for 2006:** A new, optional 240-hp 3.9L V6 and standard second-row side-impact airbags. Terraza replaces last year's 200-hp 3.5L V6 with the 3.9L and adds dual-stage driver and passenger airbags and side-impact airbags for first- and second-row outboard passengers.

OVERVIEW: The front-drive Buick Terraza, Chevrolet Uplander, Pontiac Montana SV6, and Saturn Relay are practically identical versions of the discontinued Venture. Although they have been given an optional 240-hp engine transplant and facelift, there is unfortunately a lot of the old, disappointing Venture that remains with the same suspension, steering, and transmission components. Nevertheless, all four models seat seven passengers and are loaded with standard features like 17-inch wheels, ABS, strut-type front suspension/non-independent rear suspension, an OnStar security system, and dual-stage driver and passenger front airbags. Options include a vehicle stability enhancement system, side-impact airbags, and "smart" front airbags. There's also ample cargo room, thanks to removable second and removable and flat-folding third-row seats.

These minivans have more carlike handling than GM's Astro and Safari. Seats can be folded down flat, creating additional storage space. The extended wheelbase models get more bells and whistles, including optional power slide-open passenger- and driver-side doors.

Cost analysis: Since there is very little difference between the 2005 and 2006 models, go for this year's version, which should have many of the 2005's bugs worked out and sell for about 25 percent less than its $26,620 base price. You'll also get additional passenger protection. **Best alternatives:** Other vehicles worth considering: the Honda Odyssey and the Toyota Sienna. **Options:** Be wary of the AWD option—it's unreliable. Many of these vans are equipped with Firestone and Bridgestone tires—have them removed by the dealer or ask for a $400 rebate.

Installed by the dealer, Sit-N-Lift seats work extremely well. The seat pivots, extends, and lowers to the side, allowing the passenger to get into and out of the vehicle while sitting down. The seats will support passengers weighing up to 135 kg (300 lb.), can be used in any extended-length 1997–2006 GM minivan, don't require new holes for installation, can be removed or replaced with a standard seat prior to trade-in, can be used on leased vehicles, and qualify for GM warranties and special programs.

Integrated child safety seats are generally a good idea, but make sure they can be easily installed and your child can't slip out or get tangled in the straps. Be wary of the power-assisted passenger-side sliding door; it has a reputation as a wrist-breaker and child-crusher. Consider the $235 load-levelling feature—a must-have for front-drive minivans. It keeps the weight on the front wheels, giving you better steering, traction, and braking. Other options that are worth buying: The extended wheelbase version (provides a smoother ride), traction control, power side windows, a firmer suspension, self-sealing tires, and a rear air conditioner, defroster, and heater. The $5,000 (U.S.) Sit-N-Lift electrically powered second seats for the physically challenged have performed well.

Rebates: $5,000 and zero percent financing on all models. **Delivery/PDI:** $1,200. **Depreciation:** Average. **Insurance cost:** Average. **Annual maintenance cost:** Average during the warranty period. Engine, transmission, ABS, and electrical malfunctions cause maintenance costs to soar after the warranty expires. **Parts supply/cost:** Parts are reasonably priced and not hard to find. **Warranty:** Bumper-to-bumper 3 years/60,000 km; powertrain 5 years/100,000 km; rust perforation 6 years/160,000 km. **Supplementary warranty:** A good idea, especially for the powertrain. **Highway/city fuel economy:** 9.3–13.5L/100 km with the 3.5L V6. Drivers claim they get much less.

Quality/Reliability/Safety

Con: Quality control: Below average. Just when it looked like GM had turned the corner with improved quality control, we find major engine and transmission failures returning. Owners decry engine manifold and head gasket defects along with frequent automatic transmission breakdowns and clunky shifting. Fit and finish is gaining the reputation for being "unfit and unfinished," though body components are less rattle-prone. **Reliability:** Below average. **Warranty performance:** Unacceptably bad. **Owner-reported problems:** EGR valve failures, electrical glitches, excessive front brake noise and frequent repairs (rotors and pads), early wheel bearing failure, blurry front windshield, failure-prone AC condensers, assorted body deficiencies, including poor fit and finish, paint peeling and blistering, and roof perforations caused by extensive corrosion (covered by a secret warranty). **Service bulletin problems:** Engine intake manifold leaks; poor engine and automatic transmission operation:

> I just wanted to let you know that after contacting you back in January regarding our 2001 Chevy Venture head gasket problem, I have just received my judgment through the Canadian Arbitration Program.
>
> I used the sample complaint letter as well as the judgment you have posted in the *Ford Canada v. Dufour* court case. This, combined with an avalanche of similar Chevy Venture complaints that are posted on the Internet, helped us to win a $1,700 reimbursement of the $2,200 we were looking for.
>
> The reason for our not receiving the full amount is that the arbitrator stated that GM Canada would have only replaced one head gasket instead of replacing both as we had done, and that a dealer would have supplied us with a car free of charge and therefore did not allow us the car rental expense we incurred.
>
> We are still extremely happy with the results and thank you for your books and website; you have a fan for life.
>
> D.W.

Inability to shift out of Park after installation of Sit-N-Lift device; slipping automatic transmission; transmission shudder, chuggle, hard shifting, and won't downshift; faulty front wheel bearing and assembly; defective catalytic converters that cause a rotten-egg smell in the interior may be replaced free of charge under the emissions warranty; repair tips for a faulty AC compressor; second-row seat belt won't release; static noise from radio speakers; exhaust system rattle or buzz; grinding or growling when in Park on an incline; windshield wind noise; troubleshooting assorted squeaks and rattles; power sliding door binding. Tail light/brake light and circuit board burns out from water intrusion; repair cost is covered by a "goodwill" policy. Roof rusting, leaking, or rust perforation may require a new roof under GM's "Special Policy"; and water in jack compartment. **NHTSA safety complaints:** *2005 models:* Gauge needles don't illuminate when the ignition is turned on; dash lights are dim; vehicle suddenly shuts down on the highway; stability control activates when it shouldn't; horn is difficult to activate (takes both thumbs).

> I was driving on the highway, switching lanes on dry pavement, clear day, and the traction control system or the stability control system engaged causing the vehicle to rapidly decelerate and swerve to the left. It happened to my wife and she called me crying, saying she did not want to drive the car. I did not take her seriously, until she went out of town and the vehicle did the same to me on the highway. This traction control or stability control system has a problem and is a major safety concern. I tried to disengage the system before driving it on the highway to take it to the dealer and it happened again.

•

> The consumer complained about a horn problem. The consumer has to push different spots in order to get horn to blow. It did not blow where the symbols were located on the vehicle. The consumer noticed this...on May 28, 2005. The consumer contacted the dealer, who said that they use the brakes and not the horn.

2005 *Uplander:* Vehicle will stall if it only has half a tank of fuel and is on a hill; excessive swaying and poor handling; power sliding door jammed; door ajar warning bell sounds constantly; flickering headlights and interior lights; actuating bar for windshield wipers cuts into wiring harness; brakes applied to all four wheels without driver pressing the brake pedal. *Earlier models:* Engine surging, stalling; loss of coolant; overheating; two incidents where child's wrist was fractured after elbow and hand caught between the seat and handle; tail lights fail intermittently; door opens and closes on its own while vehicle is underway; door doesn't lock into position, slides shut, and crushes all in its path:

> We are very concerned that another child, or adult, is going to be injured in this van's automatic sliding door. We were curious just how far the 2004 Venture's door would go before it would bounce back open so we put a stuffed animal in the door and hit the auto door close button. I have to say, the stuffed animal did not fare well. We also put a large carrot and a banana in the door, in an attempt to simulate a small child's arm. The carrot was sliced right in half, and the banana was smashed and oozing out of its peel. I will never purchase a Chevrolet Venture after our experience with the van.

Fire ignited under driver's seat; airbag deployed when door was slammed; airbags failed to deploy; windshield suddenly exploded outward while driving with wipers activated; Firestone tire blew out; brakes activate on their own, making it appear as if van is pulling a load; missing bolt caused steering idler arm to fall off; loose fuel tank because of loose bolts/bracket; fuel tank cracked when passing over a tree branch; plastic tube within heating system fell off and wedged behind the accelerator pedal; bracket weld pin that secures the rear split seat sheared off; faulty fuel pump causes chronic stalling; no-starts; surging; sudden acceleration; vehicle suddenly lost power while going uphill, slid back, and stalled; van will roll back while in gear on an incline; Service Engine light comes on constantly; Service Engine light remains on because transmission bearing was assembled backwards in the transmission box; premature transmission failures; power-sliding door has a gap at the base large enough to trap a child; when reversing, the door will not stop; sliding door slams shut on an incline; person's wrist broken when power-sliding door opened; broken sliding door track trim panel; centre rear lap seat belt isn't long enough to secure a rear-facing child safety seat; middle-row passenger-side seat belts jam in the retracted position; front passenger shoulder belt cuts into passenger's neck; children can slide out of the integrated child safety seat; rear seat belts failed to release; rear hatch handle broke, cutting driver's hand; electrical harness failures result in complete electrical shutdown; headlights, interior lights, gauges, and instruments fail intermittently (electrical cluster module is the prime suspect); excess padding around horn makes it difficult to depress horn button in an emergency; frequent windshield wiper motor failures; heater doesn't warm up vehicle sufficiently; antifreeze smell intrudes into the interior; and the weld that holds the lift wheel pin is not adequate to support the weight of the trailer.

 ## Road Performance

Pro: Acceleration/torque: The 3.9L is the best engine choice for smooth and responsive acceleration with good mid-range and top-end power. **Transmission:** The electronically controlled 4-speed automatic transmission usually shifts smoothly and quietly when not under load. **Routine handling:** Average, when equipped with the load-levelling option. **Braking:** Above average.

Con: Emergency handling: Below average. **Steering:** The steering is vague, slow to respond, and takes too much effort. Longer, loaded versions have a smoother ride than the base versions, which tend to be choppier. Excessive body roll in hard turns. **Acceleration/torque:** Standard engine and transmission aren't suitable for heavy towing or carrying a full passenger load. Powered by the Malibu's anemic 200-hp 3.5L V6, acceleration is barely adequate. The GM engine is hampered by less torque, making for less grunt when accelerating and frequent downshifting out of Overdrive into passing gear when climbing moderate grades. Automatic transmission doesn't hold well on hills. **Braking:** Disc/drum; watch out for excessive brake fading; the brakes progressively lose their effectiveness after repeated application.

MONTANA SV6, RELAY, TERRAZA, UPLANDER

List Price (very negotiable)	Residual Values (months)			
	24	36	48	60
Montana SV6: $24,525 (23%)	$20,000	$17,000	$14,000	$13,000
Relay: $26,995 (22%)	$21,000	$18,000	$15,500	$14,000
Terraza: $32,210 (23%)	$25,000	$22,000	$18,500	$16,000
Uplander: $23,240 (21%)	$19,000	$16,000	$13,000	$11,500

SAFETY FEATURES	STD.	OPT.
Anti-lock brakes (4W)	✓	—
Seat belt pretensioners F/R	✓	—
Side airbags	✓	—
Stability control	—	✓
Traction control	—	✓

CRASHWORTHINESS		
Head restraints F/R	[3]	[3]
Visibility F/R	[5]	[5]
Crash protection (front) D/P	[5]	[5]
Crash protection (side) F/R	[4]	[5]
Crash protection (offset)	[5]	—

General Motors/Daewoo

When is a Chevy not a Chevy? When it's a Chevy Aveo—a re-badged South Korean Daewoo. General Motors bought Daewoo's bankrupt car division in 2003, froze out the existing Daewoo dealer network, and now sells these small cars under the Chevy, Pontiac, and Suzuki banner.

GM didn't intend to keep these cars around long. They were just handy filler while the company realigned its small-car lineup and until the 2005 Cobalt and Pursuit got a surer footing. But then oil prices practically doubled and GM found itself with a mother lode of econocars that are profitable, plentiful, and no less reliable than what GM had been churning out. In fact, they are relatively well equipped, attractively styled, and reasonably priced. Quality control has also improved since the GM takeover, making these cars acceptable buys.

In Canada, Chevrolet dealers sell the entry-level Aveo (sold by Pontiac as the Wave); the Optra, a compact based on the Daewoo Lacetti; and the Epica, a mid-sized vehicle based on Daewoo's Magnos. Suzuki sells the subcompact Swift+, based on the Kalos, and the Verona.

AVEO/SHIFT+/WAVE ★★★

RATING: Average. The Aveo costs very little to own, performs urban chores and light commuting for pennies, and is better made than previous-year models. Just one nagging question: why get a car this basic to save just a bit more gas? **Strong points:** Fairly smooth engine is capable of cruising at 110 km/h; compliant suspension glides over rough spots; acceptable routine handling; good steering and braking; minimal road or powertrain noise intrudes into the cabin; soft, comfortable seats are height-adjustable to give a good view of the road; good crash scores; very few owner complaints; and side airbags added to the 2006s. **Weak points:**

The Chevrolet Aveo.

Fuel economy is disappointing for such a simple car; not much storage space; rear legroom is limited; sedan's rear corner view is obstructed by thick side pillars; very small trunk; trunk hinges intrude into the storage area; quality control is equivalent to Detroit compacts, but inferior to the Japanese competition.

OVERVIEW: The Aveo's small 103-hp 1.6L 4-cylinder engine makes it a bantamweight in the compact car division, where the Honda Civic, the Mazda3, and the Toyota Echo reign supreme. The engine is noisy and strains going uphill with its maximum four-passenger (four *small* passengers) load, but around town, the car is peppy and nimble, especially when outfitted with the 5-speed manual transmission. Nevertheless, if it's a low price you want, the Echo is more competitive, and even if you pay a few thousand dollars more for a Honda or Mazda, that difference means nothing when spread out over five years or more and refunded through a higher resale price. For your $11,795 (plus $950 freight), you also get 14-inch tires, power steering, tilt steering wheel, AM/FM radio, tachometer, intermittent wipers, split folding rear seatbacks, and dual front and side airbags. Air conditioning, a CD player with MP3 playback, power windows, power door locks, remote entry, and heated mirrors will cost you $500 more. A 4-speed automatic transmission, anti-lock brakes, power sunroof, and premium audio system will cost you another couple of thousand dollars—definitely pushing you into Honda Civic and Toyota Matrix territory. **New for 2006:** Upgraded front and side airbags, a retuned suspension for better steering control, and electronic cruise control.

TECHNICAL DATA

POWERTRAIN (FRONT-DRIVE)
Engine: 1.6L 4-cyl. (103 hp);
Transmissions: 5-speed man. • 4-speed auto.

DIMENSION/CAPACITY
Passengers: 2/3; Wheelbase: 98 in.; H: 67.4/L: 153/W: 66 in.; Headroom F/R: 5.5/2.0 in.; Legroom F/R: 40/26 in.; Cargo volume: 11.7 cu. ft.; Fuel tank: 45L/regular; Tow limit: no towing; Load capacity: 860 lb.; Turning circle: 35 ft.; Weight: 2,530 lb.

AVEO/SWIFT+/WAVE

List Price (very negotiable)	**Residual Values** (months)			
	24	**36**	**48**	**60**
Sedan: $11,795 (15%)	$ 8,000	$ 7,000	$ 5,000	$ 4,000

SAFETY FEATURES	STD.	OPT.
Anti-lock brakes (4W)	—	✓
Seat belt pretensioners F/R	✓	—
Side airbags	✓	—

CRASHWORTHINESS		
Visibility F/R	3	3
Crash protection (front) D/P	5	5
Crash protection (side) F/R	3	3
Rollover	4	—

OPTRA LS, OPTRA5 LS ★★★

The Optra LS.

RATING: Average. There's plenty of bang for your buck, at least as long as the warranty is in effect. **Strong points:** Lots of standard features, like four-wheel independent MacPherson strut suspension and four-wheel disc brakes with optional ABS, folding seatbacks, and a height-adjustable driver's seat, which includes a lumbar adjustment. Optra also has a nicely finished interior. Reasonable fuel economy (7.4–10.7L/100 km). The Optra's wagon version has a versatile interior for carrying five passengers and cargo. **Weak points:** Seating is comfortable for only four passengers, and the 119-hp engine is an embarrasment. C'mon, only 16 more horses than the entry-level Aveo? No crashworthiness testing

TECHNICAL DATA

POWERTRAIN (FRONT-DRIVE)

Engine: 2.0L 4-cyl. (119 hp);
Transmission: 5-speed man., 4-speed
auto.

DIMENSION/CAPACITY

Passengers: 2/3; Wheelbase: 102.4 in.;
H: 67.4/L: 187.3/W: 72 in.; Headroom
F/R: 5.0/3.5 in.; Legroom F/R: 42.0/36.7
in.; Cargo volume: 12.4 cu. ft.; Fuel
tank: 55L/regular; Tow limit: no towing;
Load capacity: N/A; Turning circle: N/A;
Weight: 2,765 lb.

has been carried out. Questionable long-term dependability. If GM makes enough profit from its Daewoo sales, it will improve the breed. If not, meet the new Firenza.

OVERVIEW: Costing a few thousand dollars more than the Aveo, the Optra is a compact sedan that competes with the Hyundai Elantra and the Kia Spectra. It was joined in mid-2005 by a wagon and the Optra5 hatchback—a sportier-looking, virtually identical model. For the money, you get a 119-hp 2.0L 4-cylinder engine, AM/FM/CD stereo and four speakers, front power windows and rear manual windows, power door locks, variable intermittent wipers, folding rear seats, tachometer, tilt steering wheel, 15-inch tires, and four-wheel disc brakes. You can have alloy wheels, heated mirrors, one-touch sliding glass moon roof, and rear power windows for $1,250 more.

OPTRA

List Price (very negotiable)	Residual Values (months)			
	24	36	48	60
Optra5: $14,630 (16%)	$11,000	$ 9,000	$ 7,000	$ 6,000
Wagon: $16,350 (16%)	$12,500	$10,000	$ 8,500	$ 7,500

EPICA

RATING: Average. The Epica does nothing wrong in a very competitive class where doing things right is usually accompanied with more refinement and razzle-dazzle. Long-term reliability is still unproven, however.

OVERVIEW: This mid-sized sedan is a Canadian-only Chevy-Daewoo. It competes with the Hyundai Sonata, the Kia Magentis, and the Suzuki Verona, and costs $26,605 (plus a $950 freight fee), or about $15,000 more than the cheapest Aveo. So what do you get for the extra 15 grand?

First, you get an inline 6-cylinder DOHC engine with a 4-speed automatic transmission that produces 36 more horses than the Optra's. Other standard goodies: air conditioning; AM/FM/CD player; power seats, locks, windows, and mirrors; remote entry; projector beam headlights; foglights; 15-inch tires; and four-wheel disc brakes.

Epica's 6-cylinder engine is smooth and quiet. When under load, though, it takes an inordinate amount of time to pass other cars or to merge into traffic. The ride is comfortable, thanks to standard four-wheel independent suspension (front double wishbones/rear multi-link). You also get speed-sensitive power steering, four-wheel disc brakes, with optional ABS on LS models and standard ABS on LT trim, and a passenger sensing system for the front airbags. Under GM's stewardship, the Epica's interior has been upgraded and fit and finish have improved. Front and rear headroom and legroom is sufficient for five adults.

General Motors/Saab

Another Saab Story

Beleaguered with an image that straddles the quirky and the bland, Saab sales have been stuck in Neutral for the past decade and have actually shifted into Reverse during the last few years.

Nevertheless, the company continually makes unrealistic sales forecasts that it never meets, posting important sales declines during a decade when prestige luxury cars showed unprecedented growth. So after sustaining losses of over $2 billion since 1989, GM/Saab has halved its worldwide dealer network, merged manufacturing with GM's truck division, and made plans to move manufacturing to Germany. Additionally, the automaker will compete directly against its own dealers by setting up company-owned sales sites in several prime locations.

Hmmm…that's what Peugeot, Renault, and Fiat did in North America, just before pulling out. Get the picture?

Saabs are still original, with their unique cockpit, console-mounted ignition and window switches, and innovative "night panel" that darkens all but the speedometer. Their unusual aerodynamic styling is (to put it mildly) distinctive; passenger comfort is unbeatable; and they handle very well, with precise steering and lots of road feel. But this isn't enough; lots of less expensive cars offer just as much road performance and are more reliable and easier to repair.

Saab's growth has undeniably been slowed by increased competition from European and Japanese luxury sedans that are more smartly styled, have greater market penetration, and are marketed through attractive and innovative leasing plans. In response to that competition, Saab has taken its products further upscale, dropping its bottom-end models and bringing out its own sport-utility.

Saab's reliability and servicing problems have lessened through better assembly-line quality control and more experienced mechanics in the GM network. Nevertheless, electrical system and computer module malfunctions are common and hard to troubleshoot. This means your Saab can lose power or stall at any time, despite repeated trips for servicing.

Saab 9-2X (The "Saabaru"?)

For 2006, Saab returns with its 9-2X all-wheel-drive compact, based mostly on the Subaru Impreza, except for an interior upgraded by Saab and additional interior insulation. Saab calls this its "entry-level" car and has priced it at $25,900 for the base model. Buyers would be wise to stay away from this relatively new AWD until we see how this merging of Saab and Subaru goes since GM sold its Subaru shares to Toyota last September. Crash tests have been quite positive, however. Frontal crash protection for the driver and passenger was rated four and five stars, and rollover resistance was given a a four-star rating. Only one safety related failure has been registered:

> I purchased a 2005 Saab 9-2X, and shortly after, was involved in an accident resulting in my car being totalled. The accident occurred when the steering failed to work properly, resulting in the car jumping a median and landing on its side. Shortly thereafter, the car ignited into a fire starting in the engine, which quickly spread to the interior. Luckily the passenger and I made it out quickly and safely.

RATING: Average. The 9-3 is a driver's car, with impressive braking performance, sporty handling, and sure-footed cornering. **Strong points:** Many standard safety features, comfortable seating, and lots of storage capability. Generally good build quality and exterior finish. **Weak points:** No hatchback and some turbo lag and torque steer. Convertible has minimal rear-seat room, less comfortable seating, and a tendency to shake and rattle. The servicing network is rather limited. Engine computer defects cut engine power and make the car dangerous to drive. **New for 2006:** A $36,400 SportCombi five-passenger wagon makes its appearance this year. Engine choice has changed, as well, with the debut of a base 210-hp 2.0L turbo charged 4-banger. Aero models ($41,900) will be equipped with a 250-hp turbocharged 2.8L V6.

OVERVIEW: Selling for $34,900 (plus a $1,150 freight and pre-delivery inspection fee), the 9-3 Linear Sport Sedan was totally redesigned in 2003 and got a $54,900 convertible companion for 2004. It is now set on a new platform and offers many new safety and convenience features. Rear passenger and trunk space, width, and wheelbase were also increased, although the hatchback was dropped in favour of traditional sedan styling.

The car's aerodynamic look is created by the 9-3's steeply raked front windshield and swept-back styling, two factors that limit forward visibility considerably. The standard powertrain consists of a 210-hp 2.0L 4-cylinder engine mated to either a 5- or 6-speed manual transmission, with an optional automatic 5-speed with manual shifting capability (Sentronic). The 9-3 has independent rear suspension and front MacPherson struts to give the car better-than-average handling and ride comfort. Safety has been enhanced through the use of disc brakes, electronic brake force distribution, cornering brake control, electronic stability, traction control, active head restraints, front and rear seat belt pretensioners, load limiting for all the outer seating positions, and dual-stage front airbags, seat-mounted side airbags, and side roof-rail airbags.

The 9-3 convertible is sold as either an entry-level Arc or a high-performance Aero. Both models carry the 210-hp 2.0L turbocharged engine hooked to the 5-speed manual (standard on the Arc), 6-speed manual (standard on the Aero), or optional 5-speed Sentronic automatic.

COST ANALYSIS: Inasmuch as the 2006s return with a more powerful engine and a wagon/hatchback addition, they represent the better buy, once prices are discounted a good 20 percent by year's end. **Best alternatives:** The Acura TSX, the Audi A4, and the BMW 3 Series are attractive alternatives to the 9-3 Linear Sport sedan. Keep in mind that Saabs depreciate far more quickly than the above suggested models. **Options:** Integrated child safety seats. The GPS navigation aids can be useful, but don't waste your money on the power sunroof, leather upholstery, or heated seats. **Rebates:** Rebates and discounts of at least $7,000. **Delivery/PDI:** $1,050. **Depreciation:** Faster than average. If you plan to keep your Saab for only a few years and don't want to lose much money through depreciation, choose the convertible; it keeps its value longer. **Insurance cost:** Slightly higher than average. **Parts supply/cost:** Not easily found; costly at times. **Annual maintenance cost:** Higher than average. **Warranty:** Bumper-to-bumper 4 years/80,000 km; rust perforation 6 years/unlimited km. **Supplementary warranty:** A very good idea, considering that these cars are complicated to diagnose and expensive to repair. **Highway/city fuel economy:** 8.5–11.9L/100 km with the 2.0L engine and an automatic transmission.

Quality/Reliability/Safety

Pro: Warranty performance: Above average. GM has treated Saab owners more generously than its has treated owners of cars from its other divisions, with the exception of Cadillac. **Quality control:** Average.

Con: Reliability: Worse than average, owing mainly to the cars' glitch-prone electronics. In fact, most of the 9-3's defects are electrical in nature, which tends to take lots of diagnostic time. **Owner-reported problems:** Engine malfunctions caused by defective power control modules; electrical and fuel system failures; and a rotten-egg exhaust smell. **Service bulletin problems:** Jerkiness in Drive or when upshifting; handbrake lever replacement campaign; and tips on troubleshooting an inoperative keyless entry device. **NHTSA safety complaints:** *2005 model:* Sudden engine failure:

The engine on my 2005 Saab 9-3 has failed two times within the first 4,900 miles [7,900 km] on the odometer. The first failure occurred in June of 2005 and the problem was diagnosed as a throttle body failure. The failure results in the car accelerating extremely slowly without any prior notice. The second failure occurred on July 18, 2005, when I was nearly hit making a left-hand turn. The same symptoms presented without any indication that there was a failure about to occur. I have researched the SaabNet website and it appears I am not alone in falling victim to the defective throttle body in the Saab 9-3 model. It appears to be a pervasive problem. Saab's attorney indicated that this did not rise to the level of a recall nor a problem that require replacement of the vehicle.

Other model years: Chronic stalling and loss of power caused by faulty computer hardware and software; side airbag failed to deploy; airbag warning light remains lit; aluminum hubs may not support the stress of everyday driving; emergency brake failed to hold; when passing over grooves in the road, vehicle suddenly jerks to the right or left; driver's door lock won't unlock from the inside; Pirelli tire blowout; and OnStar radio failures.

SAFETY FEATURES	STD.	OPT.	CRASHWORTHINESS		
Anti-lock brakes 4W	✓	—	Head restraints F/R	⑤	⑤
Seat belt pretensioners F/R	✓	—	Visibility F/R	❷	❶
Side airbags	✓	—			

Note: Crashworthiness hasn't been tested, except for head-restraint protection.

9-5 ★★★

RATING: Average. **Strong points:** Good acceleration, handling, road holding, and braking; "smart" head restraints; comfortable seating (lots of room for people over six feet tall in the front); lots of storage capability; improved build quality and fit and finish; good fuel economy. Excellent crashworthiness: five stars for frontal crash protection and driver-side protection; four-star rating for passenger-side protection and rollover resistance. **Weak points:** Turbo lag; the steering is over-assisted; body lean when cornering; climate controls aren't very user-friendly; servicing network is rather limited. **New for 2006:** The 260-hp turbocharged 2.3L 4-cylinder engine gets 10 additional horses. All models have restyled front and rear ends and a reworked interior; and the wagon is now called the SportCombi.

OVERVIEW: Saab's 9-5 has two body styles, a four-door sedan and wagon, equipped with a 260-hp turbocharged 2.3L 4-cylinder engine. Freight charges are $1,150. These cars all use suspension and brake parts taken from GM's Opel Vectra, with a stiffened chassis and four-wheel independent suspension. Both come with either a 5-speed manual transmission or a 5-speed automatic/manual. Standard safety features include ABS, traction control, and front head-and-torso side airbags.

9-5s are well appointed and hold the road fairly well, though there's still a lot of body lean. Cargo space is about average and there's room for five adults in a cabin that's one of the quietest you can find (except for tire noise). In addition to providing a spacious pass-through trunk, Saab pays lots of attention to detail. For example: "Smart" head restraints are specially designed to prevent neck injuries; the glove box has an air conditioning duct that keeps drinks cold; there are air vents in the back of the centre console for added comfort; rear seats fold flat for added cargo room; the cargo floor slides out for easier loading; and, for added safety, a passenger-side rear-view mirror automatically tilts down so you can get a better view when you engage Reverse.

Some things you won't like about the 9-5: an annoying turbo lag; slow downshifts with the automatic transmission; and power steering that's over-assisted

TECHNICAL DATA

POWERTRAIN (FRONT-DRIVE)
Engine: 2.3L 4-cyl. (260 hp);
Transmissions: 5-speed man.; • 5-speed man./auto.

DIMENSION/CAPACITY
Passengers: 2/3; Wheelbase: 106.4 in.; H: 57/L: 190.4/W: 70.5 in.; Headroom F/R: 3.5/3.0 in.; Legroom F/R: 41.5/28.5 in.; Cargo volume: 15.9 cu. ft.; Fuel tank: 70L/regular; Tow limit: 3,500 lb.; Load capacity: 930 lb.; Turning circle: 39 ft.; Weight: 3,470 lb.

and doesn't transmit sufficient road feel. Other minuses: Only two adults can sit comfortably in the rear; the suspension feels overly firm; low-profile tires on the Aero have poor wet-weather traction; wagons don't offer third-row seating; dash buttons are confusing; the fan-cooled seats are more gimmicky than practical; climate controls are set too low to be easily adjusted; manual-transmission-equipped cars must be shifted into Reverse before the ignition key can be removed; rear visibility is obstructed; Aero models require premium fuel; and servicing isn't widely available.

COST ANALYSIS: Best alternatives: Alternatives to the 9-5 include the Audi A4, Infiniti G35, and Lexus ES 330. **Highway/city fuel economy:** 7.5–11.7L/100 km with the manual transmission.

 ## Quality/Reliability/Safety

Pro: Quality control: Above average. Saab 9-5 owners report fewer factory-related defects than owners of the entry-level 9-3. **Reliability:** Average. **Warranty performance:** Average.

Con: Service bulletin problems: N/A. **NHTSA safety complaints:** Fuel sloshes around in fuel tank when accelerating or stopping; loss of power steering; sulfur fumes invade the interior. **Owner-reported problems:** Electrical, brake, and fuel system glitches.

9-5

List Price (negotiable)	Residual Values (months)			
	24	**36**	**48**	**60**
Base: $43,000 (30%)	$30,000	$26,000	$22,000	$19,000
Wagon: $44,500 (30%)	$33,000	$28,000	$24,000	$20,000

SAFETY FEATURES	STD.	OPT.	CRASHWORTHINESS		
Anti-lock brakes (4W)	✓	—	Visibility F/R	5	3
Seat belt pretensioners F/R	✓	—	Crash protection (front) D/P	5	5
Side airbags	✓	—	Crash protection (side) F/R	5	4
Stability control	✓	—	Rollover	4	—
Traction control	✓	—			

General Motors/Saturn

Remember the hype? Saturn would be GM's different car company. Quality would match or exceed anything offered by the Japanese. Customers would be coddled and dealers would offer fair, "no haggle" prices. Sales would soar.

This never happened.

Saturn failed to meet all of the above expectations, and the division has never made a profit. Instead, Saturn has churned out unreliable, low-quality, overpriced cars and SUVs that have sold poorly now that their novelty has worn off.

ION ★★

RATING: Below Average. There have been some improvements, but Saturn's poor-quality powertrains and uneven servicing give its Asian competitors an important advantage, and even make Chevrolet's ubiquitous Aveo, Cobalt, and Pursuit look good (actually, the Ion is built on the Cobalt platform). **Strong points:** A competent base engine hooked to a smooth-shifting manual or automatic transmission. Plenty of interior room; Quad Coupe's four doors give good rear seat access; excellent steering response and the tight turning radius is helpful in city driving; good highway stability; good visibility (sedan); and dent-resistant polymer body panels. **Weak points:** Seats on base models lack padding and side support; limited rearward visibility (coupe); suspension may be too firm for some; poor wet traction; excessive engine and road noise; and real-world fuel economy is much lower than advertised. **New for 2006:** An optional 170-hp 2.4L 4-cylinder engine and a sport-tuned suspension. The interior has been revamped to provide more front knee room and to make the sound system more accessible.

OVERVIEW: A larger, more comfortable, and more powerful vehicle than its S-series predecessor, the Ion is powered by a 140-hp 2.2L 4-cylinder engine and gives buyers the choice of either a coupe or a sedan. Other features include power steering, a 5-speed manual transmission, and an optional 4-speed automatic. Other standard features: speed-sensitive windshield wipers, split folding rear seatbacks, and plastic body side panels.

The arrival of the Red Line high-performance Ion in 2004 gave a bit of colour to an otherwise bland model lineup. Carrying a 205-hp supercharged 2.0L 4-banger hooked to a 5-speed manual transmission, this sporty variant uses its sturdier drivetrain and 17-inch alloy wheels to ratchet up the Ion's performance and handling.

TECHNICAL DATA

POWERTRAIN (FRONT-DRIVE)

Engines: 2.2L 4-cyl. (140 hp) • 2.4L 4-cyl. (170 hp) • 2.0L 4-cyl. (205 hp); Transmissions: 5-speed man. • 4-speed auto.

DIMENSION/CAPACITY

Passengers: 2/3; Wheelbase: 103 in.; H: 56/L: 185/W: 67 in.; Headroom F/R: 5.5/1.0 in.; Legroom F/R: 40/25.5 in.; Cargo volume: 14.7 cu. ft.; Fuel tank: 49.2L/regular; Tow limit: 1,000 lb.; Load capacity: 900 lb.; Turning circle: 37 ft.; Weight: 2,751 lb.

COST ANALYSIS: Go for this year's upgraded Ion. **Best alternatives:** The Honda Civic, the Hyundai Accent or Tiburon, and the Toyota Corolla; they perform better and are higher quality vehicles. **Options:** Slippery leather seats aren't worth the extra money. **Rebates:** Zero percent financing and $3,500 rebates by year's end. **Delivery/PDI:** $1,150. **Depreciation:** Average. **Insurance cost:** Average. **Parts supply/cost:** Parts are easily found and reasonably priced (with the exception of plastic body panels). **Annual maintenance cost:** Average. Estimated to increase drastically after the third year of ownership. **Warranty:** Bumper-to-bumper 3 years/60,000 km; powertrain 5 years/100,000 km; rust perforation 6 years/160,000 km. **Supplementary warranty:** A good idea in view of Saturn's poor quality control and hard-nosed attitude in treating post-warranty repair claims. **Highway/city fuel economy:** 6.7–10 L/100 km with 2.2L engine and automatic transmission.

Quality/Reliability/Safety

Con: Reliability: Below average reliability, particularly after the third year of ownership—two years earlier than when most vehicles start needing major repairs. More problems have been reported with the newer Ion than with the discontinued L-series. **Quality control:** Not up to Japanese car standards. Saturn has always been afflicted by serious quality control problems. **Warranty performance:** Great—as long as the warranty is in force, you're greeted with a smile and a handshake. Afterwards, customers report feeling abandoned. **Owner-reported problems:** Engine, transmission, power-steering, body, and electrical system glitches. **Service bulletin problems:** Engine coolant leak; no-start and hard starts; defective clutch; excessive noise from the fuel pump; sunroof rattling and flexing; inoperative HVAC blower motor; noisy; radio malfunctions; cracked rear outer door panel. **NHTSA safety complaints:** Electrical fire believed to have originated near the battery; automatic transmission shifts erratically; sudden stalling; hard starting; dash gauges fail; shifter knob came off:

> I was driving my vehicle and my shifter knob fell off in my hand. The shifter failed to go into Second and Fourth gear. I had the car towed to the dealer and the whole shifter shaft had to be replaced.

Much-vaunted plastic door panels crack:

> Door panels cracked during extreme heat; co-worker pointed out that there was a crack on my driver-side door and rear passenger-side door. The crack on the rear door eventually became a whole chunk. Vehicle has been in no accidents.

Cracked engine head; sudden engine shutdown while driving; hard starts or no-start; automatic transmission shifts harshly from Second to Third gear, or simply fails to go into gear; and many complaints of transmission slippage:

> The transmission on my 2003 Ion slips constantly. A tech from Spring Hill says this is normal for this type of transmission. Trying to turn left in front of oncoming traffic is a nightmare. This car is in the shop as we speak. The rear quarter panel is cracked and being replaced. The rear bumper is being painted because of scratches from the trunk rubbing. The front bumper is being painted because of runs in the paint. None of the body panels seem to match up. They're attempting to fix a popping noise in the front end. They're replacing the driver-side glass because it is severely scratched. It sometimes runs rough at first crank.

Horn is hard to activate; steering knuckle sheared off; airbags failed to deploy; seat belt retractor fell apart; frequent tire blowouts; steering wheel is hard to turn; turn signal lights often burn out; vehicle loses power and shakes when AC is activated; door seals improperly installed; and the key sticks in ignition.

Road Performance

Pro: Emergency handling: Excellent. **Steering:** Very little torque steer, owing to the use of equal-length driveshafts. **Acceleration/torque:** Good acceleration. **Routine handling:** Better than average. Steering has been calibrated to enhance road feel at highway speeds and effectively blocks out road harshness. **Braking:** Fairly good.

Con: Ion handling is compromised by wet pavement. **Transmission:** Excessive automatic gearbox shudder when the kickdown is engaged while passing.

ION

List Price (negotiable)	**Residual Values** (months)			
	24	**36**	**48**	**60**
Ion-1 Coupe: $13,995 (15%)	$10,000	$ 7,500	$ 5,500	$ 4,500
Red Line: $22,995 (20%)	$18,000	$14,000	$ 9,000	$ 7,000

SAFETY FEATURES	**STD.**	**OPT.**
Anti-lock brakes (4W)	✓	✓
Seat belt pretensioners F/R	✓	—
Side airbags	—	✓
Traction control	—	✓

CRASHWORTHINESS		
Head restraints F/R	4	3
Visibility F/R	5	3
Crash protection (front) D/P	5	5
Crash protection (side) F/R	4	4
4D	3	4
Rollover	4	—

General Motors/Toyota

VIBE/MATRIX ★★★

The Pontiac Vibe GT.

RATING: Average. Aimed at the youth market, these cars don't provide enough horsepower to justify their sporty pretensions, and they're hard on gas. A test-drive is essential to see if the weak engine, noise, and driving position are tolerable. **Strong points:** Brutish, edgy styling; small Matrix steering wheel

TECHNICAL DATA

POWERTRAIN (FRONT-DRIVE)

Engines: 1.8L 4-cyl. (130 hp); 1.8L
4-cyl. (123 hp) • 1.8L 4-cyl. (180 hp);
Transmissions: 5-speed man. • 4-speed
auto. • 6-speed man.

DIMENSION/CAPACITY

Passengers: 2/3; Wheelbase: 102 in.;
H: 61/L: 171.9/W: 69.9 in.; Headroom:
F/R: 6.5/5.5 in.; Legroom: F/R: 41/28
in.; Cargo volume: 28 cu. ft.; Fuel tank:
50L/reg./prem.; Tow limit: 1,500 lb.; Load
capacity: 860 lb.; Turning circle: 38 ft.;
Weight: 2,985 lb.

makes for easier cornering; refined rear suspension gives these cars impressive road manners; plenty of passenger and storage space and handy tie-downs; flexible seating; front passenger and rear seats fold completely flat to carry long cargo; 115-volt power outlet up front; well-placed interior controls and instruments; and excellent workmanship. **Weak points:** Weak, noisy, vibrating, and fuel-thirsty engines at all speeds; optional engine needs premium fuel; excessive road and engine noise; chronic rotten-egg smell in the cabin; not much low-end power for the base and XR models and even less 4×4 grunt; Vibe GT must be constantly shifted to keep accelerating; its firm suspension lets you feel every bump in the road; short occupants can barely see over the door window sill; dash instrumentation is hard to read with sunglasses and trim reflects onto the windshield; driving position may be uncomfortable over long distances; head-protecting side airbags aren't available. **New for 2006:** *Vibe:* Optional Premium interior and Sport package. *Matrix:* An improved oxygen sensor to meet stricter emissions regulations.

OVERVIEW: Officially classed as subcompact front-drive or all-wheel-drive cars, these sporty wagons are a cross between a small SUV and a station wagon and packaged like small minivans. The Vibe is built in Fremont, California, at GM's NUMMI factory. The nearly identical Toyota Matrix is manufactured in Toyota's Cambridge, Ontario, plant alongside the Toyota Corolla, whose platform it shares.

Matrix joins the Subaru Impreza in professing to provide a blend of sports-car performance, SUV versatility, and compact-car affordability. It's offered in front-drive or Toyota's V-Flex 4×4 system.

The front-drive Matrix and Vibe are equipped with a 123-/130-hp base engine (front-drive/AWD), 5-speed manual overdrive transmission, and lots of standard features, including an AM/FM CD stereo system, full instrumentation, and flip-up rear hatch glass.

The Matrix XRS and Vibe GT are the top-of-the-line performance leaders, with a 180-hp 4-cylinder engine and a high-performance 6-speed manual gearbox, plus ABS, premium six-speaker stereo, anti-theft system, 17-inch alloy wheels, and unique exterior cladding.

COST ANALYSIS: The 2006 models return this year practically unchanged. If you get the 2005, you should look for about 10 percent off and an additional break on the freight fee. Keep in mind that the Matrix is thousands of dollars cheaper than the Vibe and holds its value better. Don't get fooled by the name game. These cars are identical, except for exterior styling, options packages, and prices. These vehicles hail from factories that have garnered high quality ratings and the cars also come with similar warranties. If you really need additional horsepower, get either the XRS or GT. **Best alternatives:** Keep in mind that there are better high-performance choices out there, like the Honda Civic Si and the base Acura RSX. Other front-drives worth considering are the Chrysler PT Cruiser, the Mazda3 or Mazda5, the Hyundai Elantra or Tiburon, the Honda Civic, the Nissan Sentra, or the Toyota Corolla. The Subaru Impreza or Forester would be other good choices for the 4×4 variant. **Options:** Be wary of most options. For example, the XR option only adds side skirts, colour-keyed door handles, a leather-wrapped steering wheel, power windows, and a height-adjustable driver's seat. Of that list, 17-inch wheels that improve cornering, the windows, and the seat are worth the extra loonies. Ditch the front spoiler:

> The front spoiler on the Matrix is constantly getting scraped up on driveways. It is too low. The only way to fix the problem is to put a whole new bumper on the car, at my cost. The spoilers are listed as an option, but where I am from it is impossible to find an XR without them installed. The car is less than a year old, and already looks bad. Who would think they would design a car that would constantly get all scraped up?

Rebates: $1,500–$2,000 plus low-interest financing. **Delivery/PDI:** *Vibe:* $1,200; *Matrix:* $1,150. **Depreciation:** Much slower than average, as high fuel prices prop up resale values. **Insurance cost:** Higher than average. **Parts supply/cost:** Good availability, since many parts come from the Corolla bin. **Annual maintenance cost:** Much lower than average. **Warranty:** Bumper-to-bumper 3 years/60,000 km; powertrain 5 years/100,000 km; rust perforation 6 years/160,000 km. **Supplementary warranty:** Not needed. **Highway/city fuel economy:** 7.1–9.3L/100 km.

Quality/Reliability/Safety

Pro: Warranty performance: Another reason for choosing the Matrix over GM's Vibe. Although Toyota initially dropped the ball in handling engine oil sludge claims on other models, its warranty performance is much better than GM's, and you generally have much more leverage in pressing your claim with Toyota on Matrix models. Don't take any "show us your oil receipts" bullcrap from either company. **Quality control:** Higher than average. **Reliability:** Above average. Stainless steel exhaust system. **Safety:** Excellent visibility fore and aft, although the lower rear-window wiper housing obstructs the window area a bit. The rear wiper is particularly effective, even though the washer sometimes dribbles rather than sprays.

Con: Owner-reported problems: Owners report a rotten-egg exhaust smell intrudes into the interior. Other complaints include excessive steering wander; many reports of transmission clutch failures (see *www.matrixowners.com*); with transmission in Park, vehicle can roll away; power-steering pump failures; warped front brake rotors; excessive vibration felt in the interior during acceleration after start-up; headlight condensation; driver's seat fabric tears easily; hood popped up while car was underway; black tape covering the window frame tends to bubble; paint blisters quite easily; and gas mileage may not be up to expectations. **Service bulletin problems:** *Matrix:* Stinky exhaust can be cleaned up by replacing the catalytic converter under the emissions warranty. Loose-fitting trim panels and console door won't stay closed. *Vibe:* Driveability problems; automatic transmission slipping; and console door won't stay closed. **NHTSA safety complaints:** Front end is too low; bumper drags on the driveway; snow freezes inside low-profile rims, causing excessive vibration; chronic stalling; engine surges when braking with AC engaged; excessive steering wander; malfunction light may remain lit; dashboard reflects onto the windshield; instrument panel lights are dimmed by automatic sensor to a point where they can't be read in twilight hours; and the automatic headlights come on and go off for no apparent reason.

 Road Performance

Pro: Acceptable acceleration from start-up in First gear, but not confidence-inspiring for high-speed merging unless you have the 180-hp power plant. **Transmission:** Smooth and quiet shifting with the automatic gearbox mated to the front-drive. **Emergency handling:** Very good. The double wishbone rear suspension makes for crisp, predictable handling. **Routine handling:** Above average. **Braking:** Disc/drum; disc/disc with the XRS. Braking is good with the base set-up and better than average with the four-wheel discs.

Con: Acceleration/torque: Weak, buzzy base engine can be felt throughout the car and needs fuel-wasting high rpm to get going; 4×4 models are about 10 percent heavier and get 7 fewer horses (123) than the already power-challenged front-drive. Says *Forbes* magazine:

> [B]oth all-wheel-drive cars are saddled with a really wretched 4-speed automatic that almost has to be shifted manually to get the car moving. To put it bluntly, the AWD Vibe and Matrix are so pokey they feel like they're towing Winnebagos. To boot, the 1.8L engine doesn't hit its paltry torque peak...until a screaming 4200 rpm, at which point the vibration—did somebody say Vibe?—in the cabin is worse than a little off-putting.

The manual shift lever's upward and forward position is counterintuitive and feels a bit ragged. Steering feels a bit vague, with too much play. Both cars get blown about by sidewinds. Some torque steer (twisting) evident, especially on wet roads. Handling is not as sharp with the AWD and uneven pavement is more jolting. Small dash gauges aren't easily seen in daylight and dash trim throws a distracting reflection onto the front windshield. There's also a considerable amount of engine, wind, and road noise.

VIBE/MATRIX

List Price (negotiable) **Residual Values** (months)

	24	36	48	60
Vibe FWD: $19,900 (16%)	$15,000	$11,000	$ 9,000	$ 7,500
Vibe AWD: $23,755 (18%)	$19,000	$14,000	$12,000	$ 9,500
Vibe GT: $25,670 (20%)	$22,000	$16,000	$14,000	$11,000
Matrix FWD: $17,200 (14%)	$14,500	$11,500	$ 9,500	$ 8,000
Matrix AWD XR: $24,825 (18%)	$18,500	$15,000	$13,000	$11,000
Matrix XRS: $25,835 (18%)	$21,500	$19,000	$15,000	$13,000

SAFETY FEATURES	STD.	OPT.	CRASHWORTHINESS		
Anti-lock brakes 4W	✓	✓	Head restraints F/R	5	5
Seat belt pretensioners F/R	✓	—	Visibility F/R	3	3
Side airbags	—	✓	Crash protection (front) D/P	5	4
Stability control	—	✓	Crash protection (side) F/R	3	4
Traction control	—	✓	Rollover	4	—

ASIAN VEHICLES

Hyping the Hybrids

The savings in fuel and taxes don't do enough for me to alleviate the pain of the sticker price and the cost of a new battery down the road…. Why not buy a Civic HX that gets 44 mpg [5L/100 km] highway for $13,700 and use the extra money to plant a few hundred trees?

REILLY BRENNAN
MOTOR TREND
APRIL 2004

I have owned a '67 Ford Mustang, a slew of Mavericks, a Buick LeSabre, a Cadillac DeVille, a GMC Vandura, a Toyota Camry, and a Hyundai Elantra. I hate saying this, but it's true: Asian automakers have a lock on reliable, fuel-sipping vehicles. Whether they're cars, minivans, sport-utilities, or pickups, and whether they're built in Japan, Canada, Mexico, or the United States, Asian cars usually give you much more for your money than if you were to buy the equivalent vehicle made by DaimlerChrysler, Ford, General Motors—or most European automakers, for that matter. You can also count on Asian vehicles to be easy to repair and slow to depreciate (Kia and Daewoo being the only exceptions).

You don't always have to pay top dollar, either. You can get exceptionally good deals by purchasing Japanese vehicles that are re-badged as American models or built as co-ventures in Japanese, American, and Canadian factories— cars like the Toyota Matrix and Pontiac Vibe or the Saab 9-2X and the Subaru Impreza. The

Cash is more important than cachet. If you buy a Subaru Impreza (left) instead of Saab's 9-2X equivalent (right), you get the same car for thousands of dollars less.

Japanese counterpart is usually better supported by an indigenous dealer and servicing network.

Japanese vehicles usually sell at a 10–20 percent premium over their Detroit equivalents, although higher resale values wipe out the difference. In the past, Asian automakers have tried to keep prices down through "content-cutting" and offering fewer standard features. But this approach has produced disastrous results during the past several years. Less content led to lower quality, and manufacturers like Honda and Toyota have had to extend their powertrain warranties up to eight years to cover catastrophic engine and automatic transmission failures.

One gets the impression that Japanese automakers have become complacent after winning so many quality awards from CAA and other groups and are now coasting on their reputation. This would explain why we've seen such an upswing in safety- and performance-related defects over the past few years from such reputable companies as Nissan (200 engineers brought from Japan to fix the 2004 Quest's defects), Honda (1997–2004 models with transmission failures), and Toyota (1997–2005 models with engine sludge and stinky exhaust). It certainly has nothing to do with American versus Japanese manufacturing plants—these companies' poor-quality components have come from factories located on both sides of the Pacific.

Detroit discounting and low interest rates this year will force Japanese and Korean automakers to cut prices. Honda, Hyundai, Mitsubishi, Nissan, and Toyota have warned Detroit that they will use aggressive discounting and rebates to undercut the competition in almost every vehicle category, with particular emphasis on promoting the redesigned Honda Civic, Mazda5, Nissan Quest, and Toyota Avalon.

No market segment is safe from the Asian invasion (except possibly full-sized vans). In response to high fuel prices, Honda, Nissan, and Toyota plan to bring minicars to North America by mid-2006. Additionally, Hyundai, Mazda, and Mitsubishi will be working overtime supplying re-badged small cars to Chrysler and Ford. China, too, is expected to jump into the fray in 2006 with several small cars to be sold under the Chery banner (GM says the name sounds too much like "Chevy," and wants court protection).

Mitsubishi Motors, on the brink of bankruptcy last year, has been given a reprieve by high gas prices. It is once again in Chrysler's good graces and will likely continue to use Chrysler's dealer network to sell co-ventures, re-badged models, and its own products, like the redesigned Eclipse. Other Detroit automakers are renewing old alliances to quickly get cheap, fuel-efficient small cars to clamouring new-car buyers.

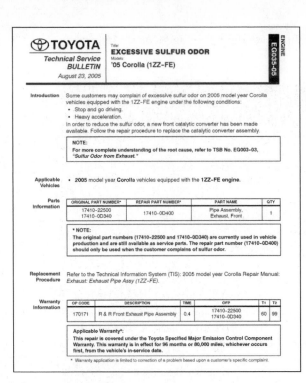

TOYOTA
Technical Service BULLETIN
August 23, 2005

Title: **EXCESSIVE SULFUR ODOR**
Models: '05 Corolla (1ZZ-FE)

ENGINE EG035-05

Introduction — Some customers may complain of excessive sulfur odor on 2005 model year Corolla vehicles equipped with the 1ZZ-FE engine under the following conditions:
- Stop and go driving.
- Heavy acceleration.

In order to reduce the sulfur odor, a new front catalytic converter has been made available. Follow the repair procedure to replace the catalytic converter assembly.

NOTE:
For more complete understanding of the root cause, refer to TSB No. EG003-03, "Sulfur Odor from Exhaust."

Applicable Vehicles — 2005 model year **Corolla** vehicles equipped with the **1ZZ-FE** engine.

Parts Information

ORIGINAL PART NUMBER*	REPAIR PART NUMBER*	PART NAME	QTY
17410-22500 17410-0D340	17410-0D400	Pipe Assembly, Exhaust, Front	1

* NOTE:
The original part numbers (17410-22500 and 17410-0D340) are currently used in vehicle production and are still available as service parts. The repair part number (17410-0D400) should only be used when the customer complains of sulfur odor.

Replacement Procedure — Refer to the Technical Information System (TIS): 2005 model year Corolla Repair Manual: Exhaust: Exhaust Pipe Assy (1ZZ-FE).

Warranty Information

OP CODE	DESCRIPTION	TIME	OFP	T1	T2
170171	R & R Front Exhaust Pipe Assembly	0.4	17410-22500 17410-0D340	60	99

Applicable Warranty*:
This repair is covered under the Toyota Specified Major Emission Control Component Warranty. This warranty is in effect for 96 months or 80,000 miles, whichever occurs first, from the vehicle's in-service date.

* Warranty application is limited to correction of a problem based upon a customer's specific complaint.

South Korean vehicles—once the laughing stock of car columnists and consumer advocates—are catching up to the Japanese competition in quality and sales. Hyundai is putting better-quality parts in its Kia subsidiary's cars, SUVs, and minivans, as Kia continues to post impressive sales gains, primarily because of its low prices and a longer base warranty. GM's Daewoo acquisition has injected serious price-cutting into the mix of entry-level small cars, as Chevrolet and GM's Suzuki partner dumps thousands of discounted and rebate-laden small Daewoos on the Canadian market. The kicker? Daewoo owners are reporting that their cars are as good as or better than the GM products they previously owned.

Acura

Acura, a division of Honda, was first off the mark in creating performance-oriented luxury-class vehicles from entry-level econocars and compact sedans like the Civic and Accord. After it launched its first car, the Legend, in 1986, and the venerable Integra a bit later, Toyota and Nissan kicked sand in Acura's face with their best-selling Lexus and Infiniti lines. Nevertheless, even without a V8 powerplant, Acura continues to distinguish itself by selling in all price ranges.

Six cars are sold under the Acura nameplate: the Canada-exclusive EL entry-level compact, the RSX Integra replacement, the TL, the RL, the NSX sports coupe (to be discontinued at the end of 2005), and the TSX, which joined the lineup two years ago, just as the CL coupe was dropped.

Acura will forego major changes or upgrades this year as it prepares for the 2007 model year, when it will bring out a new RDX sport wagon, redesign the RSX and TSX, and restyle the TL.

Acura products are mainly fully loaded Hondas with a few additional features. Despite the fact that dealers try to enforce a no-haggle policy, these cars are generally good buys because maintenance costs are low, depreciation is much slower than average, and reliability is outstanding. What few defects they have are usually related to squeaks and rattles, minor trim glitches, and to accessories, such as the navigation and sound system.

EL ★★★★★

RATING: Recommended. **Strong points:** High level of performance and comfort; lots of standard safety and convenience features; excellent fuel economy for a luxury subcompact; slow depreciation; and high-quality construction. **Weak points:** Little discounting; insufficient low-end torque; narrow interior, with rear seating for only two adults; obstructed rear visibility; and head restraints that earned a Poor rating by IIHS. **New for 2006:** Nothing significant. Big changes are due next year when the Civic is redesigned.

OVERVIEW: With a $23,500 base price ($24,700 for the Premium), the redesigned EL is Acura's best-selling car—essentially a restyled, more powerful luxury version of the Honda Civic sedan. In fact, both models are built in Honda's plant in Alliston, Ontario.

The VTEC 4-cylinder puts out 127 hp for good all-around acceleration, but maximum torque still requires high revving in the 5000-rpm range. Going uphill with a full load of passengers and baggage overwhelms the 4-banger. Honda's base 5-speed manual gearbox and optional 5-speed automatic set the standard for smooth, quiet shifts, and you get impressive fuel economy to boot (8L/100 km in the city; 6L/100 km on the highway).

Performance and handling are enhanced by a fully independent suspension, tight and responsive steering, and excellent braking, with little brake fade after successive stops.

There's good front and side visibility, thanks to the car's low hoodline and large side windows. Rear visibility is hampered a bit by the high rear deck. The interior is quieter and much more luxurious than the Civic LX sedan, plus all gauges and controls are easily seen and accessed. Both the floor-mounted trunk release and gas cap are lockable, and split folding rear seats (also lockable) allow for pass-through storage of long objects. Standard safety features include side airbags, de-powered airbags, and seat belt pretensioners.

Some of the EL's weak points include a chintzy space-saver spare tire and a relatively high price tag for what is essentially a better-equipped Civic (still, a low depreciation rate returns a greater portion of your initial investment).

COST ANALYSIS: Get the 2006, since Acura dealers seldom discount leftovers and the new version doesn't cost much more. Furthermore, some of the 2006 Civic's redesigned components are likely to find themselves in this Civic clone. **Best alternatives:** The Honda Civic Si and the Mazda3. **Options:** Nothing needed. **Rebates:** Not likely. **Delivery/PDI:** $1,280. **Depreciation:** Much slower than average. **Insurance cost:** Higher than average. **Parts supply/cost:** Moderately priced parts can be found at Acura or Honda dealers. **Annual maintenance cost:** Lower than average. **Warranty:** Bumper-to-bumper 3 years/60,000 km; powertrain 5 years/100,000 km; rust perforation 6 years/unlimited km. **Supplementary warranty:** Not needed.

TL — best buy — ★★★★★

RATING: Recommended. **Strong points:** Very good fuel economy; impressive acceleration; handles well; rides comfortably; well constructed, with quality mechanical and body components; and impressive crashworthiness scores compiled by NHTSA and IIHS. **Weak points:** Suspension may be too firm for some; not as agile as the BMW 3 Series; uncomfortable rear seating; and a wide turning circle. **New for 2006:** Lots more soundproofing and vibration dampening.

OVERVIEW: Retailing for about $41,500, the TL combines luxury and performance in a nicely styled front-drive five-passenger sedan that uses the same chassis as the Accord and CL coupe, unlike the TL which uses a slightly smaller version. The only engine available, a 258–270-hp 3.2L V6 mated to a 5-speed Sequential SportShift automatic transmission or a 6-speed manual coupled to a limited-slip differential, provides impressive acceleration (0–100 km/h in just over 8 seconds) in a smooth and quiet manner. Handling is exceptional, with the firm suspension and the responsive and precise steering making it easy to toss the TL around turns without losing control. Bumps can be a bit jarring, but this is a small price to pay for the car's high-speed stability.

Interior accommodations are better than average up front, but rear occupants may discover that legroom is a bit tight and the seat cushions lack sufficient thigh support. The cockpit layout is very user-friendly, in part because of the easy-to-read gauges and accessible controls (far-away climate controls are the only exception). Visibility fore and aft is unobstructed; however, the optional navigation system is tough to read, hard to calibrate, and subject to malfunction. Invest in maps instead.

Standard safety features include ABS, stability and traction control, front seat belt pretensioners, childproof door locks, three-point seat belts, head-protecting air-bags, and a transmission/brake interlock. Crash tests give four stars for driver and passenger crash protection in a frontal collision; four and five stars for side-impact protection; and four stars for rollover resistance. The offset crash rating is also five stars. Head restraints are given a Good rating by IIHS.

COST ANALYSIS: Get the 2005 model if it's sufficiently discounted and a bit of road noise doesn't bother you; otherwise, pay a slight premium for a 2006. **Best alternatives:** Consider the Audi A6, the Cadillac CTS, or the Infiniti G35 sedan. **Options:** Don't waste your money on the satellite navigation system; it's confusing to calibrate and hard to see. Ditch the Bridgestone tires for Michelin, Yokohama, or Pirelli. **Rebates:** $3,000 rebates; limited discounting. **Delivery/PDI:** $1,280. **Depreciation:** Much slower than average. **Insurance cost:** Higher than average. **Parts supply/cost:** Easily found and moderately priced, especially most mechanical and electronic components, but with the exception of some body parts. **Annual maintenance cost:** Less than average. **Warranty:** Bumper-to-bumper 3 years/60,000 km; powertrain 5 years/100,000 km; rust perforation

6 years/unlimited km. **Supplementary warranty:** Not needed. **Highway/city fuel economy:** 7.4–12.2L/100 km.

Quality/Reliability/Safety

Pro: Quality control: Above average. **Reliability:** Above average. **Warranty performance:** Average.

Con: Owner-reported problems: Manual and automatic transmission defects; faulty brake pads and rotors cause steering wheel "shimmy" and jerking to the right or left when braking; poor body fits; and malfunctioning accessories. **Service bulletin problems:** Engine coolant leaks; engine oil leaks; shifter stuck in Park; automatic transmission leaks repaired under warranty; vehicle pulling and drifting; headliner droops; driving position memory doesn't work; and heater blower overheats or blows the fuse. **NHTSA safety complaints:** Excessive steering wheel vibration; one accident caused by vibrating, faulty Bridgestone EL 42 Turanza tires.

TSX ★★★

RATING: Average. The 4-banger has no place in this Acura; choose a gussied-up V6-powered Accord instead. **Strong points:** Great steering and handling (outclasses the Audi A4 and Volvo S40); well laid-out instruments and controls; improved navigation system controls; well built; good fuel economy; and good crashworthiness scores compiled by NHTSA and IIHS. **Weak points:** A disappointing engine choice; premium fuel negates the small engine's fuel-sipping savings; ride is a bit firm; interior is a bit snug; low roofline hampers rear access; overly sensitive seat sensors disable the airbag even though a normal-sized adult is seated; driver's seat needs more lower back support; rear seats have insufficient thigh support; centre rear seat doesn't have a head restraint; HID low beams don't project far enough; turning circle is a bit wide; and excessive tire noise. **New for 2006:** Engine gets 10 more horses; restyled front and rear ends; an upgraded navigation system and multi-info display; memory seats; a new steering wheel; and Bluetooth wireless communication.

OVERVIEW: Essentially a more luxurious, smaller version of the Accord and the successor to the popular Integra sedan, the TSX is presented as an entry-level sports car equipped with a 205-hp 2.4L 4-cylinder engine that must compete in a luxury sedan niche where V6 power is commonplace. It gets excellent gas mileage, but requires premium fuel. It fits between the RSX and the TL in Acura's lineup and is hyped as being sportier than the TL, yet not as harsh as the high-performance RSX.

Crash tests give five stars for driver and passenger crash protection in a frontal collision; five and four stars for side-impact protection; and four stars for rollover resistance. The offset crash rating is also five stars, and head restraints are given a Good rating by IIHS.

Without a doubt, this is a cleanly styled car, both inside and out, with just a bit of a European and sporty flair in the car's interior layout. More significant, though, is the car's limited interior space. Buyers comparing the TSX with the Accord will quickly discover that the TSX has less head and shoulder room up front, and a more cramped rear-seat area. A deal breaker? Perhaps.

Nevertheless, Acura is throwing in a cornucopia of standard safety, performance, and convenience features like standard stability and traction control and head-protecting side airbags to make this $36,100 ($1,430 freight) luxury sedan attractive to shoppers who don't feel size and V6 power are everything.

Still, when you consider the TSX's price is about $10,000 more than a 4-cylinder Honda Accord, you have to wonder whether they have a lot of cachet—or nerve.

 ### Quality/Reliability/Safety

Pro: Quality control: Above average. **Reliability:** Above average. **Warranty performance:** Average.

Con: Owner-reported problems: Manual and automatic transmission defects, unstable driver's seat, poor body fits, and malfunctioning accessories. **Service bulletin problems:** Hard to engage First gear, grinds in Reverse; automatic transmission leaks repaired under warranty; heater blower overheats or blows a fuse; radio display blank; unequal AC air comes from the dash vent; and steering wheel off-centre. **NHTSA safety complaints:** Transmission suddenly failed on the highway; other reports of a grinding noise; side curtain airbag deployed inadvertently; driver's seat shifts and rocks when braking and on turns; and tire sidewall bubbling.

RL ★★★★

RATING: Above Average. **Strong points:** Good acceleration that's smooth and quiet in all gear ranges; exceptional steering and handling; comfortable ride; loaded with goodies; top-quality body and mechanical components; and a four-star front impact rating. **Weak points:** Way overpriced; head restraints rated Poor by IIHS and only Average for offset occupant protection; problematic navigation system controls. **New for 2006:** A new Technology Package that offers adaptive cruise control, run-flat tires, and a radar system that automatically provides warning and braking if the car feels a collision is imminent (Yikes!).

OVERVIEW: Retailing for about $69,000 (hmmm…the 2004 model cost only $55,800), the RL is Honda's—oh, I mean Acura's—flagship luxury sedan. It's powered by the automaker's most powerful engine, a 290-hp V6, and comes with a standard 5-speed automatic gearbox and all-wheel drive (stick shift isn't available). The RL is loaded with innovative high-tech safety and convenience features, like heated front seats, front and rear climate controls, rear-seat trunk pass-through, xenon headlights (get used to oncoming drivers flashing their headlights at you), "smart" side airbags, front seat belt pretensioners, ABS, traction control, and an anti-skid system. No other engine but the 3.5L is available, and the only option offered is Acura's ubiquitous GPS navigation system (see TL comments).

Power is delivered in a smooth and quiet manner. The car handles nicely, with a ride that's less firm than the TL's—although steering response doesn't feel as crisp. Interior accommodations for four occupants are excellent up front and in the rear because the RL uses a larger platform than the TL. All seats are well cushioned and give plenty of thigh support. Cockpit controls and instruments are easily accessed and the climate control system is efficient and easy to adjust, both fore and aft. Good all-around visibility.

COST ANALYSIS: Get the practically identical 2005 model and try to shave off some of the $13,000 price difference from the 2004 version. **Best alternatives:** Consider the BMW 5 Series and the Lexus GS 300/400. You may want to take a look at the TL sedan as well. **Options:** Forget the satellite navigation system. **Rebates:** Expect $5,000 rebates on the 2005s. **Delivery/PDI:** $1,150. **Depreciation:** Much slower than average. **Insurance cost:** Higher than average. **Parts supply/cost:** Most mechanical and electronic components are easily found and moderately priced. Body parts may be hard to come by and can be expensive. **Annual maintenance cost:** Less than average. **Warranty:** Bumper-to-bumper 3 years/60,000 km; powertrain 5 years/100,000 km; rust perforation 6 years/unlimited km. **Supplementary warranty:** Not needed. **Highway/city fuel economy:** 9.2–13.4L/100 km.

 ## Quality/Reliability/Safety

Pro: Quality control: Above average. **Reliability:** Average for all components except the manual and automatic transmissions, which are quite problematic on Acura's entire vehicle lineup. **Warranty performance:** Above average.

Con: Owner-reported problems: Chronic stalling and premature brake wear. The 6-speed transmission often misshifts to Second gear when upshifting from Third to Fourth, causing extensive engine damage. Second gear is almost impossible to access in cold weather. **Service bulletin problems:** Fuel filler cap binding, and tips on repairing automatic transmission leaks under warranty. **NHTSA safety complaints:** Vehicle suddenly stalled while exiting a freeway; dashboard display is unreadable in daylight; and in a crash, seat belt did not restrain driver.

RSX	★★★

RATING: Average. This is Acura's entry-level performance hatchback that targets drivers who want to shift fast and often, and don't mind a firm ride. **Strong points:** Well appointed; good acceleration, steering, and handling above 3000 rpm; user-friendly gauges and controls; excellent braking, especially with the Type S; updated styling; good fuel economy; first tune-up at 160,000 kilometres; low depreciation; a five-star frontal crash rating for both the driver and front-seat passenger, and four-star front side-impact rating; head restraints rated Good up front and Average in the rear by IIHS; and high-quality construction, except for transmission components. **Weak points:** So-so acceleration in lower gears; overall

TECHNICAL DATA

POWERTRAIN (FRONT-DRIVE)

Engines: 2.0L iVTEC 4-cyl. (155) • 2.0L iVTEC 4-cyl. (201 hp); Transmissions: 5-speed man. • 5-speed auto. • 6-speed man.

DIMENSION/CAPACITY

Passengers: 2/3; Wheelbase: 101.2 in.; H: 55.1/L: 172.4/W: 67.9 in.; Headroom F/R: 3.0/2.5 in.; Legroom F/R: 43.1/29.2 in.; Cargo volume: 17.8 cu. ft.; Fuel tank: 50L/reg./prem.; Tow limit: N/A; Load capacity: 850 lb.; Turning circle: 38 ft.; Weight: 2,775 lb.

acceleration compromised by the automatic transmission; limited front and rear headroom; cramped rear seating, with barely adequate knee and foot space; no sedan available; difficult rear access; high rear hatch liftover complicates loading; and excessive road and engine noise. Rearward visibility obstructed by small side windows, thick roof pillars, and a tall rear deck; rear washer fluid often just drizzles down from the nozzle at the top of the window. **New for 2006:** A slightly restyled front end.

OVERVIEW: This is a better car than the Integra it replaced for the following five reasons: It's more attractively styled, provides a higher level of driving performance, has more legroom, has a 6-percent larger cabin and a 33-percent bigger trunk, and offers more standard features. However, it's relatively pricey and only a two-door hatchback is available.

The $24,900 RSX is built on the Civic platform and is powered by a base 155-hp 2.0L twin-cam iVTEC 4-banger or a torquier 201-hp variant used by the high-performance Type S. Three transmissions are available: a 5-speed manual and 5-speed automatic offered with base models, and a 6-speed manual found on the Type S. Both engines are torquier than the power plants they replaced; however, the base engine has more useful commuting low-end torque than the so-called sportier Type S engine.

Handling and steering performance are enhanced through the use of an upgraded steering and independent suspension system, and more effective four-wheel disc brakes. Standard safety features include side airbags, front and rear seat belt pretensioners, and side-impact protection pads.

COST ANALYSIS: Since there's little that is new this year, get a discounted 2005 version, if you can find one. **Best alternatives:** Other cars worth considering are the Mazda Miata and Toyota Celica GT or GT-S. **Options:** None needed. **Rebates:** $2,000 rebates and zero percent financing on the 2006s. **Delivery/ PDI:** $1,150. **Depreciation:** Slower than average. **Insurance cost:** Higher than average. **Parts supply/cost:** It's no problem getting moderately priced parts from Acura or Honda dealers. **Warranty:** Bumper-to-bumper 3 years/60,000 km; powertrain 5 years/100,000 km; rust perforation 6 years/unlimited km. **Supplementary warranty:** Acura quality glitches aren't likely to warrant supplementary protection. **Highway/city fuel economy:** *Base engine with manual transmission:* 8.6–7.1L/100 km; *base engine with automatic:* 9.8–7.1L/100 km; *Type S:* 9.8–7.6L/100 km.

 ## Quality/Reliability/Safety

Pro: Quality control: Above average. **Reliability:** Above average for all components except the manual and automatic transmissions, which are quite problematic on Acura's entire vehicle lineup. **Warranty performance:** Above average.

Con: Owner-reported problems: Rough shifting; rotten-egg smell intrudes into the cabin; premature brake and rear strut wear; airbag light remains lit; rear bumper cover may fall off, not be aligned or flush, come loose, and chip paint; many manual and automatic transmission complaints on previous models (see *forums.clubrsx.com*); no interior hatch release; and glovebox is a bit too small. **Service bulletin problems:** Engine hesitates upon acceleration; excessive exhaust noise; tips on repairing automatic transmission leaks under warranty; heater blower motor overheats and blows a fuse; and a rotten-egg sulfur smell in the interior. **NHTSA safety complaints:** Original equipment tires are poor performers in snow, and First gear shattered upon hard acceleration.

RSX

List Price (firm)	Residual Values (months)			
	24	36	48	60
Base: $24,900 (18%)	$19,500	$16,000	$12,000	$10,000
Premium: $26,900 (18%)	$21,500	$18,000	$14,000	$12,000
Type S: $33,000 (19%)	$23,500	$20,000	$16,000	$13,500

SAFETY FEATURES			CRASHWORTHINESS		
	STD.	OPT.	Head restraints F/R	4	3
Anti-lock brakes	✓	—	Visibility F/R	5	2
Seat belt pretensioners F/R	✓	—	Crash protection (front) D/P	5	5
Side airbags	✓	—	Crash protection (side) F/R	4	—
			Rollover	4	—

NSX (2005) ★★★★

RATING: Above Average. **Strong points:** Beautifully styled; loaded with expensive performance and convenience features; handles well; rides comfortably; and is well constructed with quality mechanical and body components. **Weak points:** $142,000? Let's see...that's about five Miatas. Horsepower-challenged by other cars in this price range. Aluminum construction means fender-benders quickly become wallet busters. **New for 2006:** Nothing; this is its last year on the market.

OVERVIEW: Retailing for about $142,000, the NSX is a luxury sports car that makes no compromises. Its rear mid-mounted, "rev-happy" 290-hp 3.2L VTEC V6 is built for hard driving and taking up permanent residence at the 8000 rpm redline. There's plenty of torque throughout the gear range, and the 6-speed manual shifts flawlessly. Handling is optimized through quick and accurate steering, best-in-class brakes, and a no-surprise suspension system.

COST ANALYSIS: You will have to pay top dollar to get a leftover 2005; wait for the 2007 NSX replacement. **Best alternatives:** Also consider the BMW Z8 and the Porsche 911. **Options:** Take whatever the 2005 model comes with, since there aren't many cars available. **Rebates:** A 2005 will sell for full price without discounts or rebates. **Delivery/PDI:** $1,720. **Depreciation:** Much slower than average. **Insurance cost:** Quite high. **Parts supply/cost:** Easily found and moderately priced, especially most mechanical and electronic components, but with the exception of some body parts. **Annual maintenance cost:** Less than average. **Warranty:** Bumper-to-bumper 3 years/60,000 km; powertrain 5 years/100,000 km; rust perforation 6 years/unlimited km. **Supplementary warranty:** Not needed. **Highway/city fuel economy:** 7.4–12.2L/100 km.

Quality/Reliability/Safety

Pro: Quality control: Above average. **Reliability:** Above average for all components except the manual and automatic transmissions, which are quite problematic on Acura's entire vehicle lineup. **Warranty performance:** Above average.

Con: Owner-reported problems: Rough shifting; rotten-egg smell intrudes into the cabin; premature brake and rear strut wear. Airbag light remains lit. Rear bumper cover may fall off, not be aligned or flush, come loose, and chip paint. **Service bulletin problems:** Corrections for a hard-to-engage First gear, grinding in Reverse, and a binding fuel-filler cap. **NHTSA safety complaints/safety:** Original-equipment tires are poor performers in snow, and First gear shattered upon hard acceleration.

Honda

Like Toyota, Honda continues to post record-breaking sales and profits with every one of its cars, SUVs, and minivans. The fuel-efficient Civic, for example, is breaking sales records as oil prices hit their highest level in history and car shoppers look for an alternative to expensive hybrid fuel-sippers. As a result of this success, Honda is moving downscale and upscale at the same time by bringing out smaller vehicles in use in other countries and adding features to the Civic.

Early next year, the company will import a mini-car called either the Fit or Jazz (depending upon whether it hails from Japan or Europe). This four-door, five-passenger hatchback will have a surprisingly roomy, boxy interior and will be powered by a 1.5L 4-cylinder engine mated to a manual 5-speed transmission. Slotted below the Civic, this little economy car will also be sold as a hybrid.

The redesigned 2006 Civic goes in the other direction. It will carry a base 140-hp 1.8L 4-cylinder power plant. A high performance 197-hp Si mated to a 6-speed manual transmission will also be available.

The 2006 Hybrid Civic will also return with a slight horsepower boost (eight more horses from the engine and seven more from the electric motor).

| INSIGHT | ★★ |

RATING: Below Average. The Insight is a two-passenger econo-car that's primary purpose is to save fuel—even if it means a stiff, jerky ride, ponderous handling, and a morning commute that begins with a concert of road noises. **Strong points:** Fuel economy is estimated at a super-frugal 3.3–3.9L/100 km for highway

TECHNICAL DATA

POWERTRAIN (FRONT-DRIVE)
Engine: 1.0L 3-cyl. (73 hp);
Transmissions: 5-speed man. • CVT
DIMENSION/CAPACITY (SEDAN)
Passengers: 2; Wheelbase: 95 in.;
H: 51/L: 190/W: 72 in.; Headroom F:
3.5 in.; Legroom F: 41.5 in.; Cargo
volume: N/A; Fuel tank: 40L/regular; Tow
limit: Not rated; Load capacity: 365 lb.;
Turning circle: 34 ft.; Weight: 1,875 lb.

and city driving, though owners say they get much less. A tight turning circle is a plus in the city. **Weak points:** Not a very practical car; the 73-hp engine is way underpowered, relegating the Insight to performing light chores in the city; the battery pack gobbles up an incredible amount of interior space. Side airbags aren't available. Unreliable and expensive to service; three catalytic converters at $2,000 each (see *www.hondasucks.ca*). **New for 2006:** Carried over unchanged.

OVERVIEW: The Insight was Honda's first (half-hearted) attempt at hybrid production—and it's still a very basic machine. Although high gas prices have given the Insight its second wind, the car is so obviously outclassed by the larger, more powerful, and more refined Honda Hybrid and Toyota Prius that it is just a matter of time before this throwback to early hybrid technology is discontinued.

INSIGHT

List Price (negotiable)	Residual Values (months)			
	24	36	48	60
Base coupe: $26,000 (15%)	$19,000	$16,000	$13,000	$10,000

SAFETY FEATURES	STD.	OPT.	CRASHWORTHINESS		
Anti-lock brakes	✓	—	Head restraints F	❶	—
Seat belt pretensioners F/R	✓	—	Visibility F/R	❺	❸
			Crash protection (front) D/P	❹	❹
			Crash protection (side) F/R	❹	—
			Rollover	❹	—

All ratings on a numbered scale where ❺ is good and ❶ is bad. See page 153–154 for a more detailed description.

RATING: Average. The Civic Hybrid comes in second to the Toyota Prius, a much more refined hybrid. A good alternative is a Honda Civic HX or base Toyota Echo—two cars that cost about $12,000 less, get great gas mileage, and don't depreciate as much. The savings will buy lots of gas. **Strong points:** A fuel-sipper; smooth shifting, comfortable ride; AC can run off of the electric motor; and good front and rear visibility. **Weak points:** Fuel economy is hyped by at least 20–45 percent; cold weather performance isn't as fuel-efficient, encouraging drivers to sneak up on lights; repairs and servicing are dealer dependent; no crashworthiness data; highway rescuers are wary of cutting through the high-voltage electrical system to save occupants; there's no long-term reliability data; only average depreciation; and you have to drive several hundred thousand kilometres to amortize the hybrid's startup costs. **New for 2006:** Major powertrain improvements.

OVERVIEW: Honda was the first automaker to introduce gas-electric hybrid technology to North American consumers when it launched the Honda Insight in December 1999, followed by the Civic Hybrid in March 2002.

The Hybrid looks and feels just like a Civic, both inside and out. You should get the same high levels of reliability and durability. On top of that, its powertrain uses gasoline-electric technology that lets you travel up to 1,047 km (650 mi.) on a single tank of gas (at 4.7L/100 km or more) and the battery recharges itself as you drive.

TECHNICAL DATA

POWERTRAIN (FRONT-DRIVE)

Engines: 1.3L 3-cyl. (110 hp) • Electric motor (combined 123 hp); Transmission: CVT

DIMENSION/CAPACITY

Passengers: 2/3; Wheelbase: 106.3 in.; H: 56.5/L: 176.7/W: 69 in.; Headroom F/R: 3.0/2.0 in.; Legroom F/R: 41.5/28 in.; Cargo volume: 10.1 cu. ft.; Fuel tank: 50L/regular; Tow limit: N/A; Load capacity: 850 lb.; Turning circle: 34.8 ft.; Weight: 2,732 lb.

This five-passenger sedan is equipped with Honda's second-generation Integrated Motor Assist (IMA) system, comprising a 110-hp 1.3L gasoline engine combined with a DC brushless motor and high-tech powertrain management that reportedly gives 4.6–4.7L/100 km highway and city fuel economy—though owners claim they save much less gas.

The 2006 version's combined output, including the electric motor's output, is 110 and 123, versus last year's combined 93 and 105 horses. A continuously variable transmission replaces the 5-speed manual. Another important improvement is the addition of a motor-only drive mode, where the motor powers the car by itself during low-speed cruising.

On the downside: Owners report that similar fuel economy can be achieved with cheaper conventional Honda or Toyota small cars that aren't burdened with complex new technology. This opinion has been seconded by a report in the September 2004 issue of *Car and Driver* magazine, which concluded that one would have to drive a hybrid 266,000 km (or 165,000 mi.) to amortize its higher costs. Furthermore, the car's unique dual power plants can make for risky driving, as this Hybrid owner warns:

> [With a] 2003 Honda Civic Hybrid on a snowy road, coming over a small rise while going around a moderate curve under 40 mph [64 km/h], the battery charging function, activated by driver taking foot off the gas before cresting the hill, produced progressively stronger engine braking effect on the front wheels, equivalent to an unwanted downshift and causing fishtailing and poor response to corrective steering, so that the car slid across the road and into a snow bank and concrete abutment, causing $6,000 (U.S.) in damage. If there had been oncoming traffic, there could have been serious injuries or fatalities.

COST ANALYSIS: Get the 2006 Hybrid for the powertrain improvements. **Best alternatives:** Also consider the Toyota Prius, the Honda Civic, and the 2005 Toyota Echo. Better yet, a leftover 2005 Civic HX with its lean-burn engine will cut your gas bills and cost about half the price of the Hybrid. The VW Jetta TDI just doesn't cut it, unless engine clatter, turbo torque, and that diesel aroma are your cup of tea. **Options:** Nothing worth buying, except tires to replace the original-equipment Firestone or Bridgestone rubber. **Rebates:** Not likely, thanks to hybrid popularity. **Delivery/PDI:** $1,200. **Depreciation:** Average. Resale value after five years is less certain; it'll be a rough market for a used Civic Hybrid with an old-generation hybrid powertrain and an $5,000 battery pack that may need replacing. **Insurance cost:** Higher than average, because it's easier to "total" the car than replace its expensive, high-tech parts. **Parts supply/cost:** No data yet. **Annual maintenance cost:** Average. **Warranty:** Bumper-to-bumper 3 years/60,000 km; powertrain 5 years/100,000 km; rust perforation 6 years/unlimited km. The Hybrid's battery pack has a 10-year/160,000 km warranty; a replacement battery is estimated to cost between $4,000 and $5,000! **Supplementary warranty:** A toss-up. **Highway/city fuel economy:** 4.6–4.7L/100 km.

 ## Quality/Reliability/Safety

Pro: Quality control: Above average. **Reliability:** Above average for all components, so far. But the crunch comes this year when the original warranty expires for many owners. **Warranty performance:** Above average, but it's still early.

Con: Owner-reported problems: Much less fuel economy than promised:

> The advertised mpg of my Honda hybrid for city driving is 48 mpg [5.9L/100 km]. I have never gotten better than 38 mpg [7.4 L/100 km]. Honda says there's nothing they can do about it and just advertising that it will get 48 mpg doesn't mean it will get that actual mileage. I believe it should at least be close, not 20 percent less than advertised.

Rough shifting; rotten-egg smell intrudes into the cabin; premature brake and rear strut wear. Airbag light remains lit. Rear bumper cover may fall off, not be aligned or flush, come loose, and chip paint. Walter W., a B.C.-based engineer and *Lemon-Aid* correspondent, is concerned about the Civic's vulnerability to road debris and premature corrosion:

> During a recent major model redesign, the steering arms were moved from under the wheel axle to over the axle (according to Honda service). In order to allow the free movement of the steering arm, a section of the forward wheelwells' lining was removed. This removal allows the entry of water, gravel, and salt into the engine bay when the car wheels are off centre during a turn.

> I own both a 2002 Civic and a 2003 Civic Hybrid. Both of these cars are missing this key protection item. The result is a variety of gravel and dirt pooling in the engine bay, and frequent soaking of the engine. It appears that, other than the steering change, no changes were made to the fixtures in the bay to reflect that they are now exposed to the elements. U-beams are still facing up, bolts do not have covers, heat shields are not designed to shed gravel, and the mounting holes for the missing components are still there in the frame. In B.C. this will not be a problem, but the more eastern parts of Canada still use salt in their sand mixtures, and this material will build up in the engine bay and could cause catastrophic failures… I also learned that Honda is no longer undercoating their cars.

Service bulletin problems: Door lock cylinder sticks; clutch pedal has a notchy feel; fix for a deformed windshield moulding; and a spare tire kit is available free of charge for owners dissatisfied with receiving a can of sealant instead of a spare tire. **NHTSA safety complaints:** Airbags failed to deploy; trunk caught fire while vehicle was parked; sudden, unintended acceleration when foot was taken off of the accelerator pedal; vehicle lost all forward power while cruising on the highway; excessive brake vibration; and front wheels locked up when brakes were tapped lightly.

CIVIC HYBRID

List Price (negotiable)	Residual Values (months)			
	24	36	48	60
Base: $29,500 (15%)	$22,500	$19,000	$15,000	$12,000

SAFETY FEATURES	STD.	OPT.	CRASHWORTHINESS		
Anti-lock brakes	✓	—	Head restraints F/R	②	②
Seat belt pretensioners F/R	✓	—			
Side airbags F/R	✓	—			

CIVIC ★★★★

best buy

RATING: Recommended. The Honda Civic is one of the best performing, most dependable small cars money can buy. In its eighth redesign since 1973, the car distances itself even more from the rest of the pack. **Strong points:** Good acceleration; smooth-shifting automatic transmission; great handling; much improved steering and better cornering control; comfortable ride; good front and rear visibility; reworked dash is nicely done; a tilt/telescoping steering wheel is standard; lots of interior and trunk space; excellent resale value; and better-than-average reliability. An optional natural-gas engine is carried over. **Weak points:** Look for a price increase of about $2,000. The coupe's steeply raked front windshield cuts forward visibility; the Si suspension may be too firm for some; the latest redesign has decreased overall passenger room slightly, although outward dimesions are larger; difficult rear access; rear seat room limited to two adults; and there's a cubic foot less trunk space.

Past models have had an unusually large number of performance- and safety-related complaints that include airbag and seat belt malfunctions, sudden acceleration, transmission breakdowns, chronic stalling, and complete brake failure. Head restraints have been rated Poor by IIHS. **New for 2006:** An all-new coupe, sedan, Hybrid, and sporty Si.

OVERVIEW: The Civic is one of the most refined and competent subcompacts on the market today. Few larger and more expensive cars can match its quality, performance, and roominess. This year's improvements include more powerful base engines on the Civic, Si, and Hybrid, additional standard safety features like front, side, and head-protecting curtain side airbags, improved brakes, sleeker styling (Saturn-like up front), more interior room, and a more rigid body to reduce rattles and vibration. There are now two body styles and four models: sedan (DX, LX, and EX); coupe (LX and EX); gas-electric hybrid; and high-performance Si.

The 2006 sedans have had their wheelbase extended by 3.2 inches, and are wider and longer by 1.4 inches. Height has been reduced, however, by 0.2 inches. These models use either a 5-speed manual or a 5-speed automatic transmission coupled to a 140-hp 4-cylinder engine, while the Si gets a 197-hp 2.0L powerplant.

The coupe version uses the same powertrain as the sedan, though it is set on a wheelbase that's two inches smaller, has three inches less height, and has a front windshield with a steeper rake (tall drivers will need to stop well in back of overhanging traffic lights). The coupe's suspension is also a bit firmer than the sedan's.

COST ANALYSIS: Forget about price-dickering; these cars will be back-ordered for their first six months of production. This isn't surprising, however. New Civics in any form are very popular and usually cost a few thousand dollars more than domestic offerings. Since this year's redesigned models offer many new standard features, they are worth the extra money. Furthermore, Hondas have higher resale values, which equal or surpass what you initially spend. You may also wish to wait a half year for the early production glitches to be corrected. **Best alternatives:** Other cars worth considering that are cheaper and not as refined are the Hyundai Accent, the Mazda3, and the 2005 Toyota Echo. **Options:** Try to get a free extra set of ignition keys written into the contract; Honda's anti-start, theft-protection keys may cost as much as $150 a set. Steer clear of the standard-issue radio and Firestone or Bridgestone tires. **Rebates:** Not likely. **Delivery/PDI:** A way-too-high $1,100. **Depreciation:** Much slower than average. **Insurance cost:** A bit higher than average. **Parts supply/cost:** Reasonably priced and easily found at dealers and independent suppliers. **Annual maintenance cost:** Much less than average. **Warranty:** Bumper-to-bumper 3 years/60,000 km; powertrain 5 years/100,000 km; rust perforation 6 years/unlimited km. **Supplementary warranty:** Not needed. **Highway/city fuel economy:** 5.7–7.4L/100 km with the 2005 1.7L 4-cylinder engine.

Quality/Reliability/Safety (2005)

Pro: Quality control: Better than average, but still too many safety-related failures and annoying vibrations and rattles that will likely increase with the redesigned 2006. **Reliability:** Also better than average. **Warranty performance:** Average. Service and warranty advisors are in desperate need of attending Dale Carnegie classes.

Con: Service bulletin problems: Engine oil leaks; engine cranks, won't start; car won't move in Drive; automatic transmission fluid leaks; stalling in Reverse or Drive; manual transmission grinds when shifting into Third gear; heater blower motor overheats or blows a fuse; malfunctioning alternator; wheel bearing, brake pedal booster, clutch pedal, or master cylinder noise; A-pillar or dash rattles; sunroof rattling; binding front or rear windows; faulty door lock cylinders; doors and trunk lid hard to close; inoperable fuel door handle; and body and bumper paint peeling and cracking. **Owner-reported problems:** Oil leak from lower engine block crack; faulty main rear crankshaft seal; automatic transmission leaks, sluggish performance when it rains or when passing through a large puddle, and noisy engagement; transmission periodically wouldn't shift into Third or Fourth gear (torque converter replaced); excessive steering shimmy; and front strut leakage causes noise and difficult handling. Electrical system and fit-and-finish deficiencies include a poorly mounted driver's seat; inoperable door locks and power windows; a driver-side window that won't roll back up; a fan button that has to be turned on before the AC button will work; an erratic fuel gauge, speedometer, and tachometer; an interior light that hums as it dims; and lousy radio speakers. The vehicle produces a high magnetic field (confirmed by a Gauss meter); water leaks through the door bottoms, from the tail light into the trunk, and onto the driver-side footwell carpet; AC doesn't cool properly and AC condensate drips from under the glove compartment (heating core needs to be replaced to fix the problem); dashboard buzzing; and loose, rattling door panels and door latches. **NHTSA safety complaints:** Fire ignited in the seat belt wiring under the passenger seat; seat belts tighten up progressively when connected; child injured when he became entangled in unfastened rear centre shoulder belt, which retracted, cutting off his air; seat belts failed to lock up in a sudden panic stop; and many complaints that the airbags failed to deploy in a frontal collision:

> I hit the car in front of me going about 40 mph [64 km/h]. I do not think that my seat belt locked. My airbag did not deploy but my passenger-side airbag did. I hit the steering wheel very hard! I had to be transported to the hospital. I have severe chest contusions and neck and back sprain/strain. My insurance company believes my car may be a total loss but my airbag did not go off.... Honda was contacted the next day. Nine days later, they sent an adjuster out to inspect my car (but not an engineer). I have been told there is no reason to send an engineer out. The adjuster seemed to be more concerned with investigating me than why the airbag did not deploy. I would like to know why it is that I do not have a front end to my car on the driver's side and my airbag did not go off, but there is no damage to the front passenger side and that airbag went off!

Airbag warning light stays lit; front tie-rod broke, causing complete steering loss; sudden acceleration when AC or heater is engaged; brake and accelerator pedal are mounted too close together; sudden acceleration, particularly when braking, or when cruise control was engaged; several incidents where cellular phone triggered sudden acceleration:

> Unintended acceleration has occured three times. Put foot on brake to slow down and car accelerator starts racing. Move gearshift to Neutral. Accelerator then disengages back to normal. [The] 2005 Honda Civic LX [has] approximately 5,000 miles [8,000 km].

•

> My wife installed a Nokia 5110-to-car kit, started the engine, selected Reverse gear, and the engine started acceleration. My wife immediately shut the engine down. Now, she drives the car with the cellular phone closed. I think that a possible reason for this accident is the unintended triggering of the throttle to full open by the electromagnetic signal created by the car kit. So, this shows that the insulation of the throttle control system is weak in this model. It has to be much better insulated to screen the electromagnetic noise created by any other equipment.

Chronic stalling accompanied by steering wheel lock-up; steering lock-up while slowing for a traffic light, engine continued running; fuel leakage into the engine compartment while vehicle was underway; car has to warm up a few minutes before brake will work properly; vehicle rolls back when stopped on an incline with automatic transmission engaged; transmission surges forward when put into Reverse (blamed on transmission solenoid); automatic transmission will suddenly downshift in traffic; when accelerator pedal is tapped at less than 5 km/h, vehicle suddenly was passed from Drive to Neutral to Reverse; transmission won't easily go into First gear; steering wheel wouldn't lock when parked; steering wheel shakes when turned sharply to the left or right; taller drivers' vision blocked by non-adjustable, windshield-mounted rear-view mirror; loose driver's seat; windshield cracked suddenly; difficult to see through bottom of windshield; with AC engaged at night, film covers rear windshield (said to be either engine head gasket failure or "outgassing" from the interior's plastic trim); AC blamed for emiting toxic fumes:

> The HVAC (air conditioning/heating system/defroster) immediately started spewing toxic mold/mildew spores on a new vehicle test-driven at the dealer's. It occurs while driving, after running the air conditioning for a few minutes, turning the air conditioning off (while leaving the fan running) and waiting a few minutes. It then stinks for a few minutes and then disappears. This occurs every time this cycle is used with the air conditioning and defroster. This occurred in two almost identical vehicles (Honda Civics with different trim levels) with less than 80 miles [130 km] on them. When I asked the salesman and service advisor about it, they said that they never heard of such a thing. They said it was probably the new car smell. I had a friend concur that it was definitely a toxic mildew odour and that it would need to be treated probably every few weeks for the life of the vehicle.

Trunk springs failed; exterior and interior lights dim to an unsafe level; and Dunlop and Firestone tires have tread separation.

Road Performance

Pro: Acceleration/torque: The 2006 140-hp base engine is as smooth and responsive as before, but the extra 25 horses give the Civic more low-speed grunt and high-speed merging capability without screaming in protest. Transmission shifting is quiet and effortless with the manual and practically imperceptible with the automatic. The Si's 197-hp 2.0L 4-cylinder is a tire burner. **Emergency handling:** Much more control this year when cornering at highway speeds, thanks to the Si's new limited-slip differential and 17-inch wheels. **Steering:** Better than average power steering. **Routine handling:** Handling is excellent, and the ride is among the best in the subcompact class. The Si's larger wheels add to its handling prowess. **Braking:** Disc/drum with base models and disc/disc with the Si perform impeccably.

Con: The 2005 VTEC variant is noisier than the 2006—get a leftover Si with the VTEC option only if you enjoy constant gear shifting and intend to do a lot of highway driving, where it's most useful and less interactive. Also, stay away from last year's poorly performing 15-inch all-season tires.

CIVIC

List Price (firm) **Residual Values** (months)

	24	36	48	60
DX 2d: $18,200 (12%)	$14,000	$12,000	$ 9,000	$ 7,500
LX 2d: $20,800 (13%)	$16,000	$13,000	$10,000	$ 8,500
DX 4d: $18,400 (12%)	$14,500	$12,500	$ 9,500	$ 8,000
Si 2d: $23,000 (15%)	$18,000	$16,000	$12,500	$10,500

SAFETY FEATURES			CRASHWORTHINESS		
	STD.	**OPT.**	Head restraints F/R	❸	❷
Anti-lock brakes	✓	—	Visibility F/R	❸	❷
Seat belt pretensioners F/R	✓	—	Crash protection (front) D/P		
Side airbags	✓	—	2d	❺	❺
Stability control	✓	—	4d	❺	❺
Traction control	—	—	Crash protection (side) F/R		
			2d	❸	❹
			Hatchback	❹	❹
			4d	❹	❹
			Crash protection (offset)	❺	—
			Rollover	❹	—

S2000 ★★★★

RATING: Above Average. This vehicle steps into the void created by the Prelude's departure. **New for 2006:** Nothing significant.

OVERVIEW: This world-class sport roadster is lightweight, with a peppy 2.2L 4-cylinder 237-hp engine. Performance comes at a high price, though: $49,800 plus $1,325 PDI/transport. Furthermore, fewer than 10,000 a year are earmarked for North America (expect less than 10 percent of that figure to be sold in Canada).

The S2000 comes fully equipped with limited-slip differential, anti-lock brakes, AC, cruise control, leather seats, seat belt pretensioners, 16-inch wheels, high-intensity headlights, remote door locks with an engine immobilizer, a CD player with remote audio controls, power everything, and an air deflector.

Powered by a torquier 2.2L VTEC engine, the S2000 will reach 0–100 km/h in about the same time it takes to close the convertible roof—under 6 seconds—without straining the high-revving engine (the tachometer has an unbelievable 9000 redline). The upgraded 6-speed shifter has short throws helped by a direct link with the gearbox, rather than shift-by-wire units used in other cars. Standard features include larger wheels and wider tires. Performance drivers will immediately discover that the S2000 excels at acceleration, braking, cornering, and shifting, owing in large part to the car's powerful engine, anti-lock brakes, double wishbone body, rigid suspension, and electronically controlled rack-and-pinion steering, which enhances steering response without compromising stability. NHTSA has given the S2000 four stars for driver and passenger frontal crash protection, five stars for side protection, and five stars for rollover resistance.

Not everything is perfect, though. Rear visibility is cut a bit by the convertible top boot cover, the convertible top when it's up, and the rear plastic window *sans* defroster. The small trunk houses a temporary spare tire (shame!) and Honda doesn't include a passenger airbag shut-off switch (double shame!). The ride can be jolting, as with many convertibles. Furthermore, there are quite a few squeaks and rattles; tall drivers won't fit comfortably in the cockpit; and the cheap-sounding sound system has Lilliputian controls.

COST ANALYSIS/BEST ALTERNATIVES: Other models worth considering include the Mazda Miata or the BMW Z4.

Service bulletin problems: Noisy, notchy-feeling clutch pedal; incorrect speedometer readings; and a heater motor blower that overheats or blows a fuse.

ACCORD ★★★★

RATING: Above Average. The Accord is the benchmark for dependability and performance in the family sedan niche. It addressed most of the powertrain, performance, and comfort deficiencies of its predecessor in its redesigned 2003 model. Numerous safety-related failures and an ill-informed customer relations and service cadre aren't helpful. **Strong points:** Excellent acceleration with all three engines; 6-speed manual transmission available on more models; well equipped with user-friendly instruments and controls; easy handling, thanks to large tires and a sturdy chassis; comfortable ride; good craftsmanship; above-average reliability; and a high resale value. **Weak points:** Windshield dash reflection may be distracting. Too many owner reports of a foul-smelling exhaust entering into the cabin, airbags that explode for no reason or fail to deploy, brake failure, or sudden acceleration. Head restraint crash protection rated Poor by IIHS. **New for 2006:** A 10-hp boost in power; a new 6-speed manual transmission for the coupe; and a restyled rear end that will include the addition of LED tail lights. All 2006 Accords are now designated ultra-low-emission vehicles.

OVERVIEW: Having competed toe-to-toe for what seems like forever with the Toyota Camry and Ford Taurus/Sable, the 2006 Accord has jumped leagues ahead of the competition with its third hybrid (the Insight and Civic Hybrid are also still on the market), which mixes frugality with high performance.

If you want good fuel economy and performance with a conventional powertrain, check out these two

TECHNICAL DATA

POWERTRAIN (FRONT-DRIVE)

Engines: 2.4L 4-cyl. (166 hp) • 3.0L V6 (246 hp) • 3.0L V6 (253 hp) Hybrid; Transmissions: 5-speed man. • 5-speed auto. • 6-speed man. • CVT

DIMENSION/CAPACITY (SEDAN)

Passengers: 2/3; Wheelbase: 108 in.; H: 51/L: 190/W: 72 in.; Headroom F/R: 3.0/3.5 in.; Legroom F/R: 42/ 30.5 in.; Cargo volume: 14 cu. ft.; Fuel tank: 65L/regular; Tow limit: 1,000 lb.; Load capacity: 850 lb.; Turning circle: 39 ft.; Weight: 3,265 lb.

engines: the competent base 2.4L 166-hp 4-banger and the powerful 3.0L 246-hp V6. You want ride comfort and responsive handling? The new Accord gives you that too, through a more refined suspension and steering set-up. What about space? The Accord sedans are roomier than ever before, with interior dimensions and capacity that provide more interior space than you'll likely need.

Overall, the Honda Accord is smooth, quiet, mannerly, and predictable. Every time Honda has redesigned this line it has not only caught up with the latest advances, but also gone slightly ahead. Other strong points are ergonomics that prioritize comfort, easy driveability, and predictable handling.

Fast and nimble without a V6, this is the mid-sized sedan of choice for drivers who want maximum fuel economy and comfort along with lots of space for grocery hauling and occasional highway cruising. With the optional V6, the Accord is one of the most versatile mid-sized cars you can find. It offers something for everyone, and its top-drawer quality and high resale value mean that there's no way you can lose money buying one.

Accord Hybrid

The Accord Hybrid is equipped with a 3.0L 253-hp V6 mated to Honda's integrated electric motor-CVT transaxle unit. The engine also uses cylinder de-activation to save fuel by shutting down three cylinders during cruising and returning to 6-cylinder power when the need arises. This set-up manages to combine for the first time performance and fuel economy, and overcomes the low horsepower handicap seen with 4-cylinder hybrids. Priced at $37,000, the Hybrid will cost about $3,000 more than a conventional V6-equipped Accord.

COST ANALYSIS: Get the 4-cylinder-equipped 2005 if you want to save money on the purchase price and keep fuel consumption down. Don't go near the Hybrid unless you don't mind being tied to your dealer's service bay. **Best alternatives:** Some other vehicles worth considering in place of a standard Accord: the BMW 3 Series, the Hyundai Elantra, the Mazda6, and the Toyota Camry. There is no viable alternative to the V6-equipped Hybrid. **Options:** Choose the V6 for a smoother ride that gives you some grunt in reserve. The DVD navigation with voice control found on the EX and V6 coupe is a bit gimmicky, but easier to use and understand than most of the competition. **Rebates:** Not likely. **Delivery/PDI:** An exaggerated $1,325. Expect a six-month waiting period for the Hybrid. **Depreciation:** Slower than average for all models. **Insurance cost:** Higher than average. **Parts supply/ cost:** Good availability and moderately priced; all bets are off with the Hybrid's powertrain components. **Annual maintenance cost:** Less than average. **Warranty:** Bumper-to-bumper 3 years/60,000 km; powertrain 5 years/100,000 km; rust perforation 5 years/unlimited km. Hybrid warranty will undoubtedly be longer. **Supplementary warranty:** Not needed. Honda's base warranty and "goodwill" warranty extensions should sufficiently cover most problems.

Highway/city fuel economy: 6.9–9.0L/100 km with the base engine; 7.8–11.6L/100 km with the V6 automatic sedan. Honda says that the Hybrid's fuel economy should be similar to a 4-cylinder-equipped Civic. Don't believe it.

 ## Quality/Reliability/Safety

Pro: Reliability: Better than average, but an increase in transmission and brake failures on previous year's models, around the three-year mark, is worrisome. Still, one would imagine that Honda has learned from its mistakes and isn't putting the same failure-prone components into its 2006s. **Warranty performance:** Average. Keep in mind that Honda puts a "goodwill" clause in almost all of its service bulletins, allowing service managers to submit any claim to the company long after the original warranty has lapsed. This is a good gesture; however, the insensitive and arrogant attitude of some Honda service and warranty adminstrators is totally unacceptable.

Con: Quality control: The 2003 redesign generated almost 200 safety-related complaints when a quarter of that number would be normal. Also, following the 2003 redesign, Honda promised us better performing, more durable transmissions. It lied. Fortunately, an extended warranty now covers tranny breakdowns up to eight years. **Owner-reported problems:** Chronic hard starting caused by a faulty ignition/key; "rotten-egg" smell in the cabin; coolant in the engine oil pan; frequent hard starts; hard-shifting transmission (from First to Second gear) also shifts erratically:

> I own both a 2004 Accord EX V6 coupe and now a 2005 EX V6 sedan with automatic transmissions. Transmission gear shifter completely misses the "D" position and moves into "D3" when shifting from either Park or Neutral modes, as though that is the correct position to operate the vehicle when driving! Every other auto transmission car I've owned required extra effort to bypass the Drive position to place the shifter into another (lower) gear setting. Operating either of my vehicles in this manner may eventually cause significant damage to the transmission, engine, or both. It may even cause some unforeseen transmission behavior affecting drivability. Honda customer service was contacted and their suggestion was to be "more careful" in selecting the gear shifter position. That does not sound like a very substantial solution to an obvious mechanical problem.

Brake shuddering, grinding, and squealing; warped brake rotors; popping noise when accelerating; power-steering groan believed to be caused by the steering pump; hole in AC condenser; defective CD changer; stereo speaker hums; right-side speaker constantly blows out; windshield creaks and rattles in cold, dry weather; moon roof doesn't close all the way; pervasive rattling; windows rattle and tick; wrinkled, bubbling door window moulding; extensive paint damage; roof water leaks; and headliner sags in the rear. One owner found that falling acorns pockmarked the Accord's body, while his CR-V escaped damage. Another owner reported that the roof buckles:

> [A] 2005 Honda Accord EXL experienced a buckling roof. The consumer's wife was driving and had run over a pothole when she heard a loud noise. The consumer found the roof severely buckled. The consumer had taken the vehicle to the dealer when they found other 4-door Honda Accords with the same problem. Currently the consumer's vehicle has big buckles in the roof.... The consumer requested a refund of the purchase price, replacement of the vehicle with one with corrected design or structural condition that would prevent buckling in the future.

Service bulletin problems: Engine won't start and power windows don't work; accelerator sticking closed or difficult to depress; engine oil leaks; engine cranks, won't start; automatic transmission axle seal leaks; automatic transmission fluid leaks; manual transmission is hard to shift; accessory belt, clutch pedal, and wheel bearing noise; clicking ratching noise on right-hand turns; AC display module is too dim; AC interior water leak; inoperative AC Auto Stop; malfunctioning alternator; heater blower overheats or blows a fuse; ABS and airbag warning lights come on for no reason; brake pedal is hard to depress; trunk trim panel not fitted properly; troubleshooting ABS brake light illumination; inaccurate gauges and odometer; heating and cooling controls are not illuminated sufficiently; excessive steering vibration; noisy power-steering counter-measures; investigating owner reports of cracked windshields; seat belts slow to retract; doors don't unlock in cold weather; poor AC cooling; radio speaker doesn't work; noisy rear window regulator; rear shelf rattling; driver-side A-pillar noise; loose, noisy B-pillar trim; dash or pillar creaking or clicking; roof water leak fix; exhaust pipe rust stains; a sulfur smell invades the cabin; and troubleshooting tips for a low fuel warning when the fuel tank is a quarter full. **NHTSA safety complaints:** Sudden, unintended acceleration while car is in motion or when put into Reverse (believed to be caused by a defective cold start idle control); stalling when vehicle is accelerating; axle suddenly snapped; front wheel flew apart:

> [A driver] was driving home from work in her new 2005 Honda Accord coupe when her right front wheel came apart. Luckily, the failure did not cause any injuries or deaths; however, she was [travelling at a high speed] and the car swerved to the right and she had a hard time stopping the car since the brakes had been damaged. The parts and pieces from her wheel caused two other cars to be damaged by flat tires. The reason for filing this complaint is two-fold; to protect anyone else that may have this problem and to register a complaint against Honda Motor Company, who would not stand behind their own equipment.

Front and side curtain airbags deployed for no reason; airbag failed to deploy during collision; airbags may not work if the car is equipped with a cell phone:

We were told by the dealer that in Honda Accords, the airbag's functionality can be compromised by a cell phone being in the car! If this is the case, the cars should be recalled! There's even a special power jack between the front seats for cell phones. There's no telling how many Honda drivers are in danger if what the dealer told me is the case. How can a car manufacturer and dealer knowingly sell a vehicle whose primary safety feature deactivates because the owner is carrying a cell phone? We left the dealer with our car (8/24/05). About 2 miles [3 km] down the road, the airbag light came on again. We immediately returned to the dealer. They have the car again and are going to call Honda tech-support for advice.

Fire ignited in the insulation; severe steering pull to the right or left; console over-heats and smells burnt; keys overheat in the ignition; hard starts caused by faulty chip embedded in the key; sudden loss of braking:

I was test-driving a brand new 2005 Honda Accord LX model. During the test-drive, while approaching a traffic signal that was about to turn red, I depressed the brake pedal, but the car did not respond. I continued to depress the pedal, with no response. Because of this I was not able to stop and struck another car in the intersection.

Frequent Michelin tire blowouts; driver's seat belt won't retract; passenger-side mirror slipped off; and rear vision is obstructed by head restraints, high rear deck, and roof pillar. The original equipment tire jack is a knuckle-buster that doesn't hold up the car very well. Severe wind buffeting when driving with the rear windows open.

Road Performance

Pro: Emergency handling: Impressive. The ride is firm and well controlled, except for a rear suspension that may be too soft for some. **Steering:** Sporty and very responsive, with plenty of road feel. **Acceleration/torque:** Excellent with both the 4- and 6-cylinder engine even without this year's small horsepower boost. All engines give sparkling performance with plenty of low-end torque and minimal noise. **Transmission:** The 5- and 6-speed manual and automatic transmissions work very well, with smooth and light clutch action. **Routine handling:** Excellent handling in town and on the highway. It's also amazingly smooth and quiet. There isn't a trace of vibration throughout the operating range, including at idle. Excels in smoothness when passing over freeway expansion joints and pot-holes, where it dampens jolts better than most cars in its class. The emphasis on comfort also dominates the Accord's ride and handling. Although its chassis is as good as any, Honda's new suspension settings aren't as firm as those of the other cars in this class. **Braking:** Disc/drum and disc/disc brakes perform quite well with little fading.

Con: Hard cornering compromised a bit by softer rear suspension. Standard rear drum brakes are out of character for a car with upscale pretensions.

List Price (firm)	Residual Values (months)			
	24	36	48	60
DX Sedan: $25,000 (15%)	$20,000	$17,500	$14,500	$11,500
Accord LX-G: $26,700 (16%)	$22,000	$19,000	$16,000	$13,000
Accord EX V6: $34,000 (15%)	$26,000	$23,000	$20,000	$17,000

SAFETY FEATURES	STD.	OPT.	CRASHWORTHINESS		
Anti-lock brakes	✓	—	Head restraints F/R	❶	❶
Seat belt pretensioners F/R	✓	—	Visibility F/R	⑤	❷
Side airbags	✓	—	Crash protection (front) D/P	⑤	⑤
			Crash protection (side) F/R	④	④
			Hybrid	④	⑤
			Crash protection (offset)	⑤	—
			Rollover	④	—

ODYSSEY ★★★★★

best buy

RATING: Recommended. The upgraded 2005 model passes the Sienna in safety, performance, and convenience features. There have, however, been frequent reports of safety- and performance-related failures on previous-year Odysseys. Of particular concern are airbag malfunctions; automatic sliding-door failures; engine defects, transmission breakdowns, and erratic shifting; and sudden brake loss. **Strong points:** Plenty of power for high-speed merging; a spacious, versatile, and quiet interior; and numerous safety and convenience features. Additional

All ratings on a numbered scale where ⑤ is good and ❶ is bad. See page 153–154 for a more detailed description.

mid-range torque means less shifting when the engine is under load. Carlike ride and handling; more interior volume than the Sienna; eight-passenger seating (EX); comfortable seats; second-row middle seats can be folded down as an armrest or removed completely, much like the middle row captain's chairs, which can slide fore or aft by 25 centimetres in unison or separately; second-row power windows; and floor-stowable, 60/40 split third-row seats with eight centimetres more legroom; easy back-seat entry and exit; a convenient second driver-side door and power tailgate; most controls and displays are easy to reach and read; lots of passenger and cargo room; an extensive list of standard equipment; climate, radio, and optional navigation controls are easy to

TECHNICAL DATA

POWERTRAIN (FRONT-DRIVE)
Engine: 3.5L V6 (255 hp); Transmission: 5-speed auto.
DIMENSION/CAPACITY
Passengers: 2/3/3; Wheelbase: 118 in.; H: 68.8/L: 201/W: 77 in.; Headroom F/R1/R2: 4.5/5.5/2.0 in.; Legroom F/R1/R2: 41.5/31/28 in.; Cargo volume: 66.5 cu. ft.; Fuel tank: 80L/regular; Tow limit: 3,500 lb.; Load capacity: 1,320 lb.; Turning circle: 40 ft.; Weight: 4,615 lb.

reach (navigation voice recognition is bilingual, yippee!); air conditioning toggles with raised edges for easy flipping; and a more accessible dash-mounted gearshift. Above average quality control; better fit and finish than the Sienna; and excellent crashworthiness scores (with the exception of head restraints). The Odyssey also has standard vehicle stability-assist and traction control to prevent rollovers and enhance handling, side curtain airbags with rollover sensors for all rows, and adjustable brake and accelerator pedals. **Weak points:** Fuel consumption isn't a good as Honda promises, despite its innovative cylinder de-activation system. Unlike with the Sienna, all-wheel drive isn't available; middle-row seats don't fold flat like in other minivans, so they need to be stowed somewhere else; second-row head restraints block visibility; front-seat passenger legroom is marginal owing to the restricted seat travel; you can't slide your legs comfortably under the dash; some passengers bump their shins on the glove box; third-row seat is suitable only for children; the narrow back bench seat provides little legroom unless the middle seats are pushed far forward, inconveniencing passengers in those seats; radio control access is blocked by the shift lever, and it's difficult to calibrate the radio without taking your eyes off the road; power-sliding doors are slow to retract; some tire rumble, rattles, and body drumming at highway speeds; premium fuel is required for optimum performance; poor head restraint crashworthiness rating; and rear-seat head restraints impede side and rear visibility. The storage well won't take any tire larger than a "space saver"—meaning you'll carry your flat in the back. **New for 2006:** Carried over unchanged after last year's extensive redesign; a hybrid model may be added in 2006.

OVERVIEW: No longer simply an Accord masquerading as a minivan, the Ontario-built Odyssey is longer, wider, taller, and more powerful than before the redesign. It has a lean look, but the interior is wide and long enough to accommodate a 4' × 8' sheet of plywood laid flat. Sliding doors are offered as standard equipment, and if you buy the EX version, they will both be power-assisted.

Buyers of the redesigned model get a bigger Odyssey with a torquier 255-hp 3.5L V6, which has 15 more horses than the 2004 and more horsepower than any other minivan. The new engine uses variable cylinder de-activation to increase fuel economy up to 10 percent by automatically switching between 6-cylinder and 3-cylinder activation, depending upon engine load.

COST ANALYSIS: A new Odyssey LX sells for about $33,500, and is really the only game in town. A discounted, upgraded 2005 model would be a good choice, if you can find one. There is room for some price negotiation, with savings in the $2,000–$3,500 range, but make sure you have a specific delivery date spelled out in the contract, along with a protected price, in case there's a price increase while you're waiting for delivery. **Best alternatives:** If you want better handling and reliability, the closest competitor to the Odyssey is Toyota's Sienna minivan. The GM Montana, Relay, Terraza, and Uplander aren't in the running because of their poor reliability and limited performance. If you're looking for lots of towing "grunt," then the rear-drive GM full-sized vans would be good buys. **Options:** Remember, if you want the gimmicky video entertainment and DVD navigation system, you also have to spring for the expensive (and not-for-everyone) leather seats. Ditch the original equipment Firestone tires: You don't need the extra risk. **Rebates:** Honda has pulled back on its incentives because of higher exchange rates and the unabated popularity of its new Odyssey. Alberta is the most difficult region in which to find a bargain; don't expect any substantial incentives in that province before early 2005. **Delivery/PDI:** $1,425. **Depreciation:** Slower than average. **Insurance cost:** Higher than average. **Annual maintenance cost:** Average. **Parts supply/cost:** Moderately priced parts; availability is better than average because the Odyssey uses many generic Accord parts. CVT transmission and cylinder de-activation parts may be costly and may be available only from Honda dealers. **Warranty:** Bumper-to-bumper 3 years/60,000 km; powertrain 5 years/100,000 km; rust perforation 5 years/unlimited km. **Supplementary warranty:** Not needed. **Highway/city fuel economy:** 8.6–12.3L/100 km. Models equipped with a V6 cylinder de-activation system will alternate between 3 and 6 cylinders, depending on load and power needs. This should mean fuel savings that vary between 7 to 10 percent. Premium fuel is recommended, but the Odyssey will run on regular, with a slight loss of power (about five horses).

 ## Quality/Reliability/Safety

Pro: Reliability: Reliability has proven to be much better than average. Expect problems with the electrical system, electronics, accessories, and trim. **Safety:** Head restraints and three-point seat belts in all seven seating positions; a wide array of standard safety features is available. The Odyssey's body structure has been extensively reinforced to protect occupants from all kinds of collisions, including rollovers.

Con: Warranty performance: Comprehensive base warranty that's usually applied fairly, with lots of wiggle room that the service manager can use to apply "goodwill" adjustments for post-warranty problems. However, after-warranty assistance and dealer servicing have come in for a great deal of criticism from *Lemon-Aid* readers. Owners complain that "goodwill" refunds aren't extended to all model years with the same defect; recall repairs take an eternity to perform; and dealers exhibit an arrogant, uncaring attitude. **Quality control:** Honda is still plagued by frequent engine and automatic transmission failures. Another notable and hazardous shortcoming: failure-prone sliding doors that open when they shouldn't, don't close when they should, catch fingers and arms, get stuck open or closed, are noisy, and frequently require expensive servicing. One can only hope the Odyssey's latest redesign corrects these problems. Passenger doors may also require excessive force to open. Owners have complained of severe static electricity shocks when exiting. Other potential problems are frequent and high-cost front brake maintenance, and trim and accessory items that come loose, break away, or malfunction. **Owner-reported problems:** Transmission breakdowns; engine almost stalls out and produces a noise like valve clattering when shifting into Fourth gear; transmission gear whine at 90 km/h or when in Fourth gear (transmission sometimes replaced under new "goodwill" warranty). Front-end clunking caused by welding breaks in the front subframe; exhaust rattling or buzzing; loud fuel splashing sound in the fuel tank when coming to a stop; vehicle pulls to the right when underway; premature front brake wear; excessive brake grinding noise:

> When braking, [there's a] severe grinding noise [from the] right front. Dealer said calipers were leaking onto pads, causing noise. Replaced calipers and pads. Lasted a week, same noise, dealer again replaced pads and calipers. Said they have had a lot of complaints but don't know why it is happening. Not a safe condition.

•

> (1) We were driving today about 35 mph [55 km/h] and the signal light turned red. We proceeded to stop and our brakes started making a grinding/clunking sound. It also prevented us [from slowing down] down our van normally...in other words...increased the distance before our van stopped. (2) We just about went into the four-way intersection, but we didn't. (3) Our dealership...looked at our brakes a couple weeks ago and did not find a problem. They spoke to a couple Honda engineers who were aware of this issue with other '05 Odyssey minivans. They stated [that] Honda is working on a solution to fix this issue and the issue does not affect the vans' stopping performance. This is not true, as I have had to slam on my brakes a few weeks back due to someone pulling out in front of me and it did the same thing with the grinding/clunking. I almost hit the other car due to the increased braking distance. There are a lot of other '05 Odysseys on *www.odyclub.com/forums* that have the same braking issue. We have had this issue about seven times now. Honda needs to recall these brake pads/calipers or whatever is causing this before someone gets hurt or killed!

Sliding side door frequently malfunctions; electrical glitches; defective remote audio controls; leather seats split, crack, or discolour; and accessory items that come loose, break away, or won't work. Plastic interior panels have rough edges and are often misaligned; paint peels from the bumpers. **Service bulletin problems:** Fuel may leak from gas tank; engine oil leaks; engine cranks but doesn't start; engine stumbling, shuddering, hesitating, or momentarily surging; broken engine head bolts; free tranny repair or replacement for insufficient lubrication that can lead to heat build-up and broken gears; shift lever stuck in Park; transmission repair procedure and powertrain control module (PCM) replacement, and transmission may also lock up; rear brake noise; clunking rear brake calipers; broken alternator bracket or lower mounting bolt; right A-pillar creaking; repairing air leaks under warranty; roof rack wind noise; heater blower motor overheats or blows a fuse; power-steering noise; wheel bearing hums or growls; exhaust rattles or buzzes upon acceleration; squealing from rear quarter windows; front door howls in strong crosswind; dash or front strut creaking or ticking; broken or shattered tailgate glass; deformed windshield moulding; airbag warning indicator stays lit; inoperative centre-mount brake light; warning lights may blink on and off for no reason; and troubleshooting an off-centre steering wheel. **NHTSA safety complaints:** Seat belt unlatches, or sometimes won't unlatch; entire electrical system goes dead; faulty VSA control unit disables ABS and braking assist; vehicle won't accelerate when foot is on the gas pedal, but begins to accelerate when the brakes are applied; constant steering shimmy; driver's seat isn't level; windshield leaks; replacements are on back-order nationwide; painful noise in the cabin when rear windows are opened:

> Very loud pusating sound when rear windows open. It vibrates and is so loud I thought I had a flat tire. My ears and my children's ears hurt. It occurs when we are driving 35–40 mph [55–65 km/h].

Power sliding door opened completely while vehicle was in motion; fails to close and latch:

> 2005 Honda Odyssey EXL [with] 4,500 miles [7,200 km]. Left-side passenger power sliding door does not close and latch completely. Indicator on dash board shows door is open. Door open buzzer went on when driving. Turned off power mechanism. Door slid ajar when driving under these circumstances and with children on board—fortunately with seat belts on. Pushing did not help close and latch the door—the door closes but pops out in a couple of seconds and the lock does not work at all.

> There has been a problem with the vehicle door being loose from the track. The vehicle has been taken to dealer five times. The dealer just tightened the bolts. The problem has been reported to Honda. Upon investigation, the owner found out that others have the same problem. There have been recalls: 99V15800 and 99V159000. Honda

denied any problems. Honda stated that there were not enough complaints to cause a recall. Sometimes the child has to hold the door so it won't come open.

Automatic sliding door almost crushed child's hand; rear windshield wiper self-activates; AC condenser is easily damaged from road debris.

Road Performance

Pro: Emergency handling: Predictable and well controlled. **Acceleration/torque:** Quiet yet powerful V6 engine performance with plenty of torque throughout the power band. **Transmission:** Usually smooth and quiet shifting (note exceptions below), though a bit slow to downshift at full throttle. **Routine handling:** Better handling than most of the competition, with a short turning circle, making it quite nimble—akin to driving a large, quiet, sporty family sedan. **Braking:** Excellent braking now that rear discs have been added. Even with a full load and after repeated stops, they perform quite well—most of the time.

Con: Steering: A bit heavy at low speeds; sometimes feels over-boosted at highway speeds. **Transmission:** Column-mounted shift lever tends to slide past Drive into Third gear when shifted out of Park. Automatic transmission clunks and jolts the occupants when shifted into Reverse. The taut suspension is also a bit jolting over bumps, but the ride smoothes out as the load is increased.

ODYSSEY

List Price (negotiable)	**Residual Values** (months)			
	24	**36**	**48**	**60**
Odyssey LX: $33,200 (18%)	$25,500	$21,500	$17,500	$14,500
Odyssey EX: $35,900 (20%)	$26,500	$22,500	$18,500	$15,500

Note: The 2006 price for the new high-end Touring model is $47,600.

SAFETY FEATURES	**STD.**	**OPT.**
Anti-lock brakes (4W)	✓	—
Seat belt pretensioners F/R	✓	—
Side airbags	✓	—
Stability control	✓	—
Traction control	✓	—

CRASHWORTHINESS		
Head restraints F/R	2	2
Visibility F/R	5	1
Crash protection (front) D/P	5	5
Crash protection (side) F/R	5	5
Crash protection (offset)	4	—

Hyundai

Lemon-Aid said it four years ago: Hyundai's quality control is now much better than Detroit's and its prices are very competitive. No wonder the company is racking up impressive sales across Canada—not only for its own models, but also with its Kia division cars, SUV, and minivan. These increasing sales figures and positive quality surveys indicate the company is on a much surer footing than in the late '70s, when Hyundai Canada was run by a ragtag gang of Toronto-based auto newbies. They made money by dumping cheap but poor-quality Pony and Stellar compacts into the market to compete against equally poor-quality American small cars. At that time, Detroit iron was too expensive and not very fuel-efficient, and fuel prices were going through the roof. However, when fuel became relatively cheap again, you couldn't give a Hyundai away. So Hyundai's North American executives decided to stay alive by stretching the truth.

During the last decade, the company misled over 1.3 million owners as to their vehicles' true horsepower—in some cases boosting the reported figures by almost 10 percent. Hyundai admitted its deception in September 2002, over six months after a Vancouver Competition Bureau investigator received an anonymous tip that Hyundai was breaking the law with impunity.

Hyundai beat being charged with misleading advertising after offering buyers various forms of compensation, which ran the gamut from a $500 refund to an extended warranty. Crime doesn't pay? For Hyundai, it most certainly did.

Korean Quality?

Why not? Korean automakers have had over a decade to improve their products. Heck, even VW and Subaru were jokes when they first started out (and they're returning to that status with the VW Touareg and the Subaru Baja).

If you still have doubts as to Hyundai's car quality, check out the most recent J.D. Power survey reports or click onto NHTSA's Internet consumer complaints database (*www-odi.nhtsa.dot.gov/cars/problems/complain*). For my part, I'll add that I bought my wife a 2001 Elantra four years ago and she has only had to replace the CD changer—for free. Hyundai doesn't know from whom or where I bought the car—which probably protects both our reputations. Incidentally, there are two other nationally known auto journalists who routinely test-drive Porsches and BMWs, but go grocery shopping in the family Elantra (they know who they are).

Hyundai and Kia are copying the successful international marketing strategy employed by Japanese automakers over the past three decades. Secure a solid beachhead in one car segment and branch out from there. In fact, the two companies announced this year they intend to soon offer an expanded lineup that will be comprised of mini-cars, like the German Smart car, small minivans, like the Mazda5, luxury sedans, and small pickups. Hyundai is also sharing platforms and components with Kia in an effort to keep production costs down and raise quality. Already, preliminary owner surveys of these blended cars indicate that there has been an appreciable rise in Kia quality since the reworked 2005 models arrived.

This year, Hyundai will bring out the Entourage minivan and the Azera, a new front-drive luxury sedan that replaces the slow-selling, run-of-the-mill XG350. A surprisingly large car for Hyundai, the Azera reinforces the company's decision to leave small, cheap cars to Kia, and concentrate instead on selling upscale sedans, wagons, SUVs, and minivans. In fact, Hyundai's first minivan, the Entourage, will share Kia's Sedona platform and likely be powered by a 268-hp V6. It will be sold in the spring of 2006 as an early 2007 model.

A little larger than the Toyota Camry, the Azera will carry a 265-hp 3.8L V6 (70 more horses than the Magentis it replaces); it will be priced in the high 20s and come fully loaded with safety, performance, and convenience features. Look for it to arrive in early 2006.

ACCENT ★★★★★

best buy

TECHNICAL DATA

POWERTRAIN (FRONT-DRIVE)

Engine: 1.6L 4-cyl. (110 hp);
Transmissions: 5-speed man. • 4-speed
auto.

DIMENSION/CAPACITY

Passengers: 2/3; Wheelbase: 98 in.;
H: 57.9/L: 168.5/W: 66.7 in.; Headroom
F/R: 5.0/2.5 in.; Legroom F/R: 41.5/26
in.; Cargo volume: 12.5 cu. ft.; Fuel
tank: 45L/regular; Tow limit: N/A; Load
capacity: 850 lb.; Turning circle: 36 ft.;
Weight: 2,350 lb.

RATING: Recommended, if you're using your Accent primarily as a fuel-sipping urban dweller consigned to occasional forays on the highway. Think of it as a more refined and peppier Metro/Sprint from South Korea, built for light duty around town. **Strong points:** Reasonably priced and very well appointed; an adequate engine and acceptable automatic transmission performance in most situations; increased interior room; comfortable driving position with good visibility and height-adjustable; form-fitting bucket seats that provide plenty of support; good reliability record with few complaints relative to safety or quality control; and cheap on gas. **Weak points:** Engine could use a bit more torque and noise-vibration dampening. Ride can be too firm for some; some reports of automatic transmission flame-outs; and a high PDI and freight fee. **New for 2006:** A more-powerful 110-hp (six more horses than last year's model) 1.6L 4-cylinder engine with variable-valve timing, six airbags, ABS, improved braking, halogen headlights, a CD stereo, and XM satellite radio. The chassis' wheelbase and length are extended two inches, and the car is one inch wider and three inches taller. Two body styles will be available: a three-door hatchback and a four-door sedan.

OVERVIEW: This front-drive 4-cylinder entry-level sedan is one of the cheapest feature-laden small cars sold in North America. Carrying a homegrown 1.6L 4-cylinder engine coupled to a 5-speed manual or 4-speed automatic transmission, the Accent offers bare-bones motoring without sacrificing basic amenities, including AC, a height-adjustable driver's seat with lumbar support, and split-fold rear seats.

COST ANALYSIS: The upgraded 2006 is the Accent to buy. **Best alternatives:** Other vehicles worth considering: the Honda Civic, the Mazda3, the Nissan Sentra, and the 2005 Toyota Echo or Corolla. **Options:** An automatic transmission and power steering are essential. **Rebates:** Expect $2,500 rebates and zero percent financing on unsold 2005 models. **Delivery/PDI:** $1,200. **Depreciation:** Slower than average now that fuel prices have risen. **Insurance cost:** Average. **Parts supply/ cost:** Parts aren't hard to find, and they're reasonably priced. **Annual maintenance cost:** Average. **Warranty:** Bumper-to-bumper 3 years/60,000 km; powertrain 5 years/100,000 km; rust perforation 5 years/unlimited km. **Supplementary warranty:** A good idea, since Hyundai powertrains can be problematic. **Highway/city fuel economy:** 6.5–8.1L/100 km.

Quality/Reliability/Safety

Pro: Quality control: Average. Hyundai's complaint ratio has dropped considerably over the past few years, concomitant with the company's ditching of its failure-prone Excel and upgrading of the Sonata. Government-collected factory- and safety-related complaints have fallen to a level where they're less frequent than what you'll find recorded by Honda and Toyota owners. Repairs are straightforward because of a fairly simple design, and parts are less expensive than average. **Reliability:** Above average. **Warranty performance:** Above average.

Cons: Paint and exterior trim are not up to Honda and Toyota standards. **Service bulletin problems:** Erratic, slipping shifts and hard shifting. **Owner-reported problems:** Airbags failed to deploy; engine may burn oil; engine cooling system and cylinder head gasket failures; automatic transmission gears grind when shifting, slip, and feel like they're in no gear at all; computer fault makes the transmission suddenly downshift; front end shakes when passing over a hill; premature ignition coil failure; Check Engine light stays lit; premature front brake wear and excessive noise when braking; tiny original equipment tires decrease stability; wheel bearings, fuel system, and electrical components may also fail prematurely. **NHTSA safety complaints:** Loss of braking capability after electrical system shutdown; excessive shaking when brakes are applied; airbags failed to deploy; and transmission suddenly downshifts on its own.

 ## Road Performance

Pro: Although the 1.6L engine is no pocket rocket, it performs adequately in city traffic. **Emergency handling:** Slow, but predictable. **Steering:** The non-power steering is precise and transmits plenty of road feedback at higher speeds. **Transmission:** Surprisingly, this is one car where the automatic transmission performs better than the manual gearbox. **Routine handling:** Average. The Accent rides comfortably and handles responsively. **Braking:** Very good with the 2006 upgrades.

Con: Acceleration/torque: The manual transmission is hard to shift correctly owing to its balky linkage and long lever movements. Uneven pavement makes for a busy, jittery ride that worsens as passengers are added. Steering without the power-assist option takes a lot of effort around town and when parking.

ACCENT

List Price (negotiable)	Residual Values (months)			
	24	36	48	60
Accent GS: $12,995 (13%)	$ 8,500	$ 7,000	$ 5,500	$ 5,000
Accent GL: $14,245 (14%)	$ 9,000	$ 7,500	$ 6,500	$ 5,500
Accent GSi: $14,995 (15%)	$ 9,500	$ 8,000	$ 7,000	$ 6,000

SAFETY FEATURES	STD.	OPT.	CRASHWORTHINESS		
Seat belt pretensioners F/R	✓	—	Head restraints F/R	3	3
Side airbags	✓	—	Visibility F/R	5	5
			Crash protection (front) D/P	4	4
			Crash protection (side) F/R	5	4
			Rollover	4	—

ELANTRA ★★★★

RATING: Above Average: Less boring than a Toyota Corolla and more reliable than a Ford Focus or Fusion. **Strong points:** Peppy engine, with plenty of passing power; smooth-shifting transmission; good handling and ride quality; well appointed; plenty of interior room and comfortable seats; seatback slides far enough back to easily accommodate six-foot-plus drivers; not much interior noise; reasonably priced; and above-average crashworthiness scores. **Weak points:** Not a lot of grunt at low engine rpm; some wind noise; difficult rear entry and exit; insufficient rear-seat headroom; chronic airbag sensor failures not covered by recall; fairly rapid depreciation; and an outrageously high PDI and freight fee. **New for 2006:** Nothing important.

OVERVIEW: This Italian-designed, front-drive, conservatively styled subcompact is only marginally larger than the discontinued Excel. Nevertheless, its 138-hp 2.0L 4-cylinder power plant supplies much-needed power that you won't find with many other cars in this price range. The ride and handling are also quite good, owing mainly to the Elantra's longer wheelbase and more sophisticated suspension.

All ratings on a numbered scale where 5 is good and 1 is bad. See page 153–154 for a more detailed description.

Available as a four- and five-door sedan or as a GT hatchback and sedan, the Elantra is loaded with standard equipment, including AC and intermittent wipers, full centre console, dual remote-controlled outside mirrors, remote fuel-filler door and trunk release, reclining bucket seats, and tinted glass. Upgrading to the GT will get you leather seating, four-wheel disc brakes, high-performance suspension, larger alloy wheels, and remote keyless entry.

COST ANALYSIS: Pick an identical, discounted 2005 version. **Best alternatives:** Other cars worth considering are the Honda Civic, the Kia Spectra5, and the 2005 Toyota Echo or Corolla. **Options:** The GT is a bargain when one totes up the cost of its standard features if purchased separately. **Rebates:** $3,000 rebates and zero percent financing are coming at year's end. **Delivery/PDI:** $1,200 (this, you have to cut down!). **Depreciation:** Average. **Insurance cost:** Average. **Parts supply/cost:** Easy-to-find and reasonably priced parts, with heavy discounting by dealers and independents. **Annual maintenance cost:** Average. **Warranty:** Bumper-to-bumper 3 years/60,000 km; powertrain 5 years/100,000 km; rust perforation 5 years/unlimited km. **Supplementary warranty:** A toss-up. **Highway/city fuel economy:** 7.1–10.8L/100 km.

TECHNICAL DATA

POWERTRAIN (FRONT-DRIVE)

Engine: 2.0L 4-cyl. (138 hp); Transmissions: 5-speed man. • 4-speed auto.

DIMENSION/CAPACITY

Passengers: 2/3; Wheelbase: 103 in.; H: 56.1/L: 177.1/W: 68 in.; Headroom F/R: 2.5/2.0 in.; Legroom F/R: 40/27.5 in.; Cargo volume: 12.9 cu. ft.; Fuel tank: 55L/regular; Tow limit: 2,000 lb.; Load capacity: 850 lb.; Turning circle: 37 ft.; Weight: 2,980 lb.

Quality/Reliability/Safety

Pro: Quality control: Above average. **Reliability:** Overall reliability has been quite good except for the occasional automatic transmission failure and electrical shorts. **Warranty performance:** Above average. Hyundai staffers usually deal with customer claims in a fair and efficient manner.

Con: Owner-reported problems: Airbag Off light comes on even though the seat is occupied; many complaints that the affected vehicles weren't included in a recent recall campaign:

> While driving, the airbag warning light continuously illuminated on the dashboard. Dealership inspected vehicle several times, technician indicated to consumer the passenger had to weigh 66.4 pounds [30.1 kg] in order for the airbag light to turn off, although with people who weighed over 100 pounds [45 kg] the airbag light was still on.

Chronic stalling; excessive brake noise; passenger-side scraping noise when underway; wind howls in the interior when encountering a crosswind; while driving, a humming noise emanates from the corners of the windshield; tire thumping; window defrosting takes too long; rainwater seeps in under the door; and passenger seat back cover keeps popping out. **Service bulletin problems:** Faulty power window regulator motor; rear spoiler fastener; and free fuel pump replacement campaign. **NHTSA safety complaints:** Airbag sensors are too sensitive and disable the airbag when an average-sized adult occupies the seat; airbag failed to deploy in a collision; and airbag deployed for no reason:

> The vehicle was parked in my apartment's parking lot. My wife and I entered the vehicle. I started the engine. We both buckled our seat belts and I took off the parking brake. As I was reaching for the gearshift, the driver-side airbag deployed without warning.

Sudden, unintended acceleration:

> Travelling on the freeway, the vehicle suddenly accelerated to 80 mph [130 km/h] and would not slow down. It continued for about 15 miles [24 km] before I put the vehicle in Neutral and turned off the key (the service department at the dealer's advised me to do that). At that time, smoke poured out of the engine and I thought the vehicle was on fire. I called 911. I was able to avoid a collision; however, the policeman asked me to move the car and when I turned on the key, it started at full throttle. I was afraid so I got out and refused to move the car. When a police officer moved the car, it again started at full throttle. They towed it to the dealer. [The dealer] said there is nothing wrong with it. I am afraid to drive it.

Defective crankshaft position sensor causes the vehicle to suddenly stall out; engine surging; stalling caused by a faulty fuel pump (there's a campaign to offer a free replacement); complete loss of brakes; prematurely warped rotors and worn-out brake drums; headlights will read "dim" but will actually be on high; distracting windshield glare; and seat belts fail to lock.

 Road Performance

Pro: Acceleration/torque: Good acceleration with plenty of low-end torque. **Transmission:** Both transmissions perform well, although the automatic shifts frequently when the engine is pushed. **Emergency handling:** Better than average. **Steering:** Accurate and responsive. **Routine handling:** Independent suspension helps make for a pleasant ride, with exceptional handling and control. **Braking:** Brakes are usually quite efficient, with little fading after successive stops.

ELANTRA

List Price (negotiable)	Residual Values (months)			
	24	36	48	60
Elantra GL: $15,395 (15%)	$ 9,500	$ 7,500	$ 6,500	$ 5,500
Elentra GT: $19,895 (17%)	$12,000	$10,000	$ 8,500	$ 7,000

SAFETY FEATURES			CRASHWORTHINESS		
	STD.	OPT.			
Anti-lock brakes	—	✓	Head restraints F/R	3	3
Seat belt pretensioners F/R	✓	—	Visibility F/R	5	5
Side airbags	✓	—	Crash protection (front) D/P	5	4
Traction control	—	✓	Crash protection (side) F/R	5	4

SONATA ★★★★

RATING: Above Average. This year's refinements give the Sonata all of the safety and performance features it needs to play in the big leagues against the Japanese and Detroit family sedans. **Strong points:** A credible alternative to most Detroit-bred family sedans, and it's priced at thousands of dollars lower. Well equipped and stylish; sizzling V6 power; good handling; comfortable ride; user-friendly controls and gauges; spacious trunk and a conveniently low lift-in height; fairly quiet cabin; and much-improved quality control. **Weak points:** Prices have been boosted by a couple of thousand dollars; fuel economy isn't as good as most of the competition's;

TECHNICAL DATA

POWERTRAIN (FRONT-DRIVE)

Engines: 2.4L 4-cyl. (162 hp) • 3.3L V6 (235 hp); Transmissions: 4-speed auto./ man. • 5-speed auto./man.

DIMENSION/CAPACITY

Passengers: 2/3; Wheelbase: 107.4 in.; H: 58/L: 188.9/W: 72.1 in.; Headroom F/R: 4.0/3.0 in.; Legroom F/R: 43/37 in.; Cargo volume: 14 cu. ft.; Fuel tank: 65L/regular; Tow limit: 2,000 lb.; Load capacity: 1,100 lb.; Turning circle: 37 ft.; Weight: 3,255 lb.

steering is too sensitive for some; the suspension is somewhat bouncy; interior trim is not up to Japanese standards; and an unusually high freight fee. **New for 2006:** A redesigned Sonata with a new 4-cylinder and V6 engine, plus an expanded body that has been stretched over a larger wheelbase to enhance control and interior comfort.

OVERVIEW: This is the mid-sized sedan that Hyundai should have built years ago. Sure, incremental engine and suspension improvements over the years made the Sonata a pleasant car to own, but it lacked the refinement of a Honda or Toyota. That's no longer true.

Styled similarly to the Honda Accord, the redesigned Sonata is two inches longer, an inch wider, and two inches higher than last year's model, and has a wheelbase that is an inch longer. It meets or exceeds the engine performance standards of its competitors, although fuel economy isn't as good. The Sonata rides on a double-wishbone front suspension and a multi-link rear suspension that is more softly sprung than usual, making the car a bit "bouncier" than its competitors.

Like Hyundai's other models, the Sonata is loaded with standard features that are either optional or not found on competing makes. Some of those standard features include a 162-hp 2.4L 4-cylinder engine and a 235-hp 3.3L V6; an automatic transmission with a semi-manual mode; cruise control; four-wheel ABS; AC; tilt steering wheel; power steering; power windows, door locks and mirrors; 16-inch wheels; a stereo radio with CD player; and keyless entry with an alarm.

HYUNDAI/TOYOTA/HONDA COMPARISON

The 2006 Hyundai Sonata compares favourably with the leading mid-sized Toyota and Honda sedans.

	2006 HYUNDAI SONATA	2005 TOYOTA CAMRY	2005 HONDA ACCORD
Wheelbase	107.4 in.	107.1 in.	107.9 in.
Length	188.9 in.	189.2 in.	189.5 in.
Width	72.1 in.	70.7 in.	71.5 in.
Height	58.0 in.	58.7 in.	57.1 in.
Base engine	2.4L inline-4	2.4L inline-4	2.4L inline-4
Horsepower	162 hp @ 5800 rpm	160 hp @ 5600 rpm	160 hp @ 5500 rpm
Torque	164 lbs.-ft. @ 4250 rpm	163 lbs.-ft. @ 4000 rpm	161 lbs.-ft. @ 4500 rpm

Hyundai has again put an emphasis on safety, giving buyers a lot more safety features for their money than with competing models. For example, all new Sonatas include stability and traction control; front, side, and curtain airbags; front and rear seat belt pretensioners; an integrated rear child safety seat; and a "smart" passenger-side airbag that won't deploy if the passenger weighs less than 30 kg (66 lb.). Well, at least that's the theory—in practice, owners report the airbag is often disabled no matter what the passenger's weight.

COST ANALYSIS: Buy the redesigned 2006 model. **Best alternatives:** Other cars worth considering are the Honda Accord, the Mazda5 or Mazda6, and the Toyota Camry. **Options:** Choose the V6 engine for better performance and handling. If you get the 4-banger, keep in mind that good fuel economy means putting up with a bit more engine noise. Be wary of the sunroof; it eats up a lot of headroom and has a history of leaking. **Rebates:** Expect $3,000 rebates and zero percent financing on all leftover models. **Delivery/PDI:** A greedy $1,135. **Depreciation:** Average. **Insurance cost:** Average. **Parts supply/cost:** Easy to find and relatively inexpensive. Large engine compartment for easy servicing. **Annual maintenance cost:** Higher than average. **Warranty:** Bumper-to-bumper 3 years/60,000 km; powertrain 5 years/100,000 km; rust perforation 5 years/unlimited km. **Supplementary warranty:** Not needed. **Highway/city fuel economy:** 2005: 7.7–11.4L/100 km with the 4-cylinder and 7.9–12.3L/100 km with the V6.

Quality/Reliability/Safety

Pro: Quality control: Good quality control. Repairs are straightforward because of the Sonata's simple design. **Reliability:** Despite some past powertrain deficiencies, no serious reliability problems have taken these cars off the road. **Warranty performance:** Above average. **Owner-reported problems:** Nothing serious, but the 2006 has been on the road only since last April.

Con: Owner-reported problems: *2005:* Erratic engine performance (poor idling and stalling); vehicle loses power when going uphill; transmission leaks, clunks, and hangs up in gear; and excessive vibration when the brakes are applied. **Service bulletin problems:** Unstable idle and ABS activation. **NHTSA safety complaints:** *2006 model:* Passenger-side airbag is disabled no matter the weight of the passenger; defective automatic stability control mechanism locks the brakes and causes the car to fishtail; slight steering corrections result in unexpectedly sharp directional changes; seat belt chime is annoyingly active, sounding even if the car is a rest:

> The seat-belt warning chime on this vehicle activates the moment the driver's belt is unbuckled, even if the car is at rest, the automatic transaxle is in park, and the parking brake is set. This loud, grating chime repeats every six seconds. Although I assume the system meets current NHTSA rules per se, there is a safety threat because I have seen many posts on Internet forums from people wanting to know how to de-activate

the system because they, like most drivers, have occasion to be in the vehicle, not in traffic, with the engine running. Examples include drive-up bank teller and ATMs, drive-thru food service lanes, and in parking lots with the vehicle idling to make cell phone sales calls. Safety is threatened because if the chime is disconnected then it can't warn if the driver truly forgets once the vehicle is moved from rest or if the driver forgets the key, which would increase the risk of joy-riders stealing the vehicle. Also, shade-tree mechanics could damage the seat-belt pretensioner system wiring trying to "hot-wire" the buckle switch.

2005 and earlier models: Fuel fumes escaped from vehicle while it was parked; airbags failed to deploy; stalling caused by faulty throttle sensor; driver-side seat belt buckle released; and rear-view mirror is too big and obstructs the view.

Road Performance

Pro: Routine handling: Above average. Hyundai has changed the suspension setting to provide a more comfortable ride and better handling. **Emergency handling:** Also above average, particularly with 16-inch wheels. **Steering:** Very precise, but overly sensitive for some; predictable, with lots of road feedback. **Acceleration/torque:** Reasonably good acceleration, but the base engine's insufficient torque makes the optional V6 a prerequisite for acceptable, though not thrilling, highway cruising, especially over hilly terrain. **Transmission:** The 4- and 5-speed automatic transmissions work smoothly and are well adapted to the engine's power range. **Braking:** Disc/disc; average, with some brake fade.

Con: Ride quality deteriorates as load increases; excessive body lean in turns; and transmission sometimes shifts harshly and malfunctions.

SONATA

List Price (very negotiable)

Residual Values (months)

	24	36	48	60
GL: $21,900 (18%)	$17,500	$15,000	$12,000	$10,000
GL V6: $25,795 (19%)	$19,500	$16,000	$13,000	$11,000

SAFETY FEATURES	STD.	OPT.	CRASHWORTHINESS		
Anti-lock brakes	✓	—	Head restraints F/R	3	3
Seat belt pretensioners F/R	✓	—	Visibility F/R	5	5
Side airbags	✓	—	Crash protection (front) D/P	5	5
Stability control	✓	—	Crash protection (side) F/R	5	5
Traction control	✓	—	Crash protection (offset)	3	—
			Rollover	5	—

All ratings on a numbered scale where 5 is good and **1** is bad. See page 153–154 for a more detailed description.

RATING: Average. This sporty car delivers attractive styling with a pleasant driving experience. **Strong points:** Well equipped; impressive 2.0L performance with a manual gearbox; exceptional ride and handling; hatchback has a good amount of cargo room; and thin pillars make for good all-around visibility. Good crashworthiness scores. **Weak points:** Base 2.0L engine's passing power is seriously handicapped by the automatic transmission; manual tranny could be more precise. Ride might be too stiff for some. Excessive interior noise and vibration; uncomfortable seating—not for six-footers or portly occupants. **New for 2006:** Nothing significant. A convertible will be offered for the 2008 model year.

OVERVIEW: The Tiburon (Spanish for "shark") is a stylish, two-door spin-off of the Elantra sedan that delivers sports car thrills in a compact coupe. It's powered by a base 138-hp 2.0L 4-banger or an optional 172-hp 2.7L V6 mated to a 4-speed electronically controlled automatic or a 5- or 6-speed manual transmission. The Tiburon handles well, with gas-charged shocks inside coil springs at all four corners and front MacPherson struts. Steering is light and responsive with a minimum of body flex. Standard brakes consist of discs up front and drums in the rear; the FX package includes four-wheel discs and ABS.

COST ANALYSIS: Get an identical, discounted 2005 model. **Best alternatives:** Other vehicles worth considering: the Acura RSX, the Ford Mustang, the Honda Civic Si, the Mitsubishi Eclipse, and the Toyota

TECHNICAL DATA

POWERTRAIN (FRONT-DRIVE)
Engines: 2.0L 4-cyl. (138 hp) • 2.7L V6 (172 hp); Transmissions: 5-speed man. • 6-speed man. • 4-speed auto.

DIMENSION/CAPACITY
Passengers: 2/2; Wheelbase: 100 in.; H: 52.4/L: 173/W: 69 in.; Headroom F/R: 2.0/1.0 in.; Legroom F/R: 41.5/25 in.; Cargo volume: 14.8 cu. ft.; Fuel tank: 55L/regular; Tow limit: 1,000 lb.; Load capacity: 700 lb.; Turning circle: 38 ft.; Weight: 3,110 lb.

Corolla. **Options:** Get the V6 engine and better-gripping tires, but stay away from Firestone and Bridgestone tires; they have had serious failures in the past. **Rebates:** $3,000 rebates and low percent financing in the new year. **Delivery/PDI:** $1,200 (bargain this fee down by at least half). **Depreciation:** Average. **Insurance cost:** Higher than average. **Parts supply/cost:** Parts aren't hard to find and are less expensive than average. Repairs are straightforward because of a fairly simple design. **Annual maintenance cost:** Average. **Warranty:** Bumper-to-bumper 3 years/60,000 km; powertrain 5 years/100,000 km; rust perforation 5 years/unlimited km. **Supplementary warranty:** Not needed. **Highway/city fuel economy:** 7.4–10.5L/100 km with the base engine.

Quality/Reliability/Safety

Pro: Quality control: Above average. **Reliability:** Better than average. **Warranty performance:** Above average. **Safety:** Impressive headlight illumination and four-wheel disc brakes.

Con: Owner-reported problems: Power shutdown caused by a faulty fuel regulator; slipping clutch; faulty sunroof won't open or close; inoperative power windows and misaligned doors; premature front brake wear and excessive brake noise; hard starting; some electrical glitches; gas cap pops off when fuel tank falls below a quarter full; and paint flaking. **Service bulletin problems:** Free fuel pump replacement campaign and 2.7L V6 engine oxygen sensor change. **NHTSA safety complaints:** Hood popped up while car was underway; under-hood fire; when shifting, engine surged and smoke came out of the engine compartment; airbag deployed when it shouldn't have, didn't deploy when it should have; and the rear spoiler is distracting and cuts rearward vision.

Road Performance

Pro: The 2.0L gives respectable power, but the V6 is the preferred power plant for its reserve power. **Emergency handling:** Very good. Well controlled, with minimal body roll. **Steering:** The light, responsive steering is precise and predictable. **Transmission:** The 5-speed manual transmission shifts smoothly and is well adapted to the engine's power range. The ride is reasonably soft on good roads. **Braking:** Disc/disc; acceptable, though not impressive.

Con: Acceleration/torque: The 4-speed automatic transmission shifts roughly under full throttle and is noisy at high revs. **Routine handling:** Uneven pavement makes for a busy, jittery ride that's accentuated as passengers are added. Poor braking on wet pavement.

TIBURON

List Price (very negotiable)	**Residual Values** (months)			
	24	**36**	**48**	**60**
Base: $20,595 (17%)	$16,000	$14,000	$12,000	$ 9,000
SE: $23,895 (18%)	$17,500	$15,500	$13,000	$10,000

SAFETY FEATURES	**STD.**	**OPT.**
Anti-lock brakes	—	✓
Seat belt pretensioners F/R	✓	—
Side airbags	✓	—
Traction control	✓	—

CRASHWORTHINESS		
Head restraints F/R	3	3
Visibility F/R	5	2
Crash protection (front) D/P	5	4
Crash protection (side) F/R	4	—
Rollover	4	—

XG350 (2005) ★★★

RATING: Average; scheduled to be replaced by the Azera early in the new year. **Strong points:** Adequate acceleration; automatic transmission shifts smoothly; lots of standard features at a reasonable retail price; solid body structure; comfortable ride; good braking; plenty of front-seat room and comfort; impressive fit and finish; four-year reliability scores have been remarkably good. **Weak points:** Acceleration sometimes jerky because of the car's heavy weight and power-sapping automatic transmission; excessive body lean and front-end plowing when cornering; large turning circle; limited rear-seat headroom and footroom for tall occupants; obstructed rear corner visibility; some wind noise and tire roar intrudes into the interior; split rear seatbacks don't fold flat; and a freight fee that's way out of line. **New for 2006:** Nothing; 2005 is its last model year.

OVERVIEW: This $33,000, front-drive, four-door, five-passenger sedan has been on the market for four years, and is the closest Hyundai comes to a luxury car. XG350 designates the car's engine configuration, a 194-hp 3.5L V6. Two trim levels are offered: the base XG350 and the XG350L.

TECHNICAL DATA

POWERTRAIN (FRONT-DRIVE)

Engine: 3.5L V6 (194 hp); Transmission: 5-speed auto.

DIMENSION/CAPACITY

Passengers: 2/3; Wheelbase: 108 in.; H: 55.9/L: 192/W: 72 in.; Headroom F/R: 2.5/2.5 in.; Legroom F/R: 39/29.5 in.; Cargo volume: 14.5 cu. ft.; Fuel tank: 70L/regular; Tow limit: 2,000 lb.; Load capacity; 860 lb.; Turning circle: 41 ft.; Weight: 3,651 lb.

Well appointed and offering plenty of passenger space up front, the GX350 has a V6 engine teamed with a 5-speed automatic transmission with manual override that offers acceptable acceleration.

COST ANALYSIS: Get the 2005 model only if it's discounted by at least 25 percent. **Best alternatives:** The Honda Accord and the Toyota Avalon or Camry V6. **Options:** The L trim level isn't worth the extra money. **Rebates:** Look for $5,000 rebates, deep discounting, and low percentage financing. **Delivery/PDI:** $1,100. **Depreciation:** Average. **Insurance cost:** Higher than average. **Parts supply/cost:** Mechanical parts aren't hard to find and they're less expensive than average. Body parts are sometimes expensive and in short supply. Repair is straightforward because of a fairly simple design. **Annual maintenance cost:** Average. **Warranty:** Bumper-to-bumper 3 years/60,000 km; powertrain 5 years/100,000 km; rust perforation 5 years/unlimited km. **Supplementary warranty:** Not necessary. **Highway/city fuel economy:** 8.3–13.1L/100 km.

Quality/Reliability/Safety

Pro: Quality control: Impressive. **Reliability:** Better than average. **Warranty performance:** Above average.

Con: Owner-reported problems: Automatic transmission sometimes shifts erratically, and radio and AC/heater display is hard to see in daylight. **Service bulletin problems:** 3.5L cylinder blocks leak coolant. **NHTSA safety complaints:** Sudden, unintended acceleration; steering wheel locked up while vehicle was underway; brake calipers on both front wheels came off while driving; and brake pedal went to the floor with minimal effect.

Road Performance

Pro: The 194-hp 3.5L V6 is no tire burner, but it is competent and smooth. **Transmission:** The 5-speed automatic transmission with a manual shiftgate usually shifts smoothly and is well adapted to the engine's power range. The ride is reasonably soft on good roads. **Braking:** Disc/disc; good stopping ability with less fading after repeated application.

Con: Acceleration/torque: The automatic transmission sometimes shifts roughly under full throttle. This problem has been around since the car's debut, although to a lesser extent following each model-year upgrade. **Emergency handling:** Inadequate. Car is slow to respond and the soft suspension contributes to excessive body roll. **Routine handling:** Uneven pavement makes for a busy, jittery ride that's accentuated as passengers are added. Poor braking on wet pavement. **Steering:** Steering is vague and slow.

XG350

List Price (very negotiable)   **Residual Values** (months)

	24	36	48	60
Base: $32,995 (25%)	$23,000	$20,000	$17,000	$13,000

SAFETY FEATURES	STD.	OPT.	CRASHWORTHINESS		
			Head restraints F/R	3	3
Anti-lock brakes	✓	—	Visibility F/R	5	3
Seat belt pretensioners F/R	✓	—	Crash protection (front) D/P	5	5
Side airbags	✓	—	Crash protection (side) F/R	4	4
Traction control	✓	—	Crash protection (offset)	5	—
			Rollover	4	—

Infiniti

Unlike Toyota's Lexus division, which started out with vehicles akin to your dad's fully loaded Oldsmobile, Nissan's #1 alter ego has historically stressed performance over comfort and opulence, and has offered buyers lots of high-performance features at what were initially very reasonable prices. But the company got greedy during the mid '90s. Its Infiniti lineup became more mainstream and lost its price and performance edge, particularly after the company stripped out or downgraded the Q45's features, resurrected its embarrassingly incompetent G20, and dropped the J30 and J30t.

For 2006, Infiniti is building a more balanced, though costlier, roster of sporty luxury vehicles. It has dropped the I35 and added a rear-drive FX35/45 crossover SUV, the QX56 (Infiniti's first full-sized SUV), an all-wheel-drive G35 sedan, the V8-powered M45, and a revamped Q45.

All Infinitis come fully equipped and offer owners the prestige of driving a reliable and nicely styled luxury car with lots of standard performance and safety features. Head restraints across the entire lineup are rated Good by IIHS, and NHTSA-rated crashworthiness is fairly good.

Although Infinitis are sold and serviced by a small dealer network across Canada, this limited support base doesn't compromise either the availability or quality of servicing, since any Nissan dealer can carry out most non-warranty maintenance work.

G35 ★★★★

RATING: Above Average. This is the Infiniti with the most to offer from a price and quality perspective. **Strong points:** Smooth, responsive automatic/manual transmission works flawlessly with the sedan's powerful 280-hp V6; standard all-wheel-drive powertrain on the G35X; handles well, with good ride quality; carries a fairly large trunk; and head restraints are rated Good by IIHS. **Weak points:** Harsh ride with the Sport suspension; poorly located power seat controls aren't easily accessible and are vulnerable to cupholder spillovers; difficult rear seat access; seat cushions may be too firm for long trips; limited rear visibility with the coupes; and the trunk is hindered by a small opening. **New for 2006:** Nothing significant.

TECHNICAL DATA

POWERTRAIN (FRONT-DRIVE)
Engine: 3.5L V6 (280 hp); Transmissions: 5-speed manu-matic, 6-speed man.
• 5-speed auto.

DIMENSION/CAPACITY (SEDAN)
Passengers: 2/3; Wheelbase: 112 in.; H: 55.9/L: 187/W: 69 in.; Headroom F/R: 3.0/2.5 in.; Legroom F/R: 41.5/29 in.; Cargo volume: 12 cu. ft.; Fuel tank: 76L/premium; Tow limit: 1,000 lb.; Load capacity: 900 lb.; Turning circle: 39 ft.;

OVERVIEW: The $40,000 ($1,250 PDI and freight) G35 is Infiniti's latest rear-drive luxury sports sedan. It arrived in mid-2002 and was joined in 2003 by a slightly wider and shorter coupe sporting a more powerful engine (20 extra horses), a 6-speed manual transmission, larger tires, and smooth aerodynamic styling—all for a $45,200 base price.

The sedan doesn't come with a manual transmission, and acceleration is good, though not overwhelming. The coupe is the speed leader in this lineup thanks to its 5-speed automatic and 6-speed manual transmissions. Nevertheless, the G35 has more passenger room than a BMW 540i, Lexus IS 300, or Cadillac CTS, beats the Lexus IS 300 equipped with a manual transmission in a 0–100 km/h run, and costs less than most of the competition.

COST ANALYSIS: Get the identical 2005 G35 if it's discounted sufficiently. **Best alternatives:** Other vehicles worth considering: the Acura TL and the BMW 3 Series. **Options:** The Sports Package isn't worth the extra money. **Rebates:** $3,000+ rebates, and low-interest financing; discounts will become even more generous in mid-2006 as the competition heats up. **Delivery/PDI:** $1,250. **Depreciation:** Slower than average. **Insurance cost:** Higher than average. **Parts supply/cost:** Moderately priced parts are easily found in the Maxima parts bin. **Annual maintenance cost:** Should be much lower than average. **Warranty:** Bumper-to-bumper 4 years/100,000 km; powertrain 6 years/100,000 km; rust perforation 7 years/unlimited km. **Supplementary warranty:** Not needed. **Highway/city fuel economy:** 8.3–12.1L/100 km.

 ## Quality/Reliability/Safety

Pro: Quality control: Better then average. **Reliability:** Better than average. **Warranty performance:** Above average.

Con: Owner-reported problems: Automatic transmission sometimes shifts erratically, and radio and AC/heater display is hard to see in daylight. **Service bulletin problems:** 3.5L cylinder blocks leak coolant. **NHTSA safety complaints:** Sudden, unintended acceleration; steering wheel locked up while vehicle was underway; brake calipers on both front wheels came off while driving; and brake pedal went to the floor with minimal effect.

 ## Road Performance

Pro: Acceleration/torque: Plenty of power in all gear ranges for merging with traffic. **Transmission:** Horsepower is increased to 298-hp with the 6-speed manual gearbox. The automatic transmission is both smooth and precise. All-wheel drive is helpful in getting traction in snow or on rain-slicked roads. **Emergency handling:** Average. Cornering at high speeds produces little body roll and front-end plow. The ride is reasonably soft on good roads. All-wheel-drive assists handling in inclement weather. **Braking:** Good stopping ability with little fading after repeated stops. **Routine handling:** Above average.

Con: The automatic transmission cuts overall performance and fuel economy. As with most rear-drives, the back end has a tendency to slide out unexpectedly at high speeds, despite stability and traction control. **Steering:** Steering is vague and slow.

G35

List Price (very negotiable)	**Residual Values** (months)			
	24	**36**	**48**	**60**
Base: $40,000 (25%)	$27,000	$22,000	$19,000	$15,000

SAFETY FEATURES	**STD.**	**OPT.**
Anti-lock brakes	✓	—
Seat belt pretensioners F/R	✓	—
Side airbags	✓	—
Stability control	✓	—
Traction control	✓	—

CRASHWORTHINESS		
Head restraints F/R	[3]	[3]
Visibility F/R	[5]	[3]
Crash protection (side-IIHS) F/R	[4]	[4]

Q45 ★★★★

RATING: Above Average. A nice compromise between luxury and performance, but no match for the better-performing European competition. **Strong points:** Well appointed and stylish; impressive acceleration for a car this size; it takes on twisting roads with aplomb; smooth, quiet engine performance; improved down-shifting and less abrupt gear changes; pleasant riding; provides plenty of head- and legroom; and brakes well. Head restraints and offset crash ratings given a Good score by IIHS. **Weak points:** Bland styling, outrageously overpriced and over-engineered; average cornering ability owing to the overly soft suspension; road groove wandering; some road and wind noise; trunk space is compromised by trunk lid hinges that can crush luggage; cheap-looking flip-up door handles; no

All ratings on a numbered scale where [5] is good and [1] is bad. See page 153–154 for a more detailed description.

driver's left footrest; undersized rear-view mirrors; get used to oncoming drivers flashing their lights in reaction to your powerful xenon headlights; no NHTSA front-or side-crashworthiness data; and requires premium fuel. There's also a plethora of high-tech gadgets that will both challenge and frustrate you, while providing dealership service personnel with a secure future. **New for 2006:** A new sports sedan with standard rear active steering, an upgraded transmission and torque converter, a sport suspension, and 19-inch wheels.

OVERVIEW: Over the years, Infiniti has shifted the Q45's emphasis from performance to luxury and comfort. In fact, after the engine was downsized a few years ago from a 4.5L to a 4.1L, the Q45 designation no longer made sense. Now equipped with a base 340-hp twin-cam 4.5L V8, the Infiniti returns to its performance roots—at a price.

This $88,400 (plus a totally unjustified $1,395 freight charge) luxury rear-drive sedan comes fully loaded with lots of convenience, performance, and safety features that add to the car's complexity, drive up the cost of servicing, can be difficult to use, and may have as many drawbacks as advantages. These features include a 5-speed automatic transmission with a manual shift feature; four-wheel disc ABS with brake assist, traction control, and anti-skid capability; front side and curtain side airbags; front seat belt pretensioners; an in-dash information screen; voice-activated audio, climate, and navigation systems; and large, multi-lens projector high-intensity discharge headlights guaranteed to tick off other drivers.

Standard safety features that are a good idea include side airbags for both the driver and front passenger, dual-locking shoulder belts, and front seat belt pretensioners that activate in a crash to reduce belt slack.

COST ANALYSIS: A discounted 2005 model is the best deal, since it's practically identical to the 2006 version. **Best alternatives:** You may also consider buying a BMW 540i or a Lexus GS 430. **Options:** Auto-adjusting shock absorbers don't have much effect. Forget about the laser-guided "intelligent" cruise control. It's unproven and its failure can have disastrous consequences. The Premium package's rear-view TV system is just a gimmick—get used to turning your head. The Sports Package adds only better tires and more wood trim. **Rebates:** $5,000+ rebates and low-interest financing. **Delivery/PDI:** $1,395. **Depreciation:** Average. **Insurance cost:** Much higher than average. **Parts supply/cost:** Parts may be more expensive than other cars in this class, and they're available only from Nissan or Infiniti dealers. **Annual maintenance cost:** Much less than average. **Warranty:** Bumper-to-bumper 4 years/100,000 km; powertrain 6 years/100,000 km; rust perforation 7 years/unlimited km. **Supplementary warranty:** Not necessary. **Highway/city fuel economy:** 8.8–13.6L/100 km.

M35, M45 ★★★

The Infiniti M45.

RATING: Average. Positioned between the sporty G35 and the luxury Q45, this is the Q45's cheaper high-performance alter ego. Other cars you may wish to consider: the Acura RL V6, the Audi A6 4.2, and the BMW 540i. **Strong points:** Well appointed; superior acceleration and handling; easy entry and exit; head restraints lower into seatback; predicted low depreciation; and head restraints rated Good by IIHS. **Weak points:** Downshifts slowly when passing or merging; cruise control of limited usefulness; complicated, counterintuitive controls; confuses "sportiness" with a jolting ride; rear pillars hinder rear visibility; not much storage space; excessive tire and road noise; and requires premium fuel while delivering disappointing fuel economy. **New for 2006:** Returns relatively unchanged. Next year, the car will be much larger and have smoother styling.

OVERVIEW: The M35 and M45 are rear-drive luxury sedans that ride on a four-wheel independent suspension and carry the Q45's powerful and smooth 280-hp V6 and 335-hp V8. Essentially smaller Q45s that bridge the gap between the Q and the G35, the M cars share the Q's drivetrain, are longer than the G35, and are set on a shorter wheelbase. Because of their lighter curb weight and potent engine, these cars can do 0–100 km/h in under 6 seconds—a half-second faster than the Q45.

The M45 gives shoppers the thrills of a Q45 for about $65,400 (plus an unacceptably high $1,330 freight charge). It comes packed with all the techno-goodies car companies pile on to impress shoppers who have more money than good sense. Of particular note is its 5-speed automatic transmission, incorporating a convenient, though not very impressive, manual shift mode; a sport suspension; Vehicle Dynamics Control stability system; active head restraints; and four-wheel disc brakes supplemented by brake assist and electronic brakeforce distribution.

This isn't a pretty car. In fact, it's rather bland-looking, has an excessive rear overhang, and sports a front grille that recalls the Ford Crown Victoria.

Kia

This year, Hyundai lets Kia shine. No longer will Kia be shackled to low-tech, poor quality parts and treated like an entry-level throwaway compact. In fact, three 2006 models—the Rio, the Optima, and the Sedona—return completely redesigned, with an infusion of proven Hyundai components and platforms, more modern styling, and an array of standard safety, performance, and convenience features. Initial positive reports from buyers of the recently redesigned Spectra and Sportage minivan have led industry analysts to conclude that Hyundai's product-improvement efforts are paying off, as it uses Kia to supply entry-level small cars, minivans, and SUVs, while Hyundai churns out upscale, feature-laden cars and SUVs.

Sins of the Past

Kia has long suffered from a reputation for primitive and low-quality vehicles that are risky buys. However, over the past few years, Kia has posted impressive sales gains, thanks to low prices and a comprehensive base warranty. If fuel costs continue to rise, Kia and other small-car sales will likely be lifted by the same rising tide.

Kia's quality control, particularly when it comes to automatic transmission reliability (also a Daewoo bugaboo), has improved over the last two years. Apparently in the past the company simply used a longer base warranty as a substitute for quality control (much like Chrysler) and routinely paid warranty claims instead of improving the product. That's all changed now, says Hyundai.

For 2006, Hyundai will work at strengthening Kia's dealer network and improving quality and service. Hyundai will continue to share platforms and key components with Kia in order to put out cheap and fuel-efficient small cars, even if these cannibalize Hyundai's own sales.

RIO ★★★

RATING: Average. A good blend of economy, interior room, and useful standard features. Get the upgraded 2006 version. Keep in mind, though, that the Hyundai Accent, the Honda Civic, or the Toyota Echo may be better buys. **Strong points:** Highly manoeuvrable in city traffic, with plenty of steering feedback and a spacious trunk. Given an Acceptable rating for head restraint protection, a four-star rating for front-impact protection, and four stars for rollover resistance. Six standard airbags are provided, and passenger and cargo room have been increased on this year's model. Sharing the Accent platform and using more Hyundai components will undoubtedly improve Kia's quality; however, we don't know by how much or how long it will take. **Weak points:** An unacceptable $1,000 increase in the

2006 base price. Weak and noisy engine performance; busy, harsh ride; highway handling is slow and imprecise; problematic entry and exit; tire thumping; small audio controls and missing remote trunk release; low-budget interior materials; small door openings and limited rear headroom and legroom; trunk's small opening doesn't take bulky items and doesn't offer a pass-through for large objects; optional tilt steering wheel doesn't tilt much; poor body construction; chronic stalling caused by a defective engine control module; only two stars awarded for side crashworthiness; and depends upon a small dealer network that may complicate servicing and warranty performance. **New for 2006:** The sedan and five-door hatchback use Hyundai's Accent platform for a longer wheelbase and wider track; engine gets six more horses with variable valve timing. The Rio5 hatchback replaces the Rio Cinco5 wagon. This year's model gives additional passenger space even with its shortened body.

OVERVIEW: A bit smaller than the Sephia and Spectra, the base Rio sells for $13,295 (plus $995 freight and PDI) and is essentially a spin-off of the Ford Aspire sold from 1995–97. Base Rios are equipped with a 110-hp 1.6L 4-cylinder engine teamed with a 5-speed manual or an optional 4-speed automatic transmission. **Highway/city fuel economy:** 6.8–8.6L/100 km.

Quality/Reliability/Safety

Con: Owner-reported problems: Problems with the automatic transmission, electrical, and fuel systems; chronic stalling; power loss, owing in part to faulty engine control modules; brakes; and seat belts. **Service bulletin problems:** Hard start in cold temperatures requires a reprogramming of powertrain software; improved timing belts. **NHTSA safety complaints:** Defective fuel line ignited an under-hood fire; hood flew up and broke front windshield; side airbag failed to deploy; vehicle disengages from Overdrive because of a missing transmission control modulator; transmission jumps out of gear when brakes are applied, or is slow shifting; sudden loss of steering; brakes stick and pedal goes to the floor without stopping vehicle; brakes are noisy; excessive shaking and vibration; vehicle swerves all over the road; no-start caused by faulty computer; chronic stalling; front seat belts ride high up on the neck and rear seat belt shreds or jams; rear seat belts don't lock when a child safety seat is installed; steering binds and grinds when turned; premature tire wear; vehicle assembled without a horn; various electrical problems, including clock spring failure, cause the Check Engine light and airbag warning light to remain lit; and fuel light stays lit constantly.

SPECTRA ★★★

RATING: Average, with the potential for an Above Average rating if Kia doesn't screw up what's essentially a Hyundai Elantra with a Kia badge. Consider getting the Spectra5 hatchback for convenient loading and unloading. Other contenders: the Honda Civic, the Hyundai Elantra (which costs about $1,000 less), or the Toyota Corolla. **Strong points:** Inexpensive, and built with proven Hyundai parts; well appointed; plenty of interior room and comfortable seats; competent engine at high revs, with some reserve power and a smooth-shifting transmission; good handling and ride quality; fewer rattles and body glitches; head restraints rated Good; larger dealer network with both Kia and Hyundai providing servicing; and above-average crashworthiness scores: four stars for driver and passenger frontal crash protection; four-star driver- and three-star passenger-side protection; and four-star rollover resistance. The base warranty is quite comprehensive. **Weak points:** Could use more grunt at low engine rpm; some wind noise; fairly rapid depreciation; and a high PDI and freight fee. **New for 2006:** A redesigned 4-speed automatic transmission that is said to be lighter in weight and more durable, floormats, and a cabin air filter.

OVERVIEW: Selling for $15,995 plus $995 transport/PDI (the Spectra5 hatchback costs $4,000 more), the 2006 Spectra is available as a sedan and hatchback. It's powered by a twin-cam 138-hp 2.0L 4-cylinder engine hooked to a standard 5-speed manual or an optional 4-speed automatic transmission, set on a four-wheel independent suspension. You also get oodles of standard features, such as front-wheel disc brakes, front and rear stabilizer bars, speed-sensitive rack-and-pinion steering, front seat belt pretensioners and force limiters, a height-adjustable driver's seat, an AM/FM/CD sound system, split-fold rear seatbacks, door pockets, tinted glass, six separate airbags, and a tachometer.

The Spectra rides on Hyundai's longer wheelbase, which also adds to its height and width, smooths out the ride, and increases cargo and passenger room (Kia claims it's a third larger than the five-door it replaces).

The Spectra5 ("5" indicates it has five doors, though it's really a hatchback), is a sporty new hatchback that is actually a Kia version of the Hyundai Elantra GT. See the Hyundai Elantra section for an indication of how the Spectra is likely to perform. **Highway/city fuel economy:** 7.1–10.8L/100 km.

MAGENTIS ★★★

RATING: Average. Consider buying a competitor with more refinement and a proven history for reliability and good quality control. Three good choices: the Honda Accord, the Mazda6, and the Toyota Camry. **Strong points:** Nicely appointed; good overall visibility; plenty of front headroom; firm, supportive front bucket seats with plenty of fore-aft travel; better-than-average fuel economy with regular fuel; nice ride quality and handling; spacious trunk; four-star front and side crashworthiness rating and five stars awarded for rollover resistance; and servicing can be carried out by both Hyundai and Kia dealers. **Weak points:**

Weak 4-cylinder engine; only average V6 performance; poorly performing 4-speed automatic transmission; mediocre braking; average rear headroom; considerable body lean when turning; excessive wind and tire noise; trunk has small opening; and fit and finish not up to Honda and Toyota standard. **New for 2006:** Carried over unchanged until the redesigned 2007 model arrives in the spring of 2006.

OVERVIEW: Sold in the States as the Optima, this front-drive, five-passenger sedan was launched several years ago in Canada as the Magentis. The entry-level model sells for $22,450 (LX), $25,750 gets you an LX V6, and $28,750 is the asking price for a high-end EX V6, plus a $995 transport/PDI fee for all models. Since these models haven't been changed for 2006 and will soon be replaced, hold out for major discounting and generous rebates to cut the retail price by at least 20 percent.

Essentially a Hyundai Sonata without traction control, the Magentis comes with a twin-cam 138-hp 2.4L 4-cylinder or optional 170-hp 2.7L V6 hooked to a 4-speed automatic transmission (V6s have the Sonata's separate gate for manual shifting and four-wheel ABS). Other standard features: front seat belt pretensioners, a tilt steering column, independent double-wishbone front suspension and independent multi-link rear suspension, a 60/40 split-fold rear seat, and tinted glass.

Performance and reliability are expected to be similar to the Sonata's. Prudent shoppers should stay away from this car until it has a confidence-inspiring track record. **Service bulletin problems:** Improved engine timing belts had to be put into service. **NHTSA safety complaints:** Airbags failed to deploy; severe pulling to the left; engine surges when shifting from Second to Third gear with the manual transmission; vehicle suddenly decelerated and wouldn't go faster than 35 km/h; and horn failure.

AMANTI ★★★

RATING: Average. Drives like your father's Oldsmobile: Comfort trumps performance. Try a Toyota Avalon instead. **Strong points:** Fully loaded with safety, performance, and convenience features; acceptable V6 performance; good overall visibility; headroom and legroom beat out such key competitors as the Chrysler Concorde and the Buick LeSabre; comfortable ride; predictable handling; a spacious trunk; servicing provided by both Hyundai and Kia dealers; and received a four-star rating for rollover resistance. Very few first-year production glitches on the 2004 model. **Weak points:** The 6-cylinder engine, on par with the Toyota Camry's V6, is overwhelmed by the car's heft and doesn't have a great deal of reserve power for passing or merging. The overly soft suspension makes for a wallowing ride and lots of body lean when cornering. No frontal or side crashworthiness tests have been performed. **New for 2006:** No significant changes.

OVERVIEW: This large front-drive sedan is a $35,995 (plus a $995 PDI and freight charge) Hyundai XG350 clone, sold elsewhere as the Kia Opirus. It carries a standard 200-hp 3.5L V6 coupled to a 5-speed automatic transmission with a sequential manual mode. Ride comfort is enhanced by an independent double-wishbone front suspension with coil springs and a stabilizer bar. At the rear, there's an independent multi-link suspension with coil springs and a stabilizer bar. Overall styling is reminiscent of a Mercedes-Benz E-Class.

Amanti is no slouch in offering standard active and passive safety features, including anti-lock brakes, electronic braking distribution, brake assist, traction control, electronic stability control, and eight "smart" airbags. **Service bulletin problems:** Engine produces white smoke and runs poorly; no power to console box outlet. **NHTSA safety complaints:** Loses power while underway.

SEDONA ★ ★ ★

RATING: Average (2006); Below Average (2005). The 2005 Sedona is a competent minivan that is hard riding, poor-handling, and vulnerable to excessive wind and road noise entering into the cabin area. The 2006 version is better in almost every category and it's well worth the wait for its early 2006 arrival. **Strong points:** *2005:* Reasonably priced; well appointed; transmission shifts smoothly and quietly; low ground clearance adds to stability and helps access; low step-in; comfortable ride; convenient "walk-through" space between front seats; well laid-out, user-friendly instruments and controls; lots of storage areas; good visibility; fairly well built; minimal engine and road noise; good braking; head restraints for the 2002 model are rated Good up front, Acceptable in the rear; acceptable crashworthiness scores; and comprehensive base warranty. **Weak points:** *2005:* Slow acceleration; engine power is drained by the Sedona's heft;

10–20 percent higher fuel consumption than the V6-equipped Dodge Caravan and Toyota Sienna; poor emergency handling; vague steering and handling; excessive engine and wind noise; side doors cannot be operated electrically—which isn't such a drawback if you have children, considering the failure-prone nature of the automatic doors; and a weak dealer network. Quality control is its weakest link. **New for 2006:** Practically everything. This is the Sedona's second redesign since it was launched as a 2002 model and carried a $24,595 price tag. Scheduled to arrive in early 2006, this year's Sedona is larger in every dimension. Fuel economy should benefit from the lighter chassis and passenger space has been increased by nearly 15 percent. A more powerful V6 engine gives 45 additional horses, and the 5-speed automatic transmission has been reworked to provide smoother, more precise shifting. The new models also have a fully independent suspension with MacPherson struts up front, a multi-link set-up in the rear, and front and rear stabilizer bars. The front brake discs have been enlarged as well.

OVERVIEW: *2005 models:* Embodying typically bland minivan styling, this front-drive, seven-passenger minivan comes with a good selection of standard features, including a 195-hp 3.5L V6 engine hooked to an automatic 5-speed transmission, a low step-in height, and a commanding view of the road. For convenience, there are two sliding rear side doors (automatic doors aren't available); folding, removable second- and third-row seats; a flip-up hatchback; standard front and rear air conditioning; and a large cargo bay. Other standard amenities: 15-inch tires, AM/FM/CD stereo, power steering, power windows, power door locks, power-heated mirrors, tilt steering, rear defroster and wiper, dual airbags (side airbags not offered), and six adjustable head restraints.

COST ANALYSIS: The 2006s are the better buy as the 2005 prices edge upward. Sedonas range in price from $26,995 (LX) to $29,495 (EX). **Best alternatives:** Consider the Honda Odyssey, the Mazda MPV, or the Toyota Sienna. **Options:** Forget the EX option; it doesn't offer much for the extra cost. **Rebates:** Look for $3,500 rebates and low-financing rates by mid-2006. **Delivery/PDI:** A totally unjustified $1,150. **Depreciation:** Predicted to be a bit slower than average. **Insurance cost:** Average for an entry-level minivan. **Parts supply/cost:** Average cost; expect long delays for parts. **Annual maintenance cost:** Expected to be higher than average once first-year models lose their base warranty protection. **Warranty:** Bumper-to-bumper 5 years/100,000 km; powertrain 5 years/100,000

2005 TECHNICAL DATA

POWERTRAIN
Engine: 3.5L V6 (195 hp); Transmission: 5-speed auto.
DIMENSION/CAPACITY
Passengers: 2/3/2; Wheelbase: 115 in.; H: 69.3/L: 194/W: 75 in.; Headroom F/R1/R2: 4.0/4.5/1.0 in.; Legroom F/R1/R2: 39/28.5/30.5 in.; Cargo volume: 62 cu. ft.; Fuel tank: 75L/regular; Tow limit: 3,500 lb.; Load capacity: 1,160 lb.; Turning circle: 44 ft.; Weight: 4,802 lb.

2006 TECHNICAL DATA

POWERTRAIN
Engine: 3.8L V6 (240 hp); Transmission: 5-speed auto.
DIMENSION/CAPACITY
Passengers: 2/3/2; Wheelbase: 118.9 in.; H: 69.3/L: 202/W: 78.3 in.

km; rust perforation 5 years/unlimited km. **Supplementary warranty:** A wise buy, considering Kia's previous transmission troubles and the installation of a new set-up on the 2006. **Highway/city fuel economy:** 10.9–15.6L/100 km with the 3.5L V6. The 2006 3.8L V6 has yet to be tested.

Quality/Reliability/Safety (2005)

Pro: Quality control: Average. **Reliability:** Average. **Warranty performance:** Fairly good. **Safety:** 75 NHTSA complaints logged in on the 2004 Sedona; no reports on the 2005 or 2006 models.

Con: Service bulletin problems: AC noise, insufficient cooling, noise from speakers when using a cell phone.

SAFETY FEATURES (2005)	STD.	OPT.	CRASHWORTHINESS (2005)		
			Head restraints F/R	4	3
Anti-lock brakes	—	✓	Visibility F/R	5	5
Seat belt pretensioners F/R	✓	—	Crash protection (front) D/P	5	5
Side airbags	—	—	Crash protection (side) F/R	5	5
			Crash protection (offset)	3	—
			Rollover	4	—

SAFETY FEATURES (2006)	STD.	OPT.	CRASHWORTHINESS (2006)		
			Visibility F/R	4	5
Anti-lock brakes	✓	—			
Seat belt pretensioners F/R	✓	—			
Side airbags	✓	—			
Stability control	—	✓			
Traction control	—	✓			

Lexus

The first Lexus, an LS 400, appeared in 1989 and shared no major components with previous Toyotas. Equipped with a V8 engine and noted for its outstanding engine performance, quietness, well-appointed interior, and impressive build quality, the car was an immediate success. Now, the Lexus name has supplanted Cadillac as a term for luxury and quality, and has been chosen the most popular luxury car in Germany.

All ratings on a numbered scale where 5 is good and 1 is bad. See page 153–154 for a more detailed description.

Lexus continues to be a luxury automaker on its own merits, even though some models have mostly been dressed-up Camrys (only the ES 300/330 fit that description now). Unlike Acura and Infiniti, Lexus has become the epitome of luxury and comfort, with a small dab of performance thrown in. Lexus executives know that no matter how often car enthusiast magazines say that drivers want "road feel," "responsive handling," and "high-performance" thrills, the truth of the matter is that most drivers simply want to travel from point A to point B in safety and comfort, without interruption, in cars that are more than fully equipped Civics or warmed-over Maximas.

Although these imports do set advanced benchmarks for quality control, they don't demonstrate engineering perfection, as a recent spate of engine failures—including sludge buildup and automatic transmissions that hesitate, then surge when shifting—proves. And yes, cheaper luxury cars from Acura, Nissan, and Toyota give you almost as much comfort and reliability, but without as much cachet and resale value.

Technical service bulletins show that these cars are affected by electrical malfunctions, faulty emissions control components, computer module miscalibrations, and minor body fit and trim glitches. Most owners haven't heard of these problems, because Lexus dealers have been particularly adept at fixing many of them before they become chronic.

The Lexus lineup is geared to the luxury cruiser crowd, which prefers comfort to performance thrills. All models come with a full array of standard safety features. The company holds a winning hand, and won't make any major changes to its 2006 models, except for the launch of an RX hybrid and the redesign of the IS and the GS.

IS 250, IS 350 ★★★

RATING: Average. Better equipped than the IS 300; however, BMW is still the benchmark for high-performance handling. **Strong points:** More standard safety, performance, and convenience features than the IS 300; the car is wider, longer, and more solid-looking; a competent standard IS 350 3.5L engine; easy handling and effective braking; an upgraded interior; optional navigation screen is user-friendly and easily read; pleasant riding; low beltline provides a great view; and first-class workmanship. **Weak points:** 2006s are more expensive; the IS 250 2.5L engine provides 11 fewer horses than the IS 300's 215-hp 3.0L V6 and feels rather sluggish when pushed; handling on either model doesn't feel as sharp or responsive as BMW's, owing in large part to an intrusive Vehicle Dynamics Integrated Management system that automatically eases up on the throttle during hard cornering. Emergency braking also isn't a confidence-builder; there's no 6-speed manual transmission available with the IS 350; rear seating is still cramped

The Lexus IS 250.

for average-sized adults despite a roomier interior; the car requires premium fuel; and there's no crashworthiness data. **New for 2006:** Two new additions replace the IS 300.

OVERVIEW: Targeting BMW's 3 Series, Lexus's IS 250 and IS 350 rear-drive sports-compact sedans come with either a 204-hp 2.5L or a 306-hp 3.5L V6. The IS 250 is equipped with a standard 6-speed manual transmission; a 6-speed automatic is optional. All-wheel-drive IS 250s offer the 6-speed automatic as a standard feature. It's not possible to get the IS 350 equipped with a manual 6-speed shifter. Other important standard features include four-wheel, ABS-equipped disc brakes; front, side, and knee airbags; Electronic Brake Force Distribution; independent suspension; performance tires; front seat belt pretensioners; stability and traction control; tilt steering; air conditioning; rear seat heater ducts; and halogen headlights.

TECHNICAL DATA (250, 350)

POWERTRAIN (REAR-DRIVE)

Engines: 2.5L V6 (204 hp) • 3.5L V6 (306 hp); Transmissions: 6-speed man. • 6-speed auto.

DIMENSION/CAPACITY

Passengers: 2/3; Wheelbase: 107.4 in.; H: 56.1/L: 180.1/W: 70.1 in., 70.9 in.; Headroom F/R: N/A; Legroom F/R: 43.9/30.6 in.; Cargo volume: 13.3 cu. ft.; Fuel tank: 65L/premium; Tow limit: N/A; Load capacity: N/A; Turning circle: 33.5 ft.; Weight: 3,435 lb., 3,527 lb.

COST ANALYSIS: Forget about the 2005 IS 300; most have been sold and this year's new models are far more refined. **Best alternatives:** Other cars worth considering are the Acura TL, the BMW 3 Series, and the Infiniti G35. Audi's A4 would be a contender, were it not for a decline in quality control. **Options:** Don't waste money on the sunroof, heated seats, or leather upholstery. **Rebates:** Expect $3,000–$5,000 discounts early in the new year. **Delivery/PDI:** $1,675. **Depreciation:** Predicted to be much lower than average. **Insurance cost:** Much higher than average. **Parts supply/cost:** Average availability, though parts may be quite expensive because of a lack of independent part suppliers. **Annual**

maintenance cost: Below average. **Warranty:** Bumper-to-bumper 4 years/80,000 km; powertrain 6 years/110,000 km; rust perforation 6 years/ unlimited km. **Supplementary warranty:** Not necessary. **Highway/city fuel economy:** *IS 250:* 6.7–9.8L/100 km.; *IS 350:* 7.7–10.8L/100 km.

IS 250, IS 350

List Price (negotiable)	Residual Values (months)			
	24	36	48	60
IS 250: $36,300 (25%)	$31,000	$27,000	$23,000	$19,000
IS 250 AWD: $41,900 (26%)	$34,000	$30,000	$26,000	$21,000
IS 350: $49,000 (27%)	$39,000	$35,000	$29,000	$26,000

SAFETY FEATURES	STD.	OPT.	CRASHWORTHINESS		
Anti-lock brakes	✓	—	Head restraints F/R	❸	❸
Seat belt pretensioners F/R	✓	—	Visibility F/R	❺	❹
Side airbags	✓	—			
Stability control	✓	—			
Traction control	✓	—			

ES 330 ★★★

RATING: Average. A near-luxury sedan that's handicapped by an unreliable automatic transmission. **Strong points:** Good acceleration; pleasantly quiet ride; quiet running; top-quality components; good side crashworthiness and rollover resistance ratings; favourable accident injury claim data; and excellent quality control and warranty performance. **Weak points:** Dangerous automatic

TECHNICAL DATA

POWERTRAIN (FRONT-DRIVE)

Engine: 3.3L V6 (218 hp); Transmission: 5-speed auto.

DIMENSION/CAPACITY

Passengers: 2/3; Wheelbase: 107 in.; H: 57.3/L: 191/W: 71 in.; Headroom F/R: 2.5/2.5 in.; Legroom F/R: 41.5/27 in.; Cargo volume: 14.5 cu. ft.; Fuel tank: 70L/premium; Tow limit: N/A; Load capacity: 900 lb.; Turning circle: 39 ft.; Weight: 3,460 lb.

transmission that hesitates and surges when shifting; primarily a four-seater, as three adults can't sit comfortably in the rear. Headroom is inadequate for tall occupants. Steering feel is muted. Manual shifting system isn't very user-friendly; and overall handling isn't as nimble as its BMW or Mercedes rivals. Traction control is no longer a standard feature; you'll need the anti-skid option. Trunk space is limited (low liftover, though) and rear corner visibility is hampered by the high rear end; and no frontal crashworthiness data. **New for 2006:** Satellite radio.

OVERVIEW: A Camry clone with more standard luxury features, this $39,900 entry-level Lexus front-drive carries a 218-hp V6 mated to an electronically controlled 5-speed automatic transmission that handles the 3.3L engine's horses effortlessly, without sacrificing fuel economy. All ES 330s feature dual front and side airbags, anti-lock brakes, double-piston front brake calipers, optional Adaptive Variable Suspension, power adjustable pedals with memory setting, 60/40 split-fold rear seats, DVD navigation system, 10-way power adjustable driver's seat with memory, rain-sensing wipers, and one of the rarest features of all: a conventional spare tire.

COST ANALYSIS: Discounted 2005s are the better buy because there is nothing to justify the 2006's higher cost. The usurious freight/PDI fee should be at least halved. **Best alternatives:** An all-dressed Camry, an Acura TL, a BMW 3 Series, a Toyota Avalon, or a Volvo S40 or S60. **Options:** Anti-skid Variable Stability Control is worthwhile. I don't recommend the Adaptive Variable Suspension option; it's mostly a gimmick with little functional improvement. **Rebates:** Look for some discounting, $3,000 rebates, and zero percent financing. **Delivery/PDI:** $1,675. **Depreciation:** Much lower than average. **Insurance cost:** Much higher than average. **Parts supply/cost:** Average availability, and parts are moderately priced. **Annual maintenance cost:** Below average. **Warranty:** Bumper-to-bumper 4 years/80,000 km; powertrain 6 years/110,000 km; rust perforation 6 years/unlimited km. **Supplementary warranty:** May be needed to cover automatic transmission malfunctions. **Highway/city fuel economy:** 7.5–11.6L/100 km.

 ## Quality/Reliability/Safety

Pro: **Quality control:** Average.

Con: **Warranty performance:** Below Average. **Reliability:** Below Average. **Owner-reported problems:** Airbag sensors inadvertently disable the airbags; computer glitch causes the powertrain to jerk and drag; when slowing to a stop or coming out of a turn, transmission hesitates or feels like it's slipping; and some trim items and interior fit and finish deficiencies. **Service bulletin problems:** A stinky exhaust caused by a faulty catalytic converter; moon roof noise caused by weather-strip sticking; rear door trim panel rattle; and a remedy for the vehicle pulling to one side. **NHTSA safety complaints:** Sudden acceleration accompanied by loss of braking capability; airbag sensors disable the device in spite of an adult sitting in the seat. More than 50 complaints that the automatic transmission shifts erratically, suddenly accelerates, or slips, and hesitates before going into gear:

> 2005 ES 330 was nearly new, only 100 miles [160 km], no abnormal behavior up to that point. While shifting into Park...and with no pressure on accelerator, car suddenly lurched forward, striking concrete stancheon of parking lot light pole. This resulted in damage to the front bumper, frame, right quarter-panel, and right headlight assembly, causing over $4,000 in repair costs.

•

> Transmission is unpredictable. Sometimes it hesitates, sometimes it lurches. It shudders at times when shifting. I've had the car in to the dealer for two computer-download fixes. The first lasted a day, making the car seem like the demo I test-drove. The car was returned and another fix by computer was done with no change to the quirky, unsafe condition of this transmission. My wife was nearly broadsided in cross-traffic pattern as the car hesitated as she attempted to turn onto a side street. I have had four similar situations. These problems are at speeds up to 40 mph [64 km/h]. These problems do not seem to occur if you stomp on the accelerator from a stopped position. The general manager at the agency has driven the car "around the block" and experienced none of these problems. Yet the service department admits it's not the way this car should operate and no further manufacturer update/correction is available. They say they are working on it. The manager says per Toyota this is the normal way this car drives and they won't do anything to satisfy my complaint. These two statements are a contradiction. I've been advised by one of the techs to use premium fuel because it would help the engine/transmission work better. I've done this since that conversation and the performance is still substandard and in stop-and-go traffic still unpredictable and dangerous.

Car lurches to the left or right when the brakes are applied; rear window shattered for no apparent reason; airbag light comes on for no reason; turn signals aren't loud enough to signal they are activated; and windshield wipers fail to work intermittently.

Road Performance

Pro: Emergency handling: Very good, predictable, and easy to master. **Acceleration/torque:** Fast acceleration and lots of torque, especially with this year's power upgrade. **Transmission:** When working correctly, tranny shifts smoothly in all gear ranges; the trouble is that the tranny is very unreliable. **Routine handling:** Capable handling, with little body roll. **Braking:** Disc/disc; better-than-average braking.

Con: Considerable body lean when cornering under power. Transmission shifts and accelerates unexpectedly; kickdown when passing is slower than what one would expect. Steering is still a bit numb and over-assisted.

ES 330

List Price (negotiable)	Residual Values (months)			
	24	36	48	60
ES 330: $39,950 (23%)	$34,500	$30,500	$25,500	$20,500

SAFETY FEATURES	STD.	OPT.	CRASHWORTHINESS		
			Head restraints F/R	3	3
Anti-lock brakes	✓	—	Visibility F/R	5	2
Seat belt pretensioners F/R	✓	—	Crash protection (front) D/P	5	5
Side airbags	✓	—	Crash protection (side) F/R	5	4
Stability control	—	✓	Crash protection (offset)	5	—
Traction control	—	✓	Rollover	4	—

GS 300, GS 430 ★ ★ ★

RATING: Average. An exercise in passive driving; an abundance of electronic gadgetry cannot transform these luxury sedans into sports cars. **Strong points:** Good high-performance powertrain set-up (V6 and V8 engine get a horsepower boost of 20 and 55, respectively); pleasantly quiet ride; acceptable handling and braking; average fuel economy, though premium fuel must be used; and exceptional quality control. **Weak points:** Primarily a four-seater with limited headroom for six-footers; the Audi A6 offers eight more centimetres of rear legroom; middle-rear passengers, as usual in rear-drive sedans, get to ride the powertrain hump and thump the low roof with their head; high window line impedes rear visibility; some instruments hidden by the steering wheel; trunk and fuel-door releases hidden at the base of the dash; dash-mounted GPS navigator, climate control, and entertainment system tries to do too much; fan speed control is too recessed; mediocre FM performance and no user-friendly radio presets. Secondary controls, like power mirror and trunk and fuel releases, are hidden in a

All ratings on a numbered scale where is good and ❶ is bad. See page 153–154 for a more detailed description.

The Lexus GS 300.

small tray mounted to the left of the steering column where it is easily hit by the driver's knee; the ignition start button is counter-intuitive; and floormats are optional. No crashworthiness data available. 2006 prices have been boosted $2,600 for the GS 300 and $5,200 for the GS 430. **New for 2006:** A more powerful V6 and V8, a 6-speed automatic transmission with a semi-manual mode, AWD, upgraded stability and traction control, a new Adaptive Variable Suspension, headlights that turn with the steering, and larger 18-inch wheels.

OVERVIEW: Starting at $64,300, the GS 300 carries a 245-hp 3.0L V6 engine. For another $10,400 you can buy a GS 430 with a 300-hp 4.3L V8. Both engines have VVT-i (Variable Valve Timing with intelligence), a feature that continually changes the engine timing to achieve peak horsepower with low emissions and high fuel economy. Other innovative standard features include electronic stability and traction control, dual side airbags, and dual-zone climate controls, plus oodles of other safety, performance, and convenience features. Besides having a V8 engine, the GS 430 uses 18-inch wheels and tires, larger, more sophisticated brakes, variable-ratio steering and suspension (Normal or Sport), Vehicle Dynamics Integration Management, a feature which uses the electronics of the throttle, steering, and brakes to prevent the loss of traction, improved transmission gearing, and swiveling headlights.

COST ANALYSIS: These two GS models continue to be comfortable and polished luxury sedans, but sporty performers they are not. The Infiniti M, for example, allows for more driver input and is more satisfying to

TECHNICAL DATA

POWERTRAIN (REAR-DRIVE)

Engines: 3.0L V6 (245 hp) • 4.3L V8 (300 hp); Transmissions: 5-speed auto. • 6-speed auto.

DIMENSION/CAPACITY

Passengers: 2/3; Wheelbase: 112.2 in.; H: 56.1/L: 190/W: 71.7; Headroom F/R: 3.5/3 in.; Legroom F/R: 44.5/34.3 in.; Cargo volume: 14.8 cu. ft.; Fuel tank: 70L/premium; Tow limit: N/A; Turning circle: 37.1 ft.; Weight: 3,685 lb.

drive, owing mainly to its extra 40 horses, crisper shifts, precise steering, more predictable brakes, and a less intrusive stability system. **Best alternatives:** Other cars worth considering are the Acura RL and the BMW 5 Series. **Options:** Stay away from the in-dash navigator ($2,750 with a rear-view backup camera); it complicates the calibration of the sound system and climate controls. Other money-wasting options: a power sunshade ($250), moon roof ($1,500), the Mark Levinson stereo ($5,000), XM radio ($550), ventilated seats ($250), spoiler ($300), "Intuitive Park Assist" parking sensors ($700), and rain-sensing wipers with "Adaptive Front Lighting" swiveling headlights ($700). Finally, there's a Pre-Collision System that is a risky feature under the best of conditions. It tightens seat belts and suspension, and applies the brakes if it sees an inevitable crash. You also get Dynamic Radar Cruise Control ($3,500) that reduces your speed when cars cut you off. Adding all-wheel drive costs $2,750 and includes run-flat tires (letting you limp home up to about 180 km). **Rebates:** Expect $5,000 rebates, zero percent financing, generous leasing terms, and discounting on the MSRP by about 10 percent. Discounting and rebates will become more attractive early in the new year. **Delivery/PDI:** $1,675. **Depreciation:** Slower than average. **Insurance cost:** Much higher than average. **Parts supply/cost:** Parts aren't easily found outside of the dealer network; prices tend to be on the high side. **Annual maintenance cost:** Less than average. **Warranty:** Bumper-to-bumper 4 years/80,000 km; powertrain 6 years/110,000 km; rust perforation 6 years/ unlimited km. **Supplementary warranty:** Not necessary. **Highway/city fuel economy:** *GS 300:* 9.0–13.3L/100 km; *GS 430:* 9.4–12.9L/100 km.

Road Performance

Pro: Acceleration/torque: V6 is smooth and quiet; car runs faster than the GS 300 but doesn't burn more fuel. Hot-rod acceleration with lots of torque (0–100 km/h: 6.1 seconds with the V8). Handling is improved via sportier tires, a retuned suspension, and swiveling headlights. **Braking:** Disc/disc; exceptional—no surprise braking once you learn to apply the brakes with care.

Con: Some body shake at cruising speed, likely caused by the sporty Dunlop 17-inch tires. Numb steering. Automatic transmission's manual mode doesn't allow for much driver input and the omnipresent stability control system continually fights the driver for control. Brakes feel overly aggressive.

GS 300, GS 430

List Price (negotiable)	Residual Values (months)			
	24	36	48	60
GS 300: $64,300 (30%)	$49,500	$42,500	$37,500	$32,500
GS 430: $74,700 (30%)	$55,000	$46,000	$41,000	$36,000

All ratings on a numbered scale where ⑤ is good and ① is bad. See page 153–154 for a more detailed description.

SAFETY FEATURES			CRASHWORTHINESS		
	STD.	OPT.			
			Head restraints F/R	5	5
Anti-lock brakes	✓	—	Visibility F/R	5	2
Seat belt pretensioners F/R	✓	—	Crash protection (offset)	5	—
Side airbags	✓	—			
Traction control	✓	—			

LS 430, SC 430 ★★★★

The Lexus LS 430.

RATING: Above Average. **Strong points:** Impressive V8 acceleration; a quiet, comfortable ride; convertible is agile with no body flexing; well appointed with curtain side airbags, high-intensity headlights, and VSC anti-skid system; first-class construction and high-quality mechanical components; and better-than-average warranty performance. **Weak points:** Automatic transmission is slow to downshift when passing (a common Lexus trait); mind-numbing, complex navigation system controls and voice-activation system; sedan handling is no match for the European competition; convertible's 18-inch tires make for a jittery, wandering ride over rough pavement; and premium fuel required. No crashworthiness data available. **New for 2006:** Nothing significant.

OVERVIEW: The $85,700 LS 430 rear-drive luxury compact sedan is Lexus' response to the Audi A8 and BMW 7 Series. It carries a 290-hp twin-cam V8 engine hooked to a 6-speed automatic transmission. It's chock-full of the latest techno-gadgets to assure your comfort and safety. The $92,650 SC 430 is Lexus' first convertible, filling the void left by the discontinued SC 400. It comes equipped with the LS 430's V8 engine (with 10 additional horses) and 5-speed automatic transmission. A power-retractable metal roof is housed in the trunk (think of the old Ford Skyliner), forcing you to use the small rear seat for cargo. Capable of reaching 100 km/h in less than 6 seconds, the SC 430's double-wishbone suspension provides both a comfortable ride and precise, responsive handling. **Service bulletin problems:** *LS 430*: Automatic transmission shifts poorly and mirrors don't return to their proper position. *SC 430*: Navigation system door is hard to open or close. **NHTSA safety complaints:** Premature failure of Dunlop tires; seat belt tightened around child's neck and had to be cut away.

COST ANALYSIS: The cheaper 2005 LS 430 and SC 430 are the better buys. **Best alternatives:** Other cars worth considering are the BMW Z8 and 7 Series (if you can figure out the iDrive feature) and the Infiniti M35 or M45. Nissan's Q45 doesn't have the build quality or performance to match the LS 430. **Options:** Ultra Luxury package contains an expensive array of unnecessary features. The convertible rear spoiler isn't needed, but run-flat tires are a good idea, considering the SC 430's limited storage space. **Rebates:** $4,000, plus zero percent financing and favourable lease deals. **Delivery/PDI:** $1,675. **Depreciation:** Much lower than average. **Insurance cost:** Higher than average. **Parts supply/cost:** Predicted average availability and moderately expensive parts. **Annual maintenance cost:** Average. **Warranty:** Bumper-to-bumper 4 years/80,000 km; powertrain 6 years/110,000 km; rust perforation 6 years/unlimited km. **Supplementary warranty:** Not necessary. **Highway/city fuel economy:** *LS 430*: 8.8–12.8L/100 km; *SC 430*: 9.3–13.1L/100 km.

Mazda

Back to the Future

Mazda has come full circle. Following its debut almost four decades ago as a small automaker selling inexpensive econocars and a rotary-engine-powered 1968 R100 coupe, followed by the RX-7 roadster (1978–2002), Mazda went upmarket and almost went bankrupt in 1994. Then Ford stepped in to turn the company around (Mazda was a major Ford supplier), and two years later bought a controlling interest of the company's shares. This takeover raised expectations that Mazda would soon turn profitable through better management and an exciting new array of cars, trucks, and minivans. That didn't happen then. But it is happening now.

Mazda returns this year with its Wankel rotary engine-powered RX-8 sports car, a new Mazda5 mini-minivan, and a substantially redesigned Miata, the MX-5. The Wankel is a truly innovative engine, first bought by General Motors from bankrupt NSU, and originally destined to power the Chevrolet Vega—until the General got cold feet and sold the technology to Mazda.

Additionally, the peppy and fuel-efficient Mazda3 goes into its third model year after replacing the long-running Protegé, bringing the company back to its compact car roots and adding some performance thrills. Mazda is assembling the Mazda3 at an annual pace of about 254,000, but demand is running at an annual pace of more than 300,000, making the car hard to find at a reasonable price. The Mazda3's larger brother, the Mazda6, returns this year with a hatchback and a wagon to accom-

Mazda's MPV (above) is on its last legs...er, wheels, while the fuel-thrifty Mazda5 minivan/wagon debuts this fall.

pany its sedan version. It hasn't sold very well, so expect lots of discounting. 2006 will be the MPV's last model year.

Everyone agrees that Mazda makes high-quality, competent vehicles. Unfortunately they have always been eclipsed by Honda and Toyota because there was never enough of a performance or price difference to attract buyers to Mazda. Now, with new products anchoring both ends of its 2005 lineup, the automaker has a unique opportunity to lure back customers shopping for vehicles that are reliable, fuel-efficient, affordable, and on the cutting-edge of technology.

MAZDA5 ★★★★

RATING: Above Average. The 2006 Mazda5 is a modern version of the Nissan Axxess and Colt/Eagle Summit, both dropped more than a decade ago. It's basically a compact MPV that's based broadly on the Mazda3 and carries six passengers in three rows of seats. Used mostly for urban errands and light commuting, the "5" employs the peppy, though fuel-frugal, Mazda3's 2.3L 157-hp 4-cylinder engine hooked to a standard 5-speed manual transmission or a 4-speed automatic. So far, that engine has had few problems during the past three years it has run in Canada. Its use of a timing chain instead of a belt also lowers maintenance costs.

This is a relatively tall and narrow car, with a thick, obtrusive front A-pillar. Nevertheless, it handles well, despite some body roll and steering that's a bit vague. Drivers will find it a breeze to park, easy to manoeuvre, and fairly spacious inside. Two wide-opening sliding doors make for easy entry and exit; however, the lower door hinge can trap little feet. Headroom is adequate, legroom is limited, and the rear seat is for children only. Seats can't be removed, but they do fold forward to make a flat cargo floor.

Fuel consumption is impressively low and beats every 2005 minivan listed in *EnerGuide*'s ratings. Equipped with a 5-speed manual transmission, you can expect 10.6L/100 km in the city and 8.0L/100 km on the highway; a 4-speed automatic should average 11.2L/100 km in the city and 8.3L/100 km on the highway.

Available in European and Asian markets since 1999, these small vans are expected to have fewer first-year production bugs than usual. Interestingly, Mazda recalled the car earlier this year and sent owners $500 U.S. for their inconvenience. Yessir! Problems will likely include automatic transmission gear hunting, rapid brake wear, and electrical system shorts. These cars are likely to be in short supply, however, if Mazda sticks to its modest 5,000-unit sales allotment for Canada and keeps prices in the low-20s. The GS will retail for $19,995, the upscale GT for $22,795—a few thousand dollars less than the Chevrolet Uplander and about $7,000 below Honda's Odyssey or the Toyota Sienna.

RATING: Recommended. These cars have brought the fun back into driving. **Strong points:** Good powertrain set-up, though could use a bit more passing power; easy, predictable handling; good steering feedback; rear multi-link suspension gives the car great stability at higher speeds; spacious, easy-to-load trunk; user-friendly instruments and controls; and better-than-average workmanship. **Weak points:** Mazda3 has a history of automatic transmission malfunctions (but no more than Honda and Toyota), prematurely worn-out brake rotor and pads, and fit-and-finish deficiencies. A high deck cuts rear visibility; lots of road noise; there's limited rear footroom; trunk is small; and be wary of Mazda dealers overcharging for scheduled maintenance. **New for 2006:** The 2.0L engine gets variable-valve timing, which may improve fuel economy slightly, and adds two more horsepower; a new optional 5-speed automatic transmission will be sold with the S and five-door versions.

OVERVIEW: Going into its third year, the front-drive Mazda3 is an econobox with flair, an entry-level small car that replaces the Protegé. With considerable engineering help from Ford and Volvo, these cars use a platform that will also serve future iterations of the Ford Focus and Volvo S40.

Powered by a 150-hp 2.0L or 160-hp 2.3L 4-cylinder engine coupled to either a 5-speed manual or a 4-speed Sport mode automatic transmission, the car offers spirited acceleration and smooth, sporty shifting. Handling is enhanced with a highly rigid body structure, front and rear stabilizer bars, multi-link rear suspension,

TECHNICAL DATA

POWERTRAIN (FRONT-DRIVE)
Engines: 2.0L 4-cyl. (150 hp) • 2.3L 4-cyl. (160 hp); Transmissions: 5-speed man. • 4-speed auto.

DIMENSION/CAPACITY
Passengers: 2/3; Wheelbase: 104 in.; H: 57.7/L: 178/W: 69 in.; Headroom F/R: 5.5/2 in.; Legroom F/R: 41.5/27 in.; Cargo volume: 31.2 cu. ft.; Fuel tank: 55L/ regular; Tow limit: N/A; Load capacity: 850 lb.; Turning circle: 36 ft.; Weight: 2,815 lb.

and four-wheel disc brakes. Interior room is quite ample with the car's relatively long 263.9-centimetre (104-inch) wheelbase, extra width, and straight sides, which maximize headroom, legroom, and shoulder room.

COST ANALYSIS: Get a 2006, since most of the 2005s have been sold, and those that will be available won't be discounted. **Best alternatives:** Other cars worth considering are the Honda Civic or the Toyota Corolla. **Options:** The 5-speed automatic transmission with AC is a good start. Head-protecting side curtain airbags are essential, as the car received a Poor IIHS crash-rating without them. **Rebates:** Are you kidding? You'll be lucky if the dealer accepts the full "suggested" retail price. **Delivery/PDI:** $1,195. **Depreciation:** Much slower than average. **Insurance cost:** Average. **Parts supply/cost:** Parts are easy to find. **Annual maintenance cost:** Less than average, so far. **Warranty:** Bumper-to-bumper 3 years/80,000 km; powertrain 5 years/100,000 km; rust perforation 5 years/unlimited km. **Supplementary warranty:** Not needed. **Highway/city fuel economy:** 7.5–10.5L/100 km.

Quality/Reliability/Safety

Pro: Quality control: Incredibly good overall workmanship and quality control. **Reliability:** Better than average. **Warranty performance:** Average.

Con: Owner-reported problems: Mostly transmission and brake deficiencies. The transmission can be hard to shift, especially from Third to Fourth gear; premature wearout of brake pads and rotors; brake rotors are easily grooved; a huge accumulation of brake dust on the rear wheels. Hard starts caused by a faulty fuel pump; AC doesn't cool the car and prevents it from accelerating. **Service bulletin problems:** Engine pulley may break suddenly:

ENGINE — NOISE/SMELL/OVERHEATING/CHARGE LAMP ON
BULLETIN NO.: 01-003/05

DRIVE BELT TENSIONER PULLEY BREAKAGE/CHARGING WARNING LIGHT ON/OVERHEATING

2004–2005 Mazda3; equipped with a manual transmission and built before October 2004

DESCRIPTION: Some vehicles may experience any of the following symptoms:

- Unusual noise and/or smell from the engine compartment
- Charging system warning light is ON
- Overheating

This may be caused by a faulty drive belt auto tensioner pulley, which should be replaced along with the AC belt and drive belt.

Vehicle may be hard to start because of fouled spark plugs or debris clogging the fuel pump; Mazda will install improved plugs and replace the pump under warranty:

HARD STARTS
BULLETIN NO.: 01-013/05

2004–2005 Mazda3, equipped with 2.0 and 2.3L engines.

DESCRIPTION: Some vehicles may experience an engine with hard starting (cranks but takes 10 seconds or longer to start). The condition is more likely after vehicle sits overnight or for an extended time. Rough idle may occur just after the engine is started.

This may be caused by fouled spark plugs if the vehicle is frequently driven in stop-and-go conditions, such as in heavy traffic. In some cases, foreign debris may get stuck in the pressure regulator valve of the fuel pump, and cause fuel holding pressure to drop below specification.

Whine in the steering system; front wipers don't wipe well; loose door trim screw cap; paint stains on the roof, hood, and trunk; and front brake squeaking noise:

FRONT BRAKE SQUEAK WHEN COLD
BULLETIN NO.: 04-001/05

2004–2005 Mazda3

DESCRIPTION: When applying the brakes during slow speed driving and in a cold condition, some vehicles may have a squeak noise coming from the front brakes. This may be caused by resonance in the pad, disc, and caliper.

A modified mounting support for the front brake calipers and modified pads have been introduced to correct this concern.

NHTSA safety complaints: Sudden stalling while cruising on the highway and rolling away when parked on an incline.

MAZDA3

List Price (negotiable)	Residual Values (months)			
	24	36	48	60
GX: $16,495 (15%)	$12,000	$10,000	$ 8,000	$ 6,500
GS: $17,895 (15%)	$13,000	$11,000	$ 9,000	$ 7,000
GT: $21,545 (17%)	$15,500	$13,000	$11,000	$ 9,000

SAFETY FEATURES			CRASHWORTHINESS		
	STD.	OPT.	Head restraints F/R	④	③
Anti-lock brakes	—	✓	Visibility F/R	④	④
Seat belt pretensioners F/R	✓	—	Crash protection (front) D/P	④	④
Side airbags	—	✓	Crash protection (side) F/R	③	③
			Rollover	④	—

MAZDA6 ★★★★

Almost $40,000 is too much to pay for the Speed6's turbocharged engine, stiffer suspension, and larger brakes.

RATING: Above Average; a car enthusiast's mid-sized sedan. **Strong points:** High prices are easily bargained down; very agile; holds the road better than the Honda Accord, the Toyota Camry, and the Nissan Altima; adequate powertrain set-up; good overall handling with responsive, precise steering; all-independent suspension; impressive braking; comfortable seating; better-than-average workmanship. **Weak points:** Manual transmission shifting isn't all that smooth; hard riding over uneven pavement; some body lean in turns; torque steer (pulling) to the right when accelerating; excessive road noise intrudes into the cabin; rear spoiler blocks rear visibility; trunk opening isn't conducive to loading large objects; Mazda has a history of automatic transmission and fit-and-finish deficiencies; and watch out for scheduled maintenance overcharges. One major Mazda6 drawback may be price—there's not enough difference to lure Honda, Nissan, and Toyota buyers away. **New for 2006:** Vehicles equipped with a 4-cylinder engine get an upgraded 5-speed automatic transmission; 3.0L engines get a bit more low-end grunt, but lose five horses in the process (215 hp); and all models will be slightly restyled. The Mazda Speed6 will arrive in the late fall with a turbocharged 274-hp inline 4-cylinder engine coupled to all-wheel drive, a firmer suspension, and larger brakes. For this, we will be charged almost $37,100, freight ($1,195) included.

OVERVIEW: Blame it all on Nissan. They kicked off the family feud over mid-sized sedans by revamping their Altima a few years ago to offer a sweet combination of high performance, capacious interior, and clean aerodynamic styling. Then Toyota reworked its Camry, and Honda responded with its seventh-generation Accord. Now it's Mazda's turn, so *voilà!* We have the Mazda6.

The Mazda6 is offered with two power plants: an impressive 160-hp inline 4-cylinder that almost equals the Accord's entry-level engine, and a 215-hp V6 that trumps the Camry's 190 horses, but comes up woefully short when compared with the 244 horses unleashed by the Accord and 250 horsepower reading for the Nissan Altima. Either Mazda engine can be hooked to a 5-speed manual or automatic transmission that also offers a semi-manual "Sport Shift" feature. Early testers of the manual tranny say the MazdaSpeed manual is far more precise and doesn't get hung up as easily when shifting into Fifth gear.

Don't get the idea that this is a warmed-over 626. It's set on an entirely new platform and carries safety and convenience features never seen by its predecessor, like two-stage airbags and a chassis engineered to deflect crash forces away from occupants. Wider than the Accord, the Mazda6's interior allows for a comfortable ride, carries an unusually large 17.6 cubic foot trunk, and now offers hatchback and wagon versions. Consider getting the 2006 for the transmission upgrade. **Highway/city fuel economy:** 6.7–9.6L/100 km for the base engine and a manual transmission; 7.5–10.5L/100 km with an automatic; 8.1–12.1L/100 km with the V6 and the manual transmission; and 8.1–12.3L/100 km with the GT and the automatic transmission.

Quality/Reliability/Safety

Going into the Mazda6's fourth year on the market, there have been few owner complaints. However, some owners mention omnipresent interior clunks, a number of driveability concerns that include poor engine and transmission performance, and a rotten-egg smell that pervades the interior. **Service bulletin problems:** Engine camshaft ticking noise; clutch chatter; erratic seat-heater operation; AC fogging on the lower part of the windshield; hesitation and rough idle at high altitude; brake judder, moan; popping, clunking noise from the front

TECHNICAL DATA

POWERTRAIN (FRONT-DRIVE)
Engines: 2.3L 4-cyl. (160 hp) • 3.0 V6 (215 hp) • 2.3L Turbo-4 (274 hp); Transmissions: 5-speed man. • 6-speed man. • 5-speed auto. • 6-speed auto.
DIMENSION/CAPACITY
Passengers: 2/3; Wheelbase: 105 in.; H: 56.7/L: 187/W: 70 in.; Headroom F/R: 3/4 in.; Legroom F/R: 41/28 in.; Cargo volume: 33.5 cu. ft.; Fuel tank: 68L/ regular; Tow limit: N/A; Load capacity: 850 lb.; Turning circle: 41 ft.; Weight: 3,510 lb.

suspension; and a Special Warranty Program relating to an evaporative emission system leak monitoring failure and oxygen sensor failure. **NHTSA safety complaints:** Front airbag sensors inadvertently disable the airbag system; front airbags failed to deploy in an accident; rear windshield defroster system shorted out causing the rear windshield to shatter; fuel line detached from engine, making car stall and creating a puddle of gasoline underneath the car; sudden brake lock-up; and the automatic transmission and engine work poorly in merging situations, causing car to decelerate when it should accelerate. Several complaints that the automatic transmission continuously drops to a lower gear.

MAZDA6

List Price (negotiable)	Residual Values (months)			
	24	36	48	60
GS: $23,795 (19%)	$18,000	$15,000	$12,000	$ 9,000
GS V6: $25,995 (21%)	$19,000	$16,000	$13,000	$10,000
GT: $29,895 (23%)	$21,500	$18,500	$15,500	$11,500
GT V6: $32,795 (25%)	$23,000	$19,500	$16,000	$12,500
Speed6: $35,995 (26%)	$25,000	$21,500	$18,500	$15,000

SAFETY FEATURES			CRASHWORTHINESS		
	STD.	OPT.			
Anti-lock brakes	✓	—	Head restraints F/R	❸	❷
Seat belt pretensioners F/R	✓	—	Visibility F/R	❺	❺
Side airbags	—	✓	Crash protection (front) D/P	❺	❺
Stability control	✓	✓	Crash protection (side) F/R	❸	❹
Traction control	✓	✓	Crash protection (offset)	❺	—
			Rollover	❺	—

MX-5 (MIATA) ★★★★★

RATING: Recommended. An exceptional, reasonably priced roadster. **Strong points:** Well matched and beefier powertrain provides better-than-expected acceleration with both the manual and automatic transmissions; acceleration is about four seconds quicker than the Pontiac Solstice; one of the best-shifting manual transmissions in the industry; classic sports car handling; perfectly weighted steering with plenty of road feedback; a firm but comfortable suspension; impressive braking; mirrors are bigger and more effective than those found in most luxury sports cars; a user-friendly manually operated top; engine is fairly quiet and less road noise intrudes into the cabin; instruments and controls are easy to read and access; a slightly roomier interior; good fuel economy; no safety-

related and few performance-related complaints; and a high resale value. **Weak points:** All the things that make roadsters so much "fun": limited passenger and cargo room (still not much room for six-footers); difficult entry and exit; a bit larger turning radius; restricted rear visibility with the top up; and a can of tire sealant replaces the spare tire. **New for 2006:** A new 2.0L engine adds 28 more horses; the wheelbase is 2.6 inches longer, 1.6 inches are added to the MX-5's length, and about a half inch to its height. Upgraded chassis and suspension components are also new this year. Restyled interior and exterior.

OVERVIEW: The MX-5 Miata is a stubby, lightweight, rear-drive, two-seater convertible sports car that combines new technology with old British roadster styling reminiscent of the Triumph, the Austin-Healy, and the Lotus Elan. It comes in a variety of packages: the base model Club Spec, the MX-5, the Touring, the Sport (which comes *sans* AC and power steering), and the top-of-the line Grand Touring. All cars come with a folding softtop and heated glass rear window. A removable hardtop is available as an option.

It's amazing how well the Miata is put together, considering that it isn't particularly innovative and most parts are borrowed from Mazda's other models. For example, the 170-hp 2.0L 4-cylinder engine is borrowed from the Mazda3 and Mazda6 and the suspension is taken from the RX-8. A 5-speed manual gearbox is standard fare, and a 6-speed automatic is optional, as is the 6-speed manual. The Miata is

TECHNICAL DATA

POWERTRAIN (REAR-DRIVE)
Engine: 2.0L 4-cyl. (170 hp);
Transmissions: 5-speed man. •
6-speed man. • 6-speed auto.

DIMENSION/CAPACITY
Passengers: 2; Wheelbase: 89.2 in.;
H: 49/L: 157.1/W: 67.7 in.; Headroom:
N/A.; Legroom: 43 in.; Cargo volume:
5.3 cu. ft.; Fuel tank: 48L/regular; Tow
limit: N/A; Turning circle: 30.8 ft.; Weight:
2,440 lb.

shorter than most other sports cars; nevertheless, this is a fun car to drive, costing much less than other vehicles in its class.

COST ANALYSIS: Get a 2006. Although it may cost you $400 more, this year's improvements merit the extra loonies. **Best alternatives:** Other cars worth considering are the BMW Z4 and the Toyota MR2 Spyder. **Options:** Power steering and a limited-slip differential are only useful to the lazy and cautious. The 6-speed manual transmission is a toss-up, since the 5-speed is so smooth; the new 6-speed automatic is unproven. **Rebates:** Not likely. **Delivery/PDI:** $1,195. **Depreciation:** Much slower than average. **Insurance cost:** Higher than average. **Parts supply/cost:** Parts are easy to find, but often cost more than average. **Annual maintenance cost:** Less than average. **Warranty:** Bumper-to-bumper 3 years/80,000 km; powertrain 5 years/100,000 km; rust perforation 5 years/unlimited km. **Supplementary warranty:** Not needed. **Highway/city fuel economy:** 7.5–10.5L/100 km with the 1.8L and a manual transmission.

Quality/Reliability/Safety

Pro: Quality control: Excellent workmanship and exceptional quality. **Reliability:** Nothing reported that would take these cars out of service for an extended period of time. **Warranty performance:** Average, although a lot depends on dealer servicing. If you must carry an infant, the Miata has a factory-installed airbag cut-off switch.

Con: Owner-reported problems: Some transmission clutch shudder and front-end vibration at cruising speeds; interior tends to overheat because of the proximity of the catalytic converter to the centre console. **Service bulletin problems:** Door-rattling remedies. **NHTSA safety complaints:** Seat belts can be hard to unlock; shoulder belts may chafe your neck; and seat belt's low anchor causes the belt to pull down against the shoulder.

Road Performance

Pro: Emergency handling: No surprises. Performs emergency manoeuvres predictably and almost as quickly as the Porsche Boxster. Exceptionally responsive, with minimal body roll; the rigid chassis gives the car a solid feeling; beats the Pontiac Solstice in slalom maneuvers. **Steering:** Steering is crisp and predictable—again, better than the Solstice. **Acceleration/torque:** Brisk acceleration with a good amount of low-end torque (0–100 km/h: 8.5 seconds). **Transmission:** Easy, precise throws with the manual and smooth, quiet shifting with the automatic. The 6-speed manual makes the Miata more pleasant to drive because the engine doesn't have to rev as high while cruising. **Routine handling:** Lightness and 50/50-weight distribution make it an easy car to toss around corners without tossing your cookies. **Braking:** Disc/disc; impressive braking performance on dry pavement with little brake fading after successive stops (100–0 km/h: 31 m).

MX-5 (MIATA)

List Price (negotiable)

Residual Values (months)

	24	36	48	60
GX: $27,995 (20%)	$21,000	$17,000	$14,000	$12,500
GS: $30,995 (22%)	$23,000	$18,500	$15,500	$13,500
GT: $34,495 (25%)	$25,500	$20,500	$17,500	$15,500

SAFETY FEATURES	STD.	OPT.	CRASHWORTHINESS		
			Visibility F/R	⑤	③
Anti-lock brakes	✓	—	Crash protection (front) D/P	④	⑤
Seat belt pretensioners F/R	✓	—	Crash protection (offset)	③	—
Side airbags	✓	—	Rollover	⑤	—
Stability control	—	✓			
Traction control	—	✓			

RX-8 ★★★

RATING: Average. **Strong points:** An incredibly quiet, smooth engine that loves to chase the redline; engine's front midship layout assures competent handling; reinforced chassis reduces body-flexing squeaks, rattles, and leaks; upscale, well-appointed interior; and good rear-seat access. Impressive crash scores. Prices on the 2006s have increased only a couple of hundred dollars because of weak demand. **Weak points:** Manual shifter is a bit notchy; the 4-speed automatic dramatically reduces horsepower and doesn't mesh well with the engine; and the multi-link suspension and 18-inch tires make for a slightly harsh ride, but a bit smoother than the Nissan 350Z. Interior is somewhat cramped and large door sills add to a feeling of isolation; head restraints and side pillars obstruct outward

TECHNICAL DATA

POWERTRAIN (REAR-DRIVE)

Engines: 1.3L rotary (197 hp) • 1.3L rotary (238 hp); Transmissions: 4-speed auto. • 6-speed man.

DIMENSION/CAPACITY

Passengers: 2/2; Wheelbase: 106 in.; H: 52.8/L: 174/W: 70 in.; Headroom F/R: 1.5/1.5 in.; Legroom F/R: 40/26 in.; Cargo volume: 5.1 cu. ft.; Fuel tank: 60L/ premium; Tow limit: N/A; Load capacity: 680 lb.; Turning circle: 34.8 ft.; Weight: 3,053 lb.

visibility; entry and exit are chores; little rear legroom; small trunk opening; and chronic stalling and hard starting. The $1,195 PDI and freight charge is way out of line; $300–$500 would be more acceptable. Heavy on gas, and premium fuel is recommended. **New for 2006:** Nothing significant.

OVERVIEW: The rotary is back! After an absence of almost 10 years, Mazda has brought back its latest iteration of the Wankel-inspired rotary engine in its rear-drive, four-door RX-8 sports coupe. And this time the price is right—about $12,000 less than what the $48,795 RX-7 sold for in 1995.

The RX-8 automatic is the less powerful of the two models offered, but it still has 197 hp pushing just a little over 1,360 kg (3,000 lb.) Managing that horsepower is a 4-speed Sport AT automatic transmission, which also gives you the option of shifting through the gears yourself with special "upshift" and "downshift" paddles on the steering wheel. The Sport Package upgrades the automatic's handling ability to the level of the 6-speed model.

This car comes with two 1.3L engines: a base 197-hp version and a 238-hp variant. The more expensive 6-speed car has all the performance and handling features available. This includes the high-performance 238-hp engine, a limited-slip differential, sport-tuning for the suspension, and 18-inch wheels housing larger front brakes.

Safety features for both cars include four-wheel ventilated disc brakes with ABS, side airbags, and side air curtains. **Highway/city fuel economy:** For the 4-speed automatic transmission, 8.8–12.9L/100 km; the 6-speed manual transmission is rated at 9.2–12.8L/100 km.

Quality/Reliability/Safety

Pro: Quality control: Average. **Reliability:** Average. **Warranty performance:** Average, but the test comes when these cars come off warranty.

Con: Fuel delivery glitches are worrisome, and Mazda has been inept in handling the RX-8's starting and stalling problems. **Owner-reported problems:** Mostly stalling and frequent brake repairs. *Toronto Star* consumer columnist Ellen Roseman first alerted the public to Mazda's starting problems. **Service bulletin problems:** Special Program #MSP04 authorizes the free correction of cars that won't start or lack power; other bulletins cover no-starts and stalling:

NO-STARTS
BULLETIN NO.: 01-004/05

2004–2005 RX-8

DESCRIPTION: Some vehicles may experience difficulty starting (cranks, no-start). This occurs after driving the vehicle a short distance without engine reaching normal operating temperature. Examples: starting a vehicle and moving it to wash it, engine stall due to misapplication of clutch then restart.

A cranks, no-start condition may be caused either by flooded spark plugs or lower than normal compression due to fuel flooding. Because some early calibrations do not have the improvements to cold start performance, it is important to update the vehicle's PCM to prevent possible no-start concerns. Make sure to update the PCM to the latest calibration if the vehicle exhibits a no-start concern due to fuel flooding.

NOTE: After repairs, provide customers with DE-CHOKING PROCEDURE WHEN ENGINE CRANKS BUT DOES NOT START information (for customers to try after a "CRANKS, NO-START" condition, before towing to dealership).

ENGINE STALLS/MULTIPLE DTCS SET
BULLETIN NO.: 01-007/05

DTC(S) P0126, P0420, P0456, P2404, ENGINE QUIT, OIL LEVEL WARNING LAMP ON

2004–2005 RX-8

DESCRIPTION: Some vehicles may experience one or more of the following concerns:

- P0126 Insufficient coolant temperature for stable operation (All 2004 & 2005).
- P0456 EVAP system leak detected—very small leak (2004 All & 2005 with VINs lower than JM1FE****50149880).
- P0420 Catalyst system efficiency below threshold (2004 All & 2005 with VINs lower than JM1FE****50149880).
- P2404 EVAP system leak detection pump sensor circuit range/performance problem (2004 models only).
- Engine quits at high ambient temperatures (+100 degrees F) (2004 All & 2005 with VINs lower than JM1FE****50149880).
- Oil level warning lamp illumination when oil level is not low (2004 All & 2005 with VINs lower than JM1FE****50149880).

These concerns may be caused by incorrect logic of the PCM's software.

Poor or erratic AC performance; false Low Oil Level alert; engine cover grommets missing; and contact marks on side sills. **NHTSA safety complaints:** Car rolled away when parked on an incline; in cold weather, or when driven a short distance and shut off cold, vehicle suddenly shuts down and then won't start, as if it were flooded; premature brake wear; headlights are too bright; doors are poorly sealed against road and wind noise; hard to latch the rear seatbelt because of the high centre console.

List Price (negotiable)

Residual Values (months)

	24	36	48	60
GS: $36,995 (25%)	$28,000	$24,000	$19,000	$14,500
GT: $39, 995 (26%)	$30,000	$26,000	$21,000	$16,500

SAFETY FEATURES			CRASHWORTHINESS		
	STD.	**OPT.**	Head restraints F/R	⑤	⑤
Anti-lock brakes	✓	—	Visibility F/R	❷	❷
Seat belt pretensioners F/R	✓	—	Crash protection (front) D/P	④	⑤
Side airbags	✓	—	Crash protection (side) F/R	④	④
Stability control	✓	—	Rollover	⑤	—
Traction control	✓	—			

MPV ★★★

RATING: Average. The $20,000 Mazda5 offers much more for $8,000 less. **Strong points:** Relatively low price can be easily haggled down; well appointed (lots of gadgets); smooth-shifting 5-speed automatic transmission; comfortable ride; car-like handling is especially useful for urban travel; good driver's position; responsive steering; retractable side windows; a flat-folding rear seat; and innovative storage spots. Remarkably few factory-related defects reported to NHTSA or in the service

All ratings on a numbered scale where ⑤ is good and ❶ is bad. See page 153–154 for a more detailed description.

bulletin database. **Weak points:** The Ford-sourced 3.0L V6 is a noisy, mediocre performer, with insufficient low-end power. Stability control isn't available. Shorter and narrower than most of the competition; don't believe for a minute that the MPV will hold seven passengers in comfort—six is more like it; elbow room is at a premium, and it takes a lithe figure to move down the front- and middle-seat aisle; the last two rows of seats are cramped and uncomfortable; excessive road noise. Transport and preparation fee is excessive. Dealer servicing and head office support have been problematic in the past. **New for 2006:** Nothing major; 2006 will be the MPV's last model year.

TECHNICAL DATA

POWERTRAIN (FRONT-DRIVE)
Engine: 3.0L V6 (200 hp); Transmission: 5-speed auto.
DIMENSION/CAPACITY
Passengers: 2/2/3; Wheelbase: 112 in.; H: 68.7/L: 188/W: 72 in.; Headroom F/R1/R2: 6.5/5.0/3.0 in.; Legroom F/R1/R2: 41/27.5/27.5 in.; Cargo volume: 56 cu. ft.; Fuel tank: 75L/regular; Tow limit: 3,000 lb.; Load capacity: 1,305 lb.; Turning circle: 41 ft.; Weight: 3,925 lb.

OVERVIEW: Manufactured in Hiroshima, Japan, this small minivan offers a number of innovative features, like "theatre" seating (the rear passenger seat is slightly higher) and a third seat that pivots rearward to become a rear-facing bench seat—or folds into the floor for picnics or tailgate parties. Another feature unique among minivans is Mazda's Side-by-Slide removable second-row seats, which move fore and aft as well as side-to-side while a passenger is seated. Rarely seen sliding door crank windows are standard on the entry-level model. Windows are power-assisted on the LS and ES versions.

The MPV now uses Ford's old-tech, 200-hp 3.0L Duratec V6 found in the Taurus. It is a decent performer, though not very competitive with Honda and Toyota. The 5-speed automatic transmission makes the best use of the V6 power, but it becomes quite fuel-thirsty when pushed.

One immediate benefit: The 3.0L is able to climb hills without continuously downshifting, and Mazda's "slope control" system automatically shifts to a lower gear when the hills get very steep.

Torque is still less than the Odyssey's 3.5L or the 3.8L in top-of-the-line Chryslers, though comparable with lesser Chrysler products and GM's Venture and Montana. The engine operates more smoothly than its predecessor, though it's not as quiet as Honda's 3.5L V6. The suspension works well to decrease body roll, enhancing cornering ability, which produces a sportier ride than most other minivans. This firmness may be too much for some.

COST ANALYSIS: Go for a discounted 2005 model, since it's practically identical to the 2006 version. **Best alternatives:** Other minivans worth considering are the Honda Odyssey, the Toyota Sienna, or a second-series Mazda5 mini-minivan. **Options:** The higher trim levels don't offer much of value, except for power windows and door locks and an ignition immobilizer/alarm/keyless entry system. Rear AC and seat height-adjustment mechanisms are recommended convenience features. Also, be wary of unwarranted extra charges. Writes one *Lemon-Aid* reader:

> There are far too many "extra" charges for things (like $70 for getting Scotiabank financing) that should be included in the price of the MPV. All these extra charges add up and create friction with the dealer that doesn't need to exist.... Wheel lock bolts should be standard when buying alloy wheels. It seems very petty to add $31.50 for wheel locks to the price of the $3,000 Sport Package. How can Mazda charge an extra $105 for certain paint colours on a $30,000 vehicle? This is no way to make friends.

Rebates: Expect $3,500 rebates and zero percent financing through 2005; rebates will likely go to $5,000 in the new year as the MPV reaches the end of its run. **Delivery/PDI:** $1,310. **Depreciation:** Faster than average. **Insurance cost:** Higher than average. **Parts supply/cost:** Likely to be back ordered and cost more than average, despite Mazda's warning to dealers to keep prices in check. **Annual maintenance cost:** Average; any garage can repair these minivans. **Warranty:** Bumper-to-bumper 3 years/80,000 km; powertrain 5 years/100,000 km; rust perforation 5 years/unlimited km. **Supplementary warranty:** An extended warranty is worth having, particularly in view of the fact that powertrain problems have plagued these vehicles in the past and this is the MPV's last year on the market. **Highway/city fuel economy:** 9.6–13.6L/100 km.

 ## Quality/Reliability/Safety

Pro: Quality control: Recent models feature improved workmanship and more rugged construction. Although *Consumer Reports* put the MPV in its "less reliable" listing, *Lemon-Aid* reader feedback has been positive, with only a few exceptions.

Con: Reliability: Expect some transmission failures, ABS malfunctions, and premature wearout of the front and rear brakes. **Warranty performance:** Mediocre. Expensive scheduled maintenance and high fuel and parts costs make ownership costs higher than normal. CBC TV's *Marketplace* consumer program found Mazda dealers allegedly padding the cost of routine servicing. **Owner-reported problems:** Very few. About a half-dozen complaints of rotten-egg exhaust, stalling and surging, and some oil leakage. Owners report that the electronic computer module (ECU), automatic transmission driveshaft, upper shock mounts, front 4×4 drive axles and lash adjusters, AC core, and radiator fail within the first three years. Cold temperatures tend to fry the automatic window motor, and the paint is easily chipped and flakes off early, especially around the hood, tailgate, and front fenders; premature paint peeling afflicting white-coloured MPVs is quite common. Premature brake caliper and rotor wear and excessive vibration/pulsation are chronic problem areas (repairs are needed about every 12,000 kilometres). **Service bulletin problems:** TSB #006-94 looks into all the causes and remedies for excessive brake vibrations, and TSB #11-14-95 gives an excellent diagnostic flow chart for troubleshooting excessive engine noise; engine camshaft ticking correction:

· CAMSHAFT TICKING
BULLETIN NO: 01-043/04

2001–2005 Tribute (3.0L Only)

2003–2005 Mazda6 (3.0L Only)

2002–2005 MPV

DESCRIPTION: Some vehicles equipped with the 3.0L engine may exhibit a ticking noise from the left bank cylinder head, with the engine at normal operating temperature. Customers having this concern should have engine camshaft caps removed and re-installed.

Another TSB offers remedies for shift shock (transmission slams into gear). Serious paint peeling and delaminating will be fully covered for up to six years under a Mazda secret warranty, say owners; however, there is no service bulletin confirmation of this policy. Nevertheless, the following service bulletin summary indicates that rust is an MPV problem and should be sufficient proof to win a small claims court claim for a new paint job:

MAZDA DOOR RUST
BULLETIN: 09-006/05

2000–2005 MPVs (built before February 1, 2005)

Rust may appear on the door sash areas shown, or on the inner edges and back side of these door sash areas. Customers should have their vehicle repaired as shown here:

1. Inspect inner and outer door sashes at B- and C-pillar locations.

2. Using a local body shop, refinish all affected door sash area(s).

3. Put on door stripes (#)2, (#)3, or (#)4 to the repaired door sash areas.

• This warranty information applies only to verified customer complaints on vehicles eligible for warranty repair. Any requests for "goodwill" warranty repairs will have to be made through dealer service manager to Mazda Canada (Ed.).

• Additional diagnostic time cannot be claimed for this repair.

RUST MAY APPEAR ON THESE DOOR SASH AREAS

STRIPE #3   STRIPE #2   STRIPE #4

Troubleshooting tips for correcting wind noise around doors; tips for eliminating a musty, mildew-type AC odour; AC temperature varies between dash vents. **NHTSA safety complaints:** Rotten-egg exhaust smell; engine seized when connecting rod failed; transmission failure caused by worn shaft solenoid; transmission slippage, then failure. Blown tire sidewall; Dunlop tires tread separation; airbags failed to deploy; fuel smell emanating from the AC; sudden loss of power at highway speeds; stalling upon deceleration; engine oil leakage; sudden stalling; sliding doors don't lock in place; brake caliper bolt fell off, causing vehicle to skid; shifter obscures dash and is easily knocked about; excessive drivetrain vibration at 90 km/h; child's neck tangled in seat belt; seat belts lock up when vehicle is moving; seat belts are too short; difficult keeping child safety seat secured properly because of the anchor placement; rear visibility obstructed by high seatbacks.

MPV

List Price (negotiable)	Residual Values (months)			
	24	36	48	60
GX: $27,595 (25%)	$18,000	$15,000	$12,000	$ 9,500
GS: $29,995 (25%)	$18,500	$15,500	$13,500	$10,500
GT: $35,995 (27%)	$22,500	$18,500	$15,500	$12,500

SAFETY FEATURES	STD.	OPT.	CRASHWORTHINESS		
Anti-lock brakes (2W; 4W)	✓	✓	Head restraints F/R	②	❶
Seat belt pretensioners F/R	✓	—	Visibility F/R	⑤	③
Side airbags	✓	—	Crash protection (front) D/P	⑤	⑤
Traction control	—	✓	Crash protection (side) F/R	⑤	⑤
			Crash protection (offset)	③	—

Mitsubishi

Still Struggling

Despite some monthly gains after high fuel costs stampeded buyers to small cars, Mitsubishi sales in Canada are still in a nosedive. Through July of 2005, the company had almost 1,000 fewer sales (5,935) than in the same period last year. Mitsubishi management projected that annual sales would top 20,000 units in 2003, and breathed a collective sigh of relief when they ended up with 14,122 sales.

All ratings on a numbered scale where ⑤ is good and ❶ is bad. See page 153–154 for a more detailed description.

The company got into this mess because it sold many sub-prime loans, which were never paid, in the States; its product mix was lacklustre (except for the Eclipse); and senior management has been rocked by an ongoing scandal (they deliberately hid information about safety-related defects that led to a number of injuries and fatalities). Additionally, dealers in Canada have too few vehicles on the road to generate sufficient service and repair revenue.

But Mitsubishi may be poised for a turnaround, thanks to the increased demand for small cars this year. DaimlerChrysler, Ford, and GM are looking to Mitsubishi for manufacturing co-ventures and re-badged products. Remember, Mitsubishi launched its Canadian dealer network in 2002 by piggybacking its dealers onto Chrysler's existing dealer body.

Mitsubishi sells the following models in Canada: the compact Lancer ES ($15,998), the mid-sized Galant DE ($23,948), the Eclipse GS ($25,498), GT ($32,998), and Spyder ($34,998), and the Montero Limited ($48,598), Endeavour ($34,298), and Outlander LS ($23,998) sport-utilities. Buyers are charged $925 for PDI and freight.

All things considered, Mitsubishis are fairly good buys—mechanically. However, when you buy the product, you also buy the management, and that's a particularly risky deal for Canadians at the moment. We are presently at the mercy of dual dealerships that won't necessarily have adequately trained mechanics or large parts inventories, and the little "Mitsus" will face a more challenging environment. How lucky do you feel?

LANCER ★★★/★★★★

TECHNICAL DATA

POWERTRAIN (FRONT-DRIVE/AWD)

Engines: 2.0L 4-cyl. (120 hp) • 2.4L 4-cyl. (162 hp) • 2.0L 4-cyl. turbo (286 hp); Transmissions: 5-speed man. • 6-speed man. • 4-speed auto.

DIMENSION/CAPACITY

Passengers: 2/3; Wheelbase: 103 in.; H: 54.1/L: 179/W: 70 in.; Headroom F/R: 4.5/1.5 in.; Legroom F/R: 40.5/27.5 in.; Cargo volume: 11.3 cu. ft.; Fuel tank: 50L/regular; Tow limit: N/A; Load capacity: 825 lb.; Turning circle: 42 ft.; Weight: 3,340 lb.

RATING: Average; the high-performance O•Z Rally is Above Average. Unfortunately, Chrysler sales and service may not be as good as the car. **Strong points:** Selling price is easily bargained down. Awesome acceleration with the O•Z Rally's turbocharged engine; excellent frontal and offset crashworthiness; reasonably good workmanship; dealers are starving and welcome price-haggling. **Weak points:** Base engine is a bit horsepower-challenged, especially with the automatic transmission; expect some parts delays; and front side crashworthiness is below average. **New for 2006:** Nothing significant; the company is fighting for its life. The States-only Lancer Evolution gets a horsepower boost and a restyled interior and exterior.

OVERVIEW: These entry-level front-drive econocars offer an incredible choice of vehicles that run the gamut from the cheap and mundane ES to the high-performance Evolution AWD to a sizzling street racer called the O•Z Rally. The Evolution has over double the horsepower (286 hp) of the base ES (120 hp).

Very few owner complaints. Some problems reported involving engine stalling and stumbling; automatic transmissions that lurch, jerk, and slip; clutch failure; broken axles; windshield creaking; frequent paint defects that include swirls, scratches, and peeling; and rear bumper support rusting.

LANCER

List Price (very negotiable)	**Residual Values** (months)			
	24	**36**	**48**	**60**
Base: $15,998 (15%)	$11,000	$ 9,000	$ 7,500	$ 6,000
O•Z Rally: $21,378 (18%)	$14,000	$11,000	$ 9,500	$ 8,000

SAFETY FEATURES

	STD.	OPT.
Anti-lock brakes (4W)	✓	✓
Seat belt pretensioners F/R	✓	—
Side airbags	—	✓

CRASHWORTHINESS

Head restraints F/R	2	2
Visibility F/R	5	5
Crash protection (front) D/P	4	4
Crash protection (side) F/R	2	4
Crash protection (offset)	5	—
Rollover	4	—

All ratings on a numbered scale where 5 is good and 1 is bad. See page 153–154 for a more detailed description.

RATING: Above Average, thanks to last year's improvements. **Strong points:** Soft prices; competent 4- and 6-cylinder power plants; excellent handling and steering feedback; generally good crashworthiness scores; fairly good workmanship; price-bargaining encouraged. **Weak points:** No manual transmission to make full use of the car's spirited engines; problematic rear seat entry and exit; first-year glitches are likely to plague this model redesigned in 2005. **New for 2006:** Nothing.

OVERVIEW: The Galant, Mitsubishi's most popular car, is a mid-sized sedan that was considerably improved last year with the addition of a better-performing engine that is smoother and has about 15 extra horses. Handling is better too, thanks to the revised suspension, front and rear stabilizer bars, upgraded power steering, four-wheel disc brakes, and larger, 16-inch wheels. Higher trim levels get standard ABS brakes.

Mitsubishi's 2.4L 4-banger is a standard feature with the DS and LS models, while the LS-V6 and GTS use a smooth-running V6 engine that's torquier than the Altima's and is mated to a semi-manual gearbox. The GTS comes with performance tires and larger, 17-inch wheels. The GTZ comes with standard V6 power and firmer shock absorber valving and higher spring rates.

On 2004 models Mitsubishi brought out more powerful engines, handling enhancements, larger interior, and sleeker styling. The manual transmission was dropped, however. Overall quality control is

TECHNICAL DATA

POWERTRAIN (FRONT-DRIVE)

Engines: 2.4L 4-cyl. (160 hp) • 3.8L V6 (230 hp); Transmission: 4-speed auto./man.

DIMENSION/CAPACITY

Passengers: 2/3; Wheelbase: 108 in.; H: 54.1/L: 190/W: 72 in.; Headroom F/R: 2.5/2.0 in.; Legroom F/R: 41/29.5 in.; Cargo volume: 14.6 cu. ft.; Fuel tank: 62L/premium; Tow limit: N/A; Load capacity: 825 lb.; Weight: 3,715 lb.; Turning circle: 43 ft.

impressive, generating few owner complaints. Some of the problems that have been mentioned are: rotten-egg exhaust smell; engine hesitation; transmission and brake malfunctions; noisy, squeaking front brakes; the AC may not provide an even flow of cool air through the lower vents; and a loose driver's seat.

Technical service bulletins cover rear suspension rattling, seat adjustments, window glass freezing to the moulding, and tips on reducing brake noise.

GALANT

List Price (very negotiable)	Residual Values (months)			
	24	36	48	60
DE: $23,948 (17%)	$18,000	$16,000	$13,000	$11,000
ES: $25,068 (19%)	$18,500	$16,500	$13,500	$11,500
LS V6: $28,208 (30%)	$20,000	$17,000	$15,500	$13,500
GTS: $33,348 (30%)	$24,000	$21,000	$18,000	$16,000

SAFETY FEATURES	STD.	OPT.	CRASHWORTHINESS		
Anti-lock brakes (4W)	✓	—	Head restraints F/R	❶	❶
Seat belt pretensioners F/R	✓	—	Visibility F/R	➎	➎
Side airbags	✓	—	Crash protection (front) D/P	➎	➎
Traction control	✓	✓	Crash protection (side) F/R	➎	➎
			Crash protection (offset)	➎	—
			Rollover	➍	—

ECLIPSE ★★★

RATING: Average. This car has the looks of a strong road racer. Real capability, however, is lacking. **Strong points:** Both engines have plenty of grunt throughout their power range when mated to a manual gearbox; handling is exceptionally good on all models, but the sportier GT and Spyder are better than the rest. Front-seat occupants get a firm, comfortable ride with fairly supportive seats and adequate room. **Weak points:** Automatic transmission doesn't have the quickness needed for confident highway merging; frequent shifting with the manual transmission; real world fuel economy is much less than promised with the automatic tranny; V6 engine needs premium fuel; redesigned Eclipse is 360 pounds heavier; so-so steering with the base sedan; larger than expected turning radius for the coupe; considerable "torque steer" (a pulling to the side upon acceleration)

felt with the GT; brakes are overly aggressive; excessive engine, tire, and wind noise; difficult rear entry and exit; rear seating adequate only for children or small adults; and a weak dealer network. **New for 2006:** Redesigned with a bit more interior room, additional safety features (head-protecting side airbags), racier styling, and sportier performance. The base 2.4L get 15 more horses, while the 3.8L V6 boosts horsepower by 63, to 263.

OVERVIEW: This is a beautifully styled, reasonably priced sporty coupe whose performance lags behind its looks. There are two engine choices available: a 162-hp 2.4L 4-banger and a 263-hp V6. A manual 5-speed is standard, but the optional automatic 5-speed or the 6-speed manual are better performers. A convertible version will return next year as a 2007 model. **Highway/city fuel economy:** 7.6–10.1L/100 km with the base 2.4L engine.

TECHNICAL DATA

POWERTRAIN (FRONT-DRIVE)
Engines: 2.4L 4-cyl. (162 hp) • 3.8L V6 (263 hp); Transmissions: 5-speed man. • 5-speed auto. • 6-speed man.

DIMENSION/CAPACITY
Passengers: 2/3; Wheelbase: 101.4 in.; H: 53.5/L: 179.7/W: 72.2 in.; Headroom F/R: N/A; Legroom F/R: 42.8/29.2 in.; Cargo volume: 15.7 cu. ft.; Fuel tank: 67L/regular; Tow limit: N/A; Turning circle: 35.4/40 ft.; Weight: 3,274 lb.

ECLIPSE

List Price (very negotiable)

	Residual Values (months)			
	24	36	48	60
Coupe GS: $25,498 (18%)	$20,000	$16,000	$13,000	$10,000
Coupe GT: $32,998 (25%)	$26,000	$22,000	$18,500	$15,500

SAFETY FEATURES			CRASHWORTHINESS		
	STD.	OPT.			
Anti-lock brakes (4W)	✓	—	Head restraints F/R	②	❶
Seat belt pretensioners F/R	✓	—	Visibility F/R	④	❶
Side airbags	✓	—	Crash protection (front) D/P	④	④
Traction control	✓	✓	Crash protection (side) F/R	③	—

Nissan

Nissan—or should I say Renault's Nissan division?—has risen from the dead after having been written off by most industry pundits a scant eight years ago. Fortunately, Renault had faith in Nissan's future and promptly bought a controlling interest in the company. This action allowed the French automaker to send in

its own management teams and turn Nissan's fortunes around dramatically. Today, amid record sales and profits, Nissan is branching out with smaller cars and SUVs. In mid-2006 it will launch a fuel-thrifty subcompact called the Versa and a new entry-level Xterra.

Nissan, like Mazda, makes some dependable cars, trucks, and mini-vans (exceptions being the 2003–05 350Z and the 2004 Quest), and shoppers are now visiting Nissan showrooms to buy

Nissan's 2007 Versa subcompact will go on sale in the summer of 2006.

highly styled and reasonably priced models that combine good fuel economy with cutting-edge technology. Let's hope Nissan doesn't squander this goodwill through crappy products and unreasonable price hikes, as its bosses at Renault have done.

The latest news is that Renault has sent an edict to Nissan saying it must buy more Nissan components from Renault. *Sacre bleu!*

RATING: Not Recommended. These overpriced, unreliable sporty coupes are no longer sold at list price because word has gotten out about how poorly they perform. A reputation for poor quality control and serious safety and performance-related failures has been dogging these nicely styled sportsters for the past several years, and apparently the buying public is getting wise. Transmission, suspension, and alignment defects are particularly prevalent. Don't be reluctant to haggle the price down by at least 20 percent. If you want to get a better price, delay your purchase until early 2006, when many new competitors, like the redesigned Miata, will go on sale and rebates and discounts will be at their highest level. **New for 2006:** A restyled front end and 13 more horses (300 hp).

OVERVIEW: I remember driving the 240Z around Montreal in the early 1970s and loving the car, despite its iffy brakes (*"Non, monsieur*, the brakes are fine; it's our customers who are at fault.") and its biodegradable, rust-prone body. The car put on weight over the years and became less and less reliable and sporty before it was axed in 1996.

We returned to the Z car's roots with the debut of the 2003 350Z. A sporty, rear-drive, 287-hp V6-equipped, two-passenger hatchback or convertible, the Z is priced at $45,998 (the 1996 300ZX Turbo sold for $60,698!).

The Z car is loaded with innovative features never seen on the original 240Z. These include a Continuously Variable Valve Timing Control System, front and rear ABS-equipped disc brakes, electronic brake force distribution, drive-by-wire throttle, 6-speed manual transmission, and a unique carbon-fibre driveshaft that's said to give better acceleration and provide added crash safety. There are also many optional performance features, including a 5-speed automatic transmission (more of a non-performance option), traction control, limited-slip differential, larger wheels and grippier tires, and a vehicle stability system. In 2004, a new convertible and upgraded interior trim were added.

Quality/Reliability/Safety

Pro: Crashworthiness as tested by NHTSA is much better than average: five-star frontal crash protection for the driver and four stars for the passenger; and five-star side-impact protection and rollover resistance.

Con: First off, I'm totally disappointed in what I consider Nissan's poor handling of owner complaints for such an expensive sports car. The 350Z is a doomed car if Nissan doesn't attend to its deficiencies this year. **NHTSA safety complaints:** Airbag failures; engine surged and brakes would not respond; engine knocking and misfiring at idle (fuel injectors are often blamed); car will suddenly shut down because of a defective crank position sensor; transmission often goes into "fail safe" mode and slams into first gear, putting occupants' lives in danger; complete transmission failure; tranny doesn't always downshift as it should; transmission clanks and grinds when going into Third gear (said to be the synchronizers) and has a loose feeling; loud clutch chatter and eventual failure; steering pump failed; fuel tank replaced because gas pump constantly shut off when refuelling; inoperable gas-filler door; driver's seat doesn't lock into position; hazard warning lights can be activated inadvertently; excessive brake noise; driver hit head on the metal piece attached to the convertible top; and paint defects:

> My 2005 350Z roadster gets too many paint chips.... This is on the hood and side panels. The paint also has orange-peel texture. For a new car to chip this way so early—only two months...is a defect. Car company has stated this is only because of rocks from roadway. Unacceptable paint and needs to be investigated. My car colour is new: Ultra yellow.

Original equipment Bridgestone tires are dangerous in inclement weather:

> We have Bridgestone Potenza tires P225/50WR17 (front) and P235/50WR17 (rear) on our 2005 Nissan Z350 Touring Edition: Do we have to have people killed before this is looked into? Car has just 1,600 miles [2,500 km], yes, not even 2,000 [3,200 km]; [it's] one month old. These tires will not drive safely on this car. Snowed here in Washington, DC, area on January 19, 2005...wife could not move the car from a red light without rear end fishtailing at 3 mph [5 km/h]. Could not move...help had to hand push her to side of a road. I made it to her after 3 hours. Police wanted to give me a ticket for not having all weather tires, M/S on the car, for holding up traffic because the car would not move. I had no idea the tires were not M/S. I got in car and it would not move, even when removing the traction button. Skidding/fishtailing will get you killed; these tires will not make it in snowy parts of the U.S. Why have they not tested these tires on snow-covered roads? My wife is scared to death to drive the car now.... There is a Z350 2003 model on the lot of the dealer with Michelin M/S All Weather on it.... The dealer will tell me to go to a tire company, the tire company

already is telling me to go back to the dealer. Please, NHTSA, stop this from getting people potentially injured or killed.

•

Front Bridgestone tire wear: consumer stated the tires wore out at 7000 miles [11,000 km]. He had them replaced. Then again at 10,000 [16,000 km]. Currently, at 21,000 miles [34,000 km], they have worn out again. Dealer was aware of the problem. A class action law suit was brought against Nissan.

"Roaring" front tires wear out prematurely because of a serious suspension/ alignment factory-related defect affecting 2003–04 models ("feathering," as reported at *www.my350z.com* and *www.zcar.com*); Nissan will refund the cost of one set of tires:

> I am concerned about my Nissan 350Z suspension/tires. I have been reading a lot of bulletin board entries on *www.my350z.com* and *www.zcar.com* about vehicles manufactured before December 2002. I also visited the Nissan website and see that there is a tech bulletin posted about the wear on the tires. There appears to be an issue with the suspension set up on the 350Z that is resulting in excessive wear on the tires or feathering. There are a lot of pictures on the *www.my350Z.com* website of actual tires. The feathering seems to begin anywhere from 5,000 to 10,000 miles [8,000 to 16,000 km].

Service bulletin problems: Inoperative navigation system; brake noise reduction when braking in Reverse; softtop comes too far forward and is hard to latch; water leaks; squeaks and wind noise; front suspension clunk; rear axle clicking noise; sticking fuel-filler door; seat side finisher coming off; and door window glass doesn't drop when opening the door.

SENTRA

RATING: Recommended. Unlike many bare-bones economy cars, entry-level Sentras offer dependable motoring with lots of comfort features. **Strong points:** All three engines provide plenty of power, a comfortable ride, and easy handling. Good quality control, few safety-related or performance-related defects reported by owners; in fact, barely a third of the defects reported on the 350Z. On top of that, the cars are reasonably priced after some haggling. The 2.5L-equipped SE-R versions provide much better acceleration, handling, and ride. **Weak points:** Difficult rear access; poor highway handling in wet weather; and average crashworthiness. **New for 2006:** A slight restyling of the interior; the redesigned Nissan Sentra scheduled to arrive in mid-2006 and use a 2.0L 4-cylinder engine developed jointly by Renault SA and Nissan Motor Co.

OVERVIEW: Nissan's entry-level small sedans come in three trim levels: the XE and GXE, housing a perky 126-hp 1.8L 4-cylinder engine, and the sporty SE-R, carrying a 165-hp 2.5L 4-banger with 10 additional horses in the SE-R Spec V version. A manual 5-speed transmission is standard; a 6-speed manual or a 4-speed automatic is optional. The exterior design is part Altima and part Maxima.

The 175-hp SE-R V comes with a limited-slip differential, a sport-tuned suspension, and 17-inch wheels to compete against the Honda Civic SiR and Mazda's high-performance spin-offs. Four-wheel disc brakes are a standard feature.

COST ANALYSIS: Get the 2005 XE or GXE models; they're not much different from the 2006s, and you should save a few thousand dollars. **Best alternatives:** Sentra's engine and body dimension improvements over the past few years have made it a good competitor to the Honda Civic and the Toyota Corolla. Other worthwhile cars to consider are the Hyundai Elantra and the Mazda3. **Options:** If you do a lot of highway driving, spend the extra money for the SE-R's stronger engine, enhanced suspension, and better-grade, larger tires. **Rebates:** $3,000 rebates and low financing programs. Additional discounting very likely by early summer. **Delivery/PDI:** $1,114. **Depreciation:** Average. **Insurance cost:** Average for the base models, much higher than average for the SE-R. **Parts supply/cost:** Inexpensive parts can be found practically anywhere. SE-R parts will likely be more difficult to find and relatively expensive. **Annual maintenance cost:** Less than average. **Warranty:** Bumper-to-bumper 3 years/80,000 km;

TECHNICAL DATA

POWERTRAIN (FRONT-DRIVE)

Engines: 1.8L 4-cyl. (126 hp) • 2.5L 4-cyl. (165 hp) • 2.5L 4-cyl. (175 hp); Transmissions: 5-speed man. • 6-speed man. • 4-speed auto.

DIMENSION/CAPACITY

Passengers: 2/3; Wheelbase: 100 in.; H: 55.5/L: 178/W: 67 in.; Headroom F/R: 4.0/1.5 in.; Legroom F/R: 40/25 in.; Cargo volume: 11.6 cu. ft.; Fuel tank: 50L/reg./prem.; Tow limit: 1,000 lb.; Load capacity: 825 lb.; Turning circle: 38 ft.; Weight: 2,695 lb.

powertrain 5 years/100,000 km; rust perforation 5 years/unlimited km. **Supplementary warranty:** Not needed. **Highway/city fuel economy:** *1.8L and auto.:* 6.6–8.9L/100 km; *2.5L:* 8.5–10.2L/100 km.

Quality/Reliability/Safety

Pro: Quality control: Sentras are almost trouble-free, except for some power-train failures. First-class body assembly. **Reliability:** Overall reliability is better than average. **Warranty performance:** Above average.

Con: Owner-reported problems: Clutch, exhaust, fuel system, and electrical problems are fairly common after the first three years. A smattering of engine head gasket failures. Front brake pads and rotors wear out quickly; excessive bouncing and vibration caused by prematurely worn struts; doors vibrate noisily; passenger-side window leaks; rear bumper may fall off; excessive wind noise around the windshield moulding. **Service bulletin problems:** No-start after a cold soak may signal the need to replace the starter motor; noisy alternator; and poor shifting with the automatic transmission (see bulletin).

NHTSA safety complaints: Airbag failed to deploy; sudden, unintended acceleration; repeatedly loses all engine power; high-speed bucking (surging); chronic stalling; erratic, rough idling; early automatic transmission replacement; harsh automatic transmission shifting; ABS brake failure; brakes lock up at low

> ### HARSH 1–2 SHIFTS (AUTOMATIC TRANSMISSION)
> **BULLETIN NO.: NTB05-001   DATE: JANUARY 3, 2005**
>
> **4-SPEED AUTOMATIC TRANSMISSION HARSH 1–2 SHIFT AND/OR DTC P0745 STORED (REPLACE OR REPAIR THE SOLENOID ASSEMBLY)**
>
> 2003–2005 Altima; 2003–2005 Sentra; 2003–2004 Maxima; and 2004 Quest
>
> **IF YOU CONFIRM:** The transmission fluid is full (correct level) and in good condition (not burnt), and
>
> - There is a harsh shift from 1st to 2nd gear, and/or
> - DTC P0745 (line pressure solenoid circuit) is stored.

speed, particularly on wet roads; keyless remote doesn't work and back door doesn't open from the inside, apparently because of a short in the electrical system (vanity mirror fuse?); Continental and Firestone tire tread peels off; rotten-egg exhaust smell; and while driving, windshield wipers, turn signals, headlights, horn, and hazard lights failed.

Road Performance

Pro: Acceleration/torque: Both the 1.8L and 2.5L 4-cylinder engines provide plenty of power for all driving situations. **Transmission:** Both manual and automatic transmissions shift very smoothly. **Routine handling:** Good manoeuvrability around town. Firm but well-mannered ride on most roads. **Steering:** Predictable, with little under-steer; much better with the SE-R. **Braking:** Above average; minimal fading after successive stops.

Con: Slow steering response with the base models. SE-R version has sportier handling, but ride comfort is compromised. **Emergency handling:** XE and GXE high-speed handling is a bit sloppy, and emergency handling is sluggish. Brakes tend to lock up on wet roads.

SENTRA

List Price (very negotiable)   **Residual Values** (months)

	24	36	48	60
Sedan 1.8: $16,698 (15%)	$12,000	$10,000	$ 8,000	$ 6,500
SE-R: $21,698 (18%)	$15,000	$13,000	$11,000	$ 9,000
Spec V: $22,198 (18%)	$16,000	$14,000	$12,000	$10,000

SAFETY FEATURES	STD.	OPT.
Anti-lock brakes (4W)	—	✓
Seat belt pretensioners F/R	✓	—
Side airbags	✓	—

CRASHWORTHINESS		
Head restraints F/R	3	2
Visibility F/R	5	3
Crash protection (front) D/P	4	4
Crash protection (side) F/R	2	—
Crash protection (offset)	3	—
Rollover	4	—

ALTIMA ★★★

RATING: Average. Many quality deficiencies and problematic handling. **Strong points:** Scintillating V6 acceleration; flawless automatic transmission operation; good braking; well laid-out instruments and controls; and better-than-average interior room. **Weak points:** The 4-cylinder engine isn't as refined as the competition and is noisy when pushed. Handling is acceptable but not very agile, and a large turning radius hampers manoeuvrability. Pricier 3.5 SE models come equipped with a firmer suspension and wider tires that degrade ride comfort. Brakes tend to lock up on wet roads. Limited rear headroom; snug rear seating for three adults; obstructed rear visibility; dashboard reflects into windshield and dash gauges wash out in sunlight. Quality problems have not abated on the 2005s. **New for 2006:** Carried over practically unchanged.

OVERVIEW: Shaped like a Passat, with the heart of a Maxima, Nissan's front-drive, mid-sized sedan stakes out the territory occupied by the Honda Accord, the Mazda6, and the Toyota Camry. The car's powerful 175-hp 2.5L 4-cylinder engine is almost as powerful as the competition's V6 power plants, and the optional 260-hp 3.5L V6 has few equals among cars in this price and size class. And, when you consider that the Altima is much lighter than most of its competitors, it's obvious why this car produces sizzling (and sometimes uncontrollable) acceleration with little fuel penalty. Four-wheel independent suspension strikes the right balance between a comfortable ride and sporty handling. The SE-R and 3.5 SL add even more performance and luxury enhancements.

COST ANALYSIS: Since 2005 models are practically identical to the 2006s, and complaints have moderated, get a cheaper, second-series 2005 equipped with a V6. **Best alternatives:** Other cars worth considering are the redesigned Mazda6, the Honda Accord, and the Toyota Camry. **Options:** Watch out for option-loading after you agree to a reasonable base price. Canny Nissan sales agents pretend that some options must be purchased, or that some can't be bought without others included. **Rebates:** $5,000 rebates or discounts and zero percent financing on fully loaded models. **Delivery/PDI:** $1,190. **Depreciation:** Much slower than average, especially the much-coveted V6-equipped model. **Insurance cost:** Higher than average. **Parts supply/cost:** Slightly higher than average. **Annual maintenance cost:** Average. **Warranty:** Bumper-to-bumper 3 years/80,000 km; powertrain 5 years/100,000 km; rust perforation 5 years/unlimited km. **Supplementary warranty:** Not needed. **Highway/city fuel economy:** *4-cyl. and auto.:* 7.3–10.1L/100 km; *V6 and auto.:* 8.2–11.2L/100 km.

Quality/Reliability/Safety

Con: Quality control: Below average body assembly and powertrain components. **Warranty performance:** Below average. Nissan staffers aren't particularly generous in giving out post-warranty "goodwill." **Reliability:** Lots of powertrain and body deficiencies as these vehicles age. **Owner-reported problems:** Many

---

TECHNICAL DATA

POWERTRAIN (FRONT-DRIVE)
Engines: 2.5L 4-cyl. (175 hp) • 3.5L V6 (250 hp) • 3.5L V6 (260 hp); Transmissions: 5-speed man. • 6-speed man. • 4-speed auto. • 5-speed auto.

DIMENSION/CAPACITY
Passengers: 2/3; Wheelbase: 110 in.; H: 57.9/L: 192/W: 70 in.; Headroom F/R: 3.0/2.0 in.; Legroom F/R: 40.5/30 in.; Cargo volume: 15.6 cu. ft.; Fuel tank: 60L/regular; Tow limit: 1,000 lb.; Load capacity: 860 lb.; Turning circle: 41 ft.; Weight: 3,235 lb.

reports of engine surging, stalling, and hard starting, possibly caused by a defective engine crank sensor or throttle switch (on national back order):

> While driving down the highway, I noticed my car was not accelerating when I stepped on the gas. My "service engine light" also went on. The car stalled, and had to be towed back to the dealer. This happened one week after purchasing the car. Since then, I have had it back to the dealer six times for the same problem. The car is a 2005 Altima 2.5 SL. As I'm writing this my car is back at the dealer...again towed in!

Annoying and hazardous dash reflection onto the windshield; electrical glitches; and excessive brake wear, noise, and pulsations. Snow builds up in the small wheelwells, making steering difficult and causing excessive shimmy; clutch failure when downshifting into Fourth gear; noisy, failure-prone rear shocks; early failure of the front struts; ABS warning light stays lit; ignition noise in radio speakers or static heard whenever the rear defroster is operating; and radio readouts cannot be seen in sunlight. **Service bulletin problems:** No-starts (see bulletins here and on following page).

HARD START/MIL ON/DTC P0340/P0345

BULLETIN NO.: NTB04-063   DATE: MAY 24, 2004

2003–2005 Altima (L31) with the VQ35DE (V6)

2004 Quest

2004 Maxima

IF YOU CONFIRM:

A MIL ON with DTC P0340 (CMP Sensor Bank 1) and/or P0345 (CMP Sensor Bank 2), and/or the engine is hard to start when warm, but starts OK when the engine is cold.

NOTE: "Hard start" is engine crank time that is longer than three seconds.

ACTIONS:

- If you only have DTC P0340, replace only Bank 1 CMP (Camshaft Position) Sensor.
- If you only have DTC P0345, replace only Bank 2 CMP (Camshaft Position) Sensor.
- If you have both codes, replace both sensors.
- For a "hard to start warm" incident, replace both sensors, even if you have no codes.

Noisy alternator; free tire replacement campaign covering prematurely worn Bridgestone and Continental tires. **NHTSA safety complaints:** Right front wheel came off on the highway; sudden tire failure (Bridgestone and Continental):

> At 100 miles [160 km], a brand new Nissan Altima with Continental Touring M&S, contact as tires (P215/60R16). The sidewall blew out at 10 mph [16 km/h]. I am dealing with Nissan to get them to replace all of the tires on the car. I do not feel safe with these tires.

ELECTRICAL — ENGINE NO-CRANK IN EXTREME COLD

BULLETIN NO.: NTB04-111   DATE: OCTOBER 6, 2004

ENGINE WILL NOT CRANK (NO-START) WITH OUTSIDE TEMPERATURE BELOW 10°F

2004–2005 Altima

2004 Maxima

2004 Quest

2004 Murano

2004 350Z

2004 Titan

2004 Armada

IF YOU CONFIRM: A "No Crank" (starter doesn't work) incident under all of the following conditions:

1. The vehicle sat for several hours (cold soak) with outside temperatures below 10°F (–12°C); and

2. The vehicle was then driven for a short period of time (5–10 minutes); and

3. The engine was then turned OFF for a short time (5–10 minutes); and

4. The engine would then not crank when a restart was attempted (starter doesn't work).

NOTE: This TSB applies only if all of the above occurred.

ACTION: Replace the Intelligent Power Distribution Module.

WILL NOT SHIFT OUT OF PARK

BULLETIN NO.: NTB04-098   DATE: AUGUST 24, 2004

2005 Altima with an automatic transmission

IF YOU CONFIRM: The Automatic Transmission shifter will not move out of the Park position with the ignition ON and the brake pedal depressed.

NOTE: This incident, if it occurs, may be intermittent.

ACTION: Replace the Shift Lock Control Unit with the one listed in the Parts Information.

Airbag didn't deploy; erratic-shifting transmission when going into Second gear; hard starts and a black-smoke exhaust; constant stalling; vehicle vibrates excessively on the highway; often pulls to the right once underway:

> Car pulls to right and left, hard to control steering...took to dealer four times; they say it's the road.

Defective rear seat belt can't be adjusted while being worn and constantly tightens up; and rear windshield shattered when rear door was closed. Safety defects become more common as these cars age. Dealerships are said to be aware of Altima's tendency to catch fire: A fire erupted after a collision, ignited because of a faulty fuel injection system on another occasion, and also ignited while cruising on the highway. Airbags failed to deploy; vehicle was idling and then suddenly went into Reverse and accelerated as groceries were unloaded from the trunk (dash indicator showed car in Park); driver run over by his own car when it slipped into Reverse; sudden acceleration when brakes are applied; transmission slips and engine hesitates when accelerating; chronic stalling; windshield distortion; exhaust pipe hanger pin catches debris that may ignite; tail lights constantly fail; insufficient headlight illumination and misdirected light:

> I purchased a new 2005 Nissan Altima. The first time I drove the car at night and turned on the low-beam headlights, I noticed that the lights projected far less than I had been used to in the 1998 Altima or even the 1988 Subaru that we have. Driving at night is scary, uncomfortable, and most certainly dangerous. My wife, the second driver in our family, noticed the problem, as did a neighbour. One evening, I lined up both the 1998 Altima and the 2005 Altima side-by-side and turned on the low-beam headlights of each. The new 2005 Altima headlights projected less than two-thirds the distance as the 1998 Altima's. I contacted the dealer and manufacturer to no avail. Nissan issued me a reference complaint No. 4858724. They said that there was no problem and that it just may be the design. The design! They advised me to go to another dealer, preferably at night. The service departments close at night so that is a very remote possibility. I asked if they could recommend aftermarket bulbs that I, at my own expense, could have installed. They offered no advice. These headlights are a real danger to all night drivers, especially elderly drivers.

> •

> High beam light casts a strong beam of light straight up to the sky. This was a distraction and dangerous. At all times the high beams were visible to objects 10–15 feet [3–4.5 m] above the vehicle.

Battery suddenly blew up; seat belt fails to retract; and instrument panel gauges wash out in sunlight.

Road Performance

Pro: Acceleration/torque: Impressive acceleration with powerful V6 engines. **Transmission:** Both transmissions usually perform flawlessly. **Steering:** Precise and responsive with lots of feedback. **Emergency handling:** Handles sudden corrections quite well. **Routine handling:** Acceptable manoeuvrability around town, and highway cruising is quite comfortable. Suspension handles rough pavement without jostling passengers. **Braking:** Above average.

Con: Acceleration is hard to modulate; often accompanied by tire-spinning and excessive torque steer (twisting or pulling to the right). The 4-cylinder engine tends to be buzzy and less refined than the competition.

ALTIMA

List Price (very negotiable) — **Residual Values** (months)

List Price	24	36	48	60
2.5 S: $24,698 (20%)	$18,000	$15,000	$13,000	$11,000
3.5 S: $27,598 (22%)	$21,000	$18,000	$15,000	$13,000
3.5 SE: $29,698 (18%)	$22,000	$19,000	$16,000	$14,000

SAFETY FEATURES

	STD.	OPT.
Anti-lock brakes	✓	✓
Seat belt pretensioners F/R	✓	—
Side airbags	—	✓
Traction control	—	✓

CRASHWORTHINESS

Head restraints F/R	[3]	[2]
Visibility F/R	[4]	[2]
Crash protection (front) D/P	[5]	[5]
Crash protection (side) F/R	[3]	[3]
Crash protection (offset)	[5]	—
Rollover	[4]	—

MAXIMA ★★★

RATING: Average. You get more horsepower than with the Maxima's competitors, but the car's not backed up with the technical refinements and quality components needed for safe and pleasurable driving. This year's Maxima has been downgraded because of a rising tide of factory problems, similar to the Altima's, that haven't been attenuated by much. **Strong points:** Impressive powertrain performance and a comfortable ride. **Weak points:** Excessive pulling to the right when accelerating; the shiftgate indents aren't user-friendly; 18-inch tires produce high-speed tire whine; dashboard reflection on windshield; increased chassis dimensions don't translate into a roomier interior—tall occupants may find rear

TECHNICAL DATA

POWERTRAIN (FRONT-DRIVE)

Engine: 3.5L V6 (265 hp); Transmissions: 6-speed man. • 4-speed auto. • 5-speed auto.

DIMENSION/CAPACITY

Passengers: 2/3; Wheelbase: 111 in.; H: 58.3/L: 194/W: 72 in.; Headroom F/R: 3.0/2.5 in.; Legroom F/R: 42/29.5 in.; Cargo volume: 15.5 cu. ft.; Fuel tank: 70L/premium; Tow limit: 1,000 lb.; Load capacity: 860 lb.; Turning circle: 44 ft.; Weight: 3,545 lb.

seating a bit cramped; small trunk opening limits what luggage you can carry; premium fuel required; redesign will likely hurt quality and lead to an unusually high number of safety and performance-related failures; and many incidents of the skyview roof suddenly shattering. **New for 2006:** Nothing major.

OVERVIEW: The front-drive, mid-sized Maxima soldiers on as Nissan's luxury flagship, a luxury mini-step above the best-selling Altima. The 265-hp V6 coupled to a 6-speed manual or 4- or 5-speed automatic transmission is a real dazzler. The Maxima comes with an impressive array of standard features, and a host of performance and safety features, such as large front brakes with full brake assist, a power driver's seat, xenon headlights, and 18-inch wheels.

COST ANALYSIS: The 2005 Altima is identical to the 2006 and is a better buy if sufficiently discounted. **Best alternatives:** Other cars worthy of consideration are the 205-hp Acura TSX or 258-hp 3.2TL Type S; the BMW 3 Series; and automatic-equipped versions of the 244-hp Honda Accord V6, the 204-hp Lexus IS 250, the 5-speed Mazda6 GT V6, and the 210-hp Toyota Camry V6. **Options:** Traction control wouldn't be a bad idea if you are lead-footed; otherwise, keep things simple. You might consider swapping the 6-speed manual transmission for a 4-speed Jatco automatic with a manual shift mode at the same trim level, or even for the 5-speed Aisin automatic found in the 3.5 SL model. **Rebates:** $4,500 and low-interest financing by early 2006. **Delivery/PDI:** $1,190. **Depreciation:** Average. **Insurance cost:** Higher than average. **Parts supply/cost:** Average. **Annual maintenance cost:** Average. **Warranty:** Bumper-to-bumper 3 years/80,000 km; powertrain 5 years/100,000 km; rust perforation 5 years/unlimited km. **Supplementary warranty:** Not needed. **Highway/city fuel economy:** 7.3–11.6L/100 km with automatic transmission.

 ## Quality/Reliability/Safety

Pro: **Warranty performance:** Average.

Con: **Quality control:** Below average. The 2005 Maxima has been plagued with serious quality problems, as confirmed on the *Maxima.org* website and by internal service bulletins. **Owner-reported problems:** Electrical system and automatic transmission, brake, and suspension strut assembly failures. Other persistent malfunctions include chronic no-starts caused by defective IPDM modules:

The vehicle will crank, but would not start. While driving home, the vehicle shut down in the middle of the intersection. Vehicle was inched into a parking lot. Towed the next day. The IPDM module was found to be defective. The module part was on back order.

Constant stalling; excessive front-end vibration felt through the steering:

Purchased 2005 Maxima and have had it back to the dealer six times for the same vibrating and shimmying problem that everyone seems to complain about. If I had only seen this website before I bought one! The dealership tries their best to blame the tires/wheels. They have now put five sets of tires and wheels on my brand new car...the only person there that is truthful is the service manager. I took him for a ride in the car and finally he said [that] this is a characteristic of the car...they wish Nissan would fix it.

Leaking sunroof, paint defects, loose moulding, and assorted body squeaks, clunks, and rattles. **Service bulletin problems:** Cold upshift shock; abnormal shifting; hard start after a cold soak; front brake noise; AC gurgling noise; exhaust ticking noise and buzz; water leaks from roof; and headlight fogging. **NHTSA safety complaints:** Excessive steering-wheel shimmy; vehicle underway at 100 km/h when the steering wheel suddenly locked up and the brakes failed; while vehicle was in motion, the front wheels locked up, causing extensive undercarriage damage; vehicle suddenly swerved out of control; vehicle suddenly accelerated in Reverse when put into Drive; sudden acceleration upon start-up (a faulty air control valve is suspected); airbags fail to deploy in a collision; unable to control engine speed with the accelerator pedal; vehicle stalls without warning in cold weather (suspect the computer module); fuel leaks from seal when overfilled; excessive front-end vibrations; strong bleach-type odour permeates the interior; many complaints that the headlights are poorly designed, placing the high beams too high for adequate visibility; drivers complain they can't see between the high and low beams; trunk lid and latch are hazardous when raised; and several incidents where the skyview roof shattered:

While driving a 2004 Maxima (a rental from Enterprise) on Interstate 91 in CT. On 3/7/2004, out of nowhere, the glass roof exploded outward. Glass covered me and the backseat of the car. Nothing hit the car, I went under no overpasses, there were no other vehicles around me at the time. I nearly lost control of the car and suffered minor scratches to forehead and arm from the shattered glass. I strongly feel that this was some sort of defect and want this documented as to prevent further injury to other drivers of this vehicle make.

Sunroof opens and closes on its own; steering wheel overheats in direct sunlight; the driver-side windshield washer may not work in cold weather; and tire treads separate.

Road Performance

Pro: Acceleration/torque: The powerful and smooth standard V6 engine provides substantial power without excessive noise. **Transmission:** The smooth-shifting 4-speed automatic transmission delivers power smoothly and efficiently. **Routine handling:** Very good, with lots of control. The ride is fairly firm but comfortable, owing to the refined suspension that handles rough roads well if the car is lightly loaded. Very little brake fade after successive stops. **Emergency handling:** Takes practice (see below). **Steering:** Fairly good when not accelerating too quickly or coming out of a turn.

Con: Acceleration is hard to modulate. It's often accompanied by tire spinning and excessive torque steer (twisting or pulling to the right). The large turning circle degrades handling. The 6-speed manual transmission is a bit hard-shifting and noisy. Steering feels increasingly over-assisted as the Maxima's speed picks up. **Braking:** Extended stopping distance.

MAXIMA

List Price (very negotiable)	**Residual Values** (months)			
	24	**36**	**48**	**60**
SE: $35,098 (25%)	$27,000	$24,000	$21,000	$17,000

SAFETY FEATURES	**STD.**	**OPT.**
Anti-lock brakes	✓	—
Seat belt pretensioners F/R	✓	—
Side airbags	✓	—
Stability control	—	✓
Traction control	✓	—

CRASHWORTHINESS		
Visibility F/R	5	2
Crash protection (front) D/P	5	4
Crash protection (side) F/R	4	4
Crash protection (offset)	5	—
Rollover	4	—

QUEST ★★

RATING: Below Average. **Strong points:** Soft prices are easily bargained down; wide side sliding doors; second- and third-row seats fold flat when not used; small handgrips easily accessed by children; impressive highway performance (as long as you're not carrying a full load)—crash protection and highway stability is above reproach; easy, no-surprise, carlike handling; occupants get a comfortable ride with lots of seating choices; the 4-speed automatic transmission is particularly

All ratings on a numbered scale where 5 is good and 1 is bad. See page 153–154 for a more detailed description.

smooth and quiet; braking performance is quite good (when the brakes are working properly); plenty of passenger and cargo room: These vans are nearly 30 cm longer and 5 cm wider and higher than Chrysler's short-wheelbase minivans; and mechanical components have been tested for years on the Maxima. **Weak points:** These fuel-thirsty minivans are quite heavy, and the 3.5L 240-hp engine has to go all out to carry the extra weight. Powertrain setup trails the Odyssey in acceleration and passing. Other minuses: a quirky dash and interior styling; cheap-looking interior; instrument panel produces windshield glare; control layout can be a bit confusing; soft suspension bottoms out on rough roads; excessive engine, wind, and road noise. **New for 2006:** Nothing significant.

OVERVIEW: A totally different minivan than its predecessor, the $31,698–$45,998 2004–06 Quest is one of the most stylish, smoothest-running, and (sigh) priciest minivans on the road. Now based on the Altima/Murano platform, it offers all the standard high-tech safety, performance, and convenience features one could want. Its long wheelbase allows for the widest-opening sliding doors among front-drive minivans, rear-seating access is a breeze, and a capacious interior allows for flexible cargo and passenger configurations that can easily accommodate 4′ × 8′ objects with the liftgate closed. Standard fold-flat third-row seats and fold-to-the-floor centre-row seats allow owners to increase storage space without worrying about where to store the extra seats; head restraints must be removed before the seats can be folded away.

Although it feels a bit heavy in the city, the Quest is very carlike when driven on the highway. Ride and handling are enhanced by a new four-wheel independent suspension, along with front and rear stabilizer bars and upgraded antilock brakes.

TECHNICAL DATA

POWERTRAIN (FRONT-DRIVE)

Engine: 3.5L V6 (240 hp); Transmissions: 4-speed auto. • 5-speed auto.

DIMENSION/CAPACITY

Passengers: 2/2/3; Wheelbase: 124 in.; H: 70/L: 204/W: 78 in.; Headroom F/R1/R2: 6.5/7.5/3.0 in.; Legroom F/R1/R2: 40/28/32 in.; Cargo volume: 60 cu. ft.; Fuel tank: 76L/regular; Tow limit: 3,500 lb.; Load capacity: 1,205 lb.; Turning circle: 44 ft.; Weight: 4,410 lb.

COST ANALYSIS: A discounted second-series 2005 Quest will give you all of the 2006 features for much less money. **Best alternatives:** Other minivans worth considering are the Honda Odyssey, the Toyota Sienna, and the Mazda5. **Options:** Nothing really worthwhile. **Rebates:** $5,000 by the end of 2005. **Delivery/PDI:** $1,297. **Depreciation:** Average; much faster than average for the SEL. **Insurance cost:** Higher than average. **Parts supply/cost:** Parts are often on backorder and can be expensive. **Annual maintenance cost:** Should be less than average; though much depends upon the competence of Nissan's 200 "fix-it" engineers, who camped out at the factory for the last six months of 2004. **Warranty:** Bumper-to-bumper 3 years/80,000 km; powertrain 5 years/100,000 km; rust perforation 5 years/unlimited km. **Supplementary warranty:** An extended warranty isn't needed, yet. **Maintenance/repair costs:** Higher than average. **Highway/city fuel economy:** 8.2–12.4L/100 km.

Quality/Reliability/Safety

Pro: A large dealer network means that servicing and parts are readily available. Plenty of glass provides excellent front and rear visibility. The Quest offers a large array of standard safety features, including front and side airbags that reduce deployment force as passenger weight decreases, head airbag protection for all occupants, side-impact beams, reinforced centre pillars, front- and rear-impact-absorbing zones, rear outboard three-point safety belts, standard traction control, ABS brakes with brake assist, and a childproof door lock in the sliding door. An integrated child seat is optional.

Con: Quality control: Average. **Reliability:** Not reassuring. Early models have serious body rattles and fit-and-finish deficiencies. **Warranty performance:** Below average. **Owner-reported problems:** Early reports signal some problems with electrical malfunctions, brake noise, vibration, binding, or overheating, and premature wear of the front discs, rotors, and pads. Fit-and-finish quality has been uneven on early production models, resulting in numerous squeaks and rattles. There have also been some reports of panel and paint defects and premature rusting on the inside sliding door track. Later models have improved quality control and better fit and finish. **Service bulletin problems:** No-starts; poor shifting; low power, or won't shift out of third gear:

LOW POWER/STAYS IN THIRD GEAR	
BULLETIN NO.: NTB04-144A	DATE: FEBRUARY 7, 2005

2004–2005 Quest (V42)

IF YOU CONFIRM:

- The engine has low power, and/or the transmission doesn't shift (stays in Third gear), and
- The incident occurs just after the engine is started.

ACTION: Replace the A/T Control Module (TCM) with the new one listed in the parts information.

Inoperative navigation system; engine boom and floor vibration; sunroof and SkyView roof water leaks; sliding door won't latch; AC problems; cooling system leaks or overheats; headlight fogging; and an exhaust ticking noise. **NHTSA safety complaints:** Airbag deployed inadvertantly:

> 2004 Nissan Quest minivan had all side airbags deploy while traveling 65 mph [105 km/h] with no accident to cause the deployment. Nissan has been unable to explain the reason for deployment and has agreed to fix the van but provides no assurance that the vehicle is safe. I have repeatedly asked for the cause of the errant and unsafe deployment of all of the side airbags and expressed my concerns about the safety of the vehicle. Nissan is unresponsive to my safety concerns.

Front seat belt fails to stay buckled; windshield cracked for no reason; many sliding door complaints for almost every failing imaginable:

> Rear sliding passenger door safety mechanism for detecting limbs, etc., does not function to provide safety. This mechanism forcefully pushed a 130-lb. [59-km] adult who was applying significant pressure to stop the door before hitting a 2-year-old child. Adult unable to prevent door from closing, had to pull child out of harm in addition to self.

Sliding door trapped child; other adults also trapped; door continuously pops open; sudden, unintended acceleration; vehicle will not downshift for merging with traffic; automatic transmission stuck in Third gear; vehicle rolls away when stopped on an incline; dome light fuse blows continuously; water leaks through the front windshield; dash reflects onto windshield; windshield wiper is ineffective and spray is too low; and Goodyear tires wear out prematurely.

Road Performance

Pro: Acceleration/torque: V6 has plenty of power for all driving needs. **Transmission:** The 4-speed automatic transmission is competent; however, the SE's 5-speed delivers more mid-range grunt for passing and merging. **Routine handling:** Much improved, but still handles and manoeuvres like a large station wagon. Agile (the revised suspension helps in this area) and easy to drive on the highway; less so around town. The smooth, quiet ride on the highway isn't compromised by a full load. **Emergency handling:** Impressive highway stability even after sudden steering corrections or braking. **Steering:** Precise and predictable steering. **Braking:** Disc/disc; braking performance is excellent.

Con: The 4-speed automatic lacks mid-range grunt found in the 5-speed automatic. Don't make too much of the Quest's carlike-handling pretensions. Sure, it rides and handles much better than truck-based minivans like the GM Astro, but it can't match the quality, ride, and handling of the Honda Odyssey or the Toyota

Sienna. The Quest requires a rather wide turning circle. Towing capacity of 1,590 kg (3,500 lb.) is possible only with an optional towing package.

QUEST

List Price (very negotiable)   **Residual Values** (months)

	24	36	48	60
S: $31,898 (25%)	$21,000	$17,000	$14,000	$11,000
SL: $36,198 (27%)	$23,000	$20,000	$17,000	$14,000
SE: $46,398 (30%)	$30,000	$25,000	$22,000	$19,000

SAFETY FEATURES	STD.	OPT.	CRASHWORTHINESS		
Anti-lock brakes (4W)	✓	—	Crash protection (front) D/P	5	5
Seat belt pretensioners F/R	✓	—	Crash protection (side) F/R	5	5
Side airbags	✓	—	Crash protection (offset)	5	—
Stability control	✓	✓	Rollover	4	—
Traction control	✓	—			

Subaru

In 1995, Subaru realized it was losing the battle with Honda and Toyota for buyers of its front-drive compact cars, so it bet the farm on all-wheel-drive, versatile, and reasonably priced Outback and Forester models—and on Paul Hogan, (a.k.a. Crocodile Dundee), an Australian actor *cum* Subaru pitchman. Sales soared, with most cars selling close to the MSRP and keeping much of their value come trade-in time.

But buyers are now more discerning, and Subaru sales are suffering as shoppers turn toward cheaper AWDs from Hyundai, Kia, and other Japanese automakers. Subaru is fighting back by offering tons of non-essential standard features—making their cars even more expensive.

Subaru's overall product lineup this year reinforces its AWD capabilities as it moves upscale, adding more features and boosting prices. For 2006, the Forester gets a minor restyling, six more inches of ground clearance, a 173-hp 2.3L 4-cylinder engine, and a 230-hp 2.5L turbocharged XT Limited. The Impreza and WRX will also get restyled front ends.

General Motors just sold its 20-percent stake in Fuji Heavy Industries, owner of Subaru, effectively pulling the plug on a number of planned co-ventures involving GM, Saab, and Subaru. GM was so anxious to bail out of Fuji/Subaru that it sold its $1.5 billion in shares to Toyota and Fuji for $727 million—a little less than half what GM paid originally.

All Subarus provide full-time AWD capability, but most owners don't need the Subaru's off-road prowess; only 5 percent will ever use their Subaru for off-roading. The other 95 percent just like knowing they have the option of going wherever they please, whenever they please—no matter how much extra fuel AWD burns.

FORESTER, IMPREZA, WRX, STI ★★★/★★/★

The Subaru Forester.

RATING: *Forester:* Above Average; *Impreza:* Average; *WRX and ST:* Below Average. There is nothing remarkable about Subaru except for its use of AWD and Australian *Survivor* chic to stave off bankruptcy in the mid '90s. Now that the entry-level versions have been dropped, these overpriced little sedans and wagons have priced themselves out of the market; if you don't need the AWD capability, you're wasting your money. The Forester and WRX have been downgraded mainly because the competition has raised the performance and reliability bar while Subaru simply coasts as it adds more expensive standard features. Quality control and customer service have also declined. Choose a cheaper Japanese or South Korean SUV. **Strong points:** Some long-awaited performance and size improvements. A refined AWD drivetrain; powerful WRX and STi engines and impressive

TECHNICAL DATA

POWERTRAIN (AWD)

Engines: 2.5L 4-cyl. (173 hp) • 2.5L turbo (230 hp) • 2.5L turbo (300 hp); Transmissions: 5-speed man. • 6-speed man. • 4-speed auto.

DIMENSION/CAPACITY (FORESTER)

Passengers: 2/3; Wheelbase: 99 in.; H: 60/L: 175/W: 68 in.; Headroom F/R: 5.0/5.0 in.; Legroom F/R: 42/28 in.; Cargo volume: 35.5 cu. ft.; Fuel tank: 50L/reg./prem.; Tow limit: 2,000 lb.; Load capacity: 900 lb.; Turning circle: 38 ft.; Weight: 3,215 lb.

acceleration with the base 2.5L; competent handling, without any torque steer; well-appointed base models; Forester passengers are spoiled by the roomy cabin (check out the headroom stats); lots of storage space with the wagons; nice control layout; impressive crashworthiness; and average quality control. **Weak points:** Recent models are overpriced. Generally stiff-riding, and the Outback Sport doesn't ride as comfortably or handle as well as other Imprezas. Problematic entry and exit; the coupe's narrow rear window and large rear pillars hinder rear visibility; wagon has limited cargo volume; heater is insufficient and air distribution is inadequate; comfort compromised by WRX's short wheelbase, suspension, and 16-inch tires; front- and rear-seat legroom may be insufficient for tall drivers; small doors and entryways restrict rear access; WRX and STi require premium fuel and are the only models with standard head-protecting side airbags; and a surprisingly large number of safety-related complaints that include complete brake loss, chronic surging, and stalling. **New for 2006:** *Impreza:* A light restyling. *Forester:* Also slightly restyled this year and given six additional inches of ground clearance. The 2.5L engine gets eight more horses, and a 230-hp 2.5L turbocharged XT Limited debuts. Incidentally, the turbocharged XT adds 20 horses via a redesigned engine intake manifold that could be troublesome in the future. *WRX and STi:* Updated styling and a bare-bones WRX TR. The high-performance STi will receive an upgraded limited-slip differential and steering sensor mated to the AWD. *All models:* A retuned suspension enhances ride smoothness and handling response, and there's improved braking feel. Ground clearance has been slightly increased, an alarm system is now standard, and the 5-speed manual transmission isn't available with L.L. Bean models.

OVERVIEW: The Impreza is essentially a shorter Legacy with additional convenience features. It comes as a four-door sedan, a wagon, and an Outback Sport wagon, all powered by a 173-hp 2.5L flat-four engine or the 230-hp 2.5L. The rally-inspired WRX models have a powerful turbocharged engine: a 300-hp 2.5L variant; lots of standard performance features; a sport suspension; aluminum hood with functional scoop; and higher-quality instruments, controls, trim, and seats.

The Forester is a cross between a wagon and a sport-utility. Based on the shorter Impreza, it uses the Legacy Outback's 2.5L engine or an optional turbocharged version of the same power plant, coupled to a 5-speed manual transmission or an optional 4-speed automatic. Its road manners are more subdued and its engine provides more power and torque for off-roading.

COST ANALYSIS: Buy the upgraded 2006 Forester, Impreza, or WRX. With GM selling its 20-percent interest in Subaru, it's likely the 2006 models will go at fire-sale prices as the company looks for much needed capital. WRX versions are expensive, problematic Imprezas, but when they run right, they'll equal the sporty performance of the Audi A4 and the BMW 3 Series—cars that cost $10,000 more. **Best alternatives:** If you really don't need a 4×4, here are some front-drives also worth considering: the Honda Civic, the Hyundai Elantra, the Mazda6, and the Toyota Corolla. **Rebates:** $4,000 rebates and low-interest financing. **Options:** Larger tires to smooth out the ride. **Delivery/PDI:** Be wary of delivery/PDI "creep"; the fee is $1,380 this year, double what it once was. **Depreciation:** Slower than average. Foresters hold their value best of all. **Insurance cost:** Higher than average. **Parts supply/cost:** Parts aren't easy to find and can be costly; expect delayed recall repairs. **Annual maintenance cost:** Higher than average. Mediocre, expensive servicing is hard to overcome because independent garages can't service key AWD components. **Warranty:** Bumper-to-bumper 3 years/60,000 km; powertrain 5 years/100,000 km; rust perforation 5 years/unlimited km. **Supplementary warranty:** Budget an extra $500 or more for an extended powertrain warranty to protect you from premature and repeated clutch failures. **Highway/city fuel economy:** 7.7–10.5L/100 km with the 2.5L.

Quality/Reliability/Safety

Pro: Quality control: Fair. **Safety:** The manual transmission's "Hill Holder" clutch prevents the car from rolling backwards when starting out.

Con: Quality control: Subaru reps aren't always very helpful:

> While attempting to slow my 2003 WRX for a corner on a well groomed, dry gravel road, the ABS system of the car initiated a mode that would not allow the car's brakes to function at all. During the episode (which has been and can be recreated) pedal pressure and pedal height was maintained as during normal braking operations. The brakes would not work despite the fact that I was standing with both feet on the brake pedal. I am in the process of disconnecting my ABS. Subaru North America claims that I'm nuts.

Reliability: A history of poor engine performance, premature clutch failures, and frequent brake servicing. Numerous reports of airbags failing to deploy or injuring passengers after deployment. Servicing quality is spotty. **Warranty performance:** Unacceptably bad (especially in relation to sudden acceleration, suspension, glass shattering, brake, and clutch complaints). **Owner-reported problems:** Poor engine idling, cooling; frequent cold weather stalling; manual transmission malfunctions (mostly clutch chatter and shudder); rear wheel bearing failures; alloy wheels cause excessive vibration; rear suspension clunking (strut assembly defect):

The left rear strut of my 2005 STi has failed twice in less than 13,000 miles [21,000 km]. The first failed at around 10,000 miles [16,000 km] and the second at 12,600 miles [20,000 km]. Strut failure on a bumpy road at high speed could cause loss of vehicle control and could result in very serious injury or death. Subaru should issue a recall and remedy the problem immediately. On a website for STi owners, there are over 100 owners reporting this same problem.

Premature exhaust system rust-out and early brake wear; minor electrical short circuits; catalytic converter failures; doors don't latch properly; water leaks and condensation problems from the top of the windshield or sunroof; windshield scratches too easily; and paint peeling:

I bought an '05 WRX at the end of August. Two weeks and less than 500 miles [800 km] later there was a quarter-sized spot on the drive-side door where the paint had come off down to the metal. I noticed the spot immediately after washing my car. After speaking with the dealer, I contacted Subaru and they told me it was environmental damage and they would not cover it. For the past five weeks I have been contacting Subaru and they have agreed to repaint only the affected body panels. However, since the initial spot, there have been several other spots all over the car. I am currently trying to get them to repaint the entire car, although I would rather not have a 7-week-old car completely repainted.

Service bulletin problems: Measures to eliminate noise from the rear differential area; timing belt tensioner bracket modified to prevent knocking noise; brake vibration (diagnostic procedures). **NHTSA safety complaints:** *All models:* Sudden acceleration, stalling, transmission failures, steering loss, airbag malfunctions, brake and engine lights continually on, and front seats move fore and aft. *Impreza:* Chronic rear strut failures; fuel odour inside the cabin; windshield is easily cracked and side window shatters spontaneously:

It was a 95°F [35°C] day. Using my air conditioner and after pulling into my garage at home my driver-side rear window had an explosive failure, causing glass to fly into and out of the car. The Subaru is a month old and had not had prior impacts to the window glass. I believe that improper tempering and improper window design/installation didn't allow for thermal expansion/contraction and led to the failure.

Forester: Sudden acceleration believed to be caused by a sticking throttle:

I recently (end of November 2004) purchased a new Subaru Forester. When the car is started, maybe six times in the four months I have had the car, it immediately lurches into full speed the second the accelerator is touched, and sends you 20 or more feet [6+ m] forward (once backwards) before you can possibly brake. I have narrowly avoided several potentially fatal accidents. Today I had a real accident. When I went into dealership this morning, they would not listen to me. Told me they had never heard of such a thing ever happening to a Subaru, and that something that only happened once a month was impossible to check. The manager basically called me a liar and asked me to leave. It isn't just this accident; the car can be repaired, but this is a car defect that can certainly kill someone. On at least two occasions, once in grocery lot and once leaving my driveway, it was only by chance I didn't hit a pedestrian. I feel the car is unsafe and shouldn't be driven, but even more disturbing is Subaru's attitude that nothing can be done, and that I am a liar.

Airbag failed to deploy; vehicle wanders at highway speeds; intermittent stalling; alternator shuts down at idle:

Vehicle broke down during hurricane evacuation, thereby endangering me and my family for 32 hours. 2005 Subaru Forester has a built-in defect where the alternator automatically shuts down during engine idle, so only the battery runs until out of power, thereby leaving driver and passengers stranded on roadway.

When backing into a parking space, the "Hill Holder" feature activates, forcing the driver to use excessive throttle in Reverse; heater, defroster failure. *WRX and STi:* Windshield cracking; chronic ABS brake failures; car suddenly went out of control:

I was traveling 40–45 mph [64–72 km/h] on a two-lane road in my 2005 Subaru WRX STi. I came out of a small S-curve and went over a rough patch of road, and the tail end of the car started sliding out to the right. The next thing I knew, I had run into the bank and I was facing traffic. I hit the bank at least 40 mph; there was a car in front of me and one behind me, and one coming in the other lane of traffic. It felt like the tail of the car had tightened up and sent power to the rear wheels and kept me sliding until right before I hit the bank. It swung the car around like it had sent all power to the front, which in turn put me into the bank. Nothing worked. No airbags deployed. The seat belts did not restrain me; I hit my head on the side window because none of the safety features worked on the car. I sustained injuries including whiplash and severe headaches, and I may have a fractured a vertebra in my back. Contacted Subaru of America and they blew me off, saying that there was no defects in the car, and that they waited till the government told them to fix something before they would fix any problems.

Road Performance

Pro: Acceleration/torque: The 2.5L performs much better with the Impreza and Forester than with the Legacy Outback. It is smooth and powerful, with lots of low-end torque for serious off-road use. **Transmission:** The automatic transmission shifts smoothly. The all-wheel-drive system is a boon for people who often need extra traction, and it works well with either a manual or an automatic transmission. **Routine handling:** Smooth and nimble. Hurtles through corners effortlessly with a flat, solid stance and plenty of grip. **Emergency handling:** Better than most small cars and sport-utilities. Tight cornering at highway speeds is done with minimal body lean and no loss of control. **Steering:** Precise and predictable. **Braking:** Disc/drum and disc/disc; smooth, effective braking with no brake fade after successive stops.

Con: Uncomfortable ride with a full load. The WRX produces a choppy ride when passing over uneven pavement and has a history of poor braking.

FORESTER, IMPREZA, WRX, STI

List Price (very negotiable)	Residual Values (months)			
	24	36	48	60
Impreza: $23,495 (18%)	$17,500	$13,500	$10,500	$8,500
Forester 2.5X: $27,995 (23%)	$19,500	$15,500	$12,000	$10,000
WRX Sedan: $35,495 (25%)	$25,000	$21,000	$17,000	$13,000
WRX STi: $48,995 (27%)	$34,000	$29,000	$25,000	$19,000

SAFETY FEATURES			CRASHWORTHINESS		
	STD.	OPT.	Head restraints F/R		
Anti-lock brakes	✓	—	WRX	5	5
Seat belt pretensioners F/R	✓	—	Visibility F/R	5	4
Side airbags	✓	✓	WRX STi	5	❷
Traction control	✓	—	Crash protection (front) D/P	4	5
			Forester	5	5
			Crash protection (side) F/R	4	—
			Forester	5	5
			Crash protection (offset)	5	—
			Rollover	4	—

LEGACY, OUTBACK ★★★

RATING: Average. This car is all about full-time AWD. It handles difficult terrain without the fuel penalty or clumsiness of many truck-based SUVs. Without the AWD, the Outback is just a well-equipped, middle-of-the-road vehicle, outclassed by most of the import competition. **Strong points:** A refined and reliable AWD system; a well-balanced 6-cylinder engine; a comfortable ride; interior materials and fit and finish that have been substantially upgraded; exceptional handling if Vehicle Dynamic Control (VDC) stability system works as it should; nice-handling GT version; lots of cargo room; and better-than-average crashworthiness. **Weak points:** The VDC feature adds exponential complexity to a vehicle that is already complicated to repair; serious stalling problems; and 6-cylinder-equipped vehicles

The Subaru Legacy.

are plagued by slow downshifts. The 2.5L is a sluggish performer, undoubtedly because of the car's heft; problematic automatic transmission performance when hooked to the smaller engine; base models without VDC can be dangerously unstable at high speed—their rear ends tend to slide out as the car corners. Other minuses: excessive 4-cylinder engine noise; cramped back seat is too narrow and lacks sufficient thigh support to hold three occupants in comfort; limited rear access and rear headroom for tall passengers; seat belts may be too short for large occupants; unimpressive fuel economy; the 6-cylinder engine requires premium fuel; and these cars are very dealer dependent for parts and servicing. Sean, a *Lemon-Aid* correspondent from Calgary, reports the following anomalies on his 2005 Legacy sedan:

> The stereo is barely acceptable and if the front seat passenger decides to change the radio channel, his or her hand can easily hit the gearshift lever. Plus, when it rains, a little water gets into the trunk whenever I open it.

New for 2006: Eight more horses are added to the base model's 2.5L 4-cylinder engine; larger brakes, an anti-theft engine immobilizer, and 17-inch wheels. The 2.5i Special Edition Outback comes with a new power driver's seat and a powered sunroof.

TECHNICAL DATA

POWERTRAIN (AWD)
Engines: 2.5L 4-cyl. (175 hp) • 2.5L 4-cyl. (250 hp) • 3.0L V6 (250 hp); Transmissions: 5-speed man. • 4-speed auto. • 5-speed auto.

DIMENSION/CAPACITY
Passengers: 2/3; Wheelbase: 105 in.; H: 68/L: 186/W: 54 in.; Headroom F/R: 2.5 /2.0 in.; Legroom F/R: 41/28 in.; Cargo volume: 13 cu. ft.; Fuel tank: 60L/reg./prem.; Tow limit: 2,700 lb.; Load capacity: 850 lb.; Turning circle: 38 ft.; Weight: 3,540 lb.

OVERVIEW: A competent, full-time 4×4 performer for drivers who want to move up in size, comfort, and features. Available as a four-door sedan or five-door wagon, the Legacy is cleanly and conventionally styled, with even a hint of the Acura Legend in the rear end.

The 2.5 GT model comes with a turbocharged 250-hp 2.5L 4-cylinder engine and a hood scoop made popular by the rally-inspired Impreza WRX. Engines on all models have been mounted lower, thus lowering the centre of gravity and reducing body roll, thereby making the cars less prone to roll over. Cornering ability is also enhanced by a wide track and performance-oriented steering components and suspension geometry.

The Outback has added a turbocharger to the base 2.5L 4-cylinder engine, giving it 250 horses—equal to the 3.0L V6, which has less torque.

COST ANALYSIS: Get an upgraded 2006 model. **Best alternatives:** Front-drives worth considering: the Honda Accord and the Toyota Camry. Worthwhile 4×4s: the Honda CR-V, the Hyundai Santa Fe, and the Toyota RAV4. **Options:** Base models hooked to an automatic transmission are severely performance-challenged. Stay away from the Firestone and Bridgestone original equipment tires. Optional integrated rear child seat is worthwhile. **Rebates:** $3,500 and low-interest financing. **Delivery/PDI:** $1,380. **Depreciation:** Slower than average. **Insurance cost:** Higher than average. **Parts supply/cost:** Parts aren't easily found and can be costly. **Annual maintenance cost:** Average. **Warranty:** Bumper-to-bumper 3 years/60,000 km; powertrain 5 years/100,000 km; rust perforation 5 years/unlimited km. **Supplementary warranty:** A good idea. **Highway/city fuel economy:** 2.5L: 7.8–11L/100 km; 3.0L: 8.4–12.4L/100 km.

 Quality/Reliability/Safety

Pro: Quality control: Average, though powertrain defects have begun cropping up. Above-average body assembly and finish.

Con: Reliability: More windshield cracking as seen on the Impreza and Forester:

> The windshield has cracked a total of six different times when the vehicle is being driven. This could be dangerous because the windshield could break in the driver's face.

Powertrain defects can sideline the car for days. There are several reports of the transmission jumping out of First gear when using First to slow down or to descend a steep grade. **Warranty performance:** Not impressive. **Owner-reported problems:** Cold-weather hard starts and chronic surging and stalling;

snow gets inside of wheelwell, binding steering; and minor electrical, fuel system, and automatic transmission problems. Clutch produces a burnt sulphur smell:

> The clutch on this vehicle seems to slip during normal driving, causing the worst smell. It smells like a sewage treatment plant in the summertime, and normally dissipates after a few minutes. The clutch slips during normal driving, such as starting on a mild grade, or even during bumper-to-bumper traffic. This last one is particulary annoying, as this is an everyday occurence for many of us. Normal driving in rush hour traffic causes a prolonged overwhelming smell in the passenger compartment, causing occupants to become sick to their stomachs.

Owners report that the front brakes require more attention than on an average vehicle. Premature surface rust and exhaust system rust-out are common, and misadjusted door strikers make for hard closing and opening. Servicing can be awkward because of the crowded engine compartment, particularly on turbocharged versions. Hot air always blows out of vents. Small horn buttons may be hard to find in an emergency. **Service bulletin problems:** Engine timing belt tensioner bracket modified to prevent knocking noise; AC filtration update campaign; fuel door won't open; brake vibration (troubleshooting tips); improperly installed fuel-filler hose clamp; and the availability of a revised hood deflector. **NHTSA safety complaints:** Original equipment Bridgestone tires may be unsafe when used on wet roads:

> Vehicle: '05 Subaru GT Limited sedan purchased 11/30/04. Tire: Bridgestone, Potenza RE92 (215/45 ZR17). My wife and I skidded as we approached a stop sign on a level, snow-covered road. I broke gradually and my speed was low, about 10 mph [16 km/h] as I started braking. Instead of stopping, the car just kept going even though I applied more brake pressure. If there had been a car ahead of us, I would have rear-ended it. I discovered very negative reviews of this tire on the folllowing two customer survey bases: *tirerack.com* and *1010tires.com*. The majority of customers rated this tire as poor for wet traction and very poor (dangerous was used in some reviews) for snow traction. I have case numbers with Subaru of America and Bridgestone. They and the dealer have refused my request to credit my OE tires for new ones. Many customers (average of 2.6 out of 10) answered no when asked, "would you buy this tire again?" I am very concerned that there is a safety issue with the RE92 for wet traction, especially snow traction. Considering that Subaru AWD vehicles built a reputation as a car that will be sure-footed in inclement weather, why would SoA equip this car with tires that have a 160 tread rating? Tire dealers I've spoken to about this issue say that this tire is the equivalent of a summer tire.

Chronic surging or stalling in forward gear and in Reverse:

> At different throttle inputs, there is an engine stutter/stumble. This failure is dangerous because it happens often when accelerating. Subaru denies this is a global problem for early production vehicle as does the dealer. There are many posts about

this problem at *www.legacygt.com*, including an apparent fix/logic upgrade. Subaru claims that the logic upgrade can only be applied when there is an engine light. Numerous vehicle owners have had the fix done without an engine light and they have seen an improvement.

•

The Suburu Legacy Turbo we bought in June has a major, life-threatening safety issue. We quickly found that on turns with acceleration the power steering fails. Initially our dealer could find no problem. When we demonstrated it to them they kept the car. Unable to find anything they drove another like car from their lot and found the same issue. They told us it must be a normal feature of turbo engines with AWD. Even backing onto a parking space, I've had this happen and turning left onto a busy street I have narrowly missed causing an accident several times. It seems our dealer will (kindly) put us into some other car, without the turbo, but before someone is killed we wanted to report the problem.

Automatic transmission breakdowns; ABS brake failures; brakes feel spongy and take too much time to stop vehicle; braking pedal goes to the floor before braking effect, resulting in extended stopping distances; vehicle suddenly veers to the right when accelerating or braking; cruise control failed to disengage when brake pedal was depressed; fuel sloshes in fuel tank because there are no baffles; during a collision, airbags deployed but failed to inflate; the suspension's design causes severe pulling to one side; excessive steering and vehicle vibration when passing over uneven pavement; steering lock-up while driving; knocking and clunking noise heard when turning; vehicle's rear end bounces about when passing over bumps; hard to shift from Park to Reverse; cracked seat belt buckle; and seat belts are too short for large occupants.

 ## Road Performance

Pro: Acceleration/torque: The base 2.5L engine is a competent performer with a manual gearbox only; turbocharging makes a world of difference. The 6-cylinder is adequate, but doesn't feel like it has much in reserve. **Routine handling:** Fairly soft and comfortable ride on smooth pavement. The GT's firmer suspension exhibits above-average handling. **Steering:** Acceptable steering response. Higher-end models handle well, although there is some excessive lean when cornering. **Braking:** Disc/disc; a bit better than average. **Emergency handling:** Much improved. There is less bounce on uneven pavement, the rear end tracks well when cornering, and there's not too much body lean in turns.

Con: The 4-cylinder engine is noisy and rough running; it's tuned more for low-end torque than speedy acceleration; turbocharger wastes fuel. **Transmission:** The automatic transmission shifts into too high a gear to adequately exploit the engine's power and is reluctant to downshift into the proper gear. Manual transmission's shift linkage isn't suitable for rapid gear changes. Base models don't handle well; GT rear end breaks out at high speed; stability and traction control is only available with the Outback 3.0 VDC.

LEGACY, OUTBACK

List Price (very negotiable) **Residual Values** (months)

	24	36	48	60
Legacy 2.5i: $28,495 (23%)	$19,000	$16,000	$13,000	$10,000
Outback 2.5i: $32,995 (25%)	$23,000	$19,000	$16,000	$13,000

SAFETY FEATURES			CRASHWORTHINESS		
	STD.	OPT.			
Anti-lock brakes (4W)	✓	—	Head restraints F/R	5	3
Seat belt pretensioners F/R	✓	—	Visibility F/R	5	5
Side airbags	✓	✓	Crash protection (front) D/P	4	5
Stability control	✓	✓	Crash protection (side) F/R	3	4
Traction control	✓	✓	Wagon	4	5
			Crash protection (offset)	5	—
			Rollover	4	—

Suzuki

Suzuki has been making very good entry-level small cars and sport-utility vehicles for over a decade, but most buyers aren't familiar with the company's products because they were mostly sold under GM's name. In fact, the company makes only two mainstream vehicles in its own name: the Aerio small sedan and the Vitara sport-utility—a vehicle sold by General Motors through 2004 as the Tracker and rated Above Average in *Lemon-Aid SUVs, Vans, and Trucks 2006*.

The Name Game

GM has long had a manufacturing and retail partnership with Suzuki. In 2002, GM bought a controlling interest in the assets of bankrupt Korean automaker Daewoo, and convinced Suzuki Canada to sell several of the Daewoo cars as the Suzuki Swift+ (Aveo) and Verona (Epica). Despite the fact that most of Suzuki's products are small, entry-level products, the company has made considerable progress over the past decade in raising its quality scores to a level that rivals many Japanese models.

Unfortunately, Suzuki's re-badged Daewoo cars gave Suzuki a black eye earlier this year when J.D. Power announced that Suzuki had finished last in its 2005 Quality Study of 36 nameplates. One of the cars that contributed most to the poor quality rating was the U.S.-only Suzuki Forenza, sold in Canada by GM as the Optra. Suzuki chided GM over the Forenza/Optra poor showing and promised to keep a tight lid on its own quality control.

AERIO ★★★★

RATING: Above Average. This roomy little car is a winner because of its better-than-average overall performance, low price, and versatile five-door body style that rivals many wagons and hatchbacks. **Strong points:** On the road, the Aerio performs fairly well. Its lightweight and relatively powerful engine gets it quickly up to cruising speed. The automatic transmission shifts smoothly; ride quality is good; brakes are adequate, though a bit soft; and it has good forward visibility. Unlike the sedan's low roofline, the wagon's tall roof ensures plenty of headroom for tall passengers. There's a surprising amount of passenger and cargo room, and legroom is on par with or better than most of its competition. **Weak points:** Road and engine noise are omnipresent. Rear view is restricted by wide rear pillars. The only quality problems seen so far are aluminum wheel rims bending and cracking, airbag malfunctions, premature brake pad wearout, and paint chipping. Fuel economy is sharply reduced with the automatic transmission or AWD. The 2004 and

TECHNICAL DATA

POWERTRAIN (FRONT-DRIVE)

Engine: 2.3L 4-cyl. (155 hp);
Transmissions: 5-speed man. • 4-speed auto.

DIMENSION/CAPACITY (SEDAN)

Passengers: 2/3; Wheelbase: 98 in.;
H: 60.8/L: 171/W: 68 in.; Headroom F/R: 6.0/2.0 in.; Legroom F/R: 40.5/28 in.; Cargo volume: 14.6 cu. ft.; Fuel tank: 50L/regular; Tow limit: N/A; Load capacity: 895 lb.; Turning circle: 37 ft.; Weight: 2,715 lb.

earlier models were plagued by differential snap ring failures and poor engine performance when using regular fuel. **New for 2006:** Plans are afoot to drop the wagon.

OVERVIEW: The Aerio uses a 155-hp 2.3L 4-cylinder engine that's one of the most powerful engines found in this small-car class. It has clean, simple lines and offers more standard features than did its predecessor, the Esteem. And with the addition of all-wheel drive, the $22,985 (plus $995 delivery/PDI) Aerio AWD Fastback SX competes head-to-head with the Subaru AWDs, the Pontiac Vibe, and the Toyota Matrix. Some of the car's standard features include AC, power windows, power mirrors, tilt steering wheel, CD player, a tachometer, and split-fold rear seats.

AERIO

List Price (very negotiable)   **Residual Values** (months)

	24	36	48	60
Sedan: $18,995 (15%)	$13,000	$11,000	$ 9,000	$ 7,000
AWD GLX: $22,985 (18%)	$16,000	$14,000	$11,000	$ 9,000

SAFETY FEATURES	STD.	OPT.	CRASHWORTHINESS		
Anti-lock brakes	✓	—	Head restraints F/R	5	5
Seat belt pretensioners F/R	✓	—	Visibility F/R	5	3
Side airbags	✓	—	Crash protection (front) D/P	4	3
			Crash protection (side) F/R	3	4
			Crash protection (offset)	5	—

VERONA ★★

RATING: Below Average, mainly because of the high number of performance- and safety-related complaints logged on NHTSA's database.

OVERVIEW: An updated Daewoo Leganza that's been given a sexy Italian moniker and a bit of European styling, the Verona carries a 155-hp 2.5L inline 6-cylinder engine to power its mid-sized frame. This put it in the same league as the Honda Accord, the Nissan Altima, and Toyota models, which use more efficient 4-cylinders to do the same tasks with less fuel penalty. Its ride and handling are acceptable, but lack the refinement of its Japanese competitors. A 2006 Verona GL sells for $22,995, plus $995 for freight and PDI. **New for 2006:** Nothing significant.

Service bulletin problems: Remedy for a rough-running engine and a regional recall of the electronic control module to improve engine operation in cold weather; brake vibration (troubleshooting tips); improperly installed fuel-filler hose clamp; static on AM stations; slow seat belt retraction; and the availability of a revised hood deflector. **NHTSA safety complaints:** Airbag malfunctions; a rough-running engine; constant stalling; hesitation; and a jerky transmission:

> The transmission would jerk, then worst of all, it would just cut off, whether sitting still or in motion. In that six-month period, I had to drive six loaner vehicles. People began to ask me if I owned a car lot because I was always in a different car! I filed a lemon law claim and after six months I got a brand new Verona.
>
> But the story doesn't end there, because after a month and a half of my new Verona replacement, it cut off on me while I was driving down the street. Same problem as my first Verona. The thing that got me during my first ordeal was the fact that Suzuki did not believe me which is why I had to go file a claim. But now, from what I have been told this time around, my car along with three other Veronas, is now sitting in the shop waiting for Suzuki to come and fix it. So I am in loaner car number seven.

Car doesn't downshift when it should; seat belts unlatch themselves or tighten up progressively; rear seat belts won't retract; wiper spray doesn't reach the windshield when it's windy; key won't open vehicle; and vehicle relocks itself continuously.

NHTSA front crashworthiness test results were: three stars for the driver and four stars for the passenger; side-impact protection was rated four stars for the front seat and three stars for the rear seat passenger; resistance to rollover was given four stars. The IIHS offset crashworthiness and head restraints ratings are Average.

Toyota

Toyota on the Prowl

Toyota will likely end up owning General Motors one piece at a time. It already has so much surplus cash that it could simply take over GM today and expand the scope of its operations. However, that would be a kamikazi acquisition, considering the mountain of debt and financial obligations facing America's premier automaker—not to mention the health and pension costs, union demands, and a huge inventory of vehicles no one wants to buy.

Nope, Toyota will take a cheaper and less risky route to acquire GM through more joint ventures and re-badged vehicles, buying GM's stake in other car companies, and picking up profitable GM subsidiaries at fire-sale prices.

Earlier this year, Toyota bought part of GM's Subaru stake, and it may put in a bid for General Motors Acceptance Corp., GM's subsidiary since 1919. Successfully selling automotive financing, commercial financing, insurance and mortgage products, and real estate services, GMAC has made more profits than GM car sales has. Now, with GMAC possibly on the selling block, a Toyota takeover of the automaker's financial arm may be just around the corner.

GM's co-venture with Toyota has produced the successful Pontiac Vibe/Toyota Matrix—two similar vehicles produced in separate factories in different countries.

Toyota's image as a builder of quality vehicles has been legendary, although it did take a battering during the late '90s when angry owners refused to pay $6,000–$9,000 to repair sludged up engines on most of Toyota's lineup. The company relented and extended the engine warranty up to eight years on 3.3 million vehicles. More recently, Toyota has stonewalled owners over dangerously defective automatic transmissions possibly affecting 1999–2005 Lexus ES 300/330 and Camry models. A look at the NHTSA safety complaint database shows almost 600 complaints registered on the 2002 Camry alone—100 complaints would be normal for a 3-year-old vehicle. As of September 2004, the 2004 model had generated 135 complaints.

> Difficulty shifting my 2004 Camry from Park to Reverse, then upon shifting into drive the car accelerated uncontrollably, would not stop, collided with a mobile home, airbags did not deploy, resulting in the death of one passenger and injury of driver.

•

My 2002 Lexus ES 300's transmission gets confused when shifting into and out of the lower gears, then spends too long trying to figure out what gear to be in. This causes dangerous delays in acceleration, the effect is the same as a momentary engine stall. We have had this happen on several occasions, freeway ramp entrances are certainly the most dangerous place that this has occurred. Dealer acknowledges that there have been complaints about the shifting delays but they say no fix is available. This is our third ES 300, the previous models used a cable between the gas pedal and the throttle, this new one uses what is called "fly by wire," a position sensor on the accelerator that a computer is supposed to use to figure out what to tell the engine and transmission. It isn't working very well. If not rectified, this problem will certainly lead to a crash someday—then we'll get to see how good the safety equipment is.

Yes, it does appear that Toyota has been skating on its reputation for the past few years, while Honda, Mazda, and Hyundai have continued to improve their overall quality. The redesigned 2004 Sienna minivan is a good example of Toyota's quality decline. Hardly a year has passed since its launch and, with almost 200 complaints, it has already amassed almost four times the number of safety-related complaints one would expect:

My 2004 Sienna hesitates/fails to move forward in the following mode: after braking, when the vehicle is still moving between 5 to 15 mph [8–25 km/h], the van does not respond to accelerator pedal input; vehicle hesitates with no movement forward, then shifts hard into First gear and lurches forward. We have had two close calls, waiting for the vehicle to respond to accelerator pedal input. Also, accelerator pedal has a "dead spot." The first half-inch of pedal causes no response from vehicle. This "dead spot" along with the hesitation noted above can result in a 2-second response failure from the vehicle. This situation has put my family in harm's way on numerous occasions.

A perusal of *Lemon-Aid* readers' letters and emails as well as NHTSA reports shows that recent-model Toyotas have been plagued by engineering mistakes that put occupants' lives in jeopardy. These include engine and transmission malfunctions; fuel spewing out of cracked gas tanks; sudden, unintended acceleration; gauge lights that can't be seen in daylight; and electrical system glitches that can transform the power door into a guillotine. Consequently, I have lowered some ratings this year to reflect these dangers and to warn buyers of the potential for harm.

Several other disturbing developments involve Toyota's customer relations, among then sky-high freight/PDI charges of $1,310 (Sienna) and the company's Access dealer program, which discouraged price-haggling. After *Lemon-Aid* filed a formal complaint, Ottawa stepped in and Toyota paid a $2 million settlement.

It makes no sense for the company to pat itself on the back for keeping prices low while at the same time charging exorbitant fees. Toyota customers are not stupid—they can add. And so can Toyota dealers.

When running properly, Toyotas do hold up very well over the years, are especially forgiving of owner neglect, and cost very little to service at independent garages. But the kicker for most buyers is how little their vehicles depreciate; it's not unusual to see a 5-year-old sedan selling for almost half its original selling price—a value reached by most Detroit Big Three vehicles a bit after their second year of ownership.

Among Toyota's 2006 models, we'll see a convertible Camry Solara; a Scion tC, which replaces the Celica; a high-performance Corolla, powered by a 170-hp engine borrowed from the Celica; and a redesigned Avalon and Tacoma pickup. Production of the Celica ended in July 2005, and the model is being phased out.

From a personal, password-protected homepage on the *www.toyota.ca* website, owners can now access information on their lease and loan account, Extended Car Policy Coverage, warranty coverage service history, outstanding free service campaigns, and a recommended maintenance checklist. Owners are also given the ability to respond electronically to surveys, request service appointments and update their contact information online.

PRIUS ★★

Maybe Toyota figures that Prius' chronic stalling is a fuel-saver.

RATING: Below Average. You can buy almost two small Echos or Civics for what one Prius will cost. **Strong points:** Good fuel economy, acceptable acceleration and handling in most situations, smooth transition to battery-recharge mode, five-passenger capacity, improved cabin noise suppression, and a comprehensive powertrain warranty. **Weak points:** Retails for about $7,000 more than the non-hybrid competition; $1,160 delivery/PDI fee; battery pack will eventually cost $8,000 U.S. to replace; fuel economy may be 40 percent less than advertised, say *Consumer Reports*, Society of Automotive Engineers, and others; higher gas

TECHNICAL DATA

POWERTRAIN (FRONT-DRIVE)

Engine: 1.5L 4-cyl. (110 hp);
Transmission: CVT

DIMENSION/CAPACITY

Passengers: 2/3; Wheelbase: 106 in.;
H: 53/L: 175/W: 68 in.; Headroom
F/R: 4.0/2.0 in.; Legroom F/R: 40.5/30
in.; Cargo volume: 16.1 cu. ft.; Fuel
tank: 45L/regular; Tow limit: N/A; Load
capacity: 825 lb.; Turning circle: 37 ft.;
Weight: 2,950 lb.

consumption in colder weather; 50-percent depreciation after three years; higher than average insurance premiums; dealer-dependent servicing means higher servicing costs; underpowered for passing and merging; rear seating is cramped for three adults; rear windshield cuts visibility; sales and servicing may not be available outside of large urban areas; and the CVT transmission has a mixed reliability record and cannot be easily repaired by independent agencies. The Prius engine is stall-prone, braking isn't very precise or responsive, and the car is very unstable when hit by crosswinds. Highway rescuers are wary of the car's 500-volt electrical system and are taking special courses to avoid electrocution, and safety and reliability data is a mixed bag. Side airbags are optional. Finally, toxic battery components offset any positive environmental impact from cleaner and fewer emissions. **New for 2006:** Upgraded airbags, a tire-pressure monitoring system, and redesigned front and rear lights. More features may be added in the new year.

OVERVIEW: Following its 2004 model-year redesign, the 2006 Prius is longer, wider, and more accommodating than ever. Now sold only as a four-door hatchback, it employs both a gasoline engine and an electric motor for maximum fuel economy and power—reaching 100 km/h within 10 seconds. ABS, traction control, and a continuously variable transmission (CVT) are standard features.

This hybrid is now approaching the Camry in size, and Toyota's new Hybrid Synergy Drive is more sophisticated, powerful, and efficient than the 2003 system. Interestingly, because the car relies primarily on electrical energy, fuel economy is higher in the city than on the highway—the opposite of what one finds with gasoline-powered vehicles.

An electric motor, not the gasoline engine, is the main power source, and it uses an innovative CVT for smooth and efficient shifting. The motor is used mainly for acceleration, with the gasoline engine kicking in when needed. Once underway, the 1.5L 4-cylinder gasoline engine takes over to provide power and recharge the battery pack. Braking automatically shuts off the engine, as the electric motor acts as a generator to replenish the nickel-metal-hydride battery pack.

Toyota says the Prius is engineered to be as fuel-frugal, versatile, and hassle-free as possible. Unfortunately, Toyota has fallen far short of this goal. Some shortcomings: Acceleration is still a yawner, handling is marginal, brake feedback is average, the steering is numb, the steering wheel position takes some getting used to, and the seats could use better bolstering and lumbar support.

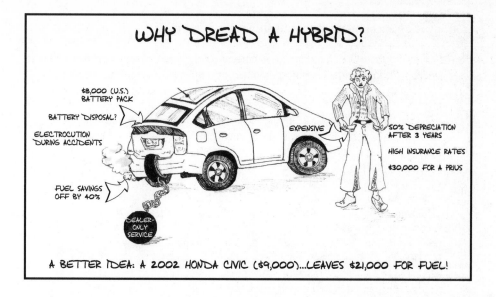

WHY DREAD A HYBRID?

$8,000 (U.S.) BATTERY PACK

BATTERY DISPOSAL?

ELECTROCUTION DURING ACCIDENTS

FUEL SAVINGS OFF BY 40%

DEALER-ONLY SERVICE

EXPENSIVE

50% DEPRECIATION AFTER 3 YEARS

HIGH INSURANCE RATES

$30,000 FOR A PRIUS

A BETTER IDEA: A 2002 HONDA CIVIC ($9,000)...LEAVES $21,000 FOR FUEL!

Going hybrid doesn't mean that drivers have to forsake modern conveniences and safety features. Each Prius comes with standard ABS (Hydraulic Anti-lock Braking System with Generative Braking Assist); traction control; front airbags; power windows, locks, and mirrors; and air conditioning. **Owner-reported problems:** Constant stalling, electrical system glitches, and tire failures. Fuel economy is nowhere near what's advertised; gas pump shuts off when refilling; inaccurate fuel gauge; vehicle runs out of gas, despite gauge showing plenty of fuel in tank. **Service bulletin problems:** Inverter coolant leak. **NHTSA safety complaints:** Eighty safety-related incidents recorded so far on the 2005 model (mostly related to chronic stalling). Driver tapped the brakes to disengage the cruise control and vehicle suddenly veered out of control to the left; extremely vulnerable to sidewinds:

> Prius had extemely poor stability at highway speeds with 25 mph [40 km/h] gusty crosswind. Directional stability was extremely poor—wind gust would shift direction of the car 10–15 degrees. Little road feedback in steering wheel, required great attention from driver to control car at 60 mph [95 km/h]. Less capable driver...probably would end up in a wreck.

Sudden acceleration when slowing down and loss of braking:

> My wife and I bought a new Prius in early March of 2005. My wife was coasting to stop (around 5 mph [8 km/h]) for a stop sign and when she put her foot on the brake the car started to accelerate. She came to a stop after hitting another car head on. Before she hit the car (she also sideswiped another car) she was able to look at her feet to confirm that she was indeed pressing on the brake pedal.

Steering failure; complete chronic stalling:

> I have a 2005 Prius that has lost all engine power on two occasions. I believe the "stalling" is intentionally designed into the software to protect the transmission. I think a design decision intended to protect the car is putting my life at risk. My Prius has "stalled" twice: once on the freeway at 80 mph [130 km/h] and again on surface streets at 30 mph [50 km/h]. In each case the transmission's internal components would be under tremendous strain unless it disengaged. In each case, all lights, headlights, indicators stayed on, the "check engine" light came on, the car continued coasting (as if put in Neutral), and the car was unresponsive to the throttle and the gearshift. In both cases I coasted to a safe spot (try crossing five lanes of 70+ mph [115 km/h] freeway traffic at night while coasting). Only after parking, turning off power, and restarting power would the car operate...at which point it operated fine. Dealer couldn't find anything wrong...in fact, the second incident was two days after my 30,000 mile [48,000 km] service! They apparently took no action regarding the concern I expressed to the service rep with respect to stalling.... I called Toyota corporate headquarters and was told they are unaware that this is a recurrent issue. This despite discussions in the press and on *hybridcars.com*. I am contacting you in case I am killed or injured before Toyota figures out that this is a serious and recurrent issue. The first incident was around January or February 2005, and the most recent was Monday, September 19, 2005.

Floormat gets stuck between pedals; accidentally bumped gearshift knob and put Prius into Dynamic Braking Mode, which almost caused a semi-truck to rear-end the car; poor emergency braking:

> While test driving a new '05 Toyota Prius, I came to the conclusion that its braking system is inadequate. Emergency braking while turning easily induces understeer because of the regenerative braking. As the aggressive brake-assist takes over there is "snap" oversteer and front wheel lockup. For average drivers this can result in complete loss of control.

Tail lights don't work; headlights will tilt down without warning; difficulty in fastening seat belts; Goodyear Integrity 185/65R/R15 tires have no traction when roads are wet.

COST ANALYSIS: All 2005s have been sold. Buying a 2006 Prius entails a six-month wait for delivery. One smart move would be to demand that the dealer give you a "protected" price to prevent last-minute price gouging. **Best alternatives:** Other small cars that represent good investments, although with less cachet, are the Honda Civic, the Hyundai Accent, and the Toyota Echo. The Civic Hybrid isn't as refined as the Prius. **Options:** Head-protecting side airbags. **Rebates:** The Prius' popularity has risen along with fuel prices, so rebates aren't likely. **Delivery/PDI:** $1,160. **Depreciation:** Faster than average. A 2001 Prius is worth less than half its original $30,000 value. **Insurance cost:** Higher than average. **Parts supply/cost:** Parts aren't easily found and can be costly. **Annual maintenance cost:** Average, so far. **Warranty:** Bumper-to-bumper 3 years/60,000 km; powertrain 5 years/100,000 km; hybrid-related components (HV battery, battery control module, inverter with converter) 8 years/160,000 km; major emission components 8 years/130,000 km; rust perforation 5 years/unlimited km. **Supplementary warranty:** Not needed. **Highway/city fuel economy**: 4.0–4.2L/100 km. Owners and industry experts say that these "official" fuel-consumption figures are way overblown.

PRIUS

List Price (very negotiable)   **Residual Values** (months)

	24	36	48	60
Prius: $30,730 (20%)	$22,000	$16,000	$13,000	$11,000

<table>
<tr><td colspan="3">SAFETY FEATURES</td><td colspan="3">CRASHWORTHINESS</td></tr>
<tr><td></td><td>STD.</td><td>OPT.</td><td></td><td></td><td></td></tr>
<tr><td>Anti-lock brakes</td><td>✓</td><td>—</td><td>Head restraints F/R</td><td>5</td><td>5</td></tr>
<tr><td>Seat belt pretensioners F/R</td><td>✓</td><td>✓</td><td>Visibility F/R</td><td>5</td><td>4</td></tr>
<tr><td>Side airbags</td><td>—</td><td>✓</td><td>Crash protection (front) D/P</td><td>5</td><td>4</td></tr>
<tr><td>Stability control</td><td>—</td><td>✓</td><td>Crash protection (side) F/R</td><td>4</td><td>4</td></tr>
<tr><td>Traction control</td><td>✓</td><td>—</td><td>Rollover</td><td>4</td><td>—</td></tr>
</table>

ECHO, YARIS ★★★★★

RATING: Recommended. Echo keeps its sedan; Yaris adds upgraded three- and five-door hatchbacks. Although the name has changed for 2006, these are remarkably practical, reliable, and cheap small cars, if you can get past the tall, function-over-form styling. **Strong points:** Plenty of usable power, excellent fuel economy, and lots of interior space for passengers, along with an incredible array of storage areas, including a huge trunk and standard 60/40 split-fold rear seats. Reasonably well equipped with good-quality materials, well-designed instruments and controls, comfortable seating, easy rear access, and excellent visibility fore and aft. Quite nimble when cornering, and very stable on the highway. Surprisingly quiet for an economy car. **Weak points:** Tall profile and light weight make the Echo vulnerable to sidewind buffeting; base tires provide poor wet traction; excessive torque steer (sudden pulling to one side when accelerating); narrow body width

The Toyota Yaris.

limits the rear bench seat to two adult passengers; and unorthodox styling is cute to some but ugly to others. **New for 2006:** Yaris debuts.

OVERVIEW: Yaris is Toyota's entry-level five-passenger econocar; it gives great fuel economy without sacrificing performance. It is essentially a spin-off of Toyota's popular Echo hatchback, a Canada-only hatch that was built specifically for the Canadian market.

Positioned between the Echo and the Corolla, the Yaris costs about $2,000 less than the Corolla and $600 more than last year's Echo hatchback. It offers about the same amount of passenger space as the Corolla, thanks to a tall roof, low floor height, and upright seating position. The Yaris has a more modern look than the Echo, and its interior improvements, like large windows, additional legroom, and high-quality trim and seats, give it the allure of a much more expensive car. The only disappointment is that the seats lack height adjustment.

Cockpit controls and instrumentation are particularly user-friendly—located high on the dash and more toward the centre of the vehicle, rather than directly in front of the driver, where many gauges and controls are hidden by the steering column. Toyota says the repositioning of the instrument cluster farther away from the driver requires less refocusing of the eyes from far to near.

TECHNICAL DATA

POWERTRAIN (FRONT-DRIVE)
Engine: 1.5L 4-cyl. (108 hp);
Transmissions: 5-speed man. • 4-speed
auto.

DIMENSION/CAPACITY (ECHO SEDAN)
Passengers: 2/3; Wheelbase: 93 in.;
H: 54.5/L: 165/W: 65 in.; Headroom F/R:
4.5/2.5 in.; Legroom F/R: 40/26 in.; Cargo
volume: 13.6 cu. ft.; Fuel tank: 45L/
regular; Tow limit: N/A; Load capacity:
775 lb.; Turning circle: 35 ft.; Weight:
2,150 lb.

The Echo and Yaris are powered by a 108-hp 1.5L DOHC 4-cylinder engine featuring Variable Valve Timing cylinder head technology. It's the same design used by Lexus to combine power and fuel economy in a low-emissions vehicle. An engine this small would provide wimpy acceleration for most cars, but thanks to the Echo's light weight, acceleration is more than adequate with a manual gearbox, and acceptable with the automatic.

Standard safety features: dual airbags, anti-whiplash seats, collapsible steering column, and ABS on RS models (optional on CE three-door and LE five-door models).

COST ANALYSIS: Get the 2006 Yaris for its richer content; it's a bargain for light commuting duties. **Best alternatives:** Other cars worth considering are the Honda Civic, the Hyundai Accent, the Suzuki Aerio, or the Mazda3. **Options:** Consider snow tires and better-quality 14-inch tires for improved traction in inclement weather. Beware of option loading, where you have to buy a host of overpriced, non-essential, impractical features in order to get one or two amenities you require. **Rebates:** Not likely. **Delivery/PDI:** $1,060. **Depreciation:** Much slower than average. **Insurance cost:** Below average. **Parts supply/cost:** Easily found and reasonably priced. **Annual maintenance cost:** Costs over the long term are predicted to be low. **Warranty:** Bumper-to-bumper 3 years/60,000 km; powertrain 5 years/100,000 km; rust perforation 5 years/unlimited km. **Supplementary warranty:** Not needed. **Highway/city fuel economy:** 5.5–7.1L/100 km with an automatic transmission.

 ## Quality/Reliability/Safety

Pro: Quality control: Remarkably well built for an entry-level subcompact; few owner complaints. This becomes harder to understand when you see the large number of safety and performance complaints registered by NHTSA against the Lexus ES 300/330 and the Toyota Camry and Sienna—vehicles costing more than twice as much. **Reliability:** No problems have turned up yet. **Warranty performance:** No problem with the Echo, because the Echo has no problems. Yaris should match that reputation.

Con: Owner complaints: Rotten-egg exhaust smell; leaking shock absorbers; electrical malfunctions; and broken door latches. **Service bulletin problems:** A Limited Service Campaign (LSC) will apply a free anti-corrosion treatment to the interior floor surface; wet front passenger foot area. **NHTSA safety complaints:** Airbag failed to deploy.

ECHO, YARIS

List Price (very negotiable)	**Residual Values** (months) 24	36	48	60
CE hatch.: $13,580 (12%)	$ 9,500	$ 7,500	$ 6,500	$ 5,500
LE hatch: $14,910 (13%)	$10,500	$ 8,500	$ 7,500	$ 6,500

SAFETY FEATURES

	STD.	OPT.
Anti-lock brakes	✓	✓
Seat belt pretensioners F/R	✓	—
Side airbags	—	✓

CRASHWORTHINESS

Head restraints F/R	[5]	[3]
Visibility F/R	[5]	[5]
Crash protection (front) D/P	[4]	[4]
Crash protection (side) F/R	[3]	[4]
Rollover	[4]	—

COROLLA ★★★★

RATING: Above Average. **Strong points:** Pleasant ride; good braking; better quality control than Detroit Big Three; improved interior ergonomics (lots more space); improved crashworthiness scores; and a high resale value. **Weak points:** Average acceleration requires constant shifting to keep in the pack; automatic transmission-equipped versions are slower still. Clumsy emergency handling; lots of high-speed wind and road noise; limited front legroom; head restraints block rear visibility; many report that these cars literally stink because of a rotten-egg exhaust smell entering the interior; some reports of airbags deploying inadvertently or failing to deploy; and high freight/PDI charges. **New for 2006:** Nothing significant.

OVERVIEW: A step up from the Echo, the Corolla has long been Toyota's conservative standard-bearer in the compact sedan class. Over the years, however, the car has

All ratings on a numbered scale where [5] is good and [1] is bad. See page 153–154 for a more detailed description.

grown in size, price, and refinement to the point where it can now be considered a small family sedan. All Corollas ride on a front-drive platform with independent suspension on all wheels. There are three variants: the value-leader CE and the more upscale S and LE. Power is supplied by a torquey 130-hp 1.8L twin-cam four, teamed with either a standard 5-speed manual gearbox or an optional 4-speed automatic.

Standard equipment includes AC, tilt steering wheel, split-fold rear seat, power mirrors, and a CD player. ABS and front side airbags are optional.

COST ANALYSIS: Buy a similarly equipped 2005 model, if you can find one sufficiently discounted. **Best alternatives:** Other small cars that represent good investments are the Honda Civic, the Hyundai Elantra or Tiburon, and the Mazda3 or Mazda6. **Options:** The optional head-protecting side airbag is essential because of the car's poor side-impact occupant-protection scores. The built-in rear child seat is also a sound buy. For better steering response and additional high-speed stability, order the optional 185/65R14 tires that come with the LE. **Rebates:** $1,000 rebates, low-interest financing, and modest discounting early in 2006. **Delivery/PDI:** $1,060. **Depreciation:** Much slower than average. **Insurance cost:** Average. **Parts supply/cost:** Parts are easily found and reasonably priced. **Annual maintenance cost:** Lower than average. **Warranty:** Bumper-to-bumper 3 years/60,000 km; powertrain 5 years/100,000 km; rust perforation 5 years/unlimited km. **Supplementary warranty:** Not needed. **Highway/city fuel economy:** 5.3–7.1L/100 km with 1.8L engine and manual transmission.

TECHNICAL DATA

POWERTRAIN (FRONT-DRIVE)
Engine: 1.8L 4-cyl. (130 hp) • 1.8L 4-cyl. (170 hp); Transmissions: 5-speed man. • 4-speed auto.

DIMENSION/CAPACITY
Passengers: 2/3; Wheelbase: 102 in.; H: 53/L: 178/W: 67 in.; Headroom F/R: 5.0/2.0 in.; Legroom F/R: 40/27 in.; Cargo volume: 14 cu. ft.; Fuel tank: 50L/regular; Tow limit: 1,500 lb.; Load capacity: 860 lb.; Turning circle: 38 ft.; Weight: 2,595 lb.

Quality/Reliability/Safety

Pro: Quality control: Good component and assembly quality. **Reliability:** Better than average; much more reliable than the Camry or Sienna. **Warranty performance:** Average. Far too often, Toyota blames owners for its own inadequacies.

Con: The Corolla has fallen from its Recommended status, owing mainly to the flurry of safety-related complaints and the insensitivity of its customer-relations staff. **Owner-reported problems:** A stinking exhaust (sulfur smell):

> Purchased 2005 Toyota Corolla in August 2004. The car has had a consistent smell of rotten eggs (sulfur), almost daily with it worse when the car idles and after car shut-off. Dealer said [to] try premium gas, which I did and no effect. Dealer said Toyota had no knowledge or suggestions about problem, although I am aware of a

5/28/04 service bulletin for 2003–2004 Corollas for the exact problem. Dealer also said it could not be the catalytic converter because the dashboard light wasn't on, yet Toyota just settled a 2 million lawsuit for the dash lights not coming on and emission defects were not being picked up with regular code testing...when I mentioned the problem with my car has persisted since late August, a week after I bought the car, the dealer suggested the smell was from bad gas and the wind probably blew it into the car. My understanding is that this smell has been a very significant problem with Corollas (and some other cars) and a number of 2005 owners on various discussion boards have also reported it. Sometimes, the smell is so strong that I have to put the window down and I wonder what the constant exposure to sulfur will do to my allergies and asthma and why I should continue to pollute the air with sulfur every day while Toyota's dealers treat me as if I am some neurotic patron.

Engine and transmission failures; a litany of airbag defects; suspension bottoms out when passing over small bumps in the road; weak climate control system; premature front and rear brake pad wear and vibrations; suspension and steering malfunctions; electrical glitches; fuel pump failures; window and dash rattles. **Service bulletin problems:** AC provides inadequate heating:

POOR HEATER PERFORMANCE	
BULLETIN NO.: AC002–05	DATE: FEBRUARY 14, 2005

2003–2005 COROLLA
INTRODUCTION: Customers in areas with extremely low ambient temperatures may complain of poor heater performance during city driving conditions. The Air Conditioner Unit Assembly has been modified to improve this condition.

Loose rear door weatherstrip; instrument panel appears off-centre; erratic airbag warning lamp operation; automatic transmission whistle, hoot; and a loose, rattling manual transmission shifter. **NHTSA safety complaints:** Loose fuel line caused fire to ignite; vehicle hesitates and then surges while cruising on the highway; sudden, unintended acceleration when parking:

While pulling into a parking space, the vehicle surged forward causing the vehicle to crash into a building. The consumer's foot was resting firmly on the brake when the incident occurred. The consumer and passenger were injured.

•

Making a half-U-turn; pulled out of parking spot and slowly drove to opposite side; put car in reverse, foot on brake, slowly backing up toward curb; foot still on brake, car standing still, turned steering wheel slightly to left to proceed, put into drive... car suddenly lurched forward at excessive speed and hit curb and bricks around a tiny tree and stopped...

Vehicle suddenly shut down while underway at 100 km/h; vehicle suddenly accelerated while cruise control was engaged; several owners report that a hole in the oil pan caused vehicle to stall; when the vehicle was parked, the parking brake was released and both airbags deployed; both airbags deployed right after driver turned on the ignition switch; airbags deployed after car passed over a bump in the road; in a rear-end collision, front airbag came out, but failed to deploy; side airbag failed to deploy in a side impact; and both airbags deployed incorrectly in a frontal collision:

> [Our] [t]hirteen-year old daughter sustained severe traumatic brain injury after [a] head-on collision. Her airbag…was completely blown apart from one side to the other, allowing her head to strike [the] dash.

> We both had seat belts on. I sustained bruising of hips and right rib. She was in [a] coma and [is] just now beginning to move [her] left side. She still cannot sit up, stand, walk, talk coherently, eat, or do anything for herself.

Faulty seat belt wiring could cause a fire; floormat catches accelerator pedal; brake failure when decelerating; when brakes are applied, pedal goes soft, resulting in extended stopping distances; when coming to a gradual stop, brakes locked up, causing extended stopping distance; rear welding broke away from the frame, resulting in complete loss of control; sudden collapse of the rear axle; rear control arm broke while driving at 110 km/h; left rear tire fell off; defective Uniroyal and Goodyear Integrity tires; warped wheels; shifter refused to go into gear while driving; transmission sometimes goes from Drive to Neutral while driving; refuses to shift out of Park; vehicle wanders all over the road and pulls to the left or right at moderate speeds; in windy conditions, vehicle becomes hard to steer, veering left or right; high beams shoot up into the sky, blind driver, and don't adequately light the highway; glow-in-the-dark inside trunk release doesn't glow in the dark because it is rarely exposed to light (owner actually crawled inside trunk to test it out); poor-quality wiper blades; poorly designed headlights have stray beams on high beam that project upward at a 45-degree angle and low-beam headlights are too dim; and sunlight washes out dash readings.

 ## Road Performance

Pro: Acceleration/torque: Adequate, though not impressive, acceleration times. **Transmission:** Both manual and automatic transmissions shift smoothly. The manual transmission gives the Corolla extra pep and uses a light clutch for effortless shifting. **Routine handling:** Average handling under normal driving conditions; the ride is busy, but comfortable. This is characteristic of Toyota products, where handling takes second place to comfort. **Braking:** Better-than-average performance without ABS.

Con: AC and an automatic transmission can seriously reduce engine horsepower. **Emergency handling:** A bit clumsy, with some body roll, and sometimes the car plows straight ahead in hard cornering. Ride quality deteriorates as the load increases. **Steering:** Not much road feel. The sedan's ABS braking isn't impressive—too much weaving and veering to one side.

COROLLA

List Price (very negotiable)	**Residual Values** (months)			
	24	**36**	**48**	**60**
CE: $15,715 (13%)	$11,500	$10,000	$ 8,500	$ 6,500
LE: $21,830 (15%)	$15,000	$13,000	$11,000	$ 9,000

SAFETY FEATURES

	STD.	OPT.
Anti-lock brakes	✓	✓
Seat belt pretensioners F/R	✓	—
Side airbags	—	✓
Stability control	—	✓
Traction control	—	✓

CRASHWORTHINESS

Head restraints F/R	[5]	[3]
Visibility F/R	[4]	[2]
Crash protection (front) D/P	[5]	[5]
Crash protection (side) F/R	[4]	[4]
Crash protection (offset)	[5]	—
Rollover	[4]	—

CAMRY, SOLARA ★★★

RATING: Average; downrated because of serious reliability problems. The Camry is coasting on its past high-quality reputation—compare its sorry quality record with those of the Avalon, Echo, and Celica. **Strong points:** *Camry:* Good powertrain set-up (V6); upgraded 4-cylinder is also a competent performer; pleasant ride; quiet interior; well-laid-out instrumentation and controls; nicely padded dash and door panels; lots of interior passenger and storage space; and a high resale value. *Solara:* A better-performing 4-cylinder engine; more firmly damped suspension; and more attractively styled than the sedan. **Weak points:** Severe, constant pulling to the left into oncoming traffic; delayed engagement of the automatic transmission makes you a sitting duck at intersections; and sudden, unintended acceleration gives you unexpected, unwanted NASCAR thrills. *Camry:* Engine horsepower isn't top in its class; V6 engines require premium fuel; suspension may be a bit too soft for some; little steering feedback; lacks a telescoping steering wheel; no rear disc brakes on 4-cylinder-equipped models (except for on the high-end XLE); seats could use much more lumbar and thigh support; annoying windshield reflections at night; and complicated navigation system controls. The

The Toyota Camry.

$1,110 transport and PDI charges are unacceptably high. Also, an unusually large number of performance- and safety-related complaints registered by government safety investigators points the finger at Toyota's cost-cutting, de-contenting strategy adopted since 1997. *Solara:* Tricky entry and exit; trunk has a small opening and high sill; limited rear visibility. **New for 2006:** A new 5-speed automatic (Solara).

OVERVIEW: The Camry is available only as a four-door sedan—gone is the station wagon. The coupe and convertibles are sold under the Solara moniker (see below). Power is supplied by a peppy 2.4L 157-hp 4-cylinder engine, a 190-hp 3.0L V6, and a 225-hp 3.3L V6. These engines can be coupled to a 5-speed manual or a 5-speed automatic. The suspension features MacPherson struts that reduce suspension noise through the use of revised springs, shocks, and an anti-sway bar. The rear suspension is similarly constructed with the addition of dual lower control arms to increase stability and reduce highway wander. Control is further maintained through speed-sensing variable power steering. V6-equipped SE and XLE models get standard four-wheel disc brakes, while the LE and 4-cylinder-equipped Camrys get discs up front and rear drums (shame!).

There's also a nice array of safety features: Traction control is standard on all V6-equipped models; rear seats have shoulder belts for the middle passenger; low

TECHNICAL DATA

POWERTRAIN (FRONT-DRIVE)
Engines: 2.4L 4-cyl. (157 hp) • 3.0L V6 (190 hp) • 3.3L V6 (225 hp); Transmissions: 5-speed man. • 5-speed auto.

DIMENSION/CAPACITY (CAMRY)
Passengers: 2/3; Wheelbase: 107 in.; H: 58.7/L: 189/W: 71 in.; Headroom F/R: 3.0/3.5 in.; Legroom F/R: 41/28.5 in.; Cargo volume: 14.1 cu. ft.; Fuel tank: 70L/reg./prem.; Tow limit: 2,000 lb.; Load capacity: 900 lb.; Turning circle: 38 ft.; Weight: 3,280 lb.

beam lights are quite bright; headlights switch on and off automatically as conditions change; and the front airbags are a third-generation de-powered design.

Camry

Camrys have fallen behind in the standard equipment offered with all of its models, obviously a result of product de-contenting to keep prices down, or as I suspect, to keep profits high. For example, the lack of a telescoping steering wheel makes it more difficult for drivers to find a comfortable driving position. MacPherson strut suspension is no match for the Honda Accord's double-wishbone suspension at all four corners.

Solara

The Solara is small, but it's not cheap. Built in Cambridge, Ontario, a base model Solara costs $27,545, but put in the Sienna and Lexus RX 330's V6 power plant and you can expect to pay $12,000 more.

Introduced in the summer of 1998, the Solara is essentially a longer, lower, barebones, two-door coupe or convertible Camry with a sportier powertrain and suspension and a more stylish exterior. But don't let this put you off. Most new Toyota model offerings, like the Sienna, Avalon, and RAV4, are also Camry derivatives.

You have a choice of either a 4- or 6-cylinder power plant. Unfortunately, if you choose the V6, you also get a gimmicky rear spoiler and a headroom-robbing moon roof. Convertibles come with a standard automatic transmission. The stiff body structure and suspension, as well as tight steering, make for easy, sporty handling, with lots of road feel and few surprises.

COST ANALYSIS: If you can find a 2005 reduced by at least $2,500, buy it. Otherwise, get the identical 2006 model for $500–$900 more than last year's version (not counting rebates and other incentives). **Best alternatives:** Other cars worth considering are the Honda Accord, the Hyundai Elantra, and the Mazda6. **Options:** The built-in child safety seat ($150) is a nice feature. Stay away from the optional moon roof; it robs you of much-needed headroom and exposes you to a deafening wind roar, rattling, and leaks. **Rebates:** $3,000 rebates, plus low-interest financing. **Delivery/PDI:** $1,160. **Depreciation:** Slower than average. **Insurance cost:** Higher than average. **Parts supply/cost:** Parts are easily found and moderately priced. **Annual maintenance cost:** Less than average. **Warranty:** Bumper-to-bumper 3 years/60,000 km; powertrain 5 years/100,000 km; rust perforation 5 years/unlimited km. **Supplementary warranty:** Not needed. **Highway/city fuel economy:** 7.8–11.9L/100 km with 3.0L engine and automatic transmission.

Quality/Reliability/Safety

Pro: Child restraint system has user-friendly anchors for easy installation, and three-point seat belts are provided in all seating positions.

Con: Quality control: On a downward trend. **Reliability:** Once one of the most reliable cars on the market; however, 2005s already have 85 safety-related defects recorded. **Warranty performance:** Terrible. Toyota has fumbled the ball with at least three major safety problems and countless other performance glitches. How sad that our own citizens park their ethics when they are hired by an automaker. **Owner-reported problems:** Camry and Solara constantly pull you to the left, into oncoming traffic:

> I have a 2004 Toyota Camry [that I] purchased in April/04. Like many others, my car drifts to the left into other lanes. This is a major safety issue as this could result in accidents and injuries. The car will not drive straight on any type of road surface. From various readings, there is a problem with the springs. This problem has existed for several years now and Toyota has been ignoring this problem. Please force Toyota to fix this problem!

Brake squeal, squeak, and grind, even though pads and calipers are replaced repeatedly; rear disc brakes cut grooves into rotors; suspension failures; heat shield rattling; squealing side window operation; and body/accessories glitches. The Solara convertible produces excessive body flexing (common to most convertibles), resulting in a creaky top. The unusually large number of safety-related complaints raises concerns that Toyota's last Camry redesign has cheapened the product. **Service bulletin problems:** Vehicle pull or drift correction:

VEHICLE PULLS/DRIFTS TO THE LEFT

BULLETIN NO.: ST002–04   DATE: FEBRUARY 4, 2004

2004 AVALON AND 2004–2005 CAMRY AND SOLARA

OP Code	Description	Time
ST3007	Preliminary Check & Road Test	0.6
Combo A	Switch Front Tire/Wheel & Road Test	0.5
Combo B	Replace Front Coil Springs	1.4
Combo C	Check Front Wheel Alignment	1.2
Combo D	Adjust Front Wheel Alignment	0.7

This repair is covered under the Toyota Comprehensive Warranty. This warranty is in effect for 36 months or 36,000 miles [58,000 km], whichever occurs first, from the vehicle's in-service date.
Confirm problem symptoms.

A. With the customer accompanying you, drive the vehicle to confirm if the customer's complaint involves vehicle pulling or drifting to the left or steering wheel off center.

B. Decide if vehicle pulling/drifting is due to tires, alignment settings, or front springs. Switch the left and right front tires, if the tires are non-unidirectional.*(continued on following page)*

Symptom	Probable Cause	Corrective Action
Vehicle pull/drift eliminated	Tire conicity	Repair complete. Vehicle pull/drift caused by tire conicity.
Vehicle pull/drift direction is reversed	Tire conicity	Refer to TSB No. ST005–01 "Repair Manual Supplement: Vehicle Pulling to One Side."
No change in vehicle pull/drift condition	1. Alignment 2. Coil Spring	1. Measure alignment and adjust. 2. Vehicle pull/drift caused by coil spring.

NOTE: Warranty Claims for Repair Procedure No. 1, use OP Code ST3007 and Combo A. only.

Engine running lean; intake manifold noise; harsh 5–4 downshift with the automatic transmission; loose, rattling manual transmission shifter; whistling from driver's side rear window; sulfur dioxide odour; erratic airbag warning lamp activation; MIL warning light constantly comes on; and ECU updated calibration. **NHTSA safety complaints:** Fire ignited in rear wheelwell; starter caught on fire in the parking lot; under-hood fire (left side) while vehicle was parked overnight; fire ignited from underneath vehicle while driving; airbags fail to deploy; sudden acceleration accompanied by brake loss:

> While the driver's foot was on the brake pedal, vehicle suddenly accelerated uncontrollably; applied the brake pedal numerous times and the vehicle continued to accelerate.

> •

> Intermittently, after coming to a complete stop, the brake pedal will sink completely to the floor after a few seconds. This has been occurring since I bought the car brand new. Once the car reached about 5,000 miles [8,000 km], it would come to a complete stop, then lunge forward several feet, stop, make a moaning sound, then lunge forward again; all while my foot was still on the brake.

> •

> Vehicle hesitated then launched forward before accelerating. Vehicle was serviced by the dealership three times. Dealership indicated technically the vehicle was performing as it should, but there was a problem with the new drive-by-wire technology

Inadvertent airbag deployment; hole in the airbag panel; faulty cruise control caused vehicle to suddenly accelerate; loss of steering control:

> While driving, steering wheel came loose, and caused loss of vehicle control. At 537 miles [860 km], while making a right-hand turn and then a left turn, as driver attempted to straighten the vehicle. Steering wheel would not respond. Vehicle

crashed into a wall. Upon impact, airbags did not deploy. Passenger sustained a broken back, and arm. Driver sustained a broken ankle and bruises.

Excessive grinding noise and long stopping distances associated with ABS braking; pedal went to floor but no braking effect; ABS brakes suddenly locked up when coming to a gradual stop; defective rear brake drum. Many owners complain of poor brake pedal design: The arm that holds up brake pedal is interfering with the driver's foot—driver stated if consumer had a large-sized foot, it could easily get wedged and stuck on brake pedal. Front right axle broke; steering U-joint bearings fell out; vehicle tends to drift to the right or veer to the left at highway speeds; excessive steering wheel vibrations at speeds over 100 km/h; entire vehicle shakes excessively when cruising; vehicle's weight is poorly distributed, causing the front end to lift up when the vehicle speed exceeds 90 km/h; suspension bottoms out too easily, damaging the undercarriage; too-compliant shock absorbers make for a rough ride over uneven terrain; rear suspension noise at low speeds; automatic transmission slippage, hesitates and then surges forward, or suddenly shifts to a lower gear:

> 2005 Toyota Camry LE V6 gradually speeds up to about 25 mph [40 km/h]. When I stop short, my transmission shifts into Neutral, and it takes about three seconds to shift back into First. When it does, I get quite a jolt. Brought car back to dealer; they are saying it is normal.

Particularly poor shifting when in Overdrive; engine was running with transmission in Park position and the car rolled down a hill—the two small girls inside the car jumped out, but one was run over; car rolled backwards after driver put it into Park and removed ignition key; vehicle parked overnight had its rear window suddenly blow out; windshield distortion is a strain on the eyes; poorly designed headlights cause a blinding glare; backup lights are too dim; floor-mounted gear shift indicator is hard to read; turn signals fail to disengage; seat belts are too tight on either side and tighten up uncomfortably with the slightest movement; airbags are disabled even when a heavy adult sits in the seat; leaking suspension struts and strut rod failure; trunk lid may suddenly collapse; faulty driver window track; driver-side door latch sticks; rotten-egg exhaust smell; fuel tank makes a sloshing noise when three-quarters full; tire-pressure monitor gives false alerts; tire jack collapsed while changing tire; high rear end cuts rear visibility; turn signal volume is too low.

 ## Road Performance

Pro: Acceleration/torque: Better than average, with sufficient reserve torque for passing. Both the 4- and 6-cylinder power plants are fairly quiet and smooth running. This car shines on long drives, and for that you must have the better-performing 3.0L or torquier 3.3L V6. **Transmission:** Smooth-shifting automatic gearbox with a dual-mode feature that allows the driver to choose either a power or economy setting. **Routine handling:** Nimble and predictable handling.

Supple but steady ride on all but the worst roads. Noise, vibration, and harshness have been reduced considerably. **Emergency handling:** Very good. Minimal body roll and front-end plow. Responds well to sudden steering corrections. **Steering:** Quick to respond and predictable. **Braking:** Better-than-average.

Con: If you want lots of driver interaction while driving, get a Honda Accord; if you want comfort, get a Camry. Neither the 4-banger nor the V6 are high-performance engines, but the Camry doesn't pretend to be a high-performance car. The overly compliant suspension makes for a busy ride when passing over bumps, even for the more tightly sprung coupes. Little road feel with power steering.

CAMRY, SOLARA

List Price (very negotiable)   **Residual Values** (months)

	24	36	48	60
LE: $24,990 (18%)	$20,000	$18,000	$15,000	$13,000
LE V6: $27,475 (20%)	$22,500	$20,500	$17,500	$15,500
XLE V6: $33,345 (22%)	$25,500	$23,500	$21,500	$19,500
Solara SE: $27,645 (20%)	$22,000	$19,500	$16,500	$14,500

SAFETY FEATURES	STD.	OPT.	CRASHWORTHINESS		
Anti-lock brakes	✓	—	Head restraints F/R	4	3
Seat belt pretensioners F/R	✓	—	Solara	3	3
Side airbags	—	✓	Visibility F/R	5	1
Stability control	—	✓	Crash protection (front) D/P	5	5
Traction control	✓	✓	Crash protection (side) F/R	4	3
			Solara	5	5
			Crash protection (offset)	5	—
			Rollover	4	—

AVALON ★★★★

RATING: Above Average. A geezer-teaser that can turn deadly through delayed shifts and engine surging. **Strong points:** Excellent powertrain performance, handling, and ride; sportier handling than the Camry; a roomy interior with plenty of storage space; large doors make for easy front- and rear-seat access; comfortable seats; a quiet interior; exceptional reliability when compared with some of Toyota's other models; and a high resale value. **Weak points:** High freight/PDI charges; rear-corner blind spots; mushy brake pedal; severe pulling into oncoming traffic; a counterintuitive navigation system; trunk space compromised by intrusion of

trunk-lid hinges and wheel housing; and a bit fuel-thirsty. **New for 2006:** An optional dealer-installed towing package.

OVERVIEW: This five-passenger near-luxury four-door offers more value and reliability than do other cars in its class that cost thousands of dollars more. A front-engine, front-drive, mid-sized sedan based on a stretched Camry platform, the Avalon is similar in size to the Ford Taurus and bigger than the rear-drive Cressida it replaced. Yet, despite its generous interior space, the car has a relatively small profile.

The Avalon comes with a 280-hp 3.5L V6 power plant, coupled to a 5-speed electronically controlled automatic transaxle. Base models offer a nice array of standard comfort and convenience features, including a tilt/telescope steering wheel with audio and climate controls, plus a split folding rear seat with reclining backrests, AC, power windows, power door locks, cruise control, and an AM/FM cassette sound system. Safety features include standard ABS, front and rear head-protecting side airbags, a driver's knee airbag, and a three-point shoulder belt for the rear centre-seat passenger.

COST ANALYSIS: Look for an identical 2005 model, discounted by about 15 percent. **Best alternatives:** Other cars you may wish to look at: the Honda Accord V6, the Mazda6, and the Toyota Camry V6. **Options:** The engine-immobilizing anti-theft system and dealer-installed towing package are worthwhile items. Stay

TECHNICAL DATA

POWERTRAIN (FRONT-DRIVE)
Engine: 3.5L V6 (280 hp); Transmission: 5-speed auto./man.

DIMENSION/CAPACITY
Passengers: 2/3; Wheelbase: 111 in.; H: 58.5/L: 197.2/W: 72.8 in.; Cargo volume: 15.9 cu. ft.; Fuel tank: 70L/ regular; Headroom F/R: N/A; Legroom F/R: 41.7/40.1 in.; Tow limit: 2,000 lb.; Turning circle: 40 ft.; Weight: 3,490 lb.

away from the navigation control system; it's a pain to program. Sonar cruise control doesn't let other drivers know you may suddenly slow down. **Rebates:** $3,000+ on the 2005s, plus low-interest financing. **Delivery/PDI:** $1,160. **Depreciation:** Slower than average. **Insurance cost:** Higher than average. **Parts supply/cost:** Parts are relatively inexpensive and easily found. **Annual maintenance cost:** Less than average. **Warranty:** Bumper-to-bumper 3 years/60,000 km; powertrain 5 years/100,000 km; rust perforation 5 years/unlimited km. **Supplementary warranty:** Not needed. **Highway/city fuel economy:** 7.4–11L/100 km.

Quality/Reliability/Safety

Pro: Quality control: Superior quality mechanical and body components, except for powertrain shifting. **Reliability:** Interestingly, there are fewer reliability or durability problems reported than with Toyota's Camry, Corolla, or Sienna. **Warranty performance:** Disappointing. Toyota plays the "blame game" in warranty disputes, often telling owners that the cars' deficiencies are "normal" or blaming owner driving or poor maintenance for breakdowns. You can easily confirm this by searching for "engine sludge" on the Internet. Fortunately, the Avalon is so well built that these kinds of disputes are rare with Avalon owners.

Con: Owner-reported problems: Engine and transmission shift delay and sudden acceleration remains a serious problem; suspension defects (left rear subframe and bushings); brakes function erratically, appear to be automatically applied, and drag the vehicle. Reports of excessive wind noise intruding into the passenger compartment, water leaks through the front door and trunk lid, and some fragile trim items. **Service bulletin problems:** Quality issue with the parking brake assembly; remedy for a severe pull to the left. **NHTSA safety complaints:** Interestingly, the 2005 redesign hasn't caused an upsurge in consumer safety-related complaints. Toyota's infamous powertrain shifting hesitation and surging (found throughout its lineup), however, continues to be a problem for the fifth year in a row:

I drive the car and make starts and stops several times without issue, then at the next stop I start out and the car seems to shift immediately to a higher gear and I have to hit the brakes to avoid hitting other cars. Other times, I will press the gas pedal and have no response for several seconds before the car takes off. It makes it very difficult to merge into traffic as I never know when the car will go or not go. There are yet other times that it will start off normally and then seem to get stuck in what seems like second gear and rev for several seconds before shifting. Previously, I have pressed the gas pedal and ended up lurching forward when the shift finally occurred.

•

I just purchased a 2005 Toyota Avalon Limited. I experience terrible transmission hesitation/slippage. It is getting dangerous when I have to enter highway ramp because of transmission hesitation. When I coast at low speed, for example, I notice a red traffic light ahead and take my foot off the gas. The car then continues forward as if in gear and after a period of time it feels as if the transmission shifts to Neutral, the rpm drop to below 1000. Then the traffic light changes when my speed is about 5–10 mph [8–16 km/h] and I slowly depress the accelerator. The engine rpm increase about 300–500 rpm but there is no acceleration. Then the transmission gets the message and we start to accelerate.

•

The real safety issue occurred yesterday, when I was the first car waiting at a train crossing for about three minutes while the train was passing. After it passed, as I was crossing the tracks, it took about 15 seconds for the car to move, again stuck and reving in low gear! I have almost been rear-ended on freeway entrances, red lights turning to green, and at numerous other times, and now on train tracks!

Sudden acceleration caused by a stuck throttle; activation of the optional sonar cruise control could also cause rear-end accidents:

I have the sonar cruise control, which works very well. [The] problem [is that] when my car slows down suddenly because of the car in front, there is no warning for the car behind me. Toyota was notified of this problem and told me not to use the sonar in heavily travelled roads. That is no solution. There should be a fix to make the brake lights go on when the car is slowed down by the sonar.

2004 models and earlier: Rear wheel seized while driving at 70 km/h; sudden acceleration with no brakes; airbag deployed for no reason; front airbags failed to deploy; side airbags failed to deploy in a side impact; airbag warning light comes on constantly; transmission failure; transmission failed to hold vehicle on a hill while waiting for a red light; fuel dampener and fuel pump failure caused fuel leak and fumes to enter interior; Bridgestone tire failure; upper steering knuckle broke; steering wheel turned to the right, yet car failed to respond; dashboard lighting reflects into the windshield; and the dashboard gear display is hard to read at night.

 Road Performance

Pro: Acceleration/torque: Brisk acceleration with the smooth, powerful, and quiet V6 engine; and there's plenty of torque for passing and traversing hilly terrain (0–100 km/h: 7.8 seconds). **Transmission:** The electronically controlled 5-speed automatic transmission is well matched to its power without sacrificing performance. In fact, the powertrain set-up is one of the smoothest, best-integrated combinations available. **Emergency handling:** Slow, but sure-footed. **Routine handling:** Better-than-average handling, thanks to the stiffened suspension. Ride quality is flawless, providing living-room comfort on virtually any kind of road. **Braking:** Disc/disc; better than average (100–0 km/h: 40 m).

Con: Steering: Power steering is over-assisted at all speeds, and the car has a tendency to oversteer. Tends to plow ahead when cornering at high speed and nosedive in abrupt stops. Navigation system is distractingly complicated to program; doesn't seem worth the effort. A bit of wind noise around the doors.

AVALON

List Price (very negotiable)	**Residual Values** (months)			
	24	**36**	**48**	**60**
Avalon XLS: $38,900 (25%)	$32,000	$26,000	$22,000	$17,000

SAFETY FEATURES	**STD.**	**OPT.**
Anti-lock brakes	✓	—
Seat belt pretensioners F/R	✓	—
Side airbags	✓	—
Stability control	✓	—
Traction control	✓	—

CRASHWORTHINESS		
Head restraints F/R	3	3
Visibility F/R	5	2
Crash protection (front) D/P	5	5
Crash protection (side) F/R	5	5
Crash protection (offset)	5	—
Rollover	4	—

CELICA (2005) ★★★★★

RATING: Recommended. One of Toyota's most dependable cars—I hate to see it phased out this year. **Strong points:** Exceptionally well-matched engine and transmission; great road holding and handling; comfortable front seating; impressive reliability; few performance- or safety-related owner complaints; reasonably priced GT; and a high resale value. **Weak points:** High freight/PDI charges; automatic transmission compromises GT engine performance; difficult rear-seat access, rear seating not for three adults, and rear bucket seats aren't suitable for long drives. Pricey GT-S; 180-hp engine is noisy at high rpm. **New for 2006:** Closing out a 33-year run in Canada.

OVERVIEW: The front-drive Celica is a four-passenger, two-door hatchback that offers benchmark reliability, good handling, and great fuel economy in an attractive sports-car package. The GT and GT-S have a firm suspension, well-equipped interior, ABS brakes, and a more sporting feel than do other versions. All handle competently and provide the kind of sporting performance expected from a car of this class. The extra performance in the higher-line versions does come at a price, but this isn't a problem given the high resale value and excellent reliability for which Celicas are known. Overall, it's one of the best choices in the sporty car field.

TECHNICAL DATA
POWERTRAIN (FRONT-DRIVE)
Engines: 1.8L 4-cyl. (140 hp) • 1.8L 4-cyl. (180 hp); Transmissions: 5-speed man. • 6-speed man. • 4-speed auto.
DIMENSION/CAPACITY
Passengers: 2/2; Wheelbase: 102 in.; H: 46/L: 170/W: 68 in.; Headroom F/R: 2.0/N/A; Legroom F/R: 41.5/24 in.; Cargo volume: 12.9 cu. ft.; Fuel tank: 55L/premium; Tow limit: 2,000 lb.; Load capacity: 725 lb.; Turning circle: 36 ft.; Weight: 2,570 lb.

COST ANALYSIS: Buy the 2005 model; there is no 2006 version. For driving pleasure and performance, the GT is your best value. There's a generous array of standard equipment, performance is excellent, and it looks much like the more expensive GT-S. **Best alternatives:** If you miss the GT version, try the Ford Mustang or the Mazda Miata. GT-S rivals include the Acura Integra GS-R and the BMW 323Ci. **Options:** The Celica comes fairly well equipped. **Rebates:** Not likely. **Delivery/PDI:** $1,160. **Depreciation:** Slower than average. **Insurance cost:** Higher than average. **Parts supply/cost:** Parts are relatively inexpensive and easily found. **Annual maintenance cost:** Less than average. **Warranty:** Bumper-to-bumper 3 years/60,000 km; powertrain 5 years/100,000 km; rust perforation 5 years/ unlimited km. **Supplementary warranty:** Not necessary. **Highway/city fuel economy:** 7.3–10.2L/100 km with an automatic transmission.

Quality/Reliability/Safety

Pro: Quality Control: Once the best among automakers, but has declined of late. **Reliability:** The Celica uses the same mechanical components that are employed on Toyota's other models, and this explains why reliability and durability fluctuate so much. **Warranty performance:** Celica warranty claims have been handled fairly, with only a few exceptions. **Safety:** Safety features include dual front airbags, height-adjustable front head restraints, impact-absorbing materials on the roof and doors, three-point seat belts with pretensioners and force limiters for front passengers, three-point seat belts for rear passengers, and rear child seat anchors. When the airbags are deployed, a sensor disconnects the fuel pump to minimize the risk of fire.

Con: Owner-reported problems: The front brakes are troublesome; some audio systems and trim items have also been failure-prone. **Service bulletin problems:** Troubleshooting tips for a sulfur rotten-egg exhaust odour. **NHTSA safety complaints:** Fuel tank leaks and hood latch failure. Rear head restraints aren't available and the audible reverse alarm isn't Toyota's brightest idea. Audible only inside the vehicle, it adds a forklift cachet to your Celica. For info on disabling this feature, log onto *www.celica.net*, an excellent site for technical advice and owners' unbiased reviews.

Road Performance

Pro: Emergency handling: Better than average. **Steering:** Responsive, predictable power steering also transmits plenty of road feel. **Acceleration/torque:** Both the 140- and 180-hp variants of the 1.8L provide plenty of high-performance thrills. GT engine has more torque at lower rpm than the GT-S, which only delivers sporty performance after hitting 6000 rpm. **Transmission:** Standard 5-speed manual transmission has easy throws and light clutch action. The GT-S' E-shift automatic transmission is very user-friendly, and shifting times are reasonably quick. **Routine handling:** Nimble and predictable handling in all conditions. Sportier handling on GT and GT-S models makes for a firm but not uncomfortable ride. **Braking:** Excellent performance (100–0 km/h: 37 m).

Con: Automatic transmission saps GT's engine performance. Suspension may be too firm for some.

CELICA

List Price (very negotiable)

	Residual Values (months)			
	24	**36**	**48**	**60**
Liftback GT: $25,000 (20%)	$19,000	$17,000	$14,000	$11,000
GT-S: $34,230 (22%)	$26,000	$23,000	$20,000	$16,000

SAFETY FEATURES	STD.	OPT.	CRASHWORTHINESS		
Anti-lock brakes	✓	✓	Head restraints F/R	5	5
Seat belt pretensioners F/R	✓	—	Visibility F/R	5	5
Side airbags	—	✓	Convertible	5	2
			Crash protection (front) D/P	4	4
			Crash protection (side) F/R	3	—
			Rollover	5	—

RATING: Above Average. There has been a resurgence of safety-related defects since the 2004 model was redesigned; however, the comfort, performance, and convenience features make it an above average buy in its class—almost as good as the Honda Odyssey. **Strong points:** Smooth powertrain (most of the time); a comfortable, stable ride; plenty of standard safety, performance, and convenience features; a fourth door; and a good amount of passenger and cargo room. **Weak points:** Unacceptably high freight and PDI charges ($1,310); V6 performance compromised by AC and automatic transmission power drain; lacks the trailer-towing brawn of rear-drive minivans; and towing capability may be much less than advertised, says this *Lemon-Aid* reader:

TECHNICAL DATA

POWERTRAIN (FRONT-DRIVE/AWD)
Engine: 3.3L V6 (230 hp); Transmission: 5-speed auto.

DIMENSION/CAPACITY (LE)
Passengers: 2/2/3; 2/3/3; Wheelbase: 119 in.; H: 69/L: 200/W: 77 in.; Headroom F/R1/R2: 3.5/4.0/2.5 in.; Legroom F/R1/R2: 40.5/31.5/25 in.; Cargo volume: 70.5 cu. ft.; Fuel tank: 79L/regular; Tow limit: 3,500 lb.; Load capacity: 1,280 lb.; Turning circle: 39 ft.; Weight: 4,365 lb.

> We have just leased a 2004 Toyota Sienna CE. Imagine our surprise when we discovered within the owner's manual a "Caution" stating that one must not exceed 72 km/h (45 mph) while towing a trailer. This limit is not stated in the promotional literature we were provided, or on the *Toyota.ca* website, or in any trailer-towing rating guide. This limit was also not mentioned at any time during our purchase negotiations. Alarmingly, Toyota defines a "Caution" as a "warning against anything which may cause injury to people if the warning is ignored." As it turns out the dealer was not aware of this speed limit.

Less efficient rear drum brakes; rear visibility obstructed by middle roof pillars and rear head restraints; low rear head-restraint effectiveness rating; the wide centre pillars make for difficult access to the middle seats; removing middle- and third-row seats is a two-person chore; radio speakers are set too low for acceptable acoustics; an unusually large number of body rattles and safety-related complaints; mediocre braking; third-row head restraints are mounted too low; and expensive options. **New for 2006:** A standard roof rack.

OVERVIEW: Toyota built the Sienna for comfort and convenience. If you want more performance and driver interaction—get a Honda Odyssey. Sienna's 230-hp 3.3L V6 turns in respectable acceleration times under nine seconds, almost as good as the Honda Odyssey. Handling is also very carlike, but again, not as agile as Honda's minivan. You will find a spacious interior, however, that accommodates up to eight passengers. All models come with standard four-wheel disc brakes and all-wheel drive is available.

Sienna offers dual power-sliding doors with optional remote controls, and its interior is well detailed. The third-row seats split and fold away, head restraints don't have to be removed when the seats are stored, and second-row bucket seats are easily converted to bench seats. Other nice interior features are a telescoping steering wheel and power-assisted second-row windows.

COST ANALYSIS: Toyota is keeping most prices near last year's levels, which isn't surprising, since the 2006 models are essentially identical, warmed-over 2005s. Base models start at $30,800 for the 7-passenger CE; the CE AWD sells for $36,700; prices for the LE start at $36,255; and the LE AWD fetches $40,665. **Best alternatives:** Other minivans worth considering are the Honda Odyssey and the Mazda MPV. Mazda minivans are catching up to Honda and Toyota in performance and reliability, while the less reliable and old-tech Ford and GM models are hardly in the running. Chrysler's extensive 7-year powertrain warranty, generous rebates, and innovative styling have kept its minivans on life-support for the past several years. Why not the Nissan Quest? The redesigned Quest has also been seriously glitch-afflicted and, like the Sienna, there's no assurance this year's model will be much improved. **Options:** Power windows and door locks, rear heater, and AC unit. Be wary of the power-sliding door. As with the Odyssey and GM minivans, these doors can injure children and pose unnecessary risks to other occupants. Go for Michelin or Pirelli original equipment tires. Don't buy Bridgestone or Dunlop run-flat tires:

> I have a 2005 Toyota Sienna XLE AWD which is equipped with Dunlop run-flat tires. This car was used for one year and had mileage of 17,800 [28,600 km] when we noticed that all four tires had the tread barrier exposed. It was exposed only on the outside and inside edges of the tires. The car was handling extremely strangely and was starting to wander on turns.... [T]he car started to wander into an oncoming traffic lane when changing to the left lane of a four-lane road. I contacted Toyota, only to be told that there was no mileage guarantee on the tires and they were $250/piece to replace. When told that they nearly caused [a] head-on accident they quickly offered to replace two of them free and then I could repair the others. They still would not guarantee the tires for any future mileage. I have since gone on the web to find that

these tires have been reported by a huge number of the owners to have a similar problem. These tires do not wear correctly, they wear much too fast, and the Toyota service rep at my dealership told me that we should run the tires at a higher-than-recommended tire pressure

Adds A.H., a *Lemon-Aid* correspondent from British Columbia:

I have had a very frustrating experience with the run-flat tires on my 2004 Toyota Sienna AWD, which does not have a spare tire. I was travelling from Calgary to Quadra Island in British Columbia, and got a puncture near Kamloops. I returned to the Kamloops dealer and requested that the punctured tire be replaced. They had to order the tire from Toronto. The tire had to be shipped to Delta near Vancouver and then re-shipped to Kamloops. It took about eight days for the tire to reach Kamloops.

After waiting for about five days in Kamloops, I requested that all four run-flat tires be replaced with ordinary Goodyear Eagles. These tires cost $700.

My vacation was ruined since I had to pay for accommodation in Kamloops as well as Quadra Island while waiting for the run-flat tires to arrive. As a result, I spent about $800 on accommodation in Kamloops.

In summary, I spent $1,500 to repair a punctured tire. It was the most expensive puncture I have ever had.

I strongly recommend that Toyota take the following action:

- Advise all owners of 2004 Siennas (with AWD) to carry a spare tire inside the van.
- Put pressure on the manufacturer of run-flat tires to make them widely available in Canada. They should be available within a day from small cities such as Kamloops.
- Recommend an alternative ordinary tire with the same performance characteristics as the run-flat tires.

Rebates: $2,000 in early 2006. **Delivery/PDI:** $1,310. **Depreciation:** Much slower than average. **Insurance cost:** A bit higher than average. **Parts supply/cost:** Excellent supply of reasonably priced parts taken from the Camry parts bin. Fuel tank components needed for recall repairs are often back-ordered, and automatic transmission torque converters may be in short supply because of Toyota's special-replacement extended warranty. Run-flat tire replacements are expensive and hard to find. **Annual maintenance cost:** Lower than average, but much higher than the 2003 and earlier Siennas. **Warranty:** Bumper-to-bumper 3 years/60,000 km; powertrain 5 years/100,000 km; rust perforation 5 years/unlimited km. **Supplementary warranty:** An extended warranty isn't really necessary. **Highway/city fuel economy:** 8.1–12.2L/100 km.

Quality/Reliability/Safety

Pro: Reliability: Better than the Detroit average, but when was that ever a compliment?

Con: Warranty performance: Infuriating. Toyota's Canadian maladministration has remained hidden because sales continue to be strong. This has allowed the company to get away with dumb moves like the Toyota Access no-haggle sales program (some called it price-fixing) that resulted in a federal probe and Toyota Canada's $2 million charitable "gift" settlement. Owners are also getting tired of being blamed for Toyota's factory defects, which include engine sludge, transmission and engine malfunctions that result in delayed shifts and then sudden acceleration, predatory sliding doors, and run-flat tire problems. Reliability concerns include stalling when the AC engages; electrical shorts; excessive brake noise; sliding door defects; premature tire wear, and various other body glitches, including excessive creaks and rattles and paint that's easily chipped. **Owner-reported problems:** Premature brake wear and noisy brakes; engine replacement because of sludge buildup; automatic transmission failures; distracting windshield reflections and distorted windshields; power-sliding door malfunctions; driver's side mirror vibrates excessively; interior squeaks and rattles; and some premature rusting.

Service bulletin problems: *All years:* Sliding door hazards, malfunctions, and noise are a veritable plague affecting all model years and generating a ton of service bulletins; owner feedback confirms that front brake pads and discs will be replaced under Toyota's "goodwill" policy if they wear out before 2 years/40,000 km; loose, poorly fitted trim panels (TSB # BO017-03 REVISED September 9, 2003). Rusting at the base of the two front doors will be repaired at no cost, usually with a courtesy car included. According to *www.siennaclub.org,* the proper fix is: Repaint inside of doors (presumably after removing paint and rust), cover with 3M film, and replace and coat inside seals with silicone grease. *2005 models:* No-start in sub-freezing temperatures; correction for the AWD transmission shifter that may become progressively harder to move; secret warranty (Limited Service Campaign) to replace power steering fluid return hoses free of charge; ECM recalibration for shifting enhancement; rear wiper improvement; fuel injector ticking noise at idle; AC compressor durability improvement and fix for AC blower motor noise; exhaust system squeak or creak. **NHTSA safety complaints:** Sudden acceleration when parking or shifting to Reverse; complete brake loss; many reports that the front and side airbags failed to deploy:

> Van was "t-boned" on passenger side by large pickup truck probably going 45 mph [70 km/h] or so. Truck hit front side panel and passenger door. Estimated damage at this point over $14,000. Passenger had to be extricated by Jaws of Life and suffered fractured pelvis and face lacerations. Neither the side curtain airbag nor side seat airbag went off.

Airbag deployed for no reason while vehicle was underway; hesitation when accelerating, then sudden acceleration; laser-controlled cruise control jerks back to former speed when the way seems clear; gear shift lever can be accidently knocked from Fourth gear to Reverse; brake pedal stiffens intermittently; run-flat tires don't signal driver when they are damaged and may catch fire:

> 2005 Toyota Sienna has Bridgestone run-flat tires and the back right passenger tire went flat then smoked and caught fire.

When the rear windows are down, the door will not stay open; sliding doors fail to latch when they are opened; sliding door continues closing even if a child or pet is in its way (similar to complaints on previous model year Siennas); automatic interior light shut-off fails intermittently, draining the battery; rear heater core leaks coolant.

Road Performance

Pro: Emergency handling: No problem. Sienna can change course abruptly without wallowing or losing directional stability. **Steering:** Excellent steering feel and quick response. **Acceleration/torque:** Toyota's V6 handles most driving chores effortlessly without noise or vibration (0–100 km/h: 10.2 seconds). **Transmission:** Quiet and smooth shifting. **Routine handling:** A pleasure. Handling is crisp and effortless. **Braking:** Average.

Con: Base engine struggles a bit when carrying a full load uphill.

SIENNA

List Price (very negotiable)	**Residual Values** (months)			
	24	**36**	**48**	**60**
CE: $30,800 (21%)	$23,500	$20,500	$16,000	$13,000
LE: $36,255 (22%)	$26,000	$24,000	$19,000	$16,000
CE AWD: $36,700 (22%)	$28,000	$25,000	$21,000	$18,000

SAFETY FEATURES

	STD.	OPT.
Anti-lock brakes (4W)	✓	—
Seat belt pretensioners F/R	✓	—
Side airbags	✓	✓
Traction control	✓	✓

CRASHWORTHINESS

Head restraints F/R	[1]	[1]
Visibility F/R	[5]	[3]
Crash protection (front) D/P	[4]	[5]
Crash protection (side) F/R	[5]	[5]
Crash protection (offset)	[5]	—
Rollover	[4]	—

EUROPEAN VEHICLES

Smart Cars Lionized

Small cars driving through a safari park in Merseyside, England, have been chased by confused lions who think they are prey. Staff at Knowsley Safari Park are monitoring smaller vehicles, including Smart cars and Mini Coopers, after the lions started paying special interest.

David Ross, park manager, told the BBC News website that a group of lionesses chased after one Smart car after being confused by its compact appearance.

"With Smart cars and sometimes Mini Coopers, the lions definitely raise an eyebrow. It sparks their interest because of their size. We had an incident of two ladies in a car being chased by lionesses."

"It must have been quite frightening for them, but we always have staff in a vehicle by the lion enclosure to deal with any problems."

BBC NEWS, UK EDITION
AUGUST 16, 2005

Mercedes Quality Declines

For years, Mercedes has cut costs in an effort to hold the line on prices. Materials that look and feel relatively cheap have been showing up even in expensive models like the S-Class sedan, but have been especially notable in the M-Class sport utility. At the same time, the revered Mercedes brand has been dropping in quality and durability rankings.

One such survey by TUV, a German auto-inspection and research association...ranked half a dozen Toyotas ahead of the highest-rated Mercedes, the SLK....

NEW YORK TIMES
FEBRUARY 24, 2002

Sell the Sizzle, Forget the Costs

European vehicles are generally a driver's delight and a frugal consumer's nightmare. They're noted for a high level of performance combined with a full array of standard comfort and convenience features. They're fun to drive, well appointed, and attractively styled. But they're also unreliable, overpriced, and a pain in the butt to service.

Many of the European vehicles we see today will be gone tomorrow. They'll bite the dust quickly or disappear through attrition after mergers with other companies. Heck, the latest owner surveys show that even Europeans don't want to buy European cars.

Why the decline in the popularity of European cars? Firstly, they can't withstand performance and durability comparisons with cheaper Asian competitors. This has been a serious VW shortcoming for years. Secondly, when times get tough, European automakers get out of town. Remember Aro, Dacia, Fiat, Peugeot, Renault, Skoda, and Yugo? And finally, they aren't that dependable and tend to be poorly serviced, with maintenance bills that rival the costs of a week at Cannes. Shoppers understandably balk at these outrageously high prices, and European automakers respond by adding non-essential, problem-prone gadgets that drive up costs even more. In effect, they are selling the sizzle because the steak is bad.

Writes British independent automotive journalist Robert Farago, on his website The Truth About Cars (*www.robertfarago.com/truth*):

> Once upon a time, a company called Mercedes-Benz built luxury cars. Not Elk aversive city runabouts [an allusion to the Smart car]. Not German taxis. Not teeny tiny hairdressers' playthings. And definitely not off-roaders.... In the process, the Mercedes brand lost its reputation for quality and exclusivity. In fact, the brand has become so devalued that Mercedes themselves abandoned it, reviving the Nazi-friendly Maybach marque for its top-of-the-range limo. Now that Mercedes has morphed with Chrysler, the company is busy proving that the average of something good and something bad is something mediocre.

You won't read this kind of straight reporting from the cowering North American motoring press as they fawn over any new techno-gadget-laden vehicle hailing from England, Germany, or Sweden. It's easy for them; they get their cars and press junkets for free.

Some European automakers, unable to hide the lousy quality of their vehicles, abandoned the U.S. and Canadian markets altogether, while others are barely hanging on. Vauxhall, Fiat (now hoping to be acquired by dummy GM), Renault, and Peugeot were the first to turn tail, while Jaguar (more Taurus bull than Jaguar cat), Saab (now sitting on GM's truck chassis and about to be relocated to Germany), and Ford's Land Rover landmine continue to struggle with losses that have drained their cash reserves for years. Ford's Volvo division is lucky—it has managed to eke out a small profit, but sales are still iffy.

Buyers aren't falling for the car ads' appeal to snobbery. They are still wary of European automakers' reputation for poor quality, high parts and servicing costs, and weak dealer networks. And they have independent data to support their misgivings. One MIT study concluded over a decade ago that European automakers built poor-quality vehicles and then, much like the Detroit Big Three, attempted to fix their mistakes at the end of the assembly line. As one reviewer of *The Machine That Changed the World*, by James P. Womack, Daniel T. Jones, and Daniel Roos (HarperCollins, November 1991), wrote:

> This study of the world automotive industry by a group of MIT academics reaches the radical conclusion that the much-vaunted Mercedes technicians are actually a throwback to the pre-industrial age, while Toyota is far ahead in costs and quality by building the automobiles correctly the first time.

Canadian drivers have their own examples of spotty European-built quality. Here's what one diesel Jetta owner wrote:

> Phil: I have a 2000 VW Jetta TDI. It has 125,000 km on it and has a long list of problems. I have printed the words "LEMON @ 125k" on the back window with the brightest yellow paint I could find. I have had about six people with Jettas or [who] had friends with Jettas stop and talk to me. I also found a website with a chat group about VWs. There seems to be a problem with either the airflow meter or some sort of sensor in the airflow. It seems to happen at the 100,000-km mark, give or take 20,000 km. Anyways, the airflow metre is a $500 part, plus installation. This problem results in a huge loss of power. On long inclines, my car cannot reach 100 km/h. If I happen to be going faster than that, my car will lose speed in a hurry.
>
> I sat outside the dealership a few Saturdays ago. With my car painted up, it took all of 10 minutes for the sales and service managers to come out. They asked me what was wrong with the car and I started my list: power-steering rack was gone, ABS system gone, car loses power going up hills. The service manager interrupted at that point, saying it was an airflow sensor. (How about that? Didn't even look at the car and he knew what it was.) I didn't get to finish my list, mind you.

J.L.

Lemon-Aid readers who own pricey European imports invariably tell me of nightmarish electrical glitches that run the gamut from the annoying to the life-threatening. A few years ago, for example, Mercedes had to repurchase 2,000 E-Class sedans from U.S. owners because of problems with the vehicle's "COMAND" (cockpit management and data system) feature. The system, which integrates the phone and navigation and entertainment systems, worked sporadically and, in some cases, short-circuited other systems and drained the battery.

Other problems noted by owners include premature brake wear and excessive brake noise, AC malfunctions, faulty computer modules leading to erratic shifting, poor driveability, hard starts, and frequent stalling. Interestingly, although Ladas were low-quality Soviet imports, their deficiencies pale in comparison to what I've seen coming out of the European luxury corral. Maybe that's the logic behind GM's co-venture with Lada to market a Cavalier-Lada 4×4 to European consumers: payback for all of those European lemons shipped to North America over the past four decades.

Engine Sludge

What do Audi, Chrysler, Mercedes, Toyota, and VW have in common? Engine sludge—and a tendency to blame owners for the ruinous effect of this problem, which is caused by cheapened engines.

Mercedes recently settled a "sludge" class action for $32 million that affects many vehicles made from 1997 through 2004. Toyota refuses to give figures for their payout, except to admit the problem may afflict up to 3.3 million Toyotas. And Audi, Chrysler, and VW have switched over to "cover your butt" mode, characterized by such inanities as "owners don't change their oil often enough," "a special oil must be used," "show us your receipts," and "okay, we'll process claims on a case-by-case basis."

No doubt these automakers will eventually do the right thing and extend their warranties for this problem as Mercedes and Toyota have done, but not before being hauled into court, kicking and screaming over "frivolous lawsuits" and "owner responsibility." These same manufacturers have assured *Lemon-Aid* that their sludge problems are history; however, there's no way for owners to confirm this. So keep your fingers crossed, and keep the local small claims court address written on a notepad.

Service with a Shrug

Have you visited a European automaker's dealership lately? Although poor servicing is usually more acute with vehicles that are new on the market, it has long been the Achilles' heel of European importers. Owners give them low ratings for mishandling complaints, inadequately training service representatives, and hiring an insufficient number of mechanics—not to mention for the abrasive, arrogant attitude typified by some automakers and dealers who bully customers because they have a virtual monopoly on sales and servicing in their region. Look at their dealer networks and you'll see that most European automakers are crowded in Ontario and on the West Coast, leaving their customers in Eastern and Western Canada to fend for themselves. This makes their chances of finding someone to do competent repairs about as likely as those of getting Bloc Québécois leader Gilles Duceppe to vote Liberal.

In light of all their shortcomings, why are some European vehicles so popular? Basically, because their well-heeled buyers have more bucks than brains. As I said before, these cars look so good and make driving so much fun and so comfortable that you quickly forget about Franz, Ingmar, and Luigi waiting in the service bay for you to top off their Canada Pension Plan.

Audi

Saddled in the early '80s with a reputation for poor-quality cars that would suddenly accelerate out of control, Audi fought back and staged a spectacular comeback with well-built, moderately priced front-drive and AWD Quattro sedans and wagons. Through an expanded lineup of sedans, coupes, and a Cabriolet, Audi has gained a reputation for making sure-footed all-wheel-drive luxury cars that are loaded with lots of high-tech bells and whistles.

The Audi TT.

As with most European makes, Audis excel in comfort and performance. But servicing and warranty support remain problematic, especially now that VW/Audi has closed down its Canadian headquarters and runs its Canadian operations from the U.S. and Germany. This absence of a regional presence delayed the settlement of the automaker's ignition-coil problems (chronic no-starts and stalling) several years ago, and will certainly make it harder to resolve engine sludge claims. The fact that Audi only warrants the powertrain up to 4 years or 80,000 kilometres is far from reassuring.

The 2006 model lineup is highlighted by a redesigned A6 and A8. The A3, a five-door hatchback that is smaller than the A4, arrived in May and is sold as a 2006. Powered by a 250-hp 3.2L V6 and AWD, its primary competitors are the Mini Cooper, the Saab 9-2X, and the Volvo S40.

Audi is my choice for the top European luxury and sports car brand. Its cars provide a fun driving experience without the fear that your wallet will be emptied by outrageous service charges and recurring product failings—as long as you watch those oil changes and electrical shorts.

RATING: Not Recommended during its first year on the market. **Strong points:** Depreciation will likely be much slower than average. The car's a superb highway performer, thanks to its powerful and smooth-running engine and transmission. Handling is crisp, steering is accurate, and cornering is accomplished with minimal body roll. Lots of safety, performance, and convenience features; and superior fit and finish. **Weak points:** Fairly expensive for an entry-level Audi hatchback; most vehicles will sell for their full price because of their popularity; premium gas is required; and insurance premiums are predicted to be higher than average. Judging by past Audi launches, the A3 will have many factory problems in its first year. Most of the first-year deficiencies will relate to the electrical system, powertrain, brakes, and accessories. No crashworthiness data.

OVERVIEW: Based on this year's redesigned Volkswagen Golf, the A3 is Audi's latest entry-level compact 4-door hatchback. It's a well-appointed, generously powered front-drive that arrived last May and sells for $33,650 for the base 2.0T and $36,500 for the top-of-the-line 2.0T Wagon. There is plenty of power available with the 2.0L turbocharged 4-cylinder engine's 200 horses, coupled to either a 6-speed manu-matic or a 6-speed manual transmission. An all-wheel-drive version equipped with a powerful 250-hp 3.2L V6 and a sequential manual transmission that also shifts automatically will arrive in mid-2006.

All models come fully equipped with anti-lock four-wheel disc brakes, anti-skid/traction control, 17-inch alloy wheels, automatic climate control, and a split folding rear seat. Front and rear seat belt pretensioners and front torso side airbags and head-protecting curtain side airbags for both seating rows ensure occupant crash protection.

Audi rates the A3 as capable of carrying five passengers; however, the three back-seat passengers will find it tight. Furthermore, torso-protecting back-seat side airbags are optional. Premium fuel is required.

COST ANALYSIS: Wait at least six months for the price to come down and factory-related defects to be corrected. **Best alternatives:** You may also wish to consider the Acura TSX and the BMW 3 Series. **Rebates:** Not likely, though prices will likely soften in late summer. **Delivery/PDI:** $1,300. **Depreciation:** Predicted to be very slow. Audi values no longer nosedive when the base warranty expires. **Insurance cost:** Higher than average. **Parts supply/cost:** Shouldn't be a problem long-term because parts are shared with the VW Golf and Jetta. Forget about saving money by getting parts from an independent supplier; they carry few Audi parts. **Annual maintenance cost:** Predicted to be slightly higher than average. **Warranty:** Bumper-to-bumper 4 years/80,000 km; powertrain 4 years/80,000 km; rust perforation 10 years/unlimited km. **Supplementary warranty:** Don't leave the dealership without it. **Highway/city fuel economy:** N/A.

A4, S4, RS4 ★★★★

The Audi A4.

RATING: Above Average. **Strong points:** Loaded with safety, performance, and convenience features; optional AWD; powerful and smooth-running base engine; comfortable ride; works exceptionally well with the continuously variable transmission (CVT), although it's not available with AWD Quattro models; exceptional handling; lots of cargo room (wagon); front and rear seat belt pretensioners; and impressive build quality and attention to detail. **Weak points:** Not as fast as its rivals; ride is stiff at low speeds; quite limited rear seatroom where the front seatbacks continually press against rear occupants' knees; climate controls mounted too low; rear centre head restraint is mounted too low; obstructed rear visibility owing to the high rear deck; some tire drumming and engine noise. **New for 2006:** Redesigned from the ground up. These models have a variety of engine and body configurations that include a turbocharged 4-cylinder, a V6, and a powerful V8, housed in either a four-door sedan or four-door wagon. The A4 Quattro gets a 6-speed manual transmission and the 3.2 front-drive sedans will henceforth use a CVT. Early in 2006, we will see the arrival of the 414-hp V8-equipped RS 4 model.

OVERVIEW: This is Audi's most popular model, probably because it comes in so many variations, including sedans, Avant wagons, and convertibles, plus high-performance variants sold under the S4 and RS4 labels. The A4 bills itself as Audi's family sport sedan and targets the BMW 3 Series and Volvo S40/S60 customer by featuring a roomy interior, a 6-speed manual or continuously variable automatic transmission (CVT) with manual-shift capability, all-wheel drive, independent suspension, low-speed traction enhancement, automatic climate control, dual and side head-protecting airbags, ABS, and two standard engines: a 170-hp 1.8L turbo 4-cylinder with the Cabriolet and a 200-hp 2.0L turbo four with the sedan. Three other engines are offered either as options or with specific models. The 340-hp V8-equipped S4 has more than enough power to take on the high-performance competition. Although the S4 is essentially an all-dressed A4, its 6-speed manual transmission and Cabriolet add more cachet and power to the mix.

COST ANALYSIS: Go for the redesigned 2006. **Best alternatives:** If you like the S4 Quattro tire-burner, also consider the BMW M3 convertible or 5 Series and the Porsche 911 Carrera. A4 alternatives are the Audi TT Coupe, the BMW 3 Series, the Lexus IS 300, the Toyota Avalon, and the Volvo S60 or V70. **Options:** An automatic transmission and all-wheel drive. Think twice about getting the power moon roof if you're a tall driver. **Rebates:** $3,000 rebates and a variety of dealer incentive plans and low-interest financing programs. **Delivery/PDI:** $1,300 (double what would be barely acceptable). **Depreciation:** Very slow. Audi values no longer nosedive when the base warranty expires and repair costs become the owner's responsibility. **Insurance cost:** Higher than average. **Parts supply/cost:** Often back ordered and expensive. Forget about saving money by getting parts from an independent supplier; they carry few Audi parts. **Annual maintenance cost:** Higher than average, but not exorbitant. **Warranty:** Bumper-to-bumper 4 years/80,000 km; powertrain 4 years/80,000 km; rust perforation 10 years/unlimited km. **Supplementary warranty:** Don't leave the dealership without it. **Highway/city fuel economy:** *1.8L:* 7.5–11.4L/100 km;

TECHNICAL DATA

POWERTRAIN (FRONT-DRIVE/AWD)

Engines: 1.8L 4-cyl. (170 hp) • 2.0L 4-cyl. (200 hp) • 3.0L V6 (220 hp) • 3.2L V6 (255 hp) • 4.2L V8 (340 hp) • 4.2L V8 (414 hp); Transmissions: 6-speed man. • 6-speed auto. • CVT

DIMENSION/CAPACITY

Passengers: 2/3; Wheelbase: 104 in.; H: 56.2/L: 179/W: 70 in.; Headroom F/R: 3.0/2.0 in.; Legroom F/R: 43/25.5 in.; Cargo volume: 13.4 cu. ft.; Fuel tank: 70L/premium; Tow limit: 2,000 lb.; Load capacity: 1,145 lb.; Turning circle: 38 ft.; Weight: 3,920 lb.

3.0L V6: 8.1–11.5L/100 km. Remember, front-drives get better gas mileage; AWD models trade fuel economy for better traction.

Quality/Reliability/Safety

Pro: Quality control: Better than average. Overall quality control has improved over the past several years, with fewer body, trim, accessory, brake, and electrical glitches than exhibited by previous models. Still, there's a lot left to be done. **Reliability:** Average. Brake and electrical problems have taken these cars out of service for extended periods in the past. **Warranty performance:** Average.

Con: Owner-reported problems: The electrical system is the car's weakest link, and it has plagued Audi's entire lineup for the past decade. Normally, this wouldn't be catastrophic; however, as the cars become more electronically complex, with more functions handled by computer modules, you're looking at some annoying glitches to say the least. Owners also report long servicing delays, some premature brake wear and grinding when in Reverse, transmission suddenly downshifting or jerking into forward gear, sudden stalling, and other powertrain glitches. **Service bulletin problems:** Engine oil leak at camshaft adjuster; misfires and moisture accumulation in the headlights. **NHTSA safety complaints:** No-starts; sudden acceleration; airbags failed to deploy; chronic complaints of delayed braking; no brakes in rainy weather; parking brake failure; premature replacement of the front brake rotors; sudden headlight failure; and complaints that the blue-white headlights blind oncoming drivers.

Road Performance

Pro: Acceleration/torque: The base 2.0L engine provides gobs of low-end torque and accelerates better with the automatic transmission than with the manual gearbox. The turbocharger works well, with no turbo delay or torque steer. **Transmission:** Both the manual and Tiptronic automatic transmission perform flawlessly. The CVT is continuously pleasurable to drive. **Routine handling:** Very good, though not as sporty as Acura's TSX. **Emergency handling:** Better than average. **Steering:** Crisp and predictable, with lots of road feedback. **Braking:** Disc/disc; impressive braking performance when the brakes are working properly.

Con: The ride is a bit firm and the car still exhibits some body roll and brake dive under extreme conditions. Braking is a bit twitchy at times.

List Price (negotiable)   **Residual Values** (months)

	24	36	48	60
A4 2.0T sedan: $35,950 (25%)	$28,000	$24,000	$20,000	$16,000
A4 3.2 AWD: $48,780 (30%)	$36,000	$31,000	$27,000	$22,000
S4 Quattro: $69,650 (30%)	$55,000	$50,000	$45,000	$40,000

SAFETY FEATURES	STD.	OPT.	CRASHWORTHINESS		
Anti-lock brakes	✓	—	Head restraints F/R	4	2
Seat belt pretensioners F/R	✓	—	Visibility F/R	5	2
Side airbags	✓	—	Crash protection (front) D/P	4	4
Traction control	✓	—	Crash protection (side) F/R	5	4
			Crash protection (offset)	5	—
			Rollover	4	—

A6 ★★★

RATING: Average. **Strong points:** A more powerful, torquier base engine; superb handling; comfortable seating; plenty of passenger and cargo room (it beats out both BMW and Mercedes in this area); easy front and rear access; and very good build quality. The Avant wagon performs like a sporty sport-utility, with side airbags, intense HID xenon headlights, and excellent outward visibility. IIHS considers offset crash protection to be Acceptable and head restraint protection to be Good. **Weak points:** V8 is a bit growly when pushed; firm suspension can make for a jittery ride; radio controls aren't easily accessed; some tire thumping and highway wind noise; the wagon's two-place rear seat is rather small; no NHTSA crashworthiness rating; limited availability of the most popular models; a chintzy powertrain warranty; and servicing can be problematic. **New for 2006:** A 3.2L V6 Avant with a Tiptronic transmission and all-wheel drive, and an A6 sedan with a CVT.

OVERVIEW: The $63,210 (plus a grossly inflated $1,300 freight/PDI) A6 3.2 is essentially a larger, fully equipped A4. It's a comfortable, spacious front-drive luxury sedan or wagon that offers standard dual front side airbags and head-protecting curtain side airbags; torso side airbags are optional. Also standard are ABS, an anti-skid system, and xenon headlights (thieves love 'em). There's also a multi-tasking joystick control for all the entertainment, navigation, and climate control functions. It's similar in function to BMW's iDrive system, which has been roundly criticized as both confusing and dangerously distracting. The sedan comes with a base 255-hp 3.2L V6 or an optional 335-hp 4.2L V6. Both engines are mated to a 6-speed automatic transmission with manual-shift capability; Audi's Quattro all-wheel drive is also available.

COST ANALYSIS: Choose the 2006 models for their more sophisticated safety features. **Best alternatives:** Other vehicles worth taking a look at are the Acura TL, the BMW 5 Series, and the Volvo V70. **Options:** All-wheel drive, if needed. Think twice about getting the power moon roof if you're a tall driver. **Rebates:** $5,000 rebates and low-interest financing. **Delivery/PDI:** $1,300. **Depreciation:** Slower than average. **Insurance cost:** Higher than average. **Parts supply/cost:** Very dealer-dependent and expensive. Independent suppliers carry few Audi parts. **Annual maintenance cost:** Low during the warranty period, then it climbs steadily. **Warranty:** Bumper-to-bumper 4 years/80,000 km; powertrain 4 years/80,000 km; rust perforation 10 years/unlimited km. **Supplementary warranty:** A prerequisite to Audi ownership, and it guarantees a good resale price. **Highway/city fuel economy:** 7.8–13.5L/100 km; *Quattro:* 8.4–13.9L/100 km.

 ## Road Performance

Pro: Acceleration/torque: Better-than-average acceleration with the upgraded base engine and automatic transmission. **Braking:** Excellent braking performance.

Con: Vehicle shakes when put into Reverse, and the front bumper catches on parking bumpers. **Service bulletin problems:** Moisture accumulation in headlights; OnStar loses vehicle location. **NHTSA safety complaints:** Airbags failed to deploy; front seat failed to stay anchored in a rear-ender; severe hesitation upon acceleration; vehicle loses power or stalls when making right turns; premature transmission failure; transmission slips from automatic to manual mode without warning; chronic hesitation at low speed; faulty gas tank sensors transmit wrong indication of remaining fuel; and distorted front windshield.

RATING: Recommended. **Strong points:** Impressive acceleration with the optional 225-hp power plant; all-wheel drive available; good handling and road holding; very well appointed and tastefully designed interior; comfortable, supportive seats; plenty of passenger and cargo space (especially with rear seatbacks folded); standard ABS; "smart" dual front airbags; five-star rating for side crashworthiness and rollover resistance; Good front head restraint protection and Average rear head restraint protection; optional Bose sound system; and a predicted high resale value. **Weak points:** Base engine lacks low-end torque; excess weight limits handling; poor rear and side visibility; ride may be too firm for some; confusing interior controls; a useless back seat; difficult rear-seat access; lots of engine and road noise; and limited availability. **New for 2006:** Carried over unchanged.

OVERVIEW: Costing an estimated $56,680 (plus $1,300 for freight/PDI), the TT Coupe 225 Quattro debuted in the spring of 1999 as a sporty front-drive hatchback with 2+2 seating and set on the same platform used by the A4, Golf, Jetta, and New Beetle. A two-seat convertible version, the TT Roadster 225 Quattro sells for $61,650. The base 180-hp 1.8L engine (lifted from the A4) is coupled to a manual 5-speed. A 225-hp 1.8L engine and 250-hp 3.2L V6, coupled to a 6-speed manual transaxle, are optional. Shorter and more firmly sprung than the A4, the TT's engines are turbocharged, though only the optional engine comes with standard AWD. A spoiler and anti-skid system are also standard.

More beautifully styled and with better handling than the Prowler, the TT comes with lots of high-tech standard features that include four-wheel disc brakes, airbags everywhere, traction control (front-drive models), a power top (Quattro), a heated-glass rear window, and a power-retractable glass windbreak between the roll bars (convertible). An alarm system employs a pulse radar system to catch prying hands invading the cockpit area.

COST ANALYSIS: Go for an identical 2005, if you can find one that's discounted. **Best alternatives:** The BMW Z Series, the Honda S2000, and the Mazda Miata. **Options:** All-wheel drive is recommended only if it's essential for your driving needs. **Service bulletin problems:** N/A. **NHTSA safety complaints:** Incredibly few consumer complaints. Xenon headlights make it difficult to see the sides of the road; central computer causes door locks to jam; windshield wipers often stop working; faulty gas tank sensors transmit wrong indication of remaining fuel; and Michelin tire tread separation.

BMW

Whew, did BMW ever dodge a bullet when it unloaded money-losing Land Rover onto a gullible Ford and kept the popular Mini Cooper for itself! BMW has finally recovered from its 1994 purchase of the Rover Group, which drained cash reserves, delayed the upgrading of its models, and weakened management through dismissals and resignations. Over the past three years, these canny Germans have bounced back by upgrading their best-selling 3 Series, 5 Series, flagship 7 Series, and profit-laden X5 sport-utility, including spinning off a smaller X3 variant earlier this year.

BMW continues to build well-appointed cars that excel at handling and driving comfort. Its vehicles have excellent road manners, depreciate slowly, and have an "I got mine!" cachet that buyers find hard to resist. Unfortunately, they also have an incredibly complicated centre-console-mounted iDrive feature that some have renamed the "iDie" controller. An article in *Popular Science*, entitled "uDrive Me Crazy," describes it this way:

> With a push, turn, or shove, this automotive supermouse controls 700 functions, which are displayed in menus on the screen above. Most features that 7 Series drivers had previously selected and modulated via switches, knobs, sliders, pushbuttons, and stalks are now operated by the knob.... It's somewhere between silly and wonderful. It's more a step sideways than a step forward—a few good ideas, a few good features, and a whole bunch of bad implementation.

Pity that BMW has installed iDrive on its redesigned 5 Series, and that Audi followed the trend with its A6 and A8 models.

Other BMW minuses: limited interior room (except in the high-end models), some quality-control deficiencies (notably the powertrain, electrical system, and notoriously soft brake pads), and its vehicles can be difficult and expensive to service. A good website that lists BMW problems and fixes is *www.roadfly.org*.

Other than cachet, there are many good reasons for buying a BMW, including good overall reliability (with just a few exceptions, like the X5 SUV); impressive, high-performance road handling; prestige value; and a low rate of depreciation. Keep in mind, though, that there are plenty of other cars that cost less, offer more interior room (Audi comes to mind), and are more reliable and better performing.

So, if you are buying a BMW, remember that the entry-level versions of these little status symbols are more show than go, and that just a few options can blow your budget. The larger, better-performing high-end models are more expensive and don't give you the same standard features as do many Japanese imports. Also, be prepared to endure long servicing waits, body and trim glitches, and brake, electrical, and accessory problems.

MINI COOPER ★★★

RATING: Average. **Strong points:** Distinctively styled; slow depreciation; offset, front, and side crash protection; crash protection and head restraint effectiveness given an Above Average rating by the IIHS. NHTSA says this little tyke merits a four-star rating for its resistance to rollovers. **Weak points:** High retail price and freight/PDI fee, mediocre ride and handling, limited front visibility, and predicted to be glitch-prone. **New for 2006:** Nothing significant. **Best alternatives:** The Mazda Miata and the Porsche Boxster.

OVERVIEW: Arriving late to the nostalgia niche dominated by the Chrysler PT Cruiser, the Ford T-Bird, and the VW New Beetle, BMW has finally let loose with its own flashback from the past—the Mini Cooper, last marketed by Austin in 1967. The front-drive, $25,800 (S version: $30,500 plus a hair-raising $1,395 freight/PDI fee) Mini Cooper returns with a new sedan Checkmate Package that includes stability control. Dealer markup is 10 percent and freight/PDI tops $1,395;

discounting isn't likely. Unlike the T-Bird, the Mini still has the distinctive looks of the original. Fortunately, it has ditched the original's 10-inch wheels for 16- and 17-inchers.

Although not as small as the original Austin Cooper, the Mini is still less than 4 metres long, with a 239-centimetre wheelbase, a width of 1.9 metres, and a height of only 1.4 metres (yes, smaller than a Chevy Metro). The 115-hp 1.6L 4-banger can be teamed to a 5-speed manual or automatic transmission and turns in a 0–100 km/h time of a leisurely 9.2 seconds. The Cooper S uses a 163-hp supercharged version of the same 1.6L motor (with more robust components, set on a sturdier frame) and a standard 6-speed manual transmission. Speed freaks can get a 200-hp variant of the same engine. Four-wheel ABS disc brakes are standard, along with a host of safety features.

Okay, so the Mini's neither cheap nor fast, but it is stylish, with its uniquely hunkered-down, *cute* look that we simply *loved* in *The Italian Job*. It has more interior space than the Austin (were we all smaller then?), there are 50/50 split folding seats for additional storage space, and the fully independent suspension carries a body that we're told is much more rigid than what's offered by the competition. Outward visibility (traffic lights excluded) is unobstructed, and the rear window includes an intermittent-running rear wiper (an essential feature for a car this low-slung). Owners put fuel economy in the 9.5L/100 km range.

So what's not to like? How about traffic-light stops? The forward-mounted windshield makes it next to impossible to see traffic lights when stopped at a corner. Take away the retro styling and you get an undersized, underperforming, and untried British import thrust into a market where many proven competitors do more for less money. When compared with the Mercedes C230, the Subaru WRX, and the VW New Beetle, the Cooper S is relatively overpriced for a car with the smallest interior and cargo area of this class. Also, it's built in England, which guarantees a plethora of quality bugs. Said the *Christian Science Monitor* in an early review:

> Quality is suspect in both [models]. Thrumming wheel bearings, whining steering, loose and missing interior parts marred two weeks of driving.

Finally, take all that high-speed handling praise with a *huge* grain of salt: Reports from professional drivers are fairly harsh. Says *Car and Driver*'s editor-in-chief:

> Turn the wheel a little bit, and as the car rolls slightly, it increases the degree of your turn by a factor of two or three times. I'm surprised no one has put this car into a ditch. Until this is fixed, the Mini is undrivable.

Service bulletin problems: Engine idle dip and poor acceleration; AC whistling, sunroof squeaking, and rear hatch/door window rattling; seat heater gets too hot or too cold; windshield stress cracks; speedometer needle vibrates; and inoperative interior lights. See *www.mini.ca* or *www.mini2.com/forum* for a good overview of ownership pros and cons. **NHTSA safety complaints:** Inaccurate speedometer and jammed passenger-side seat belt shoulder retractor. Other deficiencies mostly concern poor ergonomics, a surprising oversight for a German-engineered car. For example: Inside door handles are located too far back on the doors; getting the spare tire from under the vehicle is a chore; and shoulder belts are uncomfortable.

3 SERIES ★★★★★

best buy

RATING: Recommended. One of the best-handling sport sedans on the market. Still, many competitors deliver more interior room and standard features for less money. **Strong points:** Good acceleration (highlighted by the $73,950 M3's incredibly fast performance); excellent handling; impressive braking; and top-notch quality control. **Weak points:** Many complaints of engine overheating, sudden shutdown, and engine compartment fires; a somewhat harsh ride (the M3 is harsher than most); insufficient front headroom and seat lumbar support for tall occupants; limited rear-seat room and cargo area; tricky entry and exit, even on sedans; confusing navigation system controls; excessive tire noise, especially with the M3; and requires premium fuel. **New for 2006:** Redesigned 325i and 330i sedans, plus the sedans and wagons get optional all-wheel drive. An AWD 325xi Sport Wagon with a standard Panoramic Roof is also new this year.

TECHNICAL DATA

POWERTRAIN (REAR-DRIVE/AWD)

Engines: 2.5L 6-cyl. (184 hp) • 3.0L 6-cyl. (215 hp) • 3.0L 6-cyl. (255 hp) • 3.2L 6-cyl. (333 hp); Transmissions: 5-speed man. • 5-speed auto. • 6-speed man. • 6-speed auto. • 6-speed manumatic

DIMENSION/CAPACITY

Passengers: 2/3; Wheelbase: 108 in.; H: 55.7/L: 177/W: 70 in.; Headroom F/R: 2.0/1.5 in.; Legroom F/R: 41/25.5 in.; Cargo volume: 15 cu. ft.; Fuel tank: 62L/premium; Tow limit: 1,000 lb.; Load capacity: 1,060 lb.; Turning circle: 36 ft.; Weight: 3,460 lb.

OVERVIEW: With BMW's recent mechanical upgrades, styling changes, and increased exterior and interior dimensions, the 3 Series has come to resemble its more expensive big brothers with super-smooth powertrain performance and enhanced handling. You will find four engines, rear- or all-wheel drive, and four body styles among 10 different models. The base coupes now come with the 2.5L and 3.0L 6-cylinder engines used in BMW's entry-level sedans and standard Sport suspension. These new four-seaters are also lower, longer, and wider than their four-door equivalents, use different body panels, and present a more aerodynamic appearance. The 323 convertible and wagon versions have been made over in a similar fashion. The 333-hp 3.2L 6-cylinder engine is reserved for the unbelievably fast and nimble M3 coupe and convertible.

Recently upgraded cockpit amenities include a standard tilt/telescope steering wheel, and optional power memory seats, power lumbar adjustments, an in-dash CD player, and steering wheel, audio, and cruise controls. Traction and stability control and rear side-impact airbags are standard.

COST ANALYSIS: Most of the 2005 models return practically unchanged, so they are worth buying if they're discounted sufficiently. **Best alternatives:** Other cars worth considering are the Audi A4 and the Lexus IS 300. **Options:** If you buy a convertible, invest $1,500 in the rollover protection system that pops up from behind the rear seat. The optional Sport suspension does enhance handling and steering, but it also produces an overly harsh, jiggly ride on rough pavement. The Sport Package comes with a harsh-shifting SMG gearbox (the one you loved to hate on the M3)—it isn't worth the extra money. Wider tires compromise traction in snow. **Rebates:** Not likely. **Delivery/PDI:** $1,250. **Depreciation:** Slower than average. **Insurance cost:** Higher than average. **Parts supply/cost:** Parts are less expensive than for other cars in this class. Unfortunately, they aren't easily found outside of the dealer network, where they're often back ordered. **Annual maintenance cost:** Average until the warranty runs out; then your mechanic starts sharing your paycheque. **Warranty:** Bumper-to-bumper 4 years/80,000 km; powertrain 4 years/80,000 km; rust perforation 6 years/unlimited km. **Supplementary warranty:** Not needed. **Highway/city fuel economy:** 7.3–11.5L/100 km with the 2.5L engine.

 ## Quality/Reliability/Safety

Pro: Quality control: Better than average. Body assembly and workmanship are quite good. **Reliability:** Average, although there have always been problems with some engines self-destructing on previous sporty models. **Warranty performance:** Acceptable, most of the time. BMW usually resolves disputes through individual "goodwill" settlements; however, their handling of their engine-overheating problem was deplorably stupid.

Con: Parts are scarce outside major metropolitan areas, and independent mechanics are rare. **Owner-reported problems:** Engines, brakes, electrical system (telematics), and some body trim and accessories are the most failure-prone components. Engine overheating is a serious and most common failure on past models. *M3:* Loud clunking from the rear end when shifting or decelerating said to be caused by a faulty driveshaft attachment at the differential. **Service bulletin problems:** Delayed automatic transmission engagement; engine cylinder head oil leaks; cold weather valve cover damage; head bolt threads pull out of engine block; low-oil-level warning campaign (secret warranty); dead battery campaign (another secret warranty); intermittent exterior mirror failure; telematics control unit installation campaign; keyless entry won't lock or unlock doors; inoperative BMW Assist campaign—calls cannot be completed; AC light control module reprogramming; lighting switches off late; and a loose front turn signal light. **NHTSA safety complaints:** *All models:* Many incidents where cooling fan failure caused engine to overheat or a fire to ignite (see *www.roadfly. org*); and airbag failed to deploy. *325i:* Transmission failure within five days of purchase; transmission replaced and still downshifts harshly; rpm idle fluctuation; vehicle jerked forward when decelerating; sudden loss of power caused by computer failure; electrical system fire; right door airbag deployed even though vehicle was hit on the left; sunroof glass suddenly exploded (several incidents reported); door locks without prior warning; faulty fuel pump; and Bridgestone tire tread separation. *328:* Premature tire failure (bubbles in the tread); sudden acceleration; when accelerating, engine cuts out, then surges forward (suspected failure of the throttle assembly); severe engine vibrations after a cold start as Check Engine light comes on; if driver wears a size 12 or larger shoe, when foot is flush against the accelerator pedal, the top of the shoe rubs up against the panel above the pedal, preventing full pedal access; and rear quarter blind spot with the convertibles. *330i:* Side airbag deployed when vehicle hit a pothole; vehicle overheats in low gear; tires lose air; and vehicle slips out of Second gear when accelerating.

 Road Performance

Pro: Acceleration/torque: The 6-cylinder engines and transmissions are the essence of harmonious cooperation, even when coupled to an automatic transmission—there's not actually that much difference between the manual and the automatic from a performance perspective. **Transmission:** Light and precise gear shifting with easy clutch and shift action. **Routine handling:** Competent and predictable handling on dry surfaces. **Emergency handling:** No-surprise suspension and steering make for crisp high-speed and emergency handling. Good rear-end stability. **Steering:** Exceptionally accurate and sensitive. Lots of road feedback. **Braking:** Smooth, efficient braking produces short stopping distances.

Con: The ride is firm and occasionally uncomfortable on rough roads. Mediocre acceleration with the heavier ragtop coupled to an automatic transmission. Some body flexing and shake when the convertible is run over rough pavement.

3 SERIES

List Price (negotiable)	Residual Values (months)			
	24	36	48	60
325i sedan: $40,300 (20%)	$30,000	$23,000	$18,000	$15,000
330i: $47,900 (25%)	$38,000	$32,000	$27,000	$24,000

SAFETY FEATURES	STD.	OPT.	CRASHWORTHINESS		
			Head restraints F/R	3	3
Anti-lock brakes	✓	—	Visibility F/R	5	5
Seat belt pretensioners F/R	✓	—	Crash protection (front) D/P	4	5
Side airbags	✓	—	Crash protection (side) F/R	3	5
Traction control	✓	—	Crash protection (offset)	5	—
			Rollover	4	—

Jaguar

Jaguar is proof positive that the British can't build quality cars. Although the cars' styling, ride, handling, and comfort still entice motoring masochists full of nostalgia for the British cars of the 1960s, what Ford gives them instead is a hodgepodge of Taurus and Lincoln parts thrown together with a Jaguar badge. No wonder that Taurus-sourced powertrain, electronic, and body problems persist—problems such as sudden, unintended acceleration, automatic transmission and brake failures, shimmying, and excessive noise when driving with the rear windows open. What's all the more surprising is that even with these serious defects, insiders say these pseudo-Jags are better built than the original versions.

Still, the Jaguar's poor-quality image has been tough to accept, which may explain why these luxury cars have such a high rate of depreciation (a $90,000 1997 XK8 now sells for less than $15,000), and why prudent buyers prefer to lease rather than purchase their Jags.

When Ford bought Jaguar, it had three goals: improve quality, make the cars more affordable, and make the division profitable. Consequently, Ford has introduced

All ratings on a numbered scale where 5 is good and 1 is bad. See page 153–154 for a more detailed description.

two cheaper models, the S-Type and X-Type series, joined by the more upscale XJ8 and XK8. As far as making Jaguar profitable—forget it. Forecasts of 200,000 annual sales have been halved and Jaguar continues to lose money, recently posting a $500+ million operating loss that it blames on the economy, its workers, and unsophisticated shoppers (oh no, not on the cars!).

High-end Jaguars have excess weight that makes it necessary to install lots of complicated and difficult-to-troubleshoot devices, as well as larger engines, in order to make them decent highway performers. Entry-level Jags have a different problem—convincing buyers that their X-Types are more than gussied-up $41,995 Contours (with a larger trunk and less headroom) and that S-Types are worth $62,795 even though they have fewer luxury features than many competitors.

Leading with its chin, Jaguar offers a comprehensive 4-year/80,000 km base mechanical warranty. The automaker also provides a 6-year/unlimited km rust perforation warranty, and Jaguar Club benefits that include no-cost maintenance, roadside assistance, and trip interruption services. Spotty servicing quality is still a problem. Unfortunately, there aren't many Jaguar dealers to choose from, so if you don't find a competent and conscientious one, it's doubtful that you'll be able to go elsewhere for a second opinion, particularly if your Jag's not running.

S-TYPE ★★

RATING: Below Average. On sale since the summer of 1999, the S-Type shares its rear-drive platform with Lincoln's LS sedan. **Strong points:** Impressive engine performance; superb handling and road holding; quiet running; improved reliability; a well-appointed interior; better than average side crashworthiness scores; and a five-star rollover-resistance rating. **Weak points:** A history of very poor reliability and high maintenance costs; not much room for cargo; a cramped interior; limited dealer network and Ford mechanics unfamiliar with the model; some parts delay; and accelerated depreciation. **New for 2006:** More powerful V8s, upgraded brakes, and a slight restyling.

OVERVIEW: This is a mid-priced Jaguar built on Ford's shared platform concept that was also used with the 2000 Lincoln LS sedan. So what's not to like? How about an interior that won't hold three rear occupants in comfort? Or plastic trim instead of real wood?

The S-Type has a longer wheelbase than the XJ sedans, and is wider and taller. It's just a bit shorter in length, however. Retro styling continues at Ford with the oval grille, vertical bars, four round headlights, and bland, pinched-looking tail lights. From the side, this Jag looks like an Infiniti J30.

Aimed at the BMW 5 Series, Mercedes E-Class, and Lexus GS crowd, the S-Type is pricier than its Lincoln LS twin at $62,800 for the V6 (the same as last year's price) and $10,200 more for the V8 ($73,000).

Quality control, although improved of late, is still likely to be a long-term problem, particularly since this model is churned out by Jaguar's old manufacturing complex near Birmingham, England. The car does have four-wheel ABS, traction control, front head/chest side airbags, Ford's Duratec-based 235-hp 3.0L V6, and an optional 300-hp 4.2L V8 or supercharged 400-hp variant. The 6-speed automatic transmission is standard on all models and the 5-speed manual is a no-charge option with the 3.0L model.

Deficiencies include steering that's a bit over-assisted for high speeds (the optional Sport Package will help), limited passenger and cargo space (rear passengers sit knees-to-chin with scrunched toes), restricted rear visibility, and a confusing array of audio and climate controls.

Owner-reported problems: Poor headlight illumination; AC failure; passenger-side front wheel fell off; Continental tire blowouts; and sliding roof may not close properly or bounces open. **Service bulletin problems:** Driveline clunk or knock when downshifting; incorrect gear selection; a rear-end thump; power-steering squeaks and roof panel wind noise; telematic issues with the navigation system; and vehicle locks when closing the door ("Honest, officer, it's my car").

COST ANALYSIS: There isn't any compelling reason to buy or lease a 2005 or 2006 S-Type when the car is compared with less expensive convertibles and roadsters from BMW and Porsche. **Best alternatives:** Other more reliable luxury cars with as much or more cachet that you may wish to consider are the Lexus models, the Lincoln Town Car, and the more plebeian but much more reliable Toyota Avalon. **Options:** The voice-activation system is a pricey gadget that adds complexity without providing the promised convenience. **Rebates:** Jaguar is a low-volume seller, and discounting is quite common. Expect zero percent financing and $5,000+ rebates. **Delivery/PDI:** $700 (about half the fee charged for a Toyota Sienna). **Depreciation:** Faster than average. **Insurance cost:** Higher than average, almost usurious. **Parts supply/cost:** Parts are often back ordered because not a lot of Ford dealer inventory goes into stocking Jaguar parts. The S and X versions will be able to benefit from Ford's generic Lincoln parts, but powertrain components will still likely be back ordered. Parts are moderately expensive as well, and there are few independent suppliers to inject price competition into the equation. **Annual maintenance cost:** Predicted to be higher than average. **Warranty:** Bumper-to-bumper 4 years/80,000 km; rust perforation 6 years/ unlimited km. **Supplementary warranty:** Don't leave home without it. **Highway/ city fuel economy:** *3.0L V6:* 8.9–13.8L/100 km; *V8:* 9.1–14.2L/100 km.

S-TYPE

SAFETY FEATURES			CRASHWORTHINESS		
	STD.	**OPT.**	Head restraints F/R	5	5
Anti-lock brakes	✓	—	Visibility F/R	5	**2**
Seat belt pretensioners F/R	✓	—	Crash protection (side) F/R	4	5
Side airbags	✓	—	Rollover	5	—
Traction control	✓	—			

X-TYPE ★

bad buy

RATING: Not Recommended. Aimed at the Acura TL, Audi A4, BMW 3 Series, Mercedes C-Class, and Lexus crowd, the X-Type's $41,995 base price and $46,995 MSRP for the Sport model is a lot of money to pay for what is essentially a *faux* Jaguar competing in a very real crowd. **Strong points:** Offset crash protection and head-protecting side airbags rated Above Average by the IIHS; comfortable ride; excellent steering and handling, particularly with the AWD; and lots of trunk space. **Weak points:** This isn't a luxury car, even though it's advertised as one; Lincoln's LS 3.0L is barely adequate; limited dealer network; Ford mechanics are less familiar with this model; navigation system isn't easy to program or understand; and transmission set-up is a bit confusing and imprecise. **New for 2006:** Nothing important.

OVERVIEW: This all-wheel drive is a derivative of the Ford Mondeo and Contour, and has the same interior dimensions, except for a larger trunk and a bit less headroom. Power is supplied by the Lincoln LS-derived, 227-hp 3.0L V6, hooked to either a manual or automatic 5-speed transmission. The optional Sport Package offers a firmer suspension, dynamic stability control, 17-inch tires, and exclusive trim features.

Quality/Reliability/Safety

Service bulletin problems: Incorrect gear selection; a rear-end thump; a driveline clunk/knock when downshifting; power-steering squeaks; roof panel wind noise; telematic issues with the navigation system; and vehicle locks when closing the door. **NHTSA safety complaints:** Engine surging; sudden, unintended acceleration; chronic stalling; multiple automatic transmission failures; airbag remains de-activated, even though a full-sized adult is seated; ignition switch can be hit by driver's knee, causing the car to shut down; and tire tread/side wall peeled away.

X-TYPE

SAFETY FEATURES

	STD.	OPT.
Anti-lock brakes	✓	—
Side airbags	✓	—
Traction control	—	✓

CRASHWORTHINESS

Head restraints F/R	5	5
Crash protection (front) D/P	4	4
Crash protection (side) D/P	4	4
Crash protection (offset)	5	—
Rollover	4	—

All ratings on a numbered scale where 5 is good and 1 is bad. See page 153–154 for a more detailed description.

Mercedes-Benz

Mercedes' Quality Nosedives

Mercedes-Benz still hasn't recovered from a severe sales slump caused by increased competition from the Japanese automakers (mainly Lexus), fewer buyers of luxury cars owing to higher fuel prices, and the public perception that Mercedes quality has tanked. The irony of this situation is that Chrysler, owned by DaimlerBenz, now ranks higher than Mercedes in many quality surveys.

Mercedes' misfortune was inevitable. Except for some hapless buyers, everyone knew that Mercedes' 1998 M-Class sport-utilities were abysmally bad. You couldn't have made a worse vehicle, judging by the unending stream of desperate-sounding service bulletins sent by the head office to dealers following the official launch. Two bulletins stand out in my mind: One was an authorization for dry-cleaning payouts to dealers whose customers' clothing was stained by the dye from the burgundy-coloured leather seats. The other was a lengthy explanation as to why drivers were jolted by static electricity when entering or leaving the vehicle.

Car columnists have always known that Mercedes has made some bad cars and SUVs, but it took business reporters (not auto beat writers) from the gutsy *Wall Street Journal* to spill the beans. In a February 2, 2002, article titled "An Engineering Icon Slips," the *WSJ* cited several confidential industry-initiated surveys that showed that Mercedes' quality and customer satisfaction had fallen dramatically since 1999—to a level below that of GM's Opel, a brand that had one of the worst reputations for poor quality in Europe.

An earlier J.D. Power and Associates study of vehicle durability in the States put Mercedes 12th in its ranking, behind Lincoln, Cadillac, and (gasp!) Jaguar. Its chief failings were in the transmission and features/controls categories. Following this study, J.D. Power and Associates announced to a National Automobile Dealers Association convention that Mercedes' rating for overall quality had been lowered to "Fair" from "Good."

The quality issue surfaced first in various quality surveys and after the launch of the technically advanced E-Class in 2003. It then was reflected in slipping positions in customer-satisfaction polls. In a recent *Consumer Reports* U.S. subscriber survey, the 2004 Mercedes-Benz E-Class was the most problem-ridden car. Among 2001 models, the C-Class was the worst car and the M-Class the worst SUV.

Industry insiders tell me that Mercedes-Benz quality has been diluted by the more than doubling of its product lineup since 1997 and by the free ride it has received from a fawning press. Helpful, too, have been the company's aggressive PR campaigns and the Teutonic mindset that tends to blame the driver rather than the product—both spectacularly successful in keeping the quality myth alive in the media, until the *Wall Street Journal* broke the story. Neither mindset nor PR worked to mitigate the owner displeasure over M-B's engine sludge stonewalling, though. It cost Mercedes $32 million U.S. to settle after the company denied that there was a factory-related problem.

For a small taste of how well Mercedes manages the press circling its vehicles, look on the Internet for stories relating to the A-Class "baby Benz" (a Smart car predecessor sold mainly in Europe) flipping over during its press launching, allegations involving M-B's Holocaust involvement, its tight-lipped reaction to the above-cited quality surveys, and reports that Mercedes residual values have fallen dramatically.

SMART ★★

RATING: Below Average. Not a Smart buy unless Mercedes expands Smart sales to all of North America.

Strong points: Fuel-frugal to the extreme; slow depreciation; distinctive, cute styling; and sold in 46 out of Canada's 55 Mercedes-Benz dealerships. Vancouver gives Smart drivers cheaper parking at city-owned lots; and the city of Duncan, on Vancouver Island, offers micro-car parking spaces that allow Smarts and Mini Coopers nose-in curb parking. **Weak points:** A maxi price for a mini car; lethargic acceleration; expensive and dealer-dependent servicing (trips must be planned carefully for servicing accessibility); Mercedes won't commit to North America;

no long-term reliability figures; no NHTSA crashworthiness data; pranksters have gone from tipping over cows to tipping over Smarts; not a "green" car, as many pretend; and diesel emissions may be toxic and contain particulates that exacerbate lung disorders.

OVERVIEW: How ironic. Mercedes' most popular car is the Smart, a tiny, two-seat, French-built runabout that's based on a car that rolled over at its European press launching, isn't sold in the States, has never made a profit, and sells for $20,000—about half of what the cheapest luxury Mercedes costs. Nevertheless, Smart fever has resulted in 2,390 cars sold as of July 2005—outpacing BMW and Mercedes SUVs, Saab, Jaguar, Land Rover, and the Mini Cooper. Adding insult to Stutgart's astonishment, Smart's sales for that period equal about one-third of the sales of Mercedes' luxury lineup. Ouch!

Offered as a hardtop or convertible, the Smart arrived in Canada in the fall of 2004, after six years in Europe where it ran Mercedes into the hole to the tune of three billion dollars.

The secret behind the Smart's success in Canada is our love for small cars and fear of rising fuel prices. In fact, cheap, small cars in Canada make up 40 percent of our market, almost double the American market share.

Selling for $16,700 to $23,000, Smarts are powered by an 800-cubic-cm, 3-cylinder turbo diesel motor that produces 41 hp—nowhere near the 108 horses offered by Toyota's smallest car, the $13,000 Echo/Yaris. Furthermore, the car is only 2.5 metres long and weighs in at only 730 kg, compared to the 1,280-kg Echo. These factors combine to give the Smart a 4.4L/100 km rating, much better than the Echo's estimated city/highway fuel economy of 6.7 and 5.2L/100 km, respectively, and much more than the outrageously inaccurate fuel savings claims bandied about by Honda and Toyota when they hype their hybrids.

Why Smart may not be smart

Like Fiat, Lada, Peugeot, and Renault—four automakers who abandoned Canada after failing to expand into the States—Smart owners may be left high and dry if Mercedes decides Smart is more a drain than a gain. And Mercedes hasn't had a great record with small, entry-level "baby Benz" models, like the 190 model that was introduced over a decade ago and quickly abandoned, or the C-Class hatchback that was dropped this year. Now this wouldn't be much of a problem if Smarts were conventional small cars backed by an extensive dealer network and a large parts inventory. But that's not the case. Furthermore, unlike old MGs and Triumphs, there isn't a body of independent repairers and part suppliers who can step into the breach.

When Mercedes makes up its mind, *Lemon-Aid* will revise the Smart's rating.

C-CLASS ★★★

RATING: Average. These little entry-level cars lack the simplicity and popular pricing found in the Japanese competition; save up for an E-Class. **Strong points:** Plenty of high-tech safety features like standard "smart" airbags, side airbags, traction control, and brake assist; good powertrain matchup enhanced with AWD and a supercharger; comfortable ride; easy handling; good braking; innovative anti-theft system; and good overall crash protection. **Weak points:** The C-Class at its lower end is bereft of many standard performance and convenience features that one would expect to see in a luxury car; limited rear seat and cargo room; tight entry and exit; a choppy ride; and some tire thumping, engine, and wind noise. A weak resale value and dealer-dependent for parts and servicing. **New for 2006:** The C-Class three-door coupe has been axed, leaving just a sedan and wagon lineup that showcases a new series of V6 engines.

TECHNICAL DATA

POWERTRAIN (FRONT-DRIVE/AWD)
Engines: 2.5L V6. (201 hp) • 3.0L V6 (228 hp) • 3.5L V6 (268 hp) • 5.4L V8 (362 hp); Transmissions: 5-speed auto. • 6-speed man.

DIMENSION/CAPACITY
Passengers: 2/3; Wheelbase: 106.9 in.; H: 54.3/L: 171/W: 68 in.; Headroom F/R: N/A; Legroom F/R: 42.0/33.0 in.; Cargo volume: 9.9 cu. ft.; Fuel tank: 62L/premium; Tow limit: N/A; Load capacity: 865 lb.; Turning circle: 35.3 ft.; Weight: 3,252 lb.

OVERVIEW: These cars are Mercedes' entry-level offerings, spun off of its base four-door sedan. They include a C250 and C320 sedan and wagon, along with AMG variants.

The $36,950 (plus $1,500 freight/PDI charges) C230 sedan is the automaker's cheapest car. It carries a 201-hp 2.5L V6 base engine hooked to either a 5-speed automatic or a 6-speed manual transmission. More powerful V6 and V8 engines, including AWD, are available as you move up the model range. For example, a 228-hp 3.0L V6 powers the C280; a 268-hp 3.5L V6 is standard with the C350; and the AMG still uses a powerful 362-hp 5.4L V8 hooked to a drivetrain that was upgraded for 2006.

COST ANALYSIS: Mercedes' three-point star is sinking fast, forcing the automaker to cut prices and add incentives to move its slow-selling entry-level models. Bottom line? Take a pass on this year's entry-level offering until prices come down in the new year. **Best alternatives:** Also take a look at the Audi TT and the BMW 3 Series. Other cars worth considering are the Volvo S40, V40, V70 wagon, or V70XC. Rivals to the CLK and the SLK230 would be the BMW Z4, the Chevrolet Corvette, the Porsche Boxster, the Volvo C70 or S80, and other models in the Mercedes-Benz SL-Class stable. **Options:** The Bose sound system is a good investment. **Rebates:** $4,000–$5,000 rebates, generous leasing deals, and low-interest financing. **Delivery/PDI:** $1,495 (cut it in half through smart bargaining). **Depreciation:** Slower than average. **Insurance cost:** Higher than average. **Parts supply/cost:** Limited availability and expensive. **Annual maintenance cost:** Average. **Warranty:** Bumper-to-bumper 4 years/80,000 km; powertrain 4 years/80,000 km; rust perforation 5 years/120,000 km. **Supplementary warranty:** Not needed. **Highway/city fuel economy:** *1.8L:* 7–11.2L/100 km; *2.6L:* 8.4–13.7L/100 km; *3.2L:* 8.6–12.3L/100 km.

Quality/Reliability/Safety

Pro: Quality control: Average. **Reliability:** Average.

Con: Service bulletin problems: Crankcase oil leaks; a plethora of electrical shorts and miscalibrated electronic control modules. **NHTSA safety complaints:** *C230:* Airbags failed to deploy; many owner complaints that the vehicle suddenly loses power and then shuts down; no throttle response; vehicle shakes violently when put into gear; transmission slips in cold weather, or jerks into gear when accelerating; excessive vibration until vehicle warms up; dash gauges wash out in sunlight; driver-side seat belt buckle attachment located between the seat and console is set too far down, making it impossible for driver to latch or release buckle; blind spot between the rear window and the two back side windows; and rotten-egg exhaust smell. *240:* Airbags failed to deploy; chronic stalling; several incidents of sudden unintended acceleration; when accelerating from a stoplight, vehicle appears to stall, then surges forward, other cases where car hesitates when accelerating; and total engine failure. *320:* Dash vent reflects onto the windshield.

C-CLASS

List Price (negotiable)	Residual Values (months)			
	24	36	48	60
C230 coupe: $36,950 (25%)	$26,000	$19,000	$16,000	$13,000
C280 sedan: $42,850 (30%)	$29,000	$22,000	$19,000	$17,000
C350 Sports: $57,200 (30%)	$38,000	$34,000	$29,000	$24,000

SAFETY FEATURES	STD.	OPT.	CRASHWORTHINESS		
Anti-lock brakes	✓	—	Head restraints F/R		
Seat belt pretensioners F/R	✓	—	2d	③	③
Side airbags	✓	—	4d	⑤	⑤
Traction control	✓	—	Visibility F/R	④	❷
			Crash protection (front) D/P	④	④
			Crash protection (side) F/R	⑤	⑤
			Crash protection (offset)	⑤	—
			Rollover	④	—

E-CLASS ★★★★

RATING: Above Average. *This* is the Mercedes to buy—not some "baby Benz." Nevertheless, it too has been downrated because of a decline in quality relating to the powertrain (sludging and fuel delivery) and electrical system. **Strong points:** Strong acceleration in the higher gear ranges; well appointed with many safety, performance, and convenience features; good engine and transmission combo; 4Matic all-wheel drive operates flawlessly; easy handling; good braking; comfortable ride; roomy interior; cargo room (wagon); innovative anti-theft system; excellent quality control; a high trade-in value; four-star driver and passenger frontal crash protection; rollover resistance and side protection rated five stars; and an Above Average rating by IIHS for offset crashworthiness and head restraint effectiveness. **Weak points:** Unreasonable freight and PDI fees; handling not quite as crisp as the BMW 5 Series; suspension is a bit soft; complicated, difficult-to-use COMAND electronic control centre; navigation system controls are a pain to use; a surprisingly small trunk; and tall drivers may be bothered by the knee bolsters. The failure-prone electronics can screw up

All ratings on a numbered scale where ⑤ is good and ❶ is bad. See page 153–154 for a more detailed description.

dozens of safety and performance features. **New for 2006:** The E320 is replaced by the E350, which reflects the new 268 3.5L V6 engine.

OVERVIEW: The E-Class is your father's Oldsmobile—if he was German. Redesigned only a few times during the past decade, these family sedans and wagons are considered state-of-the-art German auto technology. E-cars do everything well, and manage to hold five people in relative comfort. They're first class in combining performance, road manners, and comfort. True, they're not the best riding, handling, or accelerating cars available, but they're able to perform each of these tasks almost as well as the best cars in each specific area, without sacrificing some other important elements in the driving equation.

These luxo-sedans and wagons are loaded with safety and performance features. The base 268-hp 3.5L V6 E350 sedan ($74,300, and $1,500 more for the CDI) comes with a 5-speed automatic transmission with manual-shift capability, traction control, and front and rear side airbags. Power is cranked up several more notches with the 302-hp 5.0L V8 used to power the E500s ($84,600). Those in the crowd who want top-drawer performance, no matter the cost, will have to make do with the $117,745 E55 AMG sedan's supercharged 469-hp 5.4L V8 mated to a 7-speed automatic transmission.

Mercedes E-Class models have front and side head-protecting airbags for all occupants, plus dual-locking shoulder belts. The front airbags are designed to deploy at higher speeds when occupants are belted than when they're unbelted. Belts in the front seat have tensioners that activate in a crash to reduce belt slack. Sensors in the seat and belt deactivate the airbags and belt pretensioner on the passenger side if no occupant is riding in this seat. The middle back seat has a lap/shoulder belt. Energy-absorbing padding between the footwell and floor carpet is designed to reduce the forces on drivers' legs in serious frontal crashes.

COST ANALYSIS: Diesel buyers should consider the carried-over 2005 turbocharged models, while performance enthusiasts will want to check out the 2005 E500's supercharged V8. All others should look for a heavily discounted second-series 2004 sedan or wagon. **Best alternatives:** Other cars worth considering are the Audi A6/all-road Quattro, the BMW 5 Series, the Lexus GS 300 or 430, and the Volvo S80, V70, or V70 XC. **Options:** Stay away from the COMAND option. **Rebates:** Look for deep discounting as leftovers are moved out to make way for the revised sedan. **Delivery/PDI:** $1,500 (double what's acceptable). **Depreciation:** Slower than average. **Insurance cost:** Higher than average. **Parts supply/cost:** Hard to find outside of the dealer network, and can be expensive at times (body parts especially). **Annual maintenance cost:** Less than average. **Warranty:** Bumper-to-bumper 4 years/80,000 km; powertrain 4 years/80,000 km; rust perforation 5 years/120,000 km. **Supplementary warranty:** Not needed. **Highway/city fuel economy:** *3.2L V6:* 7.5–11.4L/100 km; *3.2L V6 diesel:* 6.1–8.9L/100 km.

Quality/Reliability/Safety

Con: Although these cars are built for safety, their declining quality and complicated engineering can make them a nightmare to own and service. **Service bulletin problems:** Steering leaks; inoperative Parktronics system; Parking Assist system triggers for no reason; sliding roof switch cover cracks; squeaking/creaking noise suppression kit; whistling noise when brake pedal is depressed; and exhaust system noises. **NHTSA safety complaints:** *300E:* Passenger-side curtain and rear side door airbag deployed for no reason; steering suddenly locked up while turning. *320:* When accelerating, vehicle hesitates, then surges forward; intermittent stalling when decelerating; if water enters the automatic transmission control module, the transmission won't shift; stalling, hesitation, leakage, and noise caused by the failure of the transmission's electronic circuit board; malfunctioning gateway module and software causes electrical system to run haywire and the SRS light to come on; electrical shorts cause brake failures (E-Class and SL-Class); airbag failed to deploy in a collision; ABS light comes on for no reason; and faulty electrical wiring.

Road Performance

Pro: Acceleration/torque: Acceleration is better than average with the new 3.5L V6 engine, but the 5.2L V8's performance is dazzling. **Transmission:** Flawless. **Braking:** It'd be hard to find better braking with any other car in this class.

Volkswagen

While BMW and Porsche rake in the dough, VW joins Mercedes-Benz in losing money through lost sales and high warranty and marketing costs. VW's costs are too high, its labour agreements are outdated, its factories are inefficient by today's standards, and its product lineup is mediocre at best. No wonder the company is losing ground in North America, and worse, on its home ground in central Europe, where GM and Ford are staging modest comebacks. Volkswagen, like Mercedes-Benz, is also saddled with a reputation for selling poor-quality vehicles that are costly to service and require frequent repairs after the warranty expires. In fact, VW finished 34th out of 37 brands in J.D. Power's most recent annual initial-quality survey.

As with most European cars, Volkswagens are practical driver's cars and offer excellent handling and great fuel economy without sacrificing interior comfort. But overall reliability isn't very good (particularly after the fifth year of ownership), and servicing is often better and much cheaper at independent garages, which have grown increasingly popular as owners flee more expensive VW dealerships. Although parts are fairly expensive, independent repair agencies usually have no trouble finding them.

Volkswagen is trying desperately to claw its way back to profitability this year with its redesigned Golf, Jetta, and Passat. The new Jetta arrived last March, followed in September by a more luxurious GLI version, equipped with a high-performance 200-hp 2.0L 4-cylinder direct-injection gasoline engine; a wagon variant will arrive sometime in 2006.

The new Golf won't arrive until May 2006, and its GTI high-performance model debuts six months later, or three months after the Jetta equivalent arrives. Passat's redesigned 2006 model is longer, wider, and more powerful; an all-wheel drive version will debut by year's end.

NEW BEETLE ★★★

RATING: Average. Like the Mini Cooper, the New Beetle is an expensive ($23,910) trip down memory lane. Personally, I don't think it's worth it—with or without its speed-activated spoiler and dash-mounted bud vase. No matter how they stir the pot (Beetle Turbo, Turbo S, and the Beetle Convertible), the soup is cold. **Strong points:** Competent 5-cylinder engine; easy handling; sure-footed and comfortable, though firm, ride; impressive braking; most instruments and controls are user friendly; comfortable and supportive front seats with plenty of headroom and legroom; cargo area can be expanded by folding down the front seats; reasonable freight and PDI charges; upgraded head-protecting airbags and front head restraints; good crash protection scores; and top-quality mechanical components and workmanship. **Weak points:** The 2.5L engine doesn't excite; serious safety defects reported by owners; diesel engine lacks pep and produces lots of noise and vibration; easily buffeted by crosswinds; large head restraints and large front roof pillars obstruct front visibility; limited rear legroom and headroom; excessive engine noise; and skimpy interior storage and trunk space. **New for 2006:** The New Beetle is slightly restyled inside and out, and powered by a new 150-hp 2.5L

TECHNICAL DATA

POWERTRAIN (FRONT-DRIVE)

Engines: 2.5L 5-cyl. (150 hp) • 1.9L TD 4-cyl. (100 hp); Transmissions: 5-speed man. • 6-speed auto.

DIMENSION/CAPACITY

Passengers: 2/2; Wheelbase: 99 in.; H: 59.5/L: 161/W: 68 in.; Headroom F/R: 8.0/1.0 in.; Legroom F/R: 42/23.5 in.; Cargo volume: 12 cu. ft.; Fuel tank: 55L/ regular; Tow limit: N/A; Load capacity: 770 lb.; Turning circle: 37 ft.; Weight: 3,280 lb.

5-cylinder engine hooked to a 5-speed manual transmission; a 6-speed automatic is optional. Electronic stability control is standard on all models.

OVERVIEW: Why so much press coverage for the return of an ugly German import that never had a functioning heater, was declared "Small on Safety" by Ralph Nader and his Center for Auto Safety, and carried a puny 48-hp engine? The simple answer is that in its original incarnation, it was cheap and it represented the first car most of us could afford as we went through school, got our first job, and dreamed of getting a better car. Time has taken the edge off the memories of the hardships the Beetle made us endure—like having to scrape the inside windshield with our nails as our breath froze—and left us with the cozy feeling that the car wasn't that bad after all. It *was* that bad.

Now VW has resurrected the Beetle and produced a more refined and safer front engine, front-drive compact car—set on the chassis and running gear of the Golf hatchback. The 150-hp base engine is a big improvement over last year's puny powerplant (the 100-hp 1.9L turbodiesel is laughable, unless you're the one driving it). There's still not much room for rear passengers, engine noise is disconcerting, front visibility is hindered by the car's quirky design, and storage capacity is at a premium.

COST ANALYSIS: Go for the upgraded 2006 models. **Best alternatives:** Other cars worth considering are the Hyundai Elantra, the Mazda6, the Mini Cooper (if you must have cachet), and the Toyota Corolla. **Options:** Nothing important. **Rebates:** Most rebates and discounts will apply to the 2005 models, which aren't as well-equipped. **Delivery/PDI:** $1,300. **Depreciation:** Much slower than average, especially during the first two years. **Insurance cost:** Higher than average. **Parts supply/cost:** Not hard to find, since they're taken from the Golf/ Jetta parts bin, but they may be more expensive than parts for most other cars in this class. **Annual maintenance cost:** Less than average during the first three years. After this, expect repair costs to start to climb dramatically. **Warranty:** Bumper-to-bumper 2 years/40,000 km; powertrain 5 years/80,000 km; rust perforation 12 years/unlimited km. **Supplementary warranty:** A good idea. **Highway/city fuel economy:** 4.8–6.9L/100 km with the 1.9L turbodiesel.

Quality/Reliability/Safety

Pro: Quality control: Average. **Reliability:** Average. **Warranty performance:** Slow but fair treatment of warranty claims by customer service staff located in the States. **Safety:** Standard three-point seat belts and anti-theft alarm (thieves just adore these cars).

Con: Owner-reported problems: Frequent mass airflow sensor failures; intermittent automatic transmission leaks; won't shift from Reverse to Drive, slams into forward gear, or downshifts abruptly when coming to a stop; axle oil pan and oil pump failures; high-maintenance brakes because of prematurely worn pads and rotors; malfunctioning dashboard gauges; convertible top is glitch-prone; poor fit and finish accompanied by omnipresent squeaks, rattles, and buzzing; inoperative power windows; driver door and trunk won't shut; faulty radios; window regulators are often broken; and front light covers retain water and short out. **Service bulletin problems:** Hard starting or no-start; difficult Reverse gear engagement with the manual transmission; convertible top is too hard to open; passenger occupant detection system fault; inoperative radio; and front turn signal blinks too fast. **NHTSA safety complaints:** Sudden acceleration; delayed acceleration; when vehicle is cruising on the highway, it suddenly loses most of its power for about 30 seconds, and then returns to normal; steering wheel locked up when accelerating; steering wheel shakes excessively and pulls vehicle to the right; back glass suddenly exploded; rear windshield glass hard to see through; front and rear windshield distortion; chronic stalling; Check Engine light comes on for no reason; temperature gauge warning light malfunctioned and reservoir tank sensor failed, causing vehicle to overheat; side airbag deployed for no reason, injuring occupant; side-impact airbags did not deploy, resulting in death; for passengers who have seat-belt-exempting illnesses, or those who carry passengers under the weight limit, the beeper every 30 seconds is a big pain in the kazoo. In other incidents, driver-side airbag didn't deploy; airbag light wouldn't go off; driver seatback failed following a rear-end collision; busted fuel tank leaked fuel; plastic fuel tank was easily punctured because of its vulnerable low-mounted position; the headrest is 15 centimetres (6 inches) too high to fit driver's head and obstructs rear visibility; open sunroof sucks exhaust fumes into the cabin; driver-side window doesn't operate correctly; horn failure; the left front strut slipped down through the spindle, causing the spindle to hit the wheelwell; brake and turn signal lights cannot be seen by other drivers in bright sunlight because of the slope design; and windshield wipers quit working in a storm.

NEW BEETLE

List Price (negotiable)	Residual Values (months)			
	24	36	48	60
GLS: $23,910 (17%)	$17,000	$15,000	$12,000	$ 8,500
GLS TDI: $25,690 (18%)	$18,500	$16,500	$13,500	$10,000
Cvt.: $30,160 (22%)	$22,000	$19,000	$16,000	$13,000

SAFETY FEATURES			CRASHWORTHINESS		
	STD.	OPT.			
Anti-lock brakes	✓	—	Head restraints F/R	5	5
Seat belt pretensioners F/R	✓	—	Visibility F/R	2	1
Side airbags	✓	—	Crash protection (front) D/P	4	4
Stability control	✓	—	Crash protection (side) F/R	5	3
Traction control	✓	—	Crash protection (offset)	5	—
			Rollover	4	—

GOLF, JETTA ★★★★

The Volkswagen Golf.

RATING: Above Average. **Strong points:** Superb all-around front-drive performers that offer power to spare with the manual shifter and base 2.5L 5-cylinder engine; the turbocharged 200-hp 2.0L 4-cylinder engine delivers high performance thrills; first-class handling; a comfortable ride; and good fuel economy. There's also widespread discounting because of a poor sales year. **Weak points:** Difficult entry and exit; restricted rear visibility; limited rear legroom; and a high number of safety-related complaints. Many incidents reported of airbags deploying for no reason and injuring or killing occupants. Keep in mind that the $1,300 freight and PDI fee is more than double what is acceptable. Maintenance costs increase dramatically after the fifth year of ownership. **New for 2006:** New 4-and 5-cylinder engines, a 6-speed manual transmission, and standard stability and traction control.

OVERVIEW: Practical and fun to drive—that pretty well sums up the main reasons that these VWs continue to be so popular. Yet they offer much more, including lots of front interior room, plenty of power, responsive handling, great fuel economy, and better-than-average reliability over the first three years.

The Jetta is a more expensive Golf with a trunk (probably why Jettas always outsell Golfs), and the convertible (formerly called a Cabrio) is a more expensive, roofless Golf. The Golf GTI is a sporty performer that comes with lots of standard equipment, including air conditioning, an upgraded sound system, and a split folding rear seat. Jettas offer standard cruise control, power mirrors, and alloy wheels.

There are three engines available: a 100-hp 1.9L turbo diesel, a 150-hp 2.5L base 5-cylinder, and a 200-hp turbocharged 2.0L 4-cylinder. A manual 5-speed transmission is also offered as a standard feature, along with an optional 5-speed automatic and 6-speed manual.

TECHNICAL DATA

POWERTRAIN (FRONT-DRIVE)
Engines: 2.5L 5-cyl. (150 hp) • 1.9L 4-cyl. TD (100 hp) • 2.0L Turbo 4-cyl. (200 hp); Transmissions: 5-speed man. • 5-speed auto. • 6-speed man. • 6-speed auto.

DIMENSION/CAPACITY
Passengers: 2/3; Wheelbase: 101.5 in.; H: 57.5/L: 179.4/W: 69.3 in.; Headroom F/R: N/A; Legroom F/R: 41.3/33.3 in.; Cargo volume: 18 cu. ft.; Fuel tank: 55L/regular; Tow limit: 1,000 lb.; Turning circle: 35.1 ft.; Weight: 3,353 lb.

COST ANALYSIS: Don't be tempted by a discounted 2005; it will lack the refinement and power of this year's model. Also, high fuel prices have given the diesel a shot in the arm, meaning you will pay the full list price. **Best alternatives:** Other cars worth considering are the Honda Civic or Accord, the Mazda6, the Nissan Sentra, and the Toyota Corolla or Matrix. Convertible shoppers might also want to test-drive the Chrysler Sebring, the Ford Mustang, or the Mazda Miata. **Options:** Stay away from the electric sunroof; it costs a bundle to repair and offers not much more than the well-designed manual sunroof. On top of that, you lose too much headroom. The diesel option isn't a good idea unless you travel more than 30,000 km a year. Granted, there are fewer things to go wrong with diesel engines, and fuel economy is high, but gasoline-powered Japanese compacts have an excellent track record and good fuel efficiency, without the well-known diesel drawbacks. Says *Car and Driver* magazine in a recent comparison test:

> The VW gives you a little of that Peterbilt clatter and that indomitable turbo torque way down at grunting speed. You get to slog around in the ever-widening oil slick at the U-serve, too, same as real truckers, and you'll notice that clingy petro smell every time you get behind the wheel.

A lower fuel cost isn't a strong enough argument to weigh against the reduced performance of diesel engines. And diesel fuel prices have risen considerably over the past five years and are expected to go even higher—wiping out much of the fuel savings. **Delivery/PDI:** $1,300. **Rebates:** $2,000 rebates and low-interest financing on the non-diesel models. **Depreciation:** Slower than average, especially the Jetta and convertible versions. **Insurance cost:** Higher than average. **Parts supply/cost:** Not hard to find, but parts can be more expensive than most other cars in this class. **Annual maintenance cost:** Less than average while under warranty. After that, repair costs start to climb dramatically. **Warranty:**

Bumper-to-bumper 2 years/40,000 km; powertrain 5 years/80,000 km; rust perforation 12 years/unlimited km. **Supplementary warranty:** A good idea. **Highway/city fuel economy:** 4.8–6.9L/100 km with the 1.9L engine.

 ## Quality/Reliability/Safety

Pro: Quality control: Average. No rusting owing to a galvanized body and stainless steel exhaust system. **Reliability:** Good overall reliability during the first few years. **Warranty performance:** Average. **Safety:** Standard three-point seat belts and anti-theft alarm.

Con: Ownership costs rise dramatically after the fifth year of ownership. **Owner-reported problems:** The brakes and the electrical, fuel, and exhaust systems are especially troublesome; chronic stalling; many incidents where the airbag warning light stays lit or the airbag suddenly deploys; engine timing belt failure; excessive oil consumption; engine sludge buildup; automatic transmission grinding, howling, whining, erratic shifting, locking up, won't go into Fourth gear; when shifting gears, clutch goes out without warning; manual transmission slips out of gear and engages Reverse; steering moan when turning; owners report that doors are poorly hung, causing rattling and water intrusion into the cabin; and window regulators fail regularly, allowing glass to fall into door; Door Ajar light comes on for no reason; bent driver's door; instrument panel buzz; rattles are omnipresent; dashboard controls and interior and exterior trim items aren't very durable (rattles throughout the interior, dents beneath the doors, body paint scratches); and convertible top storage obstructs rear vision. **Service bulletin problems:** Inoperative air blower motor and prematurely worn rotors and rear brake pads. VW has said the company will replace pads for free up to 12 months or 19,300 km (12,000 mi.), so use that as your benchmark for negotiating a refund, regardless of the model year. **NHTSA safety complaints:** *Golf:* Airbags often deploy when the car passes over a small pothole, or they fail to deploy during a collision. Intermittent stalling; vehicle suddenly veers to one side; uncomfortable driver's seat creates excessive fatigue on long trips; horn can't be located when wheel is turned; improper lug nuts allow wheel to separate from the car. *Jetta:* Shoulder and lapbelt disengaged during a collision; restraints failed, allowing driver to hit the windshield even though the airbag deployed; vehicle was hit from all sides and neither front nor side airbags deployed; car hit the curb and airbag deployed, hitting driver's head and killing him; as with the Golf, there are many incidents where the airbag deployed for no apparent reason:

> Driving on the turnpike, the driver-side airbag deployed without any sort of impact. There is no visible damage to the vehicle, which was only two months old at the time. Fortunately the only injury was a burn from the airbag on the side of my arm. My biggest fear is knowing relatives and friends who drive Jettas and who have young children in their car. This incident could easily have been fatal. Hopefully your establishment can encourage VW where I have failed, to do something about this defect.

Passenger-side airbag deployed seconds after impact; another time, it deployed six hours after a fender-bender; and sometimes, the airbag warning light comes on for no apparent reason and shuts down the entire supplementary restraint system. Bolts from driveshaft to transmission sheared off; transmission sticks in Reverse gear; fuel tank leaks; when the brakes are released, vehicle suddenly accelerates; cruise control won't shut off; intermittent stalling when vehicle is driven at speeds over 57 km/h; no-start caused by door wiring harness failure; Check Engine light comes on, vehicle shakes violently, followed by complete brake loss; brake master cylinder failure; ABS failure; brake pedal went to the floor with no braking effect, then slowly returned to normal; brake pedal could not be pushed down; vehicle rolled down incline with emergency brake engaged; while cruising at 80 km/h, brakes suddenly engaged; moaning noise heard when turning; front seats rock front to back; and faulty heated seats are fire-prone, or as one owner so succinctly wrote to government investigators:

> My heated seats caught fire and burnt my ass....

The exhaust pipe extends underneath the bumper, revealing raw edge of pipe; trunk stainless steel protection plate at the latch cutout area is razor sharp; adhesive that secures the brake light in the rear window can melt in sunlight; gear console gives an inaccurate gear reading; inaccurate fuel reading, indicated Full when it was actually Empty; interior and instrument lights fail intermittently; headlight condensation; windshields crack or shatter from stress or temperature changes; windshield wipers shut off intermittently; window regulator failures:

> My car window failed only three days after I bought it. I was told by the dealers and a representative from the Volkswagen corporate offices that the reason they can't get it fixed in a reasonable amount of time is it is on back order from the factory because the driver-side or passenger-side window clips break in over 50 percent of new Volkswagen GTIs and Golfs within the first year.

 ## Road Performance

Pro: Acceleration/torque: The standard 2.5L 5-cylinder engine is well-suited for city driving and leisurely highway cruising, thanks mainly to the car's light weight and handling prowess. The 200-hp 4-cylinder engine is guaranteed to produce performance thrills without much of a fuel penalty. **Routine handling:** Excellent handling, though ride may be too firm for some. **Emergency handling:** Excellent now that the suspension has been firmed up this year. **Steering:** Precise and predictable. **Braking:** Acceptable.

Con: Diesel engine equipped with cruise control can't handle small hills very well, and usually drops 10–15 km/h.

GOLF, JETTA

List Price (negotiable)	Residual Values (months)			
	24	36	48	60
Golf CL: $18,530 (15%)	$13,000	$11,000	$ 8,000	$ 6,000
Jetta GLS 2.0: $24,975 (19%)	$16,000	$14,000	$11,000	$ 9,000
Jetta GLS TDI: $26,650 (20%)	$19,500	$16,000	$13,000	$11,000
1.9TDI wagon: $27,780 (20%)	$20,500	$19,000	$16,000	$14,000

SAFETY FEATURES			CRASHWORTHINESS		
	STD.	OPT.	Head restraints F/R		
Anti-lock brakes	✓	—	Golf 2d	5	5
Seat belt pretensioners F/R	✓	—	Golf 4d	3	3
Side airbags	✓	—	Jetta	3	2
Stability control	✓	—	Visibility F/R	5	2
Traction control	✓	—	Crash protection (front) D/P	5	5
			Jetta	4	4
			Crash protection (side) F/R	4	4
			Jetta	5	5
			Crash protection (offset)	5	—
			Rollover (Jetta)	4	—

PASSAT ★★★

All ratings on a numbered scale where 5 is good and 1 is bad. See page 153–154 for a more detailed description.

RATING: Average, mainly for performance, not for quality control. Its diesel engine is the Passat's strongest suit. **Strong points:** Lively acceleration with the base 4-cylinder and a manual transmission; refined road manners; sophisticated, user-friendly all-wheel drive; no turbo lag; quiet running; plenty of passenger and cargo room; impressive interior fit and finish; and exceptional driving comfort. Well appointed and holds its value well. The 2005 TDI has a range of nearly 1,000 km, making it a formidable long-range cruiser. **Weak points:** Rear corner blind spots and rear head restraints impede rear visibility; many safety and performance complaints (faulty airbags and transmissions, distorted windshields, and chronic stalling); expensive; and poor fuel economy. Diesel's environmental benefits have been over-hyped: Beyond the smoke, smell, and engine clatter, all diesel engines emit more nitrogen oxide and particulate emissions than similar-sized gasoline engines, which contribute to smog and exacerbate respiratory ailments. **New for 2006:** A new engine lineup that includes a base 200-hp 2.0L 4-cylinder and an optional 280-hp 3.6L V6. A 6-speed manual transmission is standard; the 6-speed automatic with Tiptronic is optional. Stylistically, this year's Passat has sharper lines and is 3 inches longer and 3 inches wider than before—allowing for over two extra inches of rear legroom.

OVERVIEW: Volkswagen's largest front-drive compact has become even larger and more performance-oriented for 2006. The Passat is an attractive mid-sized car that rides on the same platform as the Audi A4. It has a more stylish design than the Golf or Jetta, but still provides a comfortable, roomy interior and gives good all-around performance for highway and city driving. The car's large wheelbase and squat appearance give it a massive, solid feeling, while its aerodynamic styling makes it look sleek and clean. Most Passats come fully loaded with air conditioning, tinted glass, power-assisted disc brakes on all four wheels, front and rear stabilizer bars, full instrumentation, and even a roof rack with the wagon. An all-wheel-drive powertrain will be available in the spring.

COST ANALYSIS: Get the 2006 model for the extra room and power, but wait until mid-2006 for the prices to settle. **Best alternatives:** Other cars worth considering are the Audi A6 and the BMW 3 Series. **Options:** A good anti-theft system. The AWD is an excellent investment, if you need the extra sure-footedness and traction. **Rebates:** Not likely. **Delivery/PDI:** $1,300. **Depreciation:** Slower than average. **Insurance cost:** Higher than average. These cars are favourites with thieves—whether for radios, wheels, VW badges, or entire cars. **Parts supply/cost:** Not hard to find. Parts and service are much more expensive than

---

TECHNICAL DATA

POWERTRAIN (FRONT-DRIVE/AWD)
Engines: 2.0L 4-cyl. (200 hp) • 3.6 V6 (280 hp); Transmissions: 6-speed man. • 6-speed auto.

DIMENSION/CAPACITY
Passengers: 2/3; Wheelbase: 106 in.; H: 57.4/L: 185/W: 69 in.; Headroom F/R: 4.0/2.0 in.; Legroom F/R: 42/29 in.; Cargo volume: 15 cu. ft.; Fuel tank: 47L/premium; Tow limit: 2,000 lb.; Load capacity: 1,060 lb.; Turning circle: 38 ft.; Weight: 3,530 lb.

average. **Annual maintenance cost:** Higher than average. **Warranty:** Bumper-to-bumper 2 years/40,000 km; powertrain 5 years/80,000 km; rust perforation 12 years/unlimited km. **Supplementary warranty:** A must-have. Maintenance costs are higher than average once the warranty expires. **Highway/city fuel economy:** N/A.

 ## Quality/Reliability/Safety

Pro: Warranty performance: Average. VW staffers in the States (there's no office in Canada) have been fairly sensitive to Passat complaints. Still, I'm bothered by a company that doesn't feel that its customers merit a regional office—Suzuki and Hyundai manage it.

Con: Quality control: German build quality has been seriously overrated. Can you believe the company can't make distortion-free windshields for a $30,000–$45,000 car? **Reliability:** Below-average reliability during the first three years, judging by NHTSA database entries. The tranny complaints are all the more annoying because VW had serious Passat transmission problems in the early '90s and assured me then that the defects had been remedied at the factory. **Owner-reported problems:** An incredible number of automatic transmission malfunctions, breakdowns, and early replacements. Transmission vibration and noise; premature CV joint failure; oil pan is easily punctured owing to low ground clearance; and CV boot wears out prematurely. Frequent electrical and fuel system glitches cause chronic stalling. Gas pedal remained stuck to the floor. Premature brake wear and noisy braking. Poor fit-and-finish highlights: sunroof rattles; driver-seat memory feature fails; front spoiler and rear trim fall off; distorted windshields; seat belt latch doesn't hold the metal tongue; and heated seats that are a pain in the…well, you know. **Service bulletin problems:** N/A. **NHTSA safety complaints:** Several reports that fire ignited in the engine compartment; excess raw fuel flows out of the exhaust system; hard starts and chronic stalling; Check Engine light comes on intermittently and then engine shuts down. While cruising, vehicle speeds up, then when brakes applied, it slows down until foot is taken off the brake, when it surges again—one owner describes it this way:

> When accelerating from a stop or low speed the car hesitates and then jumps. The problem is most severe in reverse gear. The dealership has no resolution. After changing multiple parts the problem still occurs. I have talked with other 2004 Passat and Touareg owners and they have the same complaint, so it appears to be affecting more than a single vehicle.

Vehicle runs out of fuel despite the fuel gauge showing a quarter tank of gas; braking doesn't disengage cruise control; hesitation, long delays when accelerating; automatic transmission suddenly drops out of gear; airbags failed to deploy or deploy for no reason. One VW employee told U.S. federal investigators he was fired for complaining about the airbag hazard:

The driver's side head airbag (air curtain) of a 2003 Volkswagen Passat W8 sedan deployed spontaneously while I was driving the car.... A few minutes later, when the car was stopped, the steering wheel airbag deployed spontaneously.... I suffered a permanent wrist injury and am suffering from post-traumatic stress syndrome.

Airbag warning light stays lit; many complaints of windshield distortion (there's an accordion effect where letters and objects expand and contract as they pass by); passenger window suddenly exploded just after being rolled up; windshield wipers cut out and have a groove in the blade that collects snow and ice; plastic engine nose shield fell off; rear tire failure damaged the fuel-filler neck, causing a fuel leak; tire tread separation; overheated seats; and AM radio static.

Road Performance

Pro: Acceleration/torque: Impressive acceleration with the base 2.0L turbo-charged engine. **Transmission:** Great performance with the manual gearbox; smooth and quiet shifting with the automatic gearbox. The 4Motion full-time all-wheel drive shifts effortlessly into gear. **Emergency handling:** Better than average; impressive with the AWD system; no turbo lag. **Steering:** Quick, precise, and predictable. **Routine handling:** Suspension is both firm and comfortable; precise handling outclasses most of the competition.

Con: Braking: Excessive brake fade after successive stops.

PASSAT

List Price (negotiable)	Residual Values (months)			
	24	36	48	60
2.0T: $29,950 (21%)	$23,000	$19,000	$15,000	$12,000
GLS V6: $36,550 (22%)	$25,500	$22,000	$17,500	$14,000
3.6 4Motion: $45,605 (30%)	$32,000	$28,000	$23,500	$18,500

SAFETY FEATURES	STD.	OPT.	CRASHWORTHINESS		
Anti-lock brakes	✓	—	Head restraints F/R	❷	❷
Seat belt pretensioners F/R	✓	—	Visibility F/R	❺	❷
Side airbags	✓	—	Crash protection (front) D/P	❺	❺
Traction control	✓	—	Crash protection (side) F/R	❺	❹
			Crash protection (offset)	❺	—
			Rollover	❹	—

Volvo

More Mazda, Less Volvo

Volvo has always distinguished itself from the rest of the automotive pack through its much-vaunted standard safety features, crashworthiness, and engineering that emphasized function over style. But unfortunately, these noteworthy features were eclipsed by bland styling, ponderous highway performance, inconsistent quality control that compromised long-term reliability and drove up ownership costs, and chancy servicing by a small dealer network Furthermore, Asian automakers have successfully encroached upon Volvo territory by bringing out new products in smaller packages—cars that are as safe and comfortable to drive, with greater reliability thrown in.

Volvo has successfully met the Asian competition by dramatically restyling its cars and cranking up their performance capabilities several notches. Volvo has dumped its boxy station wagons and rediscovered rounded edges, all-wheel drive, and high-performance powertrains and handling. The automaker's curvy, AWD XC models are the latest example of a mindset change that is already in full swing with the company's S60, S70, S80, V70, C70 coupe, and smaller 40 Series cars.

But there are two problems that remain: pricing and quality control. All of the additional performance features are pricing Volvos out of the reach of the average car buyer. And Volvo's quality control and servicing have suffered with the mixing and matching of parts and platforms from other automakers following Ford's purchase of the company. Hopefully, Volvo's Mazda connection, facilitated by Ford, will improve quality and stabilize the brand.

S40, V50 ★★★

RATING: Average. The S40 sedan and V50 wagon represent significant quality and performance improvements over previous Volvo models, but they still have a long way to go to match cheaper alternatives from the Japanese. **Strong points:** The T5's 2.5L turbo produces better than average acceleration, accompanied by little turbo lag, thanks to its crisp and precise manual transmission, all-wheel drive, and sport suspension. Although it saps some engine power, the automatic transmission is smooth and responsive; the manual is effortless. Lots of innovative safety features that include head-protecting side airbags, dual rear integrated child booster seats, ABS, and traction control. Above average braking when brakes are functioning normally; good steering and handling; the tight turning circle is helpful for city chores; most instruments and controls are easily accessed; the standard tilt/telescope steering wheel makes it easier to find a comfortable driving

The Volvo S40.

position; sufficient front room and comfortable front seating; trunk has a low liftover; and overall Volvo reliability has improved of late (there was a decline when Ford first purchased the company). **Weak points:** The base 5-cylinder 2.4L engine, even with a manual transmission, doesn't handle long grades very well and isn't as smooth-running as a V6; suspension is fairly stiff and becomes uncomfortable when 17-inch tires are used in combination with the AWD sport suspension; and there's some wandering in panic stops. Both models lack the tossability of the Mazda3, despite sharing much of the little Mazda's chassis components. The Volvos have a bit of understeer, steering appears somewhat over-assisted, reducing road feel, and there is some front-end plowing going into corners, while the lighter Mazda3 feels like a small racer. Other minuses: engine exhaust boom and growl at high revs; entry and exit are made difficult by narrow doors; not a lot of interior width; very cramped rear seating (two adults will fit, at the most) and inadequate thigh support; when front seats are pushed back, forget about rear footroom; visibility obstructed by rear head restraints and a high rear deck lid; trunk utility hampered by its small opening and wagon's tailgate doesn't open past the roofline; limited interior storage space; busy instrument panel and controls take a while to figure out; access to the dash-mounted ignition is blocked by the windshield-wiper control stalk; serious safety-related complaints recorded by government investigators; and premium fuel is required for all engines. **New for 2006:** Carried over unchanged.

OVERVIEW: The S40/V50 ($31,120/$32,620, plus an unacceptably high $1,500 freight/PDI) are Volvo's latest small sedan and wagon built in a co-venture

TECHNICAL DATA

POWERTRAIN (FRONT-DRIVE/AWD)
Engines: 2.4L 5-cyl. (168 hp) • 2.5L Turbo 5-cyl. (218 hp); Transmissions: 6-speed man. • 6-speed auto.

DIMENSION/CAPACITY
Passengers: 2/3; Wheelbase: 104 in.; H: 51.5/L: 176/W: 70 in.; Headroom F/R: 3.0/1.5 in.; Legroom F/R: 41.5/28 in.; Cargo volume: 15 cu. ft.; Fuel tank: 47L/premium; Tow limit: 1,000 lb.; Load capacity: 950 lb.; Turning circle: 38 ft.; Weight: 3,245 lb.

with Mitsubishi Motors. The redesigned 2005 model was considerably improved with Mitsubishi's help and the 2006 version carries over these enhancements in toto. Mazda input has been crucial, inasmuch as these new Volvos use many Mazda3 components and share the Mazda3 platform (also used by the Ford Focus in Europe), though sheet metal and powertrains are quite different.

There are two 2006 models available with quite different engines: The 2.4i uses a 2.4L normally aspirated engine, and the T5 carries a slightly larger 2.5L turbo-charged engine that produces about 50 additional horses and much more power (torque) in the lower gears. A firmer suspension and larger wheels and tires are also used to enhance the T5's performance.

COST ANALYSIS: Go for the almost identical 2005 version, if you can get a good price. If not, sit tight and wait for prices on this year's models to come down early in 2006. Although 2006 prices haven't been published yet, insiders tell me prices won't increase by more than $500 on the base model and $1,000 for the turbo-charged version. **Best alternatives:** Other cars worth considering are the Acura TL and the Audi A4. **Options:** Dual integrated child booster seats are a good idea. 17-inch wheels depend upon your tolerance for a firm ride and highway rumbling. AWD means you will spend more on fuel, as well as get a stiffer ride. Leather upholstery, sunroof, and heated seats may be more trouble than they are worth. Opened-sunroof noise, especially, can be deafening. **Rebates:** Look for additional price cuts in the new year as Ford scrambles to increase market share—$4,500 rebates, lots of low-interest financing, and advantageous leasing deals. Don't let the dealer charge you an unjustified $250 "retailer participation charge" for leases. **Delivery/PDI:** $1,500. **Depreciation:** Slower than average, but other European makes may do better. *Automotive Lease Guide*, an American publication, predicts that a 2005 Volvo S40 T5 turbocharged sedan will retain 52 percent of its sticker price after 36 months, compared with a similarly priced Audi A4 sedan, which it says will retain 55 percent. **Insurance cost:** Higher than average. **Parts supply/cost:** Parts aren't hard to find, but may be much more expensive than average. **Annual maintenance cost:** Predicted to be higher than average because of a small dealer network. **Warranty:** Bumper-to-bumper 2 years/40,000 km; power-train 5 years/80,000 km; rust perforation 12 years/unlimited km. **Supplementary warranty:** A must-have in view of the car's unproven history and flurry of consumer complaints. **Highway/city fuel economy:** 6.8–10.5L/100 km.

Service bulletin problems: N/A. **NHTSA safety complaints:** *S40:* Under-hood electrical fire; cracked fuel regulator pump spilled fuel onto hot engine and spread fumes into the interior; sudden, unintended acceleration when vehicle was put into Drive; chronic stalling attributed to faulty idle control valve and air mass meter; complete loss of braking; brake pedal hard to depress, reducing brake effectiveness; brakes don't stop vehicle in a reasonable distance; brake pedal is too close to the gas pedal; brake pedal snapped, went to the floor while going downhill;

when applying the brakes in cold weather, pedal won't depress, causing extended stopping distance (dealer confirmed vacuum pump motor was defective); premature wearout of the front brake pads (around 20,000 km); vehicle pulls to the left when accelerating or coming to a stop; premature replacement of the front and rear rotors and pads; repeated automatic transmission failures that often begin with slippage from Second to Third gear; airbag light stays lit; faulty forward/backward seat adjustment; and noisy engine and sunroof.

S40, V50

List Price (negotiable)	Residual Values (months)			
	24	36	48	60
S40 2.4i: $31,120 (23%)	$23,000	$19,000	$15,000	$12,000
T5: $37,120 (25%)	$26,500	$22,000	$18,500	$15,000
T5 AWD: $39,620 (27%)	$28,000	$24,000	$21,000	$17,000
V50 2.4i: $32,620 (23%)	$24,000	$20,000	$16,000	$13,000
T5: $38,620 (25%)	$27,500	$23,000	$19,500	$16,000
T5 AWD: $41,120 (30%)	$30,000	$25,500	$22,000	$18,500

SAFETY FEATURES			CRASHWORTHINESS		
	STD.	OPT.			
Anti-lock brakes	✓	—	Head restraints F/R	5	5
Seat belt pretensioners F/R	✓	—	Visibility F/R	5	3
Side airbags	✓	—	Crash protection (front) D/P	4	5
Traction control	✓	—	Crash protection (side) F/R	5	5
			Crash protection (offset)	5	—
			Rollover	4	—

S60 ★★★

RATING: Average. Fewer owner complaints than with the smaller Volvos, but performance and standard features are outclassed by the competition. **Strong points:** Quick acceleration only with the T5's turbocharged engine; acceptable handling and braking; good array of user-friendly instruments and controls; comfortable front seating; very good head-restraint, offset, front, and side crashworthiness scores; and predicted better-than-average reliability. **Weak points:** Lots of turbo throttle hesitation and torque steer pulling when accelerating; imprecise manual shifter; ride is a bit jarring with some tire thump (worse with the T5) when passing over uneven pavement; handling isn't very agile and R version's suspension isn't as confidence-inspiring as expected; rear visibility obstructed by high parcel shelf, obtrusive head restraints, and descending roofline; rear room adequate only for

two adults and rear legroom disappears when front seats are pushed back only halfway; narrow trunk with a small opening; and all engines require premium fuel. **New for 2006:** The T5 wagon has been dropped.

OVERVIEW: The S60 is a sporty mid-range sedan version ($40,620, plus an exorbitant $1,500 freight/PDI and bogus $250 leasing charge) of the V70 wagon ($39,120). A 208-hp 2.5L 5-cylinder engine is the base power source, giving buyers optional AWD benefits without having to choose the taller, more SUV-like Cross Country. Drivers may also opt for a 257-hp 2.4L 5-cylinder, or the S60R's ($60,620) 300-hp 2.5L high-performance 5-cylinder AWD spin-off. Most engines are turbo-charged, except for the 168-hp 2.4L 5-cylinder, hooked to a 5-speed manual gearbox or "Auto-Stick" 5-speed automatic (2.5T). R versions are equipped with all-wheel drive coupled to a standard close-ratio 6-speed manual transmission or an optional 6-speed "Auto Stick." Leftover models have been deeply discounted as fuel costs have increased. Other cars worth considering are the Acura TL, the Infiniti I35, and the Lexus ES 330.

Service bulletin problems: N/A. **NHTSA safety complaints:** Right front wheel fell off; sudden stalling; automatic transmission delayed engagement and flaring; suspension (automatic stability control) glitches; ABS brakes don't work properly; head restraints obstruct rear vision; and Pirelli tire blowouts.

V70, XC70, XC90 ★★★

The Volvo V70.

RATING: Average. **Strong points:** Acceleration (T6); practical to the extreme; good handling and braking; lots of cargo room; well-designed instruments and controls are easy to read and access; many standard safety features; and excellent crashworthiness scores. **Weak points:** Too much torque steer; a jarring ride with vehicles equipped with 16- and 17-inch wheels; excessive engine, wind, and road noise; confusing navigation system controls; fuel-thirsty (turbo models); limited rear visibility; and a worrisome number of safety- and performance-related factory defects reported to the U.S. government. The XC70 is less comfortable than the V70, steering is numb and imprecise, and fuel economy suffers. Owners report that the XC70 "floats" over uneven terrain and exhibits more body roll in cornering owing to its tall body. **New for 2006:** "Instant Traction" traction control and a digital-camera-based "Blind Spot Information" feature. V70 gets an optional 6-speed automatic transmission.

OVERVIEW: The quintessential Volvo wagon and Volvo's best-selling line, the V70 has two models available: a base front-drive and an AWD. Sporty T6 versions employ front-wheel drive. Front-drives and AWD use

TECHNICAL DATA

POWERTRAIN (FRONT-DRIVE/AWD)
Engines: 2.4L 5-cyl. (168 hp) • 2.5L
5-cyl. turbo (208 hp) • 2.5L 5-cyl. turbo
(300 hp); Transmissions: 5-speed man.
• 6-speed man. • 5-speed auto. •
6-speed manu-matic

DIMENSION/CAPACITY (V70)
Passengers: 2/3/2; Wheelbase: 109 in.;
H: 52.5/L: 186/W: 73 in.; Headroom F/R:
3.5/3.5 in.; Legroom F/R: 43/28.5 in.;
Cargo volume: 35.5 cu. ft.; Fuel tank:
73L/premium; Tow limit: 3,300 lb.; Load
capacity: 1,285 lb.; Turning circle: 40 ft.;
Weight: 3,815 lb.

a 2.5L 208-hp 5-cylinder engine hooked to a 5-speed automatic. Three powertrains are offered: a 168-hp 2.4L 5-cylinder, the aforementioned 208-hp variant, and a 300-hp 2.5L 5-cylinder equipped with a high-pressure turbocharger. As expected with Volvo, these cars are loaded with safety and convenience features that include four-wheel disc brakes, head/chest front and side airbags, and high-tech seatbacks designed to minimize whiplash.

XC70, XC90

The Volvo XC70.

Essentially a renamed V70 station wagon, the XC70 is an SUV wannabe that offers five-passenger seating, high ground clearance, sleek styling, and AWD versatility—all for $47,120. Its mechanical components are practically identical to those of Volvo's other sedans. The base engine is a 168-hp (non-turbo) 2.4L 5-cylinder. The turbo version has been replaced by a 208-hp 2.5L turbocharged 5-cylinder hooked to a 5-speed automatic gearbox. A 300-hp variant is found on the V70 R. XC90 models start at $49,995 and offer seven-passenger seating, along with a base turbocharged 208-hp 2.5L 5-cylinder.

COST ANALYSIS: Discounted 2005 V70s are the best choice, since they are practically identical to the 2006 version. **Best alternatives:** Other cars worth considering are the Acura TL and the BMW 5 Series wagon. **Options:** Integrated child safety seats and a full-sized spare tire. The turbo's traction control isn't worth the extra cost. Also, take a pass on the complex Navigation System option. **Rebates:** Look for $5,000 rebates and many low-financing and discounting programs to kick in before year's end. **Delivery/PDI:** $1,500. **Depreciation:** Slower than average. **Insurance cost:** Higher than average. **Parts supply/cost:** Parts are highly dealer dependent and moderately expensive, but they aren't hard to find because of the many V70s that were sold. XC70s may have back ordered drivetrain components. **Annual maintenance cost:** Average; higher than average for the XC. Higher-than-average cost predicted for both models after their fourth year on the road. **Warranty:** Bumper-to-bumper 4 years/80,000 km; powertrain 4 years/80,000 km; rust perforation 8 years/unlimited km. **Supplementary warranty:** Recommended. The most frequent complaint concerns the brakes, an item excluded from most supplementary warranties. **Highway/city fuel economy:** 2.4L: 7.8–11L/100 km.

Quality/Reliability/Safety

Pro: Reliability: Fewer reliability problems reported than with Volvo's other models; still, chronic stalling complaints are worrisome. **Warranty performance:** Much better than average. Many warranty claims are settled through "goodwill" on a case-by-case basis. **Safety:** Standard side-impact airbags and standard traction control are a nice touch. Other safety features include rear head restraints; reinforced anti-roll bars; front and rear crumple zones; a practical roof-mounted interior cargo net that protects passengers from being hit by objects stored in the rear; and rear three-point seat belts. As with Volvo's other models, IIHS has awarded the V70 its highest rating for front and rear head restraint protection.

Con: Body assembly and paint quality are better than average, but they can't match the Japanese competition. **Owner-reported problems:** Problem areas are limited to frequent brake maintenance (rotors and pads), chronic stalling, electrical system and body faults (inoperative moon roof, door locks, and gauges), notably excessive windshield/dash glare, and side windows that won't close until control button is pressed three times. Poor fuel economy. **Service bulletin problems:** Rear shock absorber noise; the ball joint nut securing the front control arm may lose its initial tension. *XC90:* Service Campaign 135A for new and improved components; reducing false alarms when it rains; new seat belt guide to prevent second-row belt from catching in the door; and parking brake adjustment. **NHTSA safety complaints:** *V70:* Engine repeatedly stopped in traffic because of what one Volvo insider called a "weak" fuel pump that is said to affect many V70 and S80 models; same problem blamed on debris in the fuel line; vehicle runs out of gas, despite gauge showing sufficient fuel left in tank; electronic throttle hampered by a delay in fuel getting into the engine; car rolled forward down an incline despite being put into Reverse; brake and gas pedal are mounted too close together; seat belt tightens progressively; seat belt crosses at the neck; cracked sidewall of Pirelli P6 tire; fuel spews out of fuel-filler pipe; vehicle continually pulls to the right when underway; many complaints that forward visibility is seriously compromised by the dash reflecting onto the windshield (cream-beige colour the worst offender); front doors will slam shut on a moderate slope; and coffee spilled from cupholder onto airbag computer module, causing huge expense. *XC70:* Vehicle accelerated without warning; vehicle suddenly shut down on the highway; loss of brakes; vehicle rolls back when stopped on an incline; convertible top obscures visibility of the right rear side; driver's seatback locks up if it's folded toward the steering wheel; non-adjustable shoulder belt crosses at the neck; painful front seat design presses into driver's back; and xenon low-beam headlights don't give enough light when going down a hill. *XC90:* Won't start for long periods; brakes frequently lock up; original equipment Michelin tires have poor traction and are unsafe on wet roads; and hatch fell on driver's head, fracturing his neck.

Road Performance

Pro: Acceleration/torque: Plenty of high-range power with the base engine, especially with a manual gearbox. With an automatic transmission, the normally aspirated base engine has a 0–100 km/h time of 9.5 seconds. No turbo lag. The 208-hp turbocharged engine posted better-than-average acceleration times with plenty of torque. **Transmission:** Smooth and quiet automatic and manual gearboxes. **Emergency handling:** Better than average, with minimal body roll and good control. **Steering:** Predictable, rapid steering response. Handles sudden steering corrections very well. **Routine handling:** Nimble handling doesn't sacrifice passenger comfort. **Braking:** Braking performance is quite good.

Con: Moderate torque steer when accelerating. The ride deteriorates progressively as the road gets rougher and passenger weight is added.

V70, XC70, XC90

List Price (negotiable)	Residual Values (months)			
	24	36	48	60
V70 2.4: $39,120 (25%)	$26,000	$23,000	$20,000	$18,000
V70 T5: $49,120 (30%)	$32,000	$29,000	$25,000	$23,000
XC70: $47,120 (30%)	$31,000	$28,000	$24,000	$22,000
XC90: $46,995 (30%)	$31,000	$28,000	$24,000	$22,000

SAFETY FEATURES	STD.	OPT.	CRASHWORTHINESS		
			Head restraints F/R	5	5
Anti-lock brakes	✓	—	Visibility F/R	5	2
Seat belt pretensioners F/R	✓	—	Crash protection (front) D/P		
Side airbags	✓	—	XC90	5	4
Traction control	✓	—	Crash protection (side) F/R		
			XC90	5	5
			Crash protection (offset)		
			XC90	5	—
			Rollover	4	—

HELPFUL INTERNET SITES

You can find lots of information about new cars and minivans on the Internet—but it may not be true or complete. Automobile companies have their own self-serving websites that nevertheless feature details on suggested retail prices and specifications. Their sites can easily be accessed through Google's search engine by searching under the automaker's name followed by "Canada." Sometimes, the manufacturer's name followed by ".*com*" or ".*ca*" will also work. For extra fun and a more balanced presentation, put in the car model or manufacturer's name, followed by "lemon."

Consumer Protection

Alterna Services (*www.metrocu.com*)
If you're a do-it-yourself type or just getting started in your vehicle search, Alterna Services' CarFacts Centre is the place for you. Through the CarFacts Centre and Automotive Advisor you can:

- Access the latest information on automobiles and trends.
- Receive a personal consultation and have your automotive questions answered by an automotive expert.
- Take advantage of the free Used Car Referral Service, which will get you a no-haggle price on your vehicle.

In the Toronto area, the New AutoBuy Service will assist you with the purchase of your new vehicle for the lowest price. For a fee of $100, plus GST, you will learn the dealer's confidential cost price for your selected vehicle, as well as any factory rebates or special financing that may be available. The Automotive Advisor will then assist you in finding a dealer to sell you that vehicle at below the current national average selling price. You can also use the Automotive Research section for links to a wide variety of automotive related websites.

Automobile Consumer Coalition (*www.carhelpcanada.com*)
Founded by the former director of the Toronto Automobile Protection Association, Mohamed Bouchama, the ACC's Car Help Canada website provides many of the same services as the APA; however, it is especially effective in Ontario and Alberta.

Automobile Protection Association (*www.apa.ca*)

With offices in Toronto and Montreal, this consumer group fights for safer vehicles and has exposed many scams associated with new-vehicle sales, leasing, and repairs; for a small fee it will send you the invoice price for most new vehicles.

BBC TV's *Top Gear* Car Reviews (*www.topgear.beeb.com*)

Britain's automotive equivalent to Canada's CBC *Marketplace*, *Top Gear* blows the whistle on the best and worst European-sold vehicles, auto products, and industry practices.

Big Class Action (*www.bigclassaction.com/automotive.html*)

This is a useful site for using a company's class action woes in U.S. jurisdictions for leverage in settling your own Canadian claim out of court. If you decide to go the Canadian class action route, most of the legal legwork will have been done for you. The site is easy and free to search. Just type in the make of the vehicle you're investigating and read the results.

Canadian Competition Bureau (*www.competitionbureau.gc.ca*)

The Competition Bureau is responsible for administration and enforcement of the *Competition Act*, the *Consumer Packaging and Labelling Act*, the *Textile Labelling Act*, and the *Precious Metals Marking Act*. Its role is to promote and maintain fair competition so that Canadians can benefit from lower prices, increased product choice, and quality services.

Most auto-related complaints submitted to the Bureau concern price-fixing and misleading advertising. Toyota's recent $2.3 million settlement followed the Bureau's investigation into charges that the automaker rigged new car prices. Complaints can be filed online by clicking on "contact us."

Canadian Automobile Association (*www.caa.ca*)

The CAA advocates safe driving and provides services for the general public.

Canadian Driver (*www.canadiandriver.com*)

An exceptionally well-structured and current Canadian website for new- and used-vehicle reviews, MSRPs, and consumer reports. Other car magazine websites:

- *World of Wheels* (*www.autonet.ca*)
- *Automotive News* (*www.automotivenews.com*)
- *Car & Driver* (*www.caranddriver.com*)
- *Motor Trend* (*www.motortrend.com*)
- *Road and Track* (*www.roadandtrack.com*)

CBC *Marketplace* (*cbc.ca/consumers/market/files/cars/index.html*)

Marketplace has been the Canadian Broadcasting Corporation's premier national consumer show for almost three decades. Its site has extensive links and in-depth reports on Chrysler paint delamination, ABS brake failures, airbag dangers, and a host of other automotive topics.

ConsumerAffairs.com (*www.consumeraffairs.com/automotive/manufacturers. htm*)
Expecting some namby-pamby consumer affairs site? Won't find that here. A "seller beware" kind of website, where you'll find the scandals before they hit the mainstream press.

Consumer Reports and Consumers Union (*www.consumerreports.org/cro/ cars.htm*)
It costs $4.95 a month to subscribe online, but *CR*'s database is chock full of comparison tests and in-depth stories on products and services.

Protegez-Vous (Protect Yourself) (*www.protegez-vous.qc.ca*)
Quebec's French-language monthly consumer protection magazine and website is a hard-hitting critic of the auto industry. It contains dozens of test-drives and articles relating to a broad range of products and services sold in Canada.

Canadian Court Decisions (*www.canlii.org*)
Be your own legal researcher and save big bucks. Scan these websites to find court judgments from every province and territory all the way up to the Supreme Court of Canada.

Supreme Court of Canada (*www.lexum.umontreal.ca/csc-scc/en/rec/index.html*)
It's not enough to have a solid claim against a company or the government. Supporting your position with a Supreme Court decision also helps. Three pro-consumer judgments rendered in February 2002 are particularly useful:

- *Bannon v. The Corporation of the City of Thunder Bay*. An injured resident missed the deadline to file a claim against Thunder Bay; however, the Supreme Court maintained that extenuating factors, such as being under the effects of medication, extended her time to file. A good case to remember next time your vehicle is damaged by a pothole or you are injured by a municipality's negligence.
- *R. v. Guinard*. An insured posted a sign on his barn claiming the Commerce Insurance Company was unfairly refusing his claim. The municipality of St-Hyacinthe, Quebec, told him to take the sign down. He refused, maintaining that he had the right to state his opinion. The Supreme Court agreed. This judgment means that consumer protests, signs, and websites that criticize the actions of corporations cannot be shut up or taken down simply because they say unpleasant things.
- *Whiten v. Pilot Insurance Co*. The insured's home burned down and the insurance company refused to pay the claim. The jury was outraged and ordered the company to pay the $345,000 claim, plus $320,000 for legal costs and $1 million in punitive damages, making it the largest punitive damage award in Canadian history. The Supreme Court maintained the jury's decision, calling Pilot "the insurer from hell." This judgment scares the dickens out of insurers, who fear that they face huge punitive damage awards if they don't pay promptly.

Auto Safety

Airbag Killer Sites (*www.plescia.org/indexair.htm*)
Anecdotal evidence of airbag injuries and fatalities in low-speed collisions, as well as a compendium of independent research studies.

Center for Auto Safety (*www.autosafety.org*)
A Ralph Nader-founded agency that provides free online info on safety- and performance-related defects on each model vehicle.

Crashtest.com (*www.crashtest.com/netindex.htm*)
A website where crash tests from around the world can be analyzed and compared.

Drive and Stay Alive (*www.driveandstayalive.com*)
This website is run by a non-profit group that has assembled a variety of safety research papers, auto reviews, and other links that are as diverse as they are unconventional.

Insurance Institute for Highway Safety (*www.hwysafety.org*)
A dazzling site that's long on crash photos and graphs that show which vehicles are the most crashworthy in side and offset collisions and which head restraints work best.

The Safety Forum (*www.safetyforum.com*)
The Forum contains comprehensive news archives and links to useful sites, plus names of court-recognized experts on everything from unsafe Chrysler minivan latches to dangerous van conversions.

Toyota Celica Page (*celica.net/main.asp*)
An excellent site for owners' unbiased reviews and technical updates.

Transport Canada (*www.tc.gc.ca/roadsafety/Recalls/search_e.asp*)
A ho-hum site that's no way as informative as NHTSA's site. You can access recalls for 1970–2004 models, but owner complaints aren't listed, defect investigations aren't disclosed, and service bulletin summaries aren't provided. A list of used vehicles admissible for import is available at *www.tc.gc.ca/roadsafety/importation/menu.htm*, or by calling 1-888-848-8240.

U.S. National Highway Traffic Safety Administration (*www.nhtsa.dot.gov/cars/problems*)
This site has a comprehensive free database covering owner complaints, recall campaigns, crashworthiness and rollover ratings, defect investigations, service bulletin summaries, and safety research papers.

Mediation/Protest

Allpar: Chrysler, Plymouth, and Dodge Car Information (*www.allpar.com*)
This is an excellent website that's jam-packed with historical information, tips on fixing common problems inexpensively, and advice on how to deal with Chrysler representatives and dealer service managers.

Chrysler Products' Problem Web Page (*www.wam.umd.edu/~gluckman/ Chrysler*)
A resource for Chrysler owners who have had problems in dealing with Chrysler, including issues with peeling paint, transmission failure, the Chrysler-installed Bendix-10 ABS, and other maladies.

DaimlerChrysler Problems Web Page (*www.daimlerchryslervehicleproblems. com*)
This is a great site for technical info and tips on getting action from DaimlerChrysler if you have a defective Intrepid, 300M, Concorde, or LHS. SUV and truck ball joint failures are also featured.

Dead Eclipse (*www.deadeclipse.com/home.php*)
A good example of a simple but effective consumer protest website. This one targets Mitsubishi's Eclipse.

Do Not Buy a Dodge (*www.donotbuydodge.ca*)
Another excellent example of an effective and simple website set up by the Newmarket, Ontario, owner of a 2003 Caravan afflicted by water leaks, mildew, and corrosion problems.

Ford Insider Info (*www.blueovalnews.com*)
Pssst! Don't tell Ford (they've tried twice to shut down this site). Here's where you get all the latest insider info on Ford's quality problems and plans for future models.

GM Intake Manifold Defects (*www.gm-v6lemons.com*)
A 1999 GM Venture owners' campaign against leaky plastic intake gaskets affecting GM's 3.1L, 3.4L, and 3.8L V6 engines as well as the V8 used in the Tahoe, trucks, and Suburbans. Good links and technical info.

My Ford Lemon (*www.fordlemon.com/WEBSITE_netscape/home.html*)
Lots of links and caricatures relating to one Taurus owner's battle with Ford.

Neon Enthusiasts (*www.neons.org*)
Lots of technical info and troubleshooting tips. Includes service bulletins filed according to the component failure. Chrysler's head gasket service bulletin can be downloaded to buttress your small claims court claim for a free engine repair involving any Chrysler 4-cylinder engine.

Roadfly's BMW, Mini Cooper, and Porsche Message Boards (*www. roadfly.org/forums*)
Another site that's no butt-kisser. Here you'll learn about BMW fan fires, upgrades, and performance comparisons. Also contains message forums for Bentley, Cadillac, Chevy, Jaguar, Lotus, and Mercedes-Benz.

VW Lemon Page (*www.myvwlemon.com*)
Lots of venting, but enough interesting discussions to be worthwhile.

Information/Services

Alberta Vehicle Cost Calculator (*www1.agric.gov.ab.ca/app24/costcalculators/ vehicle/getvechimpls.jsp*)
Estimate and compare the ownership and operating costs of vehicles with variations in purchase price, options, fuel type, interest rates, or length of ownership.

ALLDATA Service Bulletins (*www.alldata.com/recalls/index.html*)
Free summaries of automotive recalls and technical service bulletins are listed by year, make, model, and engine option. You can access your vehicle's bulletins online by paying a $25 (U.S.) subscription fee.

The Auto Channel (*www.theautochannel.com*)
This website gives you useful, comprehensive information on choosing a new or used vehicle, filing a claim for compensation, or linking up with other owners.

The Auto Extremist (*www.autoextremist.com*)
Rantings and ravings from a Detroit insider.

Automobile News Groups

These Usenet news groups are compilations of e-mail raves and gripes that cover all makes and models. They fall into four distinct areas: *rec.autos.makers.ford* (you can substitute any automaker's name at the end); *rec.autos.tech*; *rec.autos.driving*; and *rec.autos.misc*. The easiest way to find these groups, if you don't have a news server, is to type the address into the Groups tab of the Google search engine.

Autopedia (*autopedia.com/index.html*)
An automotive encyclopedia, Autopedia offers a compendium of automotive-related information. Its legal section and lemon law listings by state are particularly helpful.

Carcostcanada.com (*www.carcostcanada.com/en*)
An impressive website for comparing Canadian MSRP prices and freight/options costs. In addition to a slew of free information on buying and leasing, you can get new vehicle invoice prices (a subscription is $39.95, which will get you five invoice prices) and referrals to dealers who will give you the best deal.

Carfax (*www.carfax.com*)
Use Carfax (Tel.: 1-888-422-7329) to see if a vehicle has been "scrapped," had flood damage, had its mileage turned back, or is stolen. You can get a Single History Vehicle Report for $19.99 or unlimited vehicle history reports for $24.99.

Cartrackers (*www.cartrackers.com*)
Used cars, consumer advice, and environmental issues are all well covered in this site, which features a terrific auto image gallery and an excellent automotive glossary.

Kelley Blue Book* and *Edmunds (*www.kbb.com, www.edmunds.com*)
Prices and technical info is American-oriented, but you'll find good reviews of almost every vehicle sold in North America, plus an informative readers' forum.

Metric Conversion Online (*www.sciencemadesimple.net/conversions.html*)
A great place to instantly convert gallons to litres, miles to kilometres, etc.

Phil Bailey's Auto World (*www.baileycar.com*)
Phil Bailey owns his own garage and specializes in the diagnosis and repair of foreign cars, particularly British ones. He's been advising Montreal motorists for years on local radio shows and has an exceptionally well-written and comprehensive website.

Straight-Six.com (*www.straight-six.com/theCrank/index.htm*)
Okay, for you high-performance aficionados, here's a website that doesn't idolize NASCAR, Earnhardt, or the Porsche Cayenne SUV (they call it the Ca-Yawn).

IBC's Vehicle Information Centre (*www.ibc.ca/vehinfo.asp*)
Part of the Insurance Bureau of Canada. VIC's website compares different model years' insurance claims experience for collision, personal injury, and theft losses.

Woman Motorist (*www.womanmotorist.com/index.php/welcome*)
Not for women only. This site's news and reviews are fresh and pertinent—and yes, women do sweat the details.

Women's Garage (*www.womensgarage.com*)
Three Canadian mechanics with a combined 100 years' experience set up this site to take the mystery out of maintaining and repairing vehicles. Don't be deterred by the site title—males will learn more than they'll care to admit.

Finally, here are a number of other websites that may be helpful:

www.bmwboard.com
www.bmwnation.com
www.cadillacsucks.net/marketshare.htm
www.carforums.com/forums

www.consumeraffairs.com/automotive/ford_transmissions.htm
www.datatown.com/chrysler
www.epa.gov/otaq/consumer/warr95fs.txt
www.flamingfords.info
www.everythingfordrivers.com/carforums.html
www.ford-trucks.com/forums
www.forum.freeadvice.com
www.hotbimmer.net
us.lexusownersclub.com
forums.mbnz.org
www.troublebenz.com/my_opinion/actions/links.htm
www.ptcruiserclub.org
www.ptcruiserlinks.com
www.vehicle-injuries.com/suv-safety-news.htm
www.worktruck.com

Appendix II
CALLING ALL CHEAPSKATES

These are volatile times, with the price of cars, fuel, and insurance going through the roof. Now's not the time to invest heavily in a vehicle that's more than you need or can afford. The following vehicle choices will help you hunker down and get reliable, safe, fuel-efficient, and inexpensive wheels that can serve as your second car, get you to school and back, or help you through that first job. Once you get on a sound financial footing, you can get that "dream machine" you've always wanted.

Consider the following tips:

1. If you really want to save money, try to buy a vehicle that's presently being used by one of your family members. Although you may risk a family squabble somewhere down the road, you'll likely get a good buy for next to nothing, you will have a good idea of how it was driven and maintained, and you can use the same repair facilities that have been repairing your family's vehicles for years. Don't worry if a vehicle is almost 10 years old—that's becoming the norm for Canadian ownership, particularly the farther west you go.
2. Get a fuel-efficient car. Be wary of diesel-equipped or hybrid cars that may require more expensive dealer servicing that could wipe out any fuel consumption savings. Don't trust hybrid fuel-economy hype: It's sometimes off by 45 percent. Also, don't buy a "lemon" simply because it's touted as being fuel-efficient: A failure-prone Ford Focus may cost you more to repair than to fuel, and a 4-cylinder minivan, though cheap to run, can make highway merging a white-knuckle affair.
3. Use *www.insurancehotline.com* to find out which cars are the cheapest to insure. Remember, having an additional licensed driver in the family places your policy in a higher risk category, with accompanying higher premiums. Not giving that extra driver permission to use the car has little bearing on your rates—you'll still pay more.
4. Used is always a better buy than new—there's little depreciation or upfront costs, and the cars have been pre-dented, pre-stained, and pre-rusted.
5. Buy privately. Look for high-mileage vehicles sold by a major rental agency like Budget, a company that offers honest money-back guarantees and reasonably priced extended warranties. Franchised new car dealers can also give you a good deal if they include all of the car's repair history. Keep the vehicle for at least 10 years and resell it privately (back to the family, perhaps?).
6. Delay buying a new car until mid-2006, when automaker and dealer clearance rebates bring down new prices and lots of inexpensive trade-ins reduce used prices as well. Also, refuse all preparation or "administration" charges.

7. Buy an entry-level Asian model or Asian/American co-venture from dealer stock for better price leverage.
8. Stay away from most American front-drives—more frequent failures and costlier repairs are a given. Besides, American automakers are now returning to rear-drives.
9. Don't buy any European models. Even the venerable *Consumer Reports* now agrees with *Lemon-Aid:* European makes are way overpriced, parts and servicing can be a problem, and quality control is declining.
10. Don't buy "nostalgia" cars: They aren't as good as the memories they invoke. New Beetles, PT Cruisers, and Ford's resurrected T-Bird are all heavily discounted. Only BMW's limited production Mini Cooper has kept a high resale value.

Frugal New and Used Buys for 2006

Okay, so I'm a cheapskate.

I can't afford the $31,045 average price for a new vehicle ($25,056 for a car and $37,855 for the average truck) quoted by Toronto auto analyst Dennis DesRosiers. Actually, that's not all we pay. DesRosiers says taxes add another 21 and 23 per cent to the suggested retail prices listed above. And fuel and insurance costs are scary, with gas prices dancing over $1 a litre and insurance premiums soaring despite a six-fold increase in insurance profits in 2003.

Yet millions of Canadians have no choice. They must have a vehicle that's safe, cheap to buy and run, and reliable, capable of taking them to work, school, or the shopping mall without breaking down or putting their lives in danger. Those last two factors are particularly important to new drivers, who usually don't have much experience with highway emergencies. Also, young drivers want vehicles that they can easily repair and customize and that will still project a "cool" cachet to their peers.

Fortunately, there are a few vehicles out there that meet the above criteria. Here are some choices that spring to mind:

Ford—2004 Mustang

Mazda—Mazda3

Suzuki—Aerio and Swift

GM—Aveo, Cavalier, and Sunfire

Chevrolet and Pontiac's Cavalier and Sunfire were heavily discounted to make room for their Cobalt and Pursuit replacements in early 2005.

Chrysler—Sebring, Avenger, and PT Cruiser

Sebring convertibles are a bargain; just be wary of automatic-transmission glitches.

Honda—Civic

A used Civic is a great buy now that the redesigned 2006 version costs almost $2,000 more.

Hyundai—Accent and Elantra

You can pay less than $6,000 for a used Accent and still benefit from Hyundai's original warranty.

Nissan—Sentra

Sentras don't look very sexy, but they give you good value for your money.

Toyota—Echo and Corolla

Next to the Honda Civic, an Echo is the best small car you can buy.

Lemon-Proofing Before You Buy

Now that you've chosen a vehicle that's priced right and seems to meet your needs, take some time to assess its interior, exterior, and highway performance by following the checklist below. Ask the dealer if you can take the vehicle home overnight in order to drive it over the same roads you would normally use in your daily activities. This will give you an important insight into how well the engine handles, all of the convenience features, how comfortable the seats are during extended driving, and whether front and rear visibility is satisfactory without your having to double up like a pretzel to avoid dash glare upon the windshield. If you can't get the vehicle for an overnight test, you may have to rent a similar one from a dealer or rental agency.

Safety Check

1. Is outward visibility good in all directions?
2. Are there large blind spots impeding vision (such as side pillars)?
3. Are the mirrors large enough for good side and rear views?
4. Does the rear-view mirror have a glare-reducing setting?
5. Is there a rear-window washer and wiper?
6. Are all instrument displays clearly visible (not washed out in sunlight), is there daytime or night-driving dash glare on the windshield, and are the controls easily reached?
7. Are the handbrake and hood release easy to reach and use?
8. Does the front seat have sufficient rearward travel to put you a safe distance from the airbag's deployment (about 25 centimetres) and still allow you to reach the brake and accelerator pedals? Are the brake and accelerator pedals spaced far enough apart?
9. Are the head restraints adjustable or non-adjustable? (The latter is better if you often forget to set them.)

10. Are the head restraints designed to permit rear visibility? (Some are annoyingly obtrusive, particularly if they're non-adjustable.)
11. Are there rear three-point shoulder belts similar to those on the front seats? (Two-point belts aren't as good.)
12. Is the seat belt latch plate easy to find and reach?
13. Does the seat belt fit comfortably across your chest without rubbing against your face or falling off your shoulder?
14. Do you feel too much pressure against you from the shoulder belt?
15. Does the seat belt release easily, retract smoothly, and use pretensioners for maximum effectiveness?
16. Are there user-friendly child seat anchorage locations?
17. Are there automatic door locks controlled by the driver or childproof rear door locks?
18. Do the rear windows roll only halfway down? When the windows are rolled down, does this create a painful cabin noise or create excessive steering/suspension vibration once the vehicle is underway?
19. Do the side airbags protect both head and torso?
20. Do the sliding minivan doors latch properly? Will they crush an object in their run channel? When the door closes can a hand or arm get trapped between the inside door handle and the interior?

Exterior Check

Tires

Don't accept Firestone or Bridgestone tires; their past performance has been far from reassuring from both a safety and durability perspective. Don't be too quick to jump on the run-flat tire bandwagon. There are still serious price, performance, and supply problems to work out.

Accident damage

Inspect the car carefully and ask for all promised corrections to be put in writing. It has been estimated that about 10 percent of new cars are damaged during delivery to the dealer, so don't be surprised at what you may find. Fortunately, you don't have to accept a new vehicle that has been dented or scratched. In British Columbia, all accidents involving more than $2,000 in repairs must be reported to buyers. In other provinces, general legal statutes protect buyers.

What to look for

1. If the vehicle has been repainted recently, check the quality of the job by inspecting the engine and trunk compartments and the inside door panels. Do it on a clear day so that you'll find any waves in the paint.
2. Check the paint—do all of the vehicle's panels match?
3. Inspect the paint for tiny bubbles. They may identify a poor priming job or premature rust.

4. Is there paint overspray or primer in the doorjambs, wheelwells, or engine compartment? These are signs that the vehicle has had body repairs.
5. Check the gaps between body panels—are they equal? Unequal gaps may indicate improper panel alignment or a bent frame.
6. Do the doors, hood, and rear hatch open and shut properly?
7. Have the bumpers been damaged or recently repaired? Check the bumper support struts for corrosion damage.
8. Test the shock absorbers by pushing hard on a corner of the vehicle. If it bounces around like a ship at sea, the shocks need replacing.
9. Look at the muffler and exhaust pipe to detect premature rust or displacement from a low-impact collision; this could channel deadly carbon monoxide into the passenger area.
10. Make sure there's a spare tire, a jack, and tools necessary for changing a flat. Can you get at the spare easily? Also look for premature rusting in the side wheelwells and for water in the rear hatch channel.
11. Look at how the vehicle sits. If one side or end is higher than the other, it could mean that the suspension is defective.
12. Ask the seller to turn on the headlights (low and high beams), turn signals, parking lights, and emergency blinking lights, and to blow the horn. From the rear, check that the brake lights, back-up lights, turn indicators, tail lights, and licence plate light all work.

Road Test

1. Start the vehicle and listen for unusual noises. Shift automatics into Park and manuals into Neutral with the handbrake engaged. Open the hood to check for fluid leaks. This test should be done with the engine running and be repeated 10 minutes after the engine has been shut down following the completion of the test-drive.
2. With the motor running, check out all dashboard controls: windshield wipers, heater and defroster, and radio.
3. If the engine stalls or races at idle, a simple adjustment may fix the trouble. Loud clanks or low oil pressure could mean potentially expensive repairs.
4. Check all ventilation systems. Are there excessive air leaks around the door handles?
5. While in Neutral, push down on the accelerator abruptly. Black exhaust smoke may require only a minor engine adjustment; blue smoke may signal major engine repairs.
6. Shift an automatic into Drive with the motor still idling. The vehicle should creep forward slowly without stalling or speeding. Listen for unusual noises when the transmission is engaged. Manual transmissions should engage as soon as the clutch is released. Slipping or stalling could require a new clutch. While driving, make absolutely sure that a 4×4 drive can be engaged without unusual noises or hesitation.
7. Shift an automatic transmission into Drive. While the motor is idling, apply the emergency brake. If the motor isn't racing and the brake is in good condition, the vehicle should stop.

8. Accelerate to 50 km/h while slowly moving through all gears. Listen for transmission noises. Step lightly on the brakes; the response should be immediate and equal for all wheels.

9. In a deserted parking lot, test the vehicle's steering and suspension by driving in figure eights at low speeds.

10. Make sure the road is clear of traffic and pedestrians. Drive at 30 km/h and take both hands off the steering wheel to see whether the vehicle veers from one side to the other. If it does, the alignment or suspension could be defective, or the vehicle could have been in an accident.

11. Test the suspension by driving over some rough terrain.

12. Stop at the foot of a small hill and see if the vehicle can climb it without difficulty.

13. On an expressway, it should take no longer than 20 seconds for most cars and minivans to accelerate from a standing start to 100 km/h.

14. Drive through a tunnel with the windows open. Try to detect any unusual motor, exhaust, or suspension sounds.

15. After the test-drive, verify the performance of the automatic transmission by shifting from Drive to Neutral to Reverse. Listen for clunking sounds during transmission engagement and treat any delayed engagement seriously; it will likely get worse.

Appendix III

TWENTY *REAL* WAYS TO SAVE ON FUEL COSTS

Before we show you how to cut your fuel costs, let's first explain why government-disseminated fuel-economy figures are a hoax.

Drivers are rightfully complaining that their real-world gas mileage is about 15 percent less than the "official" estimates given by Transport Canada and the United States Environmental Protection Agency (EPA). These figures are regularly included in published and online car guides, are posted on the window stickers of nearly every car and truck sold, and are showcased in automakers' advertising. Yet new vehicles that are tested for their energy consumption are never actually driven anywhere—much less to and from work—and their fuel-economy ratings are not ultimately based on how much fuel they consume. No wonder the government warns that "your fuel economy may vary," while hiding the fact that its own figures are misleading and dishonest.

In fact, subsequent "real world" tests conducted by the EPA on a dozen vehicles in its hybrid car fleet showed that far more fuel was burned than the EPA's own posted ratings. Differences were astonishing: the Honda Civic got 6.2L/100 km, the Insight posted 5.1L/100 km, and Toyota's Prius got 5.3L/100 km. Yet EPA continues to publish estimates that run as low as 4.6, 3.6, and 3.9L/100 km, respectively.

1. **Buy a 4-cylinder small vehicle that has a good crashworthiness and reliability rating**—Generally, a vehicle with a minimum of 100 horses will get you around town and will be suitable for light commuting duties. This choice will cut your fuel bills by a third to one-half if you are downsizing from a V8 or a 6-cylinder engine. This is assuming that you will not load up the vehicle with fuel-burning accessories. The air conditioning and other electrical accessories will put a greater load on the engine, and thus reduce a vehicle's fuel economy.

2. **Stay away from hybrids and diesels**—You have to do a lot of driving to make a diesel or hybrid pay off. If you do go diesel, stay away from the ones made by Ford and GM and go with the Chrysler Cummins, but get extra

---

RECOMMENDED FUEL-EFFICIENT VEHICLES

SMALL CARS	COMPACTS	SPORTS CARS
Chrysler Neon 2000+	Chrysler Sebring	Ford Mustang
GM Cavalier/Sunfire 2000+	Honda Accord	Mazda Miata
Honda Civic	Hyundai Elantra	
Hyundai Accent	Mazda Protégé	
Mazda 323, Mazda3	Toyota Corolla	
Suzuki Aerio	Toyota Camry	
Toyota Echo, Tercel		

---

powertrain protection. All three U.S. automakers have chronic diesel injector problems covered by secret repair warranties. Hybrids are expensive, not as frugal as they pretend to be, keep you a captive customer, can be costly to service, and may be life-threatening. For example, only 60 volts across the chest can injure or kill, and the hybrid's NiMH battery can produce 270 volts. Furthermore, in a car accident with a hybrid, if the NiMH battery cable is damaged, heavy sparking can start a fire, toxic chemicals may be released, and the EMT rescuers must put on heavy rubber gloves before touching the car to extract passengers and get the car ready for towing. Getting this important NiMH battery information about hybrids from car dealers can be very difficult. There is also an economic angle: If the NiMH battery has an 8-year warranty, its replacement cost could almost equal the cost of the gasoline saved. To save money, buy one of the cheap, used models mentioned above.

3. **Order a manual-transmission-equipped vehicle**—Manual transmissions save fuel. How much depends on factors including vehicle size, driver, and traffic conditions. Another benefit is that manual transmissions make you a more alert driver because you have to be constantly aware of traffic conditions in order to gear down to a stop and shift to accelerate. Interestingly, 12 percent of the vehicles on North American highways use manual transmissions. In Europe, it's just the opposite; over 90 percent of drivers choose a manual gearbox.

4. **Get an automatic transmission with more gears**—A 5-speed automatic saves you more fuel than a 4-speed; some high-end cars actually have 7-speed transmissions.

5. **Don't buy a 4×4 vehicle**—You will burn more fuel whether or not the 4×4 feature is engaged because of its extra weight and gearing.

6. **Be wary of the cruise control**—It's a good idea to hold a steady speed on flat terrain, but if you're driving in a hilly area, the cruise control can actually make the gas mileage worse. In hilly conditions, if traffic permits, it's better to let the vehicle slow down a little on the uphill sections, and then gain the speed back on the downhill side. If you use the cruise in these conditions, it will floor the accelerator if necessary to keep the speed constant while going uphill.

7. **Use the AC sparingly**—Don't turn on the air conditioner as a first response to the heat. Start your drive with the windows open to exhaust the hot air out

of the rear windows, and then put on the AC if needed. This will also enable the air conditioning to work faster and more efficiently when it is turned on. Having the AC off and the windows open will not save gas, however. The open windows will cause enough wind resistance to the vehicle that you could actually consume more gas than you would by driving with the windows closed and the AC on. Furthermore, driving any vehicle with a window or sunroof open will likely produce a painful roar in the cabin and cause excessive vibration in the steering.

8. **Keep your vehicle aerodynamic**—Resist the urge to attach accessories like roof racks, spoilers, and cargo carriers that hamper a vehicle's aerodynamics. Incidentally, pickup-truck drivers won't save fuel by lowering the tailgate when driving on the highway. With the gate closed, air flows across the top of the bed and does not get caught by the tailgate. The airflow patterns are less efficient with the tailgate open or removed.

9. **Use the Internet to find cheap gas**—Websites like *GasBuddy.com* will show you which stations are selling fuel that may be 10 cents less than the average price. The Internet can also be helpful in calculating your real gas mileage and savings—*www.sciencemadesimple.net/fuel_economy.php* is an easy-to-use site to try.

10. **Use regular-grade fuel**—Unless the engine "knocks," using a higher-octane fuel than is recommended by the manufacturer is foolish. Using premium fuel when the engine doesn't require it will not cause it to get better fuel economy and may damage your emissions-control system. Some high-mileage vehicles, however, may need high octane fuel if they "ping" (spark knock) heavily on regular gas. Light knocking on acceleration is not a problem, but if the knocking continues at a constant speed, or is very loud, move up to a higher-octane fuel until it stops. Persistent, heavy knocking reduces an engine's efficiency and can damage it in extreme cases.

11. **Shop price, not brand**—Gas is gas, and many different brands buy from the same refineries. Buy gasoline during the coolest time of day—early morning or late evening is best. During these times gasoline is densest. Keep in mind that gas pumps measure volumes of gasoline, not densities of fuel concentration. It is also a smart idea to use credit cards that give holders cash rebates based on a percentage of their purchases.

12. **Coddle your throttle**—New vehicles don't usually attain their top mileage until they're broken in, which occurs at about 5,000 to 8,000 km of fairly gentle driving. Avoid prolonged warming up of the engine on cold mornings—30 to 45 seconds is plenty of time. Also, don't start and stop the engine needlessly. Idling your engine for one minute consumes the amount of gas equivalent to when you start the engine. Avoid revving the engine, especially just before you switch the engine off; this wastes fuel needlessly and washes oil down from the inside cylinder walls, leading to loss of oil pressure and premature wear. Lead-footed acceleration, heavy braking, and high-speed driving all increase gas consumption. The EPA estimates that jackrabbit starts and sudden stops alone can reduce fuel economy by as much as 33 percent.

13. **Drive economically**—Driving 110 km/h instead of 90 km/h will lower your car's fuel economy by 17 percent. Driving at fast rates in low gears can

consume up to 45 percent more fuel than necessary. Keep windows closed when travelling at highway speeds—open windows cause air drag, reducing your mileage by 10 percent. Use only your right foot for both accelerating and braking. That way you can't accidentally ride the brake and use excessive gas.

14. **Get regular tune-ups and change the oil and air filter frequently**—The Car Care Council recommends changing your car's air and oil filters every three months, or 4,800 km. Fixing a car that's out of tune or has failed an emissions test can improve gas mileage dramatically: Replacing a misfiring spark plug can increase a car's fuel efficiency by as much as 30 percent. Fixing a faulty oxygen sensor may increase fuel savings by as much as 40 percent. Get tune-ups at independent garages and save a third of the cost and get a longer warranty. You can improve your car's gas mileage by 1–2 percent by using the manufacturer's recommended grade of motor oil. Opt for motor oil with the words "energy conserving" on the API performance label. This oil contains friction-reducing additives. Keep the brakes properly adjusted, since dragging brakes increases resistance. Check your gas cap—one out of every five vehicles on the road has a gas cap that is either damaged, loose, or missing altogether, which allows gas in your tank to vapourize.

15. **Be tire-smart**—Inflate all tires to the maximum limit. Each tire should be periodically spun, balanced, and checked for unevenness. Remove the spare tire; instead, keep a cell phone handy and join CAA. Changing a tire beside the road puts your life at risk and is a pain in the butt.

16. **Fight excess weight**—Remove excess weight from the trunk or the inside of the car, including extra tires, minivan back seats, and unnecessary heavy parts. Don't drive with a full fuel tank. Remember, carrying an extra 100 pounds in the trunk of your car may cut your car's fuel economy by 1–2 percent. The further you run with the tank closer to empty, the further you run in a lighter car, thereby increasing the fuel mileage. Ideally, you never want to fill your tank more than a quarter- or half-tank full.

17. **Stay away from gas-saving gadgets**—They don't work and may cancel the manufacturer's warranty. Instead, park your car in the shade to reduce fuel evaporation and buy a good windshield shade to keep the interior cool. Parking in your garage will help your car stay warm in winter and cool in summer, and you won't have to depend as much on your gas-guzzling air-conditioning or defroster when you drive.

18. **Carpool**—Carpools reduce travel monotony and gas expense—all riders chip in to help you buy. Conversation helps to keep the driver alert. Pooling also reduces traffic congestion.

19. **Consolidate trips**—Combine short errands into one trip and combine private errands with business trips as a tax write-off.

20. **Fill up in the States**—Fuel prices are hovering near $3 U.S. a gallon, but that's still a heck of a lot less than what it would cost in Canada. For example, a Chevrolet Impala or Malibu fuel tank will hold 64L (14 gallons) of gasoline. A fill-up in Canada at $1/L (Canadian) would total $64 Canadian. In the States, that same fill-up would cost $42 U.S.—a sizeable savings.

SERVICE BULLETINS YOU AREN'T SUPPOSED TO HAVE

The following confidential service bulletins have been chosen because they apply to a large number of vehicles, correct relatively expensive factory-related deficiencies, and provide undisputable proof that the automaker and dealer are jointly responsible for the correction of the problem. Use these bulletins in dealings with service managers or automakers to get free repairs for what are essentially manufacturing goofs.

Chrysler

TRANSMISSION SHUDDER WHEN TORQUE CONVERTER CLUTCH ENGAGES

BULLETIN NO.: 21-011-05 REV.   DATE: JULY 14, 2005

OVERVIEW: This bulletin involves thoroughly flushing the NAG1 (W5A580) transmission of any water contamination, replacing the transmission filter, and applying RTV sealant around the base of the transmission fill tube to prevent water intrusion past the fill tube seal.

2005–2006 300/Magnum/Charger; 2005 Grand Cherokee

SYMPTOM/CONDITION: The customer may experience a transmission shudder when shifts occur. The shudder is most noticeable with partial application of the torque converter clutch in 3rd and 4th gear.

If the customer experiences the condition perform the Repair Procedure.

NOTE: This condition may occur when only a small 0.5% concentration of water is present in the automatic transmission fluid. It will be very important to ensure that the transmission and torque converter is thoroughly flushed of any water and other possible contaminants.

TRANSMISSION FLUID WEEPAGE/LEAKS

NUMBER: 21-002-05 REV.   DATE: MAY 7, 2005

2005 300/Magnum	2005 Grand Cherokee
2004–2005 Sprinter	2004–2005 Crossfire Coupe/Crossfire Roadster

SYMPTOM/CONDITION: Transmission fluid may be wicking in the right front corner of the transmission oil pan area.

DIAGNOSIS: If the vehicle exhibits the Symptom/Condition, inspect the 13-pin connector plug guide bushing as a possible source of the transmission fluid weepage. If the weepage appears to be coming from above the transmission oil pan gasket, DO NOT REPLACE THE TRANSMISSION OIL PAN GASKET, perform the appropriate Repair Procedure.

SNOW/WATER INGESTION INTO REAR BRAKE DRUM

BULLETIN NO.: 05-003-05

DATE: JUNE 21, 2005

OVERVIEW: This bulletin involves installing a revised rear drum brake support (backing) plate and possible replacement of the rear brake shoes and drums.

2001–2005 Town & Country/Voyager/Caravan

1996–2000 Town & Country/Caravan/Voyager

SYMPTOM/CONDITION: While driving through deep or blowing snow/water, the snow/water may enter the rear brake drums causing rust to develop on the rear brake drum and shoe friction surfaces. This condition can lead to temporary freezing of the rear brake linings to the drums. This symptom is experienced after the vehicle has been parked in below freezing temperatures long enough for the snow/water to freeze inside of the rear brake drums. When the parking brake has been applied the symptom is more likely to occur.

DIAGNOSIS: If the vehicle operator describes the Symptom/Condition above, perform the appropriate Repair Procedure.

A/C POOR PERFORMANCE/ERRATIC OPERATION

BULLETIN NO.: 24-002-04

DATE: MARCH 30, 2004

A/C AND HEATER PERFORMANCE

This bulletin provides diagnostic information for A/C and heater performance complaints.

1998–2004 (LH) LHS/300M/Concorde/Intrepid

2001–04 (JR) Sebring and Stratus

NOTE: Perform customer satisfaction recall no. 857, reprogram Powertrain Control Module (PCM), for 2000 model year LH-vehicles built prior to August 30, 1999

Erratic operation of the NC and heater systems including:

- Lack of cold air
- Lack of hot air
- Unrequested mode change – Automatic Temperature Control (ATC) only
- No control of mode or temperature control
- Tapping noise from blend

CAMPAIGN — A/C DRIVE BELT TENSIONER BRACKET

CUSTOMER SATISFACTION NOTIFICATION NO.: C25

DATE: JULY 2003

A/C DRIVE BELT TENSIONER BRACKET

2003–04 (LH) Dodge Intrepid and Chrysler Concorde

This notification applies only to the above vehicles equipped with a 2.7L engine with an ENGINE build date code from 902582 through 900433.

SUBJECT: The air conditioning (A/C) compressor drive belt tensioner bracket on about 28,000 of the above vehicles may crack. If this occurs, the A/C system may not function. In addition, continued vehicle operation with a cracked tensioner bracket could damage the engine cylinder head.

REPAIR: The A/C compressor drive belt tensioner bracket must be replaced.

A/C WATER LEAKS

BULLETIN NO.: 23-010-04   **DATE: APRIL 29, 2004**

PASSENGER COMPARTMENT FLOOR WATER LEAK

OVERVIEW: This bulletin involves sealing the opening for the evaporator hose/drain tube with RTV sealer.

2001–04 Caravan, Voyager, Town & Country and Dakota

2001–03 Durango

SYMPTOM/CONDITION: Water may enter the passenger compartment between the HEVAC housing and the bulkhead. A foam seal is used to seal the heater housing to the bulkhead. Condensation from the A/C evaporator can run along the evaporator drain tube and enter the passenger compartment if the seal between the HEVAC housing and the bulkhead is not sealed properly. This will result in wet passenger compartment carpet when the air conditioning is operating.

DELAYED TRANSMISSION ENGAGEMENT

BULLETIN NO.: 21-007-04   **DATE: MAY 11, 2004**

This bulletin involves replacing the front pump assembly in the transmission and checking the Transmission Control Module (TCM) for the latest software revision level.

2004 (CS) Pacifica

2003–04 (JR) Sebring Convertible/Sebring Sedan/Stratus

2003 (KJ) Liberty

2003 (KJ) Cherokee (International Markets)

2003–04 (LH) 300M/Concorde/Intrepid

2003 (PL) Neon/SX2.0

2003 (PT) PT Cruiser

2003 (RG) Chrysler Voyager (International Markets)

2003 (RS) Town & Country/Caravan/Voyager

2003 (TJ) Wrangler

Vehicle operator may experience a delayed or temporary loss of transmission engagement after initial start up. The condition follows an extended soak (several hours) and may be accompanied by a harsh 4–3 downshift.

Ford

WATER LEAKS TO VEHICLE INTERIOR

BULLETIN NO.: 05-13-3   **DATE: 07/11/05**

2000–2005 Focus

ISSUE: Some 2000–2005 Focus vehicles may exhibit a difficult to diagnose or difficult to repair water leak or AC system condensation leak condition in the front floor area. This may be caused by sealer skips, loose grommets, mispositioned seals, or condensation leaking from the AC evaporator case.

ACTION: Determine if the concern is an AC condensation leak or a water leak and repair as necessary. Some common water leak locations and repair recommendations are listed in this article to help reduce repair time and increase repair effectiveness.

ERRATIC FLUID LEVEL READING/LEAKS AT DIPSTICK TUBE

BULLETIN NO.: 05-14-5   **DATE: 07/25/05**

2000–2005 Taurus   2000–2005 Sable
2000–2003 Windstar   2004–2005 Monterey
2004–2005 Freestar

ISSUE: Some 2000–2005 Taurus/Sable, 2000–2003 Windstar and 2004–2005 Freestar/Monterey vehicles, equipped with a 4F50N, AX4N, or AX4S transaxle, may exhibit an erratic fluid level reading on the transaxle dipstick and possible leaks around the filler tube and grommet. The condition may be due to the transaxle vent. The vent has a rubber disk under the metal cap to prevent water from entering the transaxle. This rubber disk may intermittently stick and cause improper venting.

ACTION: Replace the vent with the previous design vent stem, and rubber vent cap.

ENGINE MISFIRES

BULLETIN NO.: 04-16-1   **DATE: 08/23/04**

ENGINE MISFIRE OR ROUGH RUNNING

1996–99 Taurus SHO	1998–2002 Continental	LINCOLN:
1998–2005 Crown Victoria, Mustang	1998–2005 Town Car	1997–98 Mark VIII
2000 Taurus	2000–05 LS	
2002–05 Thunderbird	1998–2005 Navigator	
2003–05 Focus	2002–03 Blackwood	
2004–05 Taurus	2003–05 Aviator	
1997–2005 E-Series, Expedition, F-150		
1999–2005 F-Super Duty	MERCURY:	
2000–05 Excursion, F-53	1998–2005 Grand Marquis	
2001–05 Escape	2000 Sable	
2002–05 Explorer	2004–05 Sable	
	2002–05 Mountaineer	➤

ISSUE: Approximately 50% of coil on plug (COP) coils returned for warranty do not have a problem.

ACTION: The misfiring cylinder must be identified through Self-Test misfire codes or through WDS Power Balance. Rule out base engine problems, rule out fuel problems, and then look at ignition problems (be sure to rule out coil primary circuit issues). Once the above steps have been completed, and the issue is in the secondary part of the ignition system, the oscilloscope procedure outlined in this TSB can isolate the difference between a coil or spark plug problem.

COLD START KNOCKING NOISE

BULLETIN NO.: 04-2-1   **DATE: 02/09/04**

- ENGINE – EXHAUST – KNOCK DURING INITIAL COLD START
- NOISE – KNOCK DURING INITIAL COLD START

2003–04 CROWN VICTORIA

2003–04 TOWN CAR

2003–04 GRAND MARQUIS

ISSUE: Some vehicles may exhibit an engine knock during initial cold start, the knock will cease after the engine is fully warmed up.

ACTION: To service, install Exhaust Shield kit (3W7Z-5E258-AA).

LACK OF COOLING/LOW AIR FLOW FROM VENTS

BULLETIN NO.: 03-22-8   **DATE: 11/10/03**

LACK OF A/C COOLING — RESTRICTED/REDUCED AIR FLOW THROUGH VENTS — EVAPORATOR CORE ICING

2000–04 CROWN VICTORIA

2000–04 GRAND MARQUIS

ISSUE: Some vehicles may exhibit a lack of A/C cooling and restricted/reduced air flow through the A/C vents typically during extended idling conditions. This may be due to extended A/C compressor operation (lack of compressor cycling) causing icing of the evaporator core surface.

ACTION: To service, first verify that the A/C Clutch Relay is operating properly and that the contacts are not sticking closed. The A/C clutch relay contacts may stick closed due to arcing. The arcing may be caused by transient voltage from the A/C clutch field coil when the relay contacts open to turn off the AC clutch.

WIPERS/WASHERS LOSS OF INTERMITTENT OR PARK FUNCTIONS

BULLETIN NO.:TSB 04-15-2   **DATE: 08/09/04**

2002–05 Focus

Some 2002–05 Focus vehicles may exhibit concerns with the intermittent wiper function or wiper park function. Symptoms may include intermittent wipers inoperative, one sweep function stops in the middle of the glass when the stalk is released (sweep function is operational if the stalk is held), wipers jumping up when parked from the intermittent mode.

To service, replace the wiper relay. If the condition is still present, continue with normal Workshop Manual diagnosis.

SUSPENSION — CREAK, CRUNCH, GRINDING OR RATTLE NOISE

BULLETIN NO.: 04-6-1   **DATE: 04/05/04**

2000–04 FOCUS

ISSUE: Some 2000–04 Focus vehicles may exhibit a front end creaking, crunching, grinding and/or rattling noise from the front suspension while driving at slow speeds, over bumps, and/or while turning.

ACTION: Noise, vibration, harness (NVH) conditions may originate from many areas. A thorough inspection of the front suspension is necessary to determine the cause. To service, refer to the following Service Procedure and inspect the suggested areas first.

SERVICE PROCEDURE

1. Inspect front strut fasteners and confirm that they are tightened to the correct torque.
   a. Front strut to front knuckle, (one (1) driver / one (1) passenger), 90 N.m (67 lb-ft).
   b. Front strut mount to body, (three (3) driver / three (3) passenger), 30 N.m (22 lb-ft).
   c. Front strut rod to strut mount, (one (1) driver / one (1) passenger), 66 N.m (49 lb-ft).
2. Inspect for loose stabilizer bar end links.
   a. Firmly grasp the links and shake them both along the direction of the link and transverse to the link orientation in the inboard/outboard vehicle direction. If looseness is felt continue on to Step 2b, if no looseness is felt continue on to Step 3.
   b. Inspect the link end joints. If they do not appear severely corroded, torque the nuts (use anti-rotation feature to prevent ball joint damage) to 50 N.m (36 lb-ft), and repeat Step 2a. If links still feel loose after tightening or if the joint shows evidence of severe corrosion, replace the link (YS4Z-5K484-AA).
3. Inspect for the top spring sleeve coming out of position. This may cause a squeaking noise between the sleeve and indent on the ridge of the upper spring seat, or it may cause a clicking noise between the spring and upper spring seat if the sleeve is completely out of position. If the sleeve is out of position continue on to Step 3a, if the sleeve is positioned properly continue on to Step 4.
   a. Install a new rubber sleeve (1S4Z-8484-AA). Install the new rubber sleeve starting from the top of the spring coil where it contacts the spring plate.
4. If the noise is a clicking or popping from the front strut, install a service spring end cap (4S4Z-5L302-AA) on to the top spring tip. Reassemble and reinstall strut per the Workshop Manual Section 204-01.

General Motors

GAUGES DROP TO ZERO/STALLING CONDITION

BULLETIN NO.: 05-06-04-037   DATE: MAY 26, 2005

CERTAIN INSTRUMENT PANEL GAUGES GO TO ZERO AND/OR INTERMITTENT ENGINE STALL (REPAIR GROUND CONNECTIONS AND/OR REPROGRAM POWERTRAIN CONTROL MODULE (PCM))

2005 Buick Allure (Canada), LaCrosse

2004–2005 Pontiac Grand Prix with 3.8L V6 Engine

Some owners may comment that the fuel and the temperature gauge in the instrument panel intermittently go to zero while the speedometer and tachometer continue to operate normally. In addition, some may comment that the low fuel indicator is displayed in the Driver Information Center (DIC) when this occurs. In a small portion of these cases, the gauges going to zero may be followed by an engine hesitation or stall.

CAUSE: Intermittent high resistance or connection of the negative battery cable to the top of the right side frame rail may cause the I/P gauges to intermittently go to zero.

The intermittent stall condition may be caused by the following:

- An internal calculation in the Powertrain Control Module (PCM) when determining barometric values under certain engine loads. When this occurs, the engine can take several minutes to restart.
- Intermittent high resistance or connection of the negative battery cable to the top of the right side frame rail.

BODY/AC — WATER LEAKS ONTO PASSENGER FRONT FLOOR

BULLETIN NO.: 03-08-57-006B   DATE: FEBRUARY 25, 2005

WATER LEAK ON FRONT PASSENGER FLOOR (INSTALL WATER DEFLECTOR)

2005 Buick LaCrosse, Allure (Canada Only)

2004–2005 Pontiac Grand Prix

Some customers may comment on water leaking onto the front passenger carpet.

CAUSE: Water may be getting past the rubber water deflector located under the air inlet grille panel.

During diagnosis, the technician may note that the passenger compartment air filter is wet.

BODY — OUTSIDE DOOR HANDLE STICKS IN EXTREME COLD

BULLETIN NO.: 05-08-64-005   DATE: FEBRUARY 9, 2005

DOOR HANDLE STICKS WHEN AMBIENT TEMPERATURES ARE BELOW 0 DEGREES CELSIUS OR 32 DEGREES FAHRENHEIT (LUBRICATE DOOR HANDLE PAWL)

2005 Buick LaCrosse, Allure, Chevrolet Cobalt, Pontiac Pursuit

CONDITION: Some customers may comment that the outside door handle sticks.

CAUSE: This condition may be due to water freezing under the plastic sleeve on the door handle pawl causing an interference with the door handle operation.

CORRECTION: Apply lubricant to the door handle of all the doors.

UNDER-HOOD COOLANT ODORS

BULLETIN NO.: 04-06-02-010A

DATE: APRIL 19, 2005

2005 Chevrolet Equinox with 3.4L V6 Engine

CONDITION: Some customers may comment on an objectionable odor coming from under the hood. It may be found that this odor is from the engine coolant.

IMPORTANT: This repair is intended for the resolution of odor concern vehicles only. The discoloration of the coolant is normal and not related to odor. It is the result of the sealant pellets that are added to the system during production. DO NOT add sealant pellets when performing this repair.

A/T — 4T65E POOR PERFORMANCE/HARSH SHIFTS/DTCS SET

BULLETIN NO.: 02-07-30-013E

DATE: MAY 20, 2005

INCORRECT TRANSMISSION SHIFTS, POOR ENGINE PERFORMANCE, HARSH 1–2 UPSHIFTS, SLIPS 1ST AND REVERSE, TORQUE CONVERTER CLUTCH (TCC) STUCK OFF/ON, DTCS P0757, P0741, P0742, P0730, P0756

2001–2005 GM Passenger Cars with 4T65-E Automatic Transmission

2001–2005 Buick Rendezvous

2005 Buick Terraza

2001–2004 Chevrolet Venture

2005 Chevrolet Uplander

2001–2004 Oldsmobile Silhouette

2001–2005 Pontiac Aztek, Montana

2005 Saturn Relay with 4T65-F Transmission.

CONDITION: Some owners may comment on any one or more of the following conditions:

- The SES lamp is illuminated.
- The transmission slips.
- The transmission does not shift correctly, is very difficult to get the vehicle to start moving or the engine lacks the power to move the vehicle.
- Poor engine performance.

CAUSE: The most likely cause of the various conditions may be chips or debris:

All years—Pressure Reg. Valve (Bore 1) or Torque Signal Valve (Bore 4) stuck.

On 2001–2002 vehicles, a plugged orifice on the case side of the spacer plate.

On 2003–2005 vehicles, restricted movement of the 2–3 shift valves in the valve body.

On 2003–2005 vehicles, restricted movement of the 3–4 shift valves in the valve body.

HARD START/MIL ON/VARIOUS DTCS SET

BULLETIN NO.: 01-08-45-005C

DATE: MAY 02, 2005

HARD/NO-START, STALL, FUEL GAUGE INOPERATIVE/FLUCTUATES, SES/CHECK ENGINE LIGHT ON, ABS WARNING LIGHT ON, TCS WARNING LIGHT ON, TCS ACTIVATION, SERVICE TRACTION SYSTEM MESSAGE DISPLAYED, ALL-WHEEL DRIVE DISABLE MESSAGE DISPLAYED, DTCS SET (REPAIR CONNECTOR)

2002–2005 Buick Rendezvous

2005 Buick Terraza

2000–2005 Chevrolet Venture

2005 Chevrolet Uplander

2000–2004 Oldsmobile Silhouette

2000–2005 Pontiac Montana

2001–2005 Pontiac Aztek

2005 Pontiac Montana SV6

2005 Saturn Relay

CONDITION

Some customers may comment on one or more of the following conditions:

- Engine is hard to start
- Engine will not start
- Engine starts than stalls
- Fuel gauge is inoperative or fluctuates
- Service Engine Soon/Check Engine light is illuminated
- ABS Warning Light is illuminated
- TCS Warning Light is illuminated
- TCS activation
- Service Traction System message displayed

CAUSE: This condition may be due to water leaking into the interior of the vehicle, and/or spread terminals, at connector C305 that is located on the floor to the rear of the driver's seat. This connector is not sealed from the inside of the vehicle and water may enter the connector causing the terminals to become corroded. Also, the female terminals of the connector may have become spread apart causing an intermittent poor connection.

CORRECTION:

- Inspect the terminals at connector C305 for corrosion or spreading before replacing the fuel module or resistor card kit.
- Do not attempt to repair any spread female terminals as this will result in a return repair. The female terminal must be replaced.
- If the terminals show signs of corrosion, determine the source of the water leak first and repair the water leak before repairing the terminals in connector C305. Refer to Corporate Service Bulletin Number 01-01-38-009A to determine a potential source for water in the vehicle interior.
- Repair any corroded and/or spread female terminals in connector C305.

POWER SLIDING DOOR BOUNCES BACK/WON'T FULLY OPEN

BULLETIN NO.: 05-08-64-013   DATE: APRIL 28, 2005

POWER SLIDING DOOR BOUNCES WHEN IT STOPS, DOES NOT ACHIEVE FULL OPEN POSITION, DRIVER INFORMATION CENTER (DIC) MESSAGE DISPLAYED (REPROGRAM POWER SLIDING DOOR MODULE)

2005 Buick Terraza   2005 Pontiac Montana SV6

2005 Chevrolet Uplander   2005 Saturn Relay

CONDITION: Some customers may comment on one or more of the following conditions:

- A bounce of the power sliding door when it stops in the opening direction due to the fuel fill door being still open.
- The power sliding door does not achieve the full open position and stops before the hold open position.
- The Driver Information Center (DIC) displays "Passenger/Driver Sliding Door in Motion" message.
- The DIC displays "Passenger/Driver Sliding Door Obstacle Detected" message.

CORRECTION

The doors must be closed prior to programming. Wait until "Programming Complete" appears on the Tech 2(R) screen before exiting. Saturn technicians must wait for the "Programming Successful" screen on the SSS.

Technicians are to reprogram the power sliding door module with an updated software calibration. This new service calibration was released with TIS satellite data update version 4.0 available April 6, 2005 and on TIS CD-ROM version 4.0 for 2005.

ENGINE — REDESIGNED UPPER INTAKE MANIFOLD AND GASKETS

BULLETIN NO.: 04-06-01-017   DATE: MAY 26, 2004

NEW UPPER INTAKE MANIFOLD AND GASKET KITS

1995–97 Buick Riviera   2000–04 Chevrolet Impala

1995–2004 Buick Park Avenue   1995–96 Oldsmobile Ninety-Eight

1996–2004 Buick Regal   1995–99 Oldsmobile Eighty-Eight

1997–2004 Buick LeSabre   1998–99 Oldsmobile Intrigue

1998–99 Chevrolet Lumina   1995–2004 Pontiac Bonneville

1998–2004 Chevrolet Monte Carlo   1997–2003 Pontiac Grand Prix

with 3.8L V6 Engine (VIN K – RPO L36)

New upper intake manifold and gasket kits have been released. These new kits will provide the dealer with the ability to get exactly what is necessary for a correct repair. In addition some of the gaskets have been updated to a more robust design. Please reference the part numbers when ordering from GMSPO.

ENGINE SERPENTINE DRIVE BELT WEAR INFORMATION

BULLETIN NO.: 04-06-01-013   DATE: APRIL 29, 2004

SERPENTINE BELT WEAR

2004 and Prior Passenger Cars and Trucks

2003–04 and Prior HUMMER H2

All current GM vehicles designed and manufactured in North America were assembled with serpentine belts that are made with an EPDM material and should last the life of the vehicle. It is extremely rare to observe any cracks in EPDM belts and it is not expected that they will require maintenance before 10 years or 240,000 km (150,000 mi) of use.

Older style belts, which were manufactured with a chloroprene compound, may exhibit cracks depending on age. However, the onset of cracking typically signals that the belt is only about halfway through its usable life. A good rule of thumb for chloroprene-based belts is that if cracks are observed 3 mm (1/8 in) apart, ALL AROUND THE BELT, the belt may be reaching the end of its serviceable life and should be considered a candidate for changing. Small cracks spaced at greater intervals should not be considered as indicative that the belt needs changing. Any belt that exhibits chunking should be replaced.

SHAKE/VIBRATION IN STEERING WHEEL/SEAT

BULLETIN NO.: 00-03-10-007F   DATE: FEBRUARY 05, 2004

SHAKE/VIBRATION ON SMOOTH ROADS (DIAGNOSE/BALANCE TIRES/WHEELS)

1998–2004 Buick Park Avenue, Park Avenue Ultra

2000–04 Buick LeSabre

1998–2004 Cadillac Seville (SLS, STS)

2000–04 Cadillac DeVille (DTS only)

2001–03 Oldsmobile Aurora

2000–04 Pontiac Bonneville (17" Tires only)

This bulletin is being revised to add the 2004 model year and delete the screened tire program information for all tire manufacturers except for Continental General. Please discard Corporate Bulletin Number 00-03-10-007E (Section 03-Suspension).

CONDITION: Some customers may comment on shaking/vibration in the steering wheel, floor or seat while driving at highway speeds (typically between 60–72 mph (96–115 km/h)) on smooth roads.

Cause: These specific vehicles may be sensitive to various rotating mass assemblies, especially if they are considered to be out-of-balance.

CORRECTION:

Visually inspect the tires and the wheels. Inspect for evidence of the following conditions and correct as necessary:

- Missing balance weights
- Bent rim flange
- Irregular tire wear
- Incomplete bead seating
- Tire irregularities
- Mud/ice build-up in wheel
- Stones in the tire tread

Set the tire pressure to 30 psi (205 kpa) COLD.

POOR TRANSMISSION PERFORMANCE

BULLETIN NO.: 01-07-30-038B

DATE: JANUARY 26, 2004

POOR PERFORMANCE OF TRANSMISSION, SLIPPING (CLEAN TRANSMISSION VALVE BODY AND CASE OIL PASSAGES OF DEBRIS)

1999–2004 Passenger Cars and Light Duty Trucks

2003–04 HUMMER H2 with 4L60-E/4L65-E Automatic Transmission

Some customers may comment on any of the following conditions:

- The SES lamp is illuminated.
- No 3rd and 4th gear.
- The transmission does not shift correctly.
- The transmission feels like it shifts to Neutral or a loss of drive occurs.

The vehicle free wheels above 48 km/h (30 mph). High RPM needed to overcome the free wheeling. The most likely cause is chips or debris plugging the bleed orifice of the 2–3 shift solenoid (367). This will cause the transmission to stay in 2nd gear when 3rd gear is commanded and return to 1st gear when 4th gear is commanded.

- Inspect/Clean the 2–3 shift valve (368), the 2–3 shuttle valve (369) and the valve bore of debris / metal chips.
- Inspect/Clean the 2–3 shift solenoid (367) opening of debris / metal chips. While inspecting the 2–3 shift solenoid (367), look for a screen over the solenoid opening. If the solenoid DOES NOT have a screen, replace the solenoid with P/N 10478131 that does have a screen over the solenoid opening.

TRANSMISSION FLUID LEAKS/2ND, 3RD, 4TH GEARS INOPERATIVE

BULLETIN NO.: 04-07-30-025

DATE: MAY 20, 2004

TRANSMISSION FLUID LEAK, INOPERATIVE 2ND/3RD/4TH GEARS, NO MOVEMENT, CASE CRACKED OR BROKEN AT 2–4 SERVO (REPAIR TRANSMISSION AND INSTALL NEW RETAINING RING)

2004 Light Duty Trucks, including Astro and Safari minivans

CONDITION: Some customers may comment on a transmission leak, inoperative 2nd/4th gear, slipping 3rd/4th gear or no movement due to excess fluid loss.

CAUSE: This condition normally occurs at low mileage, usually under 1,600 km (1,000 mi), and investigation may show that the servo cover is loose or that the transmission case is cracked or broken at the servo bore. This condition may be caused by a servo cover retaining ring that did not retain the servo cover.

The servo retaining ring design was changed for the 2004 MY from round wire to wire with two flat faces. In mid-April 2004, the retaining ring design did revert back to a round design in production.

It is possible that the transmission case may crack at the servo cover area due to the retaining ring being incorrectly seated.

HARSH 1–2 UPSHIFT

BULLETIN NO.: 01-07-30-030A   **DATE: MAY 20, 2004**

2001–05 Passenger Cars and Light Duty Trucks with 4L60-E or 4L65-E Automatic Transmission

The following four conditions have been found to cause the majority of consistent, harsh 1–2 shift comments.

- Chips/Sediment/Debris/Contamination found in the valve body, 1–2 accumulator valve (371) bore, may cause the 1–2 accumulator valve to stick or hang-up.
- Chips/Sediment/Debris/Contamination found in the valve body, 4–3 sequence valve (383) bore, may cause the 4–3 sequence valve to stick or hang-up.
- A cracked 1–2 accumulator piston (56) that is allowing fluid to leak by.
- Mislocated/Missing valve body-to-spacer plate check balls (61).

TRANSMISSION FLUID LEAKS

BULLETIN NO.: 04-07-30-028   **DATE: JUNE 15, 2004**

TRANSMISSION LEAKS FROM REVERSE SERVO COVER (REPLACE REVERSE SERVO COVER AND SEAL)

2004 and Prior Cars and Light Duty Trucks (Automatic Transmission 4T65-E)

CONDITION: Some customers may comment on a fluid leak under the vehicle.

CAUSE: A possible cause of a transmission fluid leak usually only during cold ambient temperatures below –6.7°C (20°F) may be the reverse servo cover/seal. The reverse servo cover seal may shrink in cold ambient temperatures causing a transmission fluid leak

INACCURATE FUEL GAUGE

BULLETIN NO.: 04-08-49-018A   **DATE: JUNE 2004**

CRANKS BUT NO START, STALL, INACCURATE/INCORRECT FUEL GAUGE READING, NO FUEL, VEHICLE IS OUT OF FUEL AND FUEL GAUGE READS ABOVE EMPTY (REPLACE FUEL LEVEL SENSOR)

2001–04 Cadillac Trucks

1999–2004 Chevrolet and GMC Trucks with Gasoline Engine

CONDITION: Some customers may comment on the vehicle stalling and will not restart, vehicle ran out of fuel, vehicle appears to be out of fuel but the fuel gauge reads above empty. The fuel gauge may read 1/4 tank.

CAUSE: Contamination on the fuel sending card may cause inaccurate/incorrect fuel gauge readings.

Honda

EXHAUST/INTERIOR SULFUR SMELL

BULLETIN NO.: 03-091   DATE: APRIL 2, 2004

2003–04 Accord L4 (except vehicles equipped with mass air flow sensor)

2003–04 Accord V6

SYMPTOM: Sulfur smell in the interior (smells like rotten eggs).

PROBABLE CAUSE: Unsealed body seams are allowing a sulfur smell to enter the interior.

CORRECTIVE ACTION: Replace the catalytic converter, seal the body seams, and install flap seals.

Hyundai

ERRATIC/SLIPPING SHIFTS

BULLETIN NO.: 03-40-007-1   DATE: MARCH 2004

1996–2000 ELANTRA

1997–2001 TIBURON

1996–2004 ACCENT

DESCRIPTION: Incorrect operation of the transaxle solenoids for the 1996–2000 Elantra, 1997–2001 Tiburon and 1996–2004 Accent may result in the following symptoms:

- Erratic shift or slipping
- Transaxle held in 3rd gear Fail-safe
- Diagnostic Trouble Codes – P0740, P0741, P0742, P0743, P0745, P0747, P0748, P0750, P0752, P0753, P0755, P0757, P0758, P0760, P0765 (see DTC Information shown in this bulletin)
- MIL illuminated

Infiniti

A/T — ABNORMAL SHIFTING

BULLETIN NO.: ITB04-014   DATE: MARCH 10, 2004

ABNORMAL SHIFTING OF AUTO TRANSAXLE (RE4F04B/W)

2000–01 I30 (CA33)   2002–04 I35 (CA33)

IF YOU CONFIRM:

An Applied Vehicle equipped with an automatic transaxle has ALL of the following conditions:

- Abnormal shifting (like: slip "shift shock" no shift improper shift timing)
- Transmission fluid is not burnt
- No excessive debris in oil pan*
- The incident is listed as an A/T internal fault as per the Electronic Service Manual (ESM) diagnostic procedure

*See A/T Fluid Cooler Inspection Procedure in the appropriate ESM.

➤

SERVICE INFORMATION

Policy Change

When ESM diagnosis shows an incident is caused by an A/T internal fault for an Applied Vehicle;

- DO NOT replace the transaxle assembly.
- Instead first replace the control valve assembly (valve body) of the incident transmission. Use the latest part number shown in your Nissan Parts Catalogue.

Jaguar

ENGINE CONTROLS — LIMP HOME MODE/MIL ON

BULLETIN NO.: S303-S159   DATE: NOVEMBER 2003

ENGINE IN LIMP HOME/CHECK ENGINE MIL — WATER INGRESS INTO THROTTLE POSITION SENSOR — SERVICE ACTION S159

2003–04 S-TYPE R

ISSUE: A concern has been identified on 2003–04 MY S-TYPE R vehicles. It is possible that during washing of the vehicle by carwash or jet wash the water can run through the cowl panel grille-fixing hole into the throttle position sensor housing. This can result in the throttle position sensor failing to function, the engine management system defaults to limp home mode and a warning MIL is displayed. A sealing patch is available to prevent water flowing directly from the cowl panel grille onto the throttle position sensor.

ACTION: On 2003–04 MY S-TYPE R vehicles install a sealing patch on the mounting hole located on the suspension turret cross brace at the bracket securing it to the bulkhead.

DRIVETRAIN — THUMPING FROM REAR OF VEHICLE

BULLETIN NO.: S100-10   DATE: MARCH 2004

THUMP FROM REAR OF VEHICLE – DIFFERENTIAL MOUNT BUSHINGS – INSTALL BUSHING INSERTS

2003–04 S-TYPE

ISSUE: Customers may have concerns of the following:

- On manual transmission vehicles, a thump from the rear of the vehicle when changing gear.
- On automatic transmission vehicles, thump from the rear when accelerating after a period of deceleration.

To address this concern, two inserts have been released to restrict mounting bushing movement. These inserts fit into the bushings that support the rear of the differential in the subframe.

Mazda

SHIFT SHOCK/TCM REFLASH
BULLETIN NO.: 05-001/04

SHIFT SHOCK – TRANSMISSION CONTROL MODULE (TCM) REFLASH

2002–04 MPV

DESCRIPTION: The vehicle's automatic transaxle (ATX) may exhibit shift shock while the engine warms from cold to normal operating temperature. The symptom is intermittent, it does not occur all the time. The shift shock usually occurs during 1–2 or 2–3 upshifts, or 3–2 part throttle downshifts.

In most cases, the cause of the shift shock is from the TRANSMISSION CONTROL MODULE (TCM) software calibration. A new software calibration is available on ESI to correct the shifting concerns.

Nissan

HARD STARTS
BULLETIN NO.: NTB04-063   DATE: MAY 24, 2004

2003–05 Altima (L31) with the VQ35DE (V6) engine only

2004 Quest (V42)

2004 Maxima (A34)

IF YOU CONFIRM: The engine is hard to start when warm, but starts OK when the engine is cold. NOTE: "Hard start" is engine crank time that is longer than 3 seconds.

ACTIONS:

- If you only have DTC P0340, replace only Bank 1 CMP (Camshaft Position) Sensor.
- If you only have DTC P0345, replace only Bank 2 CMP (Camshaft Position) Sensor.
- If you have both codes, replace both sensors.
- For a "hard to start warm" incident, replace both sensors, even if you have no codes.

HARD/NO START AFTER A COLD SOAK
BULLETIN NO.: EC03-032A; NTB04-021A   DATE: APRIL 29, 2004

ENGINE CRANKS BUT HARD/NO START AFTER COLD SOAK

2004 Altima (L31) – QR25DE & VQ35DE engine, except SULEV

2004 Quest (V42) – VQ35DE engine

2004 Maxima (A34) – VQ35DE engine

IF YOU CONFIRM:

An applied vehicle has the following symptoms after a cold soak:

- Engine cranks excessively before starting
- Engine cranks but does not start

ACTION:

- Check the fuel pressure while the incident is occurring.
- If the fuel pressure is low (0–20 p.s.i.), replace the Fuel Pump Assembly.

Saturn

EXTENDED WARRANTY FOR PCM REPROGRAMMING

BULLETIN NO.: 04-I-08   DATE: JUNE 2004

WARRANTY COVERAGE CHANGE FOR EMISSION-RELATED REPROGRAMMING EVENTS

In the past, all reprogramming of vehicle controllers (powertrain control modules [PCM], engine control modules [ECM], and transmission control modules [TCM]) were covered under the New Vehicle Limited Warranty (3 years/36,000 miles [60,000 km]). Effective immediately, the coverage for emission-related reprogramming now has the same coverage as the controller under the emission warranty (8 years/80,000 miles [130,000 km]).

NO MOVEMENT IN DRIVE OR REVERSE

BULLETIN NO.: 04-07-30-024   DATE: MAY 2004

NO MOVEMENT IN DRIVE OR REVERSE

2003–04 Saturn VUE, ION Vehicles

CONDITION: Some customers may comment on the vehicle not moving in the "D" (Drive) or "R" (Reverse) gear selection positions.

In many cases, the transaxle will also produce an audible grind or whine noise when attempting to operate in drive or reverse. The Service Engine Soon Telltale (SES) may be illuminated with DTCs P1758, P1756, P1882, P0841, P0741, or P0742 recorded.

CAUSE: This condition may occur when the VT25E transaxle belt has malfunctioned and is inoperative.

CORRECTION: Flush transaxle oil cooler and replace transaxle oil cooler lines prior to replacing the VT25E Transaxle Assembly.

NO START IN COLD CONDITIONS

BULLETIN NO.: 04-08-45-005   DATE: MAY 27, 2004

NO CRANK, NO START WHEN AMBIENT TEMPERATURE IS COLD — DTCS B2960 AND OR B3033 ARE SET (REPLACE IGNITION SWITCH)

2003–04 Saturn ION Vehicles

CONDITION: Some customers may comment that their vehicle will not start when the ambient temperature is cold (usually below 32°F/0°C). This comment is referred to as a "No Crank, No Start With Complete Power". Additional comments may be as follows:

- A clicking noise is noticed when the key is first turned to the crank position, but no noise is heard after the initial start attempt.
- The "Security" light will flash immediately after trying to start the car along with the message "Service Vehicle" in the Driver Information Center.
- The vehicle will not start for at least 10 minutes after the first attempt to start the vehicle. DTCs B2960 and or B3033 may be set in history in the Body Control Module (BCM).

CAUSE: The grease in the ignition switch may have solidified to the point where the metal contacts in the ignition switch do not make complete contact with the printed circuit board containing the PASSLOCK™ resistor when the key is rotated. Therefore, the BCM does not recognize the correct PASSLOCK™ resistance from the ignition switch when the key is turned to crank. By having this incomplete contact, the PASSLOCK™ resistance voltage fluctuates, causing the BCM to see a "Valid" but "Incorrect" PASSLOCK™ voltage. This incorrect voltage causes the BCM to not allow the crank signal to be sent to the ECM.

CORRECTION: Replace ignition switch with P/N 10378752. The new ignition switch has a different grease that will not solidify at cold ambient temperatures (usually below 32°F/0°C).

CAMPAIGN — VTI A/T EXTENDED WARRANTY COVERAGE

SPECIAL POLICY ADJUSTMENT — EXTENDED TRANSMISSION WARRANTY COVERAGE FOR VARIABLE TRANSMISSION WITH INTELLIGENCE (VTI) TRANSMISSION # 04020 — (04/21/2004)

2002–04 VUE Vehicles Equipped with VTi (M75 and M16)

2004 ION Quad Coupe Vehicles Equipped with VTi (M75)

CONDITION: Saturn has determined that 2002, 2003 and 2004 VUE and 2003 and 2004 ION Quad Coupe vehicles equipped with the VTi transmission may experience certain transmission concerns that might affect customer satisfaction, and may require repair or replacement.

SPECIAL POLICY ADJUSTMENT: This special policy bulletin has been issued to extend the warranty on the VTi transmission assembly for a period of 5 years or 75,000 miles (120,000 km), whichever occurs first, from the date the vehicle was originally placed in service, regardless of ownership. The repairs will be made at no charge to the customer.

Effective immediately, vehicles covered by extended vehicle service contracts are covered by this special policy.

Toyota

TRIM PANEL DEFECTS

BULLETIN NO.: B0017-03   DATE: SEPTEMBER 9, 2003

All Models

Customers may experience an interior trim panel either loose or fitting poorly due to a deformed or missing panel attachment clips. When a trim garnish (A, B, C or D pillar garnish, door trim panel, etc.) is removed and reinstalled using the old clips, there is a possibility that the garnish may exhibit a loose condition. To prevent this condition from occurring, please use the following procedures.

INSPECTION/REPLACEMENT PROCEDURE

All Models — All trim panel attachment clips must be inspected prior to reassembly and replaced if any damage or wear is detected. If no damage is visible, the clip may be reused. Always check to make sure that the garnish is properly attached after reinstallation of all interior trim panels. ➤

2002–04 model year Camry and 2004 model year Solara — When removing the A-pillar garnish panels, replace the white plastic attachment clips (P/N 90467-A0025).

POWER SLIDING DOOR INOPERATIVE

BULLETIN NO.: EL004-04   DATE: APRIL 19, 2004

POWER SLIDING DOOR INOPERATIVE

2004 Sienna

In some instances, customers with 2004 model year Sienna vehicles may experience power sliding door inoperative conditions. A new Power Slide Door Motor, Center Bracket No. 1, and Center Hinge have been made available to improve the durability of this system.

SLIDING SIDE DOOR RATTLES

BULLETIN NO.: NV004-04   DATE: APRIL 2, 2004

SLIDING DOOR RATTLE

2004 Sienna

The sliding door front striker plate on the 2004 model year Sienna has been redesigned in order to address any customer complaints for rattles that occur under certain driving conditions. The striker plate's new coating should reduce noise from contact between the front striker plate and the sliding door lock assembly when in the closed position.

BACK DOOR LEAK AND COLD WEATHER SHUDDER IMPROVEMENT

BULLETIN NO.: B0003-04   DATE: MARCH 9, 2004

2004 Sienna

The back door stays for 2004 model year Sienna vehicles have been redesigned in order to provide improved resistance to seal damage and prevent leakage. The improvement will also address the power back door shudder that can occur when operating during cold weather conditions.

EXCESSIVE SULFUR DIOXIDE ODOR

BULLETIN NO.: EG011-04   DATE: MARCH 13, 2004

2002–04 Camry

Some customers may complain of excessive sulfur dioxide odor on 2002–04 model year Camry vehicles equipped with 1MZ-FE engines under the following conditions:

- Stop and go driving.
- Heavy acceleration.

In order to reduce the odor, a new catalytic converter has been developed.